The Family

CW01432509

Monarchy, Mass Media and the British Public, 1932–53

The Family Firm

Monarchy, Mass Media and the British Public, 1932–53

Edward Owens

LONDON
ROYAL HISTORICAL SOCIETY
INSTITUTE OF HISTORICAL RESEARCH
UNIVERSITY OF LONDON PRESS

Published in 2019 by

UNIVERSITY OF LONDON PRESS
SCHOOL OF ADVANCED STUDY
INSTITUTE OF HISTORICAL RESEARCH
Senate House, Malet Street, London WC1E 7HU

Available to download free or to purchase the hard copy edition at https://www.sas.ac.uk/publications/.

ISBNs
978-1-909646-94-0 (hardback edition)
978-1-909646-98-8 (paperback edition)
978-1-909646-95-7 (PDF edition)
978-1-909646-96-4 (ePub edition)
978-1-912702-13-8 (.mobi edition)

DOI 10.14296/1019.9781909646957

New Historical
PERSPECTIVES

Cover image: Print from a Vivex photograph of King George V (1865–1936) recording his Christmas radio broadcast at Sandringham. (RCIN 630629). Royal Collection Trust / © Her Majesty Queen Elizabeth II 2019

Contents

List of illustrations

Acknowledgements

It is with the greatest pleasure that I can finally thank all the individuals and organizations who have helped to make this book possible. To begin at the beginning: this project would never have got off the ground had it not been for the support and enthusiasm of Max Jones at the University of Manchester. Despite a difficult initial meeting in my first week as a student back in 2007, Max quickly became a trusted advisor in his role as my personal tutor and his level-three course on British heroes inspired me to think in new ways about the nature of fame and the role that public figures play in national life. Max oversaw my third-year dissertation on the aviatrix Amy Johnson and helped with the preparation of a Master's AHRC funding proposal to explore the heroic image of T. E. Lawrence. This was successful and we worked on this project together, the results of which finally made it into print in 2015. I gratefully acknowledge the support of the Arts and Humanities Research Council for funding my MA studies as well as my doctoral research – again, Max played an integral part in helping me devise a proposal for a PhD project that would examine the transformation of the British monarchy's media image in the mid twentieth century. In supervising the project, he was joined by Frank Mort, who also offered a great deal of advice at the early proposal stage. Frank is another historian whose personal kindness and patience seem to know no bounds. His insights on the monarchy's evolution have helped to smooth the rough edges off many of the arguments contained in this book and our conversations together with Max were informative and great fun in equal measure. Our meetings were also enriched by the contributions of Julie-Marie Strange and Aaron Moore, both of whom brought a unique perspective to bear on the royal family in their role as advisors on the doctoral project.

At the end of what sometimes felt like an interminable three-and-a-half years, I was very fortunate to have Penny Summerfield and David Cannadine examine the PhD thesis at the *viva voce*, which was held at the Institute of Historical Research in London. Penny and David provided me with much good advice on how to turn my doctoral research into a book and encouraged me to write a new chapter on the Second World War, which is included in the present study. In her role as co-editor of the New Historical Perspectives series, Penny has continued to shape *The Family Firm* through to completion, not only looking over final drafts of the introduction and conclusion, but also offering valuable words of advice as my final deadline drew near. This publication has been made possible by a grant from the Scouloudi Foundation in association with the Institute of Historical Research. Royal Historical Society grants also funded two month-long research trips to London while I was a PhD student. For these grants and awards, and for various other funding and job applications, Penny, David, Frank and Max have written many references (often at quite short notice!); I am grateful for their unwavering support. Back in July 2018 I met the historians who had read the first draft of *The Family Firm* at the Royal Historical Society. Jo Fox, Adrian Bingham and Richard Toye provided me with much useful feedback that has strengthened the arguments presented here. Richard has also acted as a liaison between me, the readers and the other patient individuals at the IHR and RHS involved in the production of this book, including Jane Winters, Emily Morrell, Kerry Whitston and Philip Carter. My thanks go to them all for their time and help.

Other historians who have at some point in time made me rethink my approach to the monarchy include Ina Zweiniger-Bargielowska, Sean Nixon, Matt Houlbrook, Martin Johnes, Eloise Moss, Toby Harper, Heather Jones, Christian Goeschel, Lucy Robinson, Jes Fabricius Møller and Emily Robinson – among many others. Since arriving at the University of Lincoln as a lecturer, I have further honed my ideas through in-class discussions on the royal family with the level-three students who have taken my monarchy course. My colleagues at Lincoln have also created a welcoming space where I have been able to discuss my interests. My thanks go to them all, but in particular to Chris O'Rourke, Sarah Longair, Adam Page, Helen Smith, Pietro Di Paola, Christine Grandy, Lacey Wallace, Jon Fitzgibbons, Duncan Wright, Jamie Wood, Michele Vescovi, Hope Williard, Graham Barrett, Rob Portass, Crystal Walker, Anna Marie Roos and Antonella Liuzzo Scorpo. Also with me at Lincoln, but among the friends I first made as a postgraduate at Manchester as well, are James Greenhalgh and Katherine Fennelly. They have made the transition to Lincoln a highly enjoyable one and I have learnt a great deal about history (and other things!) during our evenings spent together. Our PhD cohort at Manchester was full of 'good eggs' who not only helped me to improve as a historian but also provided much-needed fun and respite away from the grind of research. They include: Maarten Walraven-Freeling, James Corke-Webster, Gary Butler, Paula Smalley, Ben Knowles, Lee Dixon, Sarah Wood, Luke Heselwood, Stevie Spiegl, Kelly Spring, Ravi Hensman, Sean Irving, Luke Kelly, Alistair Kefford, Ben Wilcock and Jacob Bloomfield. Special thanks are also due to Ian Field – not only for sparking my interest in twentieth-century British history during my early undergraduate years, but also for providing excellent, gin-soaked company throughout my time at Manchester.

A few last thank-yous: first, to the many archivists who helped to make this project possible through their generosity of spirit, not only in replying to emails in advance of visits, but in aiding my discovery of exciting material and responding to questions on site. I am especially grateful to Katie Ankers at the BBC Written Archives Centre, Julie Crocker and her team at the Royal Archives, Fiona Courage at Mass Observation and staff at Lambeth Palace Library and the British Library's Newsroom, where the majority of the research for this book, and the PhD on which it is based, was completed. Second, I gratefully acknowledge the permission of Her Majesty Queen Elizabeth II to quote from material in the Royal Archives. Third, my thanks to all those friends outside the world of academia who have taken an interest in this project as it has developed over the course of almost eight years and particularly to those who have provided me with a bed to sleep in and a table to eat at while on my archival expeditions. I am also particularly grateful to Ben Garman and Harry Bolton for taking the time to proofread sections of this book. Fourth, my thanks to my family. My uncle, Andrew, has not only asked many important questions about this book that have shaped my thoughts as it has evolved, he has also provided a regular base in London where I have stayed during research trips to the capital. Without his hospitality, I would not have located half as much interesting material and the book would be much worse off. To my brother Andy and sister Kate, thank you for your good-natured joshing and love: you are both stars and I know you will continue to shine brightly. To my mum and dad, Debbie and Glyn – you built a home where history mattered and this fired my interest in the past. You always supported my education and encouraged me to strike my own path when I went to study and live in Manchester. You have stood by my every decision – whether or not these were right or wrong at the time! For all this I am eternally grateful. To my wife, Lisa: you have had to put up with this book (and my fraught relationship with it) since the moment we first met in 2012. Thank you for your love, patience and tireless positivity. You know better than anyone else how to put a smile on my face and this has kept me going through the bad and the good.

Finally, a special thank you to my grandmothers, Margaret (Meggie) Price and Mildred (Granny) Owens. They were the original inspiration behind the idea at the heart of *The Family Firm* and this book is therefore dedicated to them both. Meggie died twelve years ago in 2006; Granny will turn ninety-five in 2019. As women born in Britain between the wars, their early lives were influenced by some of the events discussed here. I remember Meggie talking with affection of the royal family and comparing my brother and me to Princes William and Harry when we were small children. Granny has many memories of the royal personalities discussed in this book and she remains a great admirer of the current monarch, Elizabeth II. I have always wondered how and why it was that my grandmothers, and other members of their generation, developed such strong emotional attachments to the House of Windsor. My hope is that *The Family Firm* will go some way to explaining this phenomenon.

List of abbreviations

BBCWA	BBC Written Archives Centre, Caversham
BFINA	British Film Institute National Archive, London
BOD	Bodleian Library, Oxford
BUFVC	British Universities Film and Video Council
CC	Christ Church College Archives, Oxford
JRL	John Rylands Library, Manchester
LMA	London Metropolitan Archives
LPL	Lambeth Palace Library, London
MOA	Mass Observation Archive
NPG	National Portrait Gallery, London
ODNB	*Oxford Dictionary of National Biography*
PA	Parliamentary Archive, London
RA	Royal Archives, Windsor
RCIN	The Royal Collection
TK	The Keep, University of Sussex, Brighton
TNA	The National Archives of the UK
WAL	Westminster Abbey Library, London

Introduction

> When the Labour Party comes to power we must act rapidly and it will be
> necessary to deal with the House of Lords and the influence of the City of
> London. There is no doubt that we shall have to overcome opposition from
> Buckingham Palace, and other places as well.[1]

Addressing a gathering of delegates and journalists at the annual conference
of the University of Nottingham's Labour Federation on the evening of 6
January 1934, the barrister and MP for Bristol East, Sir Stafford Cripps,
publicly bolstered his reputation as an outspoken radical who was committed
to a programme of state-led socialism when he criticized what he saw as
an obstructionist establishment, comprising bankers, peers and malign
influences at court, which he believed would oppose the implementation
of left-wing policies should the Labour party succeed in forming another
government. His oblique allusion to the machinations of the royal
household was political dynamite and ignited a national furore, with almost
every major British newspaper reproducing his words alongside articles that
questioned the speaker's motives and denounced the way he had dragged
the king's name into politics. In the days that followed, Cripps's political
opponents added their voices to the chorus of criticism, while his Labour
colleagues sought to distance themselves from the inflammatory speech. He
was then forced publicly to clarify what he had meant when he referred to
the palace and, in an attempt to explain away his earlier remarks, he told
reporters that he had not been referring to George V but to the 'officials
and other people who surround the king'.[2] He also went on to reassure his
detractors that he had full confidence in Britain's constitutional monarchy as
an essentially fair political system and, at another public meeting, he toasted
the sovereign's good health in a very deliberate act of contrition. However,
it was too late: Cripps's about-face was derided by many journalists, who
mocked his reference to the shadowy figures who lurked behind the throne

---

[1] *Morning Post*, 8 Jan. 1934, as quoted in C. Cooke, *The Life of Richard Stafford Cripps*
(London, 1957), p. 159.

[2] E.g., *Sunday Times*, 7 Jan. 1934, p. 17; *Daily Mail*, 8 Jan. 1934, p. 3; *Daily Telegraph*, 8
Jan. 1934, p. 12 and 9 Jan. 1934, p. 7; *Daily Mirror*, 8 Jan. 1934, p. 3; *Manchester Guardian*, 8
Jan. 1934, p. 9 and 10 Jan. 1934, p. 11.

'Introduction', in E. Owens, *The Family Firm: Monarchy, Mass Media and the British Public, 1932–53*
(London, 2019), pp. 1–44. License: CC-BY-NC-ND 4.0.

in their descriptions of 'royal bogeymen' and scornfully accused him of wanting to overthrow Britain's political system in order to set up a socialist dictatorship under his authority.[3]

Cripps's 'Buckingham Palace speech' (as it became known) and the media's response to his words reveal four important things. First of all, it is clear from the outrage of the press and politicians that, for the opinion-formers and law-makers, the crown occupied a near-sacred place in national life in the mid 1930s. The media and political elite revered the monarchy as the institution that had anchored Britain's evolution from feudalism to modern democracy, something which chimed with the ideas vigorously promoted by courtiers and allies of the throne that the crown stood above party politics and that the constitutional sovereign was the unifying symbol of the British people's political freedoms.[4] This mattered more than ever after 1918 because it was the year that witnessed the enfranchisement of all working-class voters for the first time following the passage of the Fourth Reform Act. In the new age of mass politics and social democracy, King George V was celebrated for his impartiality when he oversaw the formation of Britain's first Labour government in 1924; and for the way he backed constitutional progress as the shape of the nation and empire was transformed by the secession of the Free Irish State in 1922 and the emergence of a Commonwealth comprising autonomous white dominions after 1931 (Figure 0.1). Furthermore, in a very popular move that began in the years immediately before the First World War but accelerated into the interwar period, the king and his family demonstrated a keener interest in the lives of their working-class subjects and engaged with the media more readily in order to publicize their commitment to 'serving' their people.[5] The royals embarked on good-will tours of hard-hit industrial areas, sponsored charitable initiatives aimed at alleviating the material hardships that beset working-class communities and even sought to become patrons of the proletariat through visible support of their cultural pastimes and sports: for

[3] *Daily Mail*, 11 Jan. 1934, p. 11; *Daily Mirror*, 11 Jan. 1934, p. 13; *Manchester Guardian*, 11 Jan. 1934, p. 10; *The Times*, 12 Jan. 1934, p. 14; *Daily Telegraph*, 20 Jan. 1934, p. 12.

[4] J. Parry, 'Whig monarchy, whig nation: crown politics and representativeness, 1800–2000', in *The Monarchy and the British Nation 1780 to the Present*, ed. A. Olechnowicz (Cambridge, 2007), pp. 47–75, at pp. 66–9; P. Williamson, 'The monarchy and public values, 1900–1953', in Olechnowicz, *Monarchy and the British Nation*, pp. 223–57, at pp. 236–45.

[5] Williamson, 'Monarchy and public values', pp. 252–5; R. Brazier, 'The monarchy', in *The British Constitution in the Twentieth Century*, ed. V. Bogdanor (Oxford, 2007), pp. 69–98, at pp. 76–7; B. Harrison, *The Transformation of British Politics, 1860–1995* (Oxford, 1996), pp. 334–5; F. Prochaska, *Royal Bounty: the Making of a Welfare Monarchy* (New Haven, Conn., 1995), pp. 170–5.

Figure 0.1. King George
V, 1931 (RCIN 2107940).
Royal Collection Trust
/ © Her Majesty Queen
Elizabeth II 2019.

example, in 1923 the king attended a Wembley FA Cup final for the first time and presented the victors, Bolton Wanderers, with the trophy.[6]

George V's reign of almost twenty-six years (1910–36) thus witnessed the monarchy outwardly focusing its attention on the British 'masses'. When combined with the king's symbolic leadership of the nation and empire through the First World War, his close association with the cultures of commemoration and remembrance that resulted from the conflict and the royal family's more traditional role as promoters of a Christian family-centred morality, this royal 'democratization' worked to invest the House of Windsor with the sacrosanct character that was loudly championed by British public commentators in the last years of George V's reign.[7] Notably,

---

[6] Parry, 'Whig monarchy', p. 70; Williamson, 'Monarchy and public values', pp. 239–41; R. McKibbin, *Classes and Cultures: England 1918–1951* (Oxford, 1998), pp. 7–9; I. Zweiniger-Bargielowska, 'Keep fit and play the game: George VI, outdoor recreation and social cohesion in interwar Britain', *Cult. and Soc. Hist.*, xi (2014), 111–29, at p. 111.

[7] H. Jones, 'The nature of kingship in First World War Britain', in *The Windsor Dynasty 1910 to the Present: 'Long to Reign Over Us'?*, ed. M. Glencross, J. Rowbottom and M. D. Kandiah (Basingstoke, 2016), pp. 195–216; H. Jones, 'A prince in the trenches? Edward VIII

the monarchy's democratic qualities also took shape in relation to the forward march of totalitarianism in Europe. Indeed, the second key thing to acknowledge in connection with the media's response to Cripps's speech and the misleading accusation that he was planning on establishing a dictatorship of his own is the way that dissenting voices, like his, which dared to criticize the palace or question the virtues of Britain's royal democracy, were ostracized to the fringes of acceptable public debate and labelled extremist. The mainstream politics of the 1920s and 1930s were defined by a discursive emphasis on the strengths of the nation's constitutional system and on the vitality of the empire – both ideas that gained even greater traction following the emergence of continental dictatorships that were anti-democratic and intent on extending their territorial influence.[8] Thus, at the same time that journalists anxiously reported on the rise of Benito Mussolini in Italy and Adolf Hitler in Germany, they presented George V's monarchy as the benevolent, democratic antidote to totalitarianism and as the nation's constitutional safeguard against the new fascist ideology that was proving so popular in Europe.

However, the third important thing to note in relation to Cripps's speech was the way his criticism of the royal household made it clear that not everybody in Britain was convinced the monarchy had the national interest at heart in these years. In fact, George V's promotion of constitutional democracy can be interpreted in a very different light, one which contrasts with the altruistic narrative championed by his supporters. Unbeknownst to almost all of his subjects, the king and his closest advisors could best be characterized as conservative reactionaries. They privately dreaded what the future held and adapted the crown's role and public image to suit the more democratic times in an attempt to appeal to the sensibilities of working-class people whom they inherently feared and distrusted.[9] Endowed with new voting powers and a greater sense of confidence, the proletariat could, should they so choose, challenge the political status quo. The House of

---

and the First World War', in *Sons and Heirs: Succession and Political Culture in Nineteenth-Century Europe*, ed. F. L. Müller and H. Mehrkens (Basingstoke, 2016), pp. 229–46; Williamson, 'Monarchy and public values', pp. 247–51.

[8] B. Schwarz, 'The language of constitutionalism: Baldwinite Conservatism', in *Formations of Nations and People*, ed. B. Schwarz et al. (London, 1984), pp. 1–18, at pp. 11–6; P. Williamson, 'The doctrinal politics of Stanley Baldwin', in *Public and Private Doctrine: Essays in British History Presented to Michael Cowling*, ed. M. Bentley (Cambridge, 1993), pp. 181–208, at pp. 190–1; P. Mandler, *The English National Character: the History of an Idea from Edmund Burke to Tony Blair* (London, 2006), pp. 149–52; Parry, 'Whig monarchy', pp. 66–7.

[9] Prochaska, *Royal Bounty*, pp. 169–201; F. Prochaska, 'George V and republicanism, 1917–1919', *Twentieth Century British Hist.*, x (1999), 27–51.

Windsor was sensitive to these changes, having watched aghast as other European crowned heads of state were toppled by the revolutionary forces unleashed by the First World War; and it was therefore crucial that the monarchy make itself more relevant to the ordinary man, woman and child if it was to win their loyalty and affection.[10] One of the strategies implemented at the suggestion of the king's advisors witnessed the crown become 'a living power for good' among those industrial communities represented by an increasingly outspoken Labour movement.[11] Hence the royal tours of the factories and mines, the charitable schemes designed to help disabled veteran servicemen return to work, the sponsorship of hospitals for patients involved in industrial accidents and the promotion of health and fitness among working-class boys and girls – all these and other royal philanthropic initiatives can be viewed as part of a very deliberate campaign to strengthen the royalist sympathies of the masses while checking the progress of socialism among its natural supporters.

More controversially still, George V had actively tried to prop up the status quo through calculated interventions in party politics which tested the limits of his constitutional powers. In the role of mediator, the king had overseen the conferences between the three party leaders that had led to the formation of a National Government in 1931 in an effort to bring some stability to the country's finances.[12] The monarch managed to persuade his Labour prime minister, Ramsay MacDonald, to stay on and lead this cross-party alliance – an act that brought about a dramatic split in the Labour party's leadership, with the prime minister's colleagues-turned-critics interpreting his acquiescence to the king's wishes as a betrayal of the interests of working-class voters, who stood to lose from the National Government's retrenchment policies.[13] One such friend-turned-foe was Cripps, who sympathized with MacDonald's difficult position but, after politely declining the prime minister's offer of ministerial office in the new coalition administration, returned to a diminished Labour party that went on to lose the subsequent general election of October 1931 to the National Government by the greatest electoral landslide witnessed in recent British history.[14]

[10] Prochaska, 'George V', pp. 45–7.

[11] Lord Stamfordham to Bishop of Chelmsford, 25 Nov. 1918 (RA GV O1106/65), quoted in Prochaska, 'George V', p. 48.

[12] V. Bogdanor, *The Monarchy and the Constitution* (Oxford, 1995), pp. 104–12, 153, 166, 179; P. Williamson, *National Crisis and National Government: British Politics, the Economy and Empire, 1926–1932* (Cambridge, 1992), pp. 333–43.

[13] B. Pimlott, *Labour and the Left in the 1930s* (Cambridge, 1977), pp. 11–3.

[14] Collectively, the parties forming the National Government won 554 seats out of a total

The seismic political events of 1931 inevitably intensified socialist critiques of the influence that the king and his aides could bring to bear on the machinery of government. When Cripps delivered his infamous speech in 1934, he would have known from the experiences of the left-wing intellectual and politician Harold Laski, who had publicly challenged the king's actions in 1931, that to criticize the monarchy was to court controversy and invite censure.[15] Nevertheless, this did not prevent him from committing what was, by the standards of the day, a serious *faux pas*; and the sharp rebuke issued by the media was intended to defend the crown against his attack and to reestablish its inviolable character in the eyes of the public.[16] Indeed, the motivation of the journalists and news editors who sprang to the monarchy's defence is the fourth and final thing to acknowledge in relation to Cripps's ill-chosen words in 1934. It was certainly the case that many public commentators respected George V and therefore loyally promoted the idea that the monarchy was a progressive and unifying force in Britain's royal democracy. But in mocking Cripps's reference to the royal officials at work behind the scenes, reporters also downplayed the role of Buckingham Palace in government decision-making, toeing the official line that the crown was an impartial political actor, while simultaneously perpetuating the secrecy of the elite networks through which the king and his advisors sought to influence national and imperial affairs.

During and after the First World War, courtiers forged new alliances with some of the most important individuals who made up Britain's religious and political establishments. These relationships were defined by shared interests that cohered around upholding the social and economic status quo in a period marked by significant change.[17] Despite regular fears arising at court about the journalistic overexposure of the royal family, palace officials also developed a mutually beneficial alliance with the media. By the 1920s

---

of 615, while the Labour party won just 52 (Williamson, *National Crisis*, pp. 372–3, 455; R. Toye and P. Clarke, 'Cripps, Sir (Richard) Stafford', in *ODNB* <https://doi.org/10.1093/ref:odnb/32630> [accessed 12 Oct. 2018]).

[15] Bogdanor, *Monarchy and the Constitution*, p. 112; K. O. Morgan, 'The Labour party and British republicanism', *E-rea: Revue électronique d'études sur le monde Anglophone*, i (2003) <https://journals.openedition.org/erea/347> [accessed 12 Oct. 2018].

[16] Cooke, *Richard Stafford Cripps*, pp. 159–64. Cripps's knowledge of the inner workings of the royal household was not only informed by recent political events, but also by a personal knowledge inherited from his father, Sir Charles Cripps, who, as another esteemed lawyer and politician, had served as attorney general to three princes of Wales – an appointment he had taken up in 1895 under the future Edward VII, before going on to serve both George V and a young Edward VIII until 1914 (P. Williamson, 'Cripps, Charles Alfred, first Baron Parmoor', in *ODNB* <https://doi.org/10.1093/ref:odnb/32629> [accessed 12 Oct. 2018]).

[17] Prochaska, 'George V', pp. 31–48.

the monarchy was reliant on news reporters, photographers and filmmakers to publicize its activities as part of its wider campaign to transform the royal family's role and image in society. At the same time, the media operated in the belief that the activities of the House of Windsor were of interest to its audiences and thus sought access to royal events and personalities, often via private lines of communication with court officials. These opaque channels were hidden from public view behind the glowing façade of a royal family who, at least outwardly, appeared to be in touch with the interests and needs of their subjects. But they were also governed by the gentlemanly codes of discretion that characterized the upper classes – hence, social etiquette decreed that the strategic activities of courtiers were kept a closely guarded secret and the palace's campaign to democratize the monarchy's image was not openly discussed for what it was.[18]

These relationships were instrumental in the emergence of a mass media monarchy in the mid twentieth century and yet their significance has been almost entirely neglected by historians of modern Britain. Additionally, scholars have not systematically analysed how the media projected the House of Windsor's image through the various channels of publicity that existed in these decades or, more importantly still, how members of the public received and made sense of the royal media image.[19] It is with these absences in mind that *The Family Firm* sets out to map the evolution of the relationship between the monarchy, mass media and the British public from the end of George V's reign, which, as we have seen, was a period marked by an elite reverence for the crown as an institution that seemed 'popular' and 'democratic' in its reach and appeal; through the crisis years that witnessed King Edward VIII's abdication, the collapse of the conventional wisdoms that had underpinned the monarchy and the reimagining of kingship via the complex figure of King George VI; to the more egalitarian, less deferential post-war world and the beginning of the reign of the current monarch, Queen Elizabeth II.

The Family Firm shows how, beginning with George V's first Christmas radio broadcast in 1932, the royal household worked in tandem with new allies in the media and older partners from the Church of England to initiate a new phase in the House of Windsor's public relations strategy. Courtiers, clerics and news editors elevated the royal family's domesticity as a focal-point for national identification by projecting a more intimate

---

[18] M. Houlbrook, *Prince of Tricksters: the Incredible True Story of Netley Lucas, Gentleman Crook* (Chicago, Ill., 2016), pp. 223–76.

[19] For recent historical work that has begun to address this scholarly lacuna, see F. Mort, 'Love in a cold climate: letters, public opinion and monarchy in the 1936 abdication crisis', *Twentieth Century British Hist.*, xxv (2014), 30–62.

and familiar media image of the House of Windsor which was designed to engender strong emotional bonds between British subjects and their royal rulers. Negotiations between these royal 'stage-managers' were often tense and characterized by discord, especially when media coverage threatened to undermine the crown as a result of reporters' efforts to bring audiences closer to the royal family. However, the stage-managers ultimately worked to enhance the relationship between the public and the monarchy in order to unite the population around the focal point of the crown in the unstable years during and either side of the Second World War. In this way the projection of the House of Windsor's family-centred image can be interpreted as a deliberate political strategy that was comparable to earlier attempts to cultivate the loyalty of the public through new kinds of interaction, such as the highly publicized tours of industrial areas that began before 1914. But, whereas the earlier campaign was motivated by a royal fear of revolutionary socialism, the public relations strategy that developed in the 1930s and evolved through the 1940s and 1950s took shape in response to a number of key events in these decades as well as a wider range of social, cultural and political changes. It is the House of Windsor's adaptation to these dramatic developments that forms the subject of this book.

A family on the throne

The projection of the family life of the monarchy in the years between 1932 and 1953 was not entirely novel. In the mid nineteenth century Queen Victoria and her consort, Prince Albert, had sought to take on the symbolic leadership of the British middle classes by projecting that social group's particular values – including domesticity, modesty and religious piety – through new kinds of media such as collectible photographic *cartes de visite*.[20] This move to make the monarchy's public image appear more bourgeois distanced the royal family from the dissolute aristocratic legacy of the queen's Hanoverian predecessors. However, it was also motivated by the fact that many middle-class men had gained the vote in 1832, which saw them become the most influential political force in public life; and, at Albert's insistence, the monarchy thus tried to set a moral example to the rest of the nation in order to engender the loyalty and admiration of the newly empowered bourgeoisie.[21] The prince consort also helped the crown to take a crucial step forward on its journey towards modern constitutional

---

[20] J. Plunkett, *Queen Victoria: First Media Monarch* (Oxford, 2003), pp. 143–53.
[21] Bogdanor, *Monarchy and the Constitution*, pp. 16–9; J. Plunkett, 'A media monarchy? Queen Victoria and the radical press, 1837–1901', *Media History*, ix (2003), 3–18, at pp. 3–4; S. K. Kent, *Queen Victoria: Gender and Empire* (Oxford, 2016), pp. 36–59.

monarchy when he advocated that the sovereign embrace an impartial role in overseeing the day-to-day business of government, henceforth avoiding controversial entanglements with party politicians which might otherwise alienate sections of the largely middle-class electorate.[22]

Although the public image of the Victorian family monarchy encountered setbacks with Albert's untimely death in 1861 and the queen's prolonged period of mourning, the major royal events of the late nineteenth and early twentieth centuries celebrated and embellished this domestic narrative. These state occasions were also made more visible to media audiences by the emergence of a national newspaper industry in the 1880s and 1890s which superseded the localized, provincial news networks that had existed before then.[23] National daily newspapers provided the new crucial channel through which royal jubilees, funerals and coronations were projected to a nationwide readership.[24] While these events were partly staged as public spectacles that celebrated Britain's imperial power and military might, they also promoted a royal national identity that centred on identification with the figurehead of the monarch and his or her family. As historian David Cannadine first noted in his observations on the royal 'invention of tradition', this national identity was not only meant to find favour with the British middle classes but also with an increasingly restless industrial proletariat, who were encouraged to identify with the symbol of the monarchy as part of a larger national collective.[25] Indeed, the idea of the unifying family monarchy owes its origins to the essayist and political theorist Walter Bagehot, who, in his 1867 exposition on the nature of Britain's government, advised that the crown embrace its role as the 'dignified' theatrical part of the constitution. He argued that the '*family* on the throne' was an appealing symbol with which the public could identify emotionally and could thus engender adherence to the nation's parliamentary system among the masses.[26] Bagehot called himself a reformer, but he was anxious about the prospect of working-class people gaining the vote and thought that if they

[22] Bogdanor, *Monarchy and the Constitution*, pp. 19–26.

[23] M. Hampton, *Visions of the Press in Britain* (Chicago, Ill., 2004), p. 28; J. Wolffe, 'The people's king: the crowd and the media at the funeral of Edward VII, May 1910', *Court Historian*, viii (2003), 23–30.

[24] D. Cannadine, 'The context, performance and meaning of ritual: the British monarchy and the "invention of tradition", c. 1820–1977', in *The Invention of Tradition*, ed. E. Hobsbawm and T. Ranger (Cambridge, 1983), pp. 101–64, at pp. 122–5.

[25] Cannadine, 'Context, performance and meaning', pp. 122–3. See also J. Wolffe, *Great Deaths: Grieving, Religion, and Nationhood in Victorian and Edwardian Britain* (Oxford, 2000), pp. 223–6.

[26] W. Bagehot, *The English Constitution* (London, 1867), pp. 62–3 (Bagehot's italics); Bogdanor, *Monarchy and the Constitution*, p. 62.

were instead given a royal symbol to venerate it would ensure their loyalty to the socio-political hierarchy while delaying their calls for greater electoral representation.[27] He also thought that, if the monarchy fully embraced its symbolic role, this would enable politicians to exercise direct political power as part of the 'efficient' machinery of government.

Bagehot's division of royal symbolic power from the 'real' political power wielded by Britain's elected representatives has had an important influence on the way scholars have approached the history of the modern constitutional monarchy. To what extent royal officials actually heeded Bagehot's advice is unknown, but every monarch since George V is supposed to have been guided by his constitutional principles and it is notable that royal events like those mentioned above were staged more publicly, more frequently and with greater aplomb to make Britain's family monarchy more visible to the nation at a time when there was growing social and political unrest.[28] It is also significant that there developed an intense interest among media audiences in the personalities that made up the royal family in these years. Improving literacy rates and technological advancements in printing gave rise to the so-called 'new journalism', which aimed to cater to the popular tastes of an expanding working- and lower-middle-class readership.[29] One of the mainstays of new 'popular' newspapers like the *Daily Mail* and *Daily Express* were human-interest stories which presented intimate details about the lives of the rich and famous. The popular press developed a keen interest in the goings-on at court and found that readers were very receptive to coverage of the lives, loves and losses of the royal family. Hence media reports on the funeral of Queen Victoria in 1901, the coronation of King Edward VII in 1902, his death in 1910 and the coronation of his son and heir, George V, in 1911 were characterized by a focus on the human qualities of the monarchs, their distinctive characters and their family relationships.[30] Another example from George V's early reign that witnessed the new human-interest focus come together with the monarchy's nation-building role was the formal investiture of his eldest

[27] M. Taylor, 'Introduction', in W. Bagehot, *The English Constitution*, ed. M. Taylor (Oxford, 2001), pp. vii–xxx, at pp. ix–xi, xxv–xxvii.
[28] Bogdanor, *Monarchy and the Constitution*, pp. 27–41, 133; Brazier, 'The monarchy', pp. 69–83; Cannadine, 'Context, performance and meaning', p. 134.
[29] A. Bingham and M. Conboy, *Tabloid Century: the Popular Press in Britain, 1896 to the Present* (Oxford, 2015), pp. 3–10; K. Jackson, *George Newnes and the New Journalism in Britain* (Abingdon, 2018), p. 113; J. Wiener, 'How new was the new journalism?', in *Papers for the Millions: the New Journalism in Britain, 1850s to 1914*, ed. J. Wiener (New York, 1988), pp. 47–71.
[30] Plunkett, *Queen Victoria*, pp. 205, 237–8; Wolffe, *Great Deaths*, pp. 243–6; Wolffe, 'The people's king', pp. 23–30; Bingham and Conboy, *Tabloid Century*, pp. 97–130.

son, Edward, then aged seventeen, as prince of Wales in 1911. As part of an elaborate ceremony that was staged in Caernarfon castle, courtiers worked with the Liberal government, the clergy, local officials and news editors to project the investiture as an intimate act of union between the prince and his father in order to promote an inclusive British national identity that recognized Wales's distinctive cultural heritage.[31]

The image of the family monarchy was also part of the crown's public relations strategy during the First World War. At a time of national crisis that was marked by an upsurge in public criticism of the inequalities of the British class system and of the royal family's German and Russian relations, George V further democratized his dynasty's image by developing more informal relationships with those of his subjects who were serving their country, either on the Western Front or through their work in the factories, mines and hospitals back in Britain. This was achieved through tours of inspection, medal investitures and good-will visits undertaken by the monarch and his consort, Queen Mary, on Europe's battlefields and on the home front. Posing for government-sponsored newsreel crews and carefully selected groups of reporters, the royal couple engaged personally, sympathetically and without ceremony with the men and women who were contributing to the war effort.[32] It was in the fraught years of 1917–18, which witnessed a rise in industrial disorder back in Britain and an increase in anti-royal sentiment, that the king and queen also started to engage more directly with film crews, smiling and half-glancing at the camera lens in order to convey a more human image to cinema-goers who saw the newsreels.[33] However, the existential threat the crown appeared to face in this period required more drastic innovation, too, and it is significant that at the suggestion of his private secretary, Lord Stamfordham, George V took the unprecedented decision to rename his family the 'House of Windsor' in an attempt to silence those critics who had publicly condemned the Teutonic sounding 'House of Saxe-Coburg and Gotha'.[34]

George V's children also played a symbolic part in the First World War, either through philanthropic roles, like Princess Mary, who was the patron of a number of charitable schemes designed to help and hearten servicemen and their families; or as active participants, as in the case of her elder brothers, Prince Albert, later duke of York, and Edward, prince

[31] J. S. Ellis, 'Reconciling the Celt: British national identity, empire, and the 1911 investiture of the prince of Wales', *Jour. Brit. Stud.*, xxxvii (1998), 391–418.
[32] Jones, 'Nature of kingship', pp. 202–6.
[33] L. McKernan, 'The finest cinema performers we possess: British royalty and the newsreels, 1910–37', *Court Historian*, viii (2003), 59–71, at pp. 63–4.
[34] Prochaska, 'George V', pp. 37–8.

of Wales. Heather Jones has noted in her work on the monarchy's role in the war years that it was through the personality and image of Edward that the more egalitarian relationship between royalty, the media and the public came of age. The king was feted by the press when he allowed his eldest son to join Sir John French's staff on the Western Front at the end of 1914; and, although the prince was prevented from actually fighting against the enemy, he spent four years either engaged in the same hard, physical work as other servicemen or on inspections and touring trenches as his father's surrogate.[35] Media coverage of the prince's wartime activities notably highlighted the personal interest that he took in the lives and welfare of his fellow soldiers, with news reporters emphasizing how, through the horizontal bonds of military comradeship, he became a symbol of the monarchy's increasingly democratic relationship with its British and imperial subjects.

The idea that the war had a class-levelling effect in the way it brought monarchy and people together under unique circumstances was a powerful one and was carried forward into the 1920s, when, again as his father's representative, the prince of Wales toured the dominions and colonies to acknowledge their contribution and sacrifices as part of the war effort. As Frank Mort has discussed, it was during these trips that Edward established himself as a world-famous figure and consolidated his constitutional authority as a future king and the personal link that connected Britain to its far-flung empire (Figure 0.2).[36] While touring the dominions he was accompanied by journalists and film crews who presented him to media audiences back home as a democratic prince: he was handsome, smiling and willing to engage in close physical contact with the ordinary people he met. His military service earned him a special place in the lives of veterans and bereaved families in the years after 1918; and the relationships he worked to forge with these constituencies while on his imperial tours were given personal meaning through the media coverage of his informal interactions with them.[37] This was also the case back home in Britain, where Edward joined his parents and siblings in promoting and publicizing the many civic and philanthropic ventures led by the House of Windsor after the war, which aimed to foster social cohesion and deepen the royalist sympathies of the proletariat through patronage of working-class culture and the targeted alleviation of the economic hardships that afflicted the masses in the 1920s and early 1930s.[38]

---

[35] Jones, 'Prince in the trenches', pp. 233–41; Prochaska, *Royal Bounty*, pp. 179–81.

[36] F. Mort, 'On tour with the prince: monarchy: imperial politics and publicity in the prince of Wales's dominion tours 1919–20', *Twentieth Century British Hist.*, xxix (2018), 25–57.

[37] Mort, 'On tour with the prince', pp. 39–43.

[38] Prochaska, *Royal Bounty*, pp. 190–4; Zweiniger-Bargielowska, 'Keep fit', pp. 113–5.

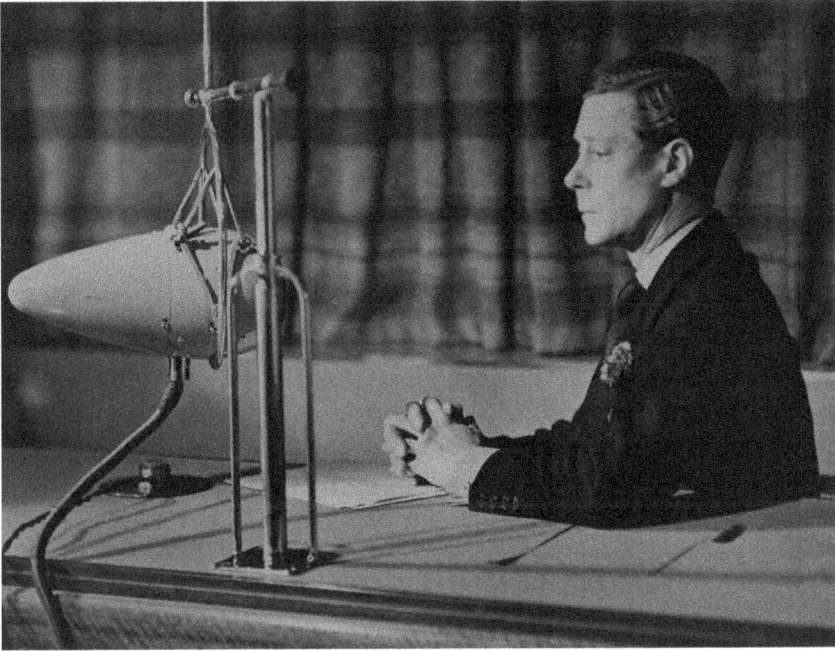

Figure 0.2. King Edward VIII as prince of Wales, April 1935
(NPG x27929). © National Portrait Gallery, London.

The legacy of the First World War also loomed large as part of George V's reputation in the years after the conflict, with his titular positions as commander-in-chief of the armed forces and supreme governor of the Church of England invested with new, powerful symbolism in a period marked by mass mourning and the commemoration of the war dead.[39] In his first years on the throne the king readily championed the Christian moral values that he had absorbed as a young Victorian man, but these took on added meaning as a result of the war. The nineteenth-century ideals of duty and self-sacrifice were of particular importance to a world that sought to understand and justify the death and destruction wrought by more than four years of conflict. As Philip Williamson has noted, the royal family spoke publicly and with increasing zeal of the 'service' they performed on behalf of their subjects as they embarked on the new activities that redefined their official roles after 1918.[40] This concept of royal service was underpinned by the idea of reciprocity: it was performed in acknowledgement of the sacrifices made by the people who had contributed to the war effort; and

---

[39] Jones, 'Nature of kingship', pp. 206–11.
[40] Williamson, 'Monarchy and public values', pp. 252–5.

was performed for their benefit now in the belief it would meet with their admiration and set a good example to the public, instructing them in the kinds of duty that they, as political citizens, also owed society.

At the same time as this public language of royal duty was taking root, the king worked to promote Christian moral values by staging the marriages of his children Princess Mary and the duke of York as national celebrations in 1922 and 1923 respectively. According to his biographers, George V was, however, troubled by the fact that his eldest son and heir, the prince of Wales, showed no such inclination to settle down; and the king's fears about the impending succession escalated after he almost died of septicaemia in the winter of 1928/29.[41] Despite the broad royalist consensus that seems to have defined British political life in the early 1930s, there were grave doubts at court and in official circles about Edward's suitability as future king.[42] Unlike his father he was not a pious man and could even be openly disdainful of religious ceremony, which infuriated the clergy.[43] More problematical still was the fact that since the end of the war the prince had, in his almost constant pursuit of the fast life, engaged in a series of reckless love affairs with married women.[44] Although he would inherit the title of supreme governor of the Church of England on becoming king, it was clear to those who knew him personally that he lacked the moral scruples required of the 'defender of the faith', given the Church's strict teachings on the indissolubility of marriage. When George V finally died on 20 January 1936 and the prince succeeded to the throne as Edward VIII, he did so as an unmarried forty-one-year-old and was ill-equipped to lead a dynasty which, as we shall see, had worked extremely hard in the early 1930s to present itself as a unifying symbol of Christian family life.

Importantly for the new king, his moral shortcomings were initially kept hidden from his subjects by a tight-lipped elite who had admired his father and who initially hoped that Edward would grow into his new role.[45] Ultimately, though, the gentlemanly codes of discretion that defined upper-class society could not withstand the pressures of the modern media exposé and, when it was finally announced less than eleven months into his reign that the king was in a relationship with an American woman called Wallis Simpson, who had already been married to two other men, both of whom were still alive, the repressive silence that had for so long guarded the crown against public criticism was instead filled with an overwhelming howl of

[41] K. Rose, *King George V* (London, 1983), pp. 308–9, 355–8.
[42] P. Ziegler, *King Edward VIII* (London, 2012), pp. 193–5.
[43] Williamson, 'Monarchy and public values', p. 250.
[44] McKibbin, *Classes and Cultures*, p. 4.
[45] Ziegler, *King Edward VIII*, pp. 281, 287.

shock, outrage and disbelief.[46] In the days that followed many of Edward's subjects wrote to him to demand that he give up the woman he loved in order to carry out his duties as king, but he opted instead to renounce the throne and marry her and was encouraged to follow his heart by other members of the public who wrote to tell him that he deserved personal happiness.[47] In order to understand the range of public responses to the events of December 1936, we need to consider the way that new kinds of journalism shaped how members of the royal family became celebrities after 1918 and the way new media technologies combined with the rise of popular cultures of domesticity and self-fulfilment to transform the emotional dimensions of modern British society. It is to these that we must now turn in order to contextualize the major historical shifts at the heart of *The Family Firm*.

Fame, family and emotion in mid twentieth-century Britain

As we have seen, the monarchy was imbued with a complex assortment of meanings in the mid 1930s: the king was the symbolic leader of a burgeoning constitutional democracy and was publicly elevated as the safeguard of the nation's political freedoms; he was the figurehead that held together an empire in a period marked by the loosening of the formal political bonds that had enabled the British government to exert control over the colonies and dominions; he and his family were at the centre of the nation's philanthropic and civic cultures; and, in promoting Christianity's teachings on marriage, service and duty, the House of Windsor had become the head of the country's morality. However, the royal family were also modern celebrities who owed their fame both to the new kinds of media exposure engineered by reporters and news editors intent on commodifying royal life for public consumption and to courtiers who discerned value in popularizing the royal personalities who made up the House of Windsor. The leading figure here was Edward, prince of Wales, who, in the years before his accession and abdication, was turned into a celebrity through the media coverage of his activities, both as the jet-setting tourist of empire and as a regular on London's fashionable nightclub scene.[48] Although part of his celebrity lay in the fact that, as heir to the throne, he was a symbol of national and imperial continuity, he was also Britain's answer to the

---

[46] Ziegler, *King Edward VIII*, pp. 308–10.

[47] Mort, 'Love in a cold climate', pp. 41–53.

[48] Mort, 'On tour with the prince'; L. N. Mayhall, 'The prince of Wales *versus* Clark Gable: anglophone celebrity and citizenship between the wars', *Cult. and Soc. Hist.*, iv (2007), 529–43.

Hollywood stars of the 1920s. A new kind of media exposure that grew out of the human-interest journalism of the early twentieth century worked to reveal, with increasing levels of intensity, the private man behind the royal public image. The result was that Edward became one of the best-known figures in the English-speaking world, with the press following his every move and at times relentlessly pursuing him for exclusive stories or photographs that would further illuminate his personality.[49]

This emphasis on royal revelation accorded with a significant shift in Britain's celebrity culture in the 1920s. Reporters and media audiences desired more intimate access to the famous because they had become accustomed to the idea that a celebrity's *public* image was just that – a manufactured fantasy created for public consumption – as opposed to an individual's 'real' self, which was deemed to exist only in private. Given how human-interest journalists regularly hounded their famous subjects for 'scoops', many celebrities found it expedient to self-expose by providing reporters and photographers with titbit stories and scenes from their personal lives which they hoped would satisfy the public's appetite for information about their private selves. Self-exposure therefore often involved celebrities revealing glimpses of their home lives and personal relationships to public view in an attempt outwardly to project what appeared to be more intimate and more 'authentic' information about themselves.[50]

The significance of this celebrity culture for the House of Windsor was that it encouraged the British public to forge para-social (one-way) emotional relationships with their royal rulers. For example, having access to information about the prince of Wales's private life, such as the fact that he enjoyed dancing with glamorous women, drinking cocktails and driving fast cars, made him seem more affable and relatable. Indeed, the close sense of proximity that developed between Edward and his subjects-turned-fans due to this kind of media coverage ensured that many felt compelled to write to him in highly personal terms at the time of his abdication.[51] However, it was the home lives of Edward's closest relatives that became essential to the way the monarchy's media image was projected to the British public

---

[49] Mort, 'On tour with the prince', pp. 46–55; Mayhall, 'The prince of Wales', pp. 532–40.

[50] C. L. Ponce de Leon, *Self-Exposure: Human-Interest Journalism and the Emergence of Celebrity in America, 1890–1940* (London, 2002), pp. 40–1; L. Beers, 'A model MP? Ellen Wilkinson, gender, politics and celebrity culture in interwar Britain', *Cult. and Soc. Hist.*, x (2013), 231–50, at pp. 238–41; E. Owens, 'The changing media representation of T. E. Lawrence and celebrity culture in Britain, 1919–1935', *Cult. and Soc. Hist.*, xii (2015), 465–88. On 'authenticity', see P. Summerfield, *Histories of the Self: Personal Narratives and Historical Practice* (London, 2019), pp. 168–72.

[51] Mort, 'Love in a cold climate', pp. 39–42.

from the early 1930s onwards. The royal household worked with its allies to elevate a family-centred vision of the House of Windsor that presented the royals as celebrities who were defined by their personal lives and domestic aspirations. As we have seen, there were precedents for this kind of public image that stretched back almost a century; and the virtuous version of bourgeois domesticity projected by Queen Victoria and Prince Albert was notably given a new lease of life in the 1920s when George V and his family posed for photographic portraits that were published by newspapers and mass-produced as souvenirs in order to foster emotional bonds between the viewer and the royal person(s) on display – a development that was mirrored in the appearance of a spate of official and unofficial royal biographies that provided readers with behind-the-scenes (but not always authentic) glimpses of life at court.[52]

However, as historians Laura King and Claire Langhamer have shown, there emerged a new, popular culture of love and domesticity in 1930s Britain, where romance, family and home life became more intrinsic to ordinary people's identities and desires.[53] This popular culture was distinguished by an increased emphasis on personal intimacy, emotional expression and the belief that self-fulfilment lay in the private domestic setting. Although this culture did not take on a truly national character until after the Second World War, the transformation of the House of Windsor's public image between the 1930s and 1950s mirrored its development, with royal men, women and children presented by officials and the media in more familial, relatable ways. Furthermore, as *The Family Firm* demonstrates, it is clear that royal stage-managers elevated the monarchy's domesticity as a focal point for popular emotional identification in a deliberate attempt to unite the British nation around the crown in a period marked by considerable social and political change.

It is also clear that the model of Christian family life promoted by the House of Windsor in this period was intended to set an example

---

[52] A. Schwarzenbach, 'Royal photographs: emotions for the people', *Contemporary European Hist.*, xiii (2004), pp. 255–80; Houlbrook, *Prince of Tricksters*, pp. 223–53.

[53] L. King, *Family Men: Fatherhood and Masculinity in Britain, 1914–1960* (Oxford, 2015), pp. 5–7; C. Langhamer, *The English in Love: the Intimate Story of an Emotional Revolution* (Oxford, 2013), pp. 6–7. See also M. Francis, *The Flyer: British Culture and the Royal Air Force 1939–1945* (Oxford, 2008); S. Szreter and K. Fisher, *Sex Before the Sexual Revolution: Intimate Life in England, 1918–1963* (Cambridge, 2010), p. 29; J. Lewis, 'Marriage', in *Women in Twentieth-Century Britain*, ed. I. Zweiniger-Bargielowska (Harlow, 2001), pp. 69–85; L. Davidoff et al., *The Family Story: Blood, Contract, and Intimacy, 1830–1960* (London, 1999), p. 18; J. Finch and P. Summerfield, 'Social reconstruction and the emergence of companionate marriage, 1945–1959', in *Marriage, Domestic Life and Social Change: Writings for Jacqueline Burgoyne*, ed. D. Clark (London, 1991), pp. 7–32.

to the public. With the exception of Edward VIII's aberration, royal domesticity provided a high moral standard that members of the public were encouraged to emulate at a time when religious and political leaders were worrying about the shape of British households.[54] As this book shows, courtiers and the media worked with the Church of England to promote Christian family life as an intrinsic part of the monarchy's public image and, in doing so, helped to popularize older religious symbols and values that would continue to shape moral attitudes well into the post-war period. Callum Brown has argued in his history of secularization in Britain that the early 1960s witnessed the sudden collapse of a Christian belief-system that had governed personal identities up until then and its replacement with a secular individualism that prized self-fulfilment ahead of everything else.[55] However, as Edward VIII's abdication made clear, as far back as the 1930s new concepts of self-fulfilment that emphasized the importance of romantic love to one's personal happiness had existed in uneasy tension with the kinds of self-denial at the heart of religious teaching. The 1936 constitutional crisis was not just a battle between a king and his ministers over who had the right to choose the monarch's wife and queen: it also witnessed a traditional royal moral code, which only tolerated love within the confines of Christian marriage, clash with a new, emotional culture that celebrated self-realization and individual happiness through the pursuit of romance, in whatever form it might take.[56]

It is also the case that the royal language of public service and self-sacrifice, so integral to George V's later reign, was at odds with the new culture of self-fulfilment. As *The Family Firm* suggests, what steadily emerged in the years from the early 1930s to the early 1950s was the idea that the royal family wished to lead emotionally enriched private lives but that their onerous public roles acted to circumscribe their individual freedom and happiness. This idea took on greater meaning with the dramatic events of December 1936, when one king gave up his 'heavy burden of responsibility' in order to marry the woman he loved and another, his younger brother, reluctantly took up the mantle in his place.[57] The increasing value that British society attached to notions of individualism and self-fulfilment thus helped to engender public sympathy for a royal family who often seemed unable

[54] P. Thane and T. Evans, *Sinners? Scroungers? Saints? Unmarried Motherhood in Twentieth-Century England* (Oxford, 2012), pp. 29–106.

[55] C. Brown, *The Death of Christian Britain: Understanding Secularisation, 1800–2000* (London, 2009), pp. 6–8.

[56] Mort, 'Love in a cold climate', pp. 34, 47–8.

[57] Edward VIII used this phrase in his abdication broadcast, which he delivered on the evening of 11 Dec. 1936 (Ziegler, *King Edward VIII*, pp. 331–3).

to realize their personal desires because of their outward commitment to religious concepts of self-sacrifice and public duty that dated back to the Victorian period.

While the idea of royal suffering may well have reflected the realities of life at court, it is clear that the royal household deliberately promoted a narrative of royal hardship in order to generate popular emotional identification with the protagonists of the House of Windsor. Just as royal officials worked to create a public image of the monarchy that highlighted the happy feelings experienced by the royal family during festive occasions like weddings, jubilees and coronations, so, too, were they responsible for creating an image that emphasized the unhappiness which could accompany life in the public eye or attended other, less joyous family events like funerals. When we think about the way royal feelings were projected via the media to the public, we can look to recent scholarship on the history of the emotions to make sense of the actions of royal stage-managers and the reactions of the media audiences on the receiving end of those royal feelings. *The Family Firm* builds on Joe Perry's study of the 'affective' dimensions of life in Nazi Germany by using three key concepts from the history of the emotions in order to explore the emotional economy that connected royal stage-managers, the media and the British population.[58] The first of these is the idea that although emotions are physiological phenomena expressed and experienced by human bodies, they are also socio-cultural constructs that are specific to time and place. An example relevant to this book, one which has already received some attention here, is love: the way love was expressed and experienced in twentieth-century Britain was constantly changing and was different to the way love was expressed and experienced by other societies at different stages of their development.[59] Notably, the emotion at the heart of the royal celebrity culture that emerged in Britain in the 1920s and 1930s was empathy, with media audiences *identifying* with the feelings of the royal family – just as they identified with the feelings of other famous people – despite the fact that they did not know these celebrities in reality and were never likely to do so. The vertical displacement of emotion onto public figures is something we take for granted in the twenty-first

---

[58] J. Perry, 'Christmas as Nazi holiday: colonising the Christmas mood', in *Life and Times in Nazi Germany*, ed. L. Pine (London, 2016), pp. 263–89.

[59] Langhamer, *The English in Love*, p. 4; J. Plamper, *The History of Emotions: an Introduction* (Oxford, 2015); S. J. Matt, 'Current emotion research in history: or, doing history from the inside out', *Emotion Rev.*, iii (2011), 117–24; W. M. Reddy, 'The rule of love: the history of Western romantic love in comparative perspective', in *New Dangerous Liaisons: Discourses on Europe and Love in the Twentieth Century*, ed. L. Passerini, L. Ellena and A. C. T. Geppert (Oxford, 2010), pp. 33–57.

century, but it is the fundamental element of a modern celebrity culture which has developed over more than three centuries and which, due to the new kinds of media exposure that emerged between the wars, restructured the relationship between the public and their royal rulers.[60]

The second idea from the history of the emotions applicable here relates to 'emotional regimes'.[61] In the role of emotional engineers, the royal household and its allies projected royal feelings in order to elicit specific emotional responses from the public. The palace's emotional regime witnessed the leading figures who made up the House of Windsor purposely displaying or vocalizing some of those aforementioned emotions – joy, sadness, love and grief – and this formed part of a public relations strategy intended to encourage ordinary British people to empathize with the royal family, thus strengthening the emotional bonds that linked them to the monarchy. Older notions of royalism were thus reconceptualized as part of more direct and more personal (imagined) relationships between British subjects and royalty. However, though royal stage-managers tried to create a top-down system of feeling that would engender loyalty to the crown through new kinds of emotional identification, their strategies were not always successful. Some members of the public were simply not affected by the new kinds of emotion mobilized by the royal family; others, meanwhile, could empathize with the emotions expressed by the personalities of the House of Windsor but at the same time experienced other feelings – such as anger or jealousy – because they took issue with royal privilege, disingenuousness or specific weaknesses.[62] As The Family Firm suggests, sometimes negative feelings won out in these emotional contests and this could translate into a deeper criticism of the monarchy – as was the case at the time of Edward VIII's abdication and George VI's succession. However, it does seem that for the most part the projection of royal emotions evoked positive responses from many members of the public, who, through the empathetic relationships they forged with the House of Windsor, came loyally to conform to the royal status quo.

---

[60] D. Giles, *Illusions of Immortality: a Psychology of Fame and Celebrity* (Basingstoke, 2000), pp. 71–4; F. Inglis, *A Short History of Celebrity* (Oxford, 2010); S. Morgan, 'Celebrity: academic "pseudo-event" or a useful concept for historians?', *Cult. and Soc. Hist.*, viii (2011), 95–114.

[61] W. M. Reddy, *The Navigation of Feeling: a Framework for the History of Emotions* (Cambridge, 2001).

[62] For the competing nature of feelings in a late twentieth-century context, see M. Billig, *Talking of the Royal Family* (London, 1992), pp. 128–30; A. Olechnowicz, '"A jealous hatred": royal popularity and social inequality', in Olechnowicz, *Monarchy and the British Nation*, pp. 280–314; J. Thomas, 'Beneath the mourning veil: Mass-Observation and the death of Diana', pp. 8–9 <http://www.massobs.org.uk/images/occasional_papers/no12_thomas.pdf> [accessed 12 Oct. 2018].

Emotional engineering was not unique to Britain. Nazi leaders sought to strengthen the hold that the Third Reich had over hearts and minds through similar kinds of manipulation of the German people's feelings.[63] Indeed, the period between the wars was a key turning point in many advanced industrial nations because new types of media enabled wide-scale emotional reprogramming from above. This brings us to the third concept from the history of the emotions which is used throughout *The Family Firm* with the aim of bridging the divide that separates the fields of mass media and affect. Barbara Rosenwein's idea of 'emotional communities' – that is, social groups which have, across time, been linked together by shared systems of feeling – can be seen on a national scale in modern mass-communication societies like Britain in the mid twentieth century.[64] Whereas Rosenwein's work focuses on medieval and early modern communities that were linked together through collective cultures of emotion that determined what feelings were expressed and experienced in these societies, new kinds of media like radio, sound newsreels and television conveyed stories about the royal family and their feelings in more immediate and vivid ways which transformed how the public empathized with royalty. Modern mass communication has, therefore, enabled the formation of what we might term *national* emotional communities, in which publics have been encouraged to share in (and conform to) a dominant system of feeling around the focal point of national events or well-known individuals like royalty. As already noted, *The Family Firm* shows that some members of the public did not feel part of, or actively resisted becoming part of, an emotional community linked around the centrepiece of the monarchy. However, as we shall see, with the start of live broadcasting British media audiences were invited to partake in royal events as part of a national collective: radio, and later television, created a heightened sense of temporal simultaneity (the sharing of time among a people) that worked to unite audiences as they imagined themselves forming part of a national emotional community knit together through the empathetic bonds they forged with the family monarchy. This kind of 'affective integration' was a distinctly modern process that not only transformed how people saw themselves in relation to the House of Windsor but also changed how they conceived of their identities in relation to the wider British nation.[65]

[63] As with the House of Windsor, the Nazis' emotional engineering met with mixed results (Perry, 'Christmas as Nazi holiday', pp. 265–6).

[64] B. Rosenwein, 'Problems and methods in the history of emotions', *Passions in Context*, i (2010), 1–32. J. Plamper noted in his recent historiographical overview of the history of emotions that very little research has been conducted on the way 'affect' and 'feeling' have been transformed by mass media in the context of the modern nation (Plamper, *History of Emotions*, pp. 285–7, 293–4).

[65] For the term 'affective integration', see Perry, 'Christmas as Nazi Holiday', p. 264.

Sources and methodology

Historians have sometimes presented George V as a sovereign who was personally averse to the press, but his actions throughout his reign suggest otherwise.[66] He oversaw the development of a mass media monarchy that relied on the new channels of publicity to convey to the British public its relevance to the modern world. Bagehot wrote of the Victorian royal family that '[t]o be invisible is to be forgotten. To be a symbol, and an effective symbol, you must be vividly and often seen'.[67] George V and his courtiers came to appreciate the validity of this statement during a long twenty-six-year reign, which not only witnessed the birth of the public relations profession in Britain but also the interconnected rise of a political culture in which politicians had to carefully manage their media images in order to have successful careers – a fact that seems initially to have been lost on Sir Stafford Cripps.[68] In presenting the first major analysis of the popular projection and reception of the monarchy's media image from the last years of George V's life to the start of his granddaughter's reign in 1953, *The Family Firm* examines how a succession of royal weddings, coronations and broadcasts were staged to familiarize the public with the lives and feelings of the individual royals who made up the House of Windsor. These events were key moments when palace, Church and media negotiated the monarchy's publicity strategy. Indeed, the first major body of sources *The Family Firm* uses are official documents which reveal, through confidential discussions between the various royal stage-managers, how courtiers sought to balance the growing demands of media audiences, who desired a more intimate knowledge of their rulers, with the need for deferential publicity that would enhance the crown's moral authority in society. Faced with a human-interest news culture that aimed to bring the royals closer to readers, listeners and viewers, the palace regularly had to fight to maintain the monarchy's dignity by resisting coverage that it deemed too informal or irreverent.

The Royal Archives provide access to files that illuminate how courtiers and members of the House of Windsor worked to stage royal family life for the audiences of mass media. Notably, these documents reveal a professionalization in the crown's public relations strategy across the period

---

[66] McKibbin, *Classes and Cultures*, pp. 8–9.

[67] *The Collected Works of Walter Bagehot*, ed. Norman St John-Stevas (15 vols., London, 1965–86), v. 419, as quoted in Bogdanor, *Monarchy and the Constitution*, p. 30.

[68] S. Anthony, *Public Relations and the Making of Modern Britain: Stephen Tallents and the Birth of a Progressive Media Profession* (Manchester, 2012), pp. 65–8; A. Taylor, 'Speaking to democracy: the Conservative party and mass opinion from the 1920s to the 1950s', in *Mass Conservatism: the Conservatives and the Public since the 1880s*, ed. S. Ball and I. Holliday (London, 2002), pp. 78–99.

in question. The position of palace press secretary was instituted in 1918, officially relinquished in 1931 and then revived in 1944.[69] However, it is clear that this post never really fell into abeyance. Rather, after 1931 there was a strengthening of the relationship that linked courtiers to sections of the media as they orchestrated royal family events for the public; and there was also a consolidation of the emotional language that members of the House of Windsor used to communicate with their subjects. Files in the Royal Archives also reveal how pressures exerted on the palace by government propagandists during the Second World War, along with the social upheaval created by the conflict, accelerated the process of professionalization, with courtiers taking on more active roles in managing the monarchy's relationship with the media in order to better promote the royal family's public image. The most important officials involved in this process in the years from 1932 to 1953 were Sir Clive Wigram, Sir Alexander Hardinge and Sir Alan Lascelles. These men each held in succession the position of principal private secretary to the monarch and all were influenced by Wigram's predecessor, Sir Arthur Bigge, also known as Lord Stamfordham, who had overseen George V's public relations strategy until his death while in office in 1931.[70] Chapter 4 uses Lascelles's published diaries, which, while often taciturn and sometimes unreliable, help to illuminate the courtier's role in managing the monarchy's media strategy from 1939 to 1945. His important influence at this time led to the restoration of the palace's press office as part of a wider wartime strategy to tighten the controls that courtiers exercised over publicity; and, throughout his career in royal service, he proved committed to strengthening the monarchy's position at the heart of the British nation, remaining in post to see Elizabeth II crowned before retiring from his royal duties in 1953 (Figure 0.3).[71]

The material from the Royal Archives examined in *The Family Firm* is rich but limited in terms of the researcher's rights of access. Documents relating to Elizabeth II's reign and early life are often judged by archivists to be too sensitive for historical research or have not yet been officially

[69] McKibbin, *Classes and Cultures*, p. 8.

[70] J. Gore, 'Wigram, Clive, 1873–1960', in *Royal Lives: Portraits of the Past Royals by Those in the Know*, ed. F. Prochaska (Oxford, 2002), pp. 557–9; F. Prochaska, 'Wigram, Clive, first Baron Wigram', in *ODNB* <https://doi.org/10.1093/ref:odnb/36890> [accessed 12 Oct. 2018]. Each of these men served as assistant private secretary to the monarch before taking up the position of principal private secretary. For a discussion of the role that courtiers played in the royal household, see D. Cannadine, 'From biography to history: writing the modern British monarchy', *Hist. Research*, lxxvii (2004), 289–312, at pp. 294–6.

[71] M. Maclagan, 'Alan Frederick Lascelles', in Prochaska, *Royal Lives*, pp. 570–2; *King's Counsellor: Abdication and War: the Diaries of Sir Alan Lascelles*, ed. D. Hart-Davis (London, 2006).

Figure 0.3. Sir Alan
Lascelles, October 1943
(NPG x169268). © National
Portrait Gallery, London.

deposited in the archive, so the later chapters of this book, which deal with the transformation of her media image as a princess and, later, as queen, have had to look further afield.[72] The BBC Written Archives Centre and the Church of England Record Centre provide historians with freer access to sources that document these institutions' links to the crown – although neither is entirely without restrictions.[73] *The Family Firm* examines communications sent by BBC editors and producers to palace officials, as well as incoming correspondence from courtiers, which reveal how both

[72] The Royal Archives do not maintain a catalogue of the Archives' holdings that is accessible to researchers. Instead, speculative requests to view material (often identified in the footnotes of royal biographers) have met with mixed results.

[73] The BBC Written Archives Centre exercises a vetting policy on all files related to the British monarchy. Many have already been opened up for research and are therefore freely accessible, but restrictions are now in place on files that have not been examined before, many of which relate to the post-1945 period. It is also the case that some sensitive documents relating to the Church's relationship with the crown have not yet been deposited in the archives of Lambeth Palace Library, or have been deliberately held back from researchers out of respect for the royal family.

parties sought to shape the monarchy's image. The Written Archives Centre also holds large files of internal production documents and memoranda that show how BBC broadcasters sought to project royal events in increasingly personal ways. Lambeth Palace Library, meanwhile, contains the papers of the archbishops of Canterbury, including those of Cosmo Gordon Lang and Geoffrey Francis Fisher. Lang is an important figure in the first half of this book because he played a significant role in developing the monarchy's family-centred public image from 1934 to the early 1940s. With his Anglo-Catholic background, he had a taste and talent for staging royal ritual and, working in tandem with George V, courtiers and other Church officials, he intensified the theatrical and spiritual elements of national royal events like weddings, jubilees and coronations.[74]

Lang acceded to the diocese of Canterbury in 1928 but before this, as archbishop of York, he had encouraged George V to embark on the first royal good-will tours of industrial Britain in 1912 in the belief that the monarch needed to spend more time among his poorest subjects, bridging class divisions by forsaking the pomp and splendour that usually attended royalty. With his strong belief in the monarchy's nation-building role, Lang became a trusted friend and spiritual counsellor to George V and later even occupied the small office within the royal household of lord high almoner. In time, the archbishop forged strong relationships with Queen Mary, George VI and his consort, Queen Elizabeth, too, and as a close ally of the throne worked with the palace in order to enhance the crown's symbolic moral role in society. Indeed, his commitment to upholding Christian family values saw him come into direct conflict with Edward VIII. Chapter 3 discusses how Lang fell out with the king and then conspired in his downfall at the time of the abdication crisis – a move that irreparably damaged the archbishop's public standing (Figure 0.4).[75]

While Geoffrey Fisher was not as influential as Lang, he was Alan Lascelles's and George VI's first choice for the position of archbishop of Canterbury after William Temple suddenly died in 1944 after only two years in office.[76] Like Lang, Fisher valued the moral symbolism of royal family life and made this felt through his involvement in the 1947 royal wedding and the 1953 coronation (Figure 0.5). Notably, documents from Westminster Abbey Library have also made it possible to examine how a coterie of other churchmen took on active roles in staging royal events for the British public

---

[74] A. Wilkinson, 'Lang, (William) Cosmo Gordon, Baron Lang of Lambeth', in *ODNB* <https://doi.org/10.1093/ref:odnb/34398> [accessed 12 Oct. 2018].

[75] R. Beaken, *Cosmo Lang: Archbishop in War and Crisis* (London, 2012), pp. 66–142.

[76] Hart-Davis, *King's Counsellor*, pp. 266–8.

Figure 0.4. Archbishop of Canterbury, Cosmo Lang (NPG x90191). © National Portrait Gallery, London.

Figure 0.5. Archbishop of Canterbury, Geoffrey Fisher (NPG x12227). © National Portrait Gallery, London.

and in managing the media's access to the 'nation's shrine'.[77] The final body
of official sources *The Family Firm* uses are government documents located
in The National Archives, Kew, which reveal how cabinet ministers and
civil servants worked with palace officials – sometimes in tandem and at
other times in tension – to project the royal family's public image.

The second main group of sources examined here are mass media
texts, including 'popular' and 'quality' national newspapers, the five main
newsreels from the period and the actual programmes broadcast by the
BBC on wireless and television. In comparison with their counterparts
in broadcasting and film, newspaper journalists and photographers were
usually the most intrepid when it came to reporting on royal family life.
This was partly due to the fact that it was easier for the curious journalist
or candid photographer – unencumbered by large pieces of technical
equipment – to spy on or even infiltrate life at court in order to provide
newspaper readers with more intimate access to the House of Windsor. This
kind of unofficial coverage could disrupt the otherwise stable public image
of the family monarchy, as was the case when Edward VIII was secretly
photographed holidaying with Wallis Simpson on the Mediterranean
coast in summer 1936, an incident that led to an eruption of international
speculation about the couple's relationship in the months before the
news broke in Britain.[78] However, the press and, in particular, popular
newspapers also sought greater access to the private lives of the House
of Windsor in these years because of the competitive news environment:
different newspapers not only vied with each other for exclusive 'scoops'
but also with newsreels and, from the early 1920s, the BBC, with film and
radio offering new kinds of access to the royal family.[79] Throughout the
period in question the press's impulse towards revelation existed in uneasy
tension with the need to maintain the monarchy's dignified public image:
if a journalist or editor overstepped the mark, he or she could be prevented
from covering future royal events. It was also the case that the elites who
controlled most of Britain's newspaper industry believed the monarchy was
a force for good. Even political rebels like the press barons Lord Northcliffe,
Lord Rothermere and the mischievous Lord Beaverbrook, each of whom
exercised significant power over the reading public between the wars and

---

[77] R. Jenkyns, *Westminster Abbey: a Thousand Years of National Pageantry* (London, 2011),
p. 148.
[78] R. Linkof, '"The photographic attack on his royal highness": the prince of Wales, Wallis
Simpson and the prehistory of the paparazzi', *Photography and Culture*, iv (2011), 277–92; N.
Hiley, 'The candid camera of the Edwardian tabloids', *History Today*, xliii (1993), 16–22.
[79] A. Bingham, *Family Newspapers? Sex, Private Life and the British Popular Press, 1918–
1978* (Oxford, 2009), pp. 239–44; Mort, 'Love in a cold climate', pp. 56–7.

who regularly challenged the policies of the nation's elected representatives, could agree that the crown was an esteemed institution that played an important role in uniting Britain and the empire at a time of widespread change.[80]

As Adrian Bingham has noted in his work on the popular press, the abdication crisis was a turning-point in the relationship between the monarchy and some of Britain's newspapers. When it was finally announced in early December 1936 that Edward VIII was in love with a married woman, the public realized that the couple's affair had been deliberately concealed from them for months by deferential Fleet Street journalists and newspaper editors who had not wanted to tarnish the crown's reputation with scandalous revelations. On recognizing they had lost the trust of their readers, some newspapers began to scrutinize the private lives of the royal family more closely, often adopting a more critical perspective on royal matters in order to re-establish public confidence in the role of the press as purveyors of truth.[81] Although the official censorship that limited the dissemination of factual information during the Second World War also strained the relationship between newspapers and the public, it is clear there was a shift towards more informal and often more irreverent kinds of royal news coverage after 1936. *The Family Firm* examines this shift and the way it mirrored a wider decline in deference among some sections of the press, which worked harder to hold the social elite to account and to sound out the diverse range of opinions of readers on the royal family. However, despite the fact that journalists were more outspoken when it came to the House of Windsor after the abdication, it is notable that the majority of newspapers continued to project royal domestic life as a national rallying point for collective emotion and unity.

The interwar years witnessed the circulation wars of the major Fleet Street dailies, which had a combined readership of more than ten million by the mid 1930s. The sample of popular and quality titles examined in *The Family Firm* reflects a wide spectrum of class and political affiliations and includes all the market-leading dailies: the *Daily Express*, *Daily Mail*, *Daily Mirror*, *News Chronicle* and the left-wing *Daily Herald*, the latter being the first to achieve a circulation of more than two million in 1932.[82] The readership of

---

[80] The belief of the press barons in the crown's sacrosanct character was evident in the gentleman's agreement arranged by Rothermere and Beaverbook at the request of Edward VIII that ensured no British newspapers revealed the king's relationship with Wallis Simpson to the public until they were eventually forced to break cover on 2 Dec. 1936.

[81] Bingham, *Family Newspapers?*, pp. 241–50.

[82] Bingham, *Family Newspapers?*, p. 19. The following 17 daily and weekly national newspapers were sampled as primary sources: *Daily Express*, *Daily Herald*, *Daily Mail*, *Daily*

these popular titles was ten times greater than that shared by the quality newspapers from the period, some of which are used here, including *The Times*, the *Daily Telegraph* and the *Manchester Guardian*. By 1940, over 80 per cent of all British families read one of the popular London dailies and this figure continued to rise after the war, with the *Daily Mirror* and Sunday *News of the World* favourites among the public.[83] In the interests of balance, *The Family Firm* also examines the only anti-royal paper from this period, the communist *Daily Worker*, which, while representing a small minority's political interests, took a leading role in opposing royal events in the inter- and early post-war periods.[84]

The royal family quickly became a mainstay of the newsreels following their arrival in the early 1910s: pre-planned royal events – be they ceremonial or more informal – made for easy filming and good watching. And, from 1917 onwards, newsreel film crews found that the royals were increasingly forthcoming as subjects: the palace saw clear potential in using the new medium to publicize the House of Windsor's official activities at home and abroad.[85] The filmic focus on the monarchy also accorded with the newsreel companies' policy of projecting what was an essentially conservative vision of Britain, which celebrated its national institutions in order to promote

---

Mirror, Daily Sketch, Daily Telegraph, Daily Worker, Manchester Guardian, News Chronicle, News of the World, Reynolds News, Sunday Express, Sunday Pictorial, Sunday Times, The Observer, The People, The Times. On sampling newspapers and British press culture, see A. Bingham, *Gender, Modernity, and the Popular Press in Inter-War Britain* (Oxford, 2004), pp. 12–5.

[83] Bingham, *Gender*, pp. 8–15; Bingham, *Family Newspapers?*, pp. 19–22; L. Beers, *Your Britain: Media and the Making of the Labour Party* (Cambridge, Mass., 2010), pp. 18–21.

[84] This author's research of newspapers initially consisted of targeted searches of digital newspaper archives; this subsequently informed the research conducted in the British Library's Newsroom. The main limitation of this study of media texts is that sources from the Celtic nations have not been systematically analysed. Rather, the focus has been on self-professed 'national' media texts: the Fleet Street press, BBC radio and television and the 5 major British newsreels. The absence of regional media forms is important because, as Bingham has discussed in relation to Scottish newspaper readers, the Celtic nations have at times proved resistant to London-based media, opting instead for regional sources of information. He has noted that, in 1935, 43% of the Scottish population purchased a Fleet Street daily, while 60% bought Scottish morning papers (Bingham, *Family Newspapers?*, p. 17). Although parts of this book examine how national media organizations mobilized an inclusive language of 'Britishness' in reports on the monarchy, further research needs to be devoted to analysing how regional media presented royal events and personalities. This research could productively explore whether these localized representations conflicted or complemented the public image of the royal family disseminated by the national media; it could also question to what extent these local images were regionally tailored to appeal to communities in the Celtic nations.

[85] McKernan, 'The finest cinema performers', pp. 59–71.

public order and prop up the socio-political hierarchy.[86] The propaganda value of newsreels was enhanced when sound entered the cinema in the late 1920s, changing how audiences experienced film.[87] Moving images of the royals undertaking visits to different parts of the country, embarking on tours to the empire or Commonwealth, delivering speeches at official functions or going about what appeared to be their everyday lives now played to soundtracks and spoken commentaries that explained their activities to audiences who were also able to absorb the atmosphere of the crowds that gathered at royal events. *The Family Firm* shows that film crews and newsreel editors developed an advanced visual language, one which combined new kinds of close-up images with panoramas and an emphasis on the wide range of sounds captured during royal occasions, as part of a deliberate strategy to convey to viewers the centrality of royal family life to the nation. This was partly achieved through the manipulation of stock footage and audio recordings, but technological innovations also enabled filmmakers to present their audiences with more intimate scenes of the House of Windsor in these years.[88] Furthermore, the royal family were often complicit in this campaign to make the crown more visually accessible. Rosalind Brunt has discussed how, after Edward VIII's reign, the newsreels switched their attention to George VI's family, presenting cinemagoers with intimate scenes of idealized domesticity in order to stabilize the House of Windsor's reputation after the moral turbulence created by the abdication.[89] As we shall see, numerous royals engaged with cameramen in order to fashion their reputations and George VI in particular sought to exercise tighter control over his filmic image in order to shore up his authority as monarch (Figure 0.6).

The five newsreels that cinemas presented to audiences in these years were distributed (under changing titles) by Pathé, Movietone, Gaumont, Paramount and Universal. The film archives of all five companies have been

---

[86] T. Aldgate, 'The newsreels, public order, and the projection of Britain', in *Impacts and Influences: Essays on Media Power in the Twentieth Century*, ed. J. Curran, A. Smith and P. Wingate (London, 1987), pp. 145–56; J. Hulbert, 'Right-wing propaganda or reporting history?: the newsreels and the Suez crisis of 1956', *Film History*, xiv (2002), 261–81; G. Turvey, 'Ideological contradictions: the film topicals of the British and Colonial Kinematograph Company', *Early Popular Visual Culture*, v (2007), 41–56, at pp. 51–3.

[87] J. Richards, 'The monarchy and film, 1900–2006', in Olechnowicz, *Monarchy and the British Nation*, pp. 258–79, at p. 262.

[88] On issues of style and technology, see N. Pronay, 'The newsreels: the illusion of actuality', in *The Historian and Film*, ed. P. Smith (Cambridge, 1976), pp. 95–119.

[89] R. Brunt, 'The family firm restored: newsreel coverage of the British monarchy 1936–45', in *Nationalising Femininity: Culture, Sexuality and British Cinema in the Second World War*, ed. C. Gledhill and G. Swanson (Manchester, 1996), pp. 140–51.

Figure 0.6. King George
VI and his family at
Windsor, April 1940 (RCIN
2108362), Royal Collection
Trust / © Her Majesty
Queen Elizabeth II 2019.

digitized and are either free to access or available via online subscription services.[90] All the newsreels used in this book have been located using the British Universities Film and Video Council's 'News on Screen' search facility, which has equipped researchers with a comprehensive database and guide to all available digital newsreel footage.[91] There is little historical scholarship on the audiences who watched newsreels, but we know that they were an important source of information among working-class people in particular, who frequented cinemas more regularly than any other social demographic in this period. In 1934 the newsreels shared a weekly audience

[90] For a discussion of the implications of the digitization of newsreel archives, see N. Hiley and L. McKernan, 'Reconstructing the news: British newsreel documentation and the British universities newsreel project', *Film History*, xiii (2001), 185–99.
[91] British Universities Film and Video Council, 'News on Screen' <http://bufvc.ac.uk/newsonscreen/search> [accessed 27 Feb. 2019]. All the newsreels examined in this book are referred to using the original titles and dates assigned to them by the BUFVC's 'News on Screen' database.

in England, Scotland and Wales of more than 18.5 million and this figure had risen to twenty million by the end of the decade, where it remained well into the 1950s despite popular concerns arising during the war regarding the government's propagandistic efforts to control newsreel content.[92]

This book also maps an important shift towards a more intimate, family-centred image in the radio and television coverage of the monarchy after 1932. The voice of a reigning sovereign was first heard by media audiences when George V and his wife, Queen Mary, recorded for gramophone an 'Empire Day message to the boys and girls of the British empire' in 1923.[93] The following year, the BBC broadcast the monarch's voice live to listeners in Britain and across the world for the first time when he delivered his speech to those who had gathered for the opening of the Wembley empire exhibition – a new kind of public performance that he would go on to repeat for BBC radio audiences at thirteen separate official events over the next decade.[94] However, this media innovation was taken one step further in 1932 when the king broadcast his first live Christmas message from Sandringham, greeting listeners gathered around radio sets in their own homes in Britain and the empire. This was a key moment in the history of the monarchy's relationship with radio and helped to create a stronger, more direct link between George V and his subjects. Ina Zweiniger-Bargielowska is among a number of historians who have studied these changes and has suggested that radio brought people closer to royalty than ever before, encouraging engaged citizenship by creating a new democratic space in which listeners could affirm their loyalty to the crown by joining in nationally shared experiences.[95] *The Family Firm* builds on this idea by examining how the emotional register of the royal public language broadcast by radio changed in this period and how listeners' feelings were transformed by the experience of hearing royal speakers talking to them. It also shows

[92] Pronay, 'Newsreels', pp. 112–3; J. Richards and D. Sheridan, *Mass-Observation at the Movies* (London, 1987), pp. 381–400; L. McKernan, 'The newsreel audience', in *Researching Newsreels: Local, National, and Transnational Case Studies*, ed. C. Chambers, M. Jönsson and M. Vande Winkel (Basingstoke, 2018), pp. 35–50.

[93] *Encyclopaedia of Recorded Sound*, ed. F. Hoffman (2 vols., New York and London, 2005), i. 1880. The recording (#19072) can be heard at <https://www.youtube.com/watch?v=3JyC6qw2D_s> [accessed 1 Feb. 2018].

[94] Richards, 'Monarchy and film', p. 263.

[95] I. Zweiniger-Bargielowska, 'Royal death and living memorials: the funerals and commemoration of George V and George VI, 1936–52', *Hist. Research*, lxxxix (2015), 158–75. See also P. P. Scannell and D. Cardiff, *A Social History of British Broadcasting*, i. *1922–1939, Serving the Nation* (Oxford, 1991), 280–1; S. Potter, *Broadcasting Empire: the BBC and the British World, 1922–1970* (Oxford, 2012), pp. 59–64; Williamson, 'Monarchy and public values', pp. 225–8.

that the BBC, the palace and religious officials specially choreographed royal ceremonial events in order to enhance the intimacy of the images carried over the airwaves. In the context of the listening cultures that characterized the inter- and post-war periods, royal family life was staged more publicly *and* personally than ever before, encouraging listeners to conceive of themselves as a national community united around the House of Windsor. Similarly, while historians have previously suggested that the focus of the 1953 coronation celebrations was Britain's relationship with the Commonwealth, this book argues that the family image of Elizabeth II was just as, if not more, important to the television coverage of the occasion and that the BBC deliberately elevated royal domesticity as part of its broadcast in order to foster new kinds of emotional identification with the queen and her family among viewers.[96]

The physical and imagined properties of new mass media like radio and television radically changed the emotional dimensions of public and private life in the mid twentieth century. The popularity of the wireless in these decades helps to explain its wide-ranging effect in engendering affective integration around the focal point of the monarchy among the population. When the BBC became a corporation in 1926 there were more than two million licence holders registered. This number climbed steeply through the 1930s and historians have estimated that, by the beginning of the Second World War, there were more than nine million licence holders, which equated to a national listenership of at least thirty-four million out of a total population of roughly forty-eight million. These numbers – estimated to be even higher by other historians – continued to climb through the war years, with radio becoming an essential part of everyday life for most of the public as cheap wireless sets made the airwaves accessible to all.[97] This increase in popularity was also driven by a significant change in the types of programme produced by broadcasters. Although the BBC remained staunchly middle-class in its tone and world view, it tried to reach out to new audiences in the late 1920s and early 1930s, in particular women and working-class people, through new programming that placed entertainment ahead of the educative impulse that shaped much of its earlier output.[98] As a patriotic institution led by elite ex-servicemen like the first director general, Sir John

---

[96] W. Webster, *Englishness and Empire, 1939–1965* (Oxford, 2005), pp. 92–118; T. Hajkowski, *The BBC and National Identity in Britain, 1922–53* (Manchester, 2010), pp. 100–4.

[97] S. Nicholas, *The Echo of War: Home Front Propaganda and the Wartime BBC, 1939–45* (Manchester, 1996), pp. 12–5; A. Briggs, *The History of Broadcasting in the United Kingdom* (5 vols., Oxford, 1965–95), ii. 253–6.

[98] Nicholas, *Echo of War*, p. 13; D. L. LeMahieu, *A Culture for Democracy: Mass Communication and the Cultivated Mind in Britain in Between the Wars* (Oxford, 1998).

Reith, the BBC loyally promoted the crown's nation-building activities in this period but also sought new kinds of access to the royal family in order to establish its own credentials as the nation's leading provider of news.

In seeking to explain why sections of the media presented royalty in the ways they did, *The Family Firm* also examines documents pertaining to the production of media texts. These include the papers of Geoffrey Dawson, editor of *The Times* newspaper, which are located in the Bodleian Library; the papers of Lord Beaverbrook, owner of the Express news group, which can be found in the Parliamentary Archives; the personal correspondence of gossip columnist and Labour MP, Tom Driberg, at Christ Church College, Oxford; and the minute books of the Newsreel Association – the newsreel companies' trade body that was set up in late 1937 – which form part of the BFI's special collections. By combining an analysis of press, newsreel and broadcasting content with an examination of the behind-the-scenes discussions that went into producing that content, this book has developed a holistic approach to Britain's media sphere in the inter- and post-war periods in response to historian Siân Nicholas's recent criticism of scholars for the way they have tended to treat different media discretely. Nicholas has noted that, by the interwar period, there existed an 'interrelated and multi-layered mass media culture' in which 'engagement in one medium routinely overlapped with others'.[99] Wherever possible, *The Family Firm* highlights how the different media of newspaper, newsreel, radio and television presented royal events and personalities; how modes of coverage either overlapped or contrasted; and how audiences responded to the different media images of the monarchy they consumed, often privileging certain sources of information ahead of others. Finally, in addition to mainstream media coverage, this book has drawn on a range of other media texts, including official photographs of royal persons and pictorial souvenirs either from the National Portrait Gallery's online archive or the Royal Collection's digital database, as well as a large number of official royal commemorative souvenirs that were published from the mid 1930s to the early 1950s with the express aim of popularizing a specific set of messages that underpinned the monarchy's public image, one of which stressed the domesticity of the House of Windsor.

As already noted above, the media tended to present the monarchy as a unifying force in British society and regularly constructed images and narratives that characterized the public as a homogenous group integrated through their loyalty to the crown. The third and final category of sources

[99] S. Nicholas, 'Media history or media histories? Re-addressing the history of the mass media in inter-war Britain', *Media History*, xviii (2012), 379–94, at p. 390.

examined here are personal testimonies, which allow us to complicate the media's representation of public feeling. In his overview of the historiography of the modern British monarchy, Andrzej Olechnowicz noted that historians have failed to engage with the popular reception of royalty in any meaningful way and advised that a future research agenda focus on the way the monarchy has been interpreted and understood by the public.[100] *The Family Firm* responds to his prompting by presenting an analysis of personal documents that show how the intimate, family-centred image of the royals worked to strengthen the emotional connections that many ordinary people forged with the House of Windsor, and how these connections took formation in relation to new concepts of fame, family life and emotional fulfilment that first arose between the wars. At the same time, it is clear that the royal family did not find favour with everyone and this book sheds some light on the discordant voices that sought to question or challenge the royal status quo. It is important to note that it is difficult to locate dissenting opinion for the period before the abdication crisis: the archival research conducted for this book did not turn up any significant body of sources that directly contradicted the popular image of George V's family monarchy. For example, the letters written by members of the public to the royal household, clergy and newspapers in relation to the royal events discussed in chapters 1 and 2 tend to be positive in tone (which may account for their archival preservation) and speak to the success of the monarchy, media and other royal stage-managers in projecting the crown's unifying role in society. It is sometimes possible to identify conflicting views by reading between the lines of sources, but we have to accept that while critical or ambivalent voices were almost certainly heard among the public, they have left little tangible trace in the historical record.

The key archive that reveals a broader complexion of public feeling after 1936 is that of the social research organization Mass Observation. The history of Mass Observation is integrally linked to that of the monarchy. Charles Madge, Humphrey Jennings and Tom Harrisson established the organization because of their concerns that the British press and politicians had misjudged and misrepresented public opinion during the abdication crisis.[101] Through ethnographic research into 'ordinary' people's lives, Mass Observation set out to investigate what the masses 'really thought' while encouraging their panel of volunteer writers to engage in the public sphere with an enhanced self-awareness. As Penny Summerfield has discussed, this

[100] A. Olechnowicz, 'Historians and the modern British monarchy', in Olechnowicz, *Monarchy and the British Nation*, pp. 6–44, at p. 44.
[101] N. Hubble, *Mass Observation and Everyday Life: Culture, History, Theory* (Basingstoke, 2006), pp. 5–7.

educative urge was characteristic of the founders' and many participants' left-of-centre desire to contribute to a movement that was working towards a better understanding of current political events.[102] Summerfield and other historians, including James Hinton, have noted that Mass Observation's respondents do not provide access to 'typical' experience in their writings but rather present accounts of everyday life that were influenced by a personal commitment to new kinds of creative self-expression.[103] Nor did the volunteer panel evenly reflect the social make-up of Britain: instead it mainly comprised lower-middle-class women and men, as well as some upper-working-class people, with most living in England and fewer contributions coming from people in the Celtic nations.[104]

In spite of the issues inherent in the sources, Mass Observation has provided historians with a unique window into the nature of public opinion in mid twentieth-century Britain, with respondents' personal testimonies telling us a great deal about the emotional worlds and social settings they inhabited.[105] Notably, many of the volunteers recorded highly personal responses to royal personalities or events either in special day diaries or in response to questionnaires sent to them by the Mass Observation organizers between 1937 and 1953. Many also noted that other people around them expressed personal thoughts and feelings about royalty, either in the crowds that gathered in British towns and cities to celebrate coronations or royal weddings, as part of special interviews conducted by Mass Observation volunteers on the public's response to royal broadcasts at the height of the Blitz, or in living rooms where media audiences gathered together first to listen to and later to watch royal events unfold as they happened. The range of material collected by the panel of volunteers poses some difficulties to the historian. When Mass Observation respondents directly engaged with, or observed, other members of the public, asking them questions about or listening into their conversations on the royal family, the public nature of these interactions inevitably shaped the kind of thing people were willing to say about the monarchy. Tom Harrisson recognized the problems of what he termed 'social sanction' – the social pressure exerted on people to

---

[102] P. Summerfield, 'Mass-Observation: social research or social movement?', *Jour. Contemp. Hist.*, xx (1985), 439–52, at p. 442.

[103] J. Hinton, *Nine Wartime Lives: Mass-Observation and the Making of the Modern Self* (Oxford, 2010), p. 17; J. Hinton, 'Self-reflections in the mass', *History Workshop Jour.*, lxxv (2013), 251–9, at pp. 256–7; Langhamer, *The English in Love*, pp. xv–xxi; Summerfield, 'Mass-Observation', pp. 441–4. See also T. Harrisson, *Living Through the Blitz* (London, 1978), p. 254.

[104] Summerfield, 'Mass-Observation', p. 441.

[105] Hinton, *Nine Wartime Lives*, p. 6.

conform to what seemed acceptable and respectable in public – and the way this prevented them from openly voicing their 'private' (real) opinions on topics like royalty, particularly at a time when, as we have seen, to criticize the monarchy was to transgress social norms.[106] *The Family Firm* is sensitive to the strands of opinion captured by Mass Observation and argues that, despite the complexity, a number of important trends can be identified to link the empathetic responses articulated by the panel of volunteer respondents and those around them in relation to the royal family. While some of the Mass Observation personal testimonies reveal indifference or hostility towards royalty, the vast majority show that people's feelings were transformed through new kinds of personal identification with the monarchy's family-centred image. Given Mass Observation's left-of-centre origins and the anti-establishment inclinations of many of its contributors, the fact that the royal family were often the recipients of positive forms of empathy suggests a much wider emotional culture existed in British society that centred on the House of Windsor.

Chapters 3 to 6 of this book either draw on previously neglected Mass Observation sources for the first time or reinterpret sources that have been discussed elsewhere. The first major study that Mass Observation organized on the monarchy recorded volunteers' responses to George VI's coronation and resulted in a published book, *May the Twelfth* (1937).[107] Coronations and royal weddings provided the Mass Observation organizers with an opportunity to gauge public reactions to events that were presented by officials and the media as important national occasions; and similar archives thus exist for the 1947 marriage of the then Princess Elizabeth and her crowning six years later. Royal biographer Philip Ziegler produced a study of some of the Mass Observation personal testimonies on the monarchy to argue that, despite persistent concerns arising about the large costs involved in staging royal events, the British population has historically warmed to, and engaged in, the celebrations.[108] His interpretation accords with the wider field of official royal biography, which has tended to perpetuate narratives of royal popularity and progressive constitutionalism at the expense of more critical approaches to the public relations campaigns developed by the royal family as part of their twentieth-century survival strategy.[109] Equally, Ziegler's work does not systematically analyse how Mass

---

[106] T. Harrisson, 'What is public opinion?', *Political Quart.*, xi (1940), 368–83.

[107] Mass Observation, *May the Twelfth: Mass Observation Day-Surveys 1937, by over Two Hundred Observers*, ed. H. Jennings et al. (London, 1937; 2nd edn., 1987).

[108] P. Ziegler, *Crown and People* (London, 1978).

[109] E.g., H. Nicolson, *King George the Fifth: His Life and Reign* (London, 1952); J. Wheeler-Bennett, *King George VI: His Life and Reign* (London, 1958); W. Shawcross, *Queen Elizabeth*

Observation respondents articulated their imagined relationships with the House of Windsor and it does not consider the large archives of school essays collected by Mass Observation on royal personalities. Chapters 2 and 6 of *The Family Firm* examine essays written by groups of schoolchildren on George V and Elizabeth II respectively. School essays are complex forms of personal testimony that reflect the dynamic processes through which young royalist identities were forged in relation to both social experiences *outside* the classroom and educative discourses *inside* the classroom.[110] They can illuminate the dominant narratives through which children and adolescents were encouraged to make sense of the monarchy and their own subject positions in relation to the crown as part of Britain's royal democracy.

School essays also reveal how emotions articulated in connection with royalty were different for boys and girls. This is perhaps unsurprising: since the nineteenth century, British women had been encouraged to nurture and express their feelings, whereas men were meant to be more emotionally reserved.[111] Equally, with the expansion of the national media in the 1880s and 1890s, the press had commodified royal human-interest stories for consumption primarily by a growing female audience. This does not mean that men and boys did not engage with these stories or feel strongly towards royalty – they frequently did, but in different ways and through different emotional registers. Gender also shaped the letters written by members of the public to the royal family, with women tending to express their inner thoughts and feelings more freely than their male counterparts. Historian Julie Gottlieb has suggested that we can explain this with reference to a wider culture of female letter writing in mid twentieth-century Britain that witnessed women trying to reach out and achieve new kinds of intimacy with otherwise remote public figures through the epistolary form.[112] But men wrote too and in increasingly informal ways, possibly inspired by modern media technologies that had encouraged a relaxation in the relationship between the public and the monarchy. *The Family Firm* draws on letters

---

the Queen Mother: the Official Biography (Basingstoke, 2009). For discussion of the merits and pitfalls of official royal biography, see Cannadine, 'From biography to history', pp. 9–15.

[110] For recent discussion regarding using school essays as sources, see H. Barron and C. Langhamer, 'Children, class, and the search for security: writing the future in 1930s Britain', *Twentieth Century British Hist.*, xxviii (2017), 367–89; H. Barron and C. Langhamer, 'Feeling through practice: subjectivity and emotion in children's writing', *Jour. Social Hist.*, li (2017), 101–23, at pp. 103–6; J. Greenhalgh, '"Till we hear the last all clear": gender and the presentation of self in young girls' writing about the bombing of Hull during the Second World War', *Gender & History*, xxvi (2014), 167–83, at pp. 169–71.

[111] T. Dixon, *Weeping Britannia: Portrait of a Nation in Tears* (Oxford, 2015), pp. 202–12.

[112] J. V. Gottlieb, '*Guilty Women*', *Foreign Policy, and Appeasement in Inter-War Britain* (Basingstoke, 2015), p. 186. See also Mort, 'Love in a cold climate', pp. 40–1.

written by both sexes in order to examine how and why readers, listeners and viewers forged emotional bonds with their royal rulers between 1932 and 1953. Taken together with the Mass Observation evidence, these personal testimonies suggest that while women may have been quicker to relate to the House of Windsor through the family-centred imagery they consumed via the media before the Second World War, by the late 1940s young men had also developed strong emotional identification with the domestic aspirations of the royals, indicative of the growth of a national culture of family life among the post-war generation.

Structure of the book

The royal weddings of the 1920s and 1930s were nation-building exercises that were designed to create loyal subjects of the crown. Chapter 1 focuses on the 1934 wedding of the duke and duchess of Kent and shows how, more than ever before, royal intimacy was staged on a spectacular scale via the new channels of mass media to foster emotional identification between the public and the House of Windsor. The lead actors – Prince George and Princess Marina of Greece – proved more willing than any previous members of the royal family to distinguish themselves as modern celebrities, publicizing an idealized romance to draw attention to their compatibility, feelings and glamour (Figure 0.7). They became the first royals to agree to filmed interviews, to wave to crowds and to kiss on camera; and their wedding in Westminster abbey was the first to be broadcast live by the BBC to listeners at home. This chapter explores how these transgressive innovations played out at the palace, with the press and among the public in a period marked by widespread social and political unrest both in Britain and in Europe.

Chapter 2 examines how George V's broadcasts recalibrated his relationship with his subjects along contours that emphasized a personal loyalty to him and the royal family. The king described his people at home and abroad as uniquely connected to him in the common enterprise of promoting social welfare, Christian family life and empire. Under the influence of the archbishop of Canterbury, Cosmo Lang, the emotional language used by the monarch to communicate publicly also changed significantly between 1932 and 1935. At a time of deep anxiety relating to the economic insecurity of large sections of the population and the failure of the League of Nations to secure a lasting peace in Europe, the king and prelate elevated a vision of a family-centred monarch dutifully committed to the care of the nation and to maintaining Britain's place in the world. Letters written to George V in his lifetime and school essays composed after his death reveal that this image of the compassionate king was internalized by

Figure 0.7. Prince George and Princess Marina, duke and duchess of Kent, 1934 (NPG x135528). © National Portrait Gallery, London.

listeners, who expressed strong emotional identification with him because of the way he had spoken to them across the airwaves.

Edward VIII's abdication and George VI's coronation in his brother's place transformed the role and public image of the monarchy in Britain. Edward's renunciation of the throne brought to an end a dynamic style of kingship based on the assertive masculinity of an individual figure and he was replaced by a monarch who seemed to take on the burdens of royal duty against his will. Chapter 3 examines the projection and reception of George VI's crowning to uncover the official and popular attitudes towards royalty following the turbulence of the abdication. It argues that the new king met with muted public enthusiasm which persisted until, and beyond, his coronation. Fortunately for him, his mother, Queen Mary, was close at hand to lend the first six months of his reign an emotional continuity with the past (Figure 0.8). The royal household also spearheaded a media campaign to generate sympathy for a monarch who, unlike his

Figure 0.8. Queen Mary,
1937 (RCIN 2808286).
Royal Collection Trust
/ © Her Majesty Queen
Elizabeth II 2019.

older brother, appeared to put public service ahead of private happiness. However, Edward's shadow loomed over the coronation; and officials and news editors had to work hard to fill the charisma vacuum created by his abdication with forceful meaning, presenting George VI as the defender of the nation's and empire's political freedoms and his crowning as a symbol of the inexorable progress of constitutional democracy, in direct contrast to continental despotism.

Since 1945 royal biographers and public commentators have mythologized the morale-boosting function played by George VI and his family on the home front during the Second World War. Chapter 4 proposes a more complex story. The king and his advisors understood the need for the monarchy to take on a more overt propaganda role at a time of national crisis and, responding to requests from government departments, agreed to a number of royal broadcasts that were designed to sustain public confidence. However, throughout the war the royal household proved determined to maintain control over the crown's media strategy, notably pursuing its own aims in launching a series of royal tours of bombed-out urban areas during the Blitz. Faced with new challenges to the established social hierarchy, not least of which was a burgeoning popular culture that valorized the wartime sacrifices of ordinary people and criticized the old ruling classes, palace officials elevated a public image of the royal family that emphasized how the exigencies of war had challenged their domesticity and that they, like other families, suffered emotionally because of the conflict. George VI's consort, Queen Elizabeth, was the leading proponent of this narrative of shared sacrifice, which was subsequently taken up by loyal media organizations and became central to the public relations campaign developed by the royal household in mythologizing the monarchy's wartime role as soon as the allied victory was secure.

The Second World War witnessed an important cultural shift among some left-wing newspapers, which became more outspoken in their criticism of the royal family. At the beginning of 1947 the press published the rumour that Princess Elizabeth – elder daughter of George VI – was engaged to Prince Philip of Greece (Figure 0.9). The *Sunday Pictorial* took the brazen and unprecedented step of polling its readers' opinions on the suitability of the match and went on to announce that the public were split over whether the prince was fit for the princess. Chapter 5 shows that the royal household and its allies were successful in generating support for Elizabeth and her fiancé by fashioning likeable media images of the couple that drew attention to the princess's commitment to her 'extraordinary' public duties and her 'ordinary' ambition as a young woman to marry someone she loved. This chapter also examines how the staging of their royal wedding strengthened the crown and Church's moral leadership of the nation by promoting an exemplary image of family life at a time when there was growing concern about the rise in cases of divorce and single mothers. Indeed, members of the public proved to be protective of this image, with many criticizing the intrusive media coverage of the royal lovers' honeymoon.

Chapter 6 focuses on emotional responses to the televised coronation of Queen Elizabeth II to argue that the new technology transformed how media audiences experienced the royal family. In the months leading up to the coronation, debates erupted in public and in private over whether or not the BBC should be able to televise the Westminster abbey service. However, the broadcaster did eventually receive permission and its coronation coverage enhanced many viewers' sense of national participation by bridging geographical divides and enabling a more intimate involvement in a royal ceremony than ever before. The 1950s culture of domesticity, which witnessed new kinds of popular consumption and home-based sociability, simultaneously undermined older, socially deferential kinds of

Figure 0.9. Princess Elizabeth and Lieutenant (Prince) Philip Mountbatten, November 1947 (RCIN 2805935). Royal Collection Trust / © Her Majesty Queen Elizabeth II 2019.

participation in royal events, such as churchgoing or community-centred activities, while strengthening the collective emotional meanings associated with the monarchy that linked media audiences together. Furthermore, the defining feature of the day was neither the Commonwealth nor national renewal, as historians have suggested. Rather, it was royal maternalism: television images of the queen separated from and then reunited with her two children – in particular, her son and heir Prince Charles – evoked powerful feelings from viewers who sympathized with the way her public role seemed to prevent her enjoying the freedoms of a normal family life (Figure 0.10).

Television portrayals of a young queen's coronation had been a long way from anyone's mind two decades previously in 1934. The queen's grandfather, by now an old man nearing the end of his life, still sat on the throne and the seismic events of the abdication crisis, the Second World War and the premature death of George VI seemed inconceivable. Yet, this was the year that the trajectory of a mass media monarchy that combined elite status and modern celebrity with personal intimacy and domestic vulnerability began and it is therefore where the story of *The Family Firm* begins.

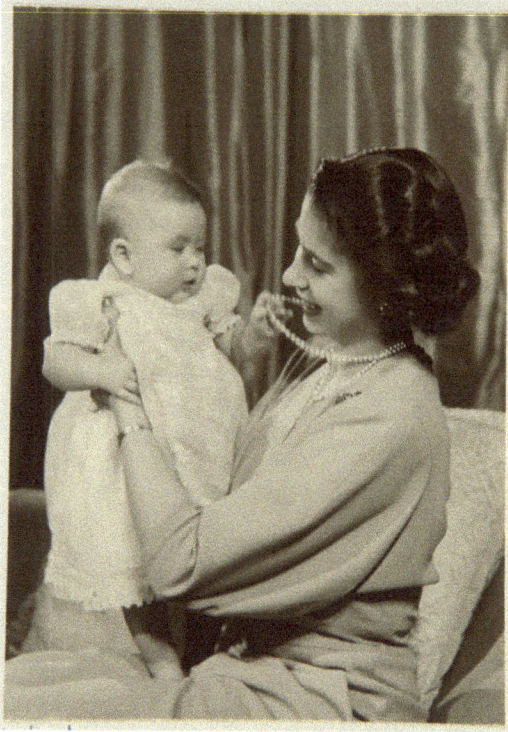

Figure 0.10. Princess Elizabeth and Prince Charles as a baby, 1949 (RCIN 2081606). Royal Collection Trust / © Her Majesty Queen Elizabeth II 2019.

1. 'All the world loves a lover': the 1934 royal wedding of Prince George and Princess Marina

More than any previous royal occasion, the 1934 wedding of Prince George, duke of Kent, to the famously glamorous Princess Marina of Greece was a spectacle driven by intimate publicity under the control of a coterie of courtiers, clerics and newsmen who were committed to elevating a 'family monarchy' as the emotional centre point of British national life.[1] The palace worked in tandem with the Church and media to orchestrate the wedding as a nation-building exercise designed to create loyal subjects of the crown. Aided by new technologies that transformed how media audiences and royalty interacted with one another, the celebration of royal domesticity engendered popular support for the House of Windsor and strengthened the monarchy's position at the centre of society in a period characterized by political turbulence at home and abroad.

At the outset the odds appeared to be stacked against the royal couple. Marina and her family had lived as exiles in Paris since 1924, having fled Greece after a series of upheavals which sprung from the First World War led to the abolition of the monarchy and its replacement with a republic. As a relatively unknown princess from a cadet branch of a politically unstable dynasty (that had only existed since 1863), and as a member of the Greek Orthodox Church, Marina could have been presented as an exotic and disruptive figure in the narrative of the domesticated British monarchy. As we shall see, special efforts were made to transform her into a popular figure with characteristics that appealed to public sensibilities. Behind closed doors, doubts also lingered about Prince George's readiness to step into the limelight as a royal celebrity and representative of his father, King George V. The prince was clever, artistic and handsome but, like his eldest brother, the prince of Wales, he was fond of the fast life. His modern pursuits and tireless pleasure-seeking contrasted with the dutiful characteristics desired of young royals by the monarch and his advisors. In 1916, aged just fourteen, George was enrolled in the Royal Naval cadets at his father's bidding and went on

---

[1] Historians have not examined the 1934 royal wedding in any detail. Rather, royal biographers have been left to retell sentimentalized accounts of the event: e.g., G. Ellison, *The Authorised Life Story of Princess Marina* (London, 1934); S. Watson, *Marina: the Story of a Princess* (London, 1997).

to spend thirteen unhappy years in the service. Eventually discharged on account of ill-health in 1929, he joined the Foreign Office as a civil servant (the first royal ever to do so), having distinguished himself as a linguist during his time in the navy; and in 1932 he became a factory inspector for the Home Office. These government roles and his attendance at royal civic events around the country increased his media visibility after a secluded time spent in the military but, as his public persona developed, his private life became increasingly tumultuous.[2] He and his eldest brother had become close friends in the mid 1920s and, living together at St. James's Palace in central London, regularly frequented the bars and nightclubs beloved of the English society set. The prince's biographer noted that, by the end of the decade, George had developed an addiction to cocaine and morphine, habits the prince of Wales helped him to overcome through vigilant nursing. He had also embarked on a series of love affairs with women and men, including the playwright and composer Noël Coward. George's various transgressions threatened to bring the monarchy into disrepute: according to diplomat and journalist Sir Robert Bruce Lockhart, around this time courtiers were forced to arrange payment to a young Frenchman in order to recover incriminating love letters George had written to him and which he had used to blackmail the prince.[3]

Fortunately for the palace, the gentlemanly codes of secrecy that governed the relationships between the royal household and British media in the 1920s and early 1930s ensured that George's frequent transgressions were kept hidden from public view.[4] Indeed, it was only with his sudden engagement to Marina in August 1934 that journalists focused their attention on the prince's private life and then they did so in order to emphasize that the royal romance was a true love match between two young, well-suited, good-looking people: there were no references whatsoever to George's bisexuality or dalliance with narcotics and, to all intents and purposes, he was, and would remain, a modern Prince Charming. The first part of this chapter picks up the royal couple's love story following the betrothal and shows how journalists were the initial driving force in creating their public images. Human-interest stories increasingly dominated the news in the late

[2] E.g., 'Royal "movie" fan', *Pathé Gazette*, 16 March 1929; 'Royal brothers arrive in Peru', *British Movietone Gazette*, 2 March 1931; 'Prince George visits pit disaster scene', *British Movietone News*, 23 Nov. 1933.

[3] C. Warwick, *George and Marina: Duke and Duchess of Kent* (London, 1988), pp. 63–72. See also L. Pickett et al., *The War of the Windsors: a Century of Unconstitutional Monarchy* (Edinburgh, 2002), pp. 54–8.

[4] M. Houlbrook, *Prince of Tricksters: the Incredible True Story of Netley Lucas, Gentleman Crook* (Chicago, Ill., 2016), pp. 226–7.

1920s and early 1930s, with reporters laying bare the personal lives of public figures in order to generate an emotional affinity between media audiences and the famous.[5] In 1934 the press exposed to the public details which were more intimate about George and Marina's romance than had been deemed acceptable in the case of earlier royal love stories. The prince and princess also proved more willing than any previous members of the royal family to distinguish themselves as modern celebrities by publicizing an idealized romance which emphasized their compatibility and glamour: they were the first royals to consent to filmed interviews, to wave at crowds and to kiss on camera. Notably, the couple's publicity strategy enabled journalists to generate the impression that their romance chimed with a new emotional culture centred on true love and personal fulfilment and it helped to divert attention away from Marina's inauspicious status as an exiled Greek princess.[6] News editors also framed their coverage of the engagement and wedding with a female audience in mind, forming part of a wider attempt by the media to discursively define modern British womanhood along contours of consumption, beauty and glamour.[7]

The second section focuses on the often fraught negotiations between the royal household, the archbishop of Canterbury and other churchmen and BBC executives as they orchestrated the first royal wedding to be broadcast live by radio to the public. These officials designed the broadcast to highlight the wedding service's religiosity while trying to appeal to a national listenership. The BBC's ambitions to broadcast the event accorded with its wider nation-building activities, which included elevating the tastes of its listeners and integrating new female and working-class audiences into the public sphere around the focal-point of the monarchy.[8] The BBC's efforts also formed part of a wider media campaign to build what seemed like a

---

[5] A. Bingham and M. Conboy, *Tabloid Century: the Popular Press in Britain, 1896 to the Present* (Oxford, 2015), pp. 97–130.

[6] C. Langhamer, *The English in Love: the Intimate Story of an Emotional Revolution* (Oxford, 2013), pp. 1–19; F. Mort, 'Love in a cold climate: letters, public opinion and monarchy in the 1936 abdication crisis', *Twentieth Century British Hist.*, xxv (2014), 30–62.

[7] I. Zweiniger-Bargielowska, 'The body and consumer culture', in *Women in Twentieth-Century Britain: Social, Cultural and Political Change*, ed. I. Zweiniger-Bargielowska (Harlow, 2001), pp. 183–97.

[8] M. Andrews, 'Homes both sides of the microphone: wireless and domestic space in interwar Britain', *Women's Hist. Rev.*, xxi (2012), 605–21, at pp. 606–7; E. Colpus, 'The week's good cause: mass culture and cultures of philanthropy at the interwar BBC', *Twentieth Century British Hist.*, xxii (2011), 305–29, at pp. 321–2; D. LeMahieu, *A Culture for Democracy: Mass Communication and the Cultivated Mind in Britain Between the Wars* (Oxford, 1998), pp. 179–80.

well-ordered nation centred on royalty.[9] At a time when public stability seemed threatened by various internal and external forces, the new media technologies of sound newsreel, photographic close-ups and wireless radio conveyed scenes of a nation united in celebration of George and Marina's wedding.

The final part of this chapter examines the public reception of the wedding. Radio brought ordinary people closer to royalty than ever before and enabled engaged citizenship by generating a democratic space in which listeners affirmed their loyalty to the crown by joining in nationally shared experiences.[10] Letters written to the organizers of the royal wedding and the British press reveal how the radio broadcast of the event worked to enhance 'affective integration' around the focal point of the monarchy: many listeners experienced a strong sense of national belonging as they joined in, and empathized with, the family story at the heart of the occasion.[11] Thus, the collaboration between the media, monarchy and Church heightened ordinary people's awareness of the centrality of the House of Windsor to national public life. Notably, this awareness was shaped by events outside Britain, too: letters reveal that media audiences internalized the imagery of a cheerful nation gathered in emotional communion around the royal wedding by comparing Britain's festive spirit with the growing disorder that troubled European politics in the early 1930s.

A surprise engagement

Journalists were primarily responsible for generating and maintaining public interest in George and Marina's engagement and wedding. In the middle of August 1934 George visited Prince Paul of Yugoslavia (Marina's brother-in-law) at his summer residence on Lake Bohinjsko [Bohinj] and there he met the Greek princess. The two had already known each other for five years and, according to the first press reports on the betrothal, 'amid the idyllic surroundings of the Slovenian Alps' their 'friendship ripened into love'.[12] However, the *Daily Mail* 'scooped' the story of the royal engagement before it was officially announced. A correspondent from the newspaper

---

[9] J. Lawrence, *Electing Our Masters: the Hustings in British Politics from Hogarth to Blair* (Oxford, 2009), pp. 97, 116–29.

[10] I. Zweiniger-Bargielowska, 'Royal death and living memorials: the funerals and commemoration of George V and George VI, 1936–52', *Hist. Research*, lxxxix (2015), 158–75.

[11] For the term 'affective integration', see J. Perry, 'Christmas as Nazi holiday: colonising the Christmas mood', in *Life and Times in Nazi Germany*, ed. L. Pine (London, 2016), pp. 263–89, at p. 264.

[12] *Daily Mail*, 29 Aug. 1934, p. 5; *Daily Mirror*, 29 Aug. 1934, p. 1; *News of the World*, 2 Sept. 1934, p. 10.

had confronted George after an opera performance in Salzburg and asked him to confirm the rumour circulated by a Viennese newspaper that he had proposed to Marina. The prince requested that the reporter deny all speculation, stating that 'there is no truth at all in these rumours'.[13] The *Mail's* revelation appears to have compelled the couple to announce their engagement officially the next day, but, in doing so, they signalled their intention to adopt a more active role than was normal for royalty by engaging with journalists in order to shape their public image. The couple agreed to a series of newspaper and newsreel interviews, as well as a number of staged film and photograph opportunities, in which they emphasized three things: their emotional fulfilment, Marina's happiness at becoming a British royal and their modern glamour.

In 1923 Lady Elizabeth Bowes-Lyon gave a reporter from the *Evening News* an 'exclusive interview' saying she was 'so very happy' following her engagement to Prince Albert, Duke of York. However, her biographer has speculated that she might have received an official warning to resist the advances of the press because after this there were no more interviews.[14] Royal protocol discouraged revelation and George's original 'denial' of his engagement typified this approach. In subsequently breaking with convention, he and Marina exercised caution in choosing whom they talked to. Reuters news agency wrote to George's equerry, Major H. W. Butler, to complain angrily that the prince had granted an interview to a Yugoslavian newspaper, having told other journalists 'that it [was] strictly forbidden for him to give interviews for the press'.[15] The couple thus engaged selectively with the media in order to publicize their story. Notably, they did grant an audience to the *Daily Express*. In what the newspaper described on its front-page as the 'First Interview with the Royal Lovers', George was recorded as explaining that the engagement was 'all very sudden and unexpected' but that he and Marina were 'very happy'. The reporter noted that, on his meeting the couple in the Hotel de l'Europe in Salzburg, they had 'been sharing a joke – and laughing consumedly over it'.[16] First-hand revelations like these seemed to provide authentic insights into the unfolding romance and conveyed the couple's emotional fulfilment and like-mindedness. Their compatibility was also communicated through large, front-page photographs with captions which highlighted their attractive physical features (Figure 1.1). Marina was described as a 'tall, beautiful' and 'charming blue-eyed

---

[13] *Daily Mail*, 27 Aug. 1934, p. 11.
[14] W. Shawcross, *Queen Elizabeth the Queen Mother: the Official Biography* (Basingstoke, 2009), pp. 154–5. See also *Daily Mirror*, 17 Jan. 1923, p. 19.
[15] RA, GDKH/WED/A01, H. D. Harrison to H. W. Butler, 3 Sept. 1934.
[16] *Daily Express*, 30 Aug. 1934, p. 1.

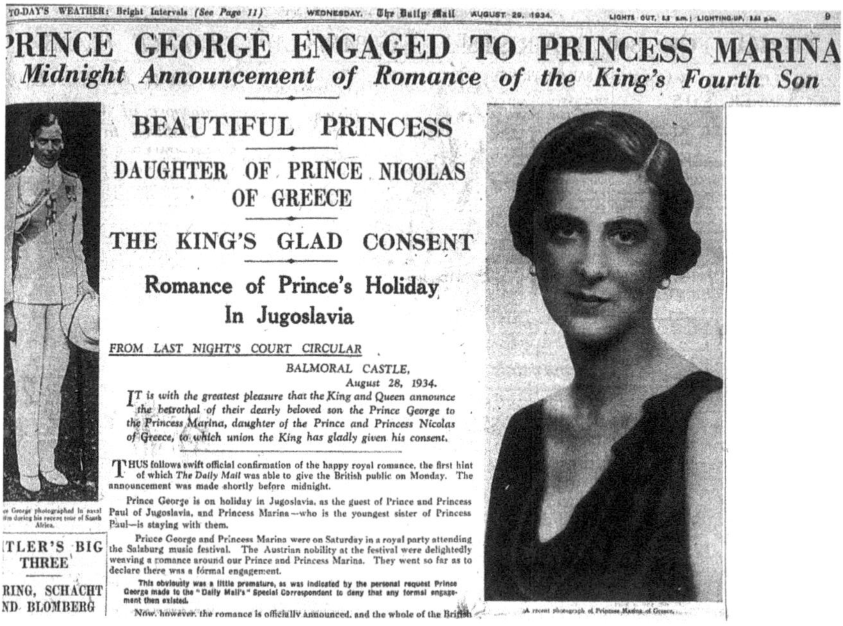

TO-DAY'S WEATHER: Bright Intervals *(See Page 11)* WEDNESDAY. The Daily Mail AUGUST 29, 1934. 9

PRINCE GEORGE ENGAGED TO PRINCESS MARINA

Midnight Announcement of Romance of the King's Fourth Son

BEAUTIFUL PRINCESS

DAUGHTER OF PRINCE NICOLAS OF GREECE

THE KING'S GLAD CONSENT

Romance of Prince's Holiday In Jugoslavia

FROM LAST NIGHT'S COURT CIRCULAR

BALMORAL CASTLE,
August 28, 1934.

IT is with the greatest pleasure that the King and Queen announce the betrothal of their dearly beloved son the Prince George to the Princess Marina, daughter of the Prince and Princess Nicolas of Greece, to which union the King has gladly given his consent.

THUS follows swift official confirmation of the happy royal romance, the first hint of which *The Daily Mail* was able to give the British public on Monday. The announcement was made shortly before midnight.

Prince George is on holiday in Jugoslavia, as the guest of Prince and Princess Paul of Jugoslavia, and Princess Marina—who is the youngest sister of Princess Paul—is staying with them.

Prince George and Princess Marina were on Saturday in a royal party attending the Salzburg music festival. The Austrian nobility at the festival were delightedly weaving a romance around our Prince and Princess Marina. They went so far as to declare there was a formal engagement.

This obviously was a little premature, as was indicated by the personal request Prince George made to the "Daily Mail's" Special Correspondent to deny that any formal engagement then existed.

Now, however, the romance is officially announced, and the whole of the British

…TLER'S BIG THREE

…RING, SCHACHT …ND BLOMBERG

Figure 1.1. 'Prince George engaged to Princess Marina', *Daily Mail*, 29 August 1934, p. 9. © The British Library Board.

brunette'. The prince was similarly 'tall, blue-eyed and good-looking' and together they formed the 'handsomest royal couple in Europe'.[17]

Romantic self-fulfilment, mutual understanding and sexual attraction became increasingly important to the way the British public viewed heterosexual relationships in this period.[18] The media's narration of the human drama of the royal engagement reflected these themes and was intended to encourage the public to empathize with the couple. The message that it was a 'true love match' also mirrored wider expectations relating to royal romance.[19] After the First World War George V strengthened the British identity of the House of Windsor by breaking with the tradition of dynastic intermarriage and allowing his relatives to marry into the English and Scottish aristocracy. Beginning with Princess Patricia of Connaught's wedding in 1919, this turn inwards towards so-called 'commoners' encouraged the belief that young royals now had the opportunity to select their spouses according to their personal desires. The king's daughter, Princess Mary, and son, Prince Albert, duke of York, married suitors apparently of their choice

[17] *Daily Express*, 29 Aug. 1934, p. 1; *News of the World*, 2 Sept. 1934, p. 10.
[18] Langhamer, *The English in Love*, pp. 1–19.
[19] *Daily Mail*, 30 Aug. 1934, p. 11; *Daily Mirror*, 30 Aug. 1934, p. 3.

in 1922 and 1923.[20] Notably, the media's response to George and Marina's romance was influenced by two Scandinavian royal love stories from the early 1930s as well. Princes Lennart and Sigvard of Sweden gave up their titles and positions in line to the throne in order to marry commoners of their choosing in 1932 and 1934 respectively. In both cases, British newsreels proclaimed ecstatically that 'all the world loves a lover' and emphasized that the princes had ignored King Gustaf V's express wishes by 'choosing to obey the dictates of [their] heart[s]'.[21] These events augmented a royal emotional culture in which love was perceived as the key to happiness and, in the Swedish cases, as more important than duty. *British Movietone News* accordingly began its first newsreel on George and Marina's betrothal by declaring that 'all the world loves a lover, especially a royal lover'.[22]

After their stay in Salzburg, the royal couple drove 200 miles by motorcar to the Bled home of Prince Paul. There they allowed *British Movietone* to record them walking in the gardens of the estate with their hosts and presented a 'film greeting' to audiences in Britain (Figure 1.2). As they stood side-by-side in front of the newsreel camera, George spoke first: 'We have received so many congratulations, we want to thank everyone for all their kindness to us'. The princess then followed suit: 'I am so very happy and looking forward to come to England [*sic*]'. This greeting was a remarkable innovation. Never before had British royalty directly addressed the public through the cinema.[23] Although the king had spoken to his subjects over the radio at Christmas for the previous two years, his messages avoided overt emotion and instead focused on social and political issues. Following the introduction of sound newsreels in the late 1920s, George and Marina were now able to record a greeting which provided viewers with what appeared to be informal glimpses into their romance. In reality, of course, these were highly choreographed scenes which most closely resembled a 1920s cinemagazine genre titled 'The Stars at Home'.[24] This film series and others

---

[20] *Daily Mirror*, 24 Nov. 1921, p. 3; 26 Apr. 1923, p. 7; 27 Apr. 1923, p. 2. See also C. Warwick, *Two Centuries of Royal Weddings* (Worthing, 1980), pp. 36–48; and J. Pope-Hennessy, *Queen Mary, 1867–1953* (London, 1959), pp. 518–19.

[21] 'A royal romance', *Pathé Super Sound Gazette*, 16 March 1931 and 'All the world loves a lover', *Pathé Super Sound Gazette*, 12 March 1934; 'Prince chooses love', *British Paramount News*, 29 Feb. 1932; and 'Love before rank', *British Paramount News*, 12 March 1934.

[22] 'Royal romance', *British Movietone News*, 30 Aug. 1934. *Pathé Gazette* first used the phrase 'all the world loves a lover' in relation to the duke of York's engagement in 1923: 'All the world loves a lover', 29 Jan. 1923.

[23] 'Prince George and Princess Marina send greetings through Movietone', *British Movietone News*, 3 Sept. 1934.

[24] E.g., 'Stars at home – Miss Nellie Wallace', *Eve and Everybody's Film Review*, 3 Nov. 1921; and 'Stars at home – Matheson Lang', *Eve and Everybody's Film Review*, 29 Sept. 1921.

Figure 1.2. 'Prince George and Princess Marina Send Greetings Through Movietone', *British Movietone News*, 3 September 1934. © AP Archive.

like it humanized famous people by exposing their home lives to public view: popular celebrities and politicians were shown in intimate surroundings engaging in everyday activities like gardening, sport or caring for pets. Given these themes, it was natural that Prince George's German Shepherd made a brief appearance in his master's arms as part of the *Movietone* film.

After their trip to Bled, George and Marina parted ways, the prince returning to Britain and the princess to her home in Paris. The French capital had been a safe haven to the Greek royal family in their exile but, rather than dwell on the princess's turbulent past, the press joined with officials in an attempt to 'naturalize' her as a member of the British royal family. On arriving back in her adoptive city, Marina agreed to another series of interviews, this time with newsreel reporters. These interviews formed part of a public relations campaign led by the princess and those close to her in order to play up her romance with George while simultaneously playing down her unfavourable status as an exiled royal. Reiterating the ideas expressed in the *Movietone* greeting, Marina emphasized how pleased she

---

See also 'Mr Bonar Law: our new premier', *Gaumont Graphic*, 23 Oct. 1922.

was to join the House of Windsor: 'I love Paris, but obviously I am so happy to go to England and to become English'.[25] Marina's father, Prince Nicholas, and Grace Ellison, who was a friend of the Greek royal family, also stressed to interviewers how 'fond of England' the princess was, that 'there [was] nothing political in the marriage' and that she 'had always made it clear that she would never marry for anything but love'.[26] These authoritative voices minimized concerns about the suitability of the love match based on Marina's inauspicious family history by highlighting instead the genuine affection which characterized the royal engagement and the princess's enthusiasm at relinquishing her association with the Greek dynasty in order to become a British royal.

The other theme which Marina emphasized to the newsreel interviewers in Paris was her famous fashion style, discussing at length the plans for her wedding dress and trousseau. Along with the front-page press reports on the couple's emotional fulfilment, coverage of the royal engagement focused on George and Marina's glamour and particularly the princess's dress sense. From the outset, it was presented as a signifier of her modernity:

> She has that indefinable quality known as "chic", and the style that she has crafted for herself has been the envy and admiration of all of Paris, where she is a well-known figure. On a formal occasion she can be royally dignified; in private life she is charming, unaffected and friendly. But always she is "chic" – on the mountainside or in the ballroom.[27]

The way the meaning of 'chic' eluded the *News of the World's* journalist shows that Marina's fashion style was highly modern, resisting classification. Royal fashion has long attracted attention and scholars have noted the princess's distinctive elegance. A new colour – Marina blue – was named after her and she wore the first royal wedding dress in which line and style were more important than decoration.[28] The ultimate recognition of this style came in a twenty-six page centrepiece feature in *Vogue* which reviewed her wedding gown and trousseau.[29] By posing for the *Vogue* photographers and by explaining to the newsreel interviewers in Paris that her wedding dress would be made by a leading British designer, Edward Molyneux, Marina helped to build a media image defined by glamour which carried

[25] 'The bride to be: Princess Marina goes shopping in Paris', *Pathé Super Sound Gazette*, 17 Sept. 1934; 'France: Princess Marina of Greece talks about her wedding plans', *British Paramount News*, 17 Sept. 1934.
[26] *Daily Mirror*, 30 Aug. 1934, p. 3; *Daily Mail*, 29 Aug. 1934, p. 5.
[27] *News of the World*, 2 Sept. 1934, p. 10.
[28] C. McDowell, *A Hundred Years of Royal Style* (London, 1985), p. 76.
[29] *Vogue*, 28 Nov. 1934, pp. 74–99.

great appeal as part of a national culture that celebrated female fashion.[30] The impact this image had on sections of the public can be detected in the many letters which accompanied gifts of shoes, dresses and other accessories sent to Marina as wedding presents by fashion retailers – each desperate for the princess's personal endorsement.[31]

With her highly modern style, the princess seemed well-matched in George and this public image of the like-minded lovers was again intended to dispel any lingering concerns regarding their suitability. The pleasure both were reported to take in dancing, art, theatre and cinema marked them out as members of a fashionable social elite renowned for its modernity.[32] Moreover, motoring and smoking became key signifiers of modernity between the wars and these activities were enjoyed by George and Marina, as illustrated in front-page photographs published after their engagement: the prince sat at the wheel of a sports car next to the princess; both held a lit cigarette (Figure 1.3).[33] Indeed, George was famed for his love of speed. The *News Chronicle* characterized him as 'ultra-modern', remarking that 'he is acknowledged as the best car driver in the Royal Family and rivals his brother, the Prince of Wales, as the best dancer'.[34] Comparisons like this one, and the news that Edward would act as George's best man, linked the younger prince to the modern masculinity of his older brother with its thrill-seeking glamour.[35] The prince of Wales had come to personify the metropolitan society set and media coverage of George and Marina made it clear that they belonged to this exclusive caste of celebrity too.[36] Reports of the couple's shared interests thus not only evoked the new culture of personal compatibility but also helped to reconfigure the kind of celebrity identity associated with the British royal family.

---

[30] G. Howell, *In Vogue: Sixty Years of Celebrities and Fashion from British Vogue* (London, 1978), p. 107.

[31] RA, GDKH/WED/C: e.g., the present of waterproof coats with a letter from Samuel Bros. of Manchester, sent to the private secretary of Princess Marina, 15 Nov. 1934; and the present of shoes and handbag with a letter from Mrs R. G. Scudamore of Brown Inc. to U. Alexander, 23 Nov. 1934.

[32] *Daily Herald*, 29 Aug. 1934, p. 1; *Daily Express*, 29 Aug. 1934, p. 2; *Daily Telegraph*, 29 Aug. 1934, p. 11.

[33] *Daily Mirror*, 30 Aug. 1934, p. 1; *Daily Express*, 30 Aug. 1934, p. 1; P. Tinkler and C. Warsh, 'Feminine modernity in interwar Britain and North America: corsets, cars, and cigarettes', *Jour. Women's Hist.*, xx (2008), 113–43.

[34] *News Chronicle*, 29 Aug. 1934, p. 2; 30 Aug. 1934, p. 4. On speed, technology and modernity, see B. Rieger, '"Fast couples": technology, gender and modernity in Britain and Germany during the nineteen-thirties', *Hist. Research*, lxxvi (2003), 364–88.

[35] *Daily Mirror*, 22 Sept. 1934, p. 1.

[36] R. McKibbin, *Classes and Cultures: England 1918–1951* (Oxford, 1998), p. 32.

THE DAILY MIRROR, Thursday, August 30, 19 34.

Broadcasting - Page 20

Daily Mirror

THE DAILY PICTURE NEWSPAPER WITH THE LARGEST NET SALE

NEW SERIAL ON MONDAY

No. 9,597. Registered at the G.P.O. as a Newspaper. THURSDAY, AUGUST 30, 1934. One Penny.

PRINCE GEORGE'S WEDDING PLANS
Ceremony in the Abbey and Full State Drive

Prince George and his fiancée, Princess Marina of Greece, with cigarettes as they drove away from Salzburg yesterday, en route for Prince Nicolas's castle in Yugoslavia. Prince George is at the wheel.

Princess Marina carrying white roses as she left a Salzburg hotel with Prince George. They smiled happily at the crowd who assembled.

PRINCESS AS A XMAS BRIDE?

From an authoritative source in London it was learned last night that Prince George proposed to Princess Marina of Greece after he had been five days at the Castle of Prince Paul in Yugoslavia. They became engaged on Sunday last, but it was two days before the necessary formalities could be completed to enable their engagement to be announced.'

Prince George has given his bride-to-be an engagement ring.

It was emphasised in Court circles that the date for the marriage ceremony will not be fixed until Prince George returns on September 7 and has seen the King and Queen at Balmoral.

One thing is practically certain — the Royal wedding will be solemnised in Westminster Abbey and there will be a drive in full state from Buckingham Palace to the Abbey and back.

As to the date, November or December — possibly a Christmas wedding—has been mentioned. A further suggestion is that the wedding might be deferred till next spring, so that it could take place in the King's Silver Jubilee year. Nothing, however, is settled.

It is thought that the King may confer a Dukedom on Prince George, either on his birthday on December 20 or just before his birthday.

WELCOME HOME NEXT WEEK TO PRINCE

London will give a great welcome to Prince George when he returns from Yugoslavia next week.

It is unlikely that Princess Marina will travel with him, but she may visit this country shortly after the Prince's return. She will then be accompanied by her parents, Prince and Princess Nicolas of Greece.

It was officially stated last night that the date for the wedding has not yet been discussed. All that is certain is that it will not take place before November.

The choice of best man has not, of course, yet been made.

It is pointed out, however, that the Prince of Wales is the only one of the royal brothers who could act as best man, as, unless the wedding is postponed until next year, the Duke of Gloucester, the only other unmarried son of the King, will be abroad on his official tour of Australia.

No plans have yet been made for the holding of a Privy Council at which the King would sanction the marriage of Prince George.

Beautiful Princess

Under the terms of the Act of Parliament which governs royal marriages, the King's consent in Council can be given at any time before the actual ceremony.

Something of Princess Marina's beauty and character was revealed yesterday by friends who saw her during her recent visits to London.

Miss Grace Ellison, the authoress, of Fitz-George-avenue, W., said :—

"I have known the Princess for a number of years. She is most beautiful, and one of the most charming girls I have met.

"What, however, will delight the people of England as much as her beauty is her culture. Prince George is, indeed, bringing a beautiful bride to England.

"Princess Marina has always been extremely fond of England; indeed, she and her family invariably use the English language in their own home.

"She has always declared that when she married it would be a love match, for Princess Marina has something of the nature of Queen Alexandra in her dislike of ostentation."

(Continued on page 3)

Figure 1.3. 'Prince George's Wedding Plans', *Daily Mirror*, 30 August 1934, p. 1. © The British Library Board.

The celebrity of George and Marina differed, however, from that of the prince of Wales in one important respect. As heir to the throne, Edward's public image was bound to his constitutional position and the British media refrained from presenting the prince of Wales in the same way as the film stars of the period: respectful of the distance between their camera lenses and the prince, they ensured that, in addition to informal images, he was presented in a more dignified manner as befitting a future king and emperor.[37] As more minor royals, the same rules did not apply to George and Marina and they broke with royal protocol by courting the media's attention through more informal displays of public intimacy. This difference was particularly evident when Marina arrived in England from France in mid September en route to Balmoral, where she would discuss her wedding plans with her fiancé and his family. According to the media descriptions of her disembarkation at Folkestone, Marina captivated the crowds who had waited to greet her: 'From the first moment she was seen – slim, beautiful and exquisitely dressed – excitedly waving a white handkerchief on the upper-deck of the cross-Channel steamer, the Princess enslaved the wildly cheering spectators massed on the pier'.[38] The press published large, front-page photographs of the princess smiling and waving to the crowds to emphasize how she had visibly interacted with spectators. These images were accompanied by the message delivered by Marina to reporters that, 'I shall love your great nation very dearly, and it seems as though your people have already some affection for me'.[39] The princess's eagerness to engage with the public by waving to them was, in fact, exceptional: the waving of an upraised arm or handkerchief was not something commonly associated with British royalty before 1934 and newspapers noted that this innovative gesture contrasted with the bowing traditionally used by the royal family to signal their appreciation of the crowd's cheers.[40]

At a time when European dictators were popularizing gestural salutes through the new media of film and photography in order to harness the support of their peoples and create visual images of disciplined nations united around the focal point of the leader, Marina's wave may have similarly intensified the personal connections between members of the public and the royal family.[41] Reporting the princess's arrival in England,

[37] F. Mort, 'On tour with the prince: monarchy, imperial politics and publicity in the Prince of Wales's dominion tours 1919–1920', *Twentieth Century British Hist.*, xxix (2018), 25–57.

[38] *Daily Mirror*, 17 Sept. 1934, p. 1.

[39] *Daily Herald*, 17 Sept. 1934, p. 1; *Daily Express*, 17 Sept. 1934, p. 1; *Daily Mirror*, 17 Sept. 1934, p. 1.

[40] *Daily Sketch*, 26 Nov. 1934, p. 12. The article was titled 'Why Princess Waves'.

[41] M. Winkler, *The Roman Salute: Cinema, History, Ideology* (Columbus, Oh., 2009), pp. 88–121.

the *News Chronicle* informed readers that 'she was soon waving both hands to [the crowd] almost as frantically as they were waving to her'.[42] According to coverage like this, Marina's wave brought her closer to the public, who were able to connect with her through new informal codes of etiquette and deportment. Both popular and quality newspapers highlighted this gestural rapport by juxtaposing photographs of the waving princess alongside images of large, excited crowds (Figure 1.4).[43] These juxtapositions presented Marina as an exalted celebrity with a mass following. The moment that best captured this imagery was when she and George became the first royals to wave from Buckingham Palace's balcony following their wedding.[44] The media coverage of the Armistice celebrations outside the palace in November 1918 had transformed the royal balcony appearance into a ritual of national significance: the public were presented as symbolically united around the focal point of the monarchy.[45] Marina modernized this ritual to suit the more emotionally expressive 1930s. According to *Pathé Gazette*, the cheering that greeted the newly-titled duke and duchess of Kent as they emerged onto the balcony with their hands upheld could be heard a mile away and represented 'a spontaneous demonstration of happy, affectionate, and loyal emotion'.[46] The many newsreel and press comments in this vein suggested that the more direct, informal modes of communication introduced by George and Marina worked to personalize the relationship between the House of Windsor and the public.

Perhaps even more significant than Marina's popularization of the royal wave was the way she and George shared the first royal kiss ever caught on camera. When Marina arrived by train from Folkestone at Victoria Station in London she and the prince embraced for a fleeting moment, George kissing her on the cheek. But to judge from press reports it was much more romantic: 'When Princess Marina stepped from the Folkestone boat train at Victoria yesterday Prince George took her in his arms and kissed her. Then she kissed him. For a moment both seemed to have forgotten everyone else'.[47]

[42] *News Chronicle*, 17 Sept. 1934, p. 1.

[43] *Daily Sketch*, 17 Sept. 1934, p. 1; *The Times*, 17 Sept. 1934, p. 16; *Daily Mirror*, 17 Sept. 1934, pp. 14–5.

[44] *News Chronicle*, 30 Nov. 1934, p. 1. Comparable photographs and newsreels from the royal weddings of the 1920s show that the couples did not wave.

[45] 'The Day: Ours', *Pictorial News*, 14 Nov. 1918; 'Germany Signs the Armistice', *Gaumont Graphic*, 14 Nov. 1918. See also D. Cannadine, 'The context, performance and meaning of ritual: the British monarchy and the "invention of tradition", *c.* 1820–1977', in *The Invention of Tradition*, ed. E. Hobsbawm and T. Ranger (Cambridge, 1983), pp. 101–64, at pp. 128 and 140–1.

[46] 'The Royal Wedding', *Pathé Gazette*, 3 Dec. 1934.

[47] *Daily Express*, 17 Sept. 1934, p. 1. See also *Daily Sketch*, 17 Sept. 1934, p. 3; *Daily Mirror*, 17 Sept. 1934, p. 3.

Figure 1.4. 'London's Warm-Hearted Welcome', *Daily Sketch*, 17 September 1934, p. 1. © The British Library Board.

Daily Mirror

THE DAILY PICTURE NEWSPAPER WITH THE LARGEST NET SALE

BIG EDITION
Broadcasting - Page 22

|| 33

CYCLIST'S DEATH: REMARKABLE INQUEST STORY — Page 5

THE DAILY MIRROR, Thursday, November 22, 1934.

No. 9,669 — Registered at the G.P.O. as a Newspaper. — THURSDAY, NOVEMBER 22, 1934 — One Penny

ROYAL LOVERS' GREETING

Duke's Kiss at Quayside—
Palace Balcony Scene

WAVING PRINCESS

ROMANCE triumphed over fog when Princess Marina—a radiant and lovely bride-elect—arrived in London yesterday for her marriage next week to the Duke of Kent. The welcome given her had three stages.

DOVER: The Duke of Kent met the Princess at the quayside, clasped her hand, kissed her and whispered a word of greeting.

LONDON: Thousands cheered Princess Marina when she drove from Victoria to Buckingham Palace after being welcomed by the King and Queen and other members of the Royal Family. Beauty, brilliance and colour marked the station scene.

THE PALACE: After a huge crowd had cheered with intervals for half an hour, Princess Marina and the Duke of Kent came out on the balcony. In the encircling fog they could only be seen as dim figures against the glow of the Palace lights, but a tumult of cheers rose towards them.

WAVE TO CROWD: Then the Duke stood aside for a moment, leaving Princess Marina to acknowledge the cheers alone by waving to the crowd. With a final wave, both withdrew.

The royal lovers, an hour later, drove to St. James's Palace and took tea with the Prince of Wales. Last night the King and Queen gave a family dinner party in their honour.

Glowing Scene Despite the Fog

By CECILIE LESLIE

Princess Marina is in London—her future home.

She arrived yesterday—three minutes early.

Here is the story of the amazing scenes which greeted her.

THOUSANDS of policemen hedged the pavement like a blue, prickly cactus fence.

Almost as much fog as policemen. A cold, white, raw blanket of fog which had not the least effect on the thousands of Londoners and country people bent on welcoming the royal bride to her future home.

Come with me to Victoria Station. You—as an unprivileged member of the public—are not allowed within 100 yards of the red carpet, the white lilies and chrysanthemums bowers prepared for Princess Marina.

It is a pity you cannot see the gloomy barrack of Victoria Station looking pleasant for once.

Twenty-five bright arc lamps shine through the grey mists and make the platform look like a first night.

It is ten to three. We are all waiting. The King and Queen are in the room behind the bower of flowers. With them is the Prince of Wales and "other members" of the Royal Family—we don't know who else yet.

Three minutes to three . . . they are going to be half an hour late, says someone . . . a faint shadow looms down the railway track . . . "Here she comes—" somebody shouts. Princess Marina is minutes early.

Mr. Tucker, engine driver of the royal train, we congratulate you! Out of the waiting-room comes the Queen. The King is by her side in a black overcoat and top-hat. There's the Prince of Wales with a red carnation in his buttonhole.

NEW FASHION

Women onlookers noticed that Princess Marina had introduced a new hat fashion.

She was wearing a flat sailor hat of beige velvet bearing lovely brown and beige ostrich feathers curling over the tiny brim and nestling over the nape of her neck.

Here are "the others." The Princess Royal, in a mink coat and an olive-green hat, with the Earl of Harewood. The Duchess of York in grey silk hat, coat and a grey fur collar, with the Duke of York . . . the whole Royal Family, in fact.

The royal coach pulls up before the red carpet. For a moment the doors remain shut, then a figure in a striking royal blue coat and hat appears—Princess Nicholas. And now—Marina !

Dressed in beige silk coat with a big soft collar about her shoulders and a tiny, jaunty hat on the side of her head, tall and slim we recognise her immediately. Cameras click. She turns her head and smiles.

Curtsy to the King

The Queen steps forward and kisses Princess Marina. Now the King has kissed her on the cheek, and Princess Marina curtsies gracefully.

More people are coming out of the coach. That's Prince Paul of Yugoslavia in the purple hat and dress and here comes the Duke of Kent.

He is trying to look as if nothing unusual is going on, but he cannot hide his pleasure.

Under the glare of the arc lamps the circle of royal friends move leisurely greeting one another.

Princess Marina never once loses her poise. Her movements are controlled and unhurried. She follows her mother, shaking hands with each person in turn.

The bright lights pick out her soft beige hat, contrasting it with the bright purple hat of Princess Paul, the ultramarine coat of Princess Nicholas, the red carnation in the Prince of Wales's lapel and the bower of white lilies glowing over the crimson carpet.

Now they pass through the arc of flowers to the crimson-carpeted corridors.

Outside the cars draw up.

The royal party hesitates. Who goes first ? The parents of bride and bridegroom, the King, the Queen and Prince and Princess Nicholas leave in the first car.

Princess Marina is about to wave her sister into the second car when the Duke motions her into the car. He gets in beside her.

As the cavalcade passes into Wilton-road a cheer goes up. Shouts follow as the Duke of Kent's car comes into sight. A man hoists a baby girl on his shoulder and she waves delightedly at everyone.

(Continued on page 3)

(Continued on page 3)

The affectionate greeting between the royal lovers at Dover. See also pages 16, 17 and 32.

Figure 1.5. 'Royal Lovers' Greeting', *Daily Mirror*, 22 November 1934, p. 1. © The British Library Board.

59

The *Daily Express* also drew attention to this description by capitalizing and emboldening its text. Despite effusive descriptions like this one, no British newspaper actually published photographs of the kiss. It is possible that this was because pictures would have failed to do justice to the press's dramatic accounts – George's peck on Marina's cheek was hardly the passionate lovers' greeting. Alternatively, it may have been that editors deemed it too risqué to publish a photograph of the kiss as it would have been the first time that the amorous gesture with its sexual connotations was visually portrayed in relation to royalty. Whatever the reasoning, the newsreels were not as reticent. *Gaumont British News* presented cinemagoers with the first onscreen royal kiss and this scoop initiated a much bolder approach to the exposure of royal intimacy, dispelling old taboos.[48] Reporting the second occasion that George welcomed his fiancé to England, a week before the wedding, the press printed front-page photographs of the couple kissing (Figure 1.5). *Pathé* went so far as to use the kiss as the backdrop to its title sequence, showing the momentary embrace twice in an attempt to attract viewers' attention.[49]

While the media drew special attention to the new kinds of intimacy which characterized the 1934 royal love story, it is important not to lose sight of George and Marina's agency in the creation of their public images. The prince seems to have understood Marina's popular appeal and he wrote to Prince Paul of Yugoslavia to describe spectators' reactions to her initial arrival in London: 'Everyone is so delighted with her – the crowd especially – 'cos when she arrived at Victoria Station they expected a dowdy princess – such as unfortunately my family are – but when they saw this lovely chic creature – they could hardly believe it and even the men were interested and shouted "Don't change – don't let them change you!"'.[50] The remark, 'Don't let *them* change you!', can be read in two ways.[51] On the one hand, it may have been intended to convey criticism of the machinations of a shadowy court and possibly those officials who Labour politician Stafford Cripps had claimed lurked behind the throne earlier in the year. On the other, and in line with Prince George's interpretation, the comment might have reflected a public concern about the potentially stifling effects that the old-fashioned British monarchy could have on the modern Marina: it certainly seems that the princess's unique glamour distinguished her from other royal women, including the duchess of York, who were less fashion-conscious. When

---

[48] 'Princess Marina at Victoria Station and Ballater', *Gaumont British News*, 20 Sept. 1934.
[49] *Daily Mirror*, 22 Nov. 1934, p. 1; *News Chronicle*, 22 Nov. 1934, p. 1; 'Royal Reception to Princess Marina', *Pathé Super Sound Gazette*, 22 Nov. 1934.
[50] Quoted in Watson, *Marina*, p. 101.
[51] This author's italics.

Figure 1.6. 'To-day's Great Abbey Wedding', *Daily Mirror*,
26 April 1923, p. 1. © The British Library Board.

Princess Alexandra of Denmark first arrived in London in anticipation of her marriage to the prince of Wales in 1863, the media feted her for her distinctive beauty and elegance.[52] Now, more than seventy years on, Marina, who was a distant relative of Alexandra through the Danish royal line, was similarly celebrated for the personal qualities she brought to British shores and her modern royal style which, according to the unparalleled press and newsreel coverage, had captured the nation's imagination.[53]

[52] J. Plunkett, *Queen Victoria: First Media Monarchy* (Oxford, 2003), pp. 51–2.
[53] For comparisons of the two royal brides, see the *Daily Mail*, 30 Aug. 1934, p. 11; H. Normanton, 'Our Danish royal bride', *The Queen*, 12 Dec. 1934, p. 13.

George was intent on promoting the popular image which he shared with the princess. During their stay together in London, he and Marina sat for English society photographer Dorothy Wilding. To date, the most informal photographs taken of a royal couple had been those of the Yorks prior to their wedding in 1923: the couple posed next to one another, although there was no physical contact; the duke, dressed in a lounge suit, rested against a table with his arms crossed so that he and his fiancée, who was wearing a dress and a pearl necklace, were positioned at a similar height (Figure 1.6).[54] Wilding helped to craft much more emotionally expressive scenes between George and Marina which emphasized their modernity and the close bond the couple ostensibly shared. In one of the Wilding photographs, Marina, dressed in a dark, sleek dress, sat in an armchair with George – in pin-striped lounge suit – perched next to her, his arm draped over her shoulder.[55] However, the most intimate Wilding photograph showed the lovers side-on, George in front, with Marina resting her chin over his shoulder (Figure 1.7). Wilding had recently photographed the Hollywood couple Gertrude Lawrence and Douglas Fairbanks Jr. in a similar pose.[56] The prince and princess's public personae thus overlapped with both the celebrity of film stars and the society set, as conveyed through the art-deco modern style associated with Wilding's portraiture in these years.[57]

George gave express permission for the widespread reproduction of the Wilding photographs. The company Raphael Tuck & Sons wrote to the prince's equerry, Major Butler, asking for George's approval to produce a series of postcards using the photographs. Desmond Tuck noted that Wilding 'made it perfectly clear that [the photographs had] not yet been passed for publication, but, with a view to the possibility that they might ultimately be, and in time for the Royal Wedding', his firm had developed negative reproductions 'in the hope that His Royal Highness may care to inspect them, and accord his sanction to us, to issue them for sale to the public'.[58] The granting or withholding of official approval was one of the main ways in which the royal household was able to control the cultural production of the monarchy's iconography.[59] Thus Butler's short reply, that 'His Royal Highness the Duke of Kent has given his consent to the

---

[54] *Daily Mirror*, 26 Apr. 1923, p. 1. For the original, see NPG x130935, Vandyk, Jan. 1923.

[55] NPG x35653, Dorothy Wilding, Oct. 1934; also NPG x33897, Wilding, Oct. 1934; NPG x46512, Wilding, Oct. 1934.

[56] NPG x33887, Wilding, Oct. 1934; NPG x46508, Wilding, Oct. 1934.

[57] V. Williams, *Women Photographers: the Other Observers 1900 to the Present* (London, 1986), p. 152.

[58] RA, GDKH/WED/A01, D. A. Tuck to H. W. Butler, 7 Nov. 1934.

[59] Houlbrook, *Prince of Tricksters*, pp. 260–2.

Figure 1.7. 'Raphael Tuck & Sons Ltd. announce Real Photo Postcards and Calendars of beautiful photographs by Dorothy Wilding of T.R.H. The Duke and Duchess of Kent', *Illustrated London News*, 1 December 1934, p. 947. © The British Library Board.

RAPHAEL TUCK & SONS LTD.
announce *Real Photo Postcards and Calendars of beautiful photographs by Dorothy Wilding*
of T.R.H. The Duke and Duchess of Kent

authorised for publication by Their Royal Highnesses
These are available as
REAL PHOTOGRAPH CALENDARS
3 subjects, 11" × 9" - - 3/6 each
3 subjects, 9" × 6¾" - - 2/- each
and
REAL PHOTOGRAPH POSTCARDS
the set of 9 subjects 2/3, or 3d. each
of all leading stationers and stores
Made in England by
RAPHAEL TUCK & SONS, LTD.
Art Publishers to their Majesties the King and Queen and H.R.H. The Prince of Wales
RAPHAEL HOUSE, MOORFIELDS, LONDON, E.C.2.

publication of the enclosed photographs', conferred legitimacy on Tuck's souvenir postcards and suggests that George approved of the intimate way in which they presented him and his fiancée.[60]

The prince's equerry played an active role in shaping George's and Marina's public images. He extended permission to the media and London restaurants to publish Wilding's photographs and he also vetted images to ensure they were appropriate.[61] The printers Valentine and Sons Ltd.

[60] RA, GDKH/WED/A01, H. W. Butler to D. A. Tuck, 8 Nov. 1934.

[61] RA, GDKH/WED/A01, the editor of *The Wireless Press* to the palace press officer, 2 Nov. 1934 and reply containing assent on 6 Nov. 1934. For press reproductions of Wilding's photographs, see *Daily Mirror*, 29 Nov. 1934, p. 1; *Daily Express*, 20 Nov. 1934, p. 8. The file LMA, 4364/02/022 contains over 20 different hotel invitations and menus which used Wilding's photographs to promote commercial events.

wrote to Butler explaining they had received instructions from the postcard distributor Messrs Carreras to supply them with a series of photographic cigarette cards 'depicting leading British popular personalities' and that they were 'particularly anxious' George and Marina should be included in this series.[62] This request reveals the extent to which the royal lovers had shot to fame on their engagement, since they were deemed to be sufficiently well-known subjects for inclusion on cigarette cards. More significant, though, was Butler's reply: 'You should allow me to see which photographs you intend to use, in case I might be able to suggest to you which ones would be suitable'.[63] This approach reveals how courtiers tried to control the visual image of the royal family and should be interpreted in light of the fact that there was a thriving trade in unofficial pictures of royalty. When Tuck originally wrote to Butler requesting permission to publish postcards of the Wilding photographs, he stated that 'there are, regrettably, on the market, produced by certain other firms, reproductions of HRH Prince George and The Princess Marina, issued, presumably without sanction, and which do anything but justice to the Royal Personages they pretend to portray'.[64] At the time of Princess Mary's wedding in 1922 courtiers had banned the commercial reproduction of royal coats of arms for fear of degrading the crown's image.[65] But twelve years on the palace adopted a more proactive role in promoting intimate pictures of George and Marina as part of an official royal visual culture which was stimulated by a growing trade in the popular image of royalty and by a mass media committed to bringing royal domesticity closer to the public.

Given George and Marina's glamour, it is perhaps unsurprising that after the prince was killed in a plane crash in 1942 a female Mass Observation respondent likened him to a Hollywood celebrity: 'He was so popular – I really think he was the most popular member of the Royal Family. His visit to any factory would create excitement. The girls used to think of him as a film star'.[66] It is certainly the case that the media reported the couple's romance to resonate with the popular themes of love, beauty and celebrity which dominated female-targeted news in this period. We should interpret the media's narration of the 1934 royal engagement and wedding as forming part of an attempt by news editors to achieve this type of audience identification and simultaneously to define modern British womanhood

[62] RA, GDKH/WED/A01, D. S. Valentine to H. W. Butler, 2 Nov. 1934.
[63] RA, GDKH/WED/A01, H. W. Butler to D. S. Valentine, 6 Nov. 1934.
[64] RA, GDKH/WED/A01, D. A. Tuck to H. W. Butler, 7 Nov. 1934.
[65] RA, LC/LCO/SPECIAL, Wedding 1922 File 19, F. S. Osgood to B. M. Shiffers, 1 Feb. 1922.
[66] MOA, File Report 1392.

along the contours of emotional fulfilment, fame and fashion.[67] Marina notably became the first member of the royal family whose style was celebrated by the media for its mass appeal. The *Daily Herald* published a photograph of 'hats which Princess Marina liked in Paris being tried on in a London store yesterday' and informed its readers that 'ones just like them will soon be on sale'.[68]

The media's efforts to appeal to the perceived tastes of British women were also evident in the way the press prioritized female journalists' insights into the royal romance. After its 'first interview' with the couple, the *Daily Express* printed an article by Winifred Loraine titled 'Princess Marina – As She Really Is'.[69] This mini-biography focused on Marina's domesticity, noting that 'she can cook and make her own dresses', in order to encourage readers to identify with her. The *Daily Mail* and *Mirror* also advertised reports prepared by their 'special woman correspondent[s]' – implying that, because of their gender, they offered a unique perspective on the love story.[70] The *News of the World* invited the romantic novelist Ruby Ayers to prepare some of its wedding coverage, her articles predictably climaxing in the kind of 'happy ending' for which she was renowned.[71] And newsreel companies also employed women specifically to deliver commentaries on the royal romance. One such voiceover preceded *British Movietone*'s recording of George and Marina's innovative 'film greeting' and the same female reporter went on to provide a number of other commentaries on the romance.[72] The shift in tone was particularly striking because all the other stories in the same newsreels were narrated by men. These strategies, then, reveal the ways in which news editors sought to tailor their coverage of the royal wedding to the perceived tastes of an expanding female audience. Equally, though, they should be interpreted as evidence of the process by which British women's interests were discursively defined in terms of love, glamour and consumerism.

---

[67] C. Grandy, *Heroes and Happy Endings: Class, Gender, and Nation in Popular Film and Fiction in Interwar Britain* (Manchester, 2014), pp. 133–76; A. Bingham, *Gender, Modernity and the Popular Press in Interwar Britain* (Oxford, 2004); pp. 78–81.

[68] *Daily Herald*, 18 Sept. 1934, p. 6; *Bolton Evening News*, 29 Nov. 1934, p. 2.

[69] *Daily Express*, 31 Aug. 1934, p. 3.

[70] *Daily Mail*, 28 Nov. 1934, p. 5; *Daily Mirror*, 30 Nov. 1934, p. 30. See A. Bingham, *Family Newspapers? Sex, Private Life and the British Popular Press, 1918–1978* (Oxford, 2009), pp. 25–6 on the marginalization of female journalists' voices in this period.

[71] *News of the World*, 25 Nov. 1934, p. 12; 2 Dec. 1934, pp. 12–3.

[72] 'Princess Marina greeted in Britain', *British Movietone News*, 22 Nov. 1934; and 'Ready for the royal wedding', *British Movietone News*, 26 Nov. 1934.

Staging a wedding, building a nation

In late 1934, the British faced the challenges of protracted socio-economic dislocation at home and growing aggression from foreign powers which seemed intent on disrupting Europe's fragile peace.[73] The threat that this kind of disorder represented to crowned heads of state was spectacularly demonstrated at the beginning of October by the assassination of King Alexander I of Yugoslavia during a diplomatic mission to France. He had been working towards a pact with the French foreign minister to unite southern Europe against Hitler when he was shot and killed by a Bulgarian revolutionary; the newsreels projected the brutality of the monarch's death around the world.[74] The courtiers who surrounded the British throne and oversaw the royal family's public relations were highly sensitive to these social and political changes. In staging George and Marina's wedding they saw an opportunity to democratize the House of Windsor's public image by presenting royal Christian family life as a focal point for national emotional identification. The scale of the media interest in George and Marina's romance distinguished it from earlier royal love stories and new media channels had helped to create a public image which was more intimate and accessible than ever before. But courtiers understood that democratization via new media existed in tension with the concern that overexposure could damage the reputation of royalty at a time when the crown's future as the leading symbol which held the nation together was by no means assured. The royal household thus sought to elevate the dignity of the royal wedding while ensuring that the British public could participate in it in innovative ways. This tension played out in the exchanges between courtiers, clerics and newsmen as they choreographed the first royal family event to be broadcast live from Westminster abbey to the nation and the world.

The first meeting at which these different interest groups came together in order to organize the royal wedding took place at the king's Scottish residence, Balmoral castle. Following their stay in London, George, Marina and the princess's parents travelled north aboard the Aberdeen express and, when they disembarked at Ballater train station, the royal lovers were given what *The Times* described as a 'real Highland welcome' by the thousands of spectators who had gathered to greet them and who crowded the roads leading to Balmoral.[75] On reaching the castle the party were met by the

---

[73] R. Overy, *The Morbid Age: Britain and the Crisis of Civilization* (London, 2010), pp. 181–6; J. Gardiner, *The Thirties: an Intimate History* (London, 2011), pp. 147–87 and 432–7; M. Ceadel, 'The first British referendum: the peace ballot, 1934–5', *Eng. Hist. Rev.*, xcv (1980), 810–39.

[74] E.g., 'Assassination', *Gaumont British News*, 11 Oct. 1934.

[75] *The Times*, 18 Sept. 1934, p. 12.

PRINCESS MARINA JOINS
IN FAMILY JOKE
AT BALMORAL

A SCOTSMAN EXPLAINS IT

Figure 1.8. 'Princess Marina Joins in Family Joke at Balmoral', *Daily Express*, 19 September 1934, p. 20. © The British Library Board.

Balmoral Highlanders in full ceremonial dress and the king's piper playing the 'Hielan' Laddie'. Then, clad in tartan country attire, George V and his consort Queen Mary received their son and their Greek guests, posing arm-in-arm for photographers (Figure 1.8). Newspapers stated that these 'delightfully informal pictures', which included Prince George in kilt and sporran, showed the royals enjoying a 'family joke' (it later emerged that the king was attempting to marshal his relatives into position for the photographers – to the amusement of all involved).[76] This was the first of several social engagements staged at the monarch's Scottish home which were widely reported on by the media. As with the extensive coverage that

---

[76] *Daily Express*, 19 Sept. 1934, p. 20; *The Times*, 19 Sept. 1934, p. 14; *The Times*, 25 Sept. 1934, p. 16.

was later devoted to stories about the gold mined for Marina's wedding ring in North Wales, descriptions of the 'Ghillies' Ball' and the 'Highland reel' danced by the prince and princess enhanced the image of a royal family that seemed to value the customs of the Celtic nations, strengthening the idea that all Britain could unite in celebrating the wedding.[77] Courtiers and the archbishop of Canterbury, who had also journeyed to Balmoral to help plan the marriage, believed the event should have this kind of inclusive appeal and two issues were of particular concern: what role could the Greek Orthodox Church – to which the princess and her family belonged – play as part of a wedding conducted in the Church of England's ceremonial centre, Westminster abbey? And would the king grant permission to the BBC to broadcast the wedding service from inside the church to listeners across Britain?

George V's private secretary, Sir Clive Wigram, had written to Archbishop Cosmo Lang from Balmoral on 4 September, noting that he was pleased the prelate and royal almoner would meet Marina and her parents as 'there is a good deal to be arranged':

> Already questions are being asked as to what part the Greek Church will take in the ceremony, or whether there will have to be some sort of a ceremony by the Greek Church before the Marriage, which presumably will take place in Westminster Abbey. The Queen, in talking to me of possibilities, said something about the Blessing by the Greek Church being given in the Private Chapel at Buckingham Palace. I am however very vague as to what is being thought of, but it seemed well to prepare you, as I know that Their Majesties will wish to discuss the matter with you when you are staying here.[78]

This letter revealed two things. First, it showed that George V and Queen Mary were concerned about the way in which royal family occasions were publicly staged and that they trusted Lang (as a long-standing friend and spiritual counsellor) to help them to plan the event.[79] Second, in referring to Queen Mary's suggestion that the Greek Orthodox Church bless the marriage in the private chapel at Buckingham Palace, the letter highlighted the potential problems a joint ceremony might create. Historians and royal biographers have presented the queen as an aloof, imperious figure of the Victorian period, but here she revealed a shrewd awareness of the importance of modern public relations in promoting the House of Windsor's position

---

[77] *Daily Mail*, 20 Sept. 1934, p. 12; 'Ballater – Princess Marina greeted in Scotland', *British Movietone News*, 20 Sept. 1934; 'Welsh gold for Princess Marina's ring', *Gaumont British News*, 8 Oct. 1934.

[78] LPL, Lang 129, fo. 311, C. Wigram to C. G. Lang, 4 Sept. 1934.

[79] R. Beaken, *Cosmo Lang: Archbishop in War and Crisis* (London, 2012), esp. ch. 4 and 5.

as a model of Christian family life.[80] In 1919 Princess Patricia had been the first member of the royal family to marry in Westminster abbey for more than five centuries.[81] The staging of her nuptials and the royal weddings of 1922 and 1923 in the abbey turned these events into spectacles of national significance by increasing the public visibility of royal domesticity. However, this visibility had far-reaching implications. Those close to the throne, including Wigram and the queen, had to consider how to organize royal weddings in order to broaden the monarchy's popular appeal while maintaining the dignity of crown and Church alike.[82]

When Lang solicited guidance from colleagues on the matter of the Greek service, Canon J. A. Douglas, general secretary of the Church of England council on foreign relations, was 'strongly of the opinion that it would be better to hold a separate ceremony so far as the Greek Orthodox Church is concerned'. Douglas agreed with Queen Mary that the Greek service 'might very well take place in Buckingham Palace's Chapel, or indeed anywhere in Buckingham Palace, before a small concourse of immediate relatives'.[83] His reasoning was rooted in a concern for the monarchy's dignity as a national symbol and for reverence for the Anglican marriage service:

> Douglas's objection to the idea of a joint ceremony in Westminster Abbey is based upon the belief that it would tend to make the whole think look ridiculous in the eyes of the Congregation and the public. At a Greek Orthodox Marriage Service the Bride and Bridegroom have to do things which in the eyes of the ordinary Britisher would appear somewhat ridiculous, e.g. wear a sort of crown,

---

[80] B. Pimlott, *The Queen: Elizabeth II and the Monarchy* (London, 2002), pp. 25, 192; Gardiner, *The Thirties*, pp. 458 and 527; Pope-Hennessy, *Queen Mary*, pp. 467–9.

[81] *Daily Mirror*, 28 Jan. 1919, p. 5; 28 Feb. 1919, p. 1. Courtiers made sure Patricia of Connaught was visible to spectators and cameramen on her wedding day, using carriages with enlarged windows in the procession to the abbey and an open-top landau on the return to Buckingham Palace.

[82] Wigram had helped to orchestrate the royal weddings of the 1920s, advising on the staging of carriage processions and on the suitability of royal ostentation at a time of industrial unrest. See RA, PS/PSO/GV/PS/MAIN/35056/B/4, Memo from C. Wigram to undisclosed recipient, 29 Jan. 1922; and RA, PS/PSO/GV/PS/MAIN/35056/B/7, Memo from C. Wigram to Lord Chamberlain, 23 Feb. 1922. Queen Mary had intervened in the preparations for her daughter Princess Mary's wedding in 1922 after the dean of Westminster had expressed concern that the ladies in attendance would not be wearing head-coverings in the abbey. He thought that the royal wedding should be used to set an example to the rest of the nation against 'eccentric and emancipated "feminists" [who had] in the last few years been trying to attend Church bare-headed'. Queen Mary suggested that 'small close-fitting caps' be worn with evening dress in order to maintain the 'reverence' of the event (RA, PS/PSO/GV/PS/MAIN/35056/B/4, Dean of Westminster to the State Chamberlain, 27 Jan. 1922); and Queen Mary to Lord Stamfordham, undated.

[83] LPL, Lang 129, fos. 314–19, A. C. Don to C. G. Lang, 17 Sept. 1934.

carry a candle, drink a glass of wine, walk round a table and so on. Poor Prince George would, I think, have the strongest objections to doing these things in the presence of the whole assembled aristocracy of the country. The whole thing would border on the ridiculous.[84]

Douglas's belief that the public would find Greek marital rituals 'ridiculous' and his sensitivity to the opinion of the 'ordinary Britisher' reflected a deeper concern within elite circles regarding the need to appeal to the 'people' as a specific social formation.[85] National culture was partly centred on what historians have termed an 'undemonstrative Protestantism' in this period; and this is clear from the way Douglas's suggestion – that British customs were incompatible with Greek religious practices – persuaded the archbishop that the Orthodox ceremony was best kept hidden from public view.[86] In conversation with the king at Balmoral, Lang presented the case against a joint service by delicately stressing that 'it would lengthen the proceedings greatly' and that the 'Orthodox ceremonies were much too elaborate for a service in the Abbey'.[87] The queen's original idea was thus adopted: it was agreed that the Greek service would take place in the private chapel at Buckingham Palace straight after the abbey ceremony and it would 'only be attended by the respective families, their suites, and any other persons specially invited'.[88] In this way Lang carefully helped to arrange a wedding which he thought would appeal to the British public's sensibilities.

The other important matter raised at the meeting between the British and Greek royal families was whether the king would permit the BBC to broadcast the wedding ceremony from Westminster abbey. On learning about the Balmoral family gathering, the controller of programmes at the BBC, Colonel Alan Dawnay, had written to Prince George's comptroller, Major Ulick Alexander, to propose the idea. Although historians have judged Dawnay's abilities as the second-in-command at the BBC (under Sir John Reith) unfavourably, his war record and patrician connections meant he was the perfect go-between to communicate with a royal household which largely comprised other ex-military men.[89] Addressing Alexander

---

[84] LPL, Lang 129, fos. 314–19, A. C. Don to C. G. Lang, 17 Sept. 1934.

[85] Houlbrook, *Prince of Tricksters*, p. 227.

[86] M. Grimley, 'The religion of Englishness: puritanism, providentialism, and "national character", 1918–1945', *Jour. Brit. Stud.*, xlvi (2007), 884–906, at p. 885; J. Wolffe, *God and Greater Britain: Religion and National Life in Britain and Ireland 1843–1945* (London, 1994), pp. 5–19.

[87] LPL, Lang 129, fos. 320–4.

[88] LPL, Lang 129, fos. 320–4.

[89] A. Briggs, *The History of Broadcasting in the United Kingdom* (5 vols., Oxford, 1965–95), ii. 411; Houlbrook, *Prince of Tricksters*, pp. 226–7.

as 'my dear Ulick' (the two were old friends having both passed through Eton and served in the Coldstream Guards together during the First World War), Dawnay explained that the BBC wanted to broadcast the wedding service, remarking that it would 'naturally be an occasion of intense interest to listeners everywhere':

> As I understand that you are going to Balmoral next week, I should be very grateful if you would discuss the matter with Wigram while you are there, and if he agrees, perhaps you could ascertain His Majesty's wishes and those of Prince George ... I am sure you will agree that it would be an excellent and a stirring thing to bring the ceremony, as it were, to the homes of people not only in this country but throughout the Empire.[90]

Dawnay's letter suggests that he viewed the monarchy as a symbol which had the potential to unite the nation and empire in these years. His approach was characteristic of a BBC which sought greater access to royal family events in order to elevate the monarchy's unifying role while simultaneously cementing its own credentials as an esteemed and internationally significant media institution.[91]

The king and Wigram also seem to have understood the importance of the crown's unifying role. Alexander was able to reply to Dawnay that he had 'brought up the question about Prince George's wedding service being broadcast' and 'there is not likely to be any objection, provided you have already obtained the permission of the Dean of Westminster to do this'.[92] Approval from the abbey authorities was, however, slow to arrive. By the time Dawnay wrote to Alexander again to explain that the dean had agreed to the broadcast and that the BBC would now like official royal consent so that it could begin its preparations, newspapers had got wind of the preliminary plans and revealed that radio listeners would be able to participate in the wedding ceremony from their homes.[93] Dawnay included a postscript in his letter noting his regret that the press had made a 'premature announcement to the effect that the ceremony will be broadcast. I can assure you that the leak has not come from here'.[94] Unfortunately for Dawnay, the leak *had* come from the BBC. In what was almost certainly a reflection of his managerial incompetence as controller of programmes,

[90] BBCWA, R34/862/1, A. Dawnay to U. Alexander, 14 Sept. 1934.

[91] T. Hajkowski, *The BBC and National Identity in Britain, 1922–53* (Manchester, 2010), pp. 83–92; S. Potter, *Broadcasting Empire: the BBC and the British World, 1922–1970* (Oxford, 2012), pp. 59–64.

[92] BBCWA, R34/862/1, U. Alexander to A. Dawnay, 24 Sept. 1934.

[93] *Daily Mail*, 10 Oct. 1934, p. 11.

[94] BBCWA, R34/862/1, A. Dawnay to U. Alexander, 10 Oct. 1934.

Dawnay had earlier instructed his director of outside broadcasts, Gerald Cock, to let the *Daily Mail*'s columnist, Collie Knox, have the scoop on the BBC's wedding preparations as soon as permission to broadcast had been acquired from the abbey.[95]

The palace and abbey authorities expressed disappointment with the BBC's indiscretion and Cock had to work hard to dispel their concerns and regain their trust.[96] This episode revealed how the organizers of the wedding had to fight to control the release of information about its planning against the pressures exerted on them by reporters hungry for disclosure. Equally, though, this chain of events showed how communications channels linking the BBC to the royal household were complicated by elite codes of etiquette, with the broadcaster negotiating court protocol in its efforts to bring royalty closer to the public.

Luckily for the BBC, George V ultimately gave his official consent to the wedding broadcast 'provided that the mechanical arrangements in connection with [the] ceremony do not obtrude on the vision'.[97] This message, written by the king's assistant private secretary, Sir Frank Mitchell, to the lord chamberlain of the royal household, again revealed a monarch who was anxious to maintain the religious significance of the service. The message was relayed to Sir Edward Knapp-Fisher, the receiver general of Westminster abbey.[98] These three men were intimately involved in maintaining the dignity of the wedding ceremony in the presence of the new form of media. Cock had to assure Knapp-Fisher that the BBC did not want to broadcast a commentary over the wedding service but, rather, that commentator Howard Marshall would describe to listeners 'scenes <u>outside</u> the Abbey'. Cock also stressed that the BBC's technical plans would enable 'a perfect reproduction of the entire service' and that no equipment would 'be visible to those in the Abbey, with the single exception of a fine wire and one microphone'.[99] Knapp-Fisher and the lord chamberlain were happy with these arrangements and it seems that the microphone placement in the abbey had the desired impact.[100] Writing to Cock after the wedding

[95] BBCWA, R30/3/644/1, BBC Internal Circulating Memo, G. Cock to A. Dawnay, 10 Oct. 1934.

[96] BBCWA, R30/3/644/1, H. Marshall to G. Cock, undated, and reply, 12 Oct. 1934; BBCWA, R30/3/644/1, G. Cock to E. Knapp-Fisher, 12 Oct. 1934; RA, LC/LCO/SPECIAL, Wedding 1934 File 14, Memo, Lord Chamberlain to F. Mitchell, 16 Oct. 1934.

[97] RA, LC/LCO/SPECIAL, Wedding 1934 File 14, Memo, F. Mitchell to the Lord Chamberlain, 17 Oct. 1934.

[98] WAL, WAM/OC/2/3, 'Broadcasting and Filming', Lord Chamberlain to E. Knapp-Fisher, 18 Oct. 1934.

[99] BBCWA, R30/3/644/1, G. Cock to E. Knapp-Fisher, 13 Oct. 1934 (Cock's emphasis).

[100] WAL, WAM/OC/2/3, 'Broadcasting and Filming', E. Knapp-Fisher to the Lord Chamberlain, 19 Oct. 1934.

THE DAILY MIRROR, Friday, November 30, 1934

Broadcasting - Page 24

Daily Mirror

THE DAILY PICTURE   NEWSPAPER WITH THE LARGEST NET SALE

ROYAL WEDDING NUMBER

No. 9,676   Registered at the G.P.O. as a Newspaper.   FRIDAY, NOVEMBER 30, 1934   One Penny

'I WILL'—VOW THAT THRILLED THE WORLD
Whole Empire as Unseen Guests at Abbey

" Never in history has a marriage been attended by so vast a company of witnesses," said the Archbishop of Canterbury in his address to the Duke of Kent and his bride. Thanks to the miracle of wireless, the whole Empire were wedding guests, for, as the Primate said, " the multitude of listening people regard the family of our beloved King and Queen as in a true sense their own." In this memorable picture the royal bridal couple are seen standing before the Archbishop during their marriage in Westminster Abbey.

Figure 1.9. '"I Will" – Vow that Thrilled the World', *Daily Mirror*, 30 November 1934, p. 1. © The British Library Board.

ceremony, the *Sunday Dispatch*'s radio correspondent, J. G. Reekie, told him: 'I listened in from my sick bed and was amazed. I don't know where the "mikes" were placed, but you certainly found the right places for them!'[101]

Knapp-Fisher also helped to control the media's access to the marriage ceremony. As with the royal weddings of the 1920s, courtiers arranged the distribution of press and photography passes to the abbey through the chairman of the Newspaper Proprietors' Association: Lord George Riddell in 1922/23 and Sir Thomas McAra in 1934.[102] However, the patrician connections which linked the palace and abbey authorities to the offices of *The Times* meant that newspaper received special consideration. Not only did the royal household entrust *The Times* with taking the official photographs of George and Marina's wedding service but the assistant editor of the paper, Robert Barrington-Ward, was also able to ask Knapp-Fisher informally if he could reserve seats for two of his reporters in the abbey.[103] The reply revealed the privileges extended to *The Times*: 'My dear Robin, the Press arrangements are in the hands of Mr Frank Mitchell of Buckingham Palace, but I should like to say that if a member of your Staff would like a roving commission in the Abbey, he would certainly be at liberty to have it. I need hardly say that Court dress would be essential for the perambulating man'.[104] The gentlemanly codes of conduct which characterized the men's relationship meant that Knapp-Fisher trusted *The Times* to maintain discretion and dignity in its coverage of the royal wedding. Indeed, the photographs of George and Marina taken by *The Times* during the service, which were subsequently distributed to other media organizations, followed the respectful, distant style of those taken at the royal weddings of the early 1920s. The couple can be seen standing in the aisle facing Archbishop Lang with their backs to the viewer (Figure 1.9). By refraining from presenting close-up photographs of their facial expressions, which would inevitably have highlighted the human emotion of the scenes, these images sought to preserve the sanctity of the pact the couple were making in front of God's representative.[105]

[101] BBCWA, R30/3/644/1, J. G. Reekie to G. Cock, 5 Dec. 1934.

[102] RA, LC/LCO/SPECIAL, Wedding 1922 File 6, Lord Riddell to the State Chamberlain, 6 Jan. 1922; RA, LC/LCO/SPECIAL, Wedding 1934 File 14, F. Mitchell to T. McAra, 26 Nov. 1934.

[103] RA, LC/LCO/SPECIAL, Wedding 1934 File 14, Lord Chamberlain to F. Mitchell, 18 Oct. 1934; WAL, WAM/OC/2/3, 'Press', R. Barrington-Ward to E. Knapp-Fisher, 18 Oct. 1934.

[104] WAL, WAM/OC/2/3, 'Press', E. Knapp-Fisher to R. Barrington-Ward, 19 Oct. 1934.

[105] *The Times*, 30 Nov. 1934, p. 22. For reproductions of the photograph in other newspapers, see *Daily Mirror*, 30 Nov. 1934, pp. 1 and 26; *Daily Express*, 30 Nov. 1934, p. 24.

The dean of Westminster, William Foxley Norris, helped Knapp-Fisher to regulate media access to the wedding service. Courtiers were particularly concerned with controlling the royal family's visual image and the idea of making a newsreel film of the wedding ceremony was out of the question. But this did not prevent newsreel companies from making unofficial advances to the abbey authorities requesting access to film the marriage service – all of which were subsequently rebuffed by the dean or receiver general.[106] There was also consternation among palace and abbey officials about the potential recording of the BBC broadcast of the service. For the previous two years, the gramophone company HMV had produced records of the king's Christmas broadcasts. On learning that HMV planned to make a recording of the royal wedding ceremony, Wigram urgently wrote to Foxley Norris asking him if he could stop it.[107] While this issue was amicably resolved by HMV withdrawing, *Universal News* recorded the section of the royal wedding broadcast in which George and Marina exchanged their marriage vows and played this audio over still photographs of the ceremony in its newsreel coverage of the event, presenting it as the 'biggest scoop for years'.[108] This recording contradicted the express wishes of Knapp-Fisher, who had earlier rejected applications from other newsreel companies to record the radio transmission; and Foxley Norris wrote to the editor of *Universal News* threatening legal action if he did not oversee the deletion of the offending soundtrack from newsreels which had been distributed to cinemas.[109]

In this way, then, the royal household and Church of England worked in tandem to try to ensure the dignity of the wedding was maintained, and not undermined, by media organizations which stood to gain commercially from exposés. Although *Universal News*'s scoop was indicative of an underhand culture of disclosure, most media organizations proved ready to toe the official line and help to popularize a respectful image of a family monarchy as the emotional centre-point of British national life. Back at Broadcasting House, Gerald Cock and his team were making arrangements for a wedding

[106] WAL, WAM/OC/2/3, 'Press', B. B. Saveall, news editor of *British Movietone News*, to W. Foxley Norris, 27 Sept. 1934, and reply, 10 Oct. 1934; R. S. Howard, editor of *Gaumont British News*, to E. Knapp-Fisher, 19 Nov. 1934, and reply, 19 Nov. 1934. See also letter from W. Foxley Norris to E. Knapp-Fisher, 5 Oct. 1934.
[107] WAL, WAM/OC/2/3, 'Broadcasting and Filming', C. Wigram to W. Foxley Norris, 19 Nov. 1934.
[108] WAL, WAM/OC/2/3, 'Broadcasting and Filming', advertisement for the *Universal News* newsreel in the *Daily Film Renter*, 1 Dec. 1934.
[109] WAL, WAM/OC/2/3, 'Broadcasting and Filming', H. W. Bishop of *Gaumont British News* to E. Knapp-Fisher, 1 Dec. 1934; W. Foxley Norris to C. R. Snape, editor of *Universal News*, 1 Dec. 1934.

broadcast which would communicate the impression that the nation had gathered to celebrate George and Marina's marriage. Earlier in the summer, the Oxford-educated Howard Marshall had achieved distinction as one of Britain's most recognizable wireless commentators with his ball-by-ball descriptions of the cricket test match series between England and Australia.[110] Marshall's recently acquired fame and background, with his low, dulcet tones and assured manner, made him the perfect choice to voice the royal wedding broadcast.[111] His royal wedding commentary was notable for the way it addressed listeners as active participants in the celebrations. A good example of this can be discerned in his closing lines after the marriage: 'It has been a great occasion, and now, as *we* take our leave of the Royal couple, I'm sure *you* will all join with *me* in wishing long life and all happiness to the Duke and Duchess of Kent'.[112] The words highlighted show how Marshall used an inclusive, personalized rhetoric to encourage his audience to feel as though they were participating in the event along with those who had gathered in London to celebrate the royal wedding.

The early 1930s were also notable for the BBC's experimentation with listener identification: the broadcaster tried to reach out to expanding female and working-class audiences through human-interest stories that appealed to the emotions.[113] The BBC's coverage of the royal wedding is a good case in point. An internal circulating memo shows that Cock's team wanted to juxtapose Marshall's commentary, with its 'privileged' perspective, alongside a 'Cockney's impressions from the crowd' as part of an evening bulletin on the royal nuptials.[114] The memo included the suggestion that 'this second speaker might be a woman'. This identification of a female, working-class voice from London as a desirable feature of the coverage should again be attributed to the way in which elite institutions including the monarchy, Church and BBC sought to engage in new ways with what they perceived as 'ordinary' people in these years. Indeed, it was between the wars that the Cockney was transformed by the media into an archetype of national working-class identity.[115] The idea that the second speaker might also be

---

[110] Briggs, *History of Broadcasting*, ii. 112.

[111] BBCWA, R30/3/644/1, H. Marshall to L. Schuster, 1 Oct. 1934. For an example of Marshall's style, see <https://www.youtube.com/watch?v=LbKHU8QdeBs> [accessed 30 May 2018].

[112] BBCWA, R30/3/644/1, H. Marshall to L. Schuster, undated (this author's italics).

[113] Colpus, 'The Week's Good Cause', pp. 321–4. See also Andrews, 'Homes Both Sides', pp. 606–8.

[114] BBCWA, R30/3/644/1, Internal Circulating Memo, Mr. Adam to Mr. Coatman, 11 Oct. 1947.

[115] G. Stedman Jones, 'The "Cockney" and the Nation', in *Metropolis: Histories and Representations since 1800*, ed. D. Feldman and G. Stedman Jones (London, 1989), pp. 272–324.

female mirrored the way the media sought to tailor its coverage of the royal wedding to the perceived tastes of women. As plans for the broadcast developed, news editor Ralph Murray took special precautions to ensure a suitable candidate provided this novel perspective:

> The crowd point of view: Cock has someone called Whittaker Wilson who he says has the right sort of contact with the crowd mentality and might suitably be dispatched into their midst to catch their comments. Or – in the abstract preferably, but practically presenting some difficulty – your solution of getting a Cockney woman in to do it herself. Miss Race could perhaps help us in getting a bright Cockney, as she has an extensive acquaintance with such people.[116]

This passage, which suggested that special care was needed to prepare for contact with working-class people, shows just how innovative the desire to reflect the 'crowd mentality' was. These negotiations also seem to point to the BBC's concern that the working-class voice should support the broadcaster's official interpretation of the royal wedding. The BBC thus saw the 1934 royal wedding as a suitable moment to explore popular opinion in order to enhance the vision of a nation united around the crown. This early example of a vox-pop interview sought to shed light on a particular version of popular opinion and anticipated Mass Observation's ethnographic intervention into national life at George VI's coronation in 1937. Royal events can thus be seen to have exerted a democratizing influence on British society by stimulating explorations of wider public attitudes.[117]

The BBC also worked to generate an image of the British nation gathered around the focal point of the marriage through its technical arrangements for the wedding broadcast. BBC editorial policy for the programme specified that listeners should be able to appreciate 'crowd noises and general effects': the engineer faded up the peal of the abbey bells and the sounds made by spectators in order to help immerse those listening in the events as they unfolded.[118] Indeed, one of the very few complaints levelled at the BBC by some listeners after the wedding was that Marshall's commentary had at times been 'too continuous to allow crowd effects etc. to stir the imagination'.[119]

---

[116] BBCWA, R30/3/644/1, Memo, R. Murray to the News Editor, 25 Oct. 1934.

[117] J. Moran, 'Vox populi?: the recorded voice and twentieth-century British history', *Twentieth Century British Hist.*, xxv (2014), 461–83, at pp. 463–5.

[118] BBCWA, R30/3/644/1, Confidential: 'Royal Wedding, 29 Nov. 1934'.

[119] BBCWA, R30/3/644/1, Anonymous handwritten memorandum: 'Royal Wedding November 29th 1934 – Criticism of Howard Marshall – Compiled from Listeners Letters'. None of the letters that criticized Marshall has survived. However, correspondence that has survived suggests the majority of letters received from listeners praised both the BBC and the commentator for their handling of the royal wedding broadcast (e.g., J. Reith to H. Marshall, 11 Dec. 1934).

This suggests that the audience wanted to engage vicariously in the event and expected to hear sounds that would help to achieve this effect. Newsreel film editors similarly understood the importance of crowd noises to the experience of their viewers and amplified the sounds of cheering which attended scenes along the procession route and outside Buckingham Palace in order to achieve symbolic auditory exaltation of the royals.[120]

The British media's emphasis on the crowds which assembled in London for the royal wedding had a deeper significance in the troubled context of the early 1930s. Before the event, news headlines reported that one million people were expected to travel to the capital from other parts of the country aboard specially chartered overnight rail services, boosting the transport industry and injecting £15 million into the tourism and hospitality sectors.[121] The *Daily Express* presented the wedding as a more direct stimulus for trade, claiming that 'hundreds will marry on November 29th' (the same day as the royal couple) as part of a 'love boom week'.[122] While the most damaging effects of the interwar economic crisis had passed by late 1934, the media clearly envisioned the royal wedding as having a positive effect on the nation's finances by bringing people together from the furthest corners of Britain. The royal household also took precautionary measures to maintain the idea that the wedding would benefit the economy. Marina had asked Edward Molyneux to create her wedding outfits in Paris, but this led to a dispute with courtiers because royal ladies were expected to set an example to the population by 'Buying British' to support the economy. In complying with this obligation, Molyneux designed her a wedding dress that would be made in London and a trousseau that would be made in Paris out of British materials. This proved a fitting *entente cordiale*, but newspapers went to special lengths to stress that British tailors would benefit from Marina's fashion choices.[123]

The media narrative that the British public's 'great invasion' of London for the wedding strengthened national ties was made even more explicitly by newspapers which claimed that the event witnessed the temporary easing of social distinctions and class animosities. Reports focused on the good-natured crowds and the degree to which people of different backgrounds

---

[120] 'The royal wedding', *Pathé Super Sound Gazette*, 29 Nov. 1934; 'The duke of Kent weds Princess Marina', *British Paramount News*, 3 Dec. 1934.

[121] *Sunday Pictorial*, 25 Nov. 1934, p. 1; *Daily Express*, 26 Nov. 1934, p. 3.

[122] *Daily Express*, 3 Nov. 1934, p. 3.

[123] E. Ehrman, 'Broken traditions: 1930–55', in *The London Look: Fashion From Street to Catwalk*, ed. C. Breward, E. Ehrman and C. Evans (London, 2004), pp. 97–117. Also see *Daily Sketch*, 29 Nov. 1934, p. 14; *Daily Telegraph*, 15 Sept. 1934, p. 8; *Daily Mirror*, 20 Nov. 1934, p. 1.

had gathered together on the procession route the night before wedding day:

> We stood there, an anxious crowd – some of us had been standing there all night – to watch the Royal Wedding. There were nearly a million of us there, and we came from all sorts and conditions of people. We were very rich, and we were very poor. We had many different political views. We did not see eye to eye by any means. But we all stood shoulder to shoulder from four to 20 deep along the kerb of the Royal route. It was a crowd now greater than any that has collected since the Armistice, and we were there to see a bride who, as the Primate so aptly put it, the British people had taken into their hearts.[124]

Likening the mood on the procession route to the public response to the Armistice in 1918, the writer Geraint Goodwin described a unique moment of cohesion which, he suggested, transcended social tensions. The same sentiment can be detected in newspaper reports which presented the wedding as 'the day that made the nation happier' and as a 'public event not, for once, depressing – as so much "news" is in these troubled times'.[125]

It is significant that there were very few dissenting media voices which offered alternative interpretations of the 1934 royal wedding. Naturally, the loudest criticism of the event came from the communist *Daily Worker*, which consistently stressed to its readership the economic disparity that separated the privileged lives of the royal family from those of the unemployed labourers who lived in Britain's depressed industrial communities. Typical was the *Worker*'s front-page coverage on royal wedding day, which claimed that the House of Windsor contributed nothing to society yet received handsome state-sponsored benefits through their civil-list payments.[126] The headline, 'Out-Of-Work Princess Signs on for Dole', conveyed this message, as did the front-page cartoon, 'Joy-Day in the Royal Rabbit-warren', which took another swipe at Marina by suggesting to readers that 'royal parasites' were welcomed in Britain, whereas they had been expelled by nations like Soviet Russia and Greece (Fig. 1.10). Interestingly, the accompanying front-page article also presented monarchy as a business operation that had specialized in exploiting 'the masses':

> To-day Marina, daughter of an unemployed 'Greek' ex-Prince, marries George, son of the head of the most prosperous branch of the firm of Royalty Unlimited – the Buckingham Palace branch of the old German family concern which

---

[124] *Daily Sketch*, 30 Nov. 1934, p. 2.

[125] *News of the World*, 2 Dec. 1934, p. 12; *Daily Mirror*, 17 Sept. 1934, p. 11. See also the cartoon 'Further Back, There!', *Daily Express*, 29 Nov. 1934, p. 17.

[126] *Daily Worker*, 29 Nov. 1934, p. 1. See also 22 Nov. 1934, p. 2; 30 Nov. 1934, pp. 1 and 4; 1 Dec. 1934, p. 6.

Figure 1.10. 'Out-Of-Work Princess Signs on for Dole', *Daily Worker*, 29 November 1934, p. 1. © The British Library Board.

supplies Europe with unwanted monarchs ... When she signs the marriage register, Marina will qualify for the handsome dole of £25,000 a year.

The *Daily Worker*'s royal wedding-day leader column reiterated this message by noting how 'bitter thoughts and feelings will be uppermost in the minds of the workers to-day, as they reflect upon the pomp, luxury and wealth that is being poured out upon two representatives of Royalty, who never in their lives have done one useful thing'.[127] The Sunday newspaper *Reynolds's Illustrated News*, which had been a strong advocate of republicanism in the nineteenth century, also presented mixed coverage of the royal wedding. While most of its content concerned British party politics, it contained some celebratory reports on the marriage, as well as readers' letters that challenged the official narrative of royal wedding day – most notably arguing that 'privileged people' would benefit from the provision of expensive seats along the marital procession route, while 'ordinary people' would have to watch through periscopes at the back of the crowds.[128] It is worth keeping in mind that the circulation of both these newspapers was low. Official estimates put the *Daily Worker*'s daily circulation in this

[127] *Daily Worker*, 29 Nov. 1934, p. 2.
[128] *Reynolds's Illustrated News*, 25 Nov. 1934, pp. 1 and 8.

period at only 15,000, whereas the popular London dailies – the *Mirror, Express, Mail, Herald* and *News Chronicle* – sold in millions.[129] Perhaps the most notable outcome of the *Daily Worker*'s critical coverage of the royal wedding was that the Home Office instigated a police investigation in to its proprietor, A. L. Morton, and cartoonist, W. D. Rowney (known by the pen name 'Maro'), and raised the possibility that criminal proceedings could be brought against both men for the way they sought to undermine the monarchy. These concerns persisted into 1935 and were renewed at the time of George V's silver jubilee following another flurry of critical articles and cartoons. However, ultimately the Home Office decided against prosecution, believing that apart from a small minority of communists, the nation was 'undivided in its devotion to the Crown' and it was therefore unnecessary to draw additional attention to what one official referred to as the 'scurrilous rubbish' of the *Daily Worker*.[130]

The mainstream media reproduced the image of a British people united around the monarchy through the dissemination of large photographs of the London crowds. While this was not a novel phenomenon, the pictures evoked a vision of a multitude of loyal subjects who had gathered to revere royalty.[131] What was new, though, was the way newsreel cameras captured scenes of surging spectators as they overcame the police cordon on the procession route outside Buckingham Palace, running towards the palace gates as if drawn to the royal family by magnetism.[132] Equally, in 1934, for the first time, the royal household permitted photographers and cameramen access to Buckingham Palace's roof, enabling them to capture vast panoramas of the crowds below.[133] Tens of thousands of faces could be seen in these images, with the geometric layout of the Mall and Victoria memorial helping to convey the orderly nature of the assembled masses. Newspapers and newsreels juxtaposed these images with scenes of the royal family standing on the balcony, the bride and groom waving to the crowds.[134] This juxtaposition was particularly striking in the *Daily*

[129] Bingham, *Family Newspapers?*, p. 19; TNA, HO 45/25480 – Anonymous memorandum, 28 June 1935.
[130] TNA, HO 45/25480 – Letter from anon to Lord Trenchard, 21 Aug. 1935.
[131] On the 19th-century popularization of crowd-centred imagery, see Plunkett, *Queen Victoria*, pp. 17, 43 and 60–7.
[132] E.g., 'The royal wedding', *British Movietone News*, 29 Nov. 1934; 'The royal wedding', *Pathé Super Sound Gazette*, 29 Nov. 1934.
[133] RA, PS/PSO/GV/PS/MAIN/55340, 'Press and Photography', F. Mitchell to the Deputy Master of the Household, 8 Nov. 1934.
[134] For these kinds of juxtaposition, see 'The royal wedding', *British Movietone News*, 29 Nov. 1934; 'The duke of Kent weds Princess Marina', *British Paramount News*, 3 Dec. 1934; *Daily Sketch*, 30 Nov. 1934, p. 25; *Daily Mirror*, 30 Nov. 1934, p. 16.

Figure 1.11. 'The Bride Waves, the Crowd Cheers', *Daily Sketch*, 30 November 1934, p. 25. © The British Library Board.

Sketch, which pictured Marina waving – the handkerchief she held aloft was imperfectly photographed and blurred to emphasize her special gestural rapport with the public (Figure 1.11). In this way the media worked with courtiers to create images of a loyal citizenry united around the family monarchy, enhancing the interwar narrative of the well-ordered British public sphere.[135]

Archbishop Lang also projected an image of a people united in their emotional connections to the House of Windsor in his royal wedding address, which he delivered to those who had gathered in Westminster abbey and to radio listeners across Britain and the world:

> Never in history, we may dare to say, has a marriage been attended by so vast a company of witnesses. For by a new and marvellous invention of science countless multitudes in every variety of place and home are joining in this Service. The whole Nation – nay, the whole Empire – are the wedding guests: and more than guests, members of the family. For this great assembly in the Abbey, the crowds waiting outside its walls, and the multitude of listening people, regard the family of our beloved King and Queen as in a true sense their own.[136]

In his opening sentences Lang reinvigorated the idea of a national family monarchy – proposed by Bagehot almost seventy years previously – modernizing the imagery of a nation joined together around the House of Windsor by stressing how new mass-communication technologies had enabled listeners to join in, and empathize with, a royal wedding. Lang encouraged his listeners to internalize the idea that the royal family were at the centre of British society and that they symbolized a Christian model of domesticity with which the nation identified. In so doing, he helped to recalibrate British citizenship through a language which stressed personal devotion to the family monarchy.

The 'Listener's Wedding'

Writing to the archbishop of Canterbury two days after the wedding, George V recorded his pleasure at the way the event had been popularly received:

> I shall never forget that beautiful service in the Abbey, so simple and yet so dignified ... Then the enormous crowds in the streets and especially the one outside this Palace, who showed their love and appreciation for us and our

---

[135] Lawrence, *Electing Our Masters*, pp. 120–27. For comparable examples in a Japanese context, see T. Fujitani, *Splendid Monarchy: Power and Pageantry in Modern Japan* (London, 1996), pp. 226–8.

[136] LPL, Lang 191, fos. 157–9, Draft of royal wedding address. See also *The Church Times*, 30 Nov. 1934, p. 598.

family, by their enthusiasm impressed us more than I can say and we deeply appreciated it. I must thank you for all that you did in arranging and carrying out the two Services, which we drew up more or less at Balmoral ... The Prime Minister and Jim Thomas both came up to me after the breakfast and said, this is a great day for England! If only the politicians would give up their party quarrels and would rally round and support the National Government, what could one not do in this country. *We* have done our best, it is now for the country to do the same.[137]

While this letter reveals the king's confidence in Ramsay MacDonald's National Government, it also suggests that officials had staged the royal wedding to help ease some of the social and political strains that afflicted British public life in late 1934. George V thanked the archbishop for his help in arranging the wedding, emphasized how they had 'done [their] best' to bring the nation together and stated how pleased he was with the dignity and simplicity of the abbey ceremony. Some social elites and ordinary members of the public shared the king's sentiment that the wedding had helped to unite Britain. Lang noted that he received many letters congratulating him on his role in the wedding and some of the correspondence he kept revealed the ways in which different sections of society had come together to celebrate the marriage.[138] Charles Wyndham described listening to the broadcast from 'an island in Parliament Square', said that he had 'heard perfectly' and that 'every word was followed most reverently by the vast crowd'. He stated that the 'climax' was Lang's address, which had been met with awe – 'you could have heard a pin drop' – and he remarked that, when the archbishop had finished, 'nobody said anything for a moment and then I heard three or 4 young artisan or clerk sort of men behind me agreeing that it was "very nice – very nice indeed"'.[139] It is entirely possible that Wyndham invented these details or that the people he claimed to have observed publicly articulated opinions under the pressures of what they deemed to be socially appropriate, thus conforming to the dominant royalist interpretation of the event. But, taken at face value, his letter implied that the different classes of people who gathered in central London to hear the broadcast over loudspeaker systems were captivated by the ceremony and, in particular, Lang's address.

Elma Paget, wife of the retired bishop of Chester, similarly wrote to Lang to share with him some of the comments made by her lodgers on hearing the royal wedding broadcast:

[137] LPL, Lang 318, fos. 21–2, King George V to C. G. Lang, 1 Dec. 1934 (the king's emphasis).
[138] LPL, Lang 191, fo. 172, Lang, note to self, 4 Dec. 1934.
[139] LPL, Lang 191, fo. 162r–v, C. Wyndham to C. G. Lang, 29 Aug. 1934.

'Lovely wasn't it and the Archbishop – wasn't he splendid, if I could have run and thanked him I'd have run miles.' 'And that oration – well I can't use no other word, so grand and so homely.' And a third 'I can't speak about it now even 'cos I'm easy touched and his words made me cry.' And the last 'Every word lovely but I could hardly listen for the lump in my throat so I turned it on again in the evening when they give [*sic*] us the record and the lump came just as bad as ever'.[140]

If Paget's words are reliable, then it would seem that the broadcast had a strong emotional impact on audiences as they listened to the wedding and that Lang rose to the occasion by combining the 'grand' with the 'homely' in his address on the family monarchy. Indeed, this idea was echoed in a letter written to Lang by Sir Samuel Hoare. He had been present in the abbey alongside Viscount Hailsham and both men agreed that 'it could not have been better. You held the balance so well between the ceremonial and the intimate'.[141] Thus, the archbishop's expert command of his audiences' feelings, both in Westminster and across the airwaves, evoked powerful responses from his listeners as they empathized with the 'ordinary' family story at the heart of the event.

This blending of the intimate with the dignified was a theme noted by radio listeners who wrote to Gerald Cock in order to congratulate the BBC. W. V. Towlett from Kent suggested that 'the pomp and splendour of the occasion, the perfect choral accompaniment and the beautiful simplicity of the Archbishop's address must have made a deep impression on many homes and recalled the "beautiful" side of life which is all too rare'.[142] E. G. from Ilford, Essex, used similar language in extending to Cock their 'heartiest congratulations on effecting a most magnificent broadcast. The simple beauty of the service was enhanced thereby'.[143] Meanwhile, Annie Maudsley from Southport was among several writers who emphasized the lucidity with which the service was broadcast. She explained that she had listened in on her portable 'Pye' wireless set and that 'the wedding service came through perfectly. Every word distinct. I don't think I should have heard so well had I been in the Abbey itself … it was just wonderful and would give millions of people the greatest pleasure'.[144] The clarity with which the service was transmitted by radio thus enabled an intimate, immersive audience experience as captured in words such as 'beautiful', 'deep' and, the

---

[140] LPL, Lang 191, fo. 171, E. K. Paget to C. G. Lang, 4 Dec. 1934. The BBC repeated its recording of the royal wedding broadcast on the evening of 29 Nov. 1934.

[141] LPL, Lang 191, fo. 164, S. Hoare to C. G. Lang, 30 Nov. 1934.

[142] BBCWA, R30/3/644/1, W. V. Towlett to G. Cock, 30 Nov. 1934.

[143] BBCWA, R30/3/644/1, E. G. to G. Cock, undated.

[144] BBCWA, R30/3/644/1, A. M. Maudsley to G. Cock, 2 Dec. 1934.

phrase of another listener from Bristol, that 'every word of the Bride's and Groom's responses was perfectly audible'.[145]

The broadcast of the royal wedding also generated temporal concurrence – the sharing of time among a people – which worked imaginatively to unite listeners as part of a national community.[146] Letter writers conveyed this sense of participation in their descriptions of the 'millions of people' and 'many homes' that joined in with the wedding. The broadcast therefore seems to have enhanced affective integration around the focal point of the monarchy, with members of the public emotionally identifying with the royal family and with a national collective as they participated in the wedding together. The language of an imagined collective which joined around the wedding broadcast also manifested itself in letters written by ordinary people to George and Marina themselves. Addressing the princess after the event, ex-serviceman Arthur Thompson from Westcliffe-on-Sea intimated that the broadcast had had a socially unifying effect on British people, bringing them together through a shared emotional identification with the lovers: 'I am sure you will not think me rude in writing you like this but I was so impressed when listening to your wedding on the wireless that I simply had to express my feelings. I am simply one of millions of my countrymen who joined in welcoming and wishing you wishes which came not only by cheering but from the Heart'.[147] Thompson articulated a strong empathy which, he emphasized, linked him intimately from his heart to the princess and he believed that he shared this feeling with his fellow Britons. Seventy-nine-year-old Reverend William Waldren from Lingfield, Surrey, expressed similar sentiments in his letter to the prince: 'We were all brightened and cheered in hearing the lovely Service by wireless from the Abbey and full of good hopes and joy for your sake – no Service I can remember seemed so exactly what it should be as this one; it was in the truest sense Divine'.[148] Waldren described his experience of the royal wedding in terms of its uplifting spiritual appeal but also remarked that the BBC's broadcast had evoked in him and those with whom he listened feelings of hope and joy for George and Marina.

The press loudly championed the idea that the broadcast had brought media audiences together. Headlines echoed Lang's address, proclaiming it the 'Listener's Wedding' and the 'Wedding Service All the World

---

[145] BBCWA, R30/3/644/1, A. M. Maudsley to G. Cock, 2 Dec. 1934. See also letters from W. H. Parr (2 Dec. 1934) and J. L. Abraham (1 Dec. 1934) to G. Cock.

[146] Fujitani, *Splendid Monarchy*, p. 28. See also B. Anderson, *Imagined Communities: Reflections on the Origin and Spread of Nationalism* (London, 1983), pp. 22–4.

[147] RA, GDKH/WED/C, A. R. Thompson to Princess Marina, 5 Dec. 1934.

[148] RA, GDKH/WED/C, W. Waldren to Prince George, 7 Dec. 1934.

Attended'.[149] As already discussed, many reports on the event presented the monarchy as the symbol which united Britain at a time of national and international instability. It is significant that the press also made a point of highlighting how people had gathered across the country to listen to the BBC broadcast together. Whereas children benefitted from a school holiday to mark the royal wedding, it was a normal working day for the rest of the population. However, this did not preclude groups assembling to hear the broadcast. The *Manchester Guardian* described how, for example, people had gone to Manchester's shops and restaurants to listen together:

> To a spectator at Lewis's [one of Manchester's leading department stores] ... it was obvious that the housewife had decided to set apart her morning in order to enjoy by the medium of the broadcast sounds and her imagination something of the great spectacle. The women seated at the tables – often with their rather puzzled children – listened attentively to the beautiful service and the voices of the bride and bridegroom. Although men listened, it was essentially a feminine occasion, as the composition of the crowds testified.[150]

The use of public listening venues like shops, as was the case here, prefigured the more intimate reception of the 1937 coronation broadcast, which most people heard in their own homes, or in the homes of friends or family.[151]

A number of letters written by readers to the press after the wedding also drew attention to the international situation in their interpretation of the event. In the weeks leading up to the marriage, newspapers were not only overwhelmed with stories on royal wedding minutiae, but also by articles on the growing unrest which characterized European politics. Along with the assassination of the king of Yugoslavia, journalists were particularly exercised by German rearmament and the threat which Hitler's dictatorship represented to the Continent's fragile peace.[152] It seems the chasm that separated Britain's ostensibly joyful mood as it prepared for the royal wedding and Europe's tumultuous politics in late 1934 helped to crystallize an image of a British people uniquely united through their emotional connections to monarchy. A letter from J. C. Fullton of London was printed by the *Daily Mirror* in its readers' correspondence section under the title 'Hailing the Throne' the day after

---

[149] *Manchester Guardian*, 30 Nov. 1934, p. 13; *News Chronicle*, 30 Nov. 1934, p. 1; *Daily Mirror*, 30 Nov. 1934, pp. 1 and 7.

[150] *Manchester Guardian*, 30 Nov. 1934, p. 13.

[151] See ch. 3.

[152] *News Chronicle*, 28 Nov. 1934, p. 1; *Daily Express*, 28 Nov. 1934, p. 1; *Daily Mirror*, 10 Oct. 1934, p. 12; *The Times*, 10 Oct. 1934, p. 16.

the royal nuptials: 'This week thousands have seen the nation "hailing" our Royal Family. What a blessing that we have a Throne to salute, instead of being obliged to "hail" some humbugging dictator!'[153] This positive appraisal of the monarchy contrasted its national symbolic importance to that of dictatorship at a time when Hitler was making disingenuous claims about building a 'peace army'.[154] The next day there followed a plethora of other letters from readers in London on the topic of the crown. P. F. Ryley stated that 'the great advantage of monarchy to any country is that the throne stands above Party. No newly raised-up Dictator, however able, can possibly command the respect due to Kingship'. Ryley opined that 'in this century we may well see a revival of monarchy, which appeared to be dying, even in England, at the end of the eighteenth century' – suggesting that the wedding had helped to revitalize the royal family's popular appeal. Meanwhile, 'S. T.' pithily described two opposing political systems: 'A dictatorship obviously doesn't go with a monarchy. If proof is wanted – look at the Dictator-run countries of Europe to-day'.[155] The crown's symbolism of political freedom and neutrality thus contrasted with the 'vulgarities of fascism' in this period.[156] Equally, it seems from letters written to newspapers and the stage-managers of the 1934 royal wedding that mass media coverage of royal events like George and Marina's romance and marriage had the effect of emphasizing the integrative, stabilizing role that the monarchy had on British national life – and that this contrasted vividly to the political uncertainty that reigned in Europe.

Conclusion

George and Marina's royal wedding had important consequences beyond 1934. Most significantly, their romance helped to shape official and popular responses to the public announcement in December 1936 that Edward VIII wanted to marry the American socialite Wallis Simpson. It was unthinkable to the clergy – and particularly Cosmo Lang, who had stressed the indissoluble nature of marriage during George and Marina's wedding ceremony only two years earlier – that the new king (who was, after all, supreme governor of the Church of England) should be permitted to marry a woman who had been divorced twice. This view was generally shared by

---

[153] *Daily Mirror*, 30 Nov. 1934, p. 13.
[154] *Daily Express*, 29 Nov. 1934, p. 10.
[155] *Daily Mirror*, 1 Dec. 1934, p. 11.
[156] J. Parry, 'Whig monarchy, whig nation: crown politics and representativeness, 1800–2000', in *The Monarchy and the British Nation, 1780 to the Present*, ed. A. Olechnowicz, (Cambridge, 2007), pp. 47–75, at pp. 55–6.

Britain's political and media elite and, together with the archbishop, they convinced the king that his regal status was compromised by his choice of wife and that he should abdicate.[157]

Under George V, the British monarchy adhered to Bagehot's idea that the royal family should act as 'the head of our *morality*'.[158] Despite George and Marina's complicated backstories, the 1934 royal wedding was celebrated as the most spectacular episode in a series of events that emphasized the domesticity and Christian fidelity of the House of Windsor. With the help of a forward-thinking BBC and that more traditional organ of societal authority, the Church of England, the royal household carefully orchestrated the marriage to enhance the national appeal of the family monarchy among media audiences, while maintaining the dignity of the crown. Edward VIII's decision to marry Wallis Simpson two years later scandalized the establishment precisely because it threatened the domestic ideal that royalty had publicly elevated in the years preceding his short reign: the moral template for monarchy diligently promoted at the time of George and Marina's romance was endangered by Edward's transgression. However, as we shall see, the king's abdication and the succession of his younger brother as George VI ultimately reinforced the moral principles that the House of Windsor championed in the 1930s, with the new monarch's moral probity and happy family life echoing those of his father and contrasting with his older brother's decadent, irreligious and childless lifestyle.[159]

Letters written to Edward VIII by his subjects at the time of the abdication crisis, however, reveal another way in which George and Marina's romance had a lasting effect on public life. More than ever before, their relationship was celebrated as a love match. The couple had worked with the British media to publicize a story that drew attention to their happiness and which resonated with the new emotional cultures of personal fulfilment and compatibility. Many of the letters Edward VIII received in December 1936 which encouraged him to follow his heart and marry the woman he loved revealed their authors' strong identification with the kind of modern romance embodied by George and Marina in 1934.[160] Female letter writers

---

[157] Beaken, *Cosmo Lang*, pp. 86–142; M. Aitken, *The Abdication of King Edward VIII: a Vivid Day-by-Day Record of the Crisis as Seen by an Insider* (London, 1966), pp. 95–105; P. Williamson, *Stanley Baldwin: Conservative Leadership and National Values* (Cambridge, 1999), pp. 326–9; J. E. Wrench, *Geoffrey Dawson and Our Times* (London, 1955), pp. 336–57.

[158] W. Bagehot, *The English Constitution* (London, 1867), p. 79 (original italics).

[159] Mort, 'Love in a cold climate', p. 61; B. Baxter, *Destiny Called to Them* (Oxford, 1939), pp. 8–12.

[160] S. Williams, *The People's King: the True Story of the Abdication* (London, 2003), p. xix; Mort, 'Love in a cold climate', p. 46 and, on women who wrote to Edward VIII, pp. 39–51.

were particularly drawn to this embryonic form of 'companionate love' with its emphasis on emotional satisfaction; and it seems likely that the female-targeted media coverage of the 1934 romance strengthened some women's imaginative investment in royal love stories. We might, therefore, interpret the 1934 romance as double-edged in its significance. On the one hand, the family monarchy assumed a truly national presence and established a virtuous domestic model for later generations of royalty to follow. On the other hand, the growing emphasis on personal fulfilment rendered the family-centred formula untenable when individual royals sought to pursue love outside the confines of Christian marriage – as in the cases of Edward VIII and, later, Princess Margaret in the 1950s and Prince Charles in the 1980s.

The 1934 royal romance had a wider political significance as well. The public was enabled through new mass media to empathize with royalty in powerful ways; and in the context of the 1930s – with the re-emergence of nationalistic politics on the Continent and the persistence of socio-economic disorder at home – the imagery of a British people united around the monarchy left an indelible impression on many who tuned in to listen to the royal wedding. Marina, in particular, was responsible for pioneering a modern and more direct relationship between royalty and the public through the use of mass media. She was motivated by a personal concern to distance herself from her past as an exiled Greek royal and she possessed a shrewd understanding of how elite institutions could democratize their public image. The princess and her inner circle drew attention to her desire to marry for love as part of a wider effort to play down her foreign origins and associations with the pre-1914 tradition of dynastic intermarriage. Meanwhile, the orchestrators of the wedding promoted its British character and this seems to have resonated with some members of the public, who wrote to the press describing how the event had strengthened their belief in the nation's constitutional system, often favourably contrasting it with European authoritarianism. George and Marina's love story unfolded at a time of growing uncertainty about the future of Britain's royal democracy and, as the next chapter on the king's Christmas broadcasts demonstrates, after 1934 the image of a nation uniquely united around the House of Windsor was promoted by the royal household and compliant mass media with greater urgency and fervour than ever before. The 1935 silver jubilee was the next stepping-stone that placed royal intimacy on a pedestal in order to bind together a nation of diverse peoples who could empathize with the protagonists of the family monarchy.

2. 'A man we understand':
King George V's radio broadcasts

In the early 1930s the British monarchy popularized a more intimate media image by means of innovative technologies that enabled members of the public to express new kinds of emotional identification with the main actors of the House of Windsor. The crown was motivated partly by a desire to generate a deeper and wider royalism among the population at a time when traditional social hierarchies were threatened by democratic change; and partly by a desire to position itself as a focal point of stability in a nation and empire convulsed by economic and political developments that were transforming the international order. The leading figure in the monarchy's public relations campaign was King George V, who, by this point, had entered the final stage of his life. Ascending the throne in 1910 against the backdrop of the constitutional stand-off between the House of Lords and House of Commons, his twenty-six-year reign was punctuated by a series of dramatic events during which the monarchy demonstrated remarkable flexibility in adjusting its role to suit the times. George V's tenure as king was defined by his highly publicized leadership of the nation and empire during the First World War; his (privately grudging) adaptation to constitutional reform; the philanthropic interest he and his consort, Queen Mary, exhibited in the lives of their most vulnerable subjects; his adherence to a Victorian code of duty; and his advocacy of Christian family values.[1] When, in 1932, he became the first British sovereign to use radio to broadcast a special Christmas greeting to his people, he did so in order to crystallize in the minds of listeners the major themes and episodes that had shaped his reign. However, the new medium also provided him with a platform to address current concerns and a chance to forge stronger emotional bonds with his subjects in a turbulent period. In 1928, aged sixty-three, the king had almost died from septicaemia and, never fully recovering his physical

---

[1] F. Prochaska, *Royal Bounty: the Making of a Welfare Monarchy* (New Haven, Conn., 1995), pp. 169–212; P. Williamson, 'The monarchy and public values, 1900–1953', in *The Monarchy and the British Nation 1780 to the Present*, ed. A. Olechnowicz (Cambridge, 2007), pp. 223–57; H. Jones, 'The nature of kingship in First World War Britain', in *The Windsor Dynasty 1910 to the Present: 'Long to Reign Over Us?*, ed. M. Glencross, J. Rowbottom and M. D. Kandiah (Basingstoke, 2016), pp. 195–216.

strength, he reduced his public activities, making way for his adult children to assume more prominent roles as his representatives. But events beyond his control compelled him to intervene in party politics again, testing the limits of his constitutional powers when he controversially facilitated the formation of a National Government in order to help steady the nation's finances in 1931. In the same year the monarchy's new relationship with the dominions was enshrined in the Statute of Westminster, which recognized their legislative autonomy while affirming their common allegiance to the crown. Meanwhile, far-reaching political and economic instability in Europe threatened to undo the fragile peace that had existed on the Continent since 1918. Thus, George V took to the microphone to emphasize the need for national and imperial unity and to urge his subjects to work together so that they might better weather the ongoing global depression and prepare for uncertain times ahead.

According to royal biographer Harold Nicolson, George V's broadcasts helped to earn him the love and respect of his subjects. Writing about how the public enthusiastically celebrated the king's silver jubilee in May 1935, Nicolson suggested that George V was like a 'friend whom they had known all their adult lives': his radio messages had transformed an 'unreal and incredible personage' into a 'human voice – intimate and paternal – speaking to them in their own living-rooms, speaking to them from a box on the table between the sewing machine and the mug'.[2] Although we should be wary of the official biographer's hagiography, it is clear from Nicolson's personal diaries that he was genuinely moved by the monarch's recorded voice.[3] His recognition of George V's talents at the microphone is all the more notable given that the biographer was often privately scathing about the king's reactionary character and limited personal interests, which outside his royal role mainly comprised shooting and stamp-collecting.[4] This chapter examines how George V's radio messages did indeed work to strengthen the emotional bonds that connected him to some members of the British public, with the new technology of broadcasting enabling affective integration around the focal point of the House of Windsor's domesticity.

---

[2] H. Nicolson, *King George the Fifth: His Life and Reign* (London, 1952), pp. 524–6. For other contemporaries' thoughts on the public's strong emotional attachment to George V, see K. Martin, *The Magic of Monarchy* (London, 1937), pp. 13–4; and LPL, MS2826, Diary of Revd. Dr. A. C. Don, 10 May 1935.

[3] *Harold Nicolson: Diaries and Letters*, i: *the Later Years, 1945–62*,ed. N. Nicolson (3 vols., London, 1968), p. 208. On the problems with official royal biography, see D. Cannadine, 'From biography to history: writing the modern British monarchy', *Hist. Research*, lxxvii (2004), 289–312, at pp. 294–8.

[4] Nicolson, *Harold Nicolson*, iii. 144 and 174.

The archbishop of Canterbury, Cosmo Lang, became royal speechwriter in 1934 and introduced a new emotional register into the king's broadcasts in order to popularize an image of George V in which his personal life and ambitions became closely entwined with the private lives and aims of his subjects. Letters written to the monarch and school essays written about him after his death in January 1936 show that Lang's personalization of royal public language intensified the imagined relationships some listeners forged with the king and his family. In a period marked by growing concerns about the prospect of another world war, the archbishop worked in tandem with the BBC and other media outlets to project George V as the empathetic, stabilizing force at the centre of imperial politics.

Philip Williamson has offered the fullest analysis of how royal public language changed during George V's reign, identifying how it became 'less elevated' and increasingly focused on a 'well recognized vocabulary and set of messages', which included constitutional progress, social cohesion, religiosity, empire and the self-denying sacrifice made by royal persons in the course of their national duty. Williamson noted that Lang scripted George V's 1934 and 1935 Christmas messages, as well as the king's silver jubilee broadcast, but he did not discuss how the archbishop transformed the emotional register of the monarch's public language.[5] Paddy Scannell and David Cardiff, meanwhile, recognized that the 'stiff and formal' style of George V's early broadcasts yielded to a more 'simple, direct and personal' mode of address to listeners who were, in turn, presented 'as individuals and friends' in his later messages. The king 'spoke of his own family as familiar [to listeners] ... of [his] personal feelings [and] of spontaneous bonds of affection which linked himself and his family to his people'. Significantly, though, Scannell and Cardiff did not identify Lang's key influence and they incorrectly suggested that the monarch's final broadcast on Christmas Day 1935 was 'the first fully to deploy an interpersonal style'.[6] Moreover, they did not attempt to explain how the changes that Lang in fact introduced in 1934 worked to redefine the king's relationship with members of the public, nor how the archbishop created an emotional template for royal public language that has endured to the present day.

This chapter uses a range of evidence to examine how George V's messages evolved between 1932 and 1935 to incorporate an emotional language which intensified the affective connections that some listeners forged with him. Sources include the royal household's correspondence

[5] Williamson, 'Monarchy and public values', esp. pp. 228–32.
[6] P. P. Scannell, and D. Cardiff, *A Social History of British Broadcasting*, i: *1922–1939, Serving the Nation* (Oxford, 1991), pp. 282–3.

with the British poet and writer Rudyard Kipling, who penned the first two Christmas broadcasts and who was responsible for introducing some of the features that Lang developed in the messages he subsequently wrote.[7] The archbishop's original drafts of the broadcasts he prepared, which are located in his papers at Lambeth Palace Library, not only reveal that he sought to strengthen the imagined bonds that connected monarch and subjects, but also show that the palace responded positively to his innovations.[8] Handwritten annotations on the typed originals and the accompanying correspondence with the king's private secretary, Sir Clive Wigram, show that Lang sent his drafts to Buckingham Palace, where they were revised and then returned to him. We can therefore detect from the drafts and revisions that the archbishop and royal household worked together to promote a more intimate vision of kingship by personalizing the language used by the monarch to address his people.

This chapter also draws on a rare surviving collection of forty letters written by members of the British public to the king or his private secretary in relation to the 1934 Christmas message – the first broadcast drafted by Lang.[9] Seven were sent in anticipation of the monarch's broadcast, the rest written in response to it and they are housed in the Royal Archives.[10] It would be wrong to generalize about national attitudes based on such a small sample of letters composed by devoted royalists, most of whom wrote to the king in order to express their admiration for him. But for the period before the advent of Mass Observation in 1937 there are very few personal testimonies like these, which have survived the last eighty years and help to reveal how ordinary people heard and responded to the monarch's radio messages. It is particularly difficult to locate discordant voices in the archive that run counter to the positive responses contained in these letters. Contrary to what the mainstream media would have had us believe at the time, it is unlikely that the public was unanimously united in adulation of George V and his family. While the worst effects of the interwar economic slump had passed by the mid 1930s, the last years of the king's reign were characterized by the same widescale working-class poverty, industrial disputes and challenges to the political status quo which had defined British society

[7] This correspondence can be located in Kipling's papers at TK, SxMs-38/2/2/2/1/2/2/5/1, King George V Christmas Broadcast, 1932; SxMs-38/2/2/2/1/2/2/5/3, King George V Christmas Broadcast, 1933.

[8] Cosmo Lang's royal drafts and the accompanying correspondence with the royal household can be found at LPL, Lang 318.

[9] All 40 letters can be found in RA, PS/PSO/GV/PS/MAIN/55357.

[10] As with Lang's draft messages, these letters have received no scholarly attention until now.

between the wars. And yet popular opposition, ambivalence or indifference to the monarchy have not left a deep impression on the historical record.[11] In the absence of other sources, be they positive or negative, the letters in the Royal Archives help to illuminate how some listeners internalized Lang's royal public language and forged strong emotional connections with George V.[12] Their very existence and intimate tone testify to the impact of radio as a 'conversational' medium that evoked personal feelings and direct, powerful responses from audiences – a phenomenon witnessed on both sides of the Atlantic during the 1930s.[13] This was the case in December 1936 at the time of the abdication crisis, as noted by Frank Mort in his analysis of the letters written by members of the public to Edward VIII.[14] A gendered divide characterized the emotional registers used by men and women to appeal to the king in 1936, with women generally writing more expressive letters that conveyed a deep personal empathy with the monarch.[15] Women tended to be more effusive in the way they addressed George V in 1934 as well, although men also drew on a wide-ranging emotional vocabulary to articulate their devotion to the king. Letter-writing was a relatively private and anonymous means by which correspondents could reach out to the monarch in the role of confidant in order to express deeply held beliefs, hopes and anxieties. At the same time, the letters to George V were epistolary performances of loyalty composed under a kind of 'social sanction' (to use Tom Harrisson's phrase) rooted in deferential politeness.

This chapter also examines a selection of school essays written in 1937 which provide glimpses into how some British children and young adults

---

[11] We know that the British media marginalized public criticism of the royal family in the first 4 decades of the 20th century out of respect for the crown, with the abdication crisis in 1936 acting as a key turning point. The absence of other oppositional voices in the historical records might also be explained by the collection and preservation policies of repositories like the Royal Archives and Lambeth Palace Library, where positive, adulatory letters from the public that commended the behaviour of the royals and the elites that surrounded them seem to have been routinely kept (possibly because the original recipients kept them), while negative correspondence has not tended to survive.

[12] The sample of letters is fairly evenly split between male and female writers. Twenty letters were written by men, 18 by women and 2 by married couples together. Of these, 6 were addressed to the king's private secretary, 5 of which were sent in anticipation of the 1934 broadcast.

[13] J. Loviglio, *Radio's Intimate Public: Network Broadcasting and Mass-Mediated Democracy* (Minneapolis, Minn., and London, 2005), pp. xiv–xvi; J. Lawrence, *Electing Our Masters: the Hustings in British Politics from Hogarth to Blair* (Oxford, 2009), pp. 96–9.

[14] F. Mort, 'Love in a cold climate: letters, public opinion and monarchy in the 1936 abdication crisis', *Twentieth Century British Hist.*, xxv (2014), 30–62, at pp. 38–9 and 51–2.

[15] See also J. V. Gottlieb, *'Guilty Women', Foreign Policy, and Appeasement in Inter-War Britain* (Basingstoke, 2015), p. 186.

developed an understanding of George V's popular reputation and the role of the monarchy in society. The essay-writers were male, working- or middle class, went to schools in the north of England and formed a specific emotional community with 'their own particular values, modes of feeling and ways to express those feelings'.[16] Their essays offer us insight into royalist identities 'in the process of formation' by revealing how boys made sense (and were encouraged to make sense) of the monarchy in the context of the classroom environment in the disorientating period that followed George V's death, the abdication of his first son and the succession of his second son.[17] Notably, many of the boys described George V in highly personal terms and several acknowledged the important role that broadcasting played in popularizing an intimate public image of the monarch which enabled them to identify with him.

This chapter offers a contextualized reading of the draft radio messages written by Lang for George V and compares his presentation of the king with the reception of the monarch's public image as articulated in the letters written by members of the public to the sovereign. Lang made four key changes to the emotional register of royal public language, each of which is addressed here in turn along with the way the innovations resonated with listeners' feelings. First of all, Lang drew attention to the king's family and home in order to emphasize that George V and his people shared a common association with the House of Windsor's domesticity. The 1930s were marked by a widening gulf between public and private modes of self-fashioning and the archbishop's focus on George V's domestic life presented the king's subjects with more intimate insights into his personal world, encouraging them to empathize with him.[18] Second, Lang seems to have intensified the relationship between George V and some of his people through a simpler, more sympathetic public language which witnessed listeners expressing loyalty to the king through emotional identification with a familiar, compassionate monarch. This also relates to the archbishop's third modification. Lang built on a theme from Kipling's earlier royal broadcasts to stress that George V and his people were united through a mutual affection rooted in the monarch's concern for his people's welfare. The archbishop's intimate style deepened this bond and drew on an

---

[16] B. H. Rosenwein, *Generations of Feeling: a History of Emotions, 600–1700* (Cambridge, 2016), p. 3.

[17] H. Barron and C. Langhamer, 'Children, class, and the search for security: writing the future in 1930s Britain', *Twentieth Century British Hist.*, xxviii (2017), 367–89.

[18] C. Langhamer, *The English in Love: the Intimate Story of an Emotional Revolution* (Oxford, 2013), esp. at pp. 1–19; L. King, *Family Men: Fatherhood and Masculinity in Britain, 1914–1960* (Oxford, 2015), pp. 5–7.

older Victorian language of service to emphasize that the burdens of royal duty impinged on the king's personal life.[19] Lang's words evoked sympathy from listeners for a sovereign who seemed committed to the welfare of his subjects and bore as his own their suffering at a time of widespread socio-economic distress.

Fourth and finally, the emotional language Lang introduced to royal broadcasts also infused Britain's imperial ties with powerful affective meaning. Supporting the BBC's aims to present Christmas as a time of imperial reunion, the first broadcast the archbishop wrote for George V forcefully projected the empire as a family of nations and was the culminating message in a carefully orchestrated relay of seasonal greetings from British and imperial representatives. Since the nineteenth century, a cult of monarchy had underpinned the empire with the sovereign recognized as head of the imperial state. The crown manifested its power through a symbolic system of governance based on hierarchical ceremonial display as powerfully demonstrated during royal tours led by the monarch or members of his or her family.[20] Following the enactment of the Statue of Westminster, George V's broadcasts sought to enhance the crown's role as the personal link that bound diverse peoples together. The king characterized the empire as a peaceful group of nations committed to upholding international order at a time of global uncertainty; and this imagery of an imperial stabilizing force was echoed in letters written to him in 1934. Furthermore, this pacific imagery was augmented by the monarch's focus on children in his messages: he publicized a kind, grandfatherly persona to encourage child listeners to become the future citizens of empire. Thus, the final part of this chapter turns to the aforementioned school essays in order to explore how this public image continued to resonate after George V's death and worked to shape royalist identities beyond his last broadcast.

'This personal link'

Historians have tended to assume that BBC radio, as with new types of visual media, increased the monarchy's popularity by substituting the 'magic of distance' with the 'magic of familiarity'.[21] While broadcasting certainly

[19] M. D. Kandiah et al., 'The ultimate Windsor ceremonials: coronations and investitures', in Glencross, Rowbottom and Kandiah, *The Windsor Dynasty*, pp. 59–86, at pp. 73–5.

[20] D. Cannadine, *Ornamentalism: How the British Saw Their Empire* (Oxford, 2002), esp. at pp. 21–2 and ch. 8; C. Kaul, 'Monarchical display and the politics of empire: princes of Wales and India, 1870–1920s', *Twentieth Century British Hist.*, xvii (2006), 464–88.

[21] T. Hajkowski, *The BBC and National Identity in Britain, 1922–53* (Manchester, 2010), p. 84. See also J. Richards, 'The monarchy and film, 1900–2006', in Olechnowicz, *The Monarchy and the British Nation*, pp. 258–79, at p. 258.

brought the monarchy *closer* to the public, the way royal voices were projected across the airwaves and internalized by listeners requires further examination. In his recent analysis of the public response to the abdication crisis, Mort identified how British people favoured radio as a more reliable medium of communication over 'the rumour mill of press journalism' after the news broke that Edward VIII might abandon the throne. Mort attributed this privileging of wireless as a source of information to its 'stronger resonances of authenticity' and the way speakers communicated directly with listeners.[22]

Politicians who used radio as a medium for campaigning between the wars benefitted from the direct channel it provided to the electorate and the sense of verisimilitude it conveyed. Prime Minister Stanley Baldwin was the undisputed master of the airwaves in Britain: heeding the advice of BBC director-general, John Reith, the Conservative leader pioneered a new kind of studio talk 'delivered as though he was sitting in the living room with his listeners', which added 'to his established image of being an honest and sincere figure without artifice or trickery'.[23] Indeed, many voters who wrote to Baldwin expressed a trust in him that sprung from the feeling he had spoken to them personally as individuals.[24] Across the Atlantic, President Franklin D. Roosevelt was using radio to similar effect in his famous 'fireside chats', which helped him to create a politically conscious American public that supported his New Deal social programme. Roosevelt's broadcasts infused his listeners' personal space and identities with a sense of national meaning and belonging, creating what Jason Loviglio has termed an 'intimate public'.[25]

Between 1932 and 1935, the emotional register of George V's broadcasts evolved as part of a royal public relations exercise that sought to project a media image of the monarch that was authentic, relatable and would work to create an 'intimate public' comprising listeners who identified with the king and his ambitions to unite his people. It took several years of persuasion from Reith and courtiers to convince the king to deliver a broadcast and, when at last he agreed, journalists welcomed the news, stressing that it

[22] Mort, 'Love in a cold climate', pp. 56–9.

[23] S. Ball, *Portrait of a Party: the Conservative Party in Britain 1918–1945* (Oxford, 2013), p. 101.

[24] Lawrence, *Electing Our Masters*, pp. 96–9. See also P. Williamson, *Stanley Baldwin: Conservative Leadership and National Values* (Cambridge, 1999), pp. 83–5; S. Nicholas, 'The construction of a national identity: Stanley Baldwin, 'Englishness' and the mass media in inter-war Britain', in *The Conservatives and British Society*, ed. M. Francis and I. Zweiniger-Bargielowska (Cardiff, 1996), pp. 127–46, at pp. 135–40.

[25] Loviglio, *Radio's Intimate Public*, pp. xiv–xvi and ch.1.

would be the first time that he would speak 'directly' to his people, noting as well that he possessed 'one of the best "wireless voices" in the world'.[26] Thus, before he even opened his mouth, the sovereign's words were ascribed great significance and his voice presented as uniquely engaging in tone and *unmediated* in its immediacy, the *Daily Express* going so far as to refer to the message as a 'heart-to-heart Christmas talk'.[27]

The novelist and poet Rudyard Kipling wrote George V's 1932 and 1933 Christmas messages. Kipling was a seasoned royal speechwriter who had previously prepared a number of messages for the king and other members of the royal family, including the prince of Wales; and he readily consented to Sir Clive Wigram's invitation to prepare the first Christmas broadcast for the monarch.[28] In both the 1932 and 1933 messages, Kipling projected an image of a monarch in open conversation with his subjects, explaining to them how they would overcome the socio-economic problems of these years while reassuring them that, through goodwill and co-operation, Britain and the empire would prevail over their troubles. For example, in his 1932 broadcast George V told listeners that 'the work to which we are all equally bound is to arrive at a reasoned tranquillity within our borders, to regain prosperity without self-seeking and to carry with us those whom the burden of past years has disheartened or overborne'.[29] Kipling's elaborate phrasing conveyed gravitas and moral seriousness through the monarch, with the press afterwards praising his 'grave and measured delivery' and his 'beautifully modulated English'.[30] However, the poet's messages were, if anything, too ornate and the style of the 1933 broadcast in particular was convoluted and complex. The first two broadcasts also lacked the deep emotional register which Cosmo Lang would incorporate into the later messages.

In drafting the king's 1934 Christmas broadcast, the first important change the archbishop introduced to George V's public language was to include in it references to other members of the royal family. He initiated this focus on family through an allusion to Prince George and Princess Marina's recent wedding, the king describing how 'the Queen and I were deeply moved' by the public's response 'a month ago at the marriage of

---

[26] *Daily Express*, 25 Nov. 1932, p. 1; *Daily Mail*, 25 Nov. 1932, p. 11. For the king's initial reluctance to broadcast, see K. Rose, *King George V* (London, 1983), p. 393.

[27] *Daily Express*, 25 Nov. 1932, p. 1.

[28] TK, SxMs-38/2/2/2/1/2/2/5/1, C. Wigram to R. Kipling, 25 Nov. 1932. For speeches written by Kipling for the prince of Wales, see SxMs-38/2/2/2/1/2/2/5/10–11.

[29] Quoted in T. Fleming, *Voices Out of the Air: the Royal Christmas Broadcasts, 1932–1981* (London, 1981), p. 11.

[30] *Daily Mirror*, 27 Nov. 1933, p. 5; *Daily Express*, 27 Nov. 1933, p. 15.

our dear son and daughter'.[31] Lang thus opened up an empathetic channel between the monarch and his listeners – the king clearly articulating his and the queen's feelings – and he elevated royal domesticity as a shared point of reference that united George V and his people. This went down well with some listeners. For example, forty-four-year-old Elizabeth Johns, who lived in Cardiff, listened to the broadcast at home and wrote a letter to both monarchs to express her gratitude for the message and her pleasure at the way the king had referred to the newlyweds:

> Dear King George and Queen Mary,
>
> I am sending you a word from my Heart to thank you for your great speech. I think it was Lovely and Good of you to think of all your Poor people and to think of your loving Son and Daughter in Law. What a lovely young couple.[32]

The king's reference to George and Marina had evoked from Johns personal identification with the royal family's relationships. This kind of empathy was echoed by Herbert Humphrey, a florist and greengrocer from Wokingham who, writing 'on behalf of [his] wife, family, and friends', stated that 'it was most pleasing to us all to hear your loving remarks respecting Their Royal Highnesses the Duke and Duchess of Kent'.[33] Here Humphrey articulated an affective affinity with the king which he felt he shared with those closest to him; and this sense of a mutual connection to royal domesticity was present in many letters that described family groups gathered in emotional communion around radio sets.

Lang's focus on other members of the royal family in George V's messages thus presented listeners with more intimate access to the king's home life; and his 1935 broadcasts, both of which were drafted by the archbishop, strengthened the image of a British people united around royal domesticity. In his silver jubilee message, George V poignantly conveyed his and Queen Mary's thanks to the public for their continuing support; he referred to the prince of Wales as 'my dear son' when praising the latter's recent philanthropic work; and, in his subsequent Christmas broadcast, he described how the 'personal link' that connected him to his subjects was partly based on a mutual appreciation of family life with its 'common joys and sorrows'.[34] A new family-centred culture was emerging in interwar Britain which placed

---

[31] LPL, Lang 318, fos. 23–31.

[32] RA, PS/PSO/GV/PS/MAIN/55357, E. Johns to King George V and Queen Mary, undated.

[33] RA, PS/PSO/GV/PS/MAIN/55357, H. Humphrey to King George V, 26 Dec. 1934.

[34] LPL, Lang 318, fos. 33–6 and fos. 40–3. Notably, the king's intimate silver jubilee broadcast coincided with the release of reports on his and the queen's home life, including that they called each other by the pet names 'Georgie' and 'May' (*Daily Express*, 3 May 1935, p. 6).

special emphasis on the personal fulfilment that could be achieved in the domestic sphere.[35] Although this culture did not take on a *truly* national and classless character until after the Second World War, the values espoused by George V closely paralleled this focus on home and family.[36] And, given that he delivered four out of five of his broadcasts to coincide with the period immediately after lunchtime on the one day in the calendar year when families came together to celebrate their kinship, the monarch's words were clearly intended for a listenership that was emotionally primed to approve of his vocal celebration of British domesticity.[37]

Whoever at Buckingham Palace was reading and revising Lang's drafts – be it a courtier or the king himself – responded positively to the archbishop's emphasis on family and deliberately edited the messages to accentuate this focus. The 1935 Christmas message was returned to Lang at Lambeth with the following revisions:

> It is this personal link between (King) **me** and **my** People which I value more than I can say. It binds us together in all our common joys and sorrows, as when this year you showed your happiness in the marriage of (another) **my** son, and your sympathy in the death of (a) **my** beloved sister. I feel (it) **this link** now as I speak to you.[38]

The intimacy of the king's references to the marriage of his son, Prince Henry, and the death of his 'beloved sister', Princess Victoria, was enhanced by the substitution of the word 'my' into Lang's original draft message, generating a stronger impression of affective attachment to the family members discussed. Similarly, the substitution of 'me' for 'King' and the inclusion of the word 'my' in front of 'People' increased the depth of meaning ascribed by George V to the 'personal link' between him and his listeners, all of whom he singled out using the word 'you' in the last sentence to try momentarily to bind them to him in acknowledgement of a national culture of domesticity exemplified by the House of Windsor.

---

[35] Langhamer, *The English in Love*, esp. pp. 1–19; King, *Family Men*, pp. 5–7; M. Johnes, *Christmas and the British: a Modern History* (London, 2016), pp. 41–2.

[36] C. Langhamer, 'The meanings of home in postwar Britain', *Jour. Contemp. Hist.*, xl (2005), 341–62; J. Finch and P. Summerfield, 'Social reconstruction and the emergence of companionate marriage, 1945–1959', in *Marriage, Domestic Life and Social Change: Writings for Jacqueline Burgoyne*, ed. D. Clark (London, 1991), pp. 7–32; S. Szreter and K. Fisher, *Sex Before the Sexual Revolution: Intimate Life in England, 1918–1963* (Cambridge, 2010), p. 29.

[37] Johnes, *Christmas and the British*, pp. 41–72. See also *Daily Mail*, 24 Dec. 1932, p. 8.

[38] LPL, Lang 318, fos. 40–3 (the palace's substitutions appear in bold, with Lang's original words in brackets).

The closing lines of the 1935 broadcast also reinforced the idea of collective domesticity. For the first time, the monarch extended festive greetings to listeners from his entire household, which created a vision of a royal family grouped around him: 'Once again as I close I send to you all, and not least to the children who may be listening to me, my truest Christmas wishes, and those of my dear wife, my children and grandchildren who are with me today. I add a heartfelt prayer that, wherever you are, God may bless and keep you always'.[39] Here, Lang's words elevated George V's persona as *paterfamilias* of the House of Windsor and symbolically conflated his position as constitutional sovereign with his role as husband, father and grandfather. We might conjecture, based on letters written to George V in 1934, that the king's greeting on behalf of his family members intensified the emotional bonds that some members of the public forged with royalty. Several listeners wrote to the royal household before the king's 1934 broadcast expressing a desire to hear the voices of other members of the royal family. Ernest Jenkins of South Croydon was typical in his appeal:

> If at the end of His Majesty's message it would be possible for Her Majesty the Queen at his invitation to speak even a single sentence of greeting it would be a dramatic and delightful surprise and would if possible add to the loyal appreciation of The King's subjects and would convey to the world at large in a still greater degree the deep interest of the Royal House in the people of all classes throughout the Empire.[40]

Jenkins believed that the power of the royal voice lay in its ability to strengthen the relationship between the monarchy and British and imperial subjects. His desire for a more personal contact with royalty was similarly articulated in letters written to the king's private secretary requesting that the daughters of the duke and duchess of York, Princesses Elizabeth and Margaret Rose, be allowed to broadcast, as well as in letters written to British newspapers and the BBC.[41]

Official correspondence shows that the king – and only the king – would speak for his family at Christmas time; other members of the House of Windsor would remain silent. A letter written by Queen Mary's private

---

[39] LPL, Lang 318, fos. 40–3.

[40] RA, PS/PSO/GV/PS/MAIN/55357, E. Jenkins to C. Wigram, 9 Nov. 1934. For other letters which expressed a desire to hear other members of the royal family speak, including the queen and the princesses, see those written by J. Abbot (to C. Wigram, 13 Dec. 1934), H. Grayson (to C. Wigram, 7 Jan. 1935), M. E. King (to C. Wigram, 1 Jan. 1935), E. Newcombe (to King George V, 1 Dec. 1934) and G. A. Whittle (to C. Wigram, 6 Dec. 1934) in the Royal Archives.

[41] E.g., *Daily Mail*, 1 Oct. 1934, p. 14; BBCWA, R34/862/1, L. B. Hyde to J. Reith, 22 Nov. 1933.

secretary, Harry Verney, to the controller of programmes at the BBC, Colonel Alan Dawnay, after the monarch had received a letter from a member of the public imploring her to broadcast reveals the palace's stance on this issue: '[T]his is a matter about which The Queen feels very strongly, and, strictly between you and me, I may say that nothing will ever induce Her Majesty to broadcast'.[42] Almost a year on, Clive Wigram clarified the palace's policy in a private letter to the editor of The Times, Geoffrey Dawson, who had forwarded to him a similar request for the queen to speak: 'I am afraid this idea is quite impracticable, and broadcasts at Christmas must be confined to the King (who speaks for the Queen as well). Otherwise we should be receiving requests for messages from all the Members of the Royal Family, including Princess Marina!'[43]

We might speculate, then, that Lang's inclusion of a Christmas greeting from the king's closest relatives at the end of the 1935 message was intended to satiate the public appetite for a more personal contact with Queen Mary and the rest of the royal family. Since the mid nineteenth century, new sorts of royal media, such as photographs, had enabled members of the public to 'consume' monarchy in new ways and offered collectors a close emotional proximity to royalty. We might interpret the desire to 'consume' the voices of the king and his family as a natural extension of this earlier culture, with the new technology of radio enabling a more intimate identification with the House of Windsor among listeners.

Kipling had included in George V's first Christmas broadcast a reference to how the monarch spoke 'from my home and from my heart to you all' and this phrase was welcomed by newspapers like the Daily Mirror for the way it enhanced the impression that the king was speaking 'personally' from the 'privacy of his Sandringham Home' to listeners.[44] Indeed, it seems probable that this was the royal household's intention. Having secured Kipling's agreement to write the 1932 message, Wigram wrote to thank him on behalf of his sovereign, noting how 'it is a wonderful innovation for the King to be able to speak to practically the whole of his Empire from his fireside in his country home'.[45] The imagery conjured by the courtier of George V delivering his message from a comfortable domestic setting was a powerful one and was incorporated by Kipling into the broadcast. However, the writer's broadcast the following year made no allusion to the king's domesticity and so it was left to Lang, who understood that Christmas was a time of home-centred celebrations, to revive the appealing image of

[42] BBCWA, R34/862/1, H. Verney to A. Dawnay, 2 Dec. 1933.
[43] RA, PS/PSO/GV/PS/MAIN/55357, C. Wigram to G. Dawson, 28 Sept. 1934.
[44] Daily Mirror, 27 Dec. 1932, pp. 3 and 11.
[45] TK, SxMs-38/2/2/2/1/2/2/5/1, C. Wigram to R. Kipling, 29 Nov. 1932.

the king talking from his own fireside to listeners in the 1934 message: 'As I sit in my own home I am thinking of the great multitudes who are listening to my voice whether they be in British homes or in far off regions of the world'.[46] These words projected a vision of George V sitting at Sandringham quietly contemplating his relationship with his people, who were similarly gathered in their homes, and the same imagery would notably reappear in both of the king's 1935 broadcasts.

Lang's emphasis on home life corresponded with wider shifts in British radio culture that were designed to create stronger resonances of verisimilitude. Accomplished broadcasters like Stanley Baldwin developed rhetorical styles that drew on the language of listeners' homes in order to connect with them.[47] The BBC's broadcasting gardener, C. H. Middleton, better known as 'Mr. Middleton', was also celebrated for his ability to convey a familiar tone across the airwaves, regularly referring to his domestic surroundings in order to link an imagined vision of his home with the physical space of his listeners' dwellings.[48] At a time when the British increasingly viewed the private sphere of home as an important locus for self-fulfilment, domestic imagery seemed to offer listeners access to the inner world of the speaker and Lang's vision of British households joined around the domesticity of the king was positively received by letter writers who commented on the 'homely' register of the king's messages.[49]

Courtiers increasingly discerned an advantage in promoting the image of the king at home as well. In 1932, they opposed the idea that the BBC publish a photograph of the microphone through which the king would speak. Ten days before George V was due to deliver his first message, his assistant private secretary, Sir Alexander Hardinge, wrote to the head of outside broadcasts, Gerald Cock, to explain that, while the sovereign did not mind the BBC photographing 'the apparatus in position in the room where the King will broadcast on Christmas Day', the picture must be 'retained for the private use of the BBC only, and … not given to the Press in any form'.[50] Just two years later, however, the palace relaxed its stance at the request of Geoffrey Dawson, who had written to Wigram to

---

[46] LPL, Lang 318, fos. 23–31.

[47] D. Cardiff, 'The serious and the popular: aspects of the evolution of style in radio talk 1928–1939', in *Media Culture and Identity: a Critical Reader*, ed. R. Collins (London, 1986), pp. 228–41, at pp. 229–30.

[48] M. Andrews, 'Homes both sides of the microphone: wireless and domestic space in inter-war Britain', *Women's History Review*, xxi (2012), 605–21, at p. 616.

[49] RA, PS/PSO/GV/PS/MAIN/55357, T. E. Bailey to King George V, 25 Dec. 1934; M. Waters to King George V, 25 Dec. 1934.

[50] BBCWA, R30, A. Hardinge to G. Cock, 14 Dec. 1932; also see reply from Cock to Hardinge, 23 Jan. 1933.

explain that *The Times* was planning a special Christmas issue and he was 'very anxious that the frontispiece should be a photograph of the King <u>at the microphone</u>'. Dawson emphasized that the special issue went 'almost entirely overseas, is bought by some 70,000 people all over the British Empire … and is of course seen and read by many thousands more. I feel that it would be an immense pleasure to them to have such a portrait of their Sovereign before them when they listen to his Christmas message'. He also explained that, because of time constraints, the king would need to sit for the photograph well before Christmas and suggested to Wigram that it would be better to take the picture at Sandringham (as opposed to Buckingham Palace) as it would 'be a little more "actual"'. He concluded his letter determinedly stating, 'I would not ask if I did not think it to the interest, not only of <u>The Times,</u> but of the Monarchy'.[51]

Dawson's royalist sentiments and his belief that the picture would bring George V into closer contact with his imperial subjects appear to have won the day and Wigram was pleased to report back that the king had agreed to the newspaper editor's wishes. Plans were then formulated for a staff photographer from *The Times* to go to Sandringham on a Sunday in mid October when, according to Wigram, 'the King would not be in shooting clothes' and to photograph the monarch in the room 'in which he generally gives the Broadcast Message'.[52] Wigram also asked that the man from *The Times* bring a microphone with him – presumably to help to maintain the illusion that the photograph showed the king speaking live to his people. Like Dawson, the king's private secretary was anxious to convey 'actuality' through the photograph, his proposals revealing his concern to elevate the king's public image as an 'ordinary man' speaking from his home on Christmas day; a picture of him in shooting dress with its elite connotations would not do. And *The Times* photographer staged the scene so that it communicated this domestic vision: the king was seated at his desk dressed in a lounge suit with the microphones in front of him and in the background was a fireplace (Figure 2.1). The photograph thus provided its viewers with a familiar representation of the monarch's domesticity that complemented the portrayals of his home life in his broadcasts and in press reports.[53]

Wigram ended his original letter to Dawson by remarking that 'in the event of this photograph being taken, I presume that it will be special for

---

[51] RA, PS/PSO/GV/PS/MAIN/55357, G. Dawson to C. Wigram, 21 Sept. 1934 (Dawson's emphasis).

[52] RA, PS/PSO/GV/PS/MAIN/55357, C. Wigram to G. Dawson, 24 Sept. 1934.

[53] E.g., *Daily Mirror*, 27 Dec. 1932, pp. 3 and 11; *The Times*, 27 Dec. 1935, p. 7.

Figure 2.1. George V at the microphone. Taken by a photographer from *The Times* in October 1934 (RCIN 630629). Royal Collection Trust / © Her Majesty Queen Elizabeth II 2019.

the "Times" and not distributed to other papers?'[54] However, George V later sanctioned the reproduction of the image as a collectible and other news editors seem to have interpreted this as enabling them to publish the image freely as part of their coverage of the 1934 Christmas broadcast.[55] Hence, whereas the king had taken exception to the publication of photographs of the microphone through which he spoke in 1932, just two years later he was prepared to pose in front of the apparatus for the camera. This shift in attitude should not only be attributed to Dawson's request, but also to the way in which the royal household and Cosmo Lang constructed an intimate image of a king who seemed happy to communicate with his subjects in an attempt to unite them around a shared idea of British home life.

'My dear friends'

Lang's second major innovation as royal speechwriter was to create a more informal relationship between the sovereign and his audience. He began by

[54] RA, PS/PSO/GV/PS/MAIN/55357, C. Wigram to G. Dawson, 24 Sept. 1934.
[55] RA, PS/PSO/GV/PS/MAIN/55357, C. Wigram to G. Dawson, 8 Nov. 1934. For examples of press reproductions of the image, see *Daily Mirror*, 24 Dec. 1934, p. 17 and *Daily Mirror*, 27 Dec. 1935, p. 5.

implementing a simpler, more cheerful rhetoric than was used by Kipling. The opening line of the 1934 Christmas broadcast established the upbeat tone of this emotional register: 'On this Christmas Day I send to all my people everywhere my Christmas greeting'.[56] This was the first time the king had begun a message by directly greeting his listeners; in previous years, he had reserved his festive wishes for the end of his broadcasts. Some listeners responded positively to this informal tone. Walter Lawrence, who was sixty-eight and from Hull, remarked in his letter to George V that he had welcomed the monarch's 'Kind Greeting on the wireless'.[57] Similarly, Mrs E. Tomlinson, from Heckington in Lincolnshire, told the king that his broadcast 'must have found a corner in the hearts of all who read and heard it. So full of good cheer and affection'.[58] She then continued: 'I dare not have presumed to express my feelings, but, that being a widow of 90 years, I might not have another opportunity'. These comments suggest that the king's friendly words could evoke intimate responses from even the most reserved listeners.

Under Lang's authorship, George V also referred to his listeners in a much more familiar way. In the 1934 message, the archbishop had the king describe his people in Britain and the empire as 'members of one Family' – an important point to which this chapter will return.[59] It suffices to say for now that in presenting the monarch as 'Head of this great and widespread Family', Lang elevated an image of George V as a symbolic father to his peoples. The archbishop reproduced this affectionate tone in the silver jubilee broadcast, with the king addressing his listeners as 'my very dear people'.[60] Lang's draft of the Christmas message he composed later that year shows that he included the same phrase in its opening line as well: 'I wish you all, my dear People, a happy Christmas'. However, once again the royal household returned his draft with revisions. This time the word 'people' was replaced with the word 'friends' and so, broadcasting on 25 December 1935, the king began his message by delivering his festive greetings to an audience who he affably characterized as 'my dear friends'.[61] Following Lang's lead, the palace clearly seems to have discerned value in promoting the public image of the familiar sovereign and, significantly, this particular version of royal informality – with the monarch referring to his or her subjects as 'friends' – has never been repeated.

---

[56] LPL, Lang 318, fos. 23–31.
[57] RA, PS/PSO/GV/PS/MAIN/55357, W. Lawrence to King George V, 26 Dec. 1934.
[58] RA, PS/PSO/GV/PS/MAIN/55357, E. Tomlinson to King George V, undated.
[59] LPL, Lang 318, fos. 23–31.
[60] LPL, Lang 318, fos. 33–6 and fos. 40–3.
[61] LPL, Lang 318, fos. 40–3.

Lang also personalized George V's public language by enhancing its sympathetic and inclusive qualities. In 1932, Wigram had written to Kipling that 'the King was wondering whether it would be possible for you to bring in a sentence [to the broadcast] that would apply to the sick and suffering and the blind, as I understand special arrangements will be made, both at home and overseas, for them to listen to His Majesty's message'.[62] It is unclear whether such arrangements were made, but the resulting sentence delivered by George V 'to those cut off from fuller life by blindness, sickness, or infirmity' projected to listeners an image of a compassionate king which resonated with his and the monarchy's long-standing association with philanthropic causes both in Britain and the empire.[63] Kipling also used the words 'our' and 'we' in his messages in order to align the king's aims with his listeners' feelings. For example, in 1932 George V stated that 'it may be that *our* future will lay upon us more than one stern test. *Our* past will have taught us how to meet it unshaken'.[64] Lang's royal public language drew more readily on personal pronouns in order to accentuate both the image of the sympathetic king, keenly interested in the welfare of his people, and the sense of a shared national experience. The archbishop created a rhetorical framework that oscillated between a highly personal register, in which George V regularly referred to himself in the first-person, and an active register that emphasized how, working together, king and people could alleviate the widespread socio-economic distress of these years and ensure Britain and the empire's future prosperity.[65]

Lang first deployed this framework in the 1934 Christmas message to enhance the sense of purpose that underpinned his vision of a family of British and imperial peoples who cared for one another:

> The world is still restless and troubled. The clouds are lifting, but *we* have still *our* own anxieties to meet. *I* am convinced that if *we* meet them in the spirit of one family *we* shall overcome them, for then private and party interests will be controlled by care for the whole community. It is as members of one family that *we* shall today, and always, remember those other members of it who are suffering from sickness or from the lack of work and hope; and *we* shall be ready to do *our* utmost to befriend them.[66]

---

[62] TK, SxMs-38/2/2/2/1/2/2/5/1, C. Wigram to R. Kipling, 16 Dec. 1932.

[63] Prochaska, *Royal Bounty*, pp. 169–212.

[64] Quoted in Fleming, *Voices Out of the Air*, p. 11 (this author's italics).

[65] For an overview of the socio-economic context of this period, see P. Williamson, *National Crisis and National Government: British Politics, the Economy and Empire, 1926–1932* (Cambridge, 1992).

[66] LPL, Lang 318, fos. 23–31 (this author's italics).

This passage shows how the archbishop's personal language punctuated George V's broadcasts by instilling in them a greater sense of purpose between the monarch and his people through collective action. Just as President Roosevelt had created politically conscious American listeners by outlining to them how they could support his New Deal programme in his fireside chats, so George V sought to convey to his subjects his concern for them and his desire that they unite in working with, and for, one another.

Many of the letters written to the king after he delivered his 1934 broadcast reveal this positive vision at work. George Pontifect from Sheen in South West London thanked the monarch for the 'inspiring message which you delivered to-day. The younger generation, to which I belong, has to face to-day hard times but we are enabled to do so with equanimity with such a ruler as you at our head'.[67] This letter shows that the king's words evoked from listeners like Pontifect an optimism about the future despite the socio-economic problems many were experiencing in the early 1930s. Another man from London, John Wm. Cooper, articulated similar sentiments:

Your Most Gracious Majesty.

Thank you for Blessed Message [*sic*]. Simple words to your people. A message that every loyal subject would understand. Sincerity that each, and every one of us, could not fail to appreciate.

Times when the majority of us are in the 'pan' to use a low expression. Times when the Politician irritates. Times when the mere mention of the word WAR is gall to us. And yet, today – Christmas Day. And any other Day of the year that our Most Gracious Majesty calls to His Subjects, the simple truth and sincerity commands.[68]

Cooper described how the king's broadcast had brought him reassurance and hope. We might also interpret the emphasis that he placed on the simplicity of the king's words as evidence of the power of Lang's more informal language in conveying a sincere and caring image of the king to listeners.

Other writers described how the king's sympathetic words had a highly personal effect on them while noting that they felt part of a larger emotional community centred on the monarchy because of the broadcast. In her letter to the king, Lilian E. Roberts, who wrote from a convalescent home in Exmouth, Devon, extended her thanks to him 'from the <u>Soul</u> for your pretty Xmas broadcast with its loving and thoughtful words of cheer for

---

[67] RA, PS/PSO/GV/PS/MAIN/55357, G. Pontifect to King George V, 25 Dec. 1934.
[68] RA, PS/PSO/GV/PS/MAIN/55357, J. W. Cooper to King George V, 25 Dec. 1934.

this happy season!'. She explained how she was 'only one of Their Majestys Big Family – needing like others in the army of suffering – more strength – but when on Xmas day I heard the King's Speech – he sounded just like a dear kind Father to us all and the voice very, very clear indeed.'[69] In this personal letter, Roberts described how the king's broadcast had had an inspiring effect on her at a time when she was ill and how the Christmas message had made her feel part of a larger family of listeners headed by a paternalistic monarch. A Mr. Saunders from Bampton in North Devon similarly wrote to George V to express his thanks 'for the uplifting help [the broadcast] gave me. For reasons of health, I am entirely alone this day; but I no longer feel lonely or unhappy after being made aware that I belong to one family of which Your Majesty is the Head. I humbly thank you from the bottom of my heart for the kind message and help'.[70] These words testify to the powerful effect that radio had in encouraging listeners to conceive of themselves as part of an imagined emotional community simultaneously linked around the focal point of the monarchy. Moreover, this sense of affective integration seems to have been acutely felt by those who listened alone to the king's broadcast or lacked actual relatives with whom to celebrate the Christmas festival.

Lang's royal public language thus worked on at least two levels: it not only resonated with some families who listened together on Christmas Day and empathized with the monarch's references to his own relatives or his home life; its kind-hearted, informal character also appealed to vulnerable people who were in need of sympathy. It is significant that the archbishop's personalized rhetoric also received widespread acclaim in the British press. As already indicated, newspapers like the *Express* and *Mirror* interpreted Rudyard Kipling's broadcasts as creating a unique link between the monarch and his people. The personal emphasis continued to inform the press coverage of Lang's messages, with newspapers stressing the intimate way in which George V characterized his audience. For example, the day after he had delivered his silver jubilee broadcast, the *Express* presented as its front-page headline the king's reference to listeners as 'my very dear people' (Figure 2.2).[71] Similarly, the *Mirror* précised George V's 1935 Christmas message with the words 'my dear friends'.[72] In this way the press helped to immortalize the image of the kind, personable sovereign, their reports

---

[69] RA, PS/PSO/GV/PS/MAIN/55357, L. E. Roberts to King George V and Queen Mary, undated (original emphasis).

[70] RA, PS/PSO/GV/PS/MAIN/55357, G. Saunders to King George V, 25 Dec. 1934.

[71] *Daily Express*, 7 May 1935, p. 1. For comparable coverage, see *Daily Mail*, 7 May 1935, p. 13.

[72] *Daily Mirror*, 27 Dec. 1935, p. 5.

Figure 2.2. 'My Very Dear People', *Daily Express*, 7 May 1935, p. 1.
© The British Library Board.

shaped by the rising influence of human-interest journalism which sought to nurture an affective affinity between media audiences and the public figures they read about in newspapers, watched in the cinema and listened to on the radio.[73]

'I dedicate myself anew'

The archbishop's third modification consolidated the personal connection between the king and his subjects. As already discussed, in Lang's messages George V spoke symbolically of a 'personal link' that united him and his people and was partly based on a shared culture of domesticity exemplified by the House of Windsor. Kipling avoided references to the king's personal life in the earlier broadcasts, but he *did* note that the monarch's relationship with his people was rooted in a bond of mutual support. For example, in the 1932 message George V stated that his 'life's aim' had 'been to serve' his people in order to improve their lives; and that their 'loyalty' and 'confidence' in him had been his 'abundant reward' for this service.[74] The king explained to listeners that he had committed himself to their welfare and that their trust in his leadership sustained him in this role. Lang's intimate public language invigorated this concept, with the monarch describing in unprecedented terms the deep mutual affection that linked him to his people.

Lang's innovation was particularly noticeable in the silver jubilee broadcast he prepared for the king. It was much more contemplative in tone than the Kipling messages and produced an image of George V reflecting on his relationship with his listeners:

> At the close of this memorable day I must speak to my people everywhere. Yet how can I express what is in my heart? As I passed this morning through cheering multitudes to and from St. Paul's Cathedral, as I thought there of all that these twenty-five years have brought to me and to my country and my Empire, how could I fail to be most deeply moved? Words cannot express my thoughts and feelings. I can only say to you, my very dear people, that the Queen and I thank you from the depth of our hearts for all the loyalty and – may I say? – the love with which this day and always you have surrounded us. I dedicate myself anew to your service for the years that may still be given to me.[75]

The highly introspective register in the opening lines of this broadcast conjured a vision of the king ruminating on his mood at the end of the jubilee celebrations. Although the monarch's allusion to the sentiment in

---

[73] L. Beers, 'A model MP? Ellen Wilkinson, gender, politics and celebrity culture in interwar Britain', *Cult. and Soc. History*, x (2013), 231–50, at pp. 238–41.

[74] Quoted in Fleming, *Voices Out of the Air*, p. 11.

[75] LPL, Lang 318, fos. 33–6.

his 'heart' had precursors in earlier messages, his rhetorical interrogation of his feelings was unprecedented and conveyed to listeners an image of a king who was able to share his deepest emotions. Then, declaring that he could not put into words his 'thoughts and feelings', implying that he was overwhelmed, he declared, in Lang's most direct and intimate linguistic flourish to date, his gratitude to his subjects for the loyalty and, extraordinarily, the love which they had supposedly shown him and Queen Mary during their reign together. Kipling had originally characterized the bond between king and people as one based on the 'public's loyalty' and 'confidence' in their monarch. Lang remodelled this bond as one founded on 'love' and it was fitting that, having stressed that the relationship between king and subjects relied on the latter's provision of emotional sustenance for the former, George V stated that he would continue, so long as he was able, to fulfil his end of this social contract, rededicating himself to the service of his people.

The idea of a British monarch sacrificing himself in return for his people's love was not new. The royal proclamation of accession and the coronation oath, which dated back more than three centuries, included phrases which emphasized that the sovereign could expect to receive his subjects' affection in return for dutiful service on their behalf.[76] And, as we know, Victorian notions of duty and service were defining features of George V's reign.[77] What was new, though, was the way the king publicly spoke of this relationship at a time when the lexicons of affection and self-sacrifice had much deeper personal resonances. Martin Francis has suggested that emotional self-restraint was key to elite male deportment in the middle decades of the twentieth century: as a man, to reveal one's feelings was to expose weakness.[78] But George V transgressed this boundary through his emotionally candid broadcasts, remodelling the image of king as a benign, loving figure whose own self-fulfilment was inhibited by his onerous position. Furthermore, this period was notable for the emergence of new understandings of the self which, above all else, prioritized personal enrichment.[79] Yet, here was a king who seemed ready to put his people's welfare ahead of his own happiness

[76] I. Bradley, *God Save the Queen: the Spiritual Dimension of Monarchy* (London, 2002), ch. 4 and 6.

[77] Williamson, 'Monarchy and public values', pp. 252–5; Glencross, Rowbottom and Kandiah, 'Ultimate Windsor ceremonials', pp. 53–5; Jones, 'The nature of kingship'.

[78] M. Francis, 'Tears, tantrums, and bared teeth: the emotional economy of three Conservative prime ministers, 1951–1963', *Jour. Brit. Stud.*, xli (2002), 354–87, at pp. 357–9.

[79] Mort, 'Love in a cold climate', pp. 52–3. Also see C. Langhamer, 'Love and courtship in mid-twentieth-century England', *Hist. Jour.*, l (2007), 173–96; J. Gardiner, *The Thirties: an Intimate History* (London, 2011), pp. 453–77.

and who told his subjects in no uncertain terms how their reciprocal love for him was compensation enough for his dedication to their care.

Lang combined this potent mix of royal self-sacrifice and popular emotional sustenance for the first time in the 1934 Christmas broadcast, with George V elaborating on the burdens of kingship: 'May I add very simply and sincerely that if I may be regarded as in some true sense the Head of this great and widespread Family, sharing its life and sustained by its affection, this will be a full reward for the long and sometimes anxious labours of my Reign of well nigh five and twenty years'.[80] Perhaps unsurprisingly, the monarch's words met with powerful responses from some listeners. John Crawley of Swaffham in Norfolk thanked the king for his message and wished him 'God's blessing in the great office to which He has called you in such difficult times as the present'.[81] Meanwhile, a vicar who ministered in the parish of Heaton Park in Newcastle-on-Tyne expressed a similar concern for George V in his letter to the king's private secretary:

> A few moments ago I stood to listen to his Majesty's broadcast message. In it he mentioned the difficulties and anxieties of his work. You may think it worthwhile to tell him of the reactions to his words of one of his humble subjects. I felt constrained to kneel down and I prayed for two things. First that God would bless and strengthen him for the great responsibilities which are his. Secondly, that I might be given grace to be worthy of his commission which I hold and have held many years.[82]

The vicar's words reveal that Lang's sentence on the 'anxious labours' of George V's reign had a sudden effect on some listeners. He expressed sympathy for the king 'for the great responsibilities which are his' and sent up a prayer in the hope that God's blessing would fortify the monarch in his role. Indeed, several religiously inspired letter writers articulated similar sentiments to the king when they emphasized that they hoped God would support him in his work.[83]

We should interpret letters like these in light of the religious content of the king's messages – he concluded each one of his broadcasts by delivering God's blessing to listeners – and also against the backdrop of the Christmas festival with its underlying symbolism of self-sacrifice.[84] Mrs Mary Munday from Hanworth in Middlesex captured the essence of this divine imagery

[80] LPL, Lang 318, fos. 23–31.
[81] RA, PS/PSO/GV/PS/MAIN/55357, J. Crawley to King George V, 25 Dec. 1934.
[82] RA, PS/PSO/GV/PS/MAIN/55357, E. King to C. Wigram, 25 Dec. 1934.
[83] RA, PS/PSO/GV/PS/MAIN/55357. See the letters written by the anonymous husband and wife from Sunderland, W. Bishop, M. Etienne, Mr. and Mrs. Perkins, L. Roberts, S. Scott, M. Waters, R. Wells and L. Wilson.
[84] Johnes, *Christmas and the British*, pp. 114–23.

in her letter to George V and, despite some awkward punctuation, it shows how Lang's royal public language awakened in her sympathy for the monarch:

> The <u>cross</u> of <u>life,</u> that is laid on us all alike both the <u>rich</u> and the <u>poor</u> each of us, 'as the same burden to carry, and your way of <u>understanding,</u> us all gives us <u>courage</u> to <u>carry</u> on as you said in your Broadcast, to us all there has been times very <u>anxious</u> for <u>you</u> and it is with <u>patience</u> that you have won through and I hope that <u>you,</u> and <u>our Beloved Queen,</u> and all the Royal <u>Family,</u> will have <u>Peace</u> of <u>Mind</u> and every <u>Happiness</u> in the coming year, to reward <u>you</u> for any <u>sorrow</u> or <u>trouble</u> that 'as come to you in the year that is nearly over, and may good <u>Health</u> <u>attend you</u> [*sic*].
>
> P.S. God Bless You.[85]

Munday's fulsome letter, with its constant underlining of words, drew on the religious imagery of the 'cross of life' and the burdens it imposed on king and subjects alike. She described how George V's '<u>understanding</u>' and 'patience' had 'won through' despite 'times very <u>anxious</u> for <u>you</u>' and she empathized with him and the royal family in expressing her hope that 1935 would prove a happy year for them all. The letter thus reveals how Lang's emphasis on the arduous nature of royal life, and specifically the idea that the monarch's function was to serve his people, resonated with some listeners, who articulated sympathy for, and gratitude to, the king.

In his last ever broadcast on Christmas Day 1935, George V publicly reflected on the difficulties of his role for a final time:

> The year that is passing – the twenty-fifth since my accession – has been to me most memorable. It called forth a spontaneous offering of loyalty – and I may say – of love, which the Queen and I can never forget. How could I fail to note in all the rejoicings not merely respect for the throne, but a warm and generous remembrance of the man himself who, may God help him, has been placed upon it?[86]

The king's implicit reference to the burdens of his office, for which he implored God's help, and his restatement of the 'love' that connected his people to him once again envisaged a bond linking monarch to subjects that was based on mutual support. By reinvoking the word 'love', Lang normalized this highly expressive vocabulary – encouraging listeners to conceive of the king in very personal terms and to envision themselves as part of a community joined together in their collective affection for him.

---

[85] RA, PS/PSO/GV/PS/MAIN/55357, M. A. Munday to King George V, 26 Dec. 1934 (original emphasis and capital letters).

[86] LPL, Lang 318, fos. 40–3.

Lang also projected this image in the oration he delivered as part of the jubilee service of commemoration on 6 May 1935 in St. Paul's cathedral when he described George V as 'a man [his subjects] could understand, respect, and trust' and celebrated the king's 'unaffected friendliness' – both of which were phrases that the press highlighted in their coverage of the event.[87]

A number of George V's listeners focused in on the king's voice in order to make sense of the burdens imposed on him by his high station. Herbert Humphrey from Wokingham noted in his letter that he and his family 'hope and trust the great strain [of the 1934 broadcast] did not inconvenience your Majesty in any way whatsoever? It was a source of thankfulness that we noticed your Majesty's voice was much stronger and also clearer than last year'.[88] Similarly, Harold G. Carlile from Fulham in West London wrote that 'my wife and family join me in begging you to accept our thanks for your wonderful words today. More welcome, still, to us all was the evidence, in your voice, of your great strength and better health'.[89] Letters like these demonstrate that some listeners paid close attention to the way the king spoke to them and reveal that the varying power of his voice encouraged audiences to empathize with him. Harold Nicolson thought George V had a 'wonderful voice – strong, emphatic, vibrant, with undertones of sentiment, devoid of all condescension, artifice or pose'.[90] Listening back to the king's broadcasts, it is instantly apparent that he did indeed deliver his messages in a measured and rhythmical way, speaking slowly and with precision to listeners. The king's other biographer, Kenneth Rose, described his accent as that of an Edwardian country gentleman.[91] While his accent would have definitely conveyed his elite status to listeners, his upper-class tones do not seem to have been deemed out-of-touch in the way that those of his granddaughter Elizabeth were twenty years on.[92] Rather, he possessed a very human radio voice: afflicted by a bronchial cough, it was gruff in character, which commentators suggested enhanced its appeal. In 1932 *The Spectator* celebrated how the king's cough had interrupted the flow of his first broadcast: 'A King who reads a message into a microphone from a manuscript may be just a King. A King who coughs is a fellow human

---

[87] *Daily Mirror*, 7 May 1935, p. 7. See also *Daily Express*, 7 May 1935, p. 2; *Daily Mail*, 7 May 1935, p. 13.

[88] RA, PS/PSO/GV/PS/MAIN/55357, H. Humphrey to King George V, 26 Dec. 1934

[89] RA, PS/PSO/GV/PS/MAIN/55357, H. G. Carlile to King George V, 25 Dec. 1934.

[90] Nicolson, *King George*, p. 526.

[91] Rose, *King George V*, p. 394.

[92] B. Pimlott, *The Queen: Elizabeth II and the Monarchy* (London, 2002), p. 282.

being'.[93] It seems likely from the letters written to George V that his coughing, which was repeated in both 1935 messages, added to the sense of spontaneity and personality he communicated over the airwaves. Moreover, in his final two broadcasts, the monarch spoke in quieter, slower tones, conjuring a vision of a more elderly gentleman in thoughtful conversation with his listeners.

'This great family'

It was partly the growing prominence of Adolf Hitler and Benito Mussolini's voices in British news reports that gave rise in the early 1930s to public concerns over whether the League of Nations could secure a lasting peace.[94] Some people clearly looked to more traditional authority figures like George V to take a lead in the movement for peace rather than place their trust in the new internationalist League. Before he delivered his Christmas broadcast in 1934, the king received several letters from members of the public suggesting that he include a new feature in his message – such as a two-minute silence or an appeal to foreign heads of state – in order to highlight his desire to secure international harmony.[95] Although these ideas were not adopted, the letters indicate that George V was perceived by some of his people as having a powerful global influence. Lang promoted this aspect of the king's persona by strengthening the vision of an imperial family linked around the focal point of the monarch in order to remodel the empire as a peaceful group of nations committed to upholding order at a time of growing uncertainty.

As the king's speechwriter, Kipling had tried to communicate through the first two Christmas broadcasts a moment of imperial union in order to strengthen the connections between Britain and its empire. The bonds that linked the motherland to the dominions had been weakened with their change in status to self-governing 'autonomous communities', as established by the Statute of Westminster in 1931. Equally, the economic tensions that sprung from the global depression and the resistance of colonial independence movements added to the strain on Britain's imperial

---

[93] Quoted in Fleming, *Voices Out of the Air*, p. 9.

[94] M. Ceadel, *Semi-Detached Idealists: the British Peace Movement and International Relations, 1854–1945* (Oxford, 2000), pp. 307–25.

[95] RA, PS/PSO/GV/PS/MAIN/55357. See, e.g., the letters written by S. Drury-Lowe and K. M. Wood. The BBC's director of outside broadcasts, Gerald Cock, also seems to have toyed briefly with the idea that George V's 1935 Christmas message could take another form, with personal tributes to the king by the heads of governments of foreign countries in what the broadcaster thought would be 'a great gesture of international amity'. See, e.g., BBCWA, R34/299/1/1a, BBC Internal Circulating Memo from G. Cock, 13 Dec. 1934.

ties.[96] Kipling's vision of unity accorded with the BBC's own aims to present Christmas as a celebration of empire reunion and built on an older tradition that saw the festival as a time when British families remembered relatives who had settled overseas in the colonies and dominions.[97] The BBC launched its new empire service in October 1932 and, working with the public broadcasting authorities in Australia, New Zealand and Canada, sought to use radio programming to promote an inclusive (although generally white Anglo-centric) idea of empire that had the monarchy at its core.[98] Notably, the controller of programmes at the BBC, Alan Dawnay, described George V's broadcasts as the 'essential climax and the most important part' of his organization's empire-themed Christmas activities.[99]

In the 1933 message Kipling characterized the empire using the metaphor of 'family' for the first time: George V told his listeners that it was his 'privilege to speak directly to all the members of our world-wide family' and that the empire formed a 'family council' that worked together 'for the benefit of the family'.[100] Writing to the speechwriter after the monarch had spoken, Clive Wigram suggested that 'the Dominions will be delighted at being taken into the "Family Council" – a very happy term'.[101] The private secretary clearly approved of the domestic image conjured by Kipling's words, although the vision of a family of different British peoples connected around the focal point of the crown was not entirely novel. At the start of the nineteenth century George III's golden jubilee was celebrated for its inclusive qualities and the monarch described as the 'Father of his People', who were, in turn, presented as 'one great family'.[102] Crucially, on taking over from Kipling, Lang drew on the poet's example and put the theme of kinship unambiguously at the centre of the 1934 Christmas broadcast to

---

[96] S. Potter, *Broadcasting Empire: the BBC and the British World, 1922–1970* (Oxford, 2012), pp. 59–64. See also M. Connelly, *Christmas: a History* (London, 2012), pp. 55–64, 118–57.

[97] Connelly, *Christmas*, pp. 118–21.

[98] Potter, *Broadcasting Empire*, pp. 55–64.

[99] BBCWA, R34/862/1, A. Dawnay to C. Wigram, 13 July 1934.

[100] Fleming, *Voices Out of the Air*, p. 12.

[101] TK, SxMs-38/2/2/1/2/2/5/3, C. Wigram to R. Kipling, 25 Dec. 1933. Interestingly, it also seems from this letter that the king was not entirely happy with the broadcast. Wigram was not as effusive in his praise of Kipling's efforts as he had been the year before (TK, SxMs-38/2/2/1/2/2/5/1, C. Wigram to R. Kipling, 27 Dec. 1932). Neither did he convey a particularly positive response from the monarch: 'The King himself is quite pleased and I am sure that in his inmost heart he realizes that this has been another success and is pouring his blessing on your head'. If the king was for some reason displeased with the 1933 message (possibly because of its over-ornate, meandering style), it would help to explain why he turned to Lang to write his broadcast the following year.

[102] L. Colley, *Britons: Forging the Nation 1707–1837* (London, 1994), pp. 230–1.

popularize the idea that the empire was a family group.[103] The archbishop sent the first draft of the message to Wigram for official approval on 10 December and the courtier replied the next day: 'His Majesty ... wishes his warmest thanks conveyed to you for all the personal trouble and thought you have bestowed upon it. The King has read your draft through once and is quite delighted with your main theme of the Family, of which His Majesty is the Head'.[104]

Wigram's response reveals that Lang had, following Kipling's lead, remodelled George V's public image to present him as head of an international family of nations. The symbolism pleased the monarch and was immediately converted into a courtly conventional wisdom. The private secretary told Lang that 'when the King has a little more time he will go carefully into each sentence, and I know you will not mind if His Majesty wishes them shortened a little, as when speaking through the microphone the King prefers short sentences'.[105] However, the archbishop's draft remained almost entirely unchanged and George V referred to the empire as a family seven separate times as part of the 1934 Christmas message. Lang thus softened the image of the British empire by infusing it with a powerful domestic imagery which was more broadly characteristic of his intimate vision of kingship. Moreover, he reaffirmed this vision of empire in the messages he wrote for George V in 1935, with the king notably describing how the imperial spirit contrasted with the increasingly worrying situation on the Continent: 'In Europe and many parts of the world anxieties surround us. It is good to think that our own family of peoples is at peace in itself and united in one desire to be at peace with other nations – the friend of all, the enemy of none'.[106]

Despite the internal and external pressures that were being exerted on the empire, the image of a united family of peoples was welcomed by some listeners who wrote to George V after his 1934 broadcast to explain how his words had brought them comfort and confidence on Christmas Day.[107] The letters suggest that listeners took the king's words to heart, with many reiterating almost verbatim the image of empire crafted by Lang. Typical was Chas Geary's letter, which he wrote to George V from his home in Leeds:

[103] LPL, Lang 318, fos. 17–20 and fos. 26–7. Lang's papers include copies of both Kipling messages, suggesting that he used them in developing his own ideas.

[104] LPL, Lang 318, fos. 26–7, C. Wigram to C. G. Lang, 11 Dec. 1934.

[105] LPL, Lang 318, fos. 26–7, C. Wigram to C. G. Lang, 11 Dec. 1934.

[106] LPL, Lang 318, fos. 40–3.

[107] RA, PS/PSO/GV/PS/MAIN/55357. See the letters written by J. W. Cooper, K. Godfrey, L. E. Roberts, G. Saunders, G. Pontifect and M. Waters.

To His Majesty the King.

This may or may not reach your Majesty's personal notice. I hope it does, for it expresses the feelings of countless thousands of your subjects who heard your Royal – your noble – wireless message yesterday.

Your Majesty condensed the very highest ideal of Empire – the Family Tie and Bond of Union. Nothing more gloriously sacred could have been said.

"The Crown" is the vital link which links Your Majesty's Subjects the world over.[108]

Geary's belief that he spoke for 'countless thousands' was a recurrent theme in the letters written to George V, which suggests that radio worked to wed some listeners to the concept of an international emotional community which was uniquely integrated around the focal point of the king.[109] T. E. Bailey, a toy and electrical shop owner from Pewsey in Wiltshire, articulated a similar sentiment:

Your Majesty, I feel as one of your most loyal and loving subjects that I must thank you for your most encouraging and homely message to us all on this Christmas day, to feel that we as an Empire have such a King to govern and guide us, is not only a proud but most thankful situation to be in. I am also sure that if your talk today appealed to others as it appealed to me there is no fear for our Old Country and Empire. God Bless you Sir.[110]

Letters like this one suggest that Lang's royal public language strengthened the monarchy's role as the link that bound disparate peoples together and show that the image of an imperial stabilizing force led by George V resonated with some listeners at a time of international uncertainty.

The metaphor of the imperial family was rapidly popularized and would notably take on even greater significance as the old empire disintegrated and was subsequently reimagined as the New Commonwealth after 1945.[111] Lang's influential role in promoting this theme is discernible from the press's response to the king's 1934 Christmas message. In an editorial titled 'One great family', the *Mirror* stated that the broadcast 'became a symbol not only of the Christmas spirit of individual family happiness, but of a

---

[108] RA, PS/PSO/GV/PS/MAIN/55357, C. Geary to King George V, 26 Dec. 1934.

[109] More research is required if we are to know whether imperial subjects in the colonies and dominions also felt part of an international emotional community united around the family monarchy.

[110] RA, PS/PSO/GV/PS/MAIN/55357, T. E. Bailey to King George V, 25 Dec. 1934.

[111] P. Murphy, *Monarchy and the End of Empire: the House of Windsor, the British Government, and the Postwar Commonwealth* (Oxford, 2013), pp. 2–5 and 17; E. Buettner, *Europe After Empire: Decolonization, Society, and Culture* (Cambridge, 2016), pp. 46–9.

worldwide Imperial fraternity'.[112] Meanwhile, an editorial in *The Times*, with its strong associations with empire, drew special attention to the way 'the head of the family' had spoken to the 'members of the British family … from his own home'.[113]

Wigram wrote to Lang again in January 1935 to convey George V's gratitude for the draft, noting that it had been 'acclaimed the most moving message that the King has delivered by wireless to his People'.[114] As well as receiving very positive reviews in national newspapers for its focus on family, the 1934 Christmas message was also commended in readers' correspondence published by the press, some of which characterized the king as the 'father of an empire family'.[115] The intimate rhetoric devised by Lang seems to have invigorated the emotional bond that connected some listeners to the king, as seen in several of the letters addressed to George V which also used the word 'father' to describe their relationships to him, despite the fact that he avoided using this word to characterize his link to his people.[116] Indeed, the royal household amended Lang's 1935 Christmas message to moderate an explicit reference to the king as a paternal figure. The archbishop's draft included the line 'my words will be very simple but spoken from the heart (like the words of the father of a family speaking to his children) **on this family festival of Christmas**'.[117] The palace's excision of Lang's original depiction of George V as 'the father of a family speaking to his children' suggests it was deemed too direct and, possibly, cloying in its description of the king's paternal qualities. It may also have been interpreted as condescending in its presentation of the subjective connection between king and people and was replaced with the allusion to the 'family festival', which gave more imaginative space to listeners to interpret his words for themselves. Instead, it was left to other commentators to highlight the king's paternal qualities – as was the case when Lang described George V as 'the Father of his people' during the sermon he delivered in honour of the king at the St. Paul's cathedral jubilee service, which was broadcast live to the nation and empire.[118]

A programme of relayed spoken greetings from across the empire preceded the king's 1934 Christmas broadcast. These 'ordinary' voices were

---

[112] *Daily Mirror*, 27 Dec. 1934, p. 11.
[113] *The Times*, 27 Dec. 1934, p. 11.
[114] LPL, Lang 318, fo. 32, C. Wigram to C. G. Lang, 30 Jan. 1935.
[115] *Daily Express*, 27 Dec. 1934, p. 8.
[116] RA, PS/PSO/GV/PS/MAIN/55357. See the letters written by K. Godfrey, L. E. Roberts and M. Waters.
[117] LPL, Lang 318, fo. 40.
[118] Quoted in the *Daily Mirror*, 7 May 1935, p. 7.

used by the BBC to augment an image of an imperial race united around the sovereign's headship. A *Daily Mirror* editorial noted that the voices 'clarified and accentuated' the meaning of empire: 'When the obscure shepherd in a Cotswold village can greet the loneliest settler far across the seas, when a Canadian fisherman can tell us of his life, when loyal voices reach us from Britons in the Dominions and natives in South Africa, the meaning of unity has a direct and personal appeal'.[119] These chains of greeting between imperial subjects had begun before the king's 1932 Christmas broadcast and, in 1933, incorporated salutations from specially selected 'ordinary' voices from around the empire for the first time, under the title 'Absent Friends'.[120] From 1934 the annual imperial relays were also designed to evoke images of the family culture supposedly shared by listeners in different parts of the empire in an effort to awaken in them a more personalized connection to the monarch. Referring again to the Cotswold shepherd who spoke as part of the 1934 broadcast, the *Daily Mail* remarked that his contribution to the relay was particularly 'moving' because, speaking in a 'typically homely way', he appealed to his long-lost brother in New Zealand to contact him if, at that point, he was listening to his voice.[121] The broadcast thus assumed greater poignancy around the informal vision of an actual family reunion, the shepherd then heralding the sovereign's message by wishing listeners a happy Christmas and bestowing the empire's blessing on his monarch. Notably, the symbolism of this relay of greetings was not lost on listeners either. Hastwell Grayson, a farmer from Great Milton in Oxfordshire, included the following in his letter to the royal household: 'The Christmas Broadcast marked a new era. The fisherman, the shepherd and the toll collector were at the microphone, officialdom was silent. The innovation met with universal applause. The broadcast culminated with His Majesty's speech on the family at home and abroad, the individual family and the family which makes the Empire'.[122] Grayson was clearly impressed by the BBC's broadcast and the way the voices of ordinary people humanized the bonds of empire. His reference to the silence of officialdom also suggests he found it refreshing that high politics was deliberately kept out of this moment of imperial fraternity.

The BBC built on Lang's 1934 vision of empire in titling its relay of greetings for the king's final Christmas message in 1935 'This great family'. BBC editorial files specified that 'the idea of the programme is to show

[119] *Daily Mirror*, 27 Dec. 1934, p. 11.

[120] *Daily Mail*, 8 Dec. 1933, p. 11. See also Potter, *Broadcasting Empire*, p. 63; Connelly, *Christmas*, pp. 146–53.

[121] *Daily Mail*, 26 Dec. 1934, p. 9.

[122] RA, PS/PSO/GV/PS/MAIN/55357, H. Grayson to King George V, 7 Jan. 1935.

the Christmas spirit in families all over the world, and to show how the whole Empire is linked together as one family by its loyalty to the King'.[123] These documents also reveal the special lengths to which broadcasters went in locating 'representative types' of voices to reflect different regional and national cultures. For example, the contribution from Sheffield would come from an 'industrial family', while a farmer would deliver Scotland's greeting. The people selected were also to be 'either a family or some group of people brought together by Christmas' and should have real 'relatives or friends' living in the empire.[124] The BBC thought that, when juxtaposed, the effect of this range of voices and dialects would be 'very pointed'.[125] Voices were thus heard from the home nations, the dominions and India, including from a family in Ottawa and a children's hospital in Aberdare, Wales; and the final segment came from two children in London calling their grandfather, who lived in New Zealand.[126]

The family-centred image conjured by the BBC's Christmas relays softened the popular vision of British imperialism in the 1930s, tempering the empire's militaristic legacy while distracting from ongoing violent disputes between colonial independence movements and the British authorities.[127] The scene of two children calling their grandfather was one of the most explicit references to the way in which empire seemed to be built on family connections that stretched over the entire world. This peaceful vision of British imperialism was also evident in George V's discussion of the personal bond which, he claimed, linked him to the empire's children. Back in 1923 the king and Queen Mary had recorded for gramophone an 'Empire Day message to the boys and girls of the British empire'; and in so doing had positioned themselves as familiar, symbolic figureheads which connected the motherland to young people in the dominions and colonies.[128] Beginning with his first Christmas message in 1932, George V ended each of

[123] BBCWA, R34/299/1/1a, Memo from Felix Felton to Director of Regional Relations, 13 Nov. 1935.
[124] BBCWA, R34/299/1/1a, Internal Circulating Memo from Felix Felton, 20 Nov. 1935
[125] BBCWA, R34/299/1/1a, Internal Circulating Memo from Felix Felton, 31 July 1935.
[126] BBCWA, R34/299/1/1a, Memo circulated by Felix Felton, 17 Dec. 1935.
[127] M. Chamberlain, 'George Lamming', in *West Indian Intellectuals, in Britain*, ed. B. Schwarz (Manchester, 2003), pp. 175–95, at p. 176; B. Bush, *Imperialism, Race and Resistance: Africa and Britain, 1919–1945* (London, 1999); W. M. Macmillan, *Warning from the West Indies: a Tract for Africa and the Empire* (London, 1936); K. A. Wagner, 'Calculated to strike terror': the Amritsar massacre and the spectacle of colonial violence', *Past & Present*, ccxxxiii (2016), 185–225.
[128] *Encyclopaedia of Recorded Sound*, ed. F. Hoffman (2 vols., New York & London, 2005), i. 1880. The recording (#19072) can be heard at <https://www.youtube.com/watch?v=3JyC6qw2D_s> [accessed 1 Feb. 2018].

his broadcasts either by making an individual reference to his child listeners or by delivering special festive wishes to the young people listening to him. Notably, in relation to Kipling's 1933 Christmas broadcast, Wigram wrote to tell the novelist that 'the little touch at the end about the children will be appreciated' – the courtier clearly valuing how the speechwriter's words would cultivate emotional bonds between the king and younger listeners.[129] The monarch's mention of children in the last lines of his 1934 broadcast inspired some of them to write to him. The Lewis children from Ridgeway, near Sheffield, wrote to inform George V how 'we three sisters have just been listening in to your Christmas greetings and we wish to thank you very much for the special message for the children'.[130] Similarly, Phoebe Cooper from West Worthing wrote that 'as the youngest member of a simple family party, I want to thank your Majesty for Your message to the Empire this afternoon, and to send to You our loyal greetings'.[131]

In his silver jubilee message George V's caring persona was communicated through a direct appeal to his young listeners:

> To the children I would like to send a special message. Let me say this to each of them whom my words may reach: the King is speaking to *you*. I ask you to remember that in days to come you will be the citizens of a great Empire. As you grow up always keep this thought before you. And when the time comes, be ready and proud to give to your country the service of your work, your mind, and your heart.[132]

Addressing his audience in the most direct register that Lang fashioned as royal speechwriter, the king presented himself as a senior relative to those children listening to him, emphasizing his personal connection to them in order to encourage them to take on active roles in the life of the empire. This message accorded with other royal attempts to promote 'good citizenship' between the wars, but the intimate nature of the jubilee appeal reveals how the king sought to integrate his subjects into the public sphere through the emotional bonds they forged with him.[133]

Importantly, a backdrop of escalating political tension in Europe enabled George V to present the empire as a pacific entity. Interpreting the 1934 Christmas broadcast as a 'peace message', the *Daily Mail* drew

---

[129] TK, SxMs-38/2/2/2/1/2/2/5/3, C. Wigram to R. Kipling, 25 Dec. 1933.

[130] RA, PS/PSO/GV/PS/MAIN/55357, Lewis children to King George V, 25 Dec. 1934.

[131] RA, PS/PSO/GV/PS/MAIN/55357, P. Cooper to King George V, 25 Dec. 1934.

[132] LPL, Lang 318, fos. 33–6. Note Lang's emphasis and also that the king placed stress on the word 'you' in his broadcast as well. See also *The Listener*, 30 Jan. 1936, p. 196.

[133] I. Zweiniger-Bargielowska, 'Keep fit and play the game: George VI, outdoor recreation and social cohesion in interwar Britain', *Cult. and Soc. History*, xi (2014), 111–29.

special attention to the king's statement that 'the clouds are lifting ... I am convinced that if we meet our anxieties in the spirit of one family we shall overcome them'.[134] The article also acknowledged that the pope and Nazi leaders had made similar 'fervent appeals in special Christmas messages that the spirit of peace might prevail throughout the world'. In this context of international disquiet, George V's later broadcasts, along with the BBC's imperial relays which preceded them, were celebrated by journalists for the way they characterized the empire as an international, stabilizing force made up of a peaceful community of peoples united by a common culture and kinship.[135] The king's image as the father figure who held this community together not only came to define the final years of his reign but also the way the British were encouraged to see themselves as a nation, which may help to explain why the public's grief appears to have been so profound when he died on 20 January 1936.[136]

'The World's Perfect Gentleman'

The Mass Observation archive houses 512 school essays titled 'The finest person who ever lived', which were written in late 1937 by working- and middle-class boys aged eight to eighteen at schools in Westhoughton, near Bolton, Lancashire and Middlesbrough in north-east England. Either under instruction or of their own volition, forty-six schoolboys wrote about George V, detailing the various characteristics they thought made him an especially 'fine' person and, in so doing, revealed some of the emotional contours along which young royalist identities were formed. The king was the second most popular choice after Jesus, on whom eighty essays were written, while Lord Nelson and Sir Francis Drake were the third and fourth most popular respectively.[137] Although there is no evidence available that sheds light on the conditions in which the essays were composed or what guidance the schoolboys received from their teachers, the large number

[134] *Daily Mail*, 26 Dec. 1934, p. 9.

[135] E.g., *Daily Mirror*, 27 Dec. 1934, p. 11; *The Times*, 27 Dec. 1934, p. 11.

[136] I. Zweiniger-Bargielowska, 'Royal death and living memorials: the funerals and commemoration of George V and George VI, 1936–52', *Hist. Research*, lxxxix (2015), 158–75.

[137] The 512 essays referred to here are the number quoted in a Mass Observation teaching handbook published to accompany this collection of essays. However, this is an approximation in that the handbook lists 45 essays on George V whereas this author has consulted the originals of the essays in the Mass Observation archive and located 46 written on him (SxMOA1/2/59/4/F-H: 'The Finest Person Who Ever Lived' handwritten essays, Westhoughton, Middlesbrough, 1937–38; Mass Observation, *Children's Essays, 1937: 'The Finest Person That Ever Lived'* (Mass Observation Teaching Booklets Series, iv, Brighton, 1988), pp. 1–30) <http://www.massobs.org.uk/images/booklets/Childrens_Essays_1937.pdf> [accessed 8 Dec. 2018].

of figures discussed suggests the boys were given some degree of choice in selecting whom they wrote about. Without knowing what kind of pedagogy took place in preparation for this exercise, we have to assume that the compositions revealed royalist identities *under construction* in response to social experiences inside and outside the classroom.[138] One of the major experiences that would certainly have shaped how the schoolboys wrote about the old king was the strange eighteen-month period that followed his death, with his charismatic eldest son relinquishing the throne to pursue true love only to be replaced by his second son who, as we shall see in the next chapter, was not a popular figure. The essay writers emphasized three positive characteristics in presenting George V as a particularly 'fine' figure and, in so doing, might have been nostalgically pointing to the qualities they thought he had embodied and were worth celebrating, knowing full well that neither of his successors had successfully carried forward their father's version of kingship.[139] The first of these qualities was the monarch's selfless dedication to serving his people irrespective of their social background: the boys expressed great admiration for the king's egalitarian character and described his relationship with his people as one rooted in intimacy. The second theme on which the essay writers focused was how George V's broadcasts had brought him closer to his subjects in Britain and the empire, crystallizing his personal link to them. Finally, the boys discussed George V's moral virtues as a family man. His domestic life impressed them and, at a time when private life was deemed to play a crucial role in the formation of a person's character, the king's ostensible love of family encouraged the schoolboys to empathize with him.[140]

The themes of selflessness and service prevailed in the essays written on the two most widely chosen figures – Jesus Christ and George V. Many of

[138] On the difficulties with using school essays as historical evidence, see J. Greenhalgh, '"Till we hear the last all clear": gender and the presentation of self in young girls' writing about the bombing of Hull during the Second World War', *Gender & History*, xxvi (2014), 167–83, at pp. 169–71; Barron and Langhamer, 'Children, class, and the search for security', pp. 369–71; H. Barron and C. Langhamer, 'Feeling through practice: subjectivity and emotion in children's writing', *Jour. Social Hist.*, li (2017), 101–23, at pp. 103–6.

[139] While it would have been easy for the schoolboys to compare George V's long reign with the much shorter, controversial reign of Edward VIII, it is notable that none of the essay writers sought to contrast the personalities of father and son, which suggests that Edward's failures as king – specifically his failure to put royal public duty ahead of self-fulfilment – did not necessarily weigh heavily on the compositions.

[140] Thirty-four of the 46 essays written on George V were numbered 1 to 34 (H1-34) and can be located in SxMOA1/2/59/4/H. One further unnumbered essay on the king can be located in file H, referred to here as 'Ho [Brass]'. Three essays on the king can be located in SxMOA1/2/59/4/F and a further 8 can be found in SxMOA1/2/59/4/G. Where identifiable, other essays are referenced using the surname of the schoolboy and relevant file letter.

the eighty essays written about Jesus discussed his self-sacrifice on behalf of his Christian followers, while over three quarters of the forty-six essays on the king focused on his caring reputation and the way he had tried in his lifetime to improve the lives of his people. While it is entirely possible that teachers instructed the boys to think in altruistic terms when writing their essays, this emphasis on the monarch's selflessness could also be revealing of the popular impact the royal public language of service had in the 1930s:

This venerable old gentleman who reigned over his beloved people for twenty-six years is in my estimation one of the finest persons whom anyone could meet. He had a quiet dignity which at once made a person feel at home in his presence and he could walk with and talk to the common people without losing any interest in them and their humble dwellings. During the fateful years of the Great War he visited the Western front and mingled freely with soldiers a thing no king has done since time of William III [sic]. He visited the wounded in the hospitals and gave them words of hope to cheer them on the long road to recovery. It was to him the nation looked for a lead and never did he fail them. The nation could only try to express their thanks in May 1935, his Silver Jubilee. The nation's mourning was expressed from all the Empire on his death for not only did he take a keen interest in home affairs but in Empire affairs ... He will be remembered as Britain's greatest King and the World's Perfect Gentleman.[141]

This teenage schoolboy's portrayal of George V was typical in the way it characterized his selfless behaviour using superlatives and hyperbole. The gentlemanly traits that the writer admired included the sovereign's 'quiet dignity' and readiness to interact with 'common people' in spite of their 'humble dwellings'. This image of the egalitarian monarch was not only projected through broadcasts in which he referred to his subjects as 'dear friends', but also harked back to the king's personal interactions with working-class people during his and the queen's tours of Britain's industrial communities before, during and after the First World War.[142] One boy, aged thirteen, commented that the monarch 'was more like ourselves rather than a King for you generally find that the kings of other countries mix very little with their fellow men'.[143] By involving himself in the lives of the poor, George V thus seems to have fashioned a reputation as a uniquely unassuming, compassionate ruler. A fifteen-year-old boy described in similar terms the monarch's affection for his people: 'He was popular with

---

[141] MOA, G. [Cranston]. Although the age of this boy is undisclosed in the essay, comparable essays written by his classmates in 'UVG' or 'U5G' contained in folder G suggest he was 14 or 15.

[142] Prochaska, *Royal Bounty*, pp. 174–5, 183–91.

[143] MOA, H14.

all classes of English because when he did a thing it was in the service of England. A king is looked upon as the Head of his country and the father of his people. George V was each of these and a great part of his time was spent among poor people in slum districts'.[144]

However, it was not just the king's interaction with working-class people that underpinned his 'service'. He was renowned for the way he had 'mingled freely with soldiers' and taken an interest in their lives during the First World War. More than half of the forty-six school essays written on George V similarly remarked that he had spent time visiting soldiers on the Western Front and initiating philanthropic schemes to aid ex-servicemen. This suggests that the legacy of the war and the king's symbolic leadership during those years, as well as his association with veterans after the conflict, endured as a key part of his reputation after his death.[145] Similarly, more than half the essays noted the monarch's charitable work on behalf of poor and sick people who were, of course, a key constituency whom he had singled out in all his broadcasts.[146] The middle- and working-class statuses of the schoolboys may well have shaped their approval of this patrician version of philanthropy and their positive identification with the king's charitable work.

While the king's ability to convey personal care for his subjects through his actions marked him out as an especially 'fine' person, the emotional expression he projected through his radio messages seems to have augmented this compassionate image. One fifteen-year-old quoted George V's last broadcast to portray the king's close link to listeners: 'He did not treat his subjects as people who were there to be taxed or not worth bothering oneself about but when he broadcast for the last time on Christmas Day 1935 he opened his speech with the words "My dear friends". He was a true Christian treating every man to whom he spoke as a personal friend'.[147] The boy's quotation in his essay of the monarch's exact opening words from his 1935 Christmas message reveals the powerful effect that the directness and familiarity of this kind of address had on some listeners: he was more a 'personal friend' than an imposing and aloof ruler. The extract also shows that the boy was comfortable describing the old king using highly personalized terms which highlighted an amity between monarch and subjects. A pupil from the same school noted the levelling effect of George V's broadcasts when he wrote that 'during his talks over the wireless on

[144] MOA, H4.
[145] MOA, F. [Rigby], G. [Archibald] and G. [Shufflebotham], H4, H6, H16, H21. On the king and the First World War, see Jones, 'Nature of kingship', pp. 195–216.
[146] MOA, F. [Ashworth], G. [Archibald], Ho [Brass], H31, H21.
[147] MOA, H2.

Christmas Day [the king] used to address us as "Fellow Countrymen"'; while another boy remarked that one of the ways the king 'showed himself to be a kind man who loved his subjects' was when he wished them 'all the best of Christmas [sic]' in his wireless broadcasts.[148] It seems quite possible that Cosmo Lang's accentuation of the emotional expression contained in George V's broadcasts helped to shape how these boys perceived the king by encouraging them to develop personal imagined relationships with him. It was certainly the case that the radio messages highlighted the king's close association with the empire. More than a quarter of all the boys mentioned George V's interest in the empire, with one fourteen-year-old boy noting that he admired the monarch's 'persistent struggle for peace which was shown by his talks to the people of his empire every Christmas'.[149]

One schoolboy in particular noted the important role of radio in enhancing the king's familiar image. He stated that 'it was at the latter part of his reign that people took more notice of him ... for, on his annual Christmas Day broadcast, millions of people, the wide world over, would listen with reverence and true sincerity. It was an act which made itself felt in the very hearts of the people'.[150] This description suggested that broadcasting had enabled a community of reverent subjects 'the wide world over' to forge new kinds of personal connections with the king. In a similar vein, a fifth of all the essays written about George V used the word 'love' to characterize the bond between king and people – the same word the monarch himself had used in his final two broadcasts. The highly personal imagery created when the boys used this affective language was typified by a fourteen-year-old in his account of how, 'when they heard of [the king's] death people were heartbroken because they each loved him as a brother'.[151] This description is one of several which illuminate the intimate register of the language used by adolescent schoolboys to convey their attachment to the king, as well as the way they thought they formed part of a larger affective community linked together by their emotional connections with the monarch.

The final aspect of the king's public image discussed in the boys' essays related to his happy Christian home life. Essays written on other individuals help to reveal the importance of domesticity in shaping the 'fine' qualities ascribed to public figures. One fifteen-year-old who weighed up the attributes

[148] MOA, H1 and G. [Hodgkinson].
[149] MOA, H11. See also G. [Hodgkinson], G. [Archibald] and G. [Shufflebotham], H5, H2 and H11.
[150] MOA, H0 [Brass].
[151] MOA, H5. For other examples, see G. [Hodgkinson], G. [Bulmer], H0, H8, H9, H12, H20 and H22.

of different men, including Jesus, Sir Francis Drake and Lord Nelson, wrote of the latter that 'in spite of his bravery and brilliant commanding power … his home life was always a tragedy to me. His lust for fame, even at the expense of his wife, seems to give him a blacker character'.[152] This boy's belief that a virtuous home life was key to defining an individual's qualities, with private virtue superseding public action, reflected the growing importance that the British public attached to the domestic sphere as the main locus where personal identities were formed and self-fulfilment found in the 1930s. In essays on the king, his marriage to Queen Mary was noted as an important aspect of his public image. Two fourteen-year-old boys wrote that she 'was a great help to him in many ways' and that 'during his reign he was helped by a faithful queen'.[153] Equally, a twelve-year-old stated that 'one of the most happy moments of [the king's] life was when he celebrated his Silver Jubilee with Queen Mary', which again shows that George V's domesticity was closely entwined with his popular appeal.[154]

A seventeen-year-old who chose to write about Jesus Christ also reflected on the importance of private life to a 'fine' character:

> All the famous men of whom we read in the annals of history or of whom we read in our newspapers are not necessarily fine. This does not mean that I do not include fame as a component of a fine character, but many of those famous men may have been evil and corrupt in the inner man. We do not know of them because we cannot read of their private lives.[155]

This schoolboy hinted that the exposure of a person's private life was important to determining their 'inner' self. This analysis corresponded closely to the increasingly popular belief that it was in the private sphere of the home where people's real identities were developed and expressed. In light of essays like this one, it would seem that George V's candid descriptions of his family life and the publicity surrounding the domesticity of the House of Windsor helped to create a personal image of the king with which members of the public could identify. Indeed, one thirteen-year-old boy articulated a knowledge of George V's loving home life when he noted that 'in his own family [the king] was extremely kind to his children and his grandchildren'.[156] The royalist identities that the school essay writers were thus forming in relation to the old monarch coalesced around some of the

---

[152] MOA, F. [Tempest].
[153] MOA, H6 and H11. For other references to Queen Mary, see G. [Archibald], G. [Wilson] and H13.
[154] MOA, H18.
[155] MOA, G. [Wilcockson].
[156] MOA, H14.

features that had, in time, come to define the monarch's reign but which he also highlighted in his final broadcasts: his close reciprocal relationship with his people; his sense of duty to serve them and improve their lives; his readiness to communicate with them in new ways; and his love of home and family. As we shall see in the next chapter, both his successors struggled to embody all of these characteristics simultaneously and, it seems, to achieve a popularity comparable to that of their father. The disparity in public affection that separated George VI from his father might have been articulated by a fourteen-year-old boy who chose to write about George V as the 'finest person who ever lived' when he stated that he hoped the new king would one day 'be as well loved' as his father:

> I am sure we will not get another king like George V for a long time, but all the same I hope that George VI will procure the love of his people, because at the moment not all the people are sincere to him, but I think that is because he did not inherit the throne from George V and will pass in time. I hope that the love of King George will linger in the hearts of his people for a very long time and that they will try to love his successors.[157]

Conclusion

Writing in his own hand to Lang five days after he had delivered his final radio broadcast to his people, George V thanked the archbishop 'for all the trouble' he had gone to in drafting the message: 'Everyone said it was the best I have done yet. What more could be said in its praise? I suppose it does give pleasure, but it is rather an effort for one. No doubt it brings me into close touch with my peoples all over the world and that of course I am very keen about'.[158] This chapter has examined how the archbishop sought to bring his monarch into closer contact with British people at home and abroad through a more intimate royal public language that heightened the affective affinity between radio listeners and the king. At a time when popular broadcasters were using more personal modes of address to connect to audiences who increasingly perceived private life as the most important site for emotional fulfilment, Lang transformed George V's broadcasts by presenting listeners with what seemed like privileged access to the personal thoughts, feelings and domestic setting of their king. Notably, the archbishop also set out to soften the empire's reputation by infusing the imagined links between monarch and imperial subjects with new emotional meaning, recasting Britain's imperial culture through family-centred, pacific imagery.

[157] MOA, H8.
[158] LPL, Lang 318, fo. 45, King George V to C. G. Lang, 30 Dec. 1935.

It seems highly likely that the positive press coverage of George V's broadcasts, combined with the letters of appreciation written by members of the public to the king like those examined here, had an affirmative effect on royal officials, confirming to them that the monarch's broadcasts were having an emotional impact on listeners. This 'positive feedback loop' can help explain the consolidation in the register of the public language projected by the monarchy in the mid 1930s, with courtiers revising Lang's 1935 drafts to accentuate their personal qualities in order to popularize the sovereign's intimate image. The letters that British subjects wrote to their king suggest that the archbishop's royal public language helped to foster public support for the monarchy by encouraging listeners to conceive of themselves as part of a national emotional community linked together by the simultaneity of radio broadcasting around the focal point of George V as head of a real and imagined family. His last Christmas broadcast also maintained the idea of mutual affection and care between sovereign and subjects, while his reference to the 'personal link between me and my people' augmented the image of a relationship in which he was sustained in his burdensome role ('may God help him!') by his people's devotion and, most notably, their 'love'.

Lang's emphasis on the burdens of kingship and the self-sacrifice made by the sovereign while enacting his or her duties has endured as one of the most resilient components of the House of Windsor's public relations strategy through to the present day. The archbishop created a template for royal public language that simultaneously championed the personal gratification associated with home and family at a time when this mattered more than ever before, but which equally stressed that royalty was forced to forgo the pleasures of ordinary life in executing their public service. Lang's messages took on powerful meaning in 1930s Britain precisely because of the way a new popular culture of self-fulfilment contrasted with the royal commitment to duty ahead of personal happiness. The idea that the royal family suffer for their station – that they are unable to live ordinary private lives without relinquishing their positions – has been linked to late twentieth-century figures like Princess Diana and her sons. However, it is clear that this idea has a longer, subtler history, specific to the period between the wars, which witnessed the emergence of a culture of family-centred self-enrichment ahead of all else.

3. 'This is the day of the people': the 1937 coronation

Seldom if ever has any British Sovereign come to the Throne with greater natural gifts for his kingship. Seldom if ever has any Sovereign been welcomed by a more enthusiastic loyalty. From God he had received a high and sacred trust. Yet by his own will he has abdicated – he has surrendered the trust. With characteristic frankness he told us his motive: it was a craving for private happiness.

Strange and sad it must be that for such a motive, however strongly it pressed upon his heart, he should have disappointed hopes so high and abandoned a trust so great. Even more strange and sad it is that he should have sought his happiness in a manner inconsistent with the Christian principles of marriage, and within a social circle whose standards and ways of life are alien to all the best instincts and traditions of his people. Let those who belong to this circle know that today they stand rebuked by the judgement of the nation which had loved King Edward.[1]

Barely had the dust stirred by the abdication crisis begun to settle when, with these words, Cosmo Lang publicly excoriated Edward VIII for his rejection of the throne in favour of personal fulfilment with his lover Wallis Simpson. The archbishop of Canterbury claimed to speak on behalf of the entire nation when he scolded the former monarch and his friends, declaring that Edward's irreligious and self-indulgent existence was incompatible with the British way of life. In this respect, he also made implicit comparisons with the version of kingship he had helped to project through the God-fearing, family-centred public image of George V, in which duty had always seemed to come before 'private happiness'. The archbishop's conciliatory suggestion that Edward had possessed all the 'natural gifts' required of a monarch not only failed to conceal the contempt he harboured for the now former king but was also disingenuous. Yes, Edward had been, *and continued to be*, extremely popular, having developed a worldwide following as a prince of Wales renowned for his globe-trotting tours of the empire, for the interest he took in the lives of the working classes and the democratic candour with

---

[1] 'Archbishop Cosmo Lang's broadcast on Edward VIII's abdication', Sunday 13 Dec. 1936 (LPL, Lang 27, fos. 209–16), quoted in R. Beaken, *Cosmo Lang: Archbishop in War and Crisis* (London, 2012), p. 244.

'"This is the day of the people": the 1937 coronation', chapter 3, E. Owens, *The Family Firm: Monarchy, Mass Media and the British Public, 1932–53* (London, 2019), pp. 133–98. License: CC-BY-NC-ND 4.0.

which he conducted himself both at home and abroad.[2] But his neglect of religion and royal protocol in favour of the fast life had put him at odds with the elderly archbishop.[3] Earlier on in the year, during a meeting with the king, Lang had also had to defend the importance of the Christian ritual involved in the coronation service when challenged by a sovereign who wanted to scale back what he perceived as the humbuggery of royal ceremonial.[4] This was just one example in a catalogue of offences which the prelate had compiled against Edward and which compelled him to help to pave the way for the removal of a monarch whose mistress, modernizing agenda and haphazard approach to public affairs posed a significant threat to the status quo.[5]

Edward's decision to pursue 'true love' resonated with the interwar emphasis on self-fulfilment and met with popular approval among sections of the public. However when it was finally announced by the British media on 3 December 1936 that the king was in a relationship with, and intended to wed, a woman who had already been married twice and whose ex-husbands were both still living, his choice of Simpson as a wife challenged the model of Christian domesticity that had been diligently promoted by the House of Windsor under George V and which had been widely celebrated as a pillar of Britain's national life. Edward was also deemed by some of his contemporaries to be too outspoken on political issues, putting him at odds with government ministers, including his prime minister, Stanley Baldwin, who gradually determined that the king lacked the dutiful and moral characteristics that his father had embodied as a constitutional figurehead. Backed by a socially conservative political and religious elite, the prime minister made it clear to the king that he would be unable to marry Simpson unless he first gave up the throne – the alternative being that his government would resign in protest because he would have directly

[2] F. Mort, 'On tour with the prince: monarchy, imperial politics and publicity in the prince of Wales's dominion tours 1919–20', *Twentieth Century British Hist.*, xxix (2018), 25–57; H. Jones, 'A prince in the trenches? Edward VIII and the First World War', in *Sons and Heirs: Succession and Political Culture in Nineteenth-Century Europe*, ed. F. L. Müller and H. Mehrkens (Basingstoke, 2016), pp. 229–46; L. N. Mayhall, 'The prince of Wales *versus* Clark Gable: anglophone celebrity and citizenship between the wars', *Cult. and Soc. Hist.*, iv (2007), 529–43.

[3] S. Bradford, *King George VI* (London, 2011), p. 213.

[4] LPL, Lang 21, fos. 24–5, 'King Edward VIII: Coronation Service', 21 July 1936.

[5] Although R. Beaken took a strong moral stance against Edward VIII's behaviour, his biographical analysis of Lang's key role in the events leading up to the abdication is excellent, particularly with regard to the archbishop's support of Prime Minister Stanley Baldwin (meeting with him on 7 occasions) as the disagreement between king and premier intensified (Beaken, *Cosmo Lang*, pp. 86–142).

disregarded his ministers' advice. Although Edward initially opposed Baldwin's position, he ultimately yielded, recognizing that because he was a constitutional monarch he had to heed the will of parliament (as relayed to him by his prime minister in this instance). Consequently, on 10 December Edward signed the instrument of abdication that saw the throne pass to his younger brother, the duke of York, who acceded as King George VI.[6]

Following a week of press-led speculation and political wrangling, Lang took to the microphone in order to offer listeners spiritual guidance on recent events. After all, Edward had already had his say: on the evening of Friday 11 December he had delivered a special abdication broadcast confessing that he had 'found it impossible to carry the heavy burden of responsibility and to discharge [his] duties as king as [he] would wish to do, without the help and support of the woman [he] love[d]'.[7] The powerful emotional appeal of this message, which did much to accelerate the idea that kingship was a burdensome enterprise, resonated with many who tuned in that night; and Lang now viewed it as a moral obligation to publicly speak out, given how the constitutional crisis had, through the *femme fatale* figure of the twice-divorced Simpson, called into question both the authority of the Church of England's teachings on the sanctity of marriage and the virtue of the House of Windsor's family life. However, with Edward taking leave of Britain for Europe and the foreseeable future, a number of commentators interpreted the archbishop's intervention as unbecoming in the way it seemed to hound out of his homeland a man who was already down.[8] Lang's chaplains had received intelligence from clergy across Britain warning of the strong loyalties that still existed for Edward among many of his former subjects, but the archbishop chose to ignore this information in speaking out and, in doing so, turned himself and the Church into targets of popular resentment.[9] In the same address he also commended Edward's

---

[6] F. Mort, 'Love in a cold climate: letters, public opinion and monarchy in the 1936 abdication crisis', *Twentieth Century British Hist.*, xxv (2014), 30–62; P. Williamson, 'The monarchy and public values, 1900–1953', in *The Monarchy and the British Nation, 1780 to the Present*, ed. A. Olechnowicz (Cambridge, 2007), pp. 223–57; P. Ziegler, 'Edward VIII: the modern monarch?', *Court Historian*, viii (2003), 73–83, at pp. 79–82; S. Williams, *The People's King: the True Story of the Abdication* (London, 2003), p. 1.

[7] Quoted in P. Ziegler, *King Edward VIII* (London, 2012), p. 331.

[8] E.g., G. Eden, 'Was Primate's Attack Unfair?', *Daily Express*, 15 Dec. 1936, p. 1. Writing in the wake of these events, the writer C. Mackenzie noted that Lang's broadcast 'dealt a disastrous blow to religious feeling throughout the country and destroyed in advance any possible effect of the Archbishop's "recall to religion" a fortnight later' (C. Mackenzie, *The Windsor Tapestry: Being a Study of the Life, Heritage and Abdication of H.R.H. the Duke of Windsor, K.G.* (London, 1938), p. 550).

[9] LPL, Lang 22, fos. 415–17, Dr. Bouquet to A. C. Don, 11 Dec. 1936. See also the diary

---

successor to listeners by praising George VI's 'happy and united' domesticity and 'high ideals of life and duty'. Then, in what the archbishop termed a 'parentheses', he added that the new king's subjects should not be put off by his speech pattern, marked as it was by 'an occasional and momentary hesitation': 'he has brought it into full control, and to those who hear, it need cause no sort of embarrassment, for it causes none to him'.[10] This was a second serious misstep on Lang's part: a British people left reeling by the sudden departure of their beloved Edward now learned that his replacement, no matter how dutiful and family orientated, was defective: George VI, with his conspicuous stammer, was a victim of his predecessors' success as broadcasters and was at a grave disadvantage compared to both his older brother and father in the age of mass communication.

This chapter picks up the abdication story in the weeks that followed Edward's sudden departure and Lang's infamous broadcast. It examines how the duke of Windsor (as Edward became known) cast a long shadow over his successor and the way George VI, aided by royal and religious officials, sought to contain the aftershocks of the events of December 1936 through to and beyond the 1937 coronation.[11] The royal public relations repair job began immediately and should be viewed as an exercise in crisis management: the human drama at the centre of the abdication had thrown into question the core values that had underpinned the monarchy in the final years of George V's reign. Under the old king, the House of Windsor was a *family monarchy* celebrated for the intimate culture of domesticity that it exemplified and, crucially, the ability of a well-known, caring sovereign to foster national unity through his concern for, and sense of duty to, his people.[12] Edward ultimately failed on both counts and it was left to his successor and those behind the throne to try to heal the deep divisions opened up by the abdication and to reunite the nation around a tarnished crown. In this respect, the royal household's construction of George VI's image and the expert orchestration of his coronation should be interpreted as part of a strategy to stabilize the monarchy's position after Edward's disastrous reign.

Contrary to the prevailing historical view that the new sovereign was warmly welcomed on his coronation day by a British people who rallied

---

of Alexander Sargent, who was another of Lang's chaplains: LPL, MS3208, 'King Edward's Abdication', 11 Dec. 1936, esp. fos. 207–8; BOD, MS. Dawson 40, fo. 183, 15 Dec. 1936.

[10] 'Archbishop Cosmo Lang's broadcast on Edward VIII's abdication', Sunday 13 Dec. 1936 (LPL, Lang 27, fos. 209–16), quoted in Beaken, *Cosmo Lang*, pp. 245–6.

[11] Whereas the abdication story is well-rehearsed, the 6-month period after Edward's impromptu departure and George VI's succession has not received sustained historical analysis before.

[12] See chs. 1 and 2.

around the media image of him as a family man and a reluctant, yet dutiful king, it is clear that George VI's personal virtues could not account on their own for the largely positive response to his crowning.[13] While these were attractive characteristics that were purposely elevated so that he better resembled his father, the media coverage of his coronation and the large body of Mass Observation reports produced in response to the occasion suggest his crowning was celebrated as a symbol of the nation's democratic vitality at a time of deep anxiety about Britain's political culture, the nature of public emotion and the growing threat of European authoritarianism.[14] Public intellectuals writing in the mid 1930s and historians writing in the present have noted that, in the last years of George V's reign, the monarchy

[13] J. Wheeler-Bennett, *King George VI: His Life and Reign* (London, 1958), pp. 296–7, 300–1, 311–4; Bradford, *George VI*, pp. 270–2, 280–3; P. Ziegler, *George VI: the Dutiful King* (London, 2014), pp. 40–6.

[14] For this chapter a complete re-examination has been undertaken of the 132 surviving reports on the 1937 coronation collected by Mass Observation that now form part of the online digital MO archive. The digitized reports are unsystematically numbered in the archive as 'day survey' files from '019' to '576'. There is another 'unidentified' day survey file that contains approximately 30 of the reports. These 132 reports can be located through the online keyword search '1937 coronation'. Three different kinds of reports were collected by Mass Observation in 1937. The first were solicited from a panel of 47 volunteers who agreed in early 1937 to make a note of their activities and observations on the 12th of each month in order to create a context against which their descriptions of the coronation celebrations on 12 May could be situated. These were labelled the 'CO' section and are referred to here in this chapter using their original CO number (1 to 47). The second were reports solicited by MO after the event through leaflets and advertisements placed in the *New Statesman* enquiring: 'Where were you on May 12th? Mass Observation wants your story'. This campaign yielded approximately 100 further reports from members of the public and these files were given the label 'CL'. While some CL files can be located in the numbered day surveys from the key word search results, most can be found in the 'unidentified' day survey file and, illogically, in day survey file '175'. They are referred to here using their original CL number. The third kind of report collected by MO were those prepared by a specially tasked 'mobile squad' of 13 'observers' in London, who took shifts in recording events in the capital as they unfolded on coronation day. Labelled 'CM', the mobile squad mainly comprised students from the University of Oxford, but also included MO co-founder Humphrey Jennings. These reports are referred to here using their original CM number. For further information on the three different types of file, see the MO publication based on the coronation reports, *May the Twelfth: Mass-Observation Day-Surveys 1937 by Over Two Hundred Observers*, ed. H. Jennings et al. (London, 1987 [1937]), pp. 89–91. Note that the number of 200 observers is misleading, as indicated by the index to the respondents' reports (pp. 439–40); and that the outline of the number of reports received and archived by MO (pp. 89–91) is also incorrect. There are, in fact, a miscellany of additional reports that were probably received later (mainly in the CL section) and were not included in *May the Twelfth*. Additionally, there are 27 further reports referred to in *May the Twelfth* that have since been lost and are not available through the digital archive. Where personal testimony from these additional reports is used in this chapter, it is referred to using *May the Twelfth*.

was widely projected as the key symbol of Britain's democracy and that this vision of the nation's political system provided a crucial liberal counter-narrative to continental dictatorship.[15] Britain's royal democracy again took centre stage on 12 May 1937, with courtiers, clergy and the media working in tandem to elevate George VI's crowning as the moment that epitomized the success of the nation's constitutional arrangement, the strength of its imperial ties and the public's devotion to the crown. Combining new kinds of coverage with more established styles of reportage, all Britain's major news outlets joined together to loudly champion to their audiences the nation's social and political evolution and the significance of the king as the figurehead of democracy. In this way the monarchy entered a new important phase. No longer was it defined by a single magnetic personality who seemed to unite the nation through emotional bonds that connected him to his subjects: rather, George VI's personal character made way on coronation day for what was instead a celebration of constitutional progress and national greatness against a troubled international backdrop. Indeed, while the king was presented as a brave stand-in for his morally flawed brother, his coronation revealed the limits of the more personal vision of kingship popularized by George V and Edward VIII, when the figure at the centre of the royal family group was a relatively unknown quantity. Fortunately for the new sovereign, his mother, Queen Mary, who was much better known to the public, was close at hand to lend proceedings a reassuring emotional continuity with the past.

'One matchless blessing'

It was common knowledge among Britain's journalists that George VI assumed the mantle of kingship unwillingly. Writing as the abdication crisis neared its climax, the London editor of the *Manchester Guardian*, James Bone, informed his boss, William Crozier, that the duke of York was 'not keen at first' to become king.[16] Royal biographers – official and unofficial – have even suggested that, in the days leading up to Edward's abdication, courtiers considered whether his youngest brother, the duke of Kent, would have been better suited to succeed him as king.[17] This was probably because

---

[15] J. Parry, 'Whig monarchy, whig nation: crown politics and representativeness, 1800–2000', in Olechnowicz, *The Monarchy and the British Nation*, pp. 47–75, at pp. 66–7; M. Houlbrook, *Prince of Tricksters: the Incredible True Story of Netley Lucas, Gentleman Crook* (Chicago, Ill., 2016), p. 225.

[16] JRL, MG/B/B220/697, J. Bone to W. Crozier, 9 Dec. 1936.

[17] D. Morrah, *Princess Elizabeth: the Illustrated Story of Twenty-One Years in the Life of the Heir Presumptive* (London, 1947), p. 62; L. Pickett, et al., *The War of the Windsors: a Century of Unconstitutional Monarchy* (Edinburgh, 2002), p. 126; M. Thornton, *Royal Feud: the Queen Mother and the Duchess of Windsor* (London, 1985), pp. 126–7.

Kent, with his Hollywood good looks, his popular wife Marina and their growing brood of children, combined a star quality comparable to Edward's with a domesticity in tune with the family-centred image of George V's monarchy. As David Cannadine has discussed, there were serious concerns about the duke of York's personality: 'lamentably ill-educated, blighted by poor health, devoid of presence or glamour, and further hampered by overwhelming shyness and a debilitating stammer, George VI was initially greeted with muted enthusiasm verging on resentful disappointment'.[18] Even the new queen consort, Elizabeth, expressed reservations about the task that lay ahead of her and her husband, telling her friend the writer Osbert Sitwell that 'I fully expect that we may be moderately unpopular for some time'.[19] Yet, George VI's biographers have tended to smooth over the disquiet regarding the king's personal qualities by presenting his coronation as the 'crucial test' through which he proved himself worthy of his role, silencing his critics and stabilizing the monarchy after his elder brother's abdication.[20] Most historians have similarly argued that, after the turbulent events of December 1936, the press and public rallied around the dutiful figure of George VI and his family.[21] While these accounts have perpetuated the royal household's own narrative of continuity, they have obscured the deep anxieties that persisted about the new king's character after his accession. Significantly, only six Mass Observation reports out of more than 150 collected by the organizers of the 1937 coronation project contained some statement of admiration for George VI and just two recorded unequivocal support for him.[22] It would be wrong to generalize about how most British people felt about the new king based on the Mass Observation reports alone, but the paucity of supportive sentiment *is* striking, especially when compared to the large body of positive comments that were recorded about both his elder brother and mother.

From the moment George VI acceded to the throne he was disadvantaged. The key motif that had suffused his father's public language on the burdens of royal duty seemed fully realized in his person. However, whereas George

---

[18] D. Cannadine, *History in Our Time* (Yale, 1998), pp. 59–60.

[19] Queen Elizabeth to O. Sitwell, 19 Feb. 1937, quoted in W. Shawcross, *Counting One's Blessings: the Selected Letters of Queen Elizabeth the Queen Mother* (Basingstoke, 2012), p. 237.

[20] Bradford, *George VI*, pp. 270–86; Wheeler-Bennett, *King George VI*, pp. 310–4; P. Ziegler, *Crown and People* (London, 1978), pp. 48 and 68.

[21] E.g., A. Bingham, *Family Newspapers? Sex, Private Life and the British Popular Press, 1918–1978* (Oxford, 2009), p. 242.

[22] For the 2 unusually positive reactions to George's actions on coronation day see respondents MOA, CL39 and CL63, both of whom were exceptional in their fervent patriotism and support for the new king. For the other four relatively positive portrayals, see CL12, CL25, CL40 and CL56.

V had offset ideas of personal suffering through his mobilization of a strong, wise and caring public image, this identity was not available to his second son, who was comparatively unknown. Equally, the dynamic, masculine persona of Edward VIII, which combined the benevolent traits of his father's image with a 'forceful and forward looking style of manhood' that many British people perceived as apposite at a time when autocratic modes of leadership were proving so successful on the Continent, was also unobtainable to George VI.[23] Indeed, the plentiful, admiring descriptions of Edward recorded by Mass Observation vividly contrasted with the lack of support logged for the new king and hinted at widespread doubts about his ability to lead a country threatened by the robust figures of the European dictators.[24] This sense of uncertainty about the new king's qualities is important because it points to the characteristics that the British had come to look for in their royal leaders in the years before the Second World War. As is addressed later, the charisma vacuum created by George VI helped to realign the monarchy with constitutional politics after its brief flirtation with a more authoritarian mode of popular sovereignty as personified by Edward VIII, but the new king's relative unpopularity compared to his brother suggests that some British people would have preferred to celebrate the version of monarchy captured in the personality cult which centred on the now duke of Windsor.

Lang's attempt to downplay concerns about the new king's infamous stammer as part of his broadcast on 13 December 1936 almost certainly had the reverse effect.[25] It marked George VI out as lacking the vocal abilities that had defined his father's public image in the final years of his reign and may even have characterized the new king as psychologically damaged. With the psychologization of science between the wars, *The Lancet* medical journal had published an exchange of 'expert' opinions on the causes of 'stammering' at the beginning of 1936; and views

[23] Mort, 'Love in a cold climate', p. 60.

[24] In his analysis of the 1937 Mass Observation study of the coronation, P. Ziegler did not fully acknowledge how the approbation that MO respondents recorded for Edward VIII compared with the lack of enthusiasm registered for George VI (Ziegler, *Crown and People*, pp. 52 and 60). Ziegler stated that 'among those who actually watched the procession such remarks as the passing of George VI provoked were generally flattering – "There's the right man for the job"' (p. 60). This is the only example Ziegler gave that presented the new king in a positive light and was, in fact, just 1 of 6 comments recorded in the MO coronation reports or *May the Twelfth* that characterized the new monarch positively.

[25] The king's biographers have agreed that Lang's broadcast had a detrimental effect on George VI's public image (Bradford, *George VI*, p. 272; Wheeler-Bennett, *King George VI*, pp. 309–10).

converged on the idea that it was a neuropathic condition that stemmed from nervousness in childhood: it was not just a 'disorder of speech, but a disorder of personality, an emotional disturbance'.[26] At a time when psychological understanding of self-development was undergoing popularization, George VI's subjects may thus have perceived him as an emotionally defective personality.[27]

But the archbishop's blunder did not deter the monarchy's image-makers from trying to project a strong and familiar kingly persona around the new sovereign. In the many biographies of George VI that newspapers published in the days and weeks after the abdication in an effort to introduce him to his people, two features predominated: he was domestic and he was dutiful.[28] Edward VIII had led the way in his abdication broadcast when he told listeners that his brother had 'one matchless blessing, enjoyed by so many of you, and not bestowed on me – a happy home with his wife and children'.[29] This point was reiterated by Lang in his post-abdication message when he commended the new king and queen's home life as a model for popular emulation.[30] The 1930s witnessed companionate love and a domesticated masculinity emerge in Britain, with men taking on more active roles in the lives of their children and spouses and finding greater pleasure in the conjugal privacy of the home.[31] The royal household, the media and the clergy promoted George VI's image along these lines, as they had done with his father in the last years of his reign. For example, the new king and his family had posed for the photographer Lisa Sheridan in June 1936 at Royal Lodge in Windsor Park and these pictures were now approved for publication, appearing on the front pages of magazines and in newspapers with captions that emphasized the monarch's loving domestic life (Figure 3.1).[32]

---

[26] 'Stammering', *The Lancet*, ccxxvii, no. 5865 (25 Jan. 1936), 208–9; 'Stammering not a speech defect', *The Lancet*, ccxxvii, no. 5869 (22 Feb. 1936), 449.

[27] M. Thomson, *Psychological Subjects: Identity, Culture, and Health in Twentieth-Century Britain* (Oxford, 2006), ch. 1.

[28] E.g., the following articles: 'Family Life at the Palace Again', *Daily Mail*, 12 Dec. 1936, p. 8; 'The New King', *The Times*, 11 Dec. 1936, p. 17; 'The Homely Family who will Lead the Empire', *Daily Mirror*, 11 Dec. 1936, pp. 16–7.

[29] Quoted in Ziegler, *King Edward VIII*, p. 331.

[30] Beaken, *Cosmo Lang*, pp. 245–6.

[31] L. King, *Family Men: Fatherhood and Masculinity in Britain, 1914–1960* (Oxford, 2015), pp. 5–7; C. Langhamer, *The English in Love: the Intimate Story of an Emotional Revolution* (Oxford, 2013). pp. 6–7; J. Lewis, 'Marriage', in *Women in Twentieth-Century Britain*, ed. I. Zweiniger-Bargielowska (Harlow, 2001), pp. 69–85.

[32] *Daily Mirror*, 11 Dec. 1936, pp. 16–7; *Daily Mail*, 11 Dec. 1936, p. 9; *Reynolds News*, 9 May 1937, p. 24.

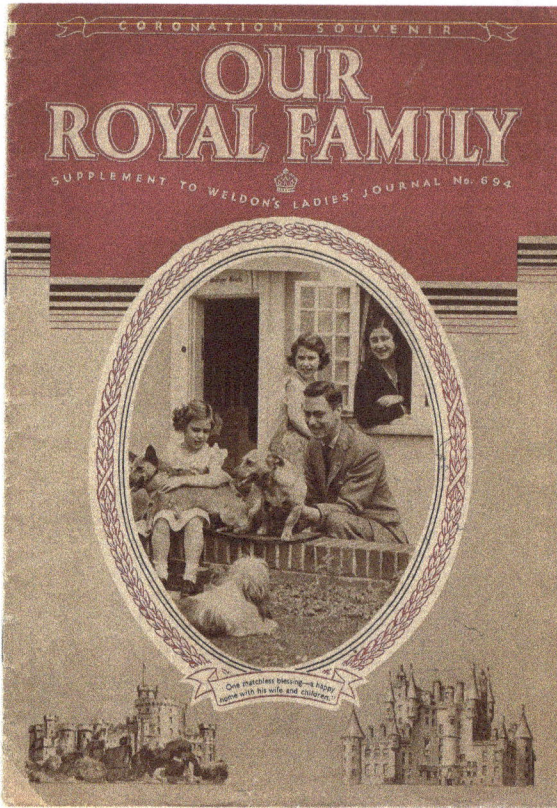

Figure 3.1. 'One Matchless Blessing – a Happy Home with His Wife and Children', *Weldon's Ladies' Journal*, dcxciv (1937), p. 1.

One photograph that was widely reproduced showed the king and his children playing with the royal corgis while the queen looked on from a window of Princess Elizabeth's life-size play cottage. This carefully arranged scene, with the king crouched in a lounge suit and the princesses in summer dresses, presented the royals as a 'normal' family group and complemented a media narrative that stressed the everyday qualities of the king. The words 'homely' – meaning ordinary – and 'intimate' predominated in reports like the one presented by the *Daily Mirror* to accompany its publication of Sheridan's photographs: 'No more homely family has ever ascended the British Throne than that of the Duke and Duchess of York. From her childhood days the new Queen has found her happiness in the simple pleasures of life … Her marriage to the Duke of York did not change her life; as these intimate pictures show, her children have inherited her simple and homely ideas'.[33]

---

[33] *Daily Mirror*, 11 Dec. 1936, pp. 16–7.

The media sustained its emphasis on the new royal family's domesticity through to, and beyond, the coronation. In February 1937 the *Guardian*'s William Crozier told his London editor that he wanted an article written on the king and queen's home life, interests and hobbies that should be 'lively and intimate'.[34] The subsequent article was one of many published by newspapers that drew attention to the pleasure the new monarch took in gardening, Sunday drives in the car with his wife and daughters and family walks.[35] This focus on the private lives of the monarchs reflected the interwar obsession with human-interest journalism, as was exemplified by a full-page report published by the *Sunday Express* three days before the coronation, titled 'Our Happy Family King', which again used Sheridan's photographs and informed readers that '[the king] is a happy man. His family life made him that. He, the Queen, and the Princesses are passionately devoted to each other. Their joy in each other is complete and perfect'.[36] This highly personal language could also be found in reports that described George VI as a 'loving husband'.[37] The media stories of the companionate, domesticated king – who had found self-fulfilment in his relationship with his wife and in his role as a father to the princesses – built on the imagery used to characterize the 1934 royal wedding and George V's happy home life in order to restore the picture of the virtuous domesticity of the House of Windsor.[38] And these reports appear to have had at least some impact on media audiences: three Mass Observation respondents positively remarked on the new king's domesticity, with one referring to the fact that her neighbours liked him 'because he is a family man'.[39]

The media also highlighted George VI's family image by focusing on the theme of dynasty and presented him in photographs and newsreels alongside his father to emphasize continuity through the order of succession.[40] *British Movietone News* produced a special 'Retrospect of the King's Life' that provided viewers with an in-depth character profile of the new ruler

[34] JRL, MG/223/24/13, W. Crozier to J. Bone, 16 Feb. 1937.

[35] *Manchester Guardian*, 3 May 1937, p. 18; *Sunday Express*, 9 May 1937, p. 1; *Daily Mirror*, 13 May 1937, p. 4; *Daily Sketch*, 13 May 1935, p. 5.

[36] *Sunday Express*, 9 May 1937, p. 9; A. Bingham and M. Conboy, *Tabloid Century: the Popular Press in Britain, 1896 to the Present* (Oxford, 2015), pp. 97–130.

[37] *Sunday Pictorial*, 9 May 1937, p. 2.

[38] We can also account for the press's candid descriptions of George VI's emotional life with reference to Edward VIII's abdication broadcast. The ex-king's public confession of love for Wallis Simpson had encouraged journalists to adopt a more intimate language in describing royal emotions and established a new precedent that continued to shape how the royal family's domesticity was publicly projected.

[39] MOA, CL12; also CL25 and CL40.

[40] E.g., *Daily Sketch*, 5 May 1937, p. 17; *Sunday Express*, 11 Apr. 1937, p. 23.

and linked his childhood through visual images to the reigns of his great-grandmother, Queen Victoria, and his grandfather Edward VII.[41] The final section of this biographical profile also presented close-up scenes of George VI's consort and daughters, the commentator stating 'how fortunate we are in this domestic family' and that the nation entertained 'great hopes … of the two princesses' – the implication being that, with the new royal family, the dynasty would continue and flourish.

Courtiers and the media worked to create a sense of continuity between George V's reign and that of his second son through an emphasis on the new king's dutiful character as well. The *Daily Mail* was typical in the way it drew readers' attention to George VI's scripted declaration at the accession meeting of the privy council after Edward VIII's abdication: 'Now that the duties of sovereignty have fallen to me I declare to you my adherence to the strict principles of constitutional government and my resolve to work before all else for the welfare of the British Commonwealth of Nations. With my wife as helpmate by my side, I take up the heavy task which lies before me. In it I look for the support of all my peoples'.[42] With these words, courtiers ensured that the public language regarding the burdens of royal duty passed seamlessly to the new king and queen. The media also discussed the monarch's history of public service – including his leadership of the duke of York's camps and the tours he had undertaken of Britain's industrial centres – and reports stressed that he had successfully adapted to his new state duties with headlines like 'The king plans [his] day like his father'.[43]

The language of royal public service was also recurrently invoked the week before the coronation in relation to the empire. On Friday 7 May the king addressed the prime ministers of the Dominions as part of an elaborate lunch meeting of the British and imperial social and political elite at Westminster hall. The editor of *The Times*, Geoffrey Dawson, described it in his diary as 'a well staged performance' that was orchestrated 'for the King to meet his Parliaments'.[44] His newspaper was typical in suggesting that the event had demonstrated the continuing strength of the relationship between the empire and the throne, with reports highlighting that 'the assembled company cheered for several minutes while the King stood obviously deeply moved by the warmth of his reception'.[45] This relationship

[41] 'A Retrospect on the King's Life', *British Movietone News*, 29 March 1937.
[42] *Daily Mail*, 14 Dec. 1936, p. 9.
[43] *Sunday Express*, 11 Apr. 1937, p. 23; *Daily Mail*, 15 Dec. 1936, p. 11.
[44] BOD, MS. Dawson 41, fo. 71.
[45] *The Times*, 8 May 1937, p. 14. Also see *Daily Mirror*, 8 May 1937, p. 3; *Daily Mail*, 8 May 1937, p. 5.

was given fuller meaning the day before the coronation when the king met with imperial representatives for a second time. Returning the addresses presented to him by the Dominion prime ministers and envoys of India and the colonies at Buckingham Palace, George VI told them that, after his father's death, it had 'pleased God to call me to be the head of this great family'. He then echoed George V's words on the burdens of royal duty: '[H]eavy are the responsibilities that have so suddenly and unexpectedly come upon me, but it gives me courage to know that I can count on your unfailing help and affection'. Having thus entreated the support of his subjects, the king offered his reciprocal service as part of the familiar moral contract that connected ruler and people: '[F]or my part I shall do my utmost to carry on my father's work for the welfare of our great Empire'.[46] The sub-heading used by the *Manchester Guardian* in its report on this meeting proclaimed the 'King Speaks as Head of a Great Family' and, in capitalized font, that he had followed 'HIS FATHER'S EXAMPLE'.[47] In this way, then, the royal household and media sought to connect George VI to the pattern of kingship established by George V, with its emphasis on imperial unity, duty and mutual assistance, in the hope that this would ensure the loyalties of the empire and Commonwealth were transferred to the new monarch, despite the fact that only six months earlier they had focused on Edward VIII as the human symbol that embodied the British imperial system.

'We have lost a good king'

The royal household applied pressure on the media in its efforts to maintain the idealized image of the new family monarchy following the abdication crisis. George VI's assistant private secretary, Sir Alan Lascelles, wrote to Dawson at *The Times* on 13 December 1936 and began his letter by criticizing Edward VIII as 'essentially a changeling, with the three dominant characteristics of changelings – no soul, no moral sense, and great personal charm'. He continued:

> The chief <u>external</u> cause of his downfall was that the public, all the world over, loved him too well & most unwisely. No man in history has ever been so fulsomely adulated as this modern Stupor Mundi, & the result was his unshakable conviction that he could get away with murder. We now have two young Princesses, who will take his place as the Pets of the world, and on one of whom, certainly, great issues will hang. In the first few pages of the Jungle Book, R. K. emphasised – what every parent knows – the immense danger of

---

[46] *Manchester Guardian*, 12 May 1937, p. 11.
[47] *Manchester Guardian*, 12 May 1937, p. 11.

praising children to their faces. Could not a concrete effort be made to stop the Tabaquis of Fleet St. from spoiling these two, at present, delightful & sensible children? It is, to me, a real danger, which I believe that you & other wise men in your part of the world could avert.[48]

Lascelles urged Dawson to help him to protect Princesses Elizabeth and Margaret from the advances of the press. He hoped that their characters would not be 'spoiled' – as he suggested had been the case with Edward. What we can also see in the letter is Lascelles's concern to preserve the sanctity of royal family life in order that the princesses – and, in particular, Elizabeth – better understood the roles they would be expected to perform in due course. Two months before the news broke that Edward was in a relationship with Wallis Simpson, the press barons Lord Beaverbrook and Lord Rothermere had, at the request of the king, co-ordinated a secretive campaign to prevent Fleet Street from publicly disclosing any information whatsoever about the royal love affair. Following the abdication crisis, some reporters expressed anger about the measures that had stopped news of the romance emerging and, fearing they had lost the trust of their readers, adopted a more irreverent approach to royalty. Journalists thus became more brazen in their attempts to expose royal private life to public view but also more critical of royal personalities for the way they behaved.[49] Lascelles seems to have anticipated the kinds of problems these new kinds of coverage could create for George VI's family and his letter to Dawson reveals that he took action in order to shelter his employers from adverse media attention.

Lascelles was wrong, however, when he assumed that Edward, now duke of Windsor, had been knocked off his pedestal as the most popular member of the royal family. The positive media coverage generated around George VI in the period from December 1936 to the coronation was complicated by news stories that continued to focus on his older brother. The popular press – in particular the *Mirror* and Beaverbrook's Express group, both of which had come out in support of Edward at the time of the abdication crisis – provided constant updates on the duke's activities and his forthcoming marriage to Wallis Simpson.[50] It is clear from Lang's and Dawson's personal papers that both men were closely monitoring Edward and viewed the press

[48] BOD, MS. Dawson 79, fos. 80–1, A. Lascelles to G. Dawson, 13 Dec. 1937.

[49] Bingham, *Family Newspapers?*, pp. 241–50.

[50] E.g., *Daily Mirror*, 5 Dec. 1936, pp. 5–6; *Daily Express*, 5 Dec. 1936, p. 10; *Daily Mirror*, 29 March 1937, p. 28; *Daily Mirror*, 8 Apr. 1937, p. 1; *Daily Mirror*, 10 Apr. 1937 p. 1; *Daily Express*, 29 March, p. 1; *Daily Express*, 12 Apr. 1937, p. 1. Beaverbrook was a strong supporter of Edward and a critic of Baldwin during the abdication crisis and both of his *Express* titles accused the prime minister of forcing a popular king off the throne (Bingham, *Family Newspapers?*, p. 242).

attention he was receiving with great apprehension: for them, he and Mrs Simpson not only provided an unwelcome distraction from the business of popularizing George VI's public image; they also represented a different version of royal authority to rival the one embodied by the new king. As was the case during the constitutional crisis, it was felt in the offices of *The Times* that a minority of newspapers had irresponsibly taken Edward's side and were championing his marriage in order to ensure he remained a popular figure. Briefing his assistant editor Robert Barrington-Ward on the weekend's news after a 'cold Easter holiday', Dawson informed him that 'the Simpson Press, as Lady Milner calls it, is getting rather busy'.[51] He enclosed with his memo a selection of articles from the day before and, although unspecified, we can speculate that this included a two-page central spread from the *Sunday Express* that was provocatively titled, 'The Case for Mrs Simpson'.[52] The article was written by the American society hostess and gossip columnist, Elsa Maxwell, who, as a 'close friend of Mrs. Simpson and the Duke of Windsor', offered readers first-hand insights into the former's personal character and love affair. This mini-biography of Simpson presented her in a generally positive light – although the *Express* tried to avoid a backlash from more critical sections of its readership by distancing itself from Maxwell's interpretation of events through an editorial précis which emphasized that the American writer and US public did not understand that the British tended to view the status of divorced persons with suspicion.

The royal household and news editors at *The Times* were also alarmed by the press coverage of Edward and Simpson's romance the week before George VI's coronation. Dawson recorded in his diary that on 6 May he had presided over a *Times* office lunch party where he had spoken with the king's private secretary, Sir Alexander Hardinge, and noted that their topics of conversation had included 'the revival of the "Simpson Press" & other gossip'.[53] Two days earlier newspapers had published stories on the duke of Windsor's looming reunion with Simpson at the Château de Candé as it was to be the lovers' first official meeting since the ex-king's abdication.[54] The most striking coverage came from the *Daily Mirror*, which noted in a leading front-page story how,

---

[51] BOD, MS. Dawson 79, fo. 126b, G. Dawson to R. Barrington-Ward, 29 March 1937. Lady Violet Milner was editor of the *National Review*. See 'Milner [*née* Maxse], Violet Georgina, Viscountess Milner', in *ONDB*, <https://doi.org/10.1093/ref:odnb/35039> [accessed 3 March 2018].

[52] *Sunday Express*, 28 March 1937, pp. 8–9.

[53] BOD, MS. Dawson 41, fo. 70, 6 May 1937. That Hardinge was present at *The Times*'s lunch party shows just how close royal courtiers and the media elite were in these years.

[54] *Daily Mirror*, 4 May 1937, p. 1.

SATURDAY, MAY 8, 1937

Daily Mirror

No. 10436   Registered at the G.P.O. as a Newspaper.   ONE PENNY

WE'RE HAPPY AT LAST

"We are always happy," said Mrs. Simpson when, yesterday, on the terrace of the Chateau de Cande, Tours, she and the Duke of Windsor posed together for the first time for photographers. Mrs. Simpson's statement came in answer to a request for "a happy picture." As she said it, Mrs. Simpson turned to the Duke and he replied, "Of course. Isn't that evident?" See page 5 for story and another picture.

Figure 3.2. 'We're Happy at Last', *Daily Mirror*, 8 May 1937, p. 1. © The British Library Board.

'laughing and joking, happier than he had been for months, the Duke of Windsor is speeding … from Austria to France – to Mrs. Simpson, at the Chateau Cande, Tours [*sic*]'.[55] A barrage of articles on the couple followed after they had been reunited as well, with large front-page photographs presenting them arm-in-arm and grinning cheerfully at one another. The accompanying captions emphasized that, at long last, the duke and Simpson were 'happy' and 'smiling' again (Figure 3.2).[56]

[55] *Daily Mirror*, 4 May 1937, p. 1.

[56] E.g., *Daily Mirror*, 8 May 1937, p. 1; *Daily Express*, 8 May 1937, p. 1; *Daily Mirror*, 8 May, p. 5; and *Daily Express*, 8 May, p. 20.

Figure 3.3. 'This is the Answer to Dictators/"Very Happy Together"',
Daily Herald, 8 May 1937, p. 1. © The British Library Board.

These upbeat portrayals of the couple's meeting were significant for two reasons. First of all, they helped to strengthen the idea that kingship was unenviable in that it did not lead to fulfilment in private life. The implication in all the reports was that it was only by relinquishing the throne that the duke had realized true happiness with the women he loved. The media fostered this narrative through indirect comparisons between the emotionally contented duke and his dutiful younger brother, as seen in the *Daily Herald*'s front-page visual juxtaposition on 8 May, four days before the coronation (Figure 3.3). The left-hand side of the page was taken up by a report on the Westminster hall meeting between George VI and the British and imperial representatives who gathered 'to do honour to the King on the eve of his crowning'. The headline described the meeting as 'The Answer to [the] Dictators' and a subheading proclaimed that 'King and Premiers [were] Pledged to Democracy'. Meanwhile, the right-hand side of the page was occupied by another smiling photograph of Edward and Mrs Simpson, with the caption 'Very Happy Together'.[57] This contrast was intended to communicate to readers the distinction between responsible (constitutional) and irresponsible (unconstitutional) kingship: the duke of Windsor had put self-gratification ahead of his national responsibility.

The second reason reports on Edward and Simpson were significant was because they seemed to celebrate the lovers' relationship and forthcoming marriage. While they may have contained veiled criticisms of the former

[57] *Daily Herald*, 8 May 1937, p. 1.

king, the stories acted as a strong reminder of the personal determination that had characterized his brief reign. Furthermore, the sheer scale of the reports on the couple's meeting distracted attention away from George VI and his family in the crucial days leading up to the coronation. Cosmo Lang and the royal household were anxious that this should not be the case. Since January the archbishop had been secretly working together with the bishop of Fulham, who exercised episcopal oversight for Anglican Churches in Europe, to try to ensure that the duke and Mrs Simpson's wedding would not be consecrated with a religious service for fear that it would endorse the actions of the ex-king and undermine the Church's teaching on marriage.[58] At the start of April 1937 the archbishop exchanged a series of letters with the now retired courtier Sir Clive Wigram about the wedding. According to the latter, 'Queen Mary … guilelessly said that she thought some kind of religious service for [Edward's] marriage would be <u>rather nice</u>'; and that in response to this the duke's friend and counsellor, Walter Monckton, had proposed that a royal chaplain officiate at the wedding. Monckton had also suggested that some of the royal family be allowed to attend the ceremony, but Wigram had told him that 'this would be a firm nail in the coffin of Monarchy'.[59] Wigram was left to deal with this issue and contacted Lang, asking for his advice in the apparent belief that if the duke were married with a religious service attended by other members of the House of Windsor, then it would not only undermine the sanctity of royal family life, but also threaten the authority of George VI by enabling his relations to demonstrate moral support for his elder brother.

Lang agreed with everything Wigram had said to Monckton. He, too, thought that the presence of members of the royal family at the wedding would legitimize the duke of Windsor's actions after the latter had damaged the crown's reputation.[60] Then, the day after the archbishop had set out his thoughts in writing to Wigram, the *Mirror* ran a front-page story that claimed Edward had asked the duke of Kent to be best man at his wedding.[61] Rumours like this one appear to have stirred the palace into action, for Wigram then wrote to tell Lang 'that the Duke of Windsor is going to be told definitely that none of his family can be present at the wedding, and

---

[58] See LPL, Lang 156. Notably, Lang and Fulham were unsuccessful: the duke and Mrs Simpson married with a religious ceremony on 3 June 1937 (Ziegler, *King Edward VIII*, p. 363).

[59] LPL, Lang 318, fos. 136–7, C. Wigram to C. G. Lang, 5 Apr. 1937; see also Ziegler, *King Edward VIII*, pp. 354–5.

[60] LPL, Lang 318, fos. 139–40, C. G. Lang to C. Wigram, 8 Apr. 1937.

[61] *Daily Mirror*, 9 Apr. 1937, p. 1.

that one of His Majesty's Chaplains cannot officiate'.[62] When this news was made public the same sections of the press that had favourably reported Edward's marriage turned on both the archbishop and the royal household. The *Daily Express* was typical in arguing that the duke was 'being treated with rather too much of a rough edge' by a Church that refused to countenance the wedding and by royal officials who had prohibited the attendance of his relations at the ceremony.[63]

Although the *Express* and *Mirror* groups developed a more irreverent approach to reporting on royalty after the abdication, other voices contested this coverage. In particular, some journalists were critical of the constant updates on Edward and Simpson's reunion and the way it cast a shadow over the coronation. The *Daily Sketch*'s Henry Newham, who wrote under the pseudonym 'Candidus', told his readers that, at the Allied Newspaper Corporation's coronation dinner, the mayor of Manchester had 'said publicly something which most of us have been thinking and many of us saying in private. There has been far too much in the newspapers about Mrs. Simpson and the Duke of Windsor'. Newham judged it was 'definitely against the public interest' and complained that Simpson had been transformed into a 'heroine' who stood 'in the light of the true heroines' – namely the new queen consort and George VI's mother, Queen Mary.[64] However, only a fraction of the public opinion recorded by the Mass Observation coronation study agreed with Newham that reports on Edward were in poor taste. One young man from Hertford wrote that, on the morning of the coronation, his 'grandmother was indignant that there was a short column about the Duke of Windsor on the front-page of the *News Chronicle*'.[65] Criticism like this was rare, though, and instead the prevailing attitude noted by the Mass Observation panel about Edward was that he was sorely missed and the coronation lacking on account of his absence.[66]

The positive reactions recorded by Mass Observation about the duke on the day of his brother's crowning pointed to the way that sections of the public preferred his version of kingship to that embodied by George VI. A member of the Mass Observation 'Mobile Squad' who was stationed in London on coronation day and tasked with recording conversations she had with the people she encountered, as well as discussions she overheard others

[62] LPL, Lang 318, fo. 141, C. Wigram to C. G. Lang, 10 Apr. 1937.

[63] *Daily Express*, 24 May 1937, p. 10.

[64] *Daily Sketch*, 7 May 1937, p. 6.

[65] MOA, CO18b. There were a small number of general criticisms aimed at the duke of Windsor. See MOA, CO38, CO41 and CL16.

[66] E.g., MOA, CM4, CO12, CO19, CO23, CO28, CO31, CO32, CO37, CO41, CO43, CO47, CL15, CL24, CL25, CL30, CL40, CL47, CL56.

having, noted that she had talked to a man she described as 'lower-middle class' and a 'strong partisan of Edward'. The man 'wanted a come-back and seemed very half-hearted about the coronation'. He complained about the lukewarm coronation service he had attended at church the previous Sunday and agreed with the Mass Observation investigator 'that many people [were] far less spontaneous about [the] coronation than [the] Jubilee'.[67] The founders of Mass Observation recognized that what was said in this kind of interview was often influenced by wider social pressures to conform to what was deemed acceptable and respectable to say out loud in public to other people – and, in the case of Mass Observation, to complete strangers. On the coronation day of George VI people might have felt it necessary to voice their loyalty to the new king and yet many, like the aforementioned interviewee, still expressed support for his elder brother, which indicates the depth of positive feeling that persisted for Edward as fostered by sections of the press like the *Express* and *Mirror*, which maintained his popular image by reporting his activities.[68]

Other people across Britain shared the belief that Edward's absence had dampened the coronation mood. A Mass Observation respondent in Birmingham heard a group of girls singing the song 'God Bless the Prince of Wales' (as Edward had been titled since 1911), which prompted the comment, '[W]e'd a seen something if it was him today'.[69] Another respondent, who sat by a 'working-class man' on a train in the Midlands, discussed with him the celebrations he had attended that afternoon in Leicester and Nottingham. This man considered that there was 'not much heart in it this time, not like the Jubilee. The Duke of Windsor was very popular … [he] took all the shine out of it … [wistfully] I practically loved him'.[70] The highly intimate language the man used to characterize his relationship with the former king reveals that Edward had, during his time as heir to the throne and as monarch, cultivated a close emotional bond with members of the public as a royal personality who willingly transgressed traditional class boundaries. This sense of closeness to the former king informed the man's regret about his abdication and detracted from his appreciation of George VI. Equally, he judged that the coronation had fared badly compared with the silver jubilee two years before. This suggests that the escalation of royal public ceremonies in the mid 1930s created a sense of anticipation in the lead up to Edward VIII's accession and that George VI's crowning in place of his brother failed to live up to expectations. The same idea was conveyed

[67] MOA, CM6.

[68] T. Harrisson, 'What is public opinion?', *Political Quart.*, xi (1940), 368–83.

[69] MOA, CO35.

[70] MOA, CO24 (only in Jennings et al., *May the Twelfth*, p. 307).

in a number of Mass Observation reports which noted that the crowds which had turned out for the coronation in London were not as large as people had expected, again implying comparison with earlier, more popular royal events.[71]

The same working-class man on board the Midlands train described how his sense of anti-climax on coronation day was compounded by his doubts about the new monarch: 'He didn't really want it. I saw him once in Halifax. He looked dreadfully tired'.[72] The belief that a strong king had been replaced with a weak one was, in fact, a common sentiment recorded by the Mass Observation panel and is unsurprising, given how some newspapers repeatedly (if indirectly) contrasted the qualities of the two brothers. A schoolgirl from Port St Mary on the Isle of Man recorded that while 'everyone [she] knew was very keen on the coronation ... there was much comparison of the present king with his brother, the Duke of Windsor, and most people seemed to agree that Edward VIII was a stronger and better king'.[73] A twenty-three-year-old schoolteacher from Wellington in Shropshire described Edward's character in similar terms:

> My mother would have been much more interested had it been Edward VIII who was crowned; she feels that he was more independent in outlook than George VI who, she thinks, will be likely to do just as he is told. We liked Edward VIII for the interest he took in social problems; at the same time we feel that George VI is both conscientious and hardworking, and that he was sincere in his dedication of himself at the Abbey.[74]

This report contained some of the rare positive remarks on George VI, here rooted in admiration for his sense of duty and his commitment to his role, something which reveals how two of the key characteristics that had defined his father's reign helped to generate support for him, too. However, both the teacher and her mother appreciated the independence Edward demonstrated during his short reign, particularly in relation to social issues, and believed that his successor would not be as outspoken. The same view was expressed by a female café proprietor in Beer, Devon, who remarked to a Mass Observation respondent: '[W]e have lost a good king – one who had sympathy with the working classes and that is largely why he had to go. They got rid of him'.[75] Several others expressed contempt for a shadowy establishment comprising royal, religious and political figures

---

[71] E.g., MOA, CM2, CO12, CO19b, CO24, CL47.
[72] MOA, CO24 (only in Jennings et al., *May the Twelfth*, p. 307).
[73] MOA, CL40.
[74] MOA, CL56.
[75] MOA, CO1.

who had forced Edward off the throne because they considered him too forthright in his opinions, while some directly accused Stanley Baldwin or Cosmo Lang of interference, with a number taking aim at the archbishop in labelling George VI his 'puppet'.[76] Reports like these reflected the scorn many harboured for Lang as a result of his disastrous broadcast after the abdication but they also implied that George VI was weak in that he could be easily manipulated by the archbishop.

After he came to the throne, a series of negative rumours encircled the new king regarding his fitness to reign, stimulated, no doubt, in part by Lang's ill-judged reference to his stammer. Notably, George VI's biographers have discounted as 'idle and malicious gossip' and 'an undercurrent of doubt' the concerns regarding his abilities, but it is clear that some media outlets devoted much more attention to these anxieties than has previously been recognized, which in turn influenced public opinion.[77] For Geoffrey Dawson, the *Daily Mirror*'s publication of a front-page headline report which proclaimed that the new king had cancelled an eight-month tour of the Dominions because he 'did not wish to be absent from Britain for any length of time during the first year of his reign' constituted a 'really monstrous performance, calculated to worry the whole Empire'.[78] The editor of *The Times* knew that the story was a fabrication – a tour had not been considered so could not be cancelled – and added the *Mirror*'s report to his 'cuttings from the Simpson Press'. The implication of stories like this one was that George VI was reluctant to take on his role as symbolic figurehead of the nation and empire; and these kinds of negative reports were compounded by rumours about the monarch's physical strength, which suddenly spiked the week before his coronation. In response to these stories an old friend of George VI spoke out publicly against what he termed the 'malicious gossip' concerning the king's health. The Reverend Robert Hyde had worked alongside the monarch at the duke of York's camps and, at a public lunch, denied that the king suffered from epileptic fits or a bad heart, or that 'he may fail at the last moment'.[79] He also sought to rid George VI of the 'rubber stamp' label that had been applied to him – that he had little power and was unable to make his own decisions – by drawing attention to the fact that he had once witnessed the monarch's bad temper, implying that he would not stand to have his opinions ignored.

---

[76] MOA, CO23, CO15, CO18, CO22, CL56.

[77] Bradford, *George VI*, pp. 270–5; Wheeler-Bennett, *King George VI*, pp. 308–10.

[78] BOD, MS. Dawson 79, fos. 126b–c, G. Dawson to R. Barrington-Ward, 31 March 1937; *Daily Mirror*, 31 March 1937, p. 1.

[79] *Daily Mirror*, 7 May 1937, p. 36; *Daily Express*, 7 May 1937, p. 1.

THE DAILY MIRROR, Fri., May 7, 1937.

Daily Mirror

Seen Sundeck, Hiawatha?

Lovely new

Bear Brand

Stocking shades

ROUGE ANGELUS

Louis Philippe

The confident choice of the world's most distinguished women

1/6

With the exclusive "Pétal-matte" principle

TO-DAY'S WEATHER
Light rain in east and north England, the Midlands and Wales. Mainly fair. High temperatures in south.
London and South-east England.— Light rain, becoming fair.

FURTHER OUTLOOK
Mainly fair; showery in the north-west.
Sea Passages.— Moderate; wind south-westerly.
Airways.— Wind moderate.
Light-up.—9.30 p.m.

'MALICIOUS GOSSIP' ABOUT THE HEALTH OF THE KING

"MALICIOUS gossip" concerning the King's health was condemned yesterday by Mr. R. R. Hyde, director of the Industrial Welfare Society, addressing the Industrial Co-Partnership Association in London.

"There is a curious failing on the part of many people," he said, "to wish to believe evil of public characters. Only yesterday at my club I was asked whether the King was epileptic.

"You may recall similar calumnies alleging that the Princesses are deaf, dumb, or imbecile; that the Queen is deaf; that there may be no Coronation because the King is so weak, that his heart is so bad, that he may fail at the last moment; and that he is a rubber-stamp king.

"My Privilege to Know Him . . ."

"It has been my privilege during the last nineteen years to have seen a great deal of the King," Mr. Hyde said, "and I speak after a long and close association with him. I have seen him in very diverse circumstances and in every mood.

"I have seen him as a Prince of State, by my own bedside in a nursing home, at his own table and fireside and with his children. I have shared with him the hospitality of peers and commoners.

"Always he is a delightful companion—very human, very lovable."

Mr. Hyde said he had known the King to be in a temper.

"I was glad of it, because it showed another side to his character," he said.

One occasion was when mounted police roughly treated a crowd of girls who clambered round his car. The King did not mind the girls there at all.

"I have shared long swims in a rough sea with the King; I have seen him play golf in different surroundings with the patience and endurance of most men. He has played a good game of tennis at Wimbledon, he has shot duck at dawn, and he has stalked deer.

"He has endured long and tiring tours of cotton mills, shipyards and mines, and once the National Anthem was played fifteen times in nine miles and he did not turn a hair.

"Never has there been any evidence of time shortcomings, or physical weaknesses, which malicious gossip has attached to him.

"Those of you who hear this gossip—do not heed it; it is unkind, unworthy and untrue."

SOMEONE RISKED HIS LIFE

. . . to put this Union Jack on top of the Radcliffe Camera, 200ft. high Oxford building—hitherto unclimbed and regarded as unclimbable. Now, all Oxford wants to know who the mountaineer is. See story on page 4.

PEER'S SON WINS SEAT

Lord Halifax's twenty-four-year-old son, the Hon. Charles Wood, retained York parliamentary seat for the National Conservatives in the by-election last night.

He defeated Mr. John Dugdale (Labour).

Figures were : Mr. Charles Wood, 22,045; Mr. John Dugdale, 17,986; majority, 4,059.

TURN TO—

AMUSEMENTS ..	28
BELINDA	30
BROADCASTING	30
CASSANDRA	10
JANE	8
P. STRONG	15
PIP AND SQUEAK	22
RUGGLES	32
SECRETS	25
SERIAL	24
STARS' MESSAGE	28

LATEST NEWS

HINDENBURGH DISASTER
(See page 1)

Mr. George Grant, of Swansea-road, Battersea, S.W.18, passenger on Hindenburg, has received a cable from his father at home saying:—"I have just received a cable saying that my father is safe."

Captain Pruss and Captain Lehmann and a number of others also reported to have survived.

ROADS TO BLAZING AIRSHIP JAMMED: SOS FOR AMBULANCES

(Continued from Page 1)

dived in flames. Then came another series of explosions.

"Through terrible flames I saw people moving amid twisted girders and smashed body-work. I saw men and women with clothes afire leap from the windows. Some left a lifeless mass below to be swallowed in the flames.

"I saw old couple clinging to one another. I saw a woman with the hair burned off her head running madly around."

Britain's worst airship disaster was the R 101, in October, 1930, while she was on a flight to India. She crashed in France with the loss of forty-eight lives. That disaster led to the discontinuance of airship building in this country.

. . . by headwinds over Newfoundland. This morning, on her arrival at Lakehurst, she again had to cruise for more than hour within sight of spectators, wai'ing for the weather to permit her mooring.

She left Frankfurt-on-Main at 8.15 p.m. on Monday with every hope of her new outside cabins booked.

On her homeward voyage, she was due to convey the last of America's visitors to the Coronation.

It is understood that it will be impossible to reach the wreckage until to-morrow morn-

. . . ing as it is still burning fiercely. Police have made a radio call for ambulances, but they are unable to get through. All roads are jammed.

Newspapermen have been barred.

Hindenburg's insurance, it was stated, was largely covered in London.

DR. ECKENER STILL HAS FAITH

BY A SPECIAL CORRESPONDENT

DR. Hugo Eckener, seventy-one-year-old designer and one-time commander of the Hindenburg, told me by telephone from his home at Friedrichshafen:—

"I am more shocked than I can say.

"In my opinion travel by a Zeppelin is just as safe as that on any other type of airship.

"Disaster cannot deter me. I still believe in airships."

When I told Dr. Eckener that there was a thunderstorm as the Hindenburg was about to land, he suggested an interesting theory.

"It is quite possible that the mooring mast acted as a conductor," he said. "The most could possibly have caused a charge of electricity."

News of the crash was 'phoned to Herr Hitler and Herr Goering, German Air Minister, shortly after the disaster.

Some idea of the size of the Hindenburg can be gained from this picture of her being manoeuvred into her hangar at Friedrichshaven.

Printed and Published by THE DAILY MIRROR NEWSPAPERS, LTD., at Geraldine House, Rolls Bldgs., Fetter-lane, London, E.C.4.—Friday, May 7, 1937. Tel. Holborn 4321.

Figure 3.4. '"Malicious Gossip" About the Health of the King', *Daily Mirror*, 7 May 1937, p. 36. © The British Library Board.

As with Lang's post-abdication broadcast, Hyde's speech probably did more harm than good, its widespread dissemination via the press fuelling the belief that the king lacked the strength of character required to fulfil his role.[80] Indeed, the story would probably have received even greater attention had British newspapers not announced that the Hindenburg zeppelin had blown up at Lakehurst in the USA on the same day. All the same, Hyde's speech was presented as the headline story on the back page of the *Daily Mirror* (Figure 3.4).[81] Contrary to the press patriotically rallying around the new king, it is clear that doubts about his abilities persisted among some news editors.[82]

The archbishop of Canterbury may have also exacerbated public concerns about the monarch's strength of character the week before the coronation. Since George VI had come to the throne, Lang had worked to reaffirm Christian public morality through his promotion of the coronation as a moment of national spiritual renewal. It seems likely that the archbishop's concerns stemmed from the duke of Windsor's continued popularity despite his 'immoral' behaviour and the knowledge that his own reputation and that of the Church of England had suffered as a result of his attack on the ex-king at the time of the abdication. Lang had, in fact, originally planned to use Edward VIII's coronation to launch a 'recall to religion', but he knew full well that his cause would be better served by George VI and Queen Elizabeth with their Christian home life.[83] However, the way the archbishop drew attention to the new king's religiosity again hinted towards a potential weakness on the part of the monarch. Lang used the *Canterbury Diocesan Gazette* as his principal vehicle for public communication, knowing that his words would subsequently be disseminated through other newspapers and periodicals. Writing at the start of May, the archbishop highlighted the coronation's religious meaning and suggested that in preparing for the event the public would 'surround and support' the new king and queen with prayers for their welfare at a special service of intercession and dedication on the Sunday night before the coronation: 'On the previous Sunday evening multitudes in their churches or in their homes throughout the land … will be remembering the King and Queen in their prayers. They will like to know that at that very time their Majesties in their own personal prayers will be associating themselves with the prayers of their people'.[84] The archbishop

---

[80] Bradford, *George VI*, p. 273; Wheeler-Bennett, *King George VI*, p. 309.

[81] *Daily Mirror*, 7 May 1937, p. 36.

[82] Bingham, *Family Newspapers?*, p. 242.

[83] LPL, MS3208, 'King Edward's Abdication', 11 Dec. 1936, fos. 193–7; Beaken, *Cosmo Lang*, pp. 77 and 97.

[84] *The Times*, 3 May 1937, p. 9.

sought to engineer this moment of spiritual communion between rulers and subjects at the behest of Cyril Bardsley, bishop of Leicester, who had suggested to him 'it would do an immense amount of good' if Lang could let it be known publicly that the king and the queen were taking part in a special service in their own private chapel at the same time as their people.[85] To amplify his vision of a nation congregated in support of their rulers, the archbishop also oversaw the publication of three special forms of service that were distributed nationally, one of which was used as part of the evening service on the Sunday before the coronation.[86] Lang went on to lead this service from the BBC concert hall and delivered a sermon titled 'The King Comes Not Alone' to an audience of special guests and, via the wireless, to British listeners gathered in their homes and at church services around the country.[87] Drawing on the language of the burdens of royal service, Lang used his address to focus his audience's attention on the responsibilities that had been laid upon the new king and his consort, not least of which was enduring a coronation service the 'whole world' would observe.[88]

As with Reverend Hyde's misjudged public intervention in defence of George VI's health, Lang's emphasis on the need for public prayer to sustain the king and queen perpetuated an image of the new monarch as physically and mentally fragile. The last time prayers of intercession were offered up for a member of the royal family had been during the grave illness of George V in the winter of 1928 to 1929. Thus the archbishop's campaign, although instigated with the best intention of generating public support for George VI, drew inadvertent attention to what seemed to be more serious shortcomings in the new king's character.

'We shall be crowning ourselves'

The sense of doubt that characterized public attitudes to George VI following his sudden accession meant that the media and the British elite chose to project more dynamic messages as the central themes of the 1937 coronation. In the lead up to 12 May journalists and members of the political establishment repeatedly stressed that the ceremony symbolized a crucial moment in the formation of the relationship between crown and people: the coronation was proof of the evolution and superiority of constitutional

[85] LPL, Lang 22, fo. 372, C. Bardsley to C. G. Lang, 16 Apr. 1937.

[86] One of the 3 main distributors claimed to have sold 1.5 million copies of the forms of service, which included servicing one tenth of all the parishes in England (LPL, Lang 22, fos. 308–9, W. K. Lowther Clarke to A. C. Don, 31 May 1937 and reply).

[87] BBCWA, R30/444/1, Confidential Memo: Coronation Week Programmes Committee.

[88] BBCWA, R30/444/1, Confidential Memo: Coronation Week Programmes Committee. For a reproduction of Lang's address, see *The Listener*, 12 May 1937, pp. 903–4 and 938.

democracy and of Britain's imperial strength at a time of international political uncertainty. Indeed, in many reports George VI was a background figure to his own crowning, with coverage instead focusing on 'the people' as the central actors in this story of democratic progress. The coronation thus witnessed a reorientation of the relationship between the king and his subjects around the symbolism of democracy after the nation's brief flirtation with a more outspoken version of popular sovereignty as embodied by Edward VIII. It was precisely because the new monarch was perceived as lacking personality that public commentators and the media were able to invest his crowning with abstract meaning, using the event to promote validatory statements about the nation's and empire's social and political character in a period when both seemed threatened by authoritarianism. Crucially, members of the public internalized these discourses of democracy and progress and reproduced them in Mass Observation reports, sometimes contrasting them directly with European fascism. In this respect we should interpret George VI's coronation as having a lasting impact in redirecting the trajectory of the monarchy's transformation in the years immediately before the Second World War.

Historians of modern Britain have discussed how the interwar period witnessed an eruption in public debates about the 'national character', led in part by the political elite: with the advent of full democracy after the Fourth and Fifth Reform Acts, they sought to maintain their hold on power through the promotion of an inclusive language of 'Englishness'. Conservative politicians like Stanley Baldwin were the most notable proponents of this creed and stressed to voters the 'common sense, good temper, ordered freedom [and] progress' that allegedly characterized the national mood.[89] Baldwin used his model 'Englishman' to try to reconcile the politically restless industrial classes to the state by uniting them through a shared sense of national heritage; and as prime minister he placed special emphasis on Britain's 'constitutional tradition', in which the new mass electorate were characterized as the keystone of parliamentary democracy and franchise reform as the core tenet of the nation's political evolution.[90] The crown played an integral role in Baldwin's story: the institution had anchored the nation's political development across time and the sovereign acted as

[89] P. Mandler, *The English National Character: the History of an Idea from Edmund Burke to Tony Blair* (London, 2006), pp. 149–51.

[90] B. Schwarz, 'The language of constitutionalism: Baldwinite conservatism', in *Formations of Nation and People*, ed. Formations Editorial Collective (London, 1984), pp. 1–18, at pp. 11–6; P. Williamson, 'The doctrinal politics of Stanley Baldwin', in *Public and Private Doctrine: Essays in British History Presented to Michael Cowling*, ed. M. Bentley (Cambridge, 1993), pp. 181–208, at pp. 190–1.

the safeguard of the individual freedoms of citizens. Against a backdrop of political volatility in Europe, the link between monarchy and democracy quickly crystallized after 1918, with a language of constitutionalism coming to define George V's later reign.[91] Baldwin's eulogy to the monarch after his death celebrated the way that he had overseen 'far-reaching constitutional and Parliamentary changes without precedent in our long history'.[92] Indeed, by January 1936 the irrepressible rise of the dictators on the Continent meant that the crown's symbolic defence of the public's political liberties and the increasing extension of these freedoms through the arteries of the Commonwealth had taken on greater meaning still.

However, the abdication crisis challenged this narrative of unceasing progress by revealing that the crown's relationship with the British public was much more fluid and unstable than the politicians and royal speechwriters would have had us believe. Letters written to Edward VIII and other key players involved in the crisis show that many sections of the public supported the king in his decision to marry Simpson and endorsed his more forthright – and more authoritarian – version of popular monarchy.[93] And, as we have seen, the belief that Edward had been a 'strong' king persisted after he had abandoned the throne. Given the deep rupture created by the abdication, it is notable that every mainstream media outlet joined with commentators from across the political spectrum to project George VI's coronation as the climax to what had otherwise been a story of unhindered evolution. One of the main themes at George V's silver jubilee in 1935 had been constitutional progress and now, two years on, the crowning of his second son was hailed as proof of the vitality of Britain's royal democracy – a message designed, at least in part, to consolidate the monarchy's power but also to re-educate subjects of the crown in the meaning of kingship following Edward VIII's temporary aberration.[94]

Behind closed doors, journalists discussed the change in direction of the monarchy. In March 1937 the *Guardian*'s editor, William Crozier, invited J. L. Hammond – one of the newspaper's most seasoned reporters – to pen the editorial leader for their coronation number 'on what we think about the monarchy ... and what we hope of the new reign'.[95] Crozier suggested

[91] Mandler, *The English National Character*, pp. 151–2.

[92] S. Baldwin, 'On the death of King George V', 21 Jan. 1936, in S. Baldwin, *Service of Our Lives: Last Speeches as Prime Minister* (London, 1938), pp. 11–20, at p. 20; for a full copy of the speech see 'A Life of Service: The Prime Minister's Tribute', *The Times*, 28 Jan. 1936, p. 25.

[93] Mort, 'Love in a cold climate', pp. 58–62.

[94] On the 1935 silver jubilee, see Williamson, 'Monarchy and public values', p. 237.

[95] JRL, MG/223/24/103, W. Crozier to J. L. Hammond, 19 March 1937.

that it was an opportunity to set the record straight after the abdication, putting across the newspaper's views 'more realistically' than they had 'hitherto done'. In a subsequent letter to Hammond, Crozier went on to admit his regret over the way the *Guardian* had previously reported on the monarchy:

> I look back with a little remorse now on all the jubilations about George V (though he was a good man) and the accession of Edward VIII but I comfort myself with the recollection that I twice in the leaders at the death of George V put in a sentence or two to the effect that we must wait and see how Edward fulfilled all the hopes that were being expressed about him. But I think that we shall in future be saying much more about the Crown and much less about its temporary owner.[96]

In Crozier's opinion, the crown had survived the personality cults of Edward VIII and his father and veneration of the monarchy would now centre more on its success as a political institution than on the characteristics of the sovereign. This can partly be explained with reference to George VI, who was found wanting in terms of personality, but the letter also betrays a belief prevalent among journalists after the abdication that the public had been wrong to place so much faith in the monarch as a national leader in the 1930s.[97] Crozier judged that, henceforward, the sovereign's personality would play second fiddle to the crown as a symbol.

The resulting leader that Hammond penned for the *Guardian* struck all the right notes while at the same time taking the view that many of the 'traditional' aspects of the coronation were antiquated and that the political freedoms which characterized British national life were yet to be fully extended to Ireland or India. The article explained the coronation by emphasizing that 'the Crown becomes more important than the King, the symbol than the man' in a ceremony which witnessed the monarch swear to 'govern his many peoples "according to their laws and customs," under a system, that is to say, by which the Ministers who represent the people take the responsibility for all the sovereign's acts'. It continued: 'The Crown is strong in popular esteem to-day because while promising government according to the law and customs of its "subjects" it stands for the same liberty to order their own life that they have gradually asserted for themselves since the days when Kings ordered it for them'.[98]

On the right of the political spectrum, the *Daily Express*'s leader drew similar attention to the long-standing bond between sovereign and subjects

[96] JRL, MG/223/24/140, W. Crozier to J. L. Hammond, 29 March 1937.
[97] K. Martin, *The Magic of Monarchy* (London, 1937).
[98] *Manchester Guardian*, 12 May 1937, p. 10.

and the idea that the monarchy had overseen the emergence of democracy in Britain. The newspaper provided a clear explanation of 'The People's Part' in the coronation:

> This is the day of the People. The people are the source of power and wealth and glory. They lift up the King to be the leader. Well the great Kings of England have understood it. We have found it convenient to take our Kings in hereditary succession when we could, but in the ultimate possession the throne of England is the property of the people of England. This day is a ceremony wherein each citizen takes his part. The King swears to defend our liberties and we take vows to make and keep him King.[99]

This simplified interpretation of how constitutional monarchy operated to guard the freedoms of British people and the way the sovereign was ultimately answerable to his or her subjects was reworked in the liberal *News Chronicle* in an explicatory article titled 'What it all means'. Acclaimed political reporter A. J. Cummings tellingly wrote that 'there is nothing wonderful (we shall freely admit) about [George VI]. We don't even know him very well ... [But] he is a modest and sensible king'. He then went on to describe to readers how the abdication crisis had proved there were 'two conditions, upon which, in a democracy, the sovereign maintains his position and popularity ... The king's mode of life must be approved by his subjects and his name must not be used for political or party advantage'.[100] The report thus presented an implicit criticism of the right-wing faction that had been led by Winston Churchill and which had sought to make political headway by taking Edward's side at the time of the abdication, with Cummings articulating the idea that the political liberty of British people was fundamentally bound to the non-partisan nature of kingship. That he also believed public approval of the king's 'mode of life' was now key to the crown's authority shows that the media's intense focus on royal private life in the 1930s had witnessed the crystallization of moral virtue as an intrinsic part of the identity of the constitutional monarch. The contingency between a common moral code, British people's political freedoms and the king's authority was also conveyed in a comment Cummings quoted from a conversation he reported having had with an unnamed 'hard-bitten Member of Parliament', who told him that 'we shall be crowning not only the King ... we shall be crowning ourselves as well'.

The left-wing *Daily Herald* offered its own distinct explanation of how the monarchy embodied the public's democratic spirit. As part of a series of articles titled 'Crown and People', the Labour peer Lord Arthur

---

[99] *Daily Express*, 12 May 1937, p. 10.
[100] *News Chronicle*, 11 May 1937, p. 8 (and the following quotations).

Ponsonby expressed his approval of the way the monarchy had overseen political progress, noting that George V had 'shown conspicuous fairness in accepting, with no trace of protest, Labour as the alternative Government'. He suggested there was 'little sign of any antagonism' between 'the tradition of monarchy and practice of Socialism'.[101] Indeed, despite the anti-imperial position the *Herald* had taken in the 1920s while it was still majority-owned by the Trades Union Congress, it would style the meeting of George VI and his Dominion prime ministers at Westminster hall as 'the answer to dictatorship', declaring that the king and his prime ministers were 'pledged to democracy'.[102] The newspaper placed special emphasis on the egalitarian quality of the Westminster hall congregation:

> They sat at lunch where Simon de Montfort assembled his first Parliament, on the spot where, century after century, Britain gradually evolved her system of Liberty – and they represented all the races, colours and creeds over which the British flag flies. A foreigner from a dictator country would have stood aghast at such an assemblage, its democracy, its friendliness, its equality.

The *Herald*'s celebration of the Commonwealth and empire in its coronation coverage accorded with a wider shift in the newspaper's editorial tone as it transformed itself into a popular tabloid after it was bought by Odhams Press in 1930. But it also revealed how pressures created by the rise of fascism in Europe ensured that even those on the political left felt it necessary to reconcile themselves to Britain's constitutional monarchy as a progressive political system.[103]

Readers had to look further afield if they wanted to find press criticism of the coronation and its imperial connotations. As at George and Marina's wedding, the communist *Daily Worker* presented the royal family as 'parasites' and criticized the coronation as a distraction from the 'real Britain' made up of economically depressed areas.[104] The newspaper was also on its own in standing with the London bus men who went on strike in coronation week, which created traffic chaos in a move that was widely condemned by the mainstream media.[105] In a front-page message, the Communist party leader Harry Pollitt drew attention to the plight of Indian workers suffering under what he perceived as an imperial system that was sustained by royal

---

[101] *Daily Herald*, 10 May 1937, p. 10.

[102] *Daily Herald*, 8 May 1937, p. 1.

[103] As historian Ben Pimlott noted: 'The Empire was unblinkingly described as if it were a democratic, almost a voluntary, association' (B. Pimlott, *The Queen: Elizabeth II and the Monarchy* (London, 2002), p. 43).

[104] *Daily Worker*, 8 May 1937, p. 4; *Daily Worker*, 12 May 1937, pp. 4–5.

[105] *Daily Worker*, 10 May 1937, p. 1; 11 May 1937, p. 1.

propaganda.[106] And the writer and renowned critic of the monarchy, George Bernard Shaw, lived up to his reputation when he criticized the coronation for creating 'illusions and idolatries'.[107] Notably, three Mass Observation respondents recorded seeing Shaw's column and two of the panel spent some of coronation day selling the *Daily Worker* in central London.[108] As with the royal wedding three years before, the newspaper went on to claim that it had enjoyed enormous sales on 12 May.[109] While this might hint at greater disaffection with monarchy than is apparent from other sources, the ideological consensus that characterized almost every other national media outlet's coverage of the coronation – namely pro-royalty, pro-constitutional democracy, pro-empire – crowded out this lone voice of dissent.

The mainstream media also consistently linked Britain's democratic freedoms to the empire's international peacekeeping role and emphasized that the crown's symbolic embodiment of the liberties of its subjects contrasted to the way European dictatorships had eroded the rights of their peoples. The *Daily Mirror* and *Mail* were typical in reproducing the coronation message of the South African imperial statesman Jan Smuts to illustrate this distinction. For him, the empire-Commonwealth was a 'league of peace', ensuring 'safety from war' and succeeding where the League of Nations had failed. Smuts described democracy in conflict with authoritarianism: 'Parliamentary government is being abandoned, personal liberty derided and the basic principle of government by consent of the governed is being replaced by the principle of dictatorship or Caesarism. Our Commonwealth stands on guard for the ideals of democracy'.[110] Smuts's appraisal resonated with the opinions voiced by some of Britain's most notable politicians in the lead-up to the coronation on the relationship between monarchy, political liberty and empire. In a series of BBC radio talks titled 'The Responsibilities of Empire' that were broadcast in April, May and June of 1937, Churchill, David Lloyd George and Prime Minister Stanley Baldwin took to the airwaves alongside a number of other statesmen to celebrate British democratic progress and its impact on the Commonwealth. The last line of Baldwin's opening broadcast was typical of what followed in the other talks and in keeping with the constitutional story he had crafted during his political career: 'The British peoples have always set before them

---

[106] *Daily Worker*, 12 May 1937, p. 1.

[107] *Daily Worker*, 12 May 1937, p. 3.

[108] On Shaw's column, see MOA, CO19b, CO36, CL64. For panel members who sold the *Daily Worker*, see MOA, CO20, CL64.

[109] *Daily Worker*, 13 May 1937, p. 1. Anecdotal evidence recorded by MO 'mobile squad' member CM7 supports this assertion.

[110] *Daily Mirror*, 13 May 1937, p. 8; *Daily Mail*, 13 May 1937, p. 2.

the ideal of freedom, and more than ever today it is their duty to maintain and to justify that ideal'.[111] Again, the radio talks bridged political divides. The Labour peer Lord Snell of Plumstead told listeners in the second of these broadcasts that his party had reconciled itself to the aims of the 'new Empire' and that he perceived it as the 'most hopeful factor of the modern world' and a 'great witness to the stabilising power of freedom'.[112]

*

Across the country, Mass Observation respondents noted that they and those around them interpreted George VI's coronation as a symbol of Britain's liberal political values and national character. They implicitly and explicitly compared the nation's freedoms with dictatorship and discussed how the Commonwealth exemplified this democratic vision. In Beer, one respondent noted a speech made by his local baker at the community's coronation celebrations. The baker had said:

> that we had gone through a unique experience that day and it reminded us that there was no country on earth where there was so much happiness, prosperity and freedom as in England and that we should show 'the foreigner' in no unmistakable terms that we valued our happiness and freedom ... There was no mention of the King and it seemed as if all mention of him was kept in the background as far as possible and when mention was made, it was in the direction of implied apology – e.g. his deeper voice, and his sincerity.[113]

The mayor of Manchester also focused on Britain's unique freedoms in his message to the city's people on coronation day. He described it as a 'great day in the history of a freedom-loving community' and declared that 'we are able to rejoice in the liberty of the subject, freedom of thought, vote, and action, in which this old country stands supreme'.[114] This emphasis on British exceptionalism intersected with a more diffuse patriotism recorded by Mass Observation respondents who noted that foreign visitors would return to their countries and 'say how impressed they were' with Britain.[115]

---

[111] S. Baldwin, 'Responsibilities of Empire', *The Listener*, xvii, 21 Apr. 1937, pp. 735–6. The original broadcast took place on 16 Apr. 1937. See also W. Churchill, 'Freedom and Progress for All', *The Listener*, xvii, 5 May 1937, pp. 849–50 and 887; D. Lloyd George, 'Peace Rests with the Empire', *The Listener*, xvii, 9 June. 1937, pp. 1121–2 and 1158.

[112] Lord Snell of Plumstead, 'Bulwark of World Peace', *The Listener*, xvii, 28 Apr. 1937, pp. 795–6.

[113] MOA, CO1.

[114] *Manchester Guardian*, 12 May 1937, p. 12.

[115] MOA, CM6, CO16, CL15, CL22, CL39.

A schoolteacher who escorted some of his pupils from Northumberland to London to see the coronation procession recorded in his report for Mass Observation that he thought the event had shown the world that national life had managed to continue after the abdication:

> From a conservative point of view the welcome given not only the King but to the people who stand for tradition and the maintenance of the status quo was most gratifying. It must have been obvious to any foreign visitor that the respect and veneration of the Crown by the people of this country had not been lessened by the unhappy events leading to the abdication of Edward VIII.[116]

The teacher conflated reverence for the monarchy with a broader respect for what he saw as 'traditional' British values and was pleased at the reception extended to George VI.

Descriptions of Britain's unique political culture also focused on the stabilizing roles played by the monarchy and empire. A retired man from County Durham wrote that the coronation benefitted the country 'as it helps us to realise the unity of the Empire with its privileges and responsibilities'.[117] The retiree was, in fact, repeating the exact words used by Baldwin in his BBC talk before the coronation, in which he had told listeners that 'ten years ago I made a broadcast speech on the Privileges of Empire' and 'tonight I am able to speak on the Responsibilities of Empire'.[118] Other respondents were more direct in conflating empire with world peace. Writing on the advantages of the coronation, a young chemist who worked in Brighton suggested that it was 'a clear factor for peace that a group of nations like the British Commonwealth should "hang together"'. Similarly, the teacher from Northumberland suggested that the king was not only doing his best to 'preserve the stability of the Crown', but also of 'the Empire and therefore the greater part of the world in these days of general lack of sound guiding principles [sic]'.[119] Positive appreciations of the nation's imperial ties as contained in personal testimonies like these indicate that the empire might have had a greater hold over British minds in this period than some historians have acknowledged.[120]

[116] MOA, CL63.

[117] MOA, CL99.

[118] I.e., the Baldwin speech delivered on 16 Apr. and published in *The Listener* 5 days later (S. Baldwin, 'Responsibilities of Empire', *The Listener*, xvii, 21 Apr. 1937, pp. 735–6.

[119] MOA, CL65 and CL63; also CM6, CL33, CL34, CL40.

[120] B. Porter, *The Absent-Minded Imperialists: Empire, Society, and Culture in Britain* (Oxford, 2004), esp. pp. 255–82; S. Potter, *Broadcasting Empire: the BBC and the British World, 1922–1970* (Oxford, 2012), pp. 14–7.

Occasionally, this pacific interpretation – which suggested that monarchy, liberty, imperialism and international peace were bound up together – coalesced with more bellicose readings of the military power of empire. For example, one of the Mass Observation mobile squad reporters who stood in the crowds on the procession route in London recorded a conversation she had overheard between a 'middle-class' man and woman, which included 'how right it was to have the Coronation at this time – foreigners would return home and say how impressed they were with England; what a move for peace this was; that the increase in armaments was an excellent thing, how stirring it was to see all the might of British arms'.[121] The topics the pair discussed and the transitions in their conversation revealed that conceptions of peace could co-exist with a belief in British military strength.[122] The conflation of Britain's peacekeeping role with imperial military power was also noted by a respondent who was a self-professed socialist and had, at the insistence of his friends at Mass Observation, taken up the opportunity to spend the day watching the procession from a stand on Oxford Street among a group of 'middle and upper class people' whom he termed 'most loyal and patriotic'. He described how a 'very large Cornishman', who was part of the group with whom he sat, exclaimed excitedly as the Household Guards marched passed: 'Look at the way they hold their rifles. Look at 'em! Now we're showing that not only Hitler can have soldiers. We'll show 'em. We'll show the World'.[123] The Cornishman was drunk but his outburst claiming the British would not be militarily upstaged by the Third Reich resonated with other views recorded by the Mass Observation panel on the way the coronation boosted the nation's confidence at a time when it seemed threatened by dictatorship.[124] While these opinions suggest that British militarism was framed through public discourse on peacekeeping and defence during these years, some of the Mass Observation panel were alarmed, one respondent recording that 'the military element is altogether too prominent; it has the psychological effect of dressing war preparations in fancy dress and making it look attractive'.[125]

One final way that perceptions of British liberty and stability were expressed on coronation day was through descriptions of the orderly character

---

[121] MOA, CM6.

[122] For a similar example, see M. Jones, '"The surest safeguard of peace": technology, the navy and the nation in boys' papers c.1905–1907', in *The Dreadnought and the Edwardian Age*, ed. R. J. Blyth, A. Lambert and J. Rüger (Farnham, 2011), pp. 109–31.

[123] MOA, CO19b.

[124] MOA, CO6, CO42, CL15, CL16, CL22, CL103.

[125] MOA, CO16. See also CO18, CO19b, CL16, CL22, CL69; D. Edgerton, *Warfare State: Britain, 1920–1970* (Cambridge, 2006), pp. 270–7.

of the crowds that assembled in central London. Since the mid nineteenth century, newspapers had focused on massed crowds at royal events as a way of conveying narratives of a popular royal consensus to media audiences.[126] The 1937 coronation was no different: between the wars the mass electorate was represented to contrast with both the rowdiness of the Edwardian years and the unruly political cultures of other nations in order to create a vision of a 'peaceful' and 'phlegmatic' citizenry.[127] In this vein, on the day of George VI's crowning *The Times* reported that the crowds that gathered in London for the celebrations were 'happy crowds': '[T]he English crowd is known to be always good-tempered and humorous, ready to snatch at any chance for a laugh and a cheer'.[128] Mass Observation reports suggest that members of the public internalized this language of a people happily united around the monarchy. Furthermore, the panel often presented British national cohesion in direct contrast with the discordance that characterized contemporary European politics. For example, one of the mobile squad who conversed with a man from Huntingdonshire and another from Wales noted that they all agreed that, compared to the British, the French were a 'very excitable' people, having been stirred up by the doctrine of republicanism.[129] Similarly, the Cornishman who watched the procession from a stand in Oxford Street was observed speaking to a Canadian woman and, gesturing 'to those massed at the edges of the processional route', said: 'Look at the crowd outside there. Look how patient and good-humoured they are. Some of them have been waiting all night, and yet they can still laugh. Why, in Russia or France there'd be no organisation; there might be disorders and fighting if they had to wait like that'.[130] This kind of opinion was also recorded in reports which noted relief that no 'fiascos [had] tak[en] place' or 'bombs ... been thrown'.[131]

Historians have suggested that the 1930s were characterized by British anxieties about the way psychological propaganda had been used in Germany to mobilize a nation in support of Hitler's Nazi regime.[132] Critics of

---

[126] On the 19th-century popularization of crowd-centred imagery, see J. Plunkett *Queen Victoria: First Media Monarch* (Oxford, 2003), pp. 17, 43, and 60–7.

[127] H. McCarthy, *The British People and the League of Nations: Democracy, Citizenship and Internationalism, c.1918–45* (Manchester, 2011), pp. 28–35; J. Lawrence, 'The transformation of British public politics after the First World War', *Past & Present*, cxc (2006), 185–216, at pp. 212–6.

[128] *The Times*, 12 May 1937, p. 13.

[129] MOA, CM8.

[130] MOA, CO19b.

[131] MOA, CO6, CO23, CO27, CL16.

[132] S. Jonsson, *Crowds and Democracy: the Idea and Images of the Masses from Revolution to Fascism* (New York, 2013), pp. 16–20, 51–4, 171–4. Jonsson has noted that mass psychology was associated with the political discourse of fascism and that it also provided left-wing

fascism, like the editor of the *New Statesman and Nation*, Kingsley Martin, had popularized psychological ways of thinking about 'the masses' as a political formation that lacked individual consciousness.[133] Given that Mass Observation's coronation project had recruited volunteer writers through advertisements in the *New Statesman*, it is perhaps unsurprising that a number of the Mass Observation panel drew on a psychological lexicon to describe the behaviour of the crowds that gathered on coronation day. In using these terms, respondents were often defining their own sense of middle-class individualism against a negative image of the 'unthinking' masses.[134] However, the way respondents focused on the emotions of the crowds also indicates that the mid 1930s were defined by a heightened sensitivity to the way 'feelings' shaped public life. Notably, the new understandings of mass behaviour that were taking root in Britain anticipated the elite obsession with the analysis of civilian morale that shaped how society was reconceptualized during the fraught years of the Blitz.[135]

While some members of the Mass Observation panel expressed reservations about the potentially destabilizing effects the masses could inflict on British society if their emotions were misdirected, most supported the idea that the coronation presented a safe and vital outlet for popular fervour, uniting the nation around the focal point of the monarchy. A teacher and farmer from Sussex described what she deemed to be the coronation's role in channelling the energies of the masses:

> I think the monarchy is to some extent a support in the maintenance of our political liberties but also it is the bulwark of class division and social privilege. A great corporate act is a powerful national experience and is good or bad as it is used. The jubilee drew the nation together in sincere admiration for a man who had lived up to a high ideal of service. Mass emotion, even if centred on a worthy object, is dangerous because it can so easily get quite out of control. For an unworthy object – e.g. anti-Jewish, it could degrade terribly. I have heard the opinion that democratic Germany made a mistake in having practically no pageantry which the Germans love and missed (they have had their fill since!!).[136]

---

intellectuals with the 'instruments' to interpret fascist ideology: a language of 'the masses' was used to understand the social disorder and violent events that disrupted interwar Europe. See also C. Borch, *The Politics of Crowds: an Alternative History of Sociology* (Cambridge, 2012), pp. 165–233.

[133] E.g., K. Martin, *Fascism, Democracy and the Press* (London, 1938), pp. 9–10.

[134] N. Hubble, *Mass Observation and Everyday Life: Culture, History, Theory* (Basingstoke, 2006), p. 2; also J. Hinton, 'Self reflections in the mass', *History Workshop Jour.*, lxxv (2013), 251–9, at p. 257.

[135] R. M. Titmuss, *Problems of Social Policy* (London, 1976), ch. 1.

[136] MOA, CO16.

This personal testimony reveals the high esteem in which the respondent held George V because of his dutiful qualities and shows that, despite her personal misgivings about the unequal social hierarchy the monarchy represented, the institution could be viewed as a safeguard against dictatorship and as a symbol of political freedom. Her criticism of the way 'mass emotion' had been exploited in Germany to foster anti-Semitism suggests that she perceived the crown, with its 'high ideal of service', as a preferable channel for mass veneration. A teenage girl from Chelsea agreed, noting that 'people must have some kind of outlet for their emotions … The English, in particular, are so bottled up in this respect, that it no doubt does them some good to have an excuse to cheer, celebrate and shout once in a while'. For her the monarchy provided a 'fairly harmless safety valve, instead of following the example of Italy or Germany'.[137]

Several other Mass Observation respondents echoed the teenager's 'safety valve' analogy and her belief that the coronation provided a vent for mass emotion which, as a 'very dangerous human characteristic', might otherwise be exploited by tyrannical politicians 'for their own advantage'.[138] Reports like these seem to indicate that the British and European political cultures of the mid 1930s, with their unique fusion of mass-mediated popular spectacle and (up until George VI) charismatic leadership, created a new sensitivity among some members of the public to the way emotion worked to legitimize political regimes. Mass Observation described a British mass society that centred on the monarchy as a democratic focal point. On the one hand, they drew on an imagery that belittled the masses by implying that they were emotionally susceptible to the draw of royal festivities. However, their descriptions also conveyed the fact that British political culture was influenced by fears about dictatorship, with respondents accepting the monarchy as a preferable system to totalitarianism. Many saw the crown as a stabilizing force, drawing together narratives of continuity, political evolution, social cohesion and peace at a time of escalating chaos elsewhere. It seems likely that in their beliefs the Mass Observation panel were influenced by the media and politicians who had, with one voice, extolled the virtues of constitutional monarchy as the defender of democracy and liberty in order to cement the crown's position at the heart of the nation and empire; and in order to re-educate subjects of the crown in the meaning of kingship following the turbulence created by the abdication crisis.

137 MOA, CO23.
138 MOA, CL1, CM2, CM10, CO29, CO38, CO41, CL8, CL15, CL22, CL46, CL66, CL101, CL107.

'Everyone likes her much more than the others'

News editors worked in tandem with royal and religious officials to perfect the performance of unity and consensus that played out on 12 May 1937. The BBC and newsreel companies were integral to the projection of the occasion, with it being the first time that radio and film crews were granted access to Westminster abbey to record a coronation service and, in the case of wireless, to broadcast the ceremony live to the nation and the world. Four elements of the coverage were of particular concern to the stage-managers. First, and in keeping with the prevailing emphasis on constitutional evolution, organizers developed a variety of strategies to convey to media audiences the impression that Britain and the empire were unified around the figurehead of the new king. Second, the coronation service was expertly choreographed to emphasize its religiosity and dignity to listeners and viewers. Third, officials worked with the media to project the ceremony in ways that fostered emotional identification between members of the public and George VI. Fourth, and last, the king's broadcast on the evening of his coronation was designed to highlight continuity with his father's reign. Nevertheless, despite the best efforts of courtiers, clergy and loyal media outlets to enhance the public image of the monarch through the careful planning and execution of coronation day, Mass Observation reports suggest that public responses to the event were mixed – with the king a particular cause for concern. Fortunately for him, his mother, Queen Mary, was close at hand to provide a reassuring emotional coherence with the past.

More than any previous royal occasion in Britain, the 1937 coronation was defined by the theme of inclusiveness. The emphasis on national and imperial participation complemented the messages of politicians and reporters on the democratic qualities of constitutional kingship and was exemplified in the way the working classes played a more visible part in the celebrations. The royal household selected four people from industrial communities across the country to attend the coronation as representatives of their class. *Gaumont British News* produced a story on the 'four guests whom the King has specially invited to the Abbey'.[139] After opening scenes of decorations going up along the Mall in central London, the film switched to the contrasting landscape of Bolsover colliery near Chesterfield, where 'pit boy' Leslie Pollard was pictured grinning, having 'been honoured' by an invitation to the ceremony. The newsreel then moved on to the three other guests: first, to a woman in a Glasgow textile factory who had helped to weave the carpet for the coronation service; then to a man based at a steelworks in South Wales who had been one of the first boys to attend

---

[139] 'Coronation Preparations', *Gaumont British News*, 8 Apr. 1937.

the duke of York's camps; and, finally, to a woman in Birmingham who, in an innovative, direct message to cinema viewers, stated how 'very proud and very happy' she was 'to be representing Birmingham and to have been chosen from such a large number of working people'.

The idea communicated through the newsreel – that the king valued all classes of his subjects, including those on the Celtic fringes – was conveyed through the government's allocation of coronation honours, too. On 11 May the *Daily Herald's* front-page headline proclaimed that 'All Classes Honoured in Coronation List'.[140] The accompanying report explained that, as well as famous individuals from 'stage, sport and literature', the honours rolls included 'railmen, clerks, housemaids [and] ship workers' from around the country. The *Herald* was among several newspapers to draw special attention to the fact that two bus men had been awarded the Order of the British Empire as well.[141] Since 1917 George V had bestowed OBEs on ordinary people in recognition of public service to the nation and empire and, as historians have noted, it was the order of chivalry of democracy signalling the crown's realization that, if it was to retain the support of the public and working-class voters in particular, it needed to reach out to them in new ways.[142] At the height of the 1937 London bus strike, the awarding of the OBE to a conductor and a driver could have appeared very calculated, but there was no criticism of this sort in the mainstream press. The propaganda value of the coronation as a socially integrative event did not escape comment entirely, though. Writing for the *Herald*, Lord Ponsonby remarked that he thought the invitation of the four working-class people to the coronation service 'a patronising sop'.[143] One Mass Observation respondent also seems to have discerned something superficial in their inclusion, sarcastically remarking on the way the BBC radio commentator characterized the four as 'honest and obedient' during the ceremony.[144]

The same *Gaumont British* newsreel that filmed the working-class guests ended in a vox-pop interview with an eighty-two-year-old woman from the East End of London. Having presented scenes of local inhabitants decorating a courtyard, the film cut to the woman, who informed viewers

[140] *Daily Herald*, 11 May 1937, p. 1.
[141] *Daily Herald*, 11 May 1937, p. 1; *Daily Mirror*, 11 May 1937, p. 3; *Daily Mail*, 11 May 1937, p. 10; *New Chronicle*, 11 May 1937, p. 8.
[142] D. Cannadine, *The Decline and Fall of the British Aristocracy* (New Haven, Conn., and London, 1990), p. 301; F. Prochaska, 'George V and republicanism, 1917–1919', *Twentieth Century British Hist.*, x (1999), 27–51, at p. 40.
[143] *Daily Herald*, 10 May 1937, p. 10.
[144] MOA, CO3.

that she was the oldest resident there and had seen Queen Victoria's jubilee and Edward VII's and George V's coronations. Placing a party hat on her head, she then told viewers that she hoped to enjoy herself at the new king's coronation with 'knees up mother brown'.[145] The mention of this famous song, with its strong associations with London's working-class drinking culture, helped to characterize the speaker and her neighbourhood. As with the BBC's interview with the 'Cockney woman' at the 1934 royal wedding, this newsreel established a new precedent by interviewing working-class people for the first time, exposing their voices and opinions in order to emphasize the scale of national involvement in a royal event. Thus, the celebration of monarchy again facilitated new (if perfunctory) modes of engagement in public life among the working-class population, witnessing the democratization of the media sphere as part of a nation-building exercise.

The traditional political representatives of the British working classes also played more visible parts in the coronation. The minutes of the committee responsible for planning the occasion show how 'Organised Labour' – consisting of trade unions and members of co-operative and friendly societies – were allocated 10,000 seats along the procession route at a reduced price to enable their delegates to participate in the event.[146] Since the rise of what courtiers had perceived as radical socialism in 1917, the monarchy had worked hard to strengthen its ties to left-wing political groups: again, many of the first recipients of the OBE had been trade-union leaders and Labour MPs as part of a deliberate move intended to counter republican sentiments among these groups.[147] In 1937 the inclusion of 'Organised Labour' can again be interpreted as tactical flattery on the part of officials to ensure that the grass roots organizations that held political influence among the working classes felt represented as part of Britain's royal democracy. Notably, the official emphasis on unity and inclusiveness extended to the empire too, as it was proposed that the Dominions should have 20,000 seats at their disposal, a presence which would help to reinforce the imperial character of the celebrations.[148]

In order to capture the sounds made by the crowds that mustered in London on 12 May, the BBC deployed the same 'atmosphere microphones' that it had used along the processional routes at the 1934 royal wedding and 1935 silver jubilee. The sound equipment was meant to help to immerse listeners in London's coronation festivities, with producers explicitly

---

[145] 'Coronation Preparations', *Gaumont British News*, 8 Apr. 1937.
[146] LPL, Lang 23, fos. 199–200, 'Coronation Joint Committee – Conclusions', 25 Jan. 1937.
[147] Prochaska, 'George V', pp. 40 and 49.
[148] LPL, Lang 23, fo. 200, 'Coronation Joint Committee – Conclusions', 25 Jan. 1937.

instructing commentators to 'let cheering speak for itself whenever possible'.[149] A number of Mass Observation respondents recorded that they, or those around them, were especially moved by the sounds of cheering crowds broadcast by the BBC as part of its coverage.[150] For some listeners, the cheering enhanced their sense of involvement by intensifying their excitement and enabling them to feel part of what they perceived as an important national occasion. One respondent listened to the radio with her mother in Sussex and they agreed that it was the BBC's 'best broadcast yet', conveying the 'scene and colour of the procession' in such a way that they enjoyed 'a bit of the thrill with the crowds'.[151] A woman who listened in from Forest Hill in London similarly described the pull of the noises that came from her radio set: 'I was surprised how much I responded to the atmosphere of the crowd, the cheering, etc. I felt a definite pride and thrill in belonging to the Empire which in ordinary life, with my political bias, is just the opposite of my true feeling ... Yet I felt a definite sense of relief that I could experience this emotion and be in and of the crowd'.[152] In portrayals like this one, the cheering crowds seem to have enlivened the writers' feelings by stimulating in them a heightened awareness of a British-imperial community and a desire to be part of that community. Although the aforementioned female respondents were both self-professed socialists and cynical about the monarchy's allure, when listening to the broadcast they experienced a kind of emotional integration around the focal point of the crown.

National simultaneity – the sharing of time among a people – has played a key role in the creation of modern national identities.[153] In this respect the BBC's coronation broadcast helped to generate a sense of unity between listeners and the events unfolding in central London through its focus on the people who assembled as part of the crowds on the processional route. The broadcaster also achieved this unifying effect through its use of an inclusive language of 'Britishness' to appeal to listeners and through its rolling coverage of the progress of the royal protagonists to and from

[149] BBCWA, R30/443/4, *World-Radio*, 7 May 1937; Schedule for Coronation Broadcast, 8 Apr. 1937, p. 9.
[150] MOA, CO14, CO16, CO23, CO33, CO41, CO43, CL7, CL8, CL11, CL34, CL64, CL101.
[151] MOA, CO16.
[152] MOA, CO41; also quoted in A. Olechnowicz, '"A jealous hatred": royal popularity and social inequality', in Olechnowicz, *The Monarchy and the British Nation*, pp. 280–314, at p. 303.
[153] T. Fujitani, *Splendid Monarchy: Power and Pageantry in Modern Japan* (London, 1996), pp. 28 and 201. See also B. Anderson, *Imagined Communities: Reflections on the Origin and Spread of Nationalism* (London, 1986), pp. 22–36.

Westminster abbey. In the first instance, BBC editorial files reveal that producers carefully selected the commentary team to ensure that English, Scottish, Irish and Welsh voices all contributed to the broadcast.[154] Producers also instructed commentators that they should not 'use "English" when [they] could use "British"' and 'always [to] keep in mind a listener who is of reasonable intelligence, who has no great education and who has never been to London' so that the broadcast would have a wide popular appeal.[155] Second, and for the first time ever, courtiers granted the BBC access to report from the forecourt of Buckingham Palace, which enabled commentators to present an eyewitness account of George VI's movements from the moment he left his London residence to the moment he returned five hours later.[156] Through a sequence of expertly managed 'handovers' between the commentary team, the BBC reported the king's journey through central London's streets right up to his disembarkation from the gold state coach at the doors of the abbey.[157] This early example of rolling media coverage increased the temporal concurrence experienced by radio listeners through the precise mapping of the movements of the royal family.

Royal and religious officials planned the 1937 coronation ceremony as a modern mass media event. This can, in part, be attributed to the influence of Edward VIII, who had wanted his coronation to be projected to the nation and the empire via the new channels of mass communication. The forward-thinking king's reign had witnessed a series of innovations in the relationship between the media and the monarchy – most notably the updating of the so-called 'ancient tradition' whereby a new sovereign addressed a special written message to his or her people. With the death of his father, Edward instead took to the airwaves to speak directly to his subjects in what he termed a 'more personal message'.[158] Similarly, he consented to the broadcasting of his coronation – a decision widely feted by

[154] BBCWA, R30/443/3, various memoranda, including Internal Circulating Memo, 1 March 1937, from S. J. de Lotbinière.
[155] BBCWA, R30/443/4, Schedule for Coronation Broadcast, 8 Apr. 1937, p. 9; BBCWA, R30/443/5, Schedule for Coronation Broadcast, 5 May 1937, p. 12. Newsreels also ensured that the 'British' character of George VI's coronation was conveyed to viewers by presenting them with scenes of the preparations taking place around the UK. The same applied to the BBC and newsreels' exhaustive coverage of the coronation tour of the Celtic fringes after the event ('The Stage is Set 1937', *Pathé Super Sound Gazette*, 10 May 1937).
[156] BBCWA, R30/443/2, S. J. de Lotbinière to Sir Hill-Child, master of the household, 4 Feb. 1937 and reply from Hill-Child to de Lotbinière on 5 Feb. 1937.
[157] BBCWA, R30/443/2, S. J. de Lotbinière to J. Edgar, 16 Jan. 1937; BBCWA, R30/443/4, Schedule for Coronation Broadcast, 8 Apr. 1937; BBCWA, R30/443/5, Schedule for Coronation Broadcast, 5 May 1937.
[158] 'The King's Broadcast', *British Movietone News*, 2 March 1936.

the press at the time – but this meant that when his shy brother unexpectedly succeeded him the new monarch had little choice but to acquiesce to the public's expectations.[159]

Cosmo Lang met with the new monarch ten days after Edward's abdication in order to explain the nature of the coronation ceremony and the role mass media would play in it. The archbishop exercised tight control over the organizations that were granted access to the service and he was particularly concerned with maintaining the dignity of the occasion. The BBC had to assure him that 'there would be no obtrusion of microphones. They would be out of sight'. The broadcaster also planned to position an 'observer' in the abbey's triforium whose job it would be to explain the ceremonial to listeners as it unfolded. The BBC's director of religion, Frederic Iremonger, who was also an honorary chaplain to the king, took on this role. Whereas the corporation had been prevented from broadcasting 'observations' from inside the abbey three years earlier at George and Marina's wedding, Iremonger's inclusion in the ceremony should be understood as an attempt by the BBC to make a complicated service meaningful to listeners through instructive commentary. Lang's only conditions were that he be permitted to vet Iremonger's script, that the director of religion must not be visible to those in the abbey and that 'no sound of his comments would be heard' inside the church walls.[160]

Iremonger was a celebrated figure at the BBC, having improved the quality of its religious output, and he seems to have understood the possibilities created by radio for strengthening listeners' religious feelings.[161] He wrote to Lang six weeks before the coronation to suggest that the 'sound-gap' created when the king and queen took communion as part of the ceremony could lead to problems: '[A] certain spiritual and emotional level will have been reached, which, if it is then lost, may never be recovered by listeners'. Iremonger suggested that the energy created by the broadcast could be sustained if the gap were covered by choral music: 'I am convinced that it would keep the reverent attention of the millions who will be listening all over the world, as nothing else would'.[162] The archbishop thought Iremonger's suggestion a good one and it was arranged for special 'wireless singers' to be accommodated in the music room of Westminster abbey for this purpose.[163]

[159] LPL, Lang 21, fos. 168–9, 'King George VI: Coronation Service', 21 Dec. 1936.
[160] LPL, Lang 21, fos. 209–12, 'Coronation Service: Broadcasting', 13 Jan. 1937.
[161] A. Briggs, *The History of Broadcasting in the United Kingdom* (5 vols. Oxford, 1965–95), ii. 217 and 226–7.
[162] LPL, Lang 22, fos. 38–9, F. A. Iremonger to C. G. Lang, 30 March 1937.
[163] LPL, Lang 22, fos. 41–3, C. G. Lang to F. A. Iremonger, 1 Apr. 1937 and reply 2 Apr. 1937.

For Lang it was imperative that, after the trauma of the abdication, the crowning of George VI should not appear at all shambolic or half-hearted. The archbishop's chaplain, Alexander Sargent, kept a coronation diary, which reveals disorganized rehearsals led by the earl marshal (the duke of Norfolk) and garter king of arms, as well as an increasingly frustrated Lang, who ultimately took charge of the occasion in order to preserve 'the atmosphere of reverence'.[164] One of the archbishop's interventions included instructing the dean of Westminster, William Foxley Norris, that the verbal acclamations shouted by the peers and bishops during the ceremony 'should be more hearty and vigorous than they were at the Rehearsal'. He typed up and distributed a note to the bishops encouraging them to take 'a lead in the Acclamation at the Recognition, after the Crowning, and after the Homage … to secure the greater reality of the Service'.[165] Lang demonstrated a similar awareness of the BBC audience's needs when, during a coronation committee meeting, he argued against a proposal tabled by the earl marshal on behalf of the ever-religious Lucy Baldwin, wife of the prime minister, 'that either at the moment when the Crown is placed on the King's head … or when he leaves the Abbey, the bells of all Churches in the country be rung'. The archbishop responded by pointing out: '[T]he ringing of Church Bells in London would greatly disturb the effective reception on the stands of the broadcast of the Service. Moreover, he knew that in many Cathedrals, Churches and Chapels throughout the United Kingdom people were arranging to assemble to listen to the broadcast service'.[166] Here was an archbishop who understood how radio had transformed the soundscape of the public sphere. He prioritized the use of mass media over more traditional customs in order to stage royal ritual for those listening on London's streets by way of loud speakers and for those who congregated to listen in religious buildings across Britain. Thus, the committee duly agreed not to approve any scheme for the ringing of church bells at the moment of the crowning or on the departure of the king from the abbey.

The international transmission of the broadcast also threw up a number of constitutional issues. Most notably, the high commissioner of Canada, Vincent Massey, had suggested to Lang in August 1936 that the Dominions be given a more prominent function in the coronation ceremony in order to recognize the evolution that had taken place between Britain and the self-governing parts of the empire.[167] In this respect, the broadcast of the service provided a new opportunity to reaffirm the symbolic bonds

---

[164] LPL, MS3208, fos. 209–20, 'The Coronation May 1937'.
[165] LPL, Lang 22, fos. 83–4, C. G. Lang to W. F. Norris, 11 May 1937.
[166] LPL, Lang 23, fo. 202, 'Coronation Joint Committee – Conclusions', 25 Jan. 1937.
[167] LPL, Lang 21, fos. 34–45, 'Coronation and the Dominions' – various memoranda.

between George VI and his subjects overseas. The result was a drawn-out series of meetings between Lang, imperial representatives, the secretary of state for Dominion affairs, Malcolm MacDonald, and constitutional experts, during which they hammered out a compromise acceptable to all the nations involved. After much deliberation (General Hertzog of South Africa proving a particularly difficult person to please) it was agreed that the coronation oath would be updated to include special references to the Dominions.[168] Baldwin's cabinet signed off on the changes and Lang would now invite the king to 'solemnly promise and swear to govern the peoples of Great Britain, Ireland, Canada, Australia, New Zealand and the Union of South Africa, of your Possessions and the other Territories to any of them belonging or pertaining, and of your Empire of India, according to their respective Laws and Customs'.[169] The revised formula of the oath both recognized the different stages of independence achieved by the Dominions and India and met with Lang's approval by ensuring that secular politics were kept at the margins of the service. While a vocal proponent of the monarch's role in imperial affairs, the archbishop impressed upon others the sanctity of the ceremonial and the need to preserve its religiosity by limiting references to the world outside the abbey.[170]

Lang's decision-making was also informed by the knowledge that the coronation was going to be filmed. As with the 1934 royal wedding, the receiver general of Westminster abbey, Sir Edward Knapp-Fisher, and Dean Foxley Norris advised on the suitability and feasibility of the newsreels' proposals. Both men had initially objected to the filming of the ceremony on the grounds that there would be insufficient space for cameramen and their apparatus and Lang agreed that it 'would be inconsistent with the dignity and reverence of the Service'.[171] However, the archbishop changed his mind – probably because he saw great potential in involving in the ceremony a wider British and imperial audience who might have otherwise felt excluded. After all, Lang was strongly of the opinion that the coronation should engender support for George VI among his peoples. The archbishop thus took a leading role in arranging how the newsreel cameramen filmed the ceremony and, in his first meeting with the new king and queen, it was agreed that their anointing and communion would

<hr/>

[168] LPL, Lang 21, fos. 215–20 and 258–60, 'The Form of the Coronation Oath', undated.

[169] LPL, Lang 21, fos. 324–6, 'The Coronation Oath', 10 Feb. 1937.

[170] Lang had initially been extremely reluctant to countenance any change to the coronation service in order to incorporate some reference to the dominions, given that it was a 'religious service not involving constitutional points' (LPL, Lang 21, fos. 34–5, 'Coronation and the Dominions').

[171] LPL, Lang 21, fo. 80, C. G. Lang to W. F. Norris, 7 Oct. 1936.

not be filmed or photographed in order to preserve the religiosity of these moments, but that all other parts of the service would be recorded.[172] Then, acting as intermediary, Lang met with representatives from Britain's newsreel companies including Neville Kearney, who was head of the film industries department, the general manager of *British Movietone News*, Sir Ernest Gordon Craig, and the managing director of *Pathé Gazette*, W. J. Gell (notably, Craig and Gell played key roles in the formation of the first newsreel trade body, the Newsreel Association, in October 1937).[173] The archbishop outlined what could and could not be filmed and stipulated to the newsreel bosses that he and the earl marshal be allowed to vet the newsreel footage before its public release. This was all agreed to and, as we shall see, Lang played an important role in the censoring of the films.

With the media plans in place, the archbishop took a number of final precautions to ensure that nothing untoward happened during the ceremony that might jeopardize either the BBC broadcast or newsreel recordings. Lang helped to arrange for the holy oil to be wiped from George VI's head with a napkin following the anointing, lest he reappear in front of the newsreel cameras with a shining brow.[174] Similarly, care was taken to accommodate the king's concerns about the weight of the crown and his fear that it might 'fall off when he walk[ed]'.[175] Finally, Lang had a small bible hastily bound following a coronation rehearsal during which the septuagenarian bishop of Norwich – who was tasked with carrying the holy book during the procession – struggled to lift the original, much larger volume that had been specially made for the occasion.[176] As high priest of modern royal ceremonial, the archbishop of Canterbury was thus intimately involved in the preparations for the one event that he, like the new king, deemed the most important of his entire life.[177]

*

Lang would have been heartened by some of the comments recorded by Mass Observation respondents about the broadcast of the coronation

---

[172] LPL, Lang 21, fos. 168–9, 'King George VI: Coronation Service', 21 Dec. 1936.

[173] LPL, Lang 22, fos. 60–1, 'Coronation Service: Films'.

[174] LPL, Lang 22, fos. 48–9 and 59, G. W. Wollaston to C. G. Lang, 8 Apr. 1937 and 20 Apr. 1937.

[175] LPL, MS3208, fos. 219–20, 'The Coronation May 1937'.

[176] LPL, Lang 22, fos. 74–6, C. G. Lang to H. Milford, 7 May 1937.

[177] LPL, Lang 223, fos. 234–56, 'Notes on the Coronation of King George VI and Queen Elizabeth'. Lang's notes provide an excellent, if partisan, account of his coronation preparations and his experience presiding over the ceremonial.

service. Several remarked on the dignity with which the ceremony was carried out or the way its sacred character had left a deep impression on them or others. For example, a man from Beer noted the reaction of a builder with whom he had discussed the service: 'It had moved him tremendously. His emotions were stirred by the ancient traditions, the setting, the music (which he was proud to think was all English except the Handel) and the religious connections of it all'.[178] A woman from North Shields who listened in with her parents similarly recorded that 'my interest [in the broadcast] was decidedly quickened as the service proceeded … I found myself surprisingly moved, until I felt I wanted to cry. That certainly surprised me as I am not easily emotionally moved by plays or novels. It might have been the music or the profound solemnity and significance of the service'.[179] One might interpret reports like these to argue that Lang's and other officials' assiduous preparations helped to ensure the sacred meaning of the coronation was communicated to listeners. Those friends and associates who wrote to congratulate the archbishop in the days and weeks after the event were also, perhaps predictably, effusive in their praise. Letters invariably remarked on the way Lang's words as celebrant had conveyed the 'deep significance of the ceremony' and left a 'deep spiritual impression' on listeners.[180] One of the leading scholarly authorities on historic coronations, Leopold G. Wickham Legge, judged that the atmosphere of the 1937 service was 'completely different' to that of Edward VII in 1901 because of its 'religious side' and the way it 'touched' the congregation as well as the unseen participants listening outside the Abbey.[181] Some members of the Mass Observation panel similarly noted the religious dimensions of the ceremony. A twenty-six-year-old woman from Bermondsey, who was a secretary to the London city council's children's care committee, suggested that the ritual had invested the new king with the spiritual power required to fulfil his role: 'The King has a very difficult task to perform. In his own strength he cannot perform it. So, by the anointing he is given special grace, to make use of if he will, just as in the sacraments of Holy Matrimony and Ordination special grace is given for special difficulties'.[182] Notably, this respondent went on to criticize the 'display of wealth in the Abbey'

---

[178] MOA, COI; see also CO36 for similar comments.

[179] MOA, CL56.

[180] LPL, Lang 22, fos. 88–125. See, e.g., letters from the archbishop of York to C. G. Lang, 22 May 1937; M. E. Carnegie to C. G. Lang, 16 May 1937; C. Strathmore to C. G. Lang, 1 June 1937.

[181] LPL, Lang 22, fos. 123–4, L. G. Wickham Legge to C. G. Lang, 31 May 1937. Wickham Legge was notably the editor of *English Coronation Records* (London, 1901).

[182] MOA, CL1.

as 'sickening' and out-of-step with 'the poverty in the distressed areas, and in [her] part of London'. While these negative sentiments reflected the writer's self-professed 'left wing' political views, her report shows how it was possible to identify positively with the sacred character of the king while simultaneously condemning the resplendent qualities of royal ceremonial.

The secretary's personal testimony is significant for a second reason. She was one of the many Mass Observation respondents who alluded in some way to the burdens of kingship. This idea, popularized in the final years of George V's reign, took on fuller form still in the figure of the new monarch. As noted in relation to the contrasting public image of the former king, Edward VIII, George VI was generally perceived by members of the public as weaker and less dynamic than his elder brother. The persistent rumour that circulated in the weeks before the coronation – that the king was ill and physically not up to the job of ruling – seems to have informed how many experienced his crowning. A large section of the Mass Observation panel remarked that the service was an 'ordeal' for its principal actor, that he would be 'tired out' by the experience, or that he might succumb to an 'epileptic fit' before it ended.[183] Sometimes concerns about the fatigue of the monarch extended to his consort, too: a farmer from King's Lynn in Norfolk said to a friend while they listened in together that he 'was sorry for the King and Queen having to go through all that ceremonial'.[184] Meanwhile, an eighteen-year-old woman from the Isle of Man noted that 'several people have said "I'm glad I'm not the King and Queen to have to go through such a ceremony without a break"'.[185] Notably, these reports, which expressed either sympathy or concern for royalty, were supplemented by descriptions from Mass Observation respondents who joined the crowds in London to cheer the gold state coach on its way to the abbey and discerned from the look on its occupant's face that he was 'uneasy' or 'nervous'.[186]

Descriptions of the difficulties faced by George VI echoed Lang's earlier broadcasts on the king's stammer and the need to support him in his burdensome role. Indeed, one wonders to what extent the archbishop consciously publicized the monarch's vulnerability knowing that it would act as a focus for public emotional identification. The media certainly helped to popularize the discourse on the burdens of the coronation. The *Sunday Express* was typical in drawing attention to the way the event would 'Play to a World Audience' with the 'modern inventions' of new mass media

[183] E.g., MOA, CM6, CO3, CO10, CO18, CO22, CO25, CO28, CO32, CL9, CL16, CL34, CL35, CL63, CL65, CL86.
[184] MOA, CO6.
[185] MOA, CL41.
[186] MOA, CL63, CL65, CO32.

'intensify[ing] a thousandfold the strain of the day for the figures around whom the pageantry is massed'. The article notably finished by stating that these were 'the penalties of those set high above their fellow men'.[187] Similarly, during and after the coronation service, the BBC commentators Howard Marshall and Frederic Iremonger presented their listeners with descriptions of a ceremony that was an uninviting and lonely experience for its lead protagonists. As George VI underwent the recognition (in which he was presented by the archbishop to the four corners of the coronation theatre), the BBC's director of religion narrated how 'standing alone he shows himself to the people' and, just before the special 'wireless singers' began singing over the section during which the king and queen took holy communion, Iremonger delivered a short prayer across the airwaves in which he beseeched God to help the royal couple stay strong 'as they spend their lives for their people'.[188] Then, once the ceremony had ended, Marshall's concluding words augmented the vulnerable public image of George VI when he described the unique 'loneliness that surrounds a king'.[189] In this vein, the *Daily Mirror* leader published the day after the coronation sustained the emphasis on the burdened monarch when it stressed that he had 'anxieties to face and delicate tasks to perform' and deserved 'all our sympathy'. Then, invoking the title of a song that had been played at the coronation, the *Mirror* hinted at both the king's suspected frailty and the public desire for robust leadership that had emerged in the crisis years of the late 1930s when it exhorted him to 'be strong and play the man!'.[190]

The disquiet expressed about the new king's physical vulnerability and inability to carry out his public role runs counter to other historical interpretations that have suggested he embodied a 'normative masculinity' rooted in physical strength and endurance in these years.[191] However, what is clear is that the predominant emotion recorded by the Mass Observation panel for the king on coronation day was sympathy and, taken together with the anxiety about his abilities, these feelings can be read as evidence of the impact of the messages peddled by the media and officials like Lang regarding his personal difficulties.[192] This type of emotion also seems

---

[187] *Sunday Express*, 9 May 1937, p. 9. For comparable coverage, see *The Sunday Times*, 16 May 1937, p. 9.

[188] BBCWA, R30/443/5, Extract from Commentary in Westminster Abbey by Howard Marshall and Commentary on the Coronation Service by Rev. F. A. Iremonger. See also <https://www.youtube.com/watch?v=cIzqrMfUzwo> [accessed 4 June 2018].

[189] H. Marshall, 'In the Abbey', *The Listener*, xvii, 19 May 1937, pp. 958 and 970.

[190] *Daily Mirror*, 13 May 1937, p. 15.

[191] I. Zweiniger-Bargielowska, 'Keep fit and play the game: George VI, outdoor recreation and social cohesion in interwar Britain', *Cult. and Soc. Hist.*, xi (2014), 111–29, at p. 113.

[192] See also Olechnowicz, '"Jealous hatred"', p. 306; D. Pocock, 'Afterword', in Jennings et

to have been specific to the large-scale royal events of the mid 1930s: in its length and elaborate ceremonial the coronation set a new precedent in terms of the pressure it exerted on its protagonist to perform as part of a mass-mediated spectacle. The image of the king who suffered under the weight of his responsibilities thus took on literal form in the figure of George VI as part of an ostensibly torturous coronation service that evoked from media audiences powerful affective responses. It is significant that the archbishop and royal household denied the BBC permission to record and transmit the ceremony live to viewers via television, knowing full well that the new medium was in its infancy and would only place added stress on the monarch.[193] Instead, the BBC's television crews were instructed that they could record sections of the procession outside the abbey and, for the first time ever, a small number of 'tele-viewers' – approximately 10,000 in London and its surrounding regions – were able to participate in a royal event through television screens.

According to Mass Observation reports, George VI's speech to Britain and the empire on the evening of the coronation met with a mixed response as well, although expressions of sympathy and uncertainty again predominated. The broadcast was forced on the new monarch because of another promise made by his elder brother while he was still on the throne.[194] Files from the Royal Archives reveal that the new king undertook secret intensive rehearsals with the help of BBC technicians and his speech therapist, Lionel Logue.[195] These files also show that concerns about George VI's ability to deliver the message were not confined to Logue and the monarch, but shared by courtiers and the BBC's John Reith. Nevertheless, in helping the king to prepare for the broadcast, the director-general proved himself as much the expert high priest of royal public relations as Cosmo Lang. For example, Reith arranged for BBC engineers to prepare a raised platform from which the monarch could speak into the microphone while standing: he preferred not to sit when delivering messages.[196] This new set-up was, of course, kept a closely guarded secret from the public lest it become another cause for concern and, in fact, the BBC's controller of public

---

al., *May the Twelfth*, pp. 415–23, at pp. 422–3.

[193] LPL, Lang 21, fos. 202 and 211, Earl Marshall to C. G. Lang, 11 Jan. 1937; 'Coronation Service: Television'. See also J. Moran, *Armchair Nation: an Intimate History of Britain in Front of the TV* (London, 2013), pp. 36–7.

[194] RA, PS/PSO/GVI/PS/COR/1000/6, A. Hardinge to J. Reith, 21 Dec. 1936.

[195] RA, PS/PSO/GVI/PS/COR/1000/8, 12 and 42, J. Reith to A. Hardinge, 30 Apr. 1937; L. Logue to J. Reith, 8 May 1937; J. Reith to C. Wigram, 25 Feb. 1937.

[196] RA, PS/PSO/GVI/PS/COR/1000/7, J. Reith to A. Hardinge, 27 Apr. 1937 and 30 Apr. 1937.

relations, Stephen Tallents, arranged for George VI to be photographed *sat* at his desk in front of a microphone in February in a pose similar to that adopted by his father when he had been photographed 'at the mic' three years previously.[197] This was to be the official photograph for the coronation speech and, while the scene differed from the reality, it provided a reassuring image of continuity with the reign of George V and was sent to newspapers across Britain and the empire in advance of the event so that they could publish it the morning after the king's broadcast.[198]

The chicanery did not stop there. Reith arranged for a pre-recording of George VI's speech to be made from the rehearsal sessions which would be broadcast via the BBC's Empire Service throughout the night of 12 May and morning of 13 May in the event that the recording of the *actual* version turned out to be poor quality because of the monarch's stammer. Reith suggested that the pre-recording could be 'cut' to create a 'perfect whole' with all 'blemishes' and 'hesitations' edited out.[199] Logue saw no harm in a 'composite record' being created 'just in case of accidents, loss of voice, etc' and it was agreed that once the composite was made all other recordings from the rehearsals would be 'destroyed' to ensure there was 'no chance of leakage' – the implication being that some unscrupulous journalist might get hold of a recording and reveal to the world the extent of the king's impediment.[200]

As with many royal speeches from these years, it is difficult to identify exactly who wrote the king's coronation broadcast, although files in the Royal Archives point to poet laureate John Masefield, who was a friend of George VI.[201] We might conjecture that Lang was too busy with his own coronation preparations to commit to the project and that Masefield, who also wrote the opening prayer for the official souvenir programme

[197] RA, PS/PSO/GVI/PS/COR/1000/36–7, S. Tallents to A. Lascelles, 9 Feb. 1937 and reply on 18 Feb. 1937.
[198] RA, PS/PSO/GVI/PS/COR/1000/45–50, various letters between S. Tallents and A. Lascelles, 4 March – 7 Apr. 1937.
[199] RA, PS/PSO/GVI/PS/COR/1000/8 and 10, J. Reith to A. Hardinge, 30 Apr. 1937 and 7 May 1937.
[200] RA, PS/PSO/GVI/PS/COR/1000/11, L. Logue to J. Reith, 8 May 1937; RA, PS/PSO/ GVI/PS/COR/1000/12, J. Reith to M. L. Alcock, 10 May 1937.
[201] RA, PS/PSO/GVI/PS/COR/1000/16–29, 'Poet Laureate's draft of the broadcast'. Under current restrictions imposed by the Royal Archives, the draft and accompanying correspondence have been removed from this file, although the index on its front cover indicates that this is the correct reference for these documents. As P. Williamson has noted, original authors of royal speeches 'observed a protocol of confidentiality and the Royal Archives preserve the convention that the words of royal persons are their own' (Williamson, 'Monarchy and public values', p. 228, n. 16).

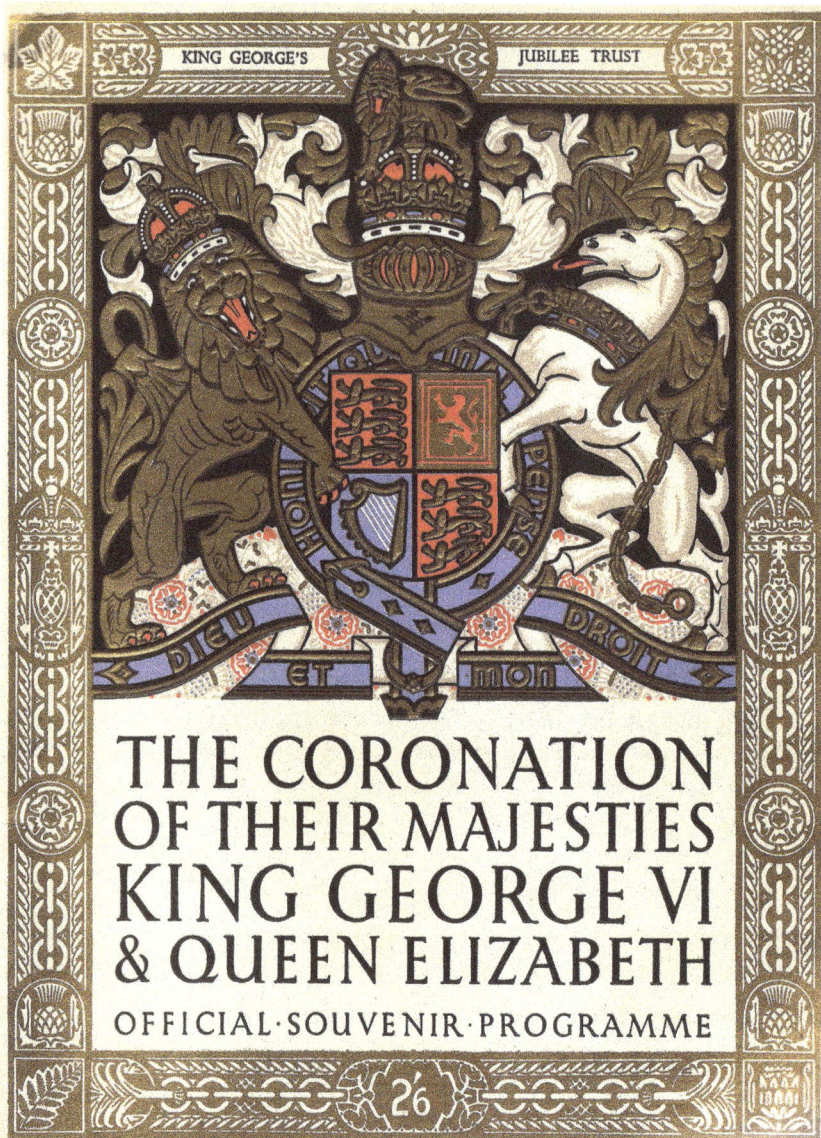

Figure 3.5. King George's Jubilee Trust, *The Coronation of Their Majesties King George VI & Queen Elizabeth: Official Souvenir Programme* (London, 1937).

published to commemorate the 1937 coronation, was deemed a fitting substitute, given that he was well-versed in the royal public language of the period.[202] It is worth briefly noting that this was the first time an official souvenir had been published to celebrate the crowning of a British sovereign (Figure 3.5). In 1935 the palace instituted a new administrative organization – King George's Jubilee Trust – set up in part to control the funding of royal charities.[203] Another key role of the trust was the preparation and publication of souvenirs, the first being produced to commemorate George V's silver jubilee.[204] The souvenirs from the 1930s and 1940s contained the same set of messages associated with the royal speeches of these years, with an emphasis on the duty and burdens of kingship, the sacrifice made by the sovereign in serving his peoples, the religiosity of the family monarchy and the strength and unity of nation and empire. In this respect we should view King George's Jubilee Trust as the new propaganda arm of the royal household, tasked with promoting royal democratic ideology to help to crystallize the meanings associated with the crown at a time of great change.

Like the broadcasts delivered by his father, George VI's coronation message was preceded by a special programme of salutations from imperial representatives, titled 'The Empire's Homage', which again symbolized the unity of Britain and the empire.[205] Then, after an extended silence, during which listeners heard some muffled whispering, the monarch began his speech with a recognizably intimate greeting: 'It is with a very full heart that I speak to you tonight. Never before has a newly-crowned King been able to talk to all his peoples in their own homes on the day of his Coronation'. George VI delivered the speech in a slow-paced monotone that was occasionally interrupted by his pausing to take breath, but it contained all the hallmarks of the royal public language that had been refined by courtiers, the archbishop of Canterbury and other writers over the previous five years. He spoke of the strength and progress of the British Commonwealth, delivered a personal greeting to those subjects 'living under the shadow of sickness or distress', expressed gratitude to listeners 'for

---

[202] King George's Jubilee Trust, *The Coronation of Their Majesties King George VI & Queen Elizabeth: Official Souvenir Programme* (London, 1937), p. 2.

[203] I. Zweiniger-Bargielowska, 'Royal death and living memorials: the funerals and commemoration of George V and George VI, *Hist. Research*, lxxxix (2015), 158–75, at pp. 168–71.

[204] King George's Jubilee Trust, *Official Programme of the Jubilee Procession* (London, 1935).

[205] RA, PS/PSO/GVI/PS/COR/1000/56, 'Synopsis of The Empire's Homage'. Again, the BBC's emphasis was on ordinary, 'representative' people's voices such as those belonging to 'a farmer, fisherman, miner'. The synopsis included the observation that 'the unofficial speakers are designed to strike a more intimate note, symbolising the unity and common humanity of the Empire on Coronation Day'.

your love and loyalty to the queen and myself', reaffirmed his dedication to serve his people and emphasized the 'grave and constant responsibility' of kingship. Then, to finish, he optimistically remarked on the important role that the empire would play in maintaining peace and drew the broadcast to a close with a familiar sign off: 'I thank you from my heart, and may God bless you all'.[206]

The media coverage of the speech was very positive, with the press publicizing a vision of the king sat at his desk speaking candidly to his peoples just as his father had done before him.[207] Mass Observation reveals a more complex public response, though. A teenager from Chelsea 'felt sorry for the man, and vaguely uncomfortable; I sat there on tenterhooks, expecting him to stutter or dry up at any minute. It moved so hesitatingly and slowly'.[208] A young man from Ilkley in Yorkshire logged similar comments that he overheard while walking home: '[W]ell he got through pretty well' and 'I was glad when he finished. It made me nervous'.[209] The discomfort some people seem to have experienced while listening to the king's speech meant that they noted a sense of relief once he 'got through it'.[210] Occasionally, the Mass Observation panel recorded more encouraging appraisals of the broadcast – although these were in the minority. For example, a speech therapist from Swansea enquired of her mother's charwoman what she had thought of the message and the older woman replied:

> "[The king] thank[ed] everyone for their kindness to him and the Queen … [He said] that he'd do his best for everyone." This was followed by a reference to the fact that he did not stutter but that he stopped periodically. "You know you'd think he'd finished and then he'd go on again … he couldn't pronounce his 'R's". She reported that several people had commented on it to her as very noticeable. She remarked however that in view of the strain of the day etc "He did very well".[211]

The sympathetic tone of the charwoman's account reveals the difficulty people had in putting forward a positive interpretation of the king's abilities. It was 'only in view of the strain of the day' that he 'did very well'. It is also clear that many who listened to George VI's broadcast were preoccupied

---

[206] Quoted in *The Times*, 13 May 1937, p. 16. For a press reference to the whispering see *News Chronicle*, 13 May 1937, p. 2.

[207] *Daily Mail*, 13 May 1937, pp. 9–10; *Daily Herald*, 13 May 1937, p. 3; *Daily Express*, 13 May 1937, p. 3; *News Chronicle*, 13 May 1937, p. 2.

[208] MOA, CO23; also CO22, CL24, CL56, CL61, CL64.

[209] MOA, CO3.

[210] See also MOA, CL1, CL35, CL107.

[211] MOA, CO28. For an almost identical response see CO32.

with the fact he managed successfully to deliver his speech, rather than concentrating on the meaning of the words he had spoken. In this respect the charwoman was unusual for noting that the king had pledged to 'do his best' in the service of his peoples.[212]

Mass Observation respondents who attended cinemas on the evening of the coronation to listen to the king's message sometimes recorded more positive experiences. One schoolmaster from west London who accompanied his family to a cinema in Hammersmith documented the fact that 'the lights lowered discriminately, and created an atmosphere of intimacy. Everyone listened intently. At the end, we stood as the National Anthem came through, being played and sung, a little too lengthily. Then the film programme was resumed'.[213] Other respondents also recorded that fellow cinema audience members listened with interest to George VI's speech.[214] The comments of the schoolmaster may help to explain the more attentive reactions in cinemas: the lights in the Hammersmith cinema were dimmed to conjure a sense of immersion and to direct the audience's attention to the aural focal point of George VI's voice. Equally, though, the silent social etiquette of cinemas and the need to behave publicly in a way that was deemed respectful of royalty seem to have combined with the spatial arrangement of auditoria to achieve a momentary unifying effect. This contrasted sharply with the experiences recorded by those who spent coronation day in other communal environments, like pubs and cafés, where other forms of social behaviour were permitted and where the attention of those present was not spatially directed towards the king's voice. They often noted that the people around them were apathetic to the events unfolding in central London: the coronation broadcast played as 'background noise' and most people paid little or no attention to the radio, engaging in regular conversation instead.[215] These accounts were also notable for descriptions of half-hearted attempts to join in with the radio coverage of the national anthem, with several respondents recording that they or those around them felt coerced into singing 'the king' (as it was also known) by minorities of stalwart patriots.[216]

---

[212] Listeners' preoccupation with George's pronunciation is reflected in various comments from the MO reports and probably accounts for the absence of any real recorded appreciation of what he had said, aside from the charwoman's recollection that he would 'do his best for everyone'. For comments on the king's voice and diction, see MOA, CO14, CO20, CO22, CO24, CO25, CO32, CL8, CL107.

[213] MOA, CO17.

[214] MOA, CM11, CO15, CO19a, CO22, CL42, CL47, CL65, CL100, CL107.

[215] MOA, CO4, CO18, CO29, CO31, CO35, CO44, CL1, CL100.

[216] MOA, CO32, CO35, CO18, CO27, CL16.

Occasionally, the Mass Observation panel noted comments which conveyed that those who listened detected a similarity between the king's voice and that of George V. One striking comment was that George VI's voice sounded 'homely, like his father's'.[217] However, in light of the other expressions of anxiety that the new monarch's speech induced in respondents and those around them, it seems likely that these optimistic reviews stemmed either from the tone of language that characterized the message or from wishful thinking and a longing to prove the media's likening of son to father true. On comparing the kings' manner of radio address, it is immediately evident that George VI sounded very different to his father: while the new sovereign spoke with the same upper-class accent as George V, he delivered his coronation broadcast in a slow and disjointed manner which lacked the measured emotional expression of his father's messages.[218]

*

There was one constant that connected the abdication of Edward VIII to the coronation of his brother George VI half a year later: the sorrowful figure of the kings' mother, Queen Mary. Since the death of her husband, the old queen's emotions had been carefully publicized in order to evoke public sympathy for her and support for the House of Windsor more generally. Lang was the architect of the queen's 'Message to the Nation and Empire', which was released by the palace and published by the press after George V's funeral. Bearing all the usual hallmarks of the archbishop of Canterbury's hand, the queen expressed her 'deepest gratitude' from 'my heart' for the compassion shown to her by her subjects and remarked that she and they 'shared' a 'personal sorrow'. She then reinforced the empathetic bond that linked her to her audience with reference to her grief and the importance of the public's support: 'God bless you, my dear people, for all the wonderful love and sympathy with which you have sustained me'.[219]

Queen Mary had remained more remote from public life than her husband, but this message after his death brought her into a closer personal relationship with British subjects. Scholars have tended to present the queen as an aloof and imperious relic of the Victorian period: old-

---

[217] MOA, CO36; also CO44, CL12, CL19, CL107.

[218] See ch. 2 and 'Radio broadcast of the Coronation of King George VI & His Majesty's Coronation Speech – 12 May 1937' <https://www.youtube.com/watch?v=CCGe_ClJqmA> [accessed 4 Feb. 2018].

[219] LPL, Lang 192, fos. 352–3 and Lang 223, fo. 233, 'The Death of King George V, 1936'. See also *Daily Mirror*, 30 Jan. 1936, p. 1; *Daily Express*, 30 Jan. 1936, p. 1.

fashioned and possessing highly conservative opinions.[220] However, while she certainly embodied the monarchy's past, she was also a potent symbol of its present and future and provided a strong physical and emotional link between the figures of her husband and the new king. As consort to George V, Queen Mary had played a visible, caring role on royal tours of industrial communities in the years before, during and after the First World War.[221] Equally, her husband's broadcasts had positioned her as an important focal point for popular emotional identification.[222] It is, therefore, somewhat unsurprising that, while public displays of affection and loyalty for George VI were muted, Queen Mary's presence elicited genuine enthusiasm among the public on coronation day.

Significantly, we should also attribute the adulation that Queen Mary met with on 12 May 1937 to an astute public relations campaign on the part of the royal household, the media and the old queen herself following the dramatic events of December 1936. The experiment of an official proclamation that illuminated the queen dowager's emotions was repeated twice more, the first of these occasions coming the morning after Edward delivered his abdication broadcast. On their front pages, under headlines that drew attention to the 'Distress That Fills A Mother's Heart', the press reproduced another message from Queen Mary that was again addressed 'to the People of the Nation and the Empire'.[223] She described once more the 'great sorrow' that had overwhelmed her after the death of her husband and how 'the sympathy and affection' that had 'sustained [her]' then were 'once again [her] strength and stay'. She told of 'the distress' that filled 'a mother's heart' because of her eldest son's abdication and then commended to readers George VI – 'summoned so unexpectedly and in circumstances so painful'. Queen Mary then commended the new queen consort, too, before

---

[220] Pimlott, *Elizabeth II*, pp. 25 and 192; J. Gardiner, *The Thirties: an Intimate History* (London, 2011), pp. 458 and 527; J. Pope-Hennessy, *Queen Mary, 1867–1953* (London, 1959), pp. 467–9. Queen Mary had kept a careful distance from over-familiar forms of public interaction. Her voice had only twice been recorded: the first time was as part of an HMV gramophone recording that she and George V made to celebrate Empire Day in 1923 <https://www.youtube.com/watch?v=3JyC6qw2D_s> [accessed 4 June 2018]. The second time was on film at the launch of the HMS Queen Mary in September 1934. She had also turned down the opportunity to deliver a radio message to the nation in the early 1930s, having been personally beseeched to do so by members of the public and the BBC (BBCWA, R34/862/1; *Daily Mail*, 10 October 1934, p. 14; 'Movietone Presents the Launch of the "Queen Mary"', *British Movietone News*, 24 Sept. 1934).

[221] F. Prochaska, *Royal Bounty: the Making of a Welfare Monarchy* (New Haven, Conn., 1995), pp. 174–5, 183–91.

[222] See ch. 2.

[223] *Daily Mirror*, 12 Dec. 1936, p. 1; *Daily Express*, 12 Dec. 1936, p. 1; *Daily Mail*, 12 Dec. 1936, p. 9; *Daily Telegraph*, 12 Dec. 1936, p. 15.

commenting that the public had 'already taken her children (Princesses Elizabeth and Margaret Rose) to [their] hearts'. The message augmented a loud chorus of voices in the media that had focused on the pain suffered by Queen Mary in 1936.[224] Moreover, these reports appear to have had some impact on the public, with one of the many readers' letters addressed to the *Daily Mirror* in the days after the abdication including the words, '[L]et us offer our sympathy to our beloved Queen Mary, whose burdens during the past year have been heavy indeed'.[225]

The second intervention relating to Queen Mary's emotions came from her youngest son, the duke of Kent, the day before the coronation. Addressing an audience at the service of intercession for George VI and his consort at Queen's hall in London, the duke declared that 'many will be thinking of the King and Queen but they will also be thinking of my mother. As a boy I can remember the Coronation of my father. She will have deeper and more personal memories of that day'. The duke's comments invoked visions of Queen Mary's own coronation in 1911 as well as the grief and anguish she had suffered over the past eighteen months. Newspapers subsequently acclaimed the duke's words as 'deeply moving' and highlighted to readers that he had asked those gathered at Queen's hall to 'think of my mother'.[226]

Thus, the palace and media's promotion of Queen Mary's popular image prior to 12 May helped to prepare members of the public to identify with her on coronation day. She represented the tangible link between George V and her second son; and her embodiment of continuity was also conveyed in press reports that linked her to her granddaughters. On 6 May she made what the *Mirror* referred to as a 'surprise visit' to Westminster abbey 'to watch coronation rehearsals in which Princess Elizabeth and Princess Margaret took part'. The report claimed that 2,000 spectators had cheered her arrival and that 'memories of her own coronation twenty-six years ago must have crowded upon [her]' during the rehearsal.[227] The queen's grandmotherly persona also drew attention to the permanence of monarchy through generational family ties and was integral to the palace's planning of the coronation procession, in which she rode alongside the two young princesses on the return leg to Buckingham Palace after their father's crowning. The media presented this as a special journey: the *Sunday Express* told readers that 'the luckiest moment of all was enjoyed by just a few hundred people in Northumberland Avenue' when there was a brief pause

[224] *Daily Mirror*, 11 Dec. 1936, p. 13.
[225] *Daily Mirror*, 12 Dec. 1936, p. 13.
[226] *Daily Sketch*, 12 May 1937, pp. 6–7; *News Chronicle*, 12 May 1937, p. 7; *Manchester Guardian*, 12 May 1937, p. 5; *Daily Mail*, 12 May 1937, p. 6.
[227] *Daily Mirror*, 7 May 1937, pp. 5 and 18; *Daily Mail*, 7 May 1937, p. 8.

and the carriage that carried Queen Mary and the princesses came to a standstill: '[F]or a minute or two it was clear they became just grandmother and grandchildren'.[228] The newspaper amplified the scene of domestic normality when it noted how 'little Margaret Rose – "just like your child or mine" – could not resist giving way to her excitement and fidgeting'.

It was also revealed to the public that Queen Mary had succumbed to tears during the coronation ceremony. A *British Movietone News* cameraman had captured scenes of her weeping in his footage inside the Abbey. On the strict instructions of Lang and the earl marshal, who oversaw the censorship of the film, these scenes were suppressed from the final edit, with the archbishop claiming they 'intruded upon [the queen's] most natural emotions'.[229] Nevertheless, journalists learnt about the incident and reported that Queen Mary had cried during the service, which possibly helped to generate sympathy for her among Mass Observation respondents who wrote about the coronation.[230] In fact, the old queen's presence at the coronation broke with royal protocol: as dowager queen (queen mother) she was not, according to tradition, meant to attend the crowning ceremony of her husband's successor. However, her biographer has suggested that she decided to break with convention and attend in order to increase the 'sense of solidarity with which the whole Royal Family was facing the new reign'.[231] It proved a shrewd modification to the programme because Mass Observation personal testimonies reveal that she was by far the most positively commented-on member of the House of Windsor to partake in the event. Notably, the new queen consort, Elizabeth, and her children were the recipients of far fewer positive comments.[232]

The unique enthusiasm that greeted Queen Mary on 12 May deserves closer historical attention. In the first instance, the response of the crowds gathered on the processional route was exceptional. A nurse and self-professed royalist from London recorded the crowd's jubilant acknowledgement of the old queen:

[228] *Sunday Express*, 16 May 1937, p. 6.
[229] LPL/Lang 218, fo. 255, 'Notes on the Coronation of King George VI and Queen Elizabeth'.
[230] *Daily Express*, 13 May 1937, pp. 1–2; *Daily Herald*, 14 May 1937, p. 1; *Daily Mail*, 13 May 1937, p. 6; *News Chronicle*, 13 May 1937, p. 5.
[231] Pope-Hennessy, *Queen Mary*, p. 584.
[232] As with George VI, there were just a few positive comments recorded about his consort, Queen Elizabeth, in the Mass Observation reports (MOA, CM6, CO32, CO36, CL25, CL40). Indeed, the new queen met with as much hostility as praise (CM3, CM4, CO27, CO30, CL8). The MO respondents recorded no criticism of either Princesses Elizabeth or Margaret. When mentioned, they were described using words such as 'sweet', 'well trained' and 'excited' (MOA, CM2, CM3, CM12, CO28, CO32, CL73).

There was a sudden stir of excitement and the Procession began. Shaving mirrors, hand mirrors small and large were held high and Periscopes appeared miraculously. I held on to mine and with its aid I saw everything quite plainly. Princess Margaret Rose looked very much a little princess from a storybook, I thought, and the Queen looked really charming. There was a real genuine excitement and feeling when our beloved Queen Mary passed through, also for Princess Marina and the Duke of Kent.[233]

As well as illuminating the high esteem in which Prince George and Princess Marina were popularly held, the nurse implied that the public shared a strong emotional bond with 'our beloved Queen Mary', noting that she was welcomed with 'real genuine' enthusiasm by the crowds. Other respondents similarly reported the unusual warmth of the greeting extended to the old queen. A female typist noted that she encountered a 'lift girl' who had spectated from the procession route and who told her, 'I think [Queen Mary] got most cheers of all, everyone likes her much more than the others'.[234] Some respondents who tuned in to listen to the coronation broadcast later recalled that they were deeply moved when they learnt that the old queen had appeared as part of the parade. A woman in her thirties from Forest Hill, London, wrote that her eyes had filled with tears as she heard the crowds, 'especially when Queen Mary appeared on the scene'. She then explained her reaction: 'I saw her recently quite close-to, and was rather repelled. She seemed just a disagreeable old lady, very bad on her feet. Nevertheless, as Queen Mother, with her children and grandchildren around her, her regal bearing, and some sort of "see-it-through" air about her, she moves me'.[235] The emphasis the respondent placed on Queen Mary's ordinary qualities, along with her motherly and grandmotherly image, reveals the impact the media's generational family-centred narrative had had on members of the public: she was the matriarchal head of the dynasty who had suffered great personal loss. In this vein, a teenage boy was overhead by one Mass Observation respondent telling his friends that 'Queen Mary is the nicest of the lot. She's had so many sorrows to bear'.[236]

Taken together, these comments indicate that Queen Mary's family-centred image engendered public support for her. Notably, other respondents suggested that her matriarchal presence bequeathed authority on the new king. One woman from Olton in Warwickshire, who listened to the coronation broadcast with her mother, recorded that, at the climactic

[233] MOA, CL25.
[234] MOA, CO33; also CO9, CL1, CL2, CL41, CL61, CL73.
[235] MOA, CO41.
[236] MOA, CO32; also CO33 and CO36.

balcony appearance at the end of the day, 'the crowd cheered when Queen Mary seemed to "present" the Royal Family to the people'.[237] This respondent invested this moment with ritualized significance: it was through the old queen's assent and 'presentation' that legitimacy was conferred on George VI and his family. Indeed, the BBC staged this moment as a crucial act of recognition between the new royal family and the assembled multitudes in order to convey a reassuring image to audience members. A number of the Mass Observation panel noted that they had listened eagerly as the large crowds that gathered outside the palace called for the king to appear on the balcony.[238] Some respondents stated they had worried that George VI would not appear at all and were overcome with a sense of relief when he and his family finally did walk out onto the balcony.[239] The sound of cheering with which the king met as he stood looking out across the thousands of faces that had massed outside the gates of his home was designed to act as an audible chorus of assent to his rule. The final scripted words of the BBC's broadcast stressed the importance of the balcony scene as an act of recognition between monarch and subjects: '[T]he long windows have been closed and still the crowd is cheering. We'll let those cheers be the last thing you hear as we leave Buckingham Palace, at the end of the Coronation ceremonies'. After these closing words the volume of the cheering was raised for fifteen seconds, after which the programme faded to silence.[240] This moment was thus stage-managed by the BBC to symbolically install the king and his family at the centre of society through what sounded like popular support.[241]

Newsreel and press photographers also presented the royal balcony appearance as the climax of the coronation celebrations. As with the visual images of the balcony set-piece after the 1934 royal wedding, editors of both media intentionally juxtaposed images of 'the masses' alongside scenes of the royal party waving from the balcony, with Queen Mary at the centre of the group, in order to create a visual dialogue in gesture between the royal family and their people (Figure 3.6).[242] One Mass Observation respondent

[237] MOA, CO14.

[238] MOA, CO14, CO16, CO33, CL15, CL34, CL40, CL56.

[239] MOA, CL56.

[240] BBCWA, R30/443/5, Schedule for Coronation Broadcast, 5 May 1937, p. 10.

[241] The BBC's expertly crafted choreography was comparable to the auditory political propaganda developed in fascist Germany and Italy in this period (C. Birdsall, *Nazi Soundscapes: Sound, Technology and Urban Space in Germany, 1933–1945* (Amsterdam, 2012); D. Thompson, *State Control in Fascist Italy: Culture and Conformity, 1925–43* (Manchester, 1991)).

[242] E.g., *Daily Mail*, 13 May 1934, p. 24; 'Pathé Gazette Has the Honour to Present the Coronation of Their Majesties King George VI and Queen Elizabeth', *Pathé Super Sound*

Figure 3.6. A balcony photograph with Queen Mary encouraging her granddaughters to wave to the crowds gathered below. Fox Photos © Getty Images .

journeyed into London on coronation evening to stand with the throng of people waiting expectantly at the palace gates for the royal family to reappear. The respondent described the very loud reception with which George VI met when he emerged, as well as the 'amazing way [that] the moment the King put up his hand in recognition of the applause the shouting suddenly became twice as enthusiastic and loud'.[243] This excerpt is testament to the power of the innovative gesture of the wave that Princess Marina had introduced just three years before in generating public enthusiasm for royalty. Most newspapers also chose to publish the picture of the five family members on the balcony, with the *Daily Express* and *Sketch* presenting it as a large front-page image.[244] This photograph was the central visual icon following weeks of coverage that had amplified the narrative of continuity through the figure of the old queen and her second son. Not only did she represent the permanence and tradition of monarchy – values briefly threatened by Edward VIII's reign – but also, as matriarch of the House of

---

Gazette, 13 May 1937.

[243] MOA, CL30.

[244] *Daily Express*, 13 May 1937, p. 1; *Daily Sketch*, 13 May 1937, p. 1; *Daily Herald*, 13 May 1937, p. 11; *Daily Mail*, 13 May 1937, p. 3; *The Times*, 13 May 1937, p. 25.

Windsor, she exemplified the idea that the essence of British kingship lay in a familiar domesticity performed by recognizable royal celebrities.

Conclusion

This chapter has shown that members of the public expressed concerns about the leadership qualities of George VI at the time of his coronation. These anxieties not only related to the sense of loss felt by some after Edward VIII's abdication but also reflected a deeper disquiet about the new king's ability to lead the nation at a time when many people desired a dynamic figure as their head of state to rival the dictators in Europe. Despite the best efforts of officials and journalists to refashion George VI's public image so that it mirrored that of his father, concerns persisted because he could neither emulate the worldly, comforting persona of George V nor embody the masculine vigour and charisma of his brother, whose romantic ambitions continued to be celebrated by vocal sections of the British press to the real consternation of palace courtiers and Cosmo Lang. Indeed, the new monarch's less dynamic personality led members of the public to channel their emotions instead towards the forlorn figure of his mother, who provided a reassuring link with the past on coronation day; and witnessed politicians and news editors on all sides of the political spectrum celebrating the king's crowning as an event that symbolized Britain and the empire's unity and constitutional evolution. The image of unity was sustained through the media's choreography of coronation day and the narrative of a nation comprising all classes and political groups uniquely joined around the House of Windsor. While this version of events distracted from the fissures created by the abdication crisis and ongoing tensions within imperial politics, it does seem to have appealed to sections of the population who internalized the messages on the vitality of British democracy and the strength of the empire, especially given the growing fears about the strong emotional appeals of fascism on the Continent.

Concerns about the new king's character notably persisted after the coronation. Mass Observation reports reveal that George VI's first Christmas broadcast in December 1937 met with mixed reactions from listeners, with a majority of respondents again focusing on his stammer rather than the meaning of the words he actually said.[245] As we shall see in the next chapter, the monarch never managed completely to rid himself of the public belief that he lacked the physicality or strength of character to lead Britain and the empire against the forces of Nazism. Nevertheless, it was partly because of this lack of vigour that the king's public image came to be defined by

---

[245] M. Johnes, *Christmas and the British: a Modern History* (London, 2016), pp. 158–9.

a new tension that has remained at the heart of the House of Windsor's public relations strategy ever since his accession. George VI's coronation demonstrated on an unprecedented scale the new kinds of pressure exerted on royal persons by modern mass media. To some extent this perception was promoted by the archbishop of Canterbury, who regularly emphasized to the public the difficulties the king and queen faced. As has also been shown here, alongside the public anxieties expressed about the new king's leadership was a sympathy for him which sprung from the way his royal duty demanded that he face up to his new position despite his own misgivings and physical inadequacies. This tension – in which the imposition of duty worked against a royal individual's private desires – was, of course, the stimulus behind Edward VIII's abdication. But, more significantly, it was embodied by George VI and, although it had first been articulated by his father in his broadcasts, the public language on the burdens of royal service became increasingly central to the crown's media strategy after 1937 and generated support for the ostensibly beleaguered figure of the new king.

As the journalist Kingsley Martin noted in the aftermath of the coronation, emotional sympathy could translate into admiration for the dutiful qualities of the monarch. In making this point, he quoted a 'north-countryman' to whom he had spoken: 'If it had been Edward the nation would have gone mad. As it is, we would still prefer to cheer Edward, but we know that we've got to cheer George. After all, it's Edward's fault he's not on the throne, and George didn't ask to get there. He's only doing his duty, and it's up to us to show that we appreciate it'.[246] Crucially, George VI became renowned for his self-denying, dutiful virtues right at the moment when new concepts of self-fulfilment – specifically within personal relationships and the domestic setting of the home – were taking off in British society.[247] This tension has persisted at the heart of the modern monarchy, but its genesis can be located in the social and political transformations of the mid 1930s. Notably, at the end of the decade, in a semi-official book entitled *Destiny Called to Them*, which celebrated the personalities of the new royal family and was written by the journalist and Conservative politician, Sir Arthur Beverley Baxter, the concept of the burdens of monarchy was immortalized as part of a now famous phrase attributed to George VI while he was still an undergraduate student at Cambridge. According to Baxter, the young Prince Albert was caught smoking while in university dress and 'an officious mentor pointed out how his offence was aggravated by his being a member of the Royal family'. To this the young prince had 'bitterly' replied that

[246] Martin, *Magic of Monarchy*, p. 107.
[247] King, *Family Men*, pp. 5–7; Langhamer, *The English in Love*, pp. 6–7.

'we're not a family ... we're a firm'.[248] Whether or not this anecdote was apocryphal, the implication was clear: to be royal was not to be envied. Royal status required of the individual that he or she set an example to others; indiscretion could not be tolerated. Royal life imposed duty where domesticity should have been: personal happiness and self-fulfilment came second to public service and self-sacrifice.

[248] A. B. Baxter, *Destiny Called to Them* (Oxford, 1939), p. 12. This phrase was recently uttered by Colin Firth in the role of George VI in the 2010 film *The King's Speech*, directed by Tom Hooper.

4. 'Now it's up to us all – not kings and queens': the royal family at war

Writing in his diary as the Second World War neared its end, King George VI's private secretary, Sir Alan Lascelles, described how he had lunched with his friend Cosmo Lang, 'whose mind is as good as ever, despite his evident physical frailty (he is eighty-one)'.[1] The old archbishop, now retired from episcopal duties, had given Lascelles what the latter termed 'good, and welcome, advice on sundry matters', with the private secretary noting: 'I asked him if, in his long life, he had noticed any tendency among Ministers, and government minions generally, to encroach on the privileges of the Crown, or in any way to circumscribe its dignity. He said, almost indignantly, that no such tendency existed – rather the contrary'.[2] In what was very likely an allusion to the way that Edward VIII's extra-constitutional behaviour at the time of the abdication crisis had threatened to undermine Stanley Baldwin's National Government, Lang dismissed out of hand the courtier's concerns about political interference in royal affairs, instead suggesting the opposite was true. Lascelles raised this topic with the ex-archbishop following five-and-a-half years of a world war during which British ministers and other state actors had tried to harness the symbolic power of the monarchy to promote the war effort. However, Lascelles, first as one of two deputies to Sir Alexander Hardinge and then, after the latter's unceremonious ousting in July 1943, as principal private secretary to the king, had managed with some success to prevent government interference in the royal household's public relations strategy.[3] While the exigencies of war had necessitated that the palace capitulate on certain points – for example, in the case of royal broadcasts at moments of national crisis – courtiers had, for the most part, carefully managed the advances of government ministers and civil servants who wanted to take advantage of the monarchy's popular appeal to suit their own agendas. Palace officials instead seized the initiative by promoting

---

[1] *King's Counsellor: Abdication and War: the Diaries of Sir Alan Lascelles*, ed. D. Hart-Davis (London, 2006), pp. 297–8.

[2] Cosmo Lang retired in 1942 and was succeeded as archbishop of Canterbury by William Temple. Lang's last official act in office was to confirm Princess Elizabeth in the Christian faith.

[3] Hart-Davis, *King's Counsellor*, pp. 138–42.

a royal public image that was distinct from government propaganda and consistent with the pre-war emphasis on a family monarchy that was at once caring, recognizable, outwardly 'exemplary' in its 'ordinariness' and yet dignified in character.

This chapter explores how from 1939 to 1945 the House of Windsor became more adept at publicizing its media image, with the interference from government and wider concerns about the monarchy's loss of status leading the palace to exert greater control over royal news coverage than ever before. In addition to this idea, this chapter develops three further points, the first being that a language of mutual emotional suffering became central to the monarchy's public relations strategy as the conflict wore on. This language built on pre-war currents of empathy that connected the public to the royal family and centred on the hardships of royal life. However, amidst the more egalitarian mood that emerged on the home front, royal publicity shifted, with members of the House of Windsor emphasizing that they shared in the emotional plight experienced by their subjects in order to conjure the image of a crown and people united by the strains of war.[4] Second, using personal testimonies, this chapter analyses how royal publicity, which emphasized that the House of Windsor and public were joined in common cause, had some positive effects on media audiences and helped to offset public criticism of perceived royal privilege at a time of national hardship. Finally, it suggests that the monarchy began actively to mythologize its wartime role long before the guns fell silent in the summer of 1945 and that this helps to account for the enduring legacy of George VI and his consort, Queen Elizabeth, as part of the popular memory of the home front.[5]

[4] The extent of social levelling brought about by the war is contested by historians, with many revisionist accounts challenging Richard Titmuss's original argument in the *Problems of Social Policy* (London, 1950) that the experience of the home front united Britain and generated an optimism and desire among all classes for progressive political change after the war had ended. See, e.g., J. Hinton, *Nine Wartime Lives: Mass-Observation and the Making of the Modern Self* (Oxford, 2010), pp. 11–4. However, some historians *have* traced a shift leftwards, however vague and incremental, towards a more egalitarian public mood, which, in part, sprung from the plans set out for post-war reconstruction by the Beveridge Report in 1942. See R. Lowe, 'The Second World War, consensus, and the foundation of the welfare state', *Twentieth Century British Hist.*, i (1990), 152–82, at pp. 158–60; M. Donnelly, *Britain in the Second World War* (Oxford, 1999), pp. 49–51; J. Gardiner, *Wartime Britain, 1939–1945* (London, 2004), pp. 581–7; A. Calder, *The People's War: Britain 1939–45* (London, 1992), pp. 525–45.

[5] M. Connelly, *We Can Take It! Britain and the Memory of the Second World War* (London, 2004), pp. 28, 63, 89, 150–2.

This chapter is structured differently to others in *The Family Firm*. Rather than focusing on a single important episode or series of connected episodes, it adopts a chronological approach in order to chart the different ways the monarchy's public image changed over the course of a dramatic six-year period. One thing that remains constant, however, is the focus on the key protagonists of the House of Windsor, as well as courtiers behind the scenes who were instrumental in staging monarchy under wartime conditions. Media and official sources illuminate how and why the royal family's public relations strategy changed, while Mass Observation personal testimonies and private letters written by the public to the House of Windsor in response to royal publicity reveal how the monarchy's image was internalized by media audiences. Notably, the British government's propaganda division, the Ministry of Information, contracted Mass Observation to collect and interpret public opinion on a range of topics during the war, including royalty, with the Mass Observation team conducting a series of investigations into popular responses to specific members of the House of Windsor and the institution of monarchy itself.[6] Under the leadership of Tom Harrisson in the first years of the war, Mass Observation shifted its stance from trying to measure *public* opinion to trying to shape *political* opinion: it promoted a socially progressive agenda by repeatedly stressing how the 'ordinary people' it studied could be better served by government.[7] Some of Mass Observation's wartime studies of public attitudes to the monarchy emphasized popular disaffection with the institution and are characterized by an alarmist tone that needs to be treated with some caution given Harrisson's aims to effect social and political change through his work in this period. Equally, the war witnessed Mass Observation focus its activities on the London area in particular, which meant that most of the studies of royalty and related topics were not representative of the nation at large.[8] However, this chapter samples relevant diary entries composed by Mass Observation's panel of regular diarists (which numbered close to 500 by the end of the war) in order to explore how people living in other parts

---

[6] These reports include File Report 247, 'The Royal Family', 4 July 1940; File Report 22, 'Newsreel Report', 28 Jan. 1940; File Report 141, 'Newsreel Report 2', 27 May 1940; File Report 444, 'Newsreel Report 3', 6 Oct. 1940; File Report 1392, 'Death of the Duke of Kent', 25 Aug. 1942; TC14/79-86; TC14/154-186; TC65/4074-4220; TC23/4419-4502.

[7] P. Summerfield, 'Mass-Observation: social research or social movement?', *Jour. Contemp. Hist.*, xx (1985), 439–52, at pp. 444–7; P. Summerfield, *Reconstructing Women's Wartime Lives: Discourse and Subjectivity in Oral Histories of the Second World War* (Manchester, 1998), pp. 4–5; N. Hubble, *Mass Observation and Everyday Life: Culture, History, Theory* (Basingstoke, 2006), p. 8; J. Hinton, *The Mass Observers: a History, 1937–1949* (Oxford, 2013), esp. pp. 153–4.

[8] Hinton, *The Mass Observers*, pp. 166–215.

of the UK articulated their thoughts and feelings on royal personalities and events between 1939 and 1945.[9]

Along with media sources, documents and pictures from The National Archives, the BBC Written Archives and the Royal Archives, this chapter draws on three additional types of evidence: the minutes of the Newsreel Association of Great Britain and Ireland (formed in late 1937), which help to illuminate how the relationship between the royal household and newsreel companies was formalized during the war; the oral testimony of the newsreel cameraman, Graham Thompson, who was officially employed as 'king's cameraman' from 1944 in order to promote the royal family's image through his coverage; and the aforementioned published diaries of Lascelles, which he began writing in June 1942.[10] Far from offering transparent access to the workings of the palace's publicity machine, the private secretary is a sometimes unreliable, and often taciturn, narrator of events.[11] It is clear from both his and the editor's comments that the diaries were eventually meant to find a public audience, but it is also apparent from his entries that Lascelles engaged in self-censorship. He thought little of those writers who used memoir or autobiography to titillate through the disclosure of intimate revelation and he had, in his other role as keeper of the Royal Archives, conspired to destroy documents that reflected badly on the private lives of his royal employers.[12] Indeed, these are the diaries of the loyal, circumspect courtier who, on inviting the writer and politician Harold Nicolson to prepare the official biography of King George V in 1948, instructed him that he was not to reveal the 'whole truth' about the monarch's life: 'It is not meant to be an ordinary biography. It is something quite different. You [Nicolson] will be writing a book about a very ancient

[9] On the MO diarists, see Summerfield, 'Mass-Observation', p. 441; Hinton, The Mass Observers, p. 140. Where diaries have been used, they have been referred to using the number assigned them by Mass Observation.

[10] The Newsreel Association's minute books are held by the BFI National Archive and offer a unique perspective on the operations and discussions that went into producing newsreel coverage of events across Britain, Europe and the rest of the world. Thompson's oral history interview was conducted in 1992 and has been made available by the British Entertainment History Project <https://historyproject.org.uk/interview/graham-thompson> [accessed 25 Apr. 2017]. Lascelles started writing his wartime diary on 2 June 1942, which unfortunately means that some of the most interesting parts of the war – notably the crisis year of summer 1940 to summer 1941 – were not documented by him.

[11] In 1944 Lascelles reinstated the palace's press office, under press secretary Captain Lewis Ritchie (see M. Maclagan, 'Alan Frederick Lascelles', in Royal Lives: Portraits of the Past Royals by Those in the Know, ed. F. Prochaska (Oxford, 2002), pp. 570–2). Before then he managed royalty's public relations alongside the king's other assistant private secretary, Sir Eric Miéville.

[12] Hart-Davis, King's Counsellor, pp. xiv, 72–3, 324–5.

national institution, and you need not descend to personalities'. Lascelles also informed him 'that [he] should not be expected to write one word that was not true. [He] should not be expected to praise or exaggerate. But [he] must omit things and incidents which were discreditable'. Writing to a friend, Nicolson apprehensively noted how, if he were to follow these strict instructions, he could 'see George V getting more and more symbolic and less real'.[13]

The private secretary's diaries illuminate the author's moral outlook as well as his approach to political affairs and the role played by the monarchy in them. Although the diaries tend discreetly to avoid the day-to-day business of managing the royal family's public image and marginalize criticism of George VI, his wife and his daughters, occasional lapses in Lascelles's focus cast some daylight on the lengths to which he went in generating and maintaining a 'good press' for his employers.[14] Indeed, the diaries reveal that their author was sensitive to the emotional pulling power of the mass media and that he understood the popular appeal of intimate royal publicity. Nevertheless, he took against what he described as the 'machine-made propaganda' of the Ministry of Information and 'artificially-inspired articles in the Press', which certain ministers and civil servants were 'constantly clamouring for' from the monarchy. For Lascelles, government propaganda lacked subtlety and instead he tried to develop a nuanced, dignified royal media image that built on pre-war traditions.[15]

The opening section of this chapter focuses on the royal family's role in the first year of the war. Surprisingly little historical work has been conducted on the monarchy's relationship with the Ministry of Information during the conflict.[16] The ministry's early wartime activities were underpinned

---

[13] *Harold Nicolson: Diaries and Letters*, iii: *the Later Years 1945–62*, ed. N. Nicolson (London, 1968), pp. 142–4.

[14] Lascelles is ever-respectful of his royal employers and (within this edited collection of diary entries) refrains from criticizing their foibles or failures. The notable exception is Edward VIII. Lascelles had worked for him when he was prince of Wales and is often at pains to disparage the ex-king's personality and actions throughout the diaries. The courtier's role in 're-inventing' the monarchy after the 1936 abdication crisis was notable for the way he sought to elevate George VI and the new royal family as everything that Edward was not – i.e., domestic, dutiful and self-sacrificing.

[15] Hart-Davis, *King's Counsellor*, pp. 81–3 and 130. Unfortunately, the selective publication of Lascelles's diaries limits the discussion of his public relations strategy. The editor of the diaries, D. Hart-Davis, is the son of one of Lascelles's closest friends and does a good job of maintaining courtly discretion while painting a positive image of his subject. This author's request (in March 2017) to view Lascelles's original wartime diaries (LASL 1/2) at the Churchill Archives Centre, Cambridge, was rejected by the Royal Archives, which had recently conducted a review of his papers and decided to keep them closed to researchers.

[16] The 2 studies that have surveyed the wartime activities of the Ministry of Information

by concerns about the British public's morale and this led to haphazard interference in a number of areas – for example, the ministry sought to regulate newspaper content and the BBC's output, giving rise to serious discontent among journalists and broadcasters.[17] However, by the summer of 1941 three ministers of information had come and gone (including Sir John Reith, the former director-general of the BBC) and the role was then taken up by the Conservative MP Brendan Bracken, who was a close political ally of Prime Minister Winston Churchill, and he remained in post until the end of the war. Compared to his predecessors, Bracken adopted a more laissez-faire approach to propaganda and, believing the public's morale to be essentially sound, he let the outside organizations through which the Ministry of Information had initially sought to convey the government's propaganda line exercise greater freedom in pursuing their own objectives. The monarchy was one such institution, but since 1939 it had resisted pressures from the ministry to become a mouthpiece of the government's wartime policy. Historians have tended to emphasize that the ministry tried to use royalty as part of its campaign to boost public confidence in the crisis years of 1940–1 during the Nazi's aerial bombardment of British cities and when invasion seemed imminent. However, it is clear that despite early attempts by the Ministry of Information to leverage the power of the king and queen's public personae by scripting radio broadcasts for them, the palace and its allies succeeded in restricting the ministry's influence over the monarchy's image by resisting changes they deemed incompatible with the royal family's pre-war reputation.

The opening section of this chapter also examines how George VI's shortcomings (as discussed in chapter 3) continued to undermine his position as Britain's symbolic figurehead; and how in response to this Queen Elizabeth adopted a more conspicuous public role at the start of the war that was generally welcomed by her subjects and helped to ensure the monarchy remained relevant at a time of uncertainty. This strategy was crucial because the duke of Windsor was set on playing an active role in the nation's war effort and his participation diverted public attention away from George VI

---

hardly mention the monarchy. See I. McLaine, *Ministry of Morale: Home Front Morale and the Ministry of Information in World War II* (London, 1979), pp. 78, 92–3; R. Mackay, *Half the Battle: Civilian Morale in Britain during the Second World War* (Manchester, 2002), pp. 63, 145–7, 163.

[17] J. Fox, 'The propaganda war', in *The Cambridge History of the Second World War* (3 vols., Cambridge, 2015), ii: *Politics and Ideology*, ed. R. J. B. Bosworth and J. A. Maiolo, pp. 91–116, at p. 94; S. Nicholas, *The Echo of War: Home Front Propaganda and the Wartime BBC, 1939–45* (Manchester, 1996), pp. 42–3, 71–2; J. Seaton, 'Broadcasting and the blitz', in *Power without Responsibility: the Press, Broadcasting and New Media in Britain*, ed. J. Curran and J. Seaton (London, 2009), pp. 120–42, at pp. 133–4.

and his consort. He was dispatched across the English Channel in a liaison role with the British army but, in summer 1940, with the Nazis' invasion of western Europe, the duke's hurried retreat across France to the Iberian peninsula led to concerns emerging among sections of the public regarding the crown's leadership in wartime: a Mass Observation file report compiled in July 1940 revealed that ordinary people's attitudes towards the monarchy were mostly ambivalent, with members of the public criticizing the duke and already articulating some of the anti-elite, 'people's war' sentiment that would come to define official wartime propaganda.[18]

The second section moves on to consider how the Blitz of 1940–1 created a much-needed role for the king and queen by providing them with an opportunity to demonstrate their sympathy for their people's plight. Courtiers orchestrated royal tours of bombed-out areas in London and the regions as informal events that brought together the royal couple and their subjects in intimate union. Once again, far from bowing to pressure from government officials to publicize widely the royal visits to blitzed communities, the royal household maintained tight control over the media arrangements for the tours, not only to ensure the king and queen's safety but in order to shape a publicity campaign that stressed the monarchs' personal sympathy for their people. This message notably gained momentum following the Luftwaffe's bombing of Buckingham Palace in September 1940: under the coordination of royal and Ministry of Information officials, the media presented it as evidence of a shared suffering that united the monarchs and their subjects. Furthermore, this narrative was projected in the broadcast delivered by Princess Elizabeth a month later when she told listeners that she and her sister, Margaret, had experienced the same kind of family separation as other British children as a result of evacuation.

The third and final part of this chapter examines a series of episodes from spring 1943 through to the VE Day celebrations of May 1945. By the end of 1942 it was widely believed by British political elites that Hitler and Nazi Germany would not win the war and that it was simply a matter of time before the Allies prevailed.[19] In keeping with these predictions, the monarchy sought to consolidate a narrative of royal leadership as part of a victorious war effort, despite the fact that there remained an undercurrent of public doubt about the royal family's role in what was now widely presented as the 'people's war'. For example, the public attitudes Mass Observation recorded in response to the sudden death of Prince George,

[18] Calder, *The People's War*, p. 138; S. O. Rose, *Which People's War? National Identity and Citizenship in Britain, 1939–1945* (Oxford, 2003), pp. 1–5, 29.

[19] Calder, *The People's War*, pp. 304–7; Hart-Davis, *King's Counsellor*, pp. 91–2, 98, 125–6.

duke of Kent, during an RAF flying mission in summer 1942 indicated that, while the House of Windsor could suffer 'the same as anyone else', they were also deemed to be privileged, with respondents noting that the royal bereaved would not experience the same material hardships as ordinary British people who lost loved ones to the fighting. And, with large swathes of the population envisioning a more equal post-war society following the publication of the Beveridge Report in late 1942, the royal household had to work hard to crystallize a vision of a king and queen united with their people in opposition to fascism and equally determined to build a better future. This final section examines how the palace elevated the royal family through a series of co-ordinated publicity campaigns in the last years of the conflict and, in so doing, initiated a process of royal myth-making that has ensured the House of Windsor's long-lasting association with the war effort.

'They're only figureheads, but they're something to look up to'

Three months before British prime minister Neville Chamberlain declared war on Nazi Germany on 3 September 1939, the recently re-formed Ministry of Information began to develop a royal public relations strategy in readiness for the outbreak of hostilities. The ministry anticipated that George VI would want to deliver some kind of message to his people in the event of war and so started in late June to prepare a number of draft broadcasts that the king might use. In so doing, civil servants were signalling their belief in the positive effects a royal message could have on British listeners, drawing as it would on the sovereign's authority as the nation's symbolic leader.[20] Officials believed that propaganda worked best when it was grafted onto comprehensible systems, hence the ministry tried to use pre-existing publicity channels such as the publishing industry, the BBC and the monarchy in order to disseminate its messages, knowing full well that the respect commanded by these institutions would also help to disguise government involvement.[21] The Ministry of Information's plans for the royal broadcast also revealed the constraints within which its propagandists operated. The ministry faced a fundamental problem in that propaganda was deemed antithetical to British values, with many officials expressing misgivings about any form of disinformation campaign. As historian Jo Fox has argued, the ministry thus drew on older 'liberal traditions' of publicity

---

[20] TNA, INF 1/670, W. R. Codling to A. P. Waterfield, 29 June 1939, 'Appendix A: Prime Minister's Broadcast'.

[21] V. Holman, 'Carefully concealed connections: the Ministry of Information and British publishing, 1939–1946', *Book History*, viii (2005), 197–226, at pp. 198–200; J. Ellul, *Propaganda: the Formation of Men's Attitudes* (New York, 1971), pp. 241–50.

– such as royal messages – to communicate the government's case for war to the public.[22] George VI had publicly endorsed his prime minister's policy of appeasement between 1938 and 1939 and it was therefore vital that he be seen to make the case for war after diplomacy had failed. However, in its efforts to refocus the royal public image in readiness for war, the Ministry of Information encountered a number of obstacles – notably an ignorance among civil servants concerning how royal public relations worked (stemming from the secrecy that enshrouded the court) and, more significantly, opposition from palace officials and allies of the royal household, who were intent on controlling the monarchy's media strategy.

Under the leadership of the civil servant A. P. Waterfield, the pre-war 'shadow' Ministry of Information also planned to produce 15 million printouts of George VI's opening wartime broadcast, including a facsimile of the king's signature, to be delivered by the Post Office to every home in Britain at a total cost of £16,000.[23] In justifying this undertaking to the Overseas and Emergency Expenditure Committee, the ministry stressed that the message would 'act as an initial stimulus to patriotism and loyalty and as a permanent reminder for fortitude in the trials ahead'.[24] For government propagandists, then, the king's words would help to generate support for the war in much the same way as his father's public image had worked to endorse mobilization and recruitment to the armed forces in 1914.[25] In this respect, an older tradition of kingship, in which the sovereign acted as both the embodiment of the state and as the rallying-point for wartime national sentiment, was reimagined by civil servants at the Ministry of Information. Yet, while George VI's message was designed to reawaken certain historic concepts, it also encapsulated contemporary concerns. Early drafts of the broadcast prepared by civil servants at the ministry reveal a preoccupation with the protection of British democracy against fascist tyranny – an ideological contest that had taken on particular significance in the mid 1930s – as well as a desire to prepare citizens for the psychological hardships to come. As with the ministry's plans for its first poster campaigns, the drafts of the king's message reflected the protracted deliberations over whether citizens on the home front needed to be readied for the horrors of aerial

---

[22] Fox, 'Propaganda war', pp. 94–6.

[23] TNA, INF 1/670, W. R. Codling to A. P. Waterfield, 29 June 1939.

[24] TNA, INF 1/670, O.E.P.E.C. Paper No. 21 – 'King's Message'. See also handwritten memorandum signed M. L. G. Balfour, 28 July 1939.

[25] H. Jones, 'The nature of kingship in First World War Britain', in *The Windsor Dynasty 1910 to the Present: 'Long to Reign Over Us'?*, ed. M. Glencross, J. Rowbottom and M. D. Kandiah (Basingstoke, 2016), pp. 195–216, at pp. 196–201.

bombardment in order to avert mass panic.[26] Indeed, it is significant that the references to the public 'standing firm' and 'carrying on' first included in the ministry's early drafts of the message found their way into the final version of George VI's broadcast, with the king instructing listeners 'to stand calm and firm and united at this time of trial'.[27]

Waterfield ultimately handed over responsibility for the drafting of the king's message to the home secretary, Sir Samuel Hoare, who oversaw the Ministry of Information's activities in the lead up to war. Waterfield recommended that other 'versions [of the message be] prepared by persons accustomed to a different outlook on public affairs from that of the Civil Service' and suggested that this might include either the archbishop of Canterbury or Stanley Baldwin.[28] Hoare subsequently forwarded the ministry's most recent draft of the king's speech to Cosmo Lang and invited him, as a longstanding royal advisor, to prepare his own version. The men's correspondence reveals that the archbishop was reluctant at first, partly because he was on holiday but also because of the difficulty involved in writing a suitable message 'in cold blood' before war had been declared. Lang found Hoare in agreement, though, that the speech should focus on Britain's 'resistance to brute force' rather than the 'defence of democratic ideals', as was the main theme of the ministry's draft. [29] The archbishop was better versed in the personalized imagery used in royal broadcasts and may have thought that the theme of democracy was too abstract for some listeners, who would rather hear their king state plainly that Hitler was a tyrant and their enemy. After a second request from Hoare, Lang agreed to write and sent the home secretary a draft that was passed on to George VI, who 'was delighted with it'.[30] The ministry then agreed some last-minute changes with the king's assistant private secretary, Alan Lascelles, who had final say over its content.[31]

The exchanges between the Ministry of Information, Hoare, Lang and courtiers reveal two things: first, that the Ministry of Information sought to harness the power of the king's public image in order to further its own

---

[26] M. Shapira, *The War Inside: Psychoanalysis, Total War, and the Making of the Democratic Self in Postwar Britain* (Cambridge, 2013), pp. 32–5.

[27] TNA, INF 1/670, 'King's Message (war-time)', undated; J. Wheeler-Bennett, *King George VI: His Life and Reign* (London, 1958), pp. 406–7. See also H. Irving, 'Keep calm and carry on – the compromise behind the slogan' <https://history.blog.gov.uk/2014/06/27/keep-calm-and-carry-on-the-compromise-behind-the-slogan> [accessed 2 Feb. 2018].

[28] TNA, INF 1/670, A. P. Waterfield to S. Hoare, 25 July 1939.

[29] LPL, Lang 318, fos. 151–4, S. Hoare to C. G. Lang, 10, 18 and 28 Aug. 1939.

[30] LPL, Lang 318, fo. 154, S. Hoare to C. G. Lang, 28 Aug. 1939.

[31] TNA, INF 1/670, handwritten memorandum from A. P. Waterfield to Miss Gilbert, 3 Sept. 1939.

aims; second, that this threw up something of a challenge to the palace, which wanted to retain control over royal publicity. The danger for the royal household was that mistakes made by the ministry could have a negative impact on the crown. This was demonstrated early on when the scheme to distribute printouts of the king's message was suddenly abandoned by the ministry due to a national paper shortage in autumn 1939, but not before the ministry's news division had broadcast a radio bulletin telling listeners that they should expect to receive a copy of the speech 'to keep … as a permanent record'.[32] George VI's private secretary, Alexander Hardinge, expressed his and the king's disappointment at this volte-face: the Ministry of Information had failed in its aims and this could only have negative repercussions on the way the public viewed the monarch.[33] Fortunately for George VI and his counsellors, when it came to the speech itself, Hoare had turned to Lang, who, as chief architect of the royal public language of the 1930s, understood precisely what the broadcast demanded, with the result being that it struck many familiar notes. Following Chamberlain's declaration of war on Sunday 3 September, the king began his first wartime speech that evening by telling listeners in words which echoed George V's radio messages that he '[spoke] with the same depth of feeling for each one of you as if I were able to cross your threshold and speak to you myself'. He went on to blame the war on Hitler's 'selfish pursuit of power' and his 'primitive doctrine of might and right'; he then emphasized the importance of protecting the political liberties that united the empire and Commonwealth; and the king ended his speech by beseeching God for support in 'whatever service or sacrifice [the war] may demand' of him and his subjects.[34]

For the Ministry of Information's Ivison Macadam, who was one of the founding members of the Council of King George's Jubilee Trust in 1935 and one of the first officials involved in drawing up plans for the re-establishment of the ministry as far back as 1937, Lang's version of the king's speech was not as good as the original draft prepared by civil servants, as it 'follow[ed] too much the general tradition of such [royal] Messages'. He thought the start of the war represented an 'occasion when we could break away from this and get something more arresting'.[35] However, in Lang's safe hands the broadcast followed the tradition of earlier royal messages and met with George VI's approval. Notably, the monarch and his advisors also insisted on having the final say over the broadcast, which ensured that

---

[32] TNA, INF 1/670, MoI News Division Evening Bulletin, 3 Sept. 1939.

[33] TNA, INF 1/670, A. Hardinge to S. Hood, 9 and 16 Oct. 1939.

[34] Wheeler-Bennett, *King George VI*, p. 406.

[35] TNA, INF 1/670, I. Macadam to A. P. Waterfield, 30 Aug. 1939.

anything unsuitable was excised: the alternative, as we shall see, was to refuse to comply with the Ministry of Information's requests altogether.

Civil servants at the ministry were certain that the British press would provide fulsome coverage of the king's speech and they were right.[36] Newspaper coverage of George VI's broadcast was extensive and unanimously positive.[37] In particular, journalists drew attention to the personal tone of the message and the domestic setting from which it was delivered. The *Daily Express* noted, for example, that the king had 'crossed the threshold' of millions of homes when he spoke to his people, while the *Daily Mail*'s report described how, 'in another room in the palace sat the Queen, listening in her own home, like millions of other wives and mothers'.[38] The other feature of the broadcast that the press highlighted was the king's instruction to his people that they 'stand firm and calm and united' in the face of danger (Figure 4.1).[39] Even the *Daily Worker*, which had been so hostile towards royalty throughout the 1930s, printed a front-page excerpt of the king's broadcast without further comment: the war against fascism clearly demanded that British newspapers from across the political spectrum form a united front.[40]

The public reaction to George VI's speech is more difficult to gauge. While Mass Observation did not conduct a formal investigation into the way listeners responded to the broadcast, a number of its regular diarists noted that they had heard it. As with George VI's pre-war speeches, media audiences tended to be preoccupied with his speech impediment. A seventeen-year-old bank clerk from Sidcup, Kent, recorded the sympathetic comments of the family members with whom he had listened: "'Poor man.' "It's a shame." "He is very courageous to do it." "Bless Him"'. The diarist stated that 'most agreed that considering his verbal shortcomings, it was a good speech'.[41] Other Mass Observation diarists were less impressed, though. A thirty-five-year-old textile warehouseman from Birmingham noted that he thought 'the Kings [*sic*] speech sounded like one of a fagged man ... He seemed to want to comfort his subjects, but knew that no words of his could cover the unpleasant wound which had been prised open in the morning'.[42] The empathetic tone of the broadcast thus seems to have resonated with this listener, but his praise was moderated by what he otherwise deemed

[36] TNA, INF 1/670, A. P. Waterfield to I. Macadam, 30 Aug. 1939.
[37] E.g., *Daily Express*, 4 Sept. 1939, p. 7; *Daily Mirror*, 4 Sept. 1939, p. 1.
[38] *Daily Mail*, 4 Sept. 1939, p. 2; *Daily Express*, 4 Sept. 1939, p.7.
[39] *Daily Mirror*, 4 Sept. 1939, p. 3; *Daily Sketch*, 4 Sept. 1939, p. 1.
[40] *Daily Worker*, 4 Sept. 1939, p. 1.
[41] MOA, 5141; also quoted in P. Ziegler, *Crown and People* (London, 1978), p. 69.
[42] MOA, 5228.

DAILY SKETCH MONDAY, SEPTEMBER 4, 1939

AND NOW MAY GOD DEFEND THE RIGHT: See P. 11

THE FASTEST EVER

Sir Malcolm Campbell
& Mr. John Cobb

both used

K·L·G
SPARKING PLUGS

DAILY SKETCH

No. 9,464   MONDAY, SEPTEMBER 4, 1939   ONE PENNY

LATEST WAR NEWS

The King's Message

"STAND calm, firm and united!" That was the keynote of the message broadcast by the King to the Empire last night.

"In this grave hour," said the King, "perhaps the most fateful in our history, I send to every household of my people, both at home and overseas, this message, spoken with the same depth of feeling for each one of you as if I were able to cross your threshold and speak to you myself.

"For the second time in the lives of most of us we are at war.

"Over and over again we have tried to find a peaceful way out of the differences between ourselves and those who are now our enemies.

"But it has been in vain. We have been forced into a conflict. For we are called, with our Allies, to meet the challenge of a principle which, if it were to prevail, would be fatal to any civilised order in the world.

"It is the principle which permits a state, in the selfish pursuit of power, to disregard its treaties and its solemn pledges; which sanctions the use of force, or threat of force, against the sovereignty and independence of other states.

Must Meet The Challenge

"Such a principle, stripped of all disguise, is surely the mere primitive doctrine that might is right; and if this principle were established throughout the world, the freedom of our own country and of the whole British Commonwealth of Nations would be in danger.

"But far more than this—the peoples of the world would be kept in the bondage of fear, and all hopes of settled peace and of the security of justice and liberty among nations would be ended.

"This is the ultimate issue which confronts us. For the sake of all that we ourselves hold dear, and of the world's order and peace, it is unthinkable that we should refuse to meet the challenge.

"It is to this high purpose that I now call my people at home and my peoples across the seas, who will make our cause their own. I ask them to stand calm, firm and united in this time of trial.

"The task will be hard. There may be dark days ahead, and war can no longer be confined to the battlefield. But we can only do the right as we see the right, and reverently commit our cause to God.

"If one and all we keep resolutely faithful to it, ready for whatever service or sacrifice it may demand, then, with God's help, we shall prevail.

"May He bless and keep us all."

A copy of the message, with a facsimile of the King's signature will be sent to every home in the land.

The King about to broadcast last night.

Britain (since 11 a.m. yesterday) and France (since 5 p.m.) at war with Germany

Lord Gort leads British Expeditionary Force

Churchill in War Cabinet as First Lord

Hitler goes to the Front

Poles invade East Prussia

Warsaw alleges Germans are dropping gas bombs

LATE MESSAGES ON BACK PAGE

Figure 4.1. 'Stand Calm, Firm and United!', *Daily Sketch*, 4 September 1939, p. 1. © The British Library Board.

an uninspiring performance. Philip Ziegler's analysis of Mass Observation diarists' responses to George VI's broadcast on 3 September tallies with the evaluation presented here: that the main reaction recorded by listeners was their focus on the monarch's stammer. Indeed, Ziegler has suggested that this emphasis on the king's delivery persisted throughout the war and that the number of diarists who tuned in to listen to his wartime broadcasts steadily declined.[43]

*

Given the problems that George VI faced as a lacklustre public speaker, it is little wonder that the Ministry of Information sought to co-opt other members of his family who were better communicators into delivering wartime public addresses. The government anticipated that the conflict would require unprecedented sacrifices on the home front both in terms of war work and also because the public would be affected as a result of attacks by enemy aircraft on British soil. The urgent need to mobilize civilians fell in part to civil servants at the Ministry of Information, who were anxious about how to prepare Britain's female population for the mass evacuation of children (and, in some cases, mothers themselves) from the towns and cities that officials thought would be targeted by the Luftwaffe.[44] Before the war, Queen Elizabeth had proven herself a competent public speaker. The final speech she delivered to the crowds that had gathered to say farewell to her and the king at the end of the 1939 royal tour of Canada and the US had been broadcast and filmed.[45] The ministry's initial plans to persuade the queen to deliver a radio message to the nation and the empire's women at

---

[43] Ziegler, *Crown and People*, pp. 69–71. Ziegler's argument regarding a declining listenership is not entirely borne out by the investigations undertaken by the BBC's listener research department. The listener research department's figures suggest that, on average, just less than two-thirds of all British adults tended to listen to the king's speech on Christmas Day during the war years. Notably, there was a small decline of approximately 10% in the early years of the war, with the 1942 broadcast heard by 56.9% of listeners. However, the figure was back in the mid 60% bracket the following year, where it remained. Winston Churchill tended to draw larger audiences with his broadcasts, regularly reaching more than 70% of adult listeners – a feat never equalled by the king. A notable case in point was the prime minister's VE Day speech, which was heard by 71.5% of the adult population according to the BBC's estimates, compared with the king's speech on the same day, which had a listenership of 68.9% (BBCWA 248/R9/1/4 Listener Research Bulletin no. 225 and 248/R9/1/5, Listener Research Bulletin no. 244).
[44] Hinton, *The Mass Observers*, p. 142.
[45] W. Shawcross, *Queen Elizabeth the Queen Mother: the Official Biography* (Basingstoke, 2009), pp. 480–1.

the outbreak of the war reveal the kind of gendered assumptions concerning the effects a speech of this kind might have on female listeners which shaped much of the ministry's wartime work.[46] At the end of August 1939 Ivison Macadam asked A. P. Waterfield for permission to seek out a writer for this task, stating 'here, almost more than anywhere, we shall want a fine piece of writing'.[47] Waterfield sought advice from the seventh earl of Perth, Eric Drummond, who later became a key advisor on the ministry's propaganda strategy. He suggested the queen should not broadcast until evacuation was complete but recommended that the ministry contact the journalist Godfrey Winn to prepare a first draft of the speech. Waterfield noted in a memo to Macadam that 'although it seems doubtful whether [Winn's] writing could ever be called fine, there is no doubt that he has an extraordinary gift for writing stuff which appeals to women. Lord Perth thinks that he is just the man for this job'.[48] Winn had distinguished himself as a women's advice columnist specializing in matters of love and relationships; and Perth's nomination of him as author of the message again reveals the kind of cultural stereotypes that shaped the Ministry of Information's attempts to appeal to a female demographic.[49]

The ministry learnt at the start of September that the BBC had also considered inviting the queen 'to broadcast a message to the mothers & children of this country & the Empire, with a special reference to the situation resulting from evacuation'. Conveying this information to Waterfield, the Ministry of Information's B. H. Needham noted that he thought 'a royal broadcast Message ought do a great deal not only to hearten the women & children generally, but to smooth over any feelings of dissatisfaction and concern which may be felt in some instances about the evacuation of the children & their separation from their parents'.[50] Needham added that he had advised the BBC to take no additional steps until the ministry had confirmed its own plans regarding the speech: in matters of royal publicity, the broadcaster now had to defer to ministry officials. Waterfield stated in his reply that he had spoken to Lascelles at the palace, who had thought it better that the ministry 'hold back for a little while'. The courtier was

[46] Rose, *Which People's War?*, pp. 131–5; S. Harper, 'The years of total war: propaganda and entertainment', in *Nationalising Femininity: Culture, Sexuality and British Cinema in the Second World War*, ed. C. Gledhill and G. Swanson (Manchester, 1996), pp. 193–212, at pp. 195–6.
[47] TNA, INF 1/670, I. Macadam to A. P. Waterfield, 30 Aug. 1939.
[48] TNA, INF 1/670, A. P. Waterfield to I. Macadam, 2 Sept. 1939.
[49] A. Bingham, 'Godfrey Herbert Winn (1906–1971)', in *ODNB* <https://doi.org/10.1093/ref:odnb/95220> [accessed 1 March 2018].
[50] TNA, INF 1/670, B. H. Needham to A. P. Waterfield, 7 Sept. 1939.

clearly wary of establishing a new precedent by having the queen deliver a direct radio message. But the civil servant thought that if the Ministry of Information waited any longer they would 'miss the evacuation boat' and an opportunity to reassure Britain's women at a time of great anxiety. His colleagues agreed and so their efforts turned to adapting Godfrey Winn's first attempt at the speech into something the queen might actually use.[51]

Annotations on Winn's original draft reveal that civil servants wanted to include 'a special appeal to all concerned to be kind to the children & mothers who have been parted by evacuation' – again signalling their belief that the queen's words could help engender stability through personal reassurance at a time of social dislocation. Winn's draft echoed the tone of earlier royal broadcasts: the queen would appeal to other wives and mothers who valued 'the security of our homes and our children' and would tell them that the 'family life' she shared with them 'ha[d] been menaced' by war.[52] The concept of a mutual suffering that united crown and people and stemmed from the forced separation of families was thus established early on by the Ministry of Information and reworked in a subsequent draft prepared by civil servants in a phrase on evacuation and how it 'affects very closely what is the dearest thing of all to us – our homes'.[53] These references to family life were also intended to resonate with a national culture that elevated domesticity as an essential part of what it was to be British. A Mass Observation report titled 'What Does Britain Mean to You?' published in September 1941 noted that 'liberty, love of home, tolerance and justice – these are some of the things which Britain has infused into her sons and daughters'.[54] As the queen's message slowly took shape, it was these things that speechwriters focused on in building a picture of an enemy who seemed to threaten all that the British held dear.

However, Ivison Macadam expressed dissatisfaction with his colleagues' efforts and invited the children's author A. A. Milne 'to have a shot'.[55] Early on, Macadam and Waterfield had discussed how the queen's message might also be targeted at children, so this could explain the choice of Milne, who was renowned for his Winnie-the-Pooh stories. But the resulting draft was mawkish and patronizing and took the idea of the queen's sympathy for

[51] TNA, INF 1/670, handwritten memorandum signed by A. P. Waterfield on 9 Sept. 1939, on original letter from B. H. Needham to Waterfield, 7 Sept. 1939.
[52] TNA, INF 1/670, 'Draft by Godfrey Winn for The Queen's Message', with handwritten annotations.
[53] TNA, INF 1/670, 'Queen's Message'.
[54] Quoted in J. Fox, 'Careless talk: tensions within British domestic propaganda during the Second World War', *Jour. Brit. Stud.*, li (2012), 936–66, at p. 948.
[55] TNA, INF 1/670, Memorandum from I. Macadam to B. H. Needham, 13 Sept. 1939.

her people along lines of mutual suffering to an extreme.[56] Milne's message addressed evacuation with the words 'many of you have had to be separated from your children; well, I am with you there. But it is only for a little time, and they will be safe, and they will come back to us'. And the message ended with the queen inviting female listeners 'to hold my hand for a moment, and to believe that with all my heart and mind and body I am thinking of you and praying for you and suffering with you'.[57] One civil servant noted in a handwritten memo that they thought the draft had 'the right "human" touch' and that the Ministry of Information should 'submit it as it stands' to the palace for review.[58] But before they could do this, Waterfield had shown Milne's draft of the broadcast to Sir Edward Grigg, now parliamentary secretary to the ministry but previously a royal advisor on the public relations of the prince of Wales's imperial tours in the 1920s.[59] Grigg adopted a more sceptical approach, akin to that of Lascelles, over the necessity of the queen's radio message in the first place, suggesting to Waterfield that such a broadcast instead 'be made to arise naturally out of an appropriate occasion [such as] the publication of the first big casualty lists or possibly the first air raid'. Waterfield also reported that Grigg 'thought the whole tone of [Milne's draft] was too "Christopher Robinish"' and would 'definitely prefer to see it re-written'.[60]

At Grigg's suggestion other authors were briefly considered, including popular novelist Storm Jameson, before the whole idea of the queen's message was temporarily shelved by the ministry. Once again, the intervention of an old royal advisor had worked to circumvent the ambitions of the Ministry of Information, which wanted to draw on the monarchy's popularity to promote its own agenda. However, the seed of the idea was firmly planted and Queen Elizabeth finally consented to broadcast on 11 November 1939, her message notably coinciding with Armistice Day and drawing on the powerful emotions associated with the memory of the First World War.[61] It is unclear why the royal household capitulated to government pressure

[56] It began: 'My Countrywomen: I am speaking to you as a wife and a mother to other wives and mothers, and as a woman to all other women' (TNA, INF 1/670, 'Draft for the Queen's Message'). See also F. Prochaska, *Royal Bounty: the Making of a Welfare Monarchy* (New Haven, Conn., 1995), p. 223.
[57] TNA, INF 1/670, 'Draft for the Queen's Message'.
[58] TNA, INF 1/670, handwritten memorandum from SFS to Lord Macmillan, 15 Sept. 1939. This civil servant could not be identified.
[59] F. Mort, 'On tour with the prince: monarchy, imperial politics and publicity in the prince of Wales's dominion tours 1919–20', *Twentieth Century British Hist.*, xxix (2018), 25–57.
[60] TNA, INF 1/670, A. P. Waterfield to the Director General, 19 Sept. 1939.
[61] Shawcross, *Queen Elizabeth the Queen Mother*, pp. 497–8.

at this point, although it is possible that they did so in the belief that the queen's broadcast would reassure parents who had consented to be separated from their children that they were doing the right thing: over the course of October, it had become apparent that the government's initial fears about mass air raids had been misplaced and a number of evacuated women and children had begun to return home to Britain's urban centres.[62]

The writer of the queen's broadcast – almost certainly Lascelles – does appear to have at least reviewed the Ministry of Information's earlier attempts at the speech as there are several passing resemblances that link the final version to the drafts prepared or commissioned by civil servants.[63] However, the end result was a tour de force in royal speechwriting and quite distinct from the ministry attempts in the way it combined a dignified, regal tone with a personal, feminine touch. As originally planned by the ministry, Queen Elizabeth addressed her words to the women of Britain and the empire. She spoke in measured terms of the importance of women's contribution to the war effort – whether it was in 'carrying on your home duties', undertaking the new kinds of 'real and vital work' *outside* the home that total war required or in putting up with seeing 'your family life broken up – your husband going off to his allotted task – your children evacuated to places of greater safety'. The author of the broadcast also clearly saw similar merits to the ministry in highlighting the shared sacrifices the war involved, as the queen then continued: 'The King and I know what it means to be parted from our children, and we can sympathise with those of you who have bravely consented to this separation for the sake of your little ones'.[64] At the start of the war the princesses had been secretly sent to Birkhall – a royal residence on the Balmoral estate in Scotland – where, out of concern for their safety, they remained until Christmas 1939.[65] The Royal Archives contain the original script of the speech and it reveals that the word 'know' was underlined (as above), in order, we might assume, to ensure that as the queen read it she placed emphasis on the one phrase which conveyed her and the king's shared sacrifice to listeners (this emphasis is also clear from the recording of the radio broadcast).[66] The empathetic language contained in

[62] See, e.g., *Daily Mail*, 13 Nov. 1939, p. 6.

[63] Although one cannot be sure this was the case without access to his papers and correspondence, Lascelles was the main royal speechwriter throughout the war. The final spoken version was also very different to the MoI drafts in The National Archives (Hart-Davis, *King's Counsellor*, pp. 118, 122, 292).

[64] RA, QEQMH/PS/SPE: BROADCASTS 11 Nov. 1939, 'Broadcast by H.M. The Queen'.

[65] B. Pimlott, *The Queen: Elizabeth II and the Monarchy* (London, 2002), pp. 56–7; M. Crawford, *The Little Princesses* (London, 1993), p. 61.

[66] 'The Queen's Broadcast Message', *Pathé Gazette*, 16 Nov. 1939. The original broadcast of the queen's message was recorded by the newsreels <https://www.youtube.com/watch?v=ohoFXRyOacI> [accessed 2 Dec. 2018] (at 04:16).

the speech thus linked the queen to her female listeners through a gendered imagery of domestic life and the associated emotions of love, happiness and concern for one's family. Notably, the broadcast's focus on maternal responsibility and national duty also tallied with government propaganda released in late 1939 that tried to dissuade evacuated mothers from returning home to British towns and cities with their children.[67]

Before delivering her broadcast, the queen had written to Cosmo Lang asking him for some last-minute help in order to ensure she included some reference to Christianity in it:

> You very kindly said today, that you would look through my broadcast, and I now send you the skeleton – I have purposely made it very simple, as I wish to speak to the simple women who are a little perplexed about this war.
>
> One thing I notice is, that I have not brought God into my few words, if you think that I should say anything about our faith in divine guidance, please do suggest a sentence or two. I think that it would be right & helpful myself – if you agree, I should be most grateful for any suggestions. It was so delightful to see you today. We always feel refreshed & strengthened when we have talked with you. I wonder if you will think my idea of a broadcast too homely. It is so difficult.[68]

It is clear from this letter that the queen was anxious about how her broadcast would be received, particularly fearing that it might come across as 'too homely' – too familiar – in tone. We do not know how Lang responded to these concerns, but he did suggest two additional sentences that made the queen's faith clear to those who tuned in. The broadcast concluded with the lines, 'We put our trust in God, who is our Refuge and Strength in all times of trouble. I pray with all my heart that He may bless and guide and keep you always'.[69] The queen's message therefore ended with a familiar religious flourish and Lang immediately wrote to her to commend her performance at the microphone:

> I couldn't refrain from saying that I have just been listening To Your Majesty's broadcast here at Canterbury where I am for the weekend, it sounded, and I knew it would, quite admirable. Your Majesty's voice was clear & full: and if I may say so, the enunciation & delivery were excellent. I could not but feel that the few closing words brought forth the final touch which would reach the hearts of all who heard. I like to think of the multitudes of women – not least

---

[67] TNA, INF 13/171, 'Don't do it, Mother – Leave your Children in the Safer Areas'.

[68] LPL, Lang 318, fos. 199–200, Queen Elizabeth to C. G. Lang, 6 Nov. 1939 (the queen's emphasis).

[69] RA, QEQMH/PS/SPE: BROADCASTS, 11 Nov. 1939, 'Broadcast by H.M. The Queen'.

the humble men – who would be cheered and encouraged by Your Majesty's heartfelt words. I offer you my real congratulations.[70]

It appears from personal testimonies that the archbishop was right to judge the queen's broadcast a success with listeners and with women in particular. As had been the case with George V in the mid 1930s, members of the public wrote to Queen Elizabeth in response to her message, expressing their personal feelings in an attempt to reach out and achieve some kind of intimacy with an otherwise remote public figure. Eluned Winifred Evans from Dolgelley in North Wales was one of these people:

Will Your Majesty please accept my sincerest appreciation and thanks for your wonderful message delivered so beautifully to the Women of the Empire. It gave me greater courage and inspiration to carry on. Your Majesty sets an example in the marvellous way you so courageously and pleasantly undertake your duties. It is a joy to read about your visits and also to see Your Majesties photographs in the press. May God Bless you and keep you and family [sic].[71]

For this writer, the queen's radio message had encouraged her 'to carry on' despite the war. She was also impressed by the public duties undertaken by the monarch and appreciated the media coverage that enabled her to keep up to date with royal activities. The personalized link that radio created between the royal family and public thus again evoked direct, empathetic responses from listeners like this one and Evans's letter notably ended with a reciprocated religious blessing. An anonymous female listener wrote to express her feelings in much the same vein:

Madam,

I do not know how to address you but I wish to thank you for the personal help you have given the women of the Empire by your moving and simple message to us last night.

There must be millions who were conscious of the love you expressed, and who were once more able to carry on because of it, so that for one person like myself to be attempting to tell you of her own experience must seem unnecessary. I just had the feeling that you would like to have a direct answer to your appeal from one of your subjects, and to definitely know that it did something.[72]

The writer's words again attest to the power of royal broadcasts in inspiring listeners and in connecting them as part of an imagined community. This

[70] RA, QEQM/PRIV/PAL/LANG, C. G. Lang to Queen Elizabeth, 11 Nov. 1939.
[71] RA, QEQM/PRIV/GEN, E. W. Evans to Queen Elizabeth, 11 Nov. 1939.
[72] RA, PS/PSO/GVI/PS/MAIN/04298, Anon. to Queen Elizabeth, 12 Nov. 1939 (original emphasis).

woman went on to describe how 'poor health and a young son in the army who seemed to have gone beyond my love and care' had left her feeling 'down and under' but that when the monarch's 'quiet words echoed in the room you seemed to speak to me, and gradually I saw how much a little home meant, and how important it was to keep on carrying on'. She ended her letter by stating that she wrote 'from my heart so I hope your secretary will be kind enough to give you my letter'. Here was a listener who thought that radio had brought her into close emotional communion with the queen and felt compelled to respond in highly intimate terms that conveyed her thanks for the monarch's uplifting words of reassurance.

These kinds of reaction extended to the queen's friends, several of whom wrote to her in order to praise the broadcast. One notable example was the letter from the old courtier Sir Clive Wigram, who thanked the queen for 'a wonderfully inspiring and encouraging message' and reported that he had attended a lunch with 'Sir John Reith and ... another prominent B.B.C. official' who 'were loud in their praises of one of the best broadcasts that have ever gone out to the world. The tone, the pace, the pronunciation, the substance with no faltering for a word were perfect'. Wigram's letter indicates that positive reactions to the queen's speech were not limited to women. Nor were these simply the toadying words of a long-time loyal servant. Wigram's sons were both in the armed forces and he confessed to the queen that:

> as a family man I felt quite emotional and it was a tonic to me. I always treasure and preserve a sentence of the late King [George V] when replying to an address from the Convocation of York in 1910 – 'The foundations of national glory are set in the homes of the people. They will only remain unshaken while the family life of our race and nation is strong, simple and pure.'

> Your Majesty's message so vividly reminded me of these sentiments. We all do indeed admire the private life of Your Majesties and the example Your Majesties set in preserving the simpleness, the strength and purity of the real home. It is always such a treat to see Your Majesties with the two Princesses and to picture what a happy family party should be.[73]

The rare glimpses into royal private life offered by Wigram's letter reveal that some of those close to the crown were also inspired by the example set by the British family monarchy. A number of personal correspondents also remarked that the queen's 'hard sacrifice of being separated from [her] children' must have meant she 'miss[ed] them dreadfully'.[74] Those who

---

[73] RA, QEQM/PRIV/PAL, C. Wigram to Queen Elizabeth, 12 Nov. 1939.

[74] RA, QEQM/PRIV/PAL, P. Mackenzie, Y. de Rothschild; and G. Weigall to Queen Elizabeth, 12/13 Nov. 1939.

knew the princesses were staying at Birkhall therefore sympathized with the queen, demonstrating that the image of royal family separation – while certainly publicized in order to evoke the identification of radio listeners – was rooted in reality and generated personal feelings of compassion among friends of the monarch, too.

Of the handful of Mass Observation diarists who recorded listening to the queen's broadcast, most did so noting their appreciation of her performance, commenting, for example, on her 'beautiful voice'.[75] She had indeed spoken with clarity and confidence and remarks like these perhaps signalled an indirect comparison with her husband's lacklustre performances as a public orator. A journalist who listened to the broadcast as it was 'rediffused' in the cinema where she was watching a film stated that 'it was received v. respectfully. Note the emphasis on the women who stay at home to do bit [*sic*], and heartily agree with the sentiment though I am not one of them'.[76] When criticism was expressed it was levelled at the press for the way they had overdramatized the story of royal family separation as alluded to by the queen. A film producer from South West London was typical in recording her disdain for the newspapers' commentaries: 'In evening listened to the queen. Quite suitable, but why must papers next day underline it "A shade of wistfulness was there when the words 'parted from our children' were spoken". No doubt, but why not trust people to appreciate that. Over-comment makes for art rather than nature'.[77] For this diarist, the press's overt focus on the queen's suffering detracted from her overall evaluation of the speech. Looking at the newspaper and newsreel reports on the broadcast, it is immediately evident that reporters and news editors did bring the human-interest elements of the message to the fore. The *Daily Telegraph* was typical in the way it presented the monarch's separation from her children:

> Sitting alone in the small room on the first floor of the Palace from which the King made his broadcast on the first day of the war, her Majesty spoke for eight minutes. The king listened at a wireless set in another room.
>
> The Queen spoke with marked confidence and fluency. Once there was a half-sigh in her voice when she said, 'The King and I know what it means to be parted from our children.'[78]

Since the beginning of the war, the press had celebrated the queen's example in agreeing to send her children out of harm's way, no doubt in part to

<hr/>

[75] MOA, 5390, 5312, 5363, 5442.
[76] MOA, 5349.
[77] MOA, 5275.
[78] *Daily Telegraph*, 13 Nov. 1939, p. 4. See also *Daily Mirror*, 13 Nov. 1939, p. 5; and *Sunday Times*, 12 Nov. 1939, p. 11.

encourage other women to make the same sacrifice. In October the *Sunday Pictorial* began a special series of weekly articles written by journalist Mavis Cox on Queen Elizabeth's daily routine in the changed circumstances of war, which included descriptions of her war work, her promotion of the women's voluntary units and her role as a domestic figure: 'We must remember, that she, too, is a mother separated from her children, and that this separation means as much to her as to the humblest mother whose kiddies have been evacuated for reasons of safety'.[79] Articles like these were addressed primarily to female readers and invoked the queen's role as a wife and mother in the context of the war effort on the home front. According to reports like these, she was a 'woman fellow-sufferer' who had bravely consented to temporary separation from her children for the good of the nation.[80]

Queen Elizabeth notably allowed a newsreel cameraman to record a version of her broadcast – the first member of the royal family to do so – and *Pathé Gazette* interspersed its subsequent film of her delivering the message with footage of mothers waving farewell to their evacuee children at train stations and scenes of host families welcoming them to their new homes in the countryside (Figure 4.2).[81] Other footage in this newsreel included the monarchs' observance of Armistice Day at the cenotaph and, as the soundtrack relayed the queen's words on the importance of women's wartime activities, the film cut to scenes of nurses and the women's auxiliary forces on parade as part of the Armistice procession. The message conveyed through innovative newsreels like this one, which saw the media of film and radio converge, was that British women had contributed to one world war and were ready to do so once again.

The media therefore used the queen's broadcast as an opportunity to stress the role that she was playing in leading women through the war. Press articles included a *Daily Mirror* piece that focused on the 'five mothers from working-class districts of Glasgow' who had listened to the monarch's broadcast from their new home on the Balmoral estate. According to the *Mirror*, these women and their children were 'guests of the queen', having been evacuated to the country – clearly implying that the royal family were

---

[79] *Sunday Pictorial*, 1 Oct. 1939, p. 7. See also 8 Oct. 1939, p. 23; 15 Oct. 1939, p. 21; 22 Oct. 1939, p. 18; 29 Oct. 1939, p. 21.

[80] S. Brown, 'Cecil Beaton and the iconography of the House of Windsor', *Photography & Culture*, iv (2011), 293–308, at p. 299; R. Brunt, 'The family firm restored: newsreel coverage of the British monarchy 1936–45', in Gledhill and Swanson, *Nationalising Femininity*, pp. 140–51, at p. 148.

[81] 'The Queen's Broadcast Message', *Pathé Gazette*, 16 Nov. 1939.

Figure 4.2. 'The King and I know what it means to be parted from
our children'. Bentley Archive/Popperfoto © Getty Images.

doing their bit in hosting city dwellers.[82] Meanwhile, a *Sunday Express* article
published the day after the queen's broadcast stated that she had 'made up
her mind to become the real as well as the titular head of Britain's women at
war' and that this involved many difficulties, not least of which was running
Buckingham Palace as a comfortable home despite the various material
restrictions that the conflict imposed on her and other 'housewives'.[83]

From the very beginning of the war, then, older ideas about the burdens of
royal public life and the national responsibilities that came with it fused with
new narratives about the hardships that the royals experienced alongside the
British public as a result of family separation and the testing circumstances
of war. These messages were readily taken up by the press, newsreels and
radio and persisted through the winter of 1939 to the summer of 1940, with
the king and queen regularly appearing in news reports that emphasized the
monarchs' keen interest in military and civilian preparations and the way
they were courageously facing up to the privations of war alongside their
people.

[82] *Daily Mirror*, 13 Nov. 1939, p. 5.
[83] *Sunday Express*, 12 Nov. 1939, p. 4.

*

We now know that the media inflated the stories of suffering faced by royalty in order to stress the 'equality of sacrifice' that supposedly characterized the war on the home front.[84] For example, in January 1940 Princess Elizabeth and Princess Margaret were moved from Birkhall to Royal Lodge in the grounds of Windsor Castle, but the narrative of a royal family separated by war was maintained despite the fact that the royal children now regularly saw their parents and, from May 1940, spent most nights with them at Windsor Castle.[85] Importantly, narratives of royal suffering appear to have had some of the desired effects on the way media audiences perceived their royal rulers, as is revealed by a Mass Observation file report that sought to illuminate public attitudes towards the House of Windsor in July 1940. The file report was based on an analysis of answers to 'indirect questioning' and a 'collection of a number of overheard remarks'. It also included a summary of 'observations made of the content of news-reels and the reactions to them'. Although by no means representative of British public opinion as a whole, the file report is interesting for the ambivalent thoughts and feelings it recorded on royalty.[86] On the positive side, it is clear the idea popularized in the 1930s that royal life was a burden worked to generate some support for the protagonists of the House of Windsor. The compiler of the study noted that 'a number of people mention that the King and Queen have a very difficult job, and it is generally considered that they do it well, in spite of difficulties'. Several comments were included to support this statement:

'They've had a pretty rotten time since they came to the throne, but they've done their job well …'

'I think they're wonderful. The King and Queen set a wonderful example to the whole country, though the King had a terrible job, suddenly being thrown into an office like that with his impediment.'

'I think they're very good you know, the King and Queen, they do what they can. It must be a terrible life.'

Members of the public also identified with the gendered personalities of the royals. Asked what they thought of the king and queen, one respondent

[84] I. Zweiniger-Bargielowska, 'Royal rations', *History Today*, xliii (1993), pp. 13–5. On the importance of the wartime language of 'equality of sacrifice', see Rose, *Which People's War?*, pp. 31–4.
[85] Pimlott, *Elizabeth II*, pp. 57–8.
[86] MOA, File Report 247, 'The Royal Family', 4 July 1940.

stated that 'they're nice homely people – and she's a wonderful mother'. Another replied: 'I think the Queen is the most popular – they both get on well with the ordinary man'. Phrases like these suggest that the official projection of the maternal side of the queen's personality and the consistent emphasis on the 'normal' qualities of royal family life helped to generate positive forms of identification with them among members of the public who saw the monarchs as 'homely', ordinary people.

These positive attitudes towards the royal family were, however, tempered by more negative comments; these were in the majority and hinted at an underlying disinterest or even disaffection with the royal family. The introduction to the report asserted that 'it was found that interest in the Royal Family had decreased during the War period, and often the subject of conversation drifted to topics more directly connected with the war'. The 'lack of interest' recorded by Mass Observation was backed up by a selection of comments, including that of a twenty-year-old middle-class man: 'I think they're quite nice people, quite harmless, but redundant – is that the word? – unnecessary. I'm not very interested in them'. Two comments that echoed this one also hinted at the way an anti-elite mood was taking hold of sections of the public as a result of official propaganda campaigns like that of broadcaster and writer J. B. Priestley, who consistently valorized the heroism of the 'little man' while denigrating older social hierarchies as part of what was fast becoming known as the 'people's war'.[87] A working-class woman aged forty-five was reported saying: 'I think it's all a bit silly – Kings and Queens in wartime. I don't think they're wanted. All them things are all right in peacetime – we like to have ceremonies, and royal robes, – but now it's up to us all – not Kings and Queens. That's what I think anyway'. A thirty-year-old male labourer thought the same: 'Kings and Queens don't make much difference when it comes to wars and so on. Ours are just figureheads, and that shows more than ever in wartime'.

The idea that royalty was relatively ineffectual – 'redundant' as one young man put it – and that they were primarily 'figureheads' was reiterated by several interviewees, one of whom alluded to both the positive and negative elements of this symbolic role: 'Well, I look at it like this – they're only figureheads, we all know that – the King doesn't 'ave any say in the Government. They're only figureheads, but they're something to look up to – you can't imagine England without a King or Queen'. The respondent highlighted the symbolism of modern kingship, which is possibly indicative of the way the constitutional, non-partisan interpretation of monarchy celebrated at the time of the 1937 coronation had taken root among the British

---

[87] Calder, *The People's War*, pp. 138–9; Nicholas, *Echo of War*, pp. 57–62, 244–5.

public.[88] However, while the king and the queen might be 'something to look up to', the fact they were simultaneously described as '*only* figureheads' is a stark reminder of the way the abdication had witnessed the replacement of a dynamic and outspoken king, renowned for his forthright leadership style, with a man whose very lack of personality meant that politicians and the media were able to cast him as the purest example of the powerless constitutional sovereign. The Mass Observation report thus hints at the way members of the public were uncertain of the leadership George VI could provide at a time of national crisis. Furthermore, the forceful presence of his older brother, the duke of Windsor, during the first months of the war not only served to highlight the king's lack of charisma (as had been the case at the time of his crowning), but also became a distraction that worked to undermine public confidence in the monarchy's wartime leadership.

As we saw in the previous chapter, far from being marginalized by the media after the abdication crisis, as some historians have suggested, Edward remained a regular fixture in the press and newsreels – in part because news editors could simply not afford to ignore him, given his enduring popularity.[89] At the beginning of the war he demanded that he be given an opportunity to participate in the fighting in some meaningful way (as had been the case in 1914) and, at the behest of his brother (who wanted him out of the public eye) and the War Office, he was sent to France in the role of a liaison as part of a British military mission to report back on the French army's preparations for the war ahead.[90] The duke's subsequent activities in the autumn of 1939 were widely reported by the media.[91] A Mass Observation study on the well-known personalities filmed by the newsreels in the first five months of the war suggested that he was the most popular member of the royal family to feature in them – that is, according to the number of times his appearance on screen was applauded by cinema viewers (which was just one of the many unscientific methods developed by Mass Observation investigators in these years to gauge how media audiences felt about public figures).[92] Although George VI and his consort appeared in a slightly higher number of newsreels in the period from September to

[88] See ch. 3.

[89] Brunt, 'The family firm restored', pp. 140–1.

[90] P. Ziegler, *King Edward VIII* (London, 1990), pp. 406–7; H. Jones, 'A prince in the trenches? Edward VIII and the First World War', in *Sons and Heirs: Succession and Political Culture in Nineteenth-Century Europe*, ed. F. L. Müller and H. Mehrkens (Basingstoke, 2016), pp. 229–46.

[91] *Daily Express*, 11 Sept. 1939, p. 4; 14 Sept. 1939, pp. 7 and 12; 2 Oct. 1939, p. 1; *Daily Mirror*, 15 Sept. 1939, p. 3; 20 Oct. 1939, p. 3; 20 Nov. 1939, p. 20.

[92] MOA, File Report 22, 'Newsreel Report', 28 Jan. 1940.

January 1940, they were applauded on far fewer occasions. If this study had any bearing on public opinion, it would seem that Edward still outshone his younger brother among some cinemagoers despite his abdication and marriage to the duchess and his dubious, highly publicized visit to Nazi Germany in October 1937.[93] It is also notable that, although he was now a former king, the newsreels which reported the duke's activities highlighted the same popular appeal and go-getting energy that had been his trademarks as monarch and prince of Wales. Commentators drew attention to the warm welcome he received on 'returning' to Britain, his pleasure at 'coming home' and his determination to fulfil his mission in France (Figure 4.3).[94]

The government and royal household secretly worked to prevent the duke from visiting British troops stationed in France, partly so that he did not upstage the king as the leading representative of the House of Windsor on the other side of the English Channel.[95] But Edward discovered this and kicked up a fuss about the way he was being treated, which led to a further souring of relations with the king. Although George VI eventually relented and allowed his brother to inspect home regiments by prior arrangement, this episode led the duke to question the importance of his role in France and his doubts escalated when German forces suddenly broke the French line in mid May 1940. He quickly travelled to the south of France, where the duchess of Windsor was staying and where he undertook a series of visits to French battalions on the Italian border. But when Italy declared war on France on 10 June, the duke was again forced to flee the enemy – this time along with his wife and retinue – first to Spain and then, at the beginning of July, to Portugal.

During this frenzied period of retreat across the Iberian Peninsula, the British government tried to work out what to do with the duke and duchess, fearing they might be captured by the Nazis and used as political pawns.[96] According to Edward's biographer, the new prime minister, Winston Churchill, proposed to arrange for transport to bring the couple back to Britain, but the duke rejected this offer on the grounds that he could stomach neither an ignominious return nor a reunion with his

[93] Ziegler, *King Edward VIII*, pp. 386–401.

[94] 'Duke and Duchess of Windsor Home', *Pathé Gazette*, 18 Sept. 1939; 'Duke and Duchess of Windsor Return Home', *Gaumont British News*, 17 Sept. 1939; 'Major-General the Duke of Windsor', *Pathé Gazette*, 9 Oct. 1939; 'Major-General the Duke of Windsor at French Headquarters', *Pathé Gazette*, 23 Oct. 1939; 'With the Army "Over There"', *Pathé Gazette*, 28 Oct. 1939.

[95] Ziegler, *King Edward VIII*, pp. 407–12.

[96] Ziegler, *King Edward VIII*, pp. 416–36. This was the period during which Edward became the focus of Nazi intrigue, although Ziegler (while often damning of the duke's character) is extremely doubtful that he ever collaborated with the enemy in any way at all.

The Duke of Windsor—home after nearly three years—motored from Portsmouth with the Duchess yesterday to Coleman's Hatch, Sussex, where they are the guests of Major E. D. Metcalfe, best man at their wedding.

The Duchess's coat was of mustard-and-black tweed.

The battery goes into action ; catches broad smiles.

EXTENDED ORDER.—The Prime Minister and Mrs. Chamberlain thread their way through a car park, taking their daily walk " somewhere in London."

Figure 4.3. 'The Duke of Windsor – Home After Nearly Three Years', *Daily Express*, 14 September 1939, p. 12. © The British Library Board.

family. The solution devised by Churchill and agreed to by George VI was that Edward and the duchess would board a ship to the Bahamas, where he would spend the rest of the war as governor of the islands. The duke eventually agreed to this plan and he and his wife set sail from Lisbon on 1 August 1940.[97]

Mass Observation reports and the media coverage of the duke's activities in summer 1940 help to explain why Churchill and George VI effectively banished Edward to the Bahamas. The duke's liaison role in France had initially kept him busy and after a while the media concerned themselves with more pressing war-related stories. A second Mass Observation study on the newsreels' coverage of popular personalities (this time in the four months from the end of January to May 1940) recorded that 'the Duke of Windsor,

[97] Ziegler, *King Edward VIII*, pp. 425–9.

the most popular of Royal figures, has not be [*sic*] observed once'.[98] British officials and royal courtiers who had viewed the duke's attention-grabbing activities at the start of the war with trepidation could content themselves in the knowledge that reporters had lost interest in Edward's inspections of allied soldiers and fortifications along the Maginot Line.[99] Indeed, this trend began at the end of 1939, right at the time that George VI undertook his own highly publicized trip to France to visit his troops. But press reports and the Mass Observation study on the monarchy from the summer of 1940 reveal why officials back in Britain had been right to worry about the potentially negative effects the duke's activities might have on both the war effort and the crown's reputation. Over the course of June and July newspapers published a spate of unfavourable reports on the duke's retreat from France across Spain to Portugal.[100] Journalists questioned whether he had deserted the British mission to which he had been attached (an accusation he refuted at the time and which has since been disproved by his biographer) and, in the case of the communist *Daily Worker*, under a cartoon that ridiculed the wartime narrative of 'equality of sacrifice', whether a private soldier would have been allowed to behave in the same way.[101] The Mass Observation file report from July 1940 on public attitudes to the monarchy similarly reveals that Edward's flight from France led to popular concerns arising about royalty's reliability in wartime. It included the comment of a forty-year-old housewife: '[T]here are some not too nice stories floating around about the Duke of Windsor. I was never particularly keen on him though, I'm glad he went'. Investigators interpreted this comment as part of a wider body of negative remarks expressed by interviewees about other European royalty, specifically regarding the Belgian king's capitulation to Nazi Germany and the rumour that the king of Romania was preparing to abdicate. Based on these comments, Mass Observation judged that 'there is a feeling well based on precedent, that Royalty is something different from the mass of people, and under present stresses, will slide off the top of the country into another country when things get tough'.[102]

---

[98] MOA, File Report 141, 'Newsreel Report 2', 27 May 1940. In fact, in this period the duke only appeared in one newsreel story: 'Duke and Duchess of Windsor Visit Famous French Fighter Squadron', *British Paramount News*, 25 March 1940.

[99] It is possible that British journalists and cameramen were prevented or dissuaded by royal officials or military authorities from reporting on Edward's activities, although evidence of this is yet to be located.

[100] *Daily Mirror*, 24 June 1940, pp. 1–2; *Daily Express*, 29 June 1940, p. 1.

[101] *Daily Express*, 8 June 1940, p. 1; *Daily Worker*, 10 July 1940, p. 3; Ziegler, *King Edward VIII*, pp. 417–18.

[102] MOA, File Report 247, 'The Royal Family', 4 July 1940.

As already noted, the same Mass Observation file report suggested that there was a cooling in public attitudes towards George VI and Queen Elizabeth, a finding which was supported by MO's data on newsreels, too: although both monarchs appeared in twice as many newsreel films in the period from the end of January to May 1940 compared to the first five months of the war, their popularity decreased according to the number of times they were applauded by cinemagoers. The Mass Observation investigators suggested this decline was 'due to the fact that they [the monarchs] are always seen visiting factories, civic centres, or the King on his own awarding medals. Every sequence is similar to the last'.[103] It is true that the royal newsreel coverage of this period was formulaic and repetitive, but the other difficulty royalty faced in 1940 was that Nazi Germany's rapid advance across Europe meant that the newsreels increasingly focused their attention on how Britain's politicians and the military were responding to the war. Indeed, all the Mass Observation studies on newsreels from 1940 recorded that Churchill was far and away the most popular personality to feature in them, having received the loudest and most consistent applause from cinemagoers both before and after becoming prime minister on 10 May.[104]

Churchill's popularity in the summer of 1940, after he had cautiously celebrated the 'miracle' of the British Expeditionary Force's evacuation from the beaches of Dunkirk and, later, the victories of 'the few' in the dramatic air battles against the Nazi Luftwaffe, needs to be considered against the apparent loss of confidence in other British leaders in this period, including royalty.[105] The July 1940 Mass Observation file report concluded by noting that the House of Windsor's prestige 'has slightly but distinctly declined in recent months', partly, it claimed, because of the failings of other royal persons, including the duke of Windsor, and partly because 'the symbolic value of Royalty has hardly been exploited since the outbreak of war'.[106] As the next section shows, the events of autumn 1940 provided the royal family with the perfect opportunity to re-establish their symbolic authority as part of Britain's war effort.

[103] MOA, File Report 141, 'Newsreel Report 2', 27 May 1940.
[104] Also see MOA, File Report 444, 'Newsreel Report 3', 6 Oct. 1940.
[105] On Churchill's popularity in summer 1940, see R. Toye, *The Roar of the Lion: the Untold Story of Churchill's World War II Speeches* (Oxford, 2013), pp. 61–72.
[106] MOA, File Report 247, 'The Royal Family', 4 July 1940.

'My sister Margaret-Rose and I feel so much for you'

Royal biographers and historians have tended to take for granted the roles played by George VI and Queen Elizabeth in supporting their people through the traumatic months of the Blitz. Scholars have interpreted the monarchs' visits to bombed out areas of London and towns and cities in the provinces as epitomizing the class-levelling experience of the war, with the king and queen willingly sharing in the suffering created by the conflict.[107] Scenes of the monarchs stood with small gatherings of their subjects among the rubble of buildings flattened by the Luftwaffe's bombing raids have become part of the popular canon of images associated with the British home front.[108] And, according to this narrative, it was through the experience of the Blitz that the king and queen came to 'know their people and their people them'.[109] The famous words supposedly uttered by the queen after Buckingham Palace had been bombed – that she was 'glad' as it meant she could 'now look the East End in the face' (as an equal) – were almost certainly apocryphal, but they perfectly encapsulate the idea that the monarchs were united with their subjects in their suffering and resilience.

While the king and queen's compassion for their subjects sprung from a genuine concern about their wellbeing, we must not lose sight of the way interactions between the monarchs and their subjects were carefully staged by royal officials and a compliant media to convey the impression of personal sympathy. The Blitz created a new and much-needed role for George VI and his consort at a time when their contribution to the war effort was being eclipsed by the fast-moving events of summer 1940. In adapting to the bombing raids, it is clear that the royal household sought to circumvent the influence of the Home Office and Ministry of Information in order to project a vision of a king and queen who were personally involved in the lives of their subjects, drawing on older forms of imagined intimacy between crown and people. Notably, the Blitz also signalled the start of a process that witnessed the monarchy become more assertive in terms of the leadership style it projected through its public relations strategy.

Official documents that detailed how Churchill's government were preparing for air raids in August 1940 (the month before the Luftwaffe's bombers began attacking Britain) also show how Buckingham Palace planned the royal visits to civil defence services that the king and queen had been undertaking across the UK since the start of the war. Importantly,

---

[107] Shawcross, *Queen Elizabeth the Queen Mother*, p. 491; S. Bradford, *King George VI* (London, 2011), pp. 427–30.

[108] Brunt, 'The family firm restored', pp. 147–8; Zweiniger-Bargielowska, 'Royal rations', p. 13.

[109] Connelly, *We Can Take It*, pp. 128 and 150–2.

these itineraries would act as the blueprint for the royal tours of blitzed areas from September 1940, with an emphasis firmly on informality and intimacy. Courtiers would liaise directly with the specific regional commissioner in charge of the civil defence service which the royals wanted to visit.[110] Then, during the visit, 'particular care is taken that the number of people presented [to the royals is] kept as small as possible and that … as little attention as possible is drawn to the visit. The opportunity is taken during the tour to present one or two individuals in an unostentatious manner, but anything in the nature of a number of formal presentations is taboo'.[111] Press arrangements for the royal civil defence service visits mirrored this emphasis on intimacy in the way they were kept to a minimum. Two specially accredited court reporters employed by two of the main news agencies – the Press Association and the Exchange Telegraph – accompanied the royal party, alongside two accredited photographers and a cameraman and producer from the newsreel company whose turn it was to film as part of the 'royal rota'.[112]

There are three reasons which help to explain why the palace exercised such tight control over the planning and execution of royal visits during the war. First and foremost, it was crucial that the king and queen remained safe. At a time when there were grave concerns among British officials about the spreading of state secrets, the palace thought that the fewer people who knew about royal visits the less likely it was that something bad would happen to the king and queen during their excursions. Second, the royal tours were clearly designed to convey to select groups of onlookers and pressmen the personal connection that ostensibly linked the king and queen to their subjects. Presentations were to be informal: the monarchs would interact with 'one or two individuals in an unostentatious manner' and any kind of ceremony was discouraged in order to signal to those watching the intimate nature of the relationship between the royals and the public – as had been the case with provincial royal tours since George V's early reign.[113] Finally, by limiting the number of journalists and cameramen who accompanied the royal couple, courtiers were able to exercise tighter control over the way newspapers and newsreels projected the tours to media audiences. Documentary evidence in the Royal Archives is fragmentary but it seems that, in late 1937, courtiers decided that the House of Windsor would benefit from having accredited court reporters who would write

---

[110] TNA, HO 186/1636, T. B. Braund to J. H. Brebner, 13 Aug. 1940.
[111] TNA, HO 186/1636, Unknown to H. V. Rhodes, 20 Aug. 1940.
[112] TNA, HO 186/1636, E. Miéville to F. N. Hillier, 25 Oct. 1940.
[113] F. Mort, 'Safe for democracy: constitutional politics, popular spectacle, and the British monarchy 1910–1914', *Jour. Brit. Stud.*, lviii (2019), 109–41.

about life at the palace and accompany members of the royal family on their public visits, thus gaining privileged access to royal news while acting as liaison with the rest of the media (similar measures had been put in place during the prince of Wales's tours of the empire and Commonwealth in the 1920s).[114] While we might conjecture that this move was intended to limit the number of journalists and photographers in constant pursuit of royalty, it also meant courtiers could better manage the media's access to the House of Windsor, which was critical in the uncertain months after George VI's coronation.

The Ministry of Home Security (which directed the civil defence services under the auspices of the Home Office) and the Ministry of Information were, to their annoyance, excluded from helping to co-ordinate royal tours during the war, but nevertheless had to deal with complaints from journalists in London and the provinces who were unable to come close to the royal visitors during their trips around Britain.[115] These tensions came to a head at the start of the Blitz. J. H. Brebner, director of the Ministry of Information's news division, wrote to T. B. Braund, a public relations officer at the Ministry of Home Security, in the hope that they could establish the protocol to be followed during royal visits of blitzed areas. Brebner wanted the Ministry of Home Security to inform the Ministry of Information's news division about all royal tours so that he could dispatch a photographer to accompany the royal party. The main problem was that the police who managed access to the blitzed areas visited by royalty did not accept the press passes distributed by the Home Office and prevented non-accredited journalists, cameramen and photographers from gaining access to the royals.[116] The Ministry of Information saw real benefits in having its own photographs of royal tours of blitzed areas which it could use as part of its propaganda campaigns and so it took up the matter directly with the palace. Two weeks later, civil servants at the Ministry of Home Security were able to confirm that press arrangements for royal visits were running much more smoothly: the royal household specified a list of news agencies, photographers and cameramen (as detailed above) to whom press passes

[114] Louis Wulff was one of these accredited court reporters. RA, PS/PSO/GVI/PS/VISUK/02428/124 refers to Wulff's being a journalist with the Press Association who was present at George VI's and Queen Elizabeth's visit to Yorkshire in 1937. RA, PS/PSO/GVI/PS/WARVIS/04648/1 refers to Wulff's being present as a PA-accredited journalist during the king and queen's visit to the Midlands on 18 and 19 April 1940. On the prince of Wales, see Mort, 'On tour with the prince', pp. 48–9.
[115] TNA, HO 186/1636, A. Lambert to T. Gardiner, 1 Aug. 1940; J. H. Brebner to T. B. Braund, 12 Sept. 1940.
[116] TNA, HO 186/1636, J. H. Brebner to T. B. Braund, 12 Sept. 1940.

were to be distributed; and the two accredited court reporters would cover the tours themselves and supervise any additional arrangements.[117] However, this was not good enough for Brebner at the Ministry of Information, who was unhappy that the two news agencies accredited by the palace controlled all information about the royal tours; and he 'strongly urge[d]' civil servants at the Ministry of Home Security to 'give the information to the Newspaper Proprietors' Association', who might then liaise with the press.[118] Once again, the Ministry of Information revealed that in the early years of the war its propaganda aims did not align with those of the palace, which sought to maintain a tight grip over the royal media image through its relationship with accredited press agencies.

As the bombing raids over London persisted through October, and under increasing pressure from disgruntled reporters who were unhappy that they were not given access to report on the royal tours of blitzed areas in Britain's towns and cities, F. N. Hillier from the Ministry of Home Security wrote to the king's other assistant private secretary, Sir Eric Miéville, to ask if he might extend the list of pressmen who could accompany the royals on their excursions. Miéville replied that it was best to stick with 'the existing plan', although under exceptional circumstances, 'by which I mean that when the visit is of particular importance', the number might be increased.[119] The palace thus stood firm in maintaining its authority over the media arrangements for the royal tours and, as far as one can tell from the historical evidence, this letter, written on 25 October 1940, signalled the end of the debate on this matter.[120]

News reports, photographs and newsreel footage of the royal tours from late 1940 to the summer of 1941 exhibit a repetitive quality that is indicative of the formulaic press arrangements which went into staging the tours for media audiences. For example, in newsreels, scenes of the king and queen arriving at blitzed sites were accompanied by soundtracks of cheering and applause as the royals moved into close proximity to grinning members of the public (Figure 4.4). The cameras regularly focused in close-up on the waving and smiles of those who gathered to greet the royal visitors and a number of key figures were regularly singled out for special attention, including civil defence volunteers, air-raid precaution wardens, nurses and mothers with

---

[117] TNA, HO 186/1636, F. N. Hillier to T. B. Braund, 24 Sept. 1940; Mr. Kirk to T. B. Braund, 15 Oct. 1940.

[118] TNA, HO 186/1636, J. H. Brebner to D. C. Bolster, 3 Oct. 1940.

[119] TNA, HO 186/1636, E. Miéville to F. N. Hillier, 25 Oct. 1940.

[120] There is no additional documentary evidence in The National Archives to suggest that the government continued to issue complaints to the royal household about access to royal tours of blitzed areas.

Figure 4.4. Royal visit to a bomb-damaged area of the East End, 23 April 1941 (RCIN 2000506). Royal Collection Trust / © Her Majesty Queen Elizabeth II 2019.

children. More often than not, commentators remarked on the reassuring smile and kind words of the queen and the camera regularly lingered on her as the emotional focal point that drew members of the public together. Commentaries also repeatedly stressed the 'personal link' that connected the monarchs to their subjects – rooted in the sympathy the royals expressed for their people and the courage and fortitude their visits supposedly inspired among the bereaved and those left homeless by the air raids.[121]

The royal household's emphasis on intimacy and informality continued to shape how royal visits to blitzed areas were staged through the summer of 1941 and again in 1944/45 with the V1 and V2 rocket attacks.[122] Regional

[121] E.g., the *Pathé Gazette* series: 'King and Queen in Raided Areas', 23 Sept. 1940; 'King and Queen Tour Merseyside', 14 Nov. 1940; 'Their Majesties in Sheffield', 13 Jan. 1941; 'Royal Tour of Bombed Areas', 20 Feb. 1941; 'Their Majesties in South Wales', 24 March 1941.

[122] TNA, HO 186/1636, H. Morrison to R. H. Jerman, 16 March 1944; Hart-Davis, *King's Counsellor*, p. 243. However, royal tours of areas affected by rocket attacks were discontinued because the missiles were landing wide of their intended targets and the British authorities did not want to draw attention to this fact (*King's Counsellor*, p. 301).

commissioners of civil defence services remained the first point of contact for the palace. They instructed courtiers on the areas that had been bombed, helped to plan the royal visits to places of interest, including other special civil defence initiatives like feeding or rest centres, and were responsible for the smooth running of the tour. For example, the regional commissioner for London was the former Antarctic explorer, Admiral Sir Edward Evans, who accompanied the king and queen on many of their trips to blitzed areas in the capital.[123] Evans played a key role in liaising with the palace to ensure that royal tours took place promptly after air raids and that all areas were covered.[124]

The tours also remained low-key affairs in terms of the way they were staged. Local dignitaries like district counsellors were deliberately excluded from itineraries and instead the royals focused their attention on the ordinary people who had endured the bombing raids.[125] Ostentatious garments like top hats were avoided at all times in order to convey to onlookers and reporters that the monarchs were 'ordinary' people, just like their subjects, and could empathize with the hardships of war.[126] Notably, the human touch that the queen mastered on these occasions became increasingly famous and mythologized, with the media and government officials regularly celebrating her role as the sympathetic focal point to which the suffering gravitated.[127]

One reason why courtiers were so determined to control the media's narrative on royal trips to blitzed communities was that the royal tourists did not always meet with a warm welcome. After the Luftwaffe's first attacks on London's East End in September 1940, it was rumoured in elite circles that the king and queen had been booed on visiting local inhabitants who had been bombed out of their homes.[128] The tours of blitzed areas, if not carefully managed, could therefore undermine the leadership role the monarchs sought to carve out for themselves in this period. The key

[123] TNA, HO 186/1636, 'Detailed List of Royal Tours Conducted by Admiral Sir Edward Evans'. Notably, the duke of Kent regularly stood in for George VI on tours of London, as this document shows.

[124] TNA, HO 186/1636, copy of memorandum by Admiral Sir Edward Evans, 17 Oct. 1940; A. Hardinge to H. U. Willink, 1 July 1941.

[125] TNA, HO 186/1636, E. Gowers to F. D. Littlewood, 28 Apr. 1941; A. Lascelles to A. S Hutchinson, 21 Oct. 1942.

[126] TNA, HO 186/1636, A. Lascelles to A. S Hutchinson, 21 Oct. 1942; Hart-Davis, *King's Counsellor*, pp. 67–8.

[127] TNA, HO 186/1636, H. U. Willink to H. Campbell, 28 June 1941. See also F. Marquis, *The Memoirs of the Rt. Hon. the Earl of Woolton* (London, 1959), pp. 222–4.

[128] *Harold Nicolson: Diaries and Letters: the War Years 1939–45*, ed. N. Nicolson (London, 1967), 114.

event that enabled the king and queen to present themselves as fellow sufferers, and which supposedly helped to quell ill-feeling among working-class victims, was the bombing of Buckingham Palace on 8 September.[129] According to an intelligence report by the Ministry of Information, up until the announcement of this news inhabitants of the East End had been complaining that 'it is always the poor that gets it' [sic] (referring to air raids).[130] This awareness of popular disaffection created some anxiety among government officials who feared social unrest, but the bombing of the palace presented the Ministry of Information with an opportunity for 'counteracting immediately the bad feeling in the East End'. The ministry contacted the royal household and arrangements were made for more than forty journalists from the British and foreign press to visit the palace grounds to see the bomb damage. As the ministry report continued: 'The theme "King with His people in the front line together" was stressed with the journalists'. The official propaganda line of shared suffering complemented the earlier idea that the royal family and their subjects endured the hardships of war together – as first articulated by the queen in her radio broadcast of November 1939. Alan Lascelles recorded in a letter to his wife that the king and queen had been photographed among the ruins of their home and that he had been responsible for conducting journalists around the bomb site.[131] It was certainly the case that the media toed the official line on the attack, with press reports stressing how the horrors of war on the home front united crown and people.[132] The newsreels also drew on the refrain of shared suffering, *Pathé News*'s commentator remarking, for example, in a film of a later royal tour of blitzed Fulham, that, 'having had their own home bombed, Their Majesties sp[oke] with understanding and sympathy [to their people]'.[133]

The Ministry of Information judged that the media coverage of the bombing of the palace 'immediately dissipated the bad feeling in the East End, led to remarkable expressions of affection for the Royal Family and aroused intense indignation throughout America'.[134] However, the Mass Observation evidence reveals a more complex picture. Investigators judged

[129] McLaine, *Ministry of Morale*, pp. 92–5.

[130] TNA, INF 1/64, Intelligence report by J. H. Brebner, MoI News Division: 'Bombing of Buckingham Palace'.

[131] Hart-Davis, *King's Counsellor*, pp. 15–6.

[132] *Daily Sketch*, 12 Sept. 1940, p. 1; *News Chronicle*, 12 Sept. 1940, p. 1; *Sunday Pictorial*, 15 Sept. 1940, p. 1.

[133] 'King and Queen in Raided Areas', *Pathé News*, 23 Sept. 1940.

[134] TNA, INF 1/64, Intelligence report by J. H. Brebner, MoI News Division: 'Bombing of Buckingham Palace'.

from the public responses recorded in the tea shop Lyons Corner House on Oxford Street that 'the attitude was almost entirely one of acute interest and curiosity; no signs of dismay or anger'. Several people expressed a desire to see the damage for themselves, while others expressed annoyance at the privileges that separated the royals from the experiences of ordinary people. One twenty-five-year-old woman was recorded as saying it was better that the Luftwaffe attack Buckingham Palace 'so they don't bomb my home'. She continued: 'It's all right for these people; they can go somewhere else. It's us working people can't go anywhere else'.[135] Another exchange between two working-class women aged thirty captures some of the anger directed by poorer people at wealthier Londoners at the start of the Blitz:

'That's the second one. Terrible, isn't it. They had a time bomb there yesterday. All over the place, aren't they.'

'They've bombed Park Lane too.'

'I don't mind about that. There are only the rich people live there.'

'There's working people there too. You can't have a place like Park Lane without working people.'

And some people seemed to experience *Schadenfreude*. One Mass Observation investigator noted that she observed a twenty-year-old woman 'calling to lorry men … hanging about at [the] side of [the] road: "They've bombed Buckingham Palace. Buckingham Palace is bombed!" She laughs excitedly the while, and the lorry men … laugh too'. As always, the Mass Observation evidence points to greater complexity in the feelings experienced and expressed by members of the public in relation to royalty. However, there were no more reports of the king and queen being booed during their visits after the first weeks of the Blitz, which might indicate that negative attitudes were indeed replaced by more positive ones.

The difficulty with which the historian has to contend in trying to gauge public opinion towards royalty in wartime is apathy. Indifference rarely makes itself heard in the archive and, given the constant hardships experienced by so many people during the conflict, one wonders to what extent they could really muster enthusiasm for the monarchy with everything else that was going on. One thing remains clear, however: the royal household and Ministry of Information actively sought to maintain the narrative of shared suffering. In spring 1942 the king and queen took a twenty-two roomed flat in Mayfair in order to free up some of their staff at a time when there was a national labour shortage and it was agreed with the War Office that

---

[135] MOA, TC23/4419-4502 (original emphasis).

the government would foot the bill for the renovation of the building. The *Sunday Pictorial* learnt about this and of the extravagant silver fittings that would feature in the newly refurbished space and prepared a report on it but, before the story could go to press, it was submitted to the censor who 'turned [it] down flat', knowing full well that it would undermine the official narrative of equality of sacrifice.[136]

*

The image of the House of Windsor suffering alongside their subjects on the home front was also promoted by a number of other institutions, most notably by that now longstanding champion of the crown, the BBC. In September 1940 the broadcaster worked with courtiers to plan Princess Elizabeth's first radio message to listeners in Britain and the English-speaking world. It is significant that the BBC did not involve the Ministry of Information in the royal broadcast but instead went straight to the palace with its idea, a decision that is indicative of the fractious relationship that developed between the broadcaster and the ministry in the first years of the war, with the latter often meddling in the BBC's output.[137] The broadcaster also had its own agenda in inviting the princess to speak. The idea originated with the director of children's hour, Derek 'Uncle Mac' McCulloch, who wanted her to inaugurate a special 'Children in Wartime' radio series due to begin in mid October. To this the director of outside broadcasts, Seymour Joly de Lotbinière, added that he thought the message could also inaugurate the BBC's new North American children's hour to be broadcast to evacuees overseas and specifically those who had been sent to the USA and Canada.[138] De Lotbinière suggested that 'the occasion would warrant a keen effort to "square" the Palace' (meaning to bring them on side), but thought that combining the two occasions would strengthen the BBC's arguments in support of its idea. It was left to the director general, Sir Frederick Ogilvie, to write to Alexander Hardinge to make the case for the princess's message. He noted that:

> such a talk, whether at the time of its first delivery or put out by records in later transmission to catch distant countries at their best listening hours, should

---

[136] R. Dudley Edwards, *Newspapermen: Hugh Cudlipp, Cecil Harmsworth King and the Glory Days of Fleet Street* (London, 2003), p. 165.

[137] B. Pimlott suggested that the MoI came up with the idea for the princess's broadcast (*Elizabeth II*, pp. 58–9); A. Briggs, *The History of Broadcasting in the United Kingdom* (5 vols. Oxford, 1965–95), iii. 28–31; Nicholas, *The Echo of War*, pp. 42–3, 71–2.

[138] BBCWA, R30/3,724/1, Memorandum by S. J. de Lotbinière: 'Princess Elizabeth in Children's Hour', 4 Sept. 1940.

be heard all over the world and notably in the United States. As Her Royal Highness's first broadcast delivered at an historic moment, it would reach the minds of the millions who heard it with a singular poignancy. I therefore convey this suggestion to you in the conviction that such a talk, however brief, would not only give world-wide pleasure but would be a unique contribution to the national cause.[139]

Historians have noted that Princess Elizabeth's message was designed to influence adult opinion in the USA at a time when Churchill's government hoped America would unite with Britain and its allies against the Axis powers.[140] To this end, Ogilvie's words clearly reveal that the BBC sought to support this 'national cause' through the broadcast. But the historical focus on the US dimension has obscured the monarchy's own urgent need to re-establish its authority in the crisis months of autumn 1940.

The significance of the innovation of having a royal child broadcast can be fully appreciated when it is considered against previous requests for similar messages. Throughout the 1930s wireless listeners had written to Buckingham Palace asking to hear other family members of the king speak to them over the airwaves. One of these listeners was T. E. Hartnoll of Cape Town, South Africa, who wrote to George V in November 1934:

> Many of us are looking forward with pleasurable anticipation to the message that your Majesty will be speaking to the world at Christmas ... Would it be allowed for the Princess Elizabeth of York to send a Xmas Greeting as well (if only a sentence) it would be most highly appreciated and give great pleasure? [sic] The Princess is well known thanks to Photography and the Press and now we should like to hear her voice.[141]

There are other letters like this one in the archives which reveal that new kinds of media exposure fostered a curiosity among sections of the public about the voices of Britain's royal personalities. Indeed, the BBC had long seen the value in broadcasting a range of royal voices and had asked courtiers whether other members of the royal family – including Queen Mary – could deliver messages.[142] However, these requests were always rebuffed by the royal household – that is, until the exigencies of war had brought in to question the leadership offered by the House of Windsor.

---

[139] RA, PS/PSO/GVI/PS/MAIN/04970, F. W. Ogilvy to A. Hardinge, 13 Oct. 1940.
[140] Pimlott, *Elizabeth II*, pp. 58–60.
[141] RA, PS/PSO/GV/PS/MAIN/55357, T. E. Hartnoll to King George V, 16 Nov. 1934. See also letters from J. Abbot, H. Grayson, G. A. Whittle and M. E. King; and Pimlott, *Elizabeth II*, p. 58.
[142] BBCWA, R34/862/1, H. Verney to A. Dawnay, 2 Dec. 1933; L. B. Hyde to J. Reith, 22 Nov. 1933.

Before this, George VI had spoken for his family; if other royals had made broadcasts they might have undermined his personal authority. Equally, as we have seen from Queen Elizabeth's private correspondence, there were concerns at the palace that other public messages might appear too informal in tone.

Once the king and queen had agreed to the princess's broadcast, Ogilvie handed over responsibility for the preparations to the BBC's new deputy director general, Stephen Tallents, a public relations expert who had previously worked on the campaigns of the General Post Office film unit and, before that, the Empire Marketing Board. Tallents knew full well that publicity worked better when driven by a 'human-interest' storyline and, in overseeing the drafting of the royal message, included a reference to the family separation the princess had endured along with other children in Britain.[143] By the autumn of 1940 Elizabeth and her sister Margaret were living at Windsor Castle, where the king and queen also spent their nights. In what was thus a misleading phrase, the BBC's first draft of the speech had the princess telling child listeners that, 'like you, my sister and I are living away from our parents, and we too try to realise that it is our duty to share some of the partings and hardships which fall to the lot of children in wartime'.[144] This image of wartime dislocation remained at the core of subsequent drafts of the broadcast and found its way into the final version spoken by the princess. Of course, the BBC maintained strict secrecy as to the actual location of the princesses lest their whereabouts be made public, which would not only have endangered them but also have undermined the narrative of royal family separation.[145]

Once again, the king's assistant private secretary, Alan Lascelles, was responsible for preparing the final draft of the princess's radio message. On 5 October Tallents wrote to him enclosing the BBC's latest effort and remarked that he knew the courtier was 'anxious to have a draft as soon as possible ... [W]e hope that this may at least give you something to work upon'. Tallents also noted in relation to the BBC's draft that:

in its closing passages it provides for a single goodnight message by Princess Margaret. So far as I know, this suggestion has not so far been considered at your end but represents only a hope on the part of our Children's Hour

[143] On Tallents, see S. Anthony, *Public Relations and the Making of Modern Britain: Stephen Tallents and the Birth of a Progressive Media Profession* (Manchester, 2012).
[144] BBCWA, R30/3,724/1, draft dated 23 Sept. 1940. See also 'Draft Layout: Announcement: Outline of Princess Elizabeth's Speech and details of rest of programme', undated.
[145] BBCWA, R30/3,724/1, unsigned memorandum marked 'Private and Confidential', 4 Oct. 1940.

Director that such a message might be found permissible. I can but say that if it were it would of course be of great programme value.[146]

Tallents's advocacy here was important because Princess Margaret did go on to say farewell at the end of her elder sister's broadcast. Clearly, Lascelles also detected value in including it and, as we shall see, he was right to: the younger princess's contribution caught some listeners off guard, delighting them in its apparent spontaneity.

In Lascelles's trusted hands, the focus of Princess Elizabeth's message became how she and her sister shared in the emotional burdens of war and empathized with the children who had been evacuated overseas. When she came to broadcast on the evening of Sunday 13 October, the princess told her listeners that:

> thousands of you in this country have had to leave your homes, and be separated from your fathers and mothers. My sister Margaret-Rose and I feel so much for you, as we know from experience what it means to be away from those we love most of all. To you living in new surroundings, we send a message of true sympathy and at the same time we would like to thank the kind people who have welcomed you to their homes in the country.[147]

Lascelles thus carefully avoided any suggestion that the princesses were *still* separated from the king and queen, should the royal deception be discovered. All references to the new 'Children in Wartime' series contained in earlier drafts were removed by the courtier, who instead focused the message on the shared emotional economy which linked the princesses to other children. The affective dimensions of the message extended to the optimism expressed by Elizabeth about the future: '[W]hen peace comes … it will be for us, the children of today, to make the world of tomorrow a better and happier place'. These lines, which alluded to an improved post-war world, concealed official concerns about the severe class tensions that affected Britain in late 1940 and demonstrate that Lascelles hoped to convey to listeners that the princesses, as young girls, shared the discomfort of other children but equally symbolized a more positive future. Elizabeth then ended by telling listeners that 'my sister is by my side and we are both going to say good night to you. Come on, Margaret'. At this point the younger princess chimed in with 'Good night children', followed by Elizabeth's final words: 'Good night and good luck to you all'.

---

[146] BBCWA, R30/3, 724/1, S. Tallents to A. Lascelles, 5 Oct. 1940. See also 'Draft Layout: Announcement: Outline of Princess Elizabeth's Speech and details of rest of programme', undated.

[147] *The Times*, 14 Oct. 1940, p. 4.

What did listeners make of the princess's broadcast? The BBC interpreted it as a propaganda triumph and reported back to the palace the ecstatic reception with which it had been received on the other side of the Atlantic.[148] Four Mass Observation investigators, each tasked with conducting interviews with people they encountered in different parts of London – including Streatham, Notting Hill Gate, Knightsbridge and Fulham – reported a more complex picture. They asked passers-by whether or not they had heard the princess's broadcast and, if so, what they thought of it.[149] The compilers of the resulting Mass Observation report noted that interviews of this kind shaped how respondents replied: '[T]his is the sort of question of which it is strongly socially done to say that Royalty was right'.[150] However, despite the problematic line of questioning, which may have suppressed interviewees' true thoughts and feelings, and the geographical limitations of the study, the replies of respondents are illuminating.

Out of a total number of fifty-seven people who were asked the questions, thirty-eight reported that they had listened to the princess's broadcast. Elizabeth had spoken at a time in the week designed to reach as many listeners as possible, which may help to explain why so many people reported hearing it.[151] There were three recurring themes to their responses. First, more than twenty of those who listened to the broadcast commented positively on how they thought it 'charming', 'sweet', 'beautiful', 'lovely' or that the princess 'spoke well' or 'was wonderful'.[152] Women tended to be more lavish in their praise than men – again revealing that it was more socially acceptable for women to express their feelings in public in this period – and several respondents described in detail the princess's diction and emotions. For example:

F30C. Yes. Very good. She was wonderful. Clear and full of confidence and she never faltered once – she was word perfect.

M65B. Yes. I think she did very well – she spoke very clearly and didn't seem at all nervous.

[148] RA, PS/PSO/GVI/PS/MAIN/04970, F. W. Ogilvie to A. Lascelles, 19 Oct. 1940.
[149] The answers to their questions can be located in MOA, TC65/4074-4220. They are included here with the identities assigned to them by the MO investigators: F/M to distinguish gender; followed by their age; followed by their class where A is upper class and D is working class.
[150] MOA, File Report 459, 18 Oct. 1940, pp. 42–3.
[151] The BBC's listener research department estimated that 50.7% of Britain's adult population tuned in to hear the princess speak. This was a sizeable increase compared to its usual Sunday children's hour adult listenership, which ranged from 7% to 11% (BBCWA, 248/R9/1/1, Listener Research Weekly Report no. 11).
[152] MOA, TC65/4074-4220.

M45B.Yes. Did you notice how she started off high and finished low. She was nervous at first.

Comments like these suggest that listeners focused intently on the princess's voice, some detecting a certain nervousness, which again shows that radio created a powerful empathetic interface between royal speakers and media audiences. The second theme that linked the Mass Observation responses was the way the princess's broadcast evoked comparisons with her mother or references to her younger sister, who, as we have seen, spoke at the end of the message:

F45C. Yes. She spoke beautifully and just like her Mother – she sounded so beautiful.

F45C. Lovely. Have you heard her mother? – just like her.

F50D. Yes. She was ever so good. I like the way she says 'Come on Margaret.'

M55C. Yes. Very good, her diction was wonderful. I liked her 'Come on Margaret'.

Comments like these indicate that the broadcast awakened in some listeners imagined connections with a larger royal family group and a desire to link the princess to her mother in order to better relate to her. Meanwhile, the comments on the princess's reference to her sister suggest that some listeners welcomed its seemingly informal tone but, as we know, it was nothing of the kind. Indeed, the third recurring theme that linked a dozen of the interviewees' responses was a criticism of the speech that sprung from a suspicion that ulterior motives lay behind it. Most stated that they did not think it was written by the princess but rather by someone else:

F40D. Yes. Didn't she sound like her mother? She did speak well. Of course it was made up for her, but still it was sweet – quite brought tears to my eyes.

F35C. It was very well spoken. I don't suppose it was her own composition. All that about 'our hosts' – just propaganda, don't you think? A child would never have thought of that.

M30D. Yes. I didn't think much of it – it's all written out for her – that sort of thing's only to keep the population quiet.

M35D. Spoke all right: but that's done for the business.

On the one hand, the criticism levelled at the princess's broadcast points to the fact that some members of the public thought the royal family usually *were* the authors of their own speeches, which is suggestive of the way that sincerity and trust underpinned the emotional bonds between British subjects and the crown. This trust seems to have been threatened by the public's growing sensitivity to, and disaffection with, official wartime propaganda, which were also revealed by the Mass Observation survey.[153] Notably, the working-class men who criticized that the broadcast was just 'done for the business' and was 'only to keep the population quiet' indicated that their distrust extended to the work that went into projecting the monarchy's media image.

Other Mass Observation evidence broadly tallied with the London interviews, although some diarists took issue with the way the princess 'told us how she had experienced the same as the refugee children'.[154] The official Mass Observation report on the broadcast that resulted from the interviews was over-negative given that most who responded tended to do so positively; and this probably has more to do with the alarmist tone that characterized Mass Observation's crusading work in the crisis months of autumn 1940 than with any reality. The one comment that investigators singled out to illustrate this negative sentiment is, however, very revealing in what it tells us about how some members of the public perceived the princess. It came from a letter written to Mass Observation by a patient in a hospital:

> The Head sister came specially in from her off period to tell me it was nearly time to tune in to Princess Elizabeth. Excitement reigned everywhere with nurses, but of four I have asked they all said it was a disappointment; [the] speech had so obviously been written for her and wasn't a 'child's' speech or child talking – so typical to so completely miss the boat with such a really good chance in their hands, she failed utterly to put across what she represents, the <u>child</u> Princess of the imagination and fairy tale, the <u>good</u> child of eternal goodwill. Instead, stereotyped Baldwin-Halifax, out of reach from working-class vocabulary stuff came drearying sterily over the air [sic].[155]

For this listener, the broadcast failed to meet expectations. Specifically, it did nothing to enhance the fairy-tale quality of the princess's image, which the hospital patient thought was so intrinsic to the way Elizabeth was perceived, but rather conveyed what the listener thought were banal political platitudes that would have little impact on the public. Clearly, Stephen Tallents's and Alan Lascelles's efforts were lost on some people.

---

[153] J. Fox, 'Winston Churchill and the "men of destiny": leadership and the role of the prime minister in wartime feature films', in *Making Reputations: Power, Persuasion and the Individual in Modern British*, ed. R. Toye and J. V. Gottlieb (London, 2005), pp. 92–108, at p. 97; Fox, 'Careless talk', pp. 950–1.

[154] MOA, 5220. See also MOA, File Report 462, 'Worcester Village Report', 20 Oct. 1940, p. 2.

[155] MOA, File Report 459, 18 Oct. 1940, pp. 42–3 (original emphasis).

Figure 4.5. Princesses Elizabeth and Margaret at the microphone,
by a photographer from *The Times* (RCIN 2002152). Royal
Collection Trust / © Her Majesty Queen Elizabeth II 2019.

The director of children's hour, Derek McCulloch, judged the broadcast
a great success, and wrote to Lascelles asking that he pass on his gratitude
to the princesses and to enquire whether they could sign copies of the
pictures taken by a photographer from *The Times* to publicize the broadcast
(Figure 4.5).[156] In fact, most leading newspapers used these pictures in their
coverage of the message, which was, needless to say, extremely positive and
highlighted its personal elements – including the shared hardships that
connected the princesses to other children and Elizabeth's likeness to her
mother.[157] The photographs also featured as stills in newsreel reproductions
of the princess's speech and, as with the queen's 1939 broadcast, *Pathé* and
Movietone imposed scenes of British children waving goodbye to their
parents at train-station platforms and arriving in the countryside where
they were to be billeted.[158] The message communicated through the newsreel
coverage of the princess's broadcast when she could be heard telling viewers
she and her sister knew what it felt like to be separated from one's parents

[156] RA, PS/PSO/GVI/PS/MAIN/04970, D. McCulloch to A. Lascelles, 21 Oct. 1940.
[157] *Daily Express*, 14 Oct. 1940, p. 3; *Daily Mirror*, 14 Oct. 1940, p. 1; *Daily Mail*, 14 Oct.
1940, p. 3; *Daily Telegraph*, 14 Oct. 1940, pp. 1 and 4; *The Times*, 14 Oct. 1940, pp. 5–6.
[158] 'Princess Elizabeth Broadcasts', *Pathé Gazette*, 17 Oct. 1940; 'Princess Elizabeth's
Message', *British Movietone News*, 17 Oct. 1940.

Figure 4.6. Marcus Adams, Princesses Elizabeth and Margaret, 9 April 1940 (RCIN 2943730). Royal Collection Trust / © Her Majesty Queen Elizabeth II 2019.

Princess Elizabeth FOURTEEN NEXT SUNDAY

Princess Elizabeth, Heir Presumptive to the Throne—pictured with her sister Margaret—will be fourteen years old on April 21. She is now five feet tall. Is clear-complexioned, strong, very healthy.—A new Marcus Adams portrait.

Figure 4.7. 'Princess Elizabeth: Fourteen Next Sunday', *Daily Express*, 17 April 1940, p. 3, with photograph by Marcus Adams. © The British Library Board.

The Princesses Grow Up

This latest photograph of the Princesses Elizabeth and Margaret Rose show how they are becoming grown-up. Their war efforts is vegetable gardening: their flower beds of peacetime are now coming up with vegetables, sown and tended by the Princesses. [Photo: Marcus Adams.]

Figure 4.8. 'The Princesses Grow Up', *Daily Mirror*, 24 April 1941, p. 5, with photograph by Marcus Adams. © The British Library Board

was, once again, that the royal children were no different to other evacuees and thus symbolic of their generation.

The image of the princesses as normal children was highlighted by the clothes they wore in photographs like the ones taken to publicize Elizabeth's broadcast in 1940. Both were dressed in matching jackets and striped jumpers – fairly ordinary-looking clothes and a far cry from the fairy-tale dresses in which they and their mother had posed for photographer Cecil Beaton before the war. Historians have argued that he played an important part in making royal femininity appear more ordinary through his wartime pictures of the princesses.[159] In fact, another photographer, Marcus Adams, was responsible for most of the portraits of Elizabeth and Margaret between 1939 and 1945 and helped to popularize the more austere iconography of the royal children in wartime (Figures 4.6, 4.7., 4.8).[160]

It is significant that apart from Elizabeth's broadcast in 1940, neither she nor her sister featured prominently as part of royal publicity in the first three years of the war. Given that they were still young, it was much easier to cast them as virtuous victims of wartime family separation than to present them as enthusiastic participants in the fight against Nazism. However, royal portraits of the princesses were commissioned every year to coincide with their birthdays. In the first three years of the war the pictorial emphasis was firmly on the girls' apparent loneliness. Elizabeth and Margaret usually posed sitting or standing together; other royals, like their mother, did not tend to feature in these images and this worked to highlight the fact that they were – to all intents and purposes – separated from their parents.[161] When the queen did feature, as was the case with one of Elizabeth's birthday portraits taken in 1941, the media's emphasis was on a fleeting family reunion and the love of a mother for her children.[162] Only later on in the war, once the princess had turned sixteen and had begun to assume a public role, and only once the threat of air attack and invasion had receded, did the royal family group begin regularly to reappear in media photographs together: it was no longer necessary to keep up the pretence of a dynasty dislocated by evacuation.[163]

---

[159] Brown, 'Cecil Beaton', pp. 293–308.

[160] On this contrast, see also Pimlott, *Elizabeth II*, pp. 60–1. Much of Adams's wartime photography of the royal family can be found under the search term 'Marcus Adams' in the online archive of the Royal Collection <https://www.royalcollection.org.uk> [accessed 5 March 2019].

[161] See also the reproduction of images in *Daily Express*, 17 Apr. 1941, p. 3; *Daily Mirror*, 21 Apr. 1941, p. 3; *Manchester Guardian*, 21 Apr. 1941, p. 6.

[162] *Daily Telegraph*, 21 Apr. 1941, p. 6.

[163] *Daily Express*, 22 Apr. 1944, p. 3; *Daily Telegraph*, 22 Apr. 1944, p. 5; *The Times*, 22 Apr. 1942, p. 6; *The Times*, 22 Apr. 1944, pp. 1 and 6.

On her turning sixteen on 21 April 1942, Elizabeth's public image changed almost overnight from that of a child to a young royal woman with duties and responsibilities much like her older relatives.[164] On the morning of her birthday, dressed like her mother in coat and floppy hat, she undertook her first inspection of a military regiment as part of a special parade at Windsor castle. The regiment were the Grenadier Guards and the princess took on an honorary role as their new colonel.[165] Her uncle Edward had served as a lieutenant of the Grenadiers during the First World War and, in so doing, had become the symbolic 'soldier prince', his service on the Western Front ensuring he came to embody the cultures of duty and sacrifice which defined the generation of men who fought in the trenches.[166] Now, the princess was projected as a symbol of her own youthful generation through her service as part of another war. She, too, wore uniform: first of all, as a sea ranger (an offshoot of the girl guides) and, from February 1945, as an auxiliary territorial service driver and mechanic. The media naturally helped to promote the image of an heir to the throne who, like her uncle Edward before her, seemed to be mucking in as part of the war effort.[167] However, by this point, the Second World War was nearing its end and we should thus interpret the media's coverage of the princess's ATS activities as forming part of a larger campaign that had been underway since 1943 to mythologize the monarchy's wartime leadership.

'We women as home-makers have a great part to play'

On 25 December 1942 George VI told those who tuned in to listen to his annual broadcast that 'it is at Christmas more than at any other time that we are conscious of the dark shadow of war'. He continued: 'Our Christmas festival today must lack many of the happy familiar features that it has had from our earliest childhood; we miss the actual presence of some of those nearest and dearest, without whom our family gathering cannot be complete'. Four months earlier the monarch's youngest brother, Prince George, duke of Kent, had been killed during a flying mission with the RAF, which demonstrated that the emotional trauma of wartime bereavement extended to the House of Windsor as well as other British families – a theme the king directly addressed in his Christmas message:

---

[164] Pimlott, *Elizabeth II*, pp. 69–70.

[165] *The Times*, 22 Apr. 1942, p. 6; *Daily Telegraph*, 22 Apr. 1942, p. 5.

[166] Jones, 'A prince in the trenches', pp. 230–5.

[167] *Daily Express*, 21 Apr. 1943, p. 4; *Daily Mirror*, 21 Apr. 1943, p. 5; *The Times*, 21 Apr. 1944, p. 6; 'Princess Elizabeth Second Subaltern', *Pathé Gazette*, 19 Apr. 1945. See also Pimlott, *Elizabeth II*, pp. 74–5.

The Queen and I feel most deeply for all of you who have lost or been parted from your dear ones, and our hearts go out to you with sorrow, with comfort, but also with pride … Suffering and hardship shared together have given us a new understanding of each other's problems. The lessons learned during the forty tremendous months behind us have taught us how to work together for victory, and we must see to it that we keep together after the war to build a worthier future.[168]

With these words, the king described how the experiences of war had generated a greater affinity among the different sections of British society, including between public and royalty. Some listeners seem to have appreciated his sentiments, too. One female Mass Observation diarist recorded in relation to the message that '[George VI] is, alas, now one with those who mourn someone near and dear in the loss of the Duke of Kent this year'.[169] The king also used the 1942 Christmas broadcast to signal that the monarchy's sights were now set firmly on what would come after the war had ended. Despite the difficulties many men, women and children across the world continued to face because of the conflict, his speech was defined by an optimism and confidence about the future that had not been present in his previous wartime Christmas messages. A year earlier the USA had joined the allied war effort and helped to tip the balance of military might against the Axis powers.[170] The crisis months of the Blitz seemed a long way off and, as Lascelles noted in his diary, British politicians were starting to turn their attention to post-war reconstruction and the question of what the Allies would do with a defeated Nazi Germany.[171]

In his Christmas broadcast George VI also spoke at length about recent allied military successes and the continued efforts of men and women on the home front in war production. It was in these two spheres that he and his consort now sought to cement their legacies as wartime leaders, the queen through her support and promotion of British women's work in factories, fields, the auxiliary services and their homes; the king through his association with national and imperial military triumphs and his ties to non-combatant men back on the home front. The gendered division that characterized the royal couple's media strategy after 1942 mirrored the kinds of public role they had carved out for themselves since the war began. The queen maintained her sympathetic public image, having regularly expressed pity for ordinary people, especially women, affected by

---

[168] T. Fleming, *Voices Out of the Air: Royal Christmas Day Broadcasts, 1932–1981* (London, 1981), pp. 36–8.
[169] M. Johnes, *Christmas and the British: a Modern History* (London, 2016), p. 158.
[170] Calder, *The People's War*, pp. 263–4, 524–5.
[171] Hart-Davis, *King's Counsellor*, pp. 91–2, 98 and 125.

the conflict. The king, while less effusive with his emotions, nevertheless proved determined to consolidate a public image as a war leader that was rooted in a more direct kind of relationship between monarch and subjects. The House of Windsor's publicity strategy in the period from the spring of 1943 through to May 1945 was therefore designed to strengthen a narrative of royal leadership in wartime that would come to underpin the monarchy's reputation after the conflict had ended. These years witnessed a shift left in the nation's political mood, with the war demonstrating how government could play a more active role in organizing the lives of civilians. The Beveridge Report, published in November 1942, encapsulated this new awareness of the population's needs in its recommendations for new kinds of social insurance and state welfare, many of which were welcomed by the public at the time and later implemented by Clement Attlee's post-war Labour government.[172] Despite continued public criticism of the privileges enjoyed by the royal family in the later years of the war, the palace sought to maintain the idea of shared experience in order to appeal to the increasingly egalitarian mood while at the same time elevating a vision of a post-war world that was centred on a popular family monarchy.

Although the sudden loss of the duke of Kent was a personal tragedy for the House of Windsor, it presented journalists with the perfect opportunity to highlight the mutual sacrifices of war that seemed to unite crown and people. With one voice, newspapers and newsreels celebrated Prince George's public service and emphasized that his death had demonstrated that no section of society was immune to wartime bereavement, focusing in particular on the grieving figures of his wife, Princess Marina, and three young children through the reproduction of large front-page photographs (Figure 4.9).[173] However, the public reaction to his death recorded by Mass Observation suggests that the monarchy had some work to do if it was to convince the population that royalty shared evenly in the hardships of the conflict with the rest of the nation. For several diarists and a number of those people who were asked about the duke for a special Mass Observation file report, the belief persisted that the House of Windsor was very different from other British families. While on the one hand respondents described the duke as just another casualty of war (signalling the class-levelling experience of wartime bereavement), they often added that his wife and children would not suffer the same material hardships as other families who

[172] Calder, *The People's War*, pp. 525–45. See also n. 4.

[173] On the duke's death, see *Daily Sketch*, 26 Aug. 1934, p. 1; *Daily Herald*, 26 Aug. 1934, p. 1; *News Chronicle*, 26 Aug. 1934, p. 2; *Daily Express*, 26 Aug. 1934, pp. 1 and 4; *Daily Mirror*, 26 Aug. 1934, p. 1; 'In Memory: HRH The Duke of Kent', *British Movietone News*, 27 Aug. 1942; 'The Death of the Duke of Kent', *Universal News*, 3 Sept. 1942.

had lost loved ones to the fighting. The words of a forty-year-old clerk and housewife from Sheffield in Yorkshire capture this kind of double-edged response:

> So, the Duke of Kent is killed. Well, the old queen has 4 sons so if she had come thru' this war with all 4, she wd. have been lucky. This will give Royalty a leg-up as what with Buckingham Palace bombed and now a son killed, the ignorant will feel so sorry for the Royal family, unmindful of the fact that for 3 years now there have been women getting that news daily, thousands of them now. I'm sorry for the old queen as a mother but no more than any other mother, and I'm sorry for the Greek wife with her so young baby, but hers will be fat sorrow, more easy to bear than lean sorrow. I reserve most of my pity for the widow who has to exist with kiddies on the widows' pension.[174]

This personal testimony reveals that people could feel sympathy for the relatives of the dead (in this case Queen Mary, Marina and her children) while at the same time expressing frustration at the way the House of Windsor was better placed to cope with the prince's death than other families because of their privileged circumstances. The respondent condescendingly expressed her annoyance at the way the so-called 'ignorant' failed to appreciate the differences that separated royal life from the experiences of ordinary people, indicating her deeper awareness of the royal public relations strategy that stressed mutual suffering. Other respondents expressed similar kinds of sympathy for Queen Mary and Marina and were probably inspired to do so by the media coverage of the prince's death, which focused on the sorrow of both women and the way they shared in the emotional burdens of war.[175]

One thirty-nine-year-old diarist from Glasgow notably took exception to the criticism levelled by other people at royal privilege. She noted that:

> there is much sympathy with the Duchess, but Queen Mary is singled out again and again. There is the usual type of envious remark that is constantly getting levelled against royalty, e.g. that Marina and the three children will have plenty to live on ... Of course, the royal family don't feel any differently from other bereaved families, but the emphasis is always in a nasty sense.[176]

This diary entry reveals the enduring popularity of Queen Mary as the recipient of public sympathy but also that there was a regularity to the 'envious' remarks purportedly levelled at the monarchy in these years. This may point to the way a deeper disaffection with royal privilege had

---

[174] MOA, 5447. See also MOA, 5277, 5324; and MOA, File Report 1392, 'Death of the Duke of Kent', 25 Aug. 1942.

[175] E.g., *Sunday Pictorial*, 30 Aug. 1942, p. 3.

[176] MOA, 5390.

Figure 4.9. 'The Duke of Kent Killed', *Daily Sketch*, 26 August 1942, p. 1. © The British Library Board.

gained traction during the war.[177] Of course, Mass Observation naturally uncovered opinions that ran counter to this idea as well. A forty-five-year-old man quoted in the file report on the duke's death told the interviewer: 'I don't think we've ever had a better Royal Family – the King and Queen have been with us in all the bad blitzes, even though they could very well have hidden themselves in the country – they're one of us'.[178] For this man, the royal tours of blitzed areas had engendered his loyalty to the House of Windsor. And, despite the cynicism articulated by several respondents, Mass Observation investigators concluded that 'the chief reaction was that [the duke's death] showed how this war was the same for everyone, even the Royal Family. Probably the death of the Duke of Kent has done more for the popularity of the Royal Family than any other single event could have done'. While this was a simplified rendering of the varied opinions recorded by Mass Observation, the one factor that linked many of the responses was an appreciation that wartime bereavement affected all sections of society, even if some families were in better positions to cope with this loss than others.

*

Queen Elizabeth spoke of the far-reaching consequences of the war for the female population in the second broadcast she delivered to Britain's women in April 1943. In so doing, she presented herself as their leader and someone to whom they could all relate. The plans for this message were not instigated by the queen, but rather pressure was brought to bear on her by government officials who saw value in another royal broadcast. In December 1941 the government instituted the National Service (No. 2) Act, which mobilized British women into new kinds of war work on an unprecedented scale.[179]

---

[177] Zweiniger-Bargielowska, 'Royal rations', pp. 14–5.
[178] MOA, File Report 1392, 'Death of the Duke of Kent'.
[179] H. L. Smith, 'The effect of the war on the status of women', in *War and Social Change: British Society in the Second World War*, ed. H. L. Smith (Manchester, 1986), pp. 208–29, at p. 214. According to A. Lascelles, at the time when older women were compelled to register for war work, he discussed with George VI whether or not the queen should register with her 'age-group'. The courtier came down against the idea, reasoning that she had already dedicated herself to a lifetime of service in the national cause in her coronation vows and it would appear farcical, possibly even undermining the government's scheme. The fact that this conversation took place does, however, show how seriously the king took his and the queen's public roles as exemplars of the nation's war effort and the idea that they should at least be seen to share in the burdens brought about by the conflict (Hart-Davis, *King's Counsellor*, pp. 39–40).

Some women enjoyed the new opportunities that opened up for them as a result of employment, while others did not, instead resenting that they had to combine their domestic roles with part-time paid work or had to leave their homes altogether following conscription into 'essential' industries in other parts of the UK.[180] The size of the female workforce peaked in 1943 after the government had introduced new forms of compulsion the previous year, witnessing an increase in the number of women who had to balance war work with domestic responsibilities.[181] The minister for labour, Ernest Bevin, was anxious about maintaining morale among disaffected female conscripts and his desire to have their contribution to the war effort formally recognized led to his proposal to Buckingham Palace that the queen broadcast a message of encouragement and gratitude to women who were engaged in work outside the home.[182] As was usually the case with special royal broadcasts, the road to convincing the palace of its value was a difficult one. Bevin first wrote to Alexander Hardinge at the start of December 1942, but four months before this the Ministry of Information had contacted the king's private secretary, suggesting that the queen deliver a special message to British housewives. The idea had first come from the BBC and the Ministry of Information was in agreement that housewives had 'a great deal to put up with that is both irritating and tiring in the normal conduct of their lives' and that 'a public appreciation of their efforts … would stimulate and encourage them to carry on during the coming winter'.[183] Hardinge replied doubtfully (although tellingly, in terms of his attitudes to innovation): 'My personal view on broadcasts by The King and Queen is that they should be reserved for special occasions. Admittedly the housewives of this country are having a difficult and somewhat wearing time. It may, however, become considerably more difficult and wearing if the Germans resume their intensive bombing of our large towns'.[184] Although Hardinge responded negatively, the queen was consulted on the idea of another broadcast and she composed a handwritten message to the courtier in mid August informing him that she 'might think of making a broadcast to women in the late autumn or early winter, but not to any section in particular. The housewife would naturally be included'.[185] This is

[180] P. Summerfield, *Women Workers in the Second World War: Production and Patriarchy in Conflict* (London, 2013), pp. 53–6; G. Braybon and P. Summerfield, *Out of the Cage: Women's Experiences in Two World Wars* (London, 2013), pp. 235–56.

[181] Smith, 'The effect of the war', p. 216.

[182] RA, PS/PSO/GVI/PS/MAIN/03959/C, E. Bevin to A. Hardinge, 3 Dec. 1942.

[183] RA, PS/PSO/GVI/PS/MAIN/03959/C, C. J. Radcliffe to A. Hardinge, 8 Aug. 1942.

[184] RA, PS/PSO/GVI/PS/MAIN/03959/C, A. Hardinge to C. J. Radcliffe, 10 Aug. 1942.

[185] RA, PS/PSO/GVI/PS/MAIN/03959/C, handwritten memorandum from Queen Elizabeth to A. Hardinge, 15 Aug. 1942.

significant because Queen Elizabeth seems to have seen in the broadcast an opportunity to lay claim to representation of all British women, not just housewives, and in so doing to convey to them her own understanding of the requirements of womanhood in wartime.

The minister of labour's approach came next. Stating that he also wrote on behalf of the minister of information, Brendan Bracken, and the minister of production, Oliver Lyttelton, Bevin argued that a royal message 'of appreciation and cheer' to the 'women of this country … whether they have been engaged in factories, in the Services, or in the work of the home … would be very encouraging to them'.[186] Bevin had befriended the king and Hardinge earlier on in the war and his appeal seems to have struck a chord.[187] When the private secretary came to reply to the minister he noted that the king and queen had 'renewed [their] consideration' of the proposed broadcast and that 'the idea … [they] are contemplating now, is that Her Majesty might do the kind of broadcast that you suggest in February. That is, as a rule, a particularly unpleasant time of the year; and perhaps an expression of gratitude and encouragement then would be especially effective'.[188] Clearly the palace wanted the broadcast to have as great an impact as possible given the difficult winter they thought lay ahead. Bevin continued to apply pressure on the royal household and tried to convince them that the message would be better received if it was delivered as part of a New Year's greeting. But the palace stood firm on the proposed date of a Sunday in February, asserting that the king thought a New Year's address would follow too soon after his own Christmas message.[189] And, in actual fact, after further deliberations the date for the queen's broadcast was pushed back to mid April: she would speak when, and only when, she was ready to speak.[190]

Having been reassured by the palace that the broadcast would definitely go ahead, Bevin set about making arrangements to ensure the widest possible female audience for the queen's message. The Ministry of Information and BBC instructed him that the optimum time for its transmission would be 9 pm on a Sunday evening but Bevin complained in a letter to Hardinge that even then 'a great many of the women to whom the proposed message would be addressed would be unable to listen to it'. He therefore suggested

[186] RA, PS/PSO/GVI/PS/MAIN/03959/C, E. Bevin to A. Hardinge, 3 Dec. 1942.
[187] Hart-Davis, *King's Counsellor*, p. 68.
[188] RA, PS/PSO/GVI/PS/MAIN/03959/C, A. Hardinge to E. Bevin, 7 Dec. 1942.
[189] RA, PS/PSO/GVI/PS/MAIN/03959/C, E. Bevin to A. Hardinge, 18 Dec. 1942 and reply on 21 Dec. 1942.
[190] RA, PS/PSO/GVI/PS/MAIN/03959/C, handwritten memorandum from A. Lascelles to A. Hardinge, 25 Jan. 1943; A. Hardinge to B. Bracken, 31 March 1943.

that a film be made of the queen while she was broadcasting, which would 'enable Her Majesty's message to reach women in the factories, the Services, and throughout the Empire, who might not otherwise hear it'.[191] The queen declined Bevin's invitation to have her actual broadcast filmed – no doubt out of fear that something could go wrong during the live transmission – but she agreed to a 'special sitting' for a separate film recording that could be shown as part of newsreels.[192] This was organized by Bracken and the Ministry of Information's film division, which worked with *British Paramount News* (the company appointed according to the royal rota) to record a version of the broadcast to be used by the newsreels. The palace notably insisted that it retain ultimate control over the film, with courtier Eric Miéville instructing *Paramount* that 'should the pictures not be considered satisfactory by The Queen, they will not be shown'.[193]

It appears from internal palace memoranda that some members of the royal household were unhappy about the pressure being brought to bear on the queen by Bevin. After Bracken took over at the Ministry of Information in 1942, it relaxed the control it had previously sought to exert over institutions like the BBC and the monarchy, instead enabling them to pursue their own propaganda objectives. But now courtiers had to deal with a stubborn minister for labour who had his own specific agenda to promote. Lascelles told Hardinge the queen hoped that, once the final date for the broadcast had been settled, 'the Ministry of Labour [would] fade out of the picture'.[194] Once again, then, it seems that while the royal family were quite prepared to support the government's aims during the war, they preferred to do so on their own terms and resisted ministerial interference in royal public relations. Nevertheless, Bevin was a useful ally to the palace given his extensive knowledge of the work that women were undertaking as part of the war effort and Hardinge thought 'it would be both politic and appreciated' to ask him whether there were any 'special points' worth including in the queen's broadcast.[195] The minister replied with a list of notes that highlighted what women working in different roles stood both to gain and to lose as a result of their occupations. For example, in relation to the 'Women in the Services', he noted positives that included 'companionship,

[191] RA, PS/PSO/GVI/PS/MAIN/03959/C, E. Bevin to A. Hardinge, 15 Jan. 1943.
[192] RA, PS/PSO/GVI/PS/MAIN/03959/C, handwritten memorandum from A. Lascelles to A. Hardinge, 25 Jan. 1943; A. Hardinge to B. Bracken, 26 Jan. 1943.
[193] RA, PS/PSO/GVI/PS/MAIN/03959/C, E. C. Miéville to G. T. Cummins, 9 Apr. 1943.
[194] RA, PS/PSO/GVI/PS/MAIN/03959/C, handwritten memorandum from A. Lascelles to A. Hardinge, 25 Jan. 1943.
[195] RA, PS/PSO/GVI/PS/MAIN/03959/C, handwritten memorandum from A. Hardinge to the private secretary of the queen, 14 Feb. 1943.

[their] direct contribution to the war, "seeing the world"' and negatives such as 'separation from families, communal living and discipline'. He compiled this kind of Ciceronian decomposition for civil defence workers, factory workers, nurses, housewives, women in the country and the women's land army. And in line with the government's policy of encouraging more women to take on responsibilities outside the home in this period, Bevin included two additional points 'which at the present stage of mobilization of women power it is important to us to stress'. These were that Queen Elizabeth might address 'the continued and still more pressing need for those women who can to be willing to leave their homes and go to the big centres of war production' and that there was a 'need for married women to take over the work which these women leave behind, dull and uninteresting and far removed from the war as it may seem'.[196]

The final version of the queen's speech did not include a direct appeal to female listeners to take on additional work – probably because the monarch would be heard overtly espousing government policy through such exhortation. The royal public relations strategy was subtler than this and the palace sought to distance royal public language from official propaganda. Nevertheless, the queen did refer to all the different occupations that women were employed in according to Bevin's list, which suggests that, in preparing the message, Lascelles and his collaborators may have taken some of their cues from the minister of labour.[197] The other contributors to the broadcast were Edward Woods (bishop of Lichfield and successor to Cosmo Lang as lord high almoner in the royal household) and Winston Churchill.[198] Exactly what these two contributed is unclear from the many drafts contained in the Royal Archives, but the final result was a wide-ranging broadcast that went further than any previous royal message in stressing the personal bonds that connected a member of the House of Windsor to the public while also outlining a vision of a future Britain centred on the family monarchy. That neither the Ministry of Information nor the BBC played any part in the drafting process is also revealing of the fact that, by 1943, the palace had managed to wrest back control over royal speech-writing in order to circumvent outside interference.

[196] RA, PS/PSO/GVI/PS/MAIN/03959/C, list that accompanied letter from E. Bevin to A. Hardinge, 10 March 1943.

[197] RA, PS/PSO/GVI/PS/MAIN/03959/C, handwritten memorandum from A. Hardinge to the private secretary of the queen, 14 Feb. 1943; A. Hardinge to E. Bevin, 1 March 1943.

[198] See copies of the speech in RA, QEQMH/PS/SPE: BROADCASTS, 11 Apr. 1943 and GVI/PS/3959(1)C. See also Shawcross, *Queen Elizabeth the Queen Mother*, p. 564 and Hart-Davis, *King's Counsellor*, p. 122.

The tone of the message was particularly intimate. The words spoken by the queen and the highly informal imagery she conjured as she delivered the broadcast set a new precedent for royal public language. She began by directly addressing female listeners:

> I would like, first of all, to try to tell you just why I am speaking to you to-night – to you my fellow-countrywomen all over the world. It is not because any special occasion calls for it; it is not because I have any special message to give you. It is because there is something that, deep in my heart, I know ought to be told you; and probably I am the best person to do it.

Annotations on the final draft of the message are in Lascelles's handwriting and, through deliberate underlining (as above), instructed the queen to place emphasis on personal pronouns such as 'you', 'your' and 'our' in order to stress to listeners both her personal connection to them and also the shared experience of war.[199] The queen went on to describe the 'quiet heroism' of the women who had engaged, supposedly uncomplainingly, in war work. The image of a female workforce stoically serving the nation echoed government propaganda and the popular idea that all members of society were doing their bit to win the 'people's war'.[200] The disaffection that caused Bevin so much concern was marginalized: instead, the queen described how women workers were keeping cheerful despite sometimes physically hard or dangerous jobs. She remarked that she admired the 'pluck' of the women workers whom she had encountered during her tours of the nation and that she had 'heard them say, "Oh, well, it's not much. I'm just doing my best to help us win the war"'. This self-deprecating image of the Englishwoman resonated with older ideas of the national character which were also captured in the queen's comment that the courage of women workers was reinforced 'by one of the strongest weapons in our national Armory – a sense of humour that nothing can daunt'.[201]

The queen then went on to address, indirectly, all the different female groups listed by Bevin that were engaged in war work, emphasizing that it was 'just as valuable' as 'that which is done by the bravest soldier, sailor, or airman who actually meets the enemy in battle'. She continued:

[199] See copy of the speech in RA, QEQMH/PS/SPE: BROADCASTS, 11 Apr. 1943. Again, this emphasis can be heard in the filmed recording of the message: 'Her Majesty's Broadcast', *British Movietone News*, 15 Apr. 1943 <https://www.youtube.com/watch?v=Mlju36D_Vno> [accessed 3 Apr. 2018].
[200] Rose, *Which People's War?*, pp. 107–9.
[201] P. Mandler, *The English National Character: the History of an Idea from Edmund Burke to Tony Blair* (London, 2006), pp. 168–70.

And have you not met that enemy too? You have endured his bombs; you have helped to put out the fires that he has kindled in our homes; you have tended those he has maimed; brought strength to those he has bereaved; you have tilled our land; you have, in uniform or out of it, given help to our fighting forces, and made for them those munitions without which they would be powerless; in a hundred ways you have filled the places of the men who have gone away to fight; and, coping uncomplainingly with all the tedious difficulties of war-time – you the housewives, many doing whole-time, and many part-time, jobs – you have kept their homes for them against the blessed day when they come back.

This passage was the core of the broadcast through which the queen described the varied experiences of British women in wartime to listeners, but simultaneously stressed that she and they were committed to winning the war, having endured its hardships together. As with her husband's message on Christmas Day 1942, the queen then drew her broadcast to a close by projecting an optimistic vision of post-war reconstruction that focused on pre-war imagery of a nation united by its domesticity:

All of us women love family life, our homes and our children, and you may be sure that our men overseas are thinking just as wistfully of these homes as we are – some – of the dear and familiar homes they left behind, others of the new homes they mean to make for the young wives of the future. These men – both at home and abroad – are counting on us at all times to be steadfast and faithful. I know that we shall not fail them, but, fortified by the great experience in this war, of our strength in unity, go forward with them, undismayed, into the future.

I feel that in all the thinking and planning which we are doing for the welfare of our country and Empire – yes, and concern for other countries too – we women as home-makers have a great part to play, and, speaking as I do tonight from my own dearly loved home, I must say that I keenly look forward to a great re-building of family life as soon as the war ends. I would like to add, with my fullest conviction, that it is on the strength of our spiritual life that the right re-building of our national life depends.

At a time when the government was worried about the impact of adultery on the home front and the damage it could do to fighting men's spirits, the queen's instruction to women to stay true to their husbands was meant to resonate with listeners, but not everyone reacted positively.[202] One Mass Observation diarist recorded that she and her companions 'were most amused at [the queen's] reference to the duty of wives to be faithful to their

<hr>

[202] Braybon and Summerfield, *Out of the Cage*, p. 272; C. Langhamer, *The English in Love: the Intimate Story of an Emotional Revolution* (Oxford, 2013), pp. 70–1.

husbands overseas – it must be serious or she certainly wouldn't have referred to it'.[203] The other moral message contained in the last segment of the broadcast was that the rebuilding of family life would lead to national renewal, with the monarch encouraging women to set an example after war had ended. As the queen's biographer has noted, she was socially and politically conservative and believed that women should step down from their wartime jobs when peace arrived.[204] Her message thus sought to resolve one of the major tensions at the heart of government policy towards women in wartime: namely, whether work outside the domestic sphere should take precedence over home-making. In the queen's message, both kinds of work were celebrated as having equal value, the queen (and her speechwriters) striking a balance in appealing to different female constituencies. And yet, the monarch presented work outside the domestic sphere as temporary and something that would inevitably come to an end for women when the war was over. The queen advocated a return to the kind of family life promoted by the monarchy before the war, underpinned as it was by a faith in God that would 'help us to carry the moral responsibilities which history is placing upon our shoulders'. And, in addition to this familiar reference to the need for divine guidance, she ended her message by returning to the well-worn idea of the burdens of royal duty by remarking that 'the King and I are grateful to think that we and our family are remembered in your prayers. We need them and try to live up to them'.

Although the aforementioned Mass Observation diarist and her friends found the queen's reference to marital infidelity amusing, most of those who recorded hearing the broadcast stated they were impressed by the moral substance of the message. The same housewife and clerk from Sheffield who had criticized 'the ignorant' for pitying royalty at the time of the duke of Kent's death recorded that the queen's broadcast was 'very pleasing' and that she was 'glad [the monarch] put emphasis on the need for [a] spiritual outlook'. This diarist also appreciated the apparently impromptu qualities of the message: 'Nice that she spoke to us just because she felt she wanted to, and for no particular reason'.[205] A thirty-three-year-old restaurant owner from Edinburgh agreed:

> Very much impressed this evening with the Queen's speech: such a charming impression of sincerity and the slight nervousness only enhanced it. I admit to sometimes thinking that having Royalty is perhaps a little old-fashioned and 'dated' in the world as it now is, but then something like this happens to prove to me once more that no other system could possibly be so satisfactory.[206]

[203] MOA, 5443.
[204] Shawcross, *Queen Elizabeth the Queen Mother*, pp. 563–4.
[205] MOA, 5447.
[206] MOA, 5415.

For this woman, the broadcast reaffirmed her belief in the whole concept of monarchy and she detected an emotion in the queen's voice that only added to the authenticity of the message. A fifty-four-year-old teacher from Surrey felt similarly inspired. He described how the monarch spoke with 'a clean and very sympathetic voice, very attractive to listen to' (here possibly implying that George VI's voice was anything but easy to listen to). He went on: 'The Queen's charm is so particularly <u>within</u> her. I have a great admiration for them both [referring to the king too] ... this is built upon respect and, in a way, gratitude I think'.[207] He then described his 'moral respect' for the monarchs, the broadcast having strengthened his appreciation of the example set by the royal family to the nation. A fifty-six-year-old nurse from Bristol also shared in this outlook, writing in her diary that 'the Queen's broadcast to women must have comforted and inspired thousands'.[208]

Not everyone agreed. A forty-three-year-old teacher from Sussex recorded that while she thought the speech 'pleasant tho' over-religious' the head of her school 'thought it awful – so gloomy. How lacking in vigour & dynamism compared with Churchill'. She recorded that her colleagues '[had] started making fun of it early on, then got the giggles. She is really good at the "be active & efficient" line, stand up for women's rights etc. But that wd. be no good if one of the family were e.g. killed in the war & the Queen was speaking to many who are anxious, sad etc. A very big number of Sussex men are prisoners'.[209] Not everyone, therefore, believed the queen's words to be sincere. The teacher noted that her colleagues thought the appeal to women workers was just a propaganda 'line' and did not think the encouragement offered by the monarch would resonate with listeners who had lost loved ones to the war or those who had family members interred in prisoner-of-war camps.

In reporting the broadcast, newspapers again drew attention to the queen's interest in the lives of her female subjects. According to the *Daily Sketch*, she 'made the broadcast at her suggestion, largely as a result ... of the experiences she has had seeing women at war work in all parts of the

---

[207] MOA, 052. For the same sentiment see MOA, 5176.

[208] MOA, 5283. The BBC's listener research department estimated that 66.5% of the adult population heard the queen's broadcast. Investigators noted that the responses of three-quarters of interviewees who had heard it were 'extremely favourable', while the other quarter were mostly 'favourable'. According to the BBC's interviewees, the speech was a success because it was considered 'noble and uplifting' and the queen's manner was appreciated, being described as 'pleasant, homely, and sincere' (BBCWA, 248/R9/1/3, Listener Research Weekly Bulletin, no. 135).

[209] MOA, 5376.

country'.[210] Reports like this one misleadingly asserted that the monarch was the instigator of the message, which consolidated her public image as the leader of Britain's women who wanted to acknowledge their important contribution to the war effort. The other main theme the press emphasized was Queen Elizabeth's reference to the importance of domesticity to post-war reconstruction, thus reiterating her view that women would leave their wartime jobs in favour of home when the conflict finally ended.[211] Meanwhile, the newsreels that used footage from the film recording of the queen's broadcast (which, incidentally, passed palace inspection) interspersed scenes of her speaking from behind a desk with stock footage of women from across Britain engaged in various types of war work, which included the auxiliary services, factory work and housewifery.[212] As with the newsreels of earlier royal wartime broadcasts, the words of the speaker were contextualized by reference to scenes of the way in which the war had transformed the lives of the public, with the visual illustration creating a direct link between the words spoken by royalty and ordinary people's experiences, reaffirming a vision of the House of Windsor's national leadership in wartime.

*

While Queen Elizabeth promoted a vision of the nation's future that was family-centred and mirrored the kind of domesticity the British monarchy had publicly elevated in the 1930s, George VI and his advisors proved determined that he should be seen as the man who had led the nation and the empire to victory over their enemies. Since May 1940 he had faced stiff competition from his prime minister, Winston Churchill, whose command of the mass media and often inspiring rhetoric won him popular acclaim among sections of the public.[213] Although a number of commentators observed a strengthening in George VI's character and style of leadership during the war, Churchill projected a 'forceful and visceral personality' which the king could never hope to imitate with his stammer. As an anti-appeaser, Churchill had been marginalized from frontline politics in the

---

[210] *Daily Sketch*, 12 Apr. 1943, p. 1.

[211] *Daily Express*, 12 Apr. 1943, p. 3; *Daily Sketch*, 12 Apr. 1943, p. 5; *Daily Herald*, 12 Apr. 1943, p. 3; *News Chronicle*, 12 Apr. 1943, p. 3.

[212] 'Her Majesty's Broadcast', *British Movietone News*, 15 Apr. 1943; 'Her Majesty's Broadcast', *British Paramount News*, 15 Apr. 1943.

[213] See n. 43 above. As Richard Toye has noted, Churchill's speeches were not always received well and his rhetoric was by no means always inspiring (Toye, *The Roar of the Lion*).

1930s, but his leadership during the crisis years of 1940/41 restored what historian Martin Francis has termed his 'militaristic and imperial vision of national identity to the foreground of official discourse'.[214]

Churchill could be extravagantly courteous to his royal superiors but often kept government secrets hidden from the king, which annoyed the latter. Furthermore, the prime minister regularly disregarded royal protocol in political affairs. For example, he liked to send off congratulatory messages to British and imperial military officials when this was very much the prerogative of the king.[215] As Lascelles noted in his diary, the effect of this misconduct was a growth in what he termed the 'silly talk' that 'Winston [was] trying to steal the King's thunder, or (to use a more homely metaphor) to push the Crown under the bed'.[216] The private secretary downplayed the 'silly talk', but was sufficiently concerned by it to orchestrate a number of press exclusives intended to raise the profile of the king in relation to the allied military victories in North Africa in May 1943 by positioning the monarch in the limelight alongside his first minister, who had devised the campaign.[217]

George VI's biographer, Sarah Bradford, has noted that Lascelles talked to confidantes of his annoyance at Churchill's behaviour and she quotes a personal friend of the royals who reported that the king and queen also felt the prime minister overshadowed them.[218] On 6 June 1944 – the evening of the D-Day landings – George VI delivered a broadcast to Britain at the insistence of the queen, who thought that he, and not his prime minister, should be the one to speak to them.[219] The radio message came after a week's wrangling between the king and Churchill over whether the prime minister should be allowed to watch the D-Day landings from a British cruiser anchored off the French coast. After a series of furious exchanges between the royal household and 10 Downing Street, the prime minister was eventually dissuaded from going. Lascelles described Churchill's behaviour as selfish and vain; and the king was forced to write to his prime minister pointing out that it would be unfair, given that the latter had expressly advised the monarch against crossing the Channel to watch the invasion out of concern

[214] M. Francis, 'Tears, tantrums, and bared teeth: the emotional economy of three Conservative prime ministers, 1951–1963', *Jour. Brit. Stud.*, xli (2002), 354–87, at p. 374. For comments on the king's stronger leadership style, see Hart-Davis, *King's Counsellor*, pp. 172 and 177.

[215] D. Cannadine, 'Churchill and the British monarchy', *Trans. Royal Hist. Soc.*, xi (2001), 249–72, at pp. 262–3; Hart-Davis, *King's Counsellor*, p. 125; Bradford, *King George VI*, p. 449.

[216] Hart-Davis, *King's Counsellor*, p. 130.

[217] Hart-Davis, *King's Counsellor*, p. 130.

[218] Bradford, *King George VI*, pp. 449–50.

[219] Shawcross, *Queen Elizabeth the Queen Mother*, p. 581.

for his safety, for him then to go himself and 'steal all the thunder'.[220] This was the most fraught exchange in a series of rows between monarch and prime minister that stretched over five years, but it is important to note that, despite the fractious temperaments of both men, their relationship did warm into a close friendship over the course of the Second World War, as evidenced by both Churchill's admiring descriptions of the king in his history of the conflict and other official sources.[221]

George VI did not attend the D-Day landings on 6 June, but he did undertake a highly publicized trip to the beaches of Normandy shortly afterwards in order to inspect his troops and, in so doing, stake his claim to the symbolic leadership of the nation's war effort.[222] This was followed shortly afterwards by an expedition to Italy to inspect the British and imperial troops involved in the northward advance through the country.[223] Tasked with accompanying the monarch's party on this trip was the *British Movietone News* cameraman Graham Thompson and it was on their return to London that the latter was asked to become 'king's cameraman'.[224] At the time Thompson was part of the newsreel crew responsible for recording all the film footage for the 'royal rota'. The five newsreel companies had used rota systems throughout the 1930s in order to save on costs. Rotas were mutually beneficial in that they involved the pooling of resources: one cameraman at a location shot the film for all five companies, with the same footage then being shared among editors. While this meant that newsreels were often formulaic and repetitive in character, the rota system worked well when applied to the monarchy. Not only were the royal family spared the ignominy of having to pose for numerous different camera crews, but having one cameraman film all their activities meant that others were not competing for intimate royal exclusives, which might have led to intrusive coverage.[225] The royal rota was instituted when the Newsreel Association (NRA) first formed in October 1937. It involved the

[220] Hart-Davis, *King's Counsellor*, pp. 224–8.

[221] W. S. Churchill, *The Second World War: Abridged Edition with an Epilogue on the Years 1945 to 1957* (London, 2002), pp. 219, 365–6; Shawcross, *Queen Elizabeth the Queen Mother*, pp. 514–5; Cannadine, 'Churchill and the British monarchy', pp. 263–4.

[222] 'Beyond the Beaches: The King Visits Normandy While Troops Press On', *Gaumont British News*, 22 June 1944; 'The King Sees Invasion Going Well', *British Paramount News*, 22 June 1944.

[223] Hart-Davis, *King's Counsellor*, pp. 242, 247–9.

[224] Interview with G. Thompson, 28 Jan. 1992, side 2 (03:55–05:00) <https://historyproject.org.uk/interview/graham-thompson> [accessed 25 Apr. 2017]. See also L. McKernan, 'The finest cinema performers we possess: British royalty and the newsreels, 1910–37', *Court Historian*, viii (2003), 59–71, at pp. 68–9.

[225] Mort, 'On tour with the prince', pp. 50–1.

newsreel companies taking turns (initially on a three-month and later a six-month rolling basis) to provide a camera crew to undertake all filming of royal events.[226] However, following the royal excursion to Italy, Thompson was invited to Buckingham Palace and offered a post that would see him become the royal family's full-time cameraman for the next six years.[227] Talking as part of an oral history interview in 1992, Thompson remarked that, in mid 1944, 'it was pretty obvious we were going to win the war by this time and Churchill had stolen all the thunder. It was time our royal household got a bit more publicity I think … It was thought that a more intimate coverage by film for the newsreel could be made if one man were nominated'.[228] Thompson's words again point to concerns at the palace that Churchill had overshadowed George VI and his family and indicate that the royal household felt a need to generate favourable publicity around the monarch. Although Thompson's initial secondment was only for three months, the palace's new press secretary, Captain Lewis Ritchie, explained to the committee of the NRA that the king had requested the cameraman be made 'a permanency'.[229] Securing the NRA's agreement was difficult, but the committee eventually decided that 'it would be impolitic to question in any way the personal request of H.M. The King'.[230] Thompson was thus accredited to the palace full-time and, along with the two official court reporters from the Press Association and Exchange Telegraph, controlled the flow of royal media coverage to the outside world.[231] Indeed, the newsreel films of royalty from August 1944, when Thompson began in his new role, are characterized by a high level of intimacy: having gained the trust of

[226] For more information on the NRA, see J. Hulbert, 'The Newsreel Association of Great Britain and Northern Ireland' <http://bufvc.ac.uk/wp-content/media/2009/06/newsreel_association.pdf> [accessed 1 Feb. 2018].

[227] Indeed, the NRA minutes show that Howard Thomas of *Pathé News* complained that Thompson was no longer beholden to the newsreel companies for whom he worked but instead had switched his allegiances to the royal household, 'becoming more a Palace official, and less a newsreel cameraman', doing exactly what courtiers told him (BFINA, NRA vol. 4, m.2665 'Royal Cameraman', 28 Oct. 1948). See also McKernan, 'The finest cinema performers', pp. 68–9. Thompson was replaced in 1950 by P. J. Turner, who remained in the post until 1962 (J. Turner, *Filming History: the Memoirs of John Turner, Newsreel Cameraman* (London, 2001)).

[228] Thompson, Interview <https://historyproject.org.uk/interview/graham-thompson>, side 2 (04:00–05:00).

[229] Thompson, Interview <https://historyproject.org.uk/interview/graham-thompson>, side 2 (05:00–06:00).

[230] BFINA, NRA vol. 3, m.1756, 'Cameraman Accredited to Buckingham Palace', 1 Nov. 1944; see also m.1643.

[231] Thompson, Interview <https://historyproject.org.uk/interview/graham-thompson>, side 2 (08:00–08:55).

the king and his family, it is clear that they let him record scenes of them at closer proximity than was normal.[232] This new access even extended to letting Thompson join them on the palace balcony, along with Churchill, during the VE Day celebrations on 8 May 1945 so that he could film the group waving to the crowds gathered outside the gates below.[233]

The famous scene of the prime minister flanked by the king and queen and the princesses on the balcony – reproduced in large front-page photographs by the majority of British newspapers – provided a reassuring image of monarch and prime minister united in victory and served to disguise the tensions that had at times characterized their relationship, as well as the royal household's ongoing concerns that Churchill had outshone the king as the nation's war leader (Figure 4.10).[234] We know these images were the result of a co-ordinated effort on the part of courtiers and the media to elevate the House of Windsor as the centre point of the celebrations, as had been the case after the armistice was declared on 11 November 1918 at the end of the First World War. Anticipating victory a month before VE Day was finally announced, Lascelles had instructed Sir Piers Legh, master of the household, 'to be ready with floodlighting apparatus in Buckingham Palace, in case the King has, at short notice, to show himself to cheering crowds from the balcony'.[235] Similarly, the committee of the Newsreel Association and Ministry of Information put in a special request to the Ministry of Works that they erect a large rostrum for filming on the Victoria memorial, 'in view of the considerable importance attaching to the "shooting" of happenings in and around Buckingham Palace'.[236] And, on the evening of

[232] E.g., 'Royal Tour of Scotland', *British Movietone News*, 28 Sept. 1944; 'His Majesty on the Continent', *Pathé Gazette*, 23 Oct. 1944; 'King Tours Lancashire', *British Paramount News*, 19 March 1945; 'Princess Elizabeth Second Subaltern', *Pathé Gazette*, 19 Apr. 1945.

[233] It is unclear whether these scenes were, in fact, released for screening as part of a newsreel. They can be seen at (01.47) in unissued footage from the *Pathé* archive, 'VE Day London' <https://www.youtube.com/watch?v=m5ZerMjt9nw> [accessed 2 Feb. 2018]. Notably, Thompson can be glimpsed walking out onto the balcony with the royal family before disappearing out of shot in 'The Fruits of Victory', *Pathé News*, 17 May 1945 <https://www.britishpathe.com/video/the-fruits-of-victory> (06:15). See also 'V.E. Day in London', *British Movietone News*, 14 May 1945 <https://www.youtube.com/watch?v=NEavcsrMoMw>; and 'Royal Family Celebrates V.E. Day', 14 May 1945, *Gaumont British News*, in which Princess Elizabeth can be seen talking to Thompson, who is out of shot. This experiment of inviting a cameraman onto the balcony has not been trialled again since.

[234] *Daily Mail*, 9 May 1945, p. 1; *Daily Telegraph*, 9 May 1945, p. 1; *Daily Sketch*, 9 May 1945, p. 1; *Daily Herald*, 9 May 1945, p. 2; *Daily Express*, 9 May 1945, p. 3. Interestingly, the *Daily Mirror* did not reproduce the image, which was indicative of the increasingly anti-elite stance it would adopt in the immediate post-war years.

[235] Hart-Davis, *King's Counsellor*, p. 307.

[236] BFINA, NRA vol. 3, m.1910 'Coverage of "V.E. Day"', 26 Apr. 1945.

Figure 4.10. 'Nation's VE Outburst of Joy', *Daily Telegraph*,
9 May 1945, p. 1. © The British Library Board.

VE Day, amid the celebrations in central London, it was made known to the press – probably at Lascelles's instruction – that Princesses Elizabeth and Margaret, 'escorted by Guards' officers, left the Palace after nightfall to mingle with the great crowds outside' – a final innovation that once again signalled to media audiences that the war had brought crown and people together in unique union.[237]

However, to judge from Mass Observation personal testimonies, it seems that the war had raised a number of questions about the place of the monarchy in modern Britain that refused to go away, no matter how well co-ordinated royal publicity was in the last years of the conflict. At the beginning of December 1944, in response to a broadcast delivered by the king in acknowledgement of the home guard's service after the defence organization's disbandment, Mass Observation conducted a series of impromptu interviews with members of the public in several parts of London, including Chelsea, Battersea and Hampstead. Interviewees were asked what they made of George VI's speech and what they thought of the royal family. There are only thirty-three sets of answers to be found in the archive, but they include people from all social backgrounds and are

---

[237] *Daily Telegraph*, 9 May 1945, pp. 1 and 6; Hart-Davis, *King's Counsellor*, p. 322.

notable for the diverse range of attitudes expressed.[238] Just over a third of respondents said that they had listened to the king's broadcast and most who had focused their replies on the fact that he had spoken much better than he usually did: again, people were clearly preoccupied with the monarch's delivery ahead of the actual meaning of his words.[239] Those who spoke in admiring terms of the king or his family echoed various comments that had been captured by Mass Observation in earlier studies, including that the royals 'do a lot of good', 'work hard', that they were 'conscientious' and had 'done much to keep up the morale of the civilian population by their visits of bombed areas'.[240] A fifty-year-old man, whom the Mass Observation investigator judged to be lower-middle class, drew on the vocabulary of the burdens of royal status in describing the House of Windsor: 'When you think of it, it must be an awful life – a rotten job – I wouldn't change places – your life would never be your own. A human sacrifice, you might call it'.[241] Meanwhile, some interviewees remarked on the symbolic significance of the crown's 'stabilising influence' in national and imperial politics and others maintained that royalty and constitutional monarchy were 'better than the alternative', which reflected a heightened sensitivity to the evils of dictatorship while also echoing comments captured by MO's 1937 coronation study that favourably compared British democracy to European fascism.[242]

However, while there were some approving descriptions of the strengths of Britain's political system, other interviewees – notably all identified by the investigators as working class – commented that they thought the monarchy was 'out of date', that it had 'outlived' its use and that a presidential system, like the one in the USA, was preferable because it was more meritocratic and democratic as the head of state had to be voted into power.[243] While these comments suggest that members of the public had thought about the USA's constitution and compared it favourably to their own political system, their criticisms were often bound up with references to the social inequality intrinsic to the British monarchical model. A twenty-five-year-old woman maintained that 'a President like Roosevelt does much more good than Royalty – they're chosen by the people they are. Royalty only grab for themselves, and if they didn't get so much for instance, that money

[238] MOA, TC/14 154-186 and TC/14 79-86.
[239] MOA, TC/14 154-186, F45B, F40C, F55D (all p. 2).
[240] MOA, TC/14 79-86, M40B (p. 6); TC/14 154–186, F45B (p. 2), F55D, M50C (p. 3).
[241] MOA, TC/14 154-186, M50C (p. 3).
[242] MOA, TC/14 79-86, M50C (p. 5), M40B, F30B (p. 6), TC/14 154-186, F45B, F40C (p. 2), M60D (p. 4).
[243] MOA, TC/14 79-86, M30D, M35C (p. 5), M40C, F25D, M45D, M50D (p. 7).

could go to charity ... They don't care for the likes of us – they pretend they do, but they don't really. They're only interested in their own class'.[244] Other interviewees similarly remarked on the economic inequities that separated their lives from those of the royal family, which points to the way that the material hardships of the war had raised popular consciousness about the injustices of Britain's class system. Certainly, the aforementioned woman was not taken in by the expressions of sympathy used by the royal family to present themselves as fellow sufferers. Instead, she believed that the royals were disingenuous in the way they 'pretend[ed]' to care for their people and a forty-year-old man expressed similar cynicism about the pretence at the heart of the monarchy's public relations strategy when he remarked: 'I've not got a lot of feeling about the Royal Family – our Grinning queen and the rest'.[245]

Positive comments on the king and royal family were just exceeded in number by negative ones. Alongside these were apathetic statements too: a seventy-year-old working-class woman was typical when she described how she had not 'much time to think of royalty these days – there's so much to do with washing and ironing and lodgers complaining and one thing and another'.[246] A sixty-year-old man who stated that, 'before the war, what royalty did was the only news we got – now all the news is war news so we don't hear much about them', also pointed to the way the conflict had witnessed the sidelining of the monarchy.[247] What is clear from the range of opinions articulated by interviewees was that the royal family's standing in society was certainly neither as strong nor as popular as they and the media claimed was the case: disaffection with the social and economic inequalities that separated royalty from the bulk of society was prominent in these responses – just as it had been in many of the personal testimonies collected by Mass Observation in relation to the monarchy throughout the war.

Conclusion

Despite the mixed picture that characterized public responses to the royal family, the official emphasis in the months immediately after VE Day was on a nation and empire united around the monarchy and its legacy of wartime leadership. In November Lascelles attended a lunch party organized by the King George V Jubilee Trust at St. James's Palace to launch

---

[244] MOA, TC/14 79-86, F25D (p. 7). Also see TC/14 79-86, F30C, M30D, M35C (p. 5), M45D (p. 7).
[245] MOA, TC/14 79-86, M40C (p. 7).
[246] MOA, TC/14 79-86, F70D (p. 3).
[247] MOA, TC/14 79-86, M60C (p. 3).

the official souvenir book, *The Royal Family in Wartime*.[248] This piece of royal propaganda reiterated the key messages that had come to underpin the monarchy's public image since George VI's accession to the throne: he and the queen were, first and foremost, the dutiful servants of their people, who had been forced to take on the burdens imposed on royalty in order to ensure national and imperial continuity following the abdication of Edward VIII. According to the book's narrative and the photographs that illustrated it, the monarchs had developed a close bond with their subjects during the Second World War, engaging with them more intimately and sympathetically than any royals had hitherto done. They had shared in the emotional suffering of their people – be it through separation from their children, as a result of their home being bombed or through the loss of a loved one on active service. But despite these hardships the king and queen had continued, undeterred, to lead the men, women and children of Britain towards victory alongside an outspoken and charismatic prime minister, who nevertheless loyally deferred to his royal superiors. And, in looking to the future, the monarchs had projected a vision of post-war reconstruction that was underpinned by the Christian family life which the House of Windsor had promoted throughout the 1930s.

The Royal Family in Wartime was the outcome of an expert public relations operation that had been developed by the royal household in the aftermath of the coronation and over the course of a six-year global conflict. Lascelles and other courtiers had managed to retain control over the royal public image despite the best efforts of external actors, including civil servants and government ministers, to exploit it to their own ends. This was something Lascelles resented, as he indicated to his friend and collaborator, Cosmo Lang, as the war drew to a close.[249] Two weeks after the launch of the new royal commemorative book, the former archbishop died aged eighty-one after collapsing from a heart attack while on the way to Kew Gardens underground station, near to where George VI had given him a grace-and-favour home in acknowledgement of all he had done for the House of Windsor.[250] However, his service on behalf of the monarchy was complete: he had worked with the palace to elevate a set of messages that would come to define the royal family's public image for the remainder of the twentieth century. And, fortunately for Lascelles, a new high priest of royal publicity had made himself known, having prepared what the king's private secretary described as an 'admirable foreword on that threadbare theme, the duties of

[248] Hart-Davis, *King's Counsellor*, pp. 369–70; King George V Jubilee Trust, *The Royal Family in Wartime* (London, 1945).
[249] See nn. 1 and 2.
[250] R. Beaken, *Cosmo Lang: Archbishop in War and Crisis* (London, 2012), pp. 231–3.

a monarch', for *The Royal Family in Wartime*.[251] As we shall see, *The Times*'s Dermot Morrah would go on to work closely with the royal household in trying to maintain a stable and popular image of the crown in the face of growing public criticism regarding decisions made by members of the royal family and the privileged position occupied by the House of Windsor in an increasingly democratic British society.

[251] Hart-Davis, *King's Counsellor*, pp. 369–70.

5. 'A happy queen is a good queen': the 1947 royal love story

The 1947 royal wedding of Princess Elizabeth to Prince Philip of Greece has received more scholarly attention than the interwar marriages of King George V's children. Historians have situated Elizabeth's marriage against the backdrop of post-war austerity and the imperial set-back of Indian independence, while royal biographers have supported Winston Churchill's characterization of the wedding as a 'splash of colour' that brightened hard economic times and represented a British propaganda triumph against Soviet totalitarianism at the beginning of the Cold War.[1] Historians who have looked at Mass Observation records and opinion polls conducted before the wedding have noted some popular dissent, including initial indifference and criticism of the event's anticipated cost at a time of strict rationing and controls.[2] As the last chapter demonstrated, this strain of public hostility was characteristic of a growing opposition to royal privilege that had gained ground during the Second World War because many British people faced very real material privation. While members of the public might have empathized with the family-centred story of suffering projected by the House of Windsor during the conflict, they were less convinced by the 'fair shares for all' narrative which officials manufactured around the royals and distrust persisted into peacetime, with sections of the media and population questioning whether money should be spent on royal events at a time of continued national hardship.[3]

This chapter offers the first major examination of the media coverage of Elizabeth and Philip's romance, the staging of their wedding and public responses to the event in 360 Mass Observation reports that have never

---

[1] J. Wheeler-Bennett, *King George VI: His Life and Reign* (London, 1958), pp. 75–24; R. Lacey, *Majesty: Elizabeth II and the House of Windsor* (London, 1979), pp. 202–3; S. Bradford, *George VI* (London, 2011), pp. 559–62; B. Pimlott, *The Queen: Elizabeth II and the Monarchy* (London, 2002), pp. 110–1, 132–3 and 142–3.

[2] P. Ziegler, *Crown and People* (London, 1978), pp. 69–79 and 80–4; I. Zweiniger-Bargielowska, 'Royal rations', *History Today*, xliii (1993), pp. 13–5; D. Kynaston, *Austerity Britain: 1945–51* (London, 2008), pp. 243–5.

[3] Zweiniger-Bargielowska, 'Royal rations', pp. 14–5.

been analysed before.[4] The 1947 royal love story initially met with a very mixed response from a less deferential media and public who opposed royal decision-making in new ways; and this threw up a challenge to the palace, which, in response, worked to popularize a romantic and egalitarian image of the princess and prince that was designed to appeal to popular sensibilities. The royal household was largely successful in creating an image of the royal lovers that engendered strong, positive forms of empathy with them among media audiences, an empathy which, in turn, worked to offset criticism of the suitability of the relationship and the material costs involved in the wedding. Courtiers also viewed the romance as an opportunity to re-energize the monarchy's moral influence in Britain: the 1940s were characterized by deep concerns that the nation's family life was in decline and so the palace worked in tandem with the Church of England and journalists to project Elizabeth and Philip's domesticity as an antidote to moral decay.[5] They were presented as exemplars of Christian family life and representatives of their generation in terms of their personalities, hopes and desires in order to encourage popular emotional identification and emulation by the rest of the nation.

The first part of this chapter examines the pioneering opinion poll conducted by the *Sunday Pictorial* in January 1947 which sought to assess the public response to early rumours of a royal engagement. Framing its investigation into the romance as part of its self-professed democratic duty to represent the views of the British people, the newspaper championed the role of the media as the key arbitrator in the sounding of post-war public opinion and, as such, it marked a significant break with the way Britain's political elite had previously managed and interpreted the public's views

---

[4] More than 360 MO respondents answered the question, 'How do you feel about the royal wedding?' It was the last question in a 4-part directive sent out to the MO panel in December 1947 which also included questions on the topics of the cost of living, funny jokes and Christmas festivities. As is always the case with MO, it seems likely that answering these initial questions, especially the one on the respondent's financial resources, affected how participants answered the question on the royal wedding. This might account for some of the concerns expressed by more than 60 respondents about the cost of the wedding. The directive replies can be located in the online Mass Observation archive using the keyword search '1947 royal wedding' and are filed under 'Directive Questionnaire December 1947'. They are referred to here using their respondent numbers. The responses can also be found as hard copies in the MO archive at The Keep (University of Sussex): see SxMOA1/3/106.

[5] G. G. Field, *Blood, Sweat, and Toil: Remaking the British Working Class, 1939–1945* (Oxford, 2011), pp. 183–216; C. Langhamer, 'The meanings of home in postwar Britain', *Jour. Contemp. Hist.*, xl (2005), 341–62, at pp. 345–7; P. Thane, 'Unmarried motherhood in twentieth-century England', *Women's Hist. Rev.*, xx (2011), 11–29, at pp. 19–21.

before 1945.[6] The *Pictorial's* poll identified some concern about Philip's suitability as husband to the future queen, with criticism aimed at his Greek background and association with a disreputable dynasty that had ties to fascism. These dissenting voices were ultimately drowned out by a loud chorus of approval for the princess's desire to marry someone she loved. The examination presented here of the enthusiasm for the love story thus substantiates the idea that romantic self-fulfilment was deemed to be a fundamental tenet of personal development in post-war Britain.[7] Moreover, the fact that a majority of the poll's respondents thought Elizabeth's emotional enrichment was more important than the constitutional implications of her marriage to a Greek prince reveals the strength of the empathetic bonds that members of the public forged with her in this period.

Although love won out over politics in the *Pictorial's* poll, royal officials proved to be more responsive to public opinion than before the war and were shaken into action by the criticism of the monarchy unearthed by the newspaper. The second part of this chapter examines how, working in close collaboration with journalists, the royal household elevated a public image of the princess that stressed her 'ordinary' ambition to find true love and happy domesticity as a young woman, as well as the heavy burdens of the royal duties imposed on her by birth that limited her ability to live a 'normal' life. These deliberately conflicting messages, which placed Elizabeth's *ordinary* desires in tension with her *extraordinary* responsibilities, worked to evoke the sympathy of media audiences in the run-up to the official announcement of her engagement to Philip in mid July. Meanwhile, the prince's leading supporter, his uncle Louis Mountbatten, had been busily engaging with Fleet Street journalists in order to secure his nephew a good write-up, which led to the transformation of Philip's public image: newspapers and newsreels presented him as a likeable young man who exercised an innovative common touch and was more English than foreigner. Mass Observation reports show that the public internalized these public images of the prince and princess and, when their betrothal was finally announced, the media maintained its positive coverage of the couple by presenting them as exemplars of a post-

---

[6] A. Bingham, *Family Newspapers? Sex, Private Life, and the British Popular Press, 1918–1978* (Oxford, 2009), pp. 241–6; L. Beers, 'Whose opinion? Changing attitudes towards opinion polling in British politics, 1937–1964', *Twentieth Century British Hist.*, xvii (2006), 177–205, at pp. 185–90; D. Hucker, *Public Opinion and the End of Appeasement in Britain and France* (Farnham, 2011), pp. 10–2; J. Thompson, *British Political Culture and the Idea of 'Public Opinion', 1867–1914* (Cambridge, 2013).

[7] C. Langhamer, *The English in Love: the Intimate Story of an Emotional Revolution* (Oxford, 2013), pp. 3–7 and 23–5; C. Langhamer, 'Love, selfhood and authenticity in post-war Britain', *Cult. and Soc. History*, ix (2012), 277–97, esp. at pp. 277–82.

war culture of love in order to emphasize that the relationship was a true romance and not a political move.

The third section examines how courtiers, the new archbishop of Canterbury, Geoffrey Fisher, and loyal media organizations choreographed Elizabeth's royal wedding to communicate an image of the royal couple as archetypes of a post-war generation with whom members of the public could identify. Partly by design and partly as a result of the constraints imposed on the orchestrators by austerity, the young lovers were projected as symbols of an intimate, family-centred national culture underpinned by Christian morality, with new media technologies working to bring this image closer to readers, listeners and viewers than ever before. Again, this narrative appealed to many Mass Observation respondents and women, in particular, who were targeted by the media, with many elements of the wedding specifically presented to appeal to feminine sensibilities as in the interwar years. The final section takes these ideas one step further by exploring how the Mass Observation panel perceived the royal lovers' lives as unenviable. The intrusive media coverage of Elizabeth and Philip's honeymoon generated sympathy for them among respondents, who believed that they, like every other young couple, were entitled to a private domestic life. Although some writers expressed anger or envy at the way the princess and prince had enjoyed an elaborate and expensive wedding, these feelings came second to the compassion many felt for the lovers because of the invasion of their privacy, with the media's more intrusive approach to royal family life leading to the emergence of a new version of the oppressed, suffering royal.

'Should our future queen wed Philip?'

Rumours of a marriage between Elizabeth and Philip had first arisen in 1941 when Henry 'Chips' Channon, Tory politician, gossip and man-about-town, commented on a story circulated by the Greek royal family that the prince was intended for the princess.[8] A friendship had blossomed between the couple in 1943, with the ambitious Lord Mountbatten staging meetings between his nephew (Philip was his sister's son) and Elizabeth, heiress presumptive to the throne. Mountbatten also made the prince apply for British citizenship and, as Philip had enjoyed a distinguished career in the Royal Navy during the war, he was a strong candidate for British nationality.

---

[8]   For an excellent discussion of the Greek royal family's reputation in this period and the negotiations between the British government, the House of Windsor and Lord Mountbatten regarding Prince Philip's naturalization, see B. Pimlott, *The Queen: Elizabeth II and the Monarchy* (London, 2002), pp. 94–101.

However, when the government discussed the prince's naturalization in October 1945, British Balkan diplomacy prevented his application from progressing. If he had been naturalized, it might have been construed either as an act in support of the Greek royalists, who were then engaged in a civil war with Greek communists, or as a sign that the Greek royal family wanted to flee abroad. On 1 September 1946 a plebiscite officially reinstated the Greek monarchy, but the vote only drew attention to George II of Greece's authoritarian reputation, further complicating any union with the Greek royal family and once again delaying Philip's naturalization.

Royal biographer William Shawcross has suggested it was in the autumn of 1946 that Elizabeth and Philip became 'unofficially engaged' during a holiday at Balmoral.[9] Rumours of a royal betrothal soon appeared in newspaper gossip columns and it was immediately clear from the press's reaction to these reports that British news editors were more willing to challenge royal decision-making than they had been before 1939.[10] The liberal newspapers called for greater transparency in relation to what they interpreted as a proposed marriage alliance with the Greek monarchy, the *Manchester Guardian* stating that if 'such an engagement were contemplated the Government would have to consider the political implications, and at present these would be vexatious since Greek affairs are the subject of so much controversy'. It stressed that Prime Minister Clement Attlee had to make his government's views known to George VI and that the dominions needed to be consulted too.[11] The *News Chronicle*'s respected political columnist A. J. Cummings smuggled a similar critique of the rumoured betrothal into a report under cover of safeguarding the 'strong links of mutual confidence' between Britain and the dominions and added that the royals would welcome their subjects' thoughts on the engagement: '[T]he King and Queen, it cannot be doubted, are fully conscious of the wisdom of learning in due course what is the public sentiment on the proposal of the Heiress Presumptive'.[12]

In a post-war world where the behaviour of the ruling elite was to be held up to greater scrutiny by the media, this appeal to 'public sentiment' created a real problem for the House of Windsor. It threatened to expose anti-royal feeling among the public, which could in turn undermine the narrative of inclusive royal populism that had been diligently promoted by

[9] W. Shawcross, *Queen Elizabeth the Queen Mother: an Official Biography* (Basingstoke, 2009), p. 625.
[10] For one of the first press rumours regarding the engagement, see *Daily Express*, 9 Nov. 1946, p. 2.
[11] *Manchester Guardian*, 2 Jan. 1947, p. 4.
[12] *News Chronicle*, 3 Jan. 1947, as quoted in *Sunday Pictorial*, 5 Jan. 1947, p. 1.

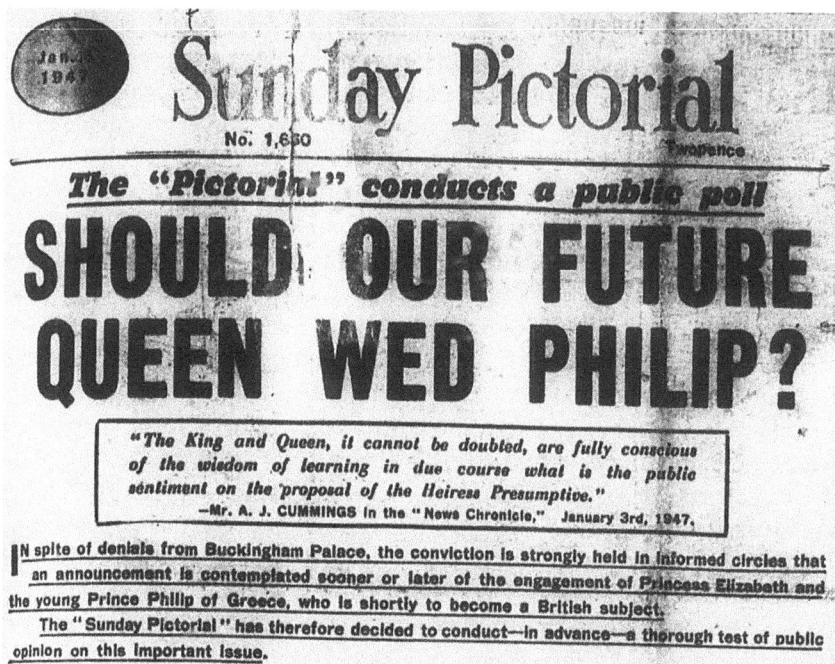

Figure 5.1. 'Should Our Future Queen Wed Philip?', *Sunday Pictorial*, 5 January 1947, p. 1. © The British Library Board.

the mainstream media before and during the war. The 1930s had witnessed the first experiments with 'public sentiment' as a barometer for testing issues of national interest and the *News Chronicle* had been the first newspaper to publish British Institute of Public Opinion surveys under the heading 'What Britain Thinks' in 1938.[13] The commercialization of the popular press after 1945 and the political parties' growing interest in the demographics they claimed to represent combined to increase the influence of public opinion in post-war Britain.[14] Moreover, as historian Adrian Bingham has noted, after the abdication of Edward VIII the left-wing *Daily Mirror* and its sister paper the *Sunday Pictorial* became more critical of the monarchy and other established hierarchies, which they accused of impeding social progress and of misrepresenting public views.[15] Against this backdrop of declining deference, the *Pictorial* decided to respond to the *Chronicle's* invitation to test public opinion on the princess's rumoured betrothal and

[13] Bingham, *Family Newspapers?*, pp. 97–8.
[14] Beers, 'Whose opinion?', p. 195.
[15] Bingham, *Family Newspapers?*, p. 244.

took the unprecedented step of conducting a royal public poll, which it announced to readers in a daring front-page headline: 'SHOULD OUR FUTURE QUEEN WED PHILIP?'[16] (Figure 5.1).

It was the first time that a British newspaper had purposely canvassed readers' opinions on a royal issue but, despite its provocative headline, the *Pictorial* was cautious in presenting any criticism of the crown, its guarded approach indicative of how unusual media scrutiny of the monarchy was in this period. It hid behind the *Guardian* and *Chronicle*'s earlier editorials by quoting them at length and backed their 'demand for a franker approach to the whole question' of the rumoured engagement. In establishing its motives for testing public opinion, the *Pictorial* also referred to a *Guardian* article that had quoted Prime Minister Stanley Baldwin's speech from the House of Commons debate on Edward's abdication ten years previously, when the prime minister had remarked that 'the King's wife was different from the position of the wife of any other citizen in the country; it was part of the price which the King has to pay'.[17] The *Pictorial* thus signalled its agreement with the *Guardian* that the same rules applied to the heiress presumptive to the throne and, again citing Baldwin, that 'it is essentially a matter in which the voice of the people must be heard'.

In discussing the constitutional issue of Elizabeth's engagement, the *Pictorial* highlighted 'the political consequences of so strong a link between the British and Greek Royal House at this stage'.[18] There was, of course, recent precedent of inter-marriage between the dynasties with Prince George and Princess Marina's wedding in 1934. But the international situation had changed by 1947 and, conscious of the onset of the Cold War, the *Pictorial* worried about the Soviet Union's reaction to the engagement. As already noted, Greek royalists were embroiled in a civil war with Greek communists at this time and it was felt that a betrothal between Elizabeth and Philip would signal British support for the Greek king and his authoritarian legacy, offending the Soviets in the 'game of Power Politics'.[19] However, while the left-wing *Pictorial* recognized in the royal betrothal the same political complexities as the liberal *Guardian* and *Chronicle*, it also raised the possibility that it was a true romance between two young lovers: '[M]any people believe that if the Princess and Prince are in love, then nothing should be allowed to stand in the way of their marriage'. The *Pictorial* thus established the social binaries through which the public would consistently be invited to make sense of the 1947 royal romance and wedding: true love

---

[16] *Sunday Pictorial*, 5 Jan. 1947, p. 1.
[17] *Sunday Pictorial*, 5 Jan. 1947, p. 1.
[18] *Sunday Pictorial*, 5 Jan. 1947, p. 1.
[19] *Sunday Pictorial*, 5 Jan. 1947, p. 1.

was presented as reason enough to overlook the constitutional implications of the relationship.

The special significance that the *Pictorial* attributed to a romance fitted with a post-war emotional culture in which love was fast becoming central to concepts of self-fulfilment.[20] Of course, this trade-off between love and public duty had a longer history, too, in a royal context, echoing the duke of Windsor's romance with Wallis Simpson a decade earlier. However, while Baldwin had deliberately marginalized public support for Edward in 1936, the *Pictorial* adopted the stance that 'above all, the loyal people over whom the young Princess will one day rule as Queen must also be afforded the opportunity of expressing their views'. Using bold capital letters to emphasize its point, the newspaper asserted that the public's views needed to be determined 'NOT AFTER THE EVENT, AS WAS THE CASE WITH ANOTHER ROYAL CRISIS IN 1936, BUT BEFORE IT'.[21]

As Bingham has noted, this was 'a powerful rhetoric of popular democracy' and typical of the way the *Pictorial* and the *Mirror* campaigned for a more equal society in which 'the palace and the politicians would not be able to ignore the voice of the people'.[22] Before the war the mainstream media had introduced 'ordinary' and 'representative' voices to news coverage in an attempt to create an image of a British people contentedly united around the focal point of the monarchy. But the *Pictorial*'s ground-breaking 1947 poll promised more complex insights into public attitudes towards royalty; and the uproar it caused on Fleet Street can be interpreted as evidence of its radical ambition. The proprietor of the *Picture Post*, Edward Hulton, was 'one of those appalled by the exercise': 'The journalism of the Sunday Pictorial has reached a new low. It is difficult to write with any restraint about this latest effort by this self-appointed voice of the people, which is as genuinely mischievous and politically harmful as it is in gross bad taste, and infinitely wounding to the feelings of all those concerned'.[23] The language Hulton used to criticize the *Pictorial* reflected the high esteem in which he held the royal family's private life and his belief that ordinary people had no right to cast judgement on their social superiors. The royalist *Daily Mail* also criticized the *Pictorial*'s decision to canvass public opinion on a royal family matter, downplaying the international elements of the story when it remarked that 'the days are past when dynastic marriages meant Power politics … The King and Queen … can surely be trusted to safeguard the

---

[20] Langhamer, *The English in Love*, pp. 3–5.
[21] *Sunday Pictorial*, 5 Jan. 1947, p. 1.
[22] Bingham, *Family Newspapers?*, pp. 244–5.
[23] Quoted in Bingham, *Family Newspapers?*, p. 245.

Figure 5.2. 'The Princess and the People', *Sunday Pictorial*,
12 January 1947, p. 1. © The British Library Board.

future of their elder daughter, who will one day be our Queen'.[24] However,
members of the public *did* want their voices heard, believing that it was
not simply a private royal issue: within a week, 6,100 letters had poured
into the offices of the *Pictorial* from all sections of society and, on the
following Sunday, the newspaper was able to announce to its readers that
55 per cent of respondents favoured the marriage on the grounds that it
was indeed a love match, 40 per cent were opposed to it, and 5 per cent
believed Elizabeth should not be prevented from marrying the Greek prince

[24] *Daily Mail*, 6 Jan. 1947, p. 2.

281

for political reasons but should renounce her right to the throne if she chose this course of action (Figure 5.2).[25]

Once again, the *Pictorial* was careful in the way it communicated criticism of royalty. Both the headline of the report, 'The Princess and the People', and the large photograph of Philip smiling next to it conveyed the impression that the public had agreed he was suitable for Elizabeth. The opening lines of the article also softened the newspaper's critique of the crown: 'The huge number of letters received confirms beyond all question the immense popularity of the Royal Family as a whole and of the Princess in particular'. The newspaper also announced that it had omitted fifty-seven 'irresponsibly anti-Royalist' letters to signal its pro-monarchy stance and, in defending its polling exercise, argued that it was 'among the functions of a newspaper in an ordered democracy' to present 'the truest reflection of public opinion on the controversies of the day'.[26]

Over a central double-page spread the *Pictorial* also offered 'a full analysis of the results so far achieved' and published a 'representative sample' of the letters it had received. According to its analysis, women formed an 'overwhelming majority' of those who supported the marriage – 'provided the two young people are in love' – and this 'feminine support' mainly came from those aged fourteen to thirty and older than fifty. The newspaper stated that 'strong objection is taken by the majority of those readers [in favour] to any "appeasement" of foreign Powers in this "purely domestic" issue'; and it noted that phrases such as 'the right to live their own lives', 'a purely private matter' and 'no interference in the dictates of Princess Elizabeth's heart' recurred in many letters.[27] These sorts of phrases suggest that supporters of the engagement believed the princess's role as a political figurehead should not impinge upon her private life.

The 'representative' letters published by the *Pictorial* in support of a betrothal also reveal that some respondents adopted a liberal, egalitarian attitude to the engagement. The mayor and mayoress of Winchester, Mr and Mrs Charles Sankey, advised 'let Royalty be the same as their subjects in "affairs of the heart" – let them choose for themselves'. Nancy Harman

[25] *Sunday Pictorial*, 12 Jan. 1947, p. 1. This number of letters is quoted in a letter from A. Christiansen to Lord Beaverbrook, 17 Jan. 1947 (PA, BBK/H/120).

[26] *Sunday Pictorial*, 12 Jan. 1947, p. 1.

[27] *Sunday Pictorial*, 12 Jan. 1947, pp. 4–5. It is possible that the *Pictorial* fabricated the results it published, either to make the betrothal seem more contentious than it actually was or to disguise overwhelming hostility to the marriage in order to avoid the royal household's disapproval. However, given the sensitivity of the topic, it seems likely the newspaper would not have risked excessive manipulation for fear of discovery and the results have therefore been interpreted at face value.

from Hastings agreed, stating that the princess 'should be able to marry the man she loves whether he be of Royal Birth or a commoner' and included the caveat that 'in her choice of a husband she should be guided only by her father and mother'. Mrs D. Morson of the London suburb Thornton Heath neatly summarized this view when she compared Elizabeth to her own kin, describing how, as a family, they had agreed that she 'should have the same privileges as our own daughters – of choosing her own husband with her parents' advice and consent'.[28] The parallels these letter writers drew between the princess and other young women show what great importance was attached to choosing one's partner, with Elizabeth's ability to marry for love conforming to wider post-war codes of feminine desire.

Other respondents contested this domestic, depoliticized version of the rumoured betrothal. The *Pictorial* stated that the letters it received opposing the engagement had mainly been written by 'politically-minded people, men just outnumbering women'. Of the 40 per cent against the marriage, 'one letter in six was from a soldier or an ex-Serviceman who has fought overseas', often writing on behalf of barracks or clubs to declare 'let's have no more foreigners in England'.[29] We can interpret comments like these as indicative of the wave of xenophobia that gripped much of Britain in the immediate aftermath of the war but they should also be viewed as part of a deeper strain of criticism that targeted the crown's European ties, which dated back to the nineteenth century.[30] Other respondents were particularly against allying with Greece or any foreign dynasty and argued that the days of royal inter-marriage were over, with an 'impressive majority' claiming the engagement was a 'political move'.[31] In this way opponents also seemed to be committed to a love match – just not with a foreign prince. They did not believe that Elizabeth was in love and advised that she 'follow in the footsteps of her father' by marrying a commoner.

Letters from respondents averse to the engagement were printed to support this position. While some critics expressed prejudice and opposed the relationship on grounds of Philip's 'foreignness', others took aim at the political standing of Greece, noting that it 'will always be in trouble with someone' or that a marriage was unwise 'in view of the present world situation'. For example, one man from London echoed the *Pictorial*'s original concern about the Soviet Union's attitude when he stated that any link

[28] *Sunday Pictorial*, 12 Jan. 1947, p. 4.
[29] *Sunday Pictorial*, 12 Jan. 1947, p. 4.
[30] T. Kushner, *We Europeans? Mass-Observation, 'Race' and British Identity in Twentieth-Century Britain* (Oxford, 2004), pp. 166–88; D. M. Craig, 'The crowned republic? Monarchy and anti-monarchy in Britain, 1760–1901', *Hist. Jour.*, xlvi (2003), 167–85, at p. 179.
[31] *Sunday Pictorial*, 12 Jan. 1947, p. 4.

with the Greek royal family would be 'eyed with suspicion' abroad, creating international tension'.[32] This writer believed that 'the ruler of England and the British Empire has to make certain personal sacrifices for the benefit of the people. Where a match such as this one occurs the choice for Princess Elizabeth will be to sacrifice love for the future of her people'.

This writer formulated a critique of the betrothal that resonated with the popular idea that royal status was burdensome, an idea which also linked to the abdication story: the princess's future position as the nation's symbolic figurehead demanded that she sacrifice her personal fulfilment. However, many respondents in favour of the engagement took the exact opposite view, namely, that her personal happiness was paramount to her ability to perform her public role. A teenage girl from Portsmouth decided with her friends that Elizabeth 'should be free to marry whom she pleases if she loves him [because] we think a happy queen is a good queen'.[33] Phyllis Jones of London similarly noted that 'if her private life is happy it is reasonable to suppose that Princess Elizabeth will make a better Queen than if she were unhappily married'.[34] Comments like these reveal how the post-war culture of romantic realization worked to frame Elizabeth's constitutional position as part of a powerful emotional discourse: only by finding true love and happiness would she achieve her full potential as future monarch.

In scrutinizing the results it had gathered after the first week of the poll, the *Pictorial* reaffirmed the divide along which the royal betrothal would be judged: it was a story of true love versus duty. The newspaper emphasized the importance of romantic fulfilment when it continued its poll a second week and, aiming to obtain 'the truest possible reflection of mass opinion', issued readers with a coupon that gave them two answers from which to choose: 'Princess Elizabeth and Prince Philip should marry if they are in love and no obstacle should be placed in their way'; or, 'There should be no royal marriage between Princess Elizabeth and Prince Philip of Greece'.[35] This narrowing of options crystallized a story split between romance and constitutional politics, which was again amplified when the newspaper disclosed the final results the following Sunday: 64 per cent of respondents supported the marriage if it was a love match and 32 per cent opposed it.[36] The *Pictorial* published a selection of mainly positive letters from the 'thousands upon thousands' it claimed to have received 'from all classes'

[32] *Sunday Pictorial*, 12 Jan. 1947, p. 5.
[33] *Sunday Pictorial*, 12 Jan. 1947, p. 5.
[34] *Sunday Pictorial*, 12 Jan. 1947, p. 4.
[35] *Sunday Pictorial*, 12 Jan. 1947, p. 5.
[36] *Sunday Pictorial*, 19 Jan. 1947, p. 1.

to reiterate the same set of messages from the previous week.[37] One letter again focused on the idea that Elizabeth's personal fulfilment would make up for the demanding tasks she faced, Mrs M. I. Tebble from Shropshire presenting love as a reward for royal duty:

> If Princess Elizabeth and Prince Philip are in love and wish to marry they should be allowed to do so. Princess Elizabeth, both now and later as a ruling Queen, will have to give up much of her time to State affairs and will also be expected to have children as heirs to the Throne. Therefore her home life should be as *happy* as possible. Prince Philip seems a healthy, intelligent man. If he is allowed to marry the Princess and can fulfil his duties as well as the Duchess of Kent he will no doubt become very popular with the British people.[38]

As well as noting the high regard in which she held Princess Marina, Mrs Tebble expressed the view that Elizabeth's personal fulfilment would compensate for a life of public service. One of the main duties she identified was the requirement to produce heirs, revealing how the princess's gender shaped the public's constitutional expectations of her. Indeed, as a young woman who entertained domestic aspirations, Elizabeth may have been better placed to have her way in these circumstances than a male heir apparent would have been. Emotional control was deemed to be vital to public deportment in the masculine world of high politics and a male heir might have been expected to forsake love and place politics ahead of personal fulfilment.[39]

What clearly emerged from the *Pictorial*'s poll was the belief that Elizabeth's role was unenviable and that her future happiness hinged on her finding love. This consolatory motif became increasingly important to the official projection and public reception of the romance as it played out over the course of 1947. The empathy expressed by members of the public for the princess had its roots in the romantic culture of the interwar period, but in the more democratic atmosphere of the post-war years it became more important than ever before that royalty was perceived as engaging in the same 'companionate' forms of love that were valued by the rest of society.[40] In this way, then, self-fulfilment in domestic life became closely

---

[37] *Sunday Pictorial*, 19 Jan. 1947, p. 7.

[38] *Sunday Pictorial*, 19 Jan. 1947, p. 7. The newspaper included this italicized emphasis.

[39] M. Francis, 'Tears, tantrums, and bared teeth: the emotional economy of three Conservative prime ministers, 1951–1963', *Jour. Brit. Stud.*, xli (2002), 354–87, esp. at pp. 358–63.

[40] Langhamer, *The English in Love*, p. 6. See also J. Finch and P. Summerfield, 'Social reconstruction and the emergence of companionate marriage, 1945–1959', in *Marriage, Domestic Life and Social Change: Writings for Jacqueline Burgoyne*, ed. D. Clark (London, 1991), pp. 7–32.

integrated into the constitutional identities of the protagonists of the House of Windsor.

The *Pictorial* praised its readers for rendering a 'valuable service to our democratic system [having] provided the authorities with a gauge of popular feeling should a marriage with Prince Philip be contemplated'.[41] Notably, its poll initiated a new wave of media scrutiny of the monarchy's national role. When the engagement was officially announced later in July, the popular press interrogated other potentially contentious aspects of the wedding arrangements via the same medium of public opinion. The *Daily Express* 'invited' its readers to take part in a 'national poll' asking 'Should the Princess's wedding day be selected as the first postwar occasion to restore to Britain the traditional gaiety of a gala public event' or 'Should the Princess be an austerity bride?'.[42] Four days later the newspaper declared that for every six replies it received 'overwhelmingly in favour of a gala wedding', it received just one against it.[43] The battle lines were thus drawn. Shortly afterwards the much less deferential *Daily Mirror* published its own interpretation of public opinion when it presented a selection of readers' letters that questioned the expense of the wedding, protested at the civil-list annuities that were to be granted Elizabeth and Philip and expressed concern that the princess would receive additional ration coupons from the government for her wedding dress.[44] To judge from the Mass Observation reports compiled at the end of 1947, it seems that many of these material concerns persisted. More than thirty respondents opposed the royal wedding on the basis of the amount of money spent on it, while a further twenty expressed unease with either the new home, allowances or wedding presents given to the bridal couple. These writers believed that the privileges enjoyed by royalty did not suit the hardships that characterized the austerity of the immediate post-war years.[45]

'I couldn't marry a man I didn't love'

It seems that the *Pictorial*'s royal poll spurred the monarchy's image-makers into action to counter the negative public opinion that the newspaper had uncovered. The royal household and the media built on the positive reactions to the rumoured engagement by projecting a public image of the princess that focused on how her personal fulfilment would make up for the

[41] *Sunday Pictorial*, 19 Jan. 1947, p. 7.
[42] *Daily Express*, 11 July 1947, p. 4.
[43] *Daily Express*, 15 July 1947, p. 4.
[44] *Daily Mirror*, 16 July 1947, p. 2 and 21 July 1947, p. 2.
[45] E.g., MOA, 1079, 2427, 3848, 3116, 3827, 3820, 4213, 4022, 3524, 3808, 3653, 3667, 4301.

demanding nature of her royal duties. Mass Observation evidence reveals that this compensatory message worked to foster popular support for her choice of husband. The most notable instance when officials mobilized this idea was in the broadcast the princess delivered to coincide with her twenty-first birthday. At the end of January 1947 Elizabeth left London with her family for a four-month tour of the Union of South Africa. They arrived in Cape Town in mid February and embarked on an extensive trip around South Africa in an effort to calm the rising tide of nationalism that had undermined the country's political stability. The tour demonstrated what royal biographer Ben Pimlott described as the crown's value as a 'link in an association of nations and territories whose ties had become tenuous, because of war, British economic weakness, and nascent nationalism'.[46] As a youthful symbol of the strength of the monarchy, Princess Elizabeth, like her uncle Edward, who had toured the white dominions as his father's ambassador, helped to promote an image of the House of Windsor as the personal link that bound together disparate imperial peoples.[47] The princess's twenty-first birthday fell on 21 April, three days before she was due to return to England. As the climax to the royal visit she broadcast a special message to the Commonwealth and empire, which Pimlott has suggested became the most important public address of her life.[48] The message was written for Elizabeth by the journalist and royal chronicler Dermot Morrah, who reported on the South African tour for *The Times* while acting as unofficial royal speechwriter. Morrah had distinguished himself for his writing on royal events in the eighteen months after George V's death, penning a series of important leader articles on Edward VIII's abdication and George VI's coronation for editor Geoffrey Dawson that helped to set the high moral tone of *The Times*'s coverage of the monarchy.[49] As the newspaper's constitutional expert, Morrah had a keen understanding of the crown's modern symbolism as well as its relationship with the empire and he seems to have known exactly what was required of him when it came to writing the princess's 1947 broadcast. George VI's private secretary, Alan Lascelles, remarked in a letter to Morrah that he could 'not recall one [draft broadcast] that has so completely satisfied me and left me feeling

[46] Pimlott, *Elizabeth II*, p. 118.

[47] F. Mort, 'On tour with the prince: monarchy, imperial politics and publicity in the prince of Wales's dominion tours 1919–20', *Twentieth Century British Hist.*, xxix (2018), 25–57.

[48] Pimlott, *Elizabeth II*, p. 115.

[49] BOD, MS. Dawson 40, fos. 19, 22, 180 (diary entries on 21 and 27 Jan., 9 Dec. 1936); MS. Dawson 40, fo. 70 (diary entry on 5 May 1937).

that no single word should be altered'.[50] Indeed, the broadcast bore all the hallmarks of the royal public language which Lascelles and Cosmo Lang had carefully crafted throughout the 1930s and early 1940s.

As well as being transmitted by radio, a version of the princess's birthday broadcast was recorded by the newsreels and Graham Thompson was once again behind the film camera, having accompanied the royal party to South Africa at the king's request.[51] In the message Elizabeth thanked her subjects for their good wishes and, speaking on behalf of all the young men and women of the Commonwealth and empire, told her listeners and viewers that they needed to work together to ensure the prosperity of the constituent nations of the British world. Then, in a manner reminiscent of both her father and grandfather, the princess pledged her life to the empire and its people before stressing that she required their mutual support in order to fulfil her role:

> I declare before you all that my whole life, whether it be long or short, shall be devoted to your service and the service of our great Imperial family to which we all belong, but I shall not have the strength to carry out this resolution alone unless you join in with me, as I now invite you to do. I know that your support will be unfailingly given. God help me to make good my vow and God bless all of you who are willing to share in it.[52]

Pimlott suggested that the princess's account of the enduring vitality of imperial relations inspired British audiences who were 'exasperated by restrictions, and worn out after the added hardships of a terrible winter'.[53] However, he did not address the way in which the message was designed to engender public support for the princess in anticipation of the announcement of her engagement to Philip on her return home. The language used by Morrah sought to evoke empathy from media audiences for Elizabeth, inviting them to support her in her burdensome role. As Lascelles confided in Morrah before the princess delivered her pledge, 'the speaker herself told me that it had made her cry. Good, said I, for if it makes

---

[50] A. Lascelles to D. Morrah, 10 March 1947, in T. Utley, 'Grandad's words made Churchill and the Queen cry. How sad Beardy misquoted them this week …', *Daily Mail*, 8 June 2012 <http://www.dailymail.co.uk/debate/article-2156173/Grandads-words-Churchill-Queen-How-sad-Beardy-misquoted-week-.html> [accessed 21 Feb. 2017].

[51] Interview with G. Thompson, *British Movietone News*, 28 Jan. 1992, side 2 (24:45–29:04) <https://historyproject.org.uk/interview/graham-thompson> [accessed 25 Apr. 2017]. For Thompson's coverage, see 'Princess's Birthday Message', *British Movietone News*, 24 Apr. 1947.

[52] Quoted in Pimlott, *Elizabeth II*, p. 117. The speech can be heard at <https://www.youtube.com/watch?v=RUIToHE_27U> [accessed 27 March 2019].

[53] Pimlott, *Elizabeth II*, p. 118.

you cry now, it will make 200 million other people cry when they hear you deliver it, and that is what we want'.[54] With these words the courtier demonstrated that he was conscious of the intimate register of the princess's broadcast and believed it would stir strong feelings among its audiences.

One woman from Watford who responded to the Mass Observation directive on the 1947 royal wedding noted that she was so moved by Elizabeth's broadcast from South Africa that she felt the princess deserved a happy home life: 'I find the Princess Elizabeth and the Duke of Edinburgh an attractive couple, I believe it is a love match and I feel that after her "dedication" of herself to our service on the occasion of her 21st birthday the Princess is deserving of the best that this country and its people can give her. Theirs is no enviable task and the public is very thoughtless in its demands'.[55] This quotation suggests that the princess's 'dedication' to serve her subjects evoked in the writer sympathy for Elizabeth and identification with her difficult role. Indeed, this respondent was one of more than forty Mass Observation writers who noted that they perceived the princess's 'life of service' and 'trying public duties' as unenviable and therefore supported the royal marriage and Elizabeth's desire to marry the man she loved.[56] Two respondents even went so far as to characterize the princess and her family as 'public servants'.[57] Phrases like these reveal the enduring legacy of the language of the burdens of royal duty first formulated by Lang, Lascelles and other officials in the 1930s. However, the frequency of sentiments like these in the 1947 Mass Observation personal testimonies is evidence of the way this language was both forcefully promoted by the palace in the lead up to the announcement of the princess's engagement and readily taken up and recirculated by the British media.

Notably, the royal household also tasked Morrah with preparing a biography of Elizabeth – published by Odhams Press in collaboration with the Council of King George's Jubilee Trust – to celebrate her twenty-first birthday.[58] As with the official souvenir the Trust produced to commemorate the royal family's wartime activities and the 1937 coronation, we should view this book as a public manual on monarchy and as evidence of the way the House of Windsor wished to project its image outwardly.[59] The blurb

[54] Lascelles to Morrah, 10 March 1947, in Utley, 'Grandad's words'.

[55] MOA, 3418.

[56] MOA, 3388. For other examples, see MOA, 1061, 4186, 4299, 4221, 4223, 4241, 1095, 4235, 3434, 1034, 4161, 4279, 3900, 2511.

[57] MOA, 3426 and 3945.

[58] D. Morrah, *Princess Elizabeth: the Illustrated Story of Twenty-One Years in the Life of the Heir Presumptive* (London, 1947).

[59] See chs. 3 and 4.

inside the book's dust jacket captures the tone and content of this piece of official propaganda:

> The year 1947 is of special significance in the life of H.R.H. Princess Elizabeth. On 21st April she celebrates her twenty-first birthday, and with the attainment of her majority, she will be called upon to assume greater responsibilities and take a still more active part in the affairs of the Empire.
>
> The duties of a princess of the Blood Royal, especially when she stands next in succession to the throne, are many and arduous, and only by years of careful training and self-discipline has she been fitted for this great task. The Empire is fortunate in having as its future queen a young woman who possesses the necessary qualities in such high degree.
>
> The Princess is the foremost representative of the younger generation, and the youth of the Empire look to her for a lead in all aspects of the nation's life. They see in her the personification of their youthful aspirations and ideals, and as such she will exercise a profound and far-reaching influence upon the lives of all people of her own age.
>
> This book gives an authoritative account of the Princess's life up to her twenty-first year. Containing some 35,000 words and more than 100 photographs, it sets out for the reader her historical background, the sort of life she has lived and is living. From its pages he will learn that the life of a real princess bears very little relation to that of a princess in fairy tale or fable. It will enable him to watch her with interest, sympathy and admiration, as she steps across the threshold of life into the world that lies before her.

Throughout the biography there is an emphasis on the demanding nature of royal public life and the concluding section explores the 'steady programme of duty' on which the princess had already embarked.[60] This analysis of the demands of royal public life was complemented by other, more explicit references to Elizabeth's burdens. Morrah told his readers that the king had been reluctant 'to sentence his daughter to the unremitting service, without hope of retirement even in old age'; and explained, in words echoing the birthday broadcast that he had prepared for the princess, that 'she needs the personal sympathy of all those who will one day be her subjects. The task that awaits her in life is as exacting as can confront any human being; she can only discharge it with the constant goodwill and support of all peoples in whose cause it is undertaken'.[61]

As well as stressing Elizabeth's duty and self-discipline, Morrah impressed upon his readers her 'normal' qualities and suggested that she was

[60] Morrah, *Princess Elizabeth*, pp. 93–128.
[61] Morrah, *Princess Elizabeth*, pp. 12 and 62.

representative of all women her age: 'simple, warm-hearted, hard-working, painstaking, cultivated, humorous and above all friendly', she was 'a typical daughter of the Britain of her time'.[62] He explained that she had 'to sum up for her future subjects all that is most characteristic of their own lives, the normal life of normal people'. Photographs and other descriptions helped to convey the impression that she had a 'natural, homely' upbringing, that she enjoyed 'ordinary' pleasures and was 'unpretentious' in her interests, having developed a liking for dancing, the theatre and sport.[63] Morrah's biography thus oscillated between the image of a princess who desired an ordinary life and an image that highlighted the challenges of her extraordinary public role, implicitly signalling to readers that it was impossible for her to lead the kind of 'normal' existence she purportedly craved. Royal officials and their allies worked to transform Elizabeth into a symbol of self-sacrifice set apart from a national culture in which self-fulfilment was prized more highly than ever before. This self-denying image was powerful and designed to elicit the empathy of British subjects, as it had done for her grandfather and father, but it was against the backdrop of a post-war emotional culture in which love was deemed to be central to personal fulfilment that the princess's sacrifice took on added meaning because of her rumoured romance with Prince Philip.

Morrah's biography became the authoritative source on Elizabeth's personality, with the media taking its cues from his portrayal of her in their birthday messages to the princess. The *Daily Mail* praised the biography and quoted Morrah in characterizing Elizabeth as 'a girl of the age' who enjoyed modern pastimes such as dancing, the cinema and dining out.[64] It also impressed upon readers that the princess 'faces a vocation and a career without parallel in the world today'. The other leading royalist newspaper, the *Daily Express*, similarly noted that 'the happiness of being a lovely young woman in an admiring world will be tempered more and more by the demands of the office for which she is destined'.[65] Newsreels were even more direct in juxtaposing Elizabeth's desire for self-fulfilment with accounts of the oppressive nature of her royal station. In its birthday coverage, *Pathé News* extended its congratulations to the princess and explained that Philip had been linked to her as a suitor but that Buckingham Palace had denied all rumours. The story ended by focusing on the burdens that lay ahead of the princess:

---

[62] Morrah, *Princess Elizabeth*, p. 128.
[63] Morrah, *Princess Elizabeth*, pp. 7, 46, 62, 112.
[64] *Daily Mail*, 21 Apr. 1947, p. 2.
[65] *Daily Express*, 21 Apr. 1947, p. 2.

Increasingly heavy public duties fall upon the shoulders of the heir presumptive to the throne [*sic*]. Britain and the Empire know that she will discharge these duties as her parents have done in the service of her people. We hope, too, that she may be allowed to find her own personal happiness. We salute the young girl who accepts such world-wide responsibilities.[66]

In this way, then, loyal newsreels and newspapers worked to engender public support for Elizabeth and, tacitly, her decision to marry Philip, offsetting the public criticism of the latter that had been exposed by the *Sunday Pictorial's* poll in January.

*

Back in Britain, Lord Mountbatten had managed to have his nephew naturalized as a British subject and was now secretly overseeing a media campaign to publicize a likeable, egalitarian and Anglicized public image of Philip.[67] Since August 1946 Mountbatten had been corresponding with the Labour MP and *Reynolds News* gossip columnist Tom Driberg, asking that he give Philip a good write-up. Addressing Driberg as 'My dear Tom', he wrote that 'it is most kind of you to say that you will help to give the right line in the Press when the news of [Philip's] naturalisation is officially announced'.[68] Mountbatten was concerned about the negative impact the Greek civil war would have on his nephew's image and encouraged Driberg to dissuade other writers on the political left from criticizing Philip's connections to the Greek royal family: '[A]nything you can do to get your Left Wing friends to realise that [Philip] has absolutely nothing whatever to do with the political set-up in Greece, or any of our reactionaries, will be to the good, provided this is done verbally and not in your newspaper'.[69] He stressed to Driberg that he should focus instead on his nephew's 'English' credentials – 'I have tried to show that he really is more English than any other nationality' – and provided the columnist with a biographical information pack that outlined the fact that the prince had spent most of his early and educational life in the United Kingdom before joining the British navy, where he had enjoyed a stellar career.[70]

[66] 'Princess Elizabeth is 21: The Girl Who Will Be Queen', *Pathé News*, 21 Apr. 1947; 'Heiress to the Throne', *British Paramount News*, 21 Apr. 1947.

[67] Pimlott, *Elizabeth II*, pp. 99–101.

[68] CC, SOC. Driberg Supplementary 4, Lord Mountbatten to T. Driberg, 14 Aug. 1946.

[69] CC, SOC. Driberg Supplementary 4, Lord Mountbatten to T. Driberg, 4 Dec. 1946.

[70] CC, SOC. Driberg Supplementary 4, Lord Mountbatten to T. Driberg, 14 Aug. 1946 and 'Notes on Prince Philip'.

Writing to his boss, Lord Beaverbrook, in December 1946, just as the first rumours of a royal engagement were gaining traction, the editor of the *Daily Express*, Arthur Christiansen, expressed astonishment at the success of Mountbatten's lobbying of British journalists and in particular Driberg:

> You are quite right in your cable about the Mountbattens. Never has a campaign of nobbling gone so well. Why, in Reynolds News this week, even Tom Driberg came out in defence of Prince Philip in almost the precise words that were used to Robertson, Gordon and myself.

> Tom said that Prince Philip was an intelligent, broad-minded, fair, good-looking young man, that he could not even speak Greek, having left Greece as an infant. And he wound up by saying that, whatever his views on Greek politics may be, it was fair to interpret his request for British citizenship as a desire, in part, to be disentangled from them permanently.

> All this, of course, is probably quite true – but it comes strangely from the pen of Tom Driberg.[71]

Christiansen's words indicate that Mountbatten had also reached out to him, along with John Gordon, the editor of the *Sunday Express*, and E. J. Robertson, who was Beaverbrook's general manager of Express News. The Driberg article to which Christiansen referred had been published the previous Sunday in *Reynolds News* and repeated almost verbatim the profile prepared by Mountbatten as part of his biographical information pack.[72] The extent of Mountbatten's campaign suggests he knew Philip's foreignness would sit uncomfortably with some sections of the British public, but his lobbying may have also concealed a deeper uncertainty regarding his nephew's chances with Princess Elizabeth. According to royal biographers, concerns about Philip were not restricted to the political left and members of the public: George VI and Queen Elizabeth were also initially worried about his character.[73] Sarah Bradford quotes a courtier who claimed that 'the family were at first horrified when they saw that Prince Philip was making up to Princess Elizabeth. They felt he was rough, ill-mannered, uneducated and would probably not be faithful'.[74] Indeed, during their courtship, Philip penned several letters to the princess's mother apologizing for his behaviour during their stays together. In late 1946 he wrote to the queen, contrite for a 'rather heated discussion' he had started at dinner with the

---

[71] PA, BBK/H/115, A. Christiansen to Lord Beaverbrook, 12 Dec. 1946.
[72] *Reynolds News*, 8 Dec. 1946, p. 3. Driberg penned a follow-up article which was published in the *Reynolds News* on 15 Dec. 1946, p. 4.
[73] On the royal family's attitude to Philip, see Bradford, *George VI*, pp. 556–9; Pimlott, *Elizabeth II*, pp. 86–105; and Shawcross, *Queen Elizabeth the Queen Mother*, pp. 623–6.
[74] Bradford, *George VI*, p. 556.

Figure 5.3. 'The King Has Gladly Given Consent', *Daily Express*,
10 July 1947, p. 1. © The British Library Board.

family, stating that he hoped she did not think him 'violently argumentative and an exponent of socialism'.[75] Yet, while forthright and progressive in his views, the Greek prince's good looks, common touch and matter-of-fact demeanour suited the more democratic times and proved very popular with the media when, on 9 July 1947, it was officially announced that he and the princess were engaged.

The press reaction was very positive, with nearly every newspaper publicizing the engagement in front-page headlines (Figure 5.3).[76] The only notable exception was the *Daily Mirror*, which, in keeping with its own and the *Pictorial*'s less deferential attitude towards old hierarchies, published a front-page editorial calling on readers to work together in order to save the economy – the implication being that Britain was run by its people, not the social elite.[77] The press and newsreels otherwise tended to overlook the

---

[75] Shawcross, *Queen Elizabeth the Queen Mother*, p. 625.

[76] E.g., *News Chronicle*, 10 July 1947, p. 1; *Daily Sketch*, 10 July 1947, p. 1; *Daily Herald*, 10 July 1947, p. 1.

[77] *Daily Mirror*, 10 July 1947, p. 1.

expressions of opposition to the match that had arisen six months earlier. On becoming a British national Philip had renounced his royal title, given up his claim to the Greek throne and had taken his uncle Louis's name to become Lieutenant Philip Mountbatten. Newspapers now referred to him using only his new name and, as was the case with his first cousin Marina in 1934, journalists repeatedly stressed that he was an anglophile. However, whereas Marina had, as a figure on the fringe of the royal family, been able to remain a member of the Greek Orthodox Church, this was not an option for Philip, who was marrying the future supreme governor of the Church of England. As Pimlott noted, in September 1947 Philip's 'transmogrification into an Englishman was completed with his formal reception into the Anglican Church by the Archbishop of Canterbury in the chapel at Lambeth Palace'.[78]

The news coverage of Philip was informed by the biographical information that Mountbatten had supplied to journalists. Newspapers toed the line that he was British in all but birth, the *Daily Sketch* typical in its analysis: while at school at Gordonstoun in Scotland he had 'always attended Church of England services, and regard[ed] himself as a good member of the Church … Although he was born on the island of Corfu, that is his only real link with Greece'.[79] Despite its criticism of the rumoured engagement back in January, the *Guardian* similarly noted Philip's Greek origins, only to stress that he was 'half English and half Danish, and has enjoyed a typically English education to which his career in the Royal Navy in which he holds a permanent commission, is a natural and fitting outcome'.[80] The press also reproduced photographs of him in which he smilingly posed in his naval uniform. One of these photographs formed part of a series of six pictures used by the *Daily Express* to map the prince's development from infancy to manhood. The other pictures included Philip as a baby; as a schoolboy performing in a typically British re-enactment of Macbeth; alongside Elizabeth at a social engagement; and playing skittles with men at his local pub, the Methuen Arms, which was close to his shore station in Corsham, Wiltshire (Figure 5.4).[81]

---

[78] Pimlott, *Elizabeth II*, p. 137. Current restrictions on the archbishop of Canterbury Geoffrey Fisher's files in Lambeth Palace regarding Elizabeth II and Prince Philip prohibit any deep investigation of the official discussions concerning the latter's reception into the Church of England. The only reference to it is in LPL, Fisher 34, fo. 54, A. Lascelles to G. Fisher, 29 July 1947.

[79] *Daily Sketch*, 10 July 1947, p. 12. For similar examples, see *Daily Telegraph* 10 July 1947, p. 4; and *Daily Herald*, 10 July 1947, p. 2.

[80] *Manchester Guardian*, 10 July 1947, p. 3. The *News Chronicle* similarly softened its original criticism of the rumoured royal betrothal in January (*News Chronicle*, 10 July 1947, p. 2).

[81] *Daily Express*, 10 July 1947, p. 2; *Daily Telegraph*, 10 July 1947, p. 1.

Figure 5.4. 'The Man She Will Marry', *Daily Express*, 10 July 1947, p. 3. © The British Library Board.

We should interpret the press's emphasis on Philip's Britishness as indicative of the lengths to which news editors were willing to go in responding to Mountbatten's concerns that members of the public would criticize his nephew because of his past. Notably, his biographical pack also helped to remodel the kind of celebrity associated with the House of Windsor. Mountbatten emphasized that his nephew was very down-to-earth by stating that, on first meeting Philip, other sailors did not believe he was royal on account of his unpretentious personality.[82] This image of the classless prince who easily traversed social boundaries was also projected in the final scenes of a *Pathé* newsreel story on the royal engagement. A cameraman and reporter had journeyed to the Methuen Arms to interview some of the villagers who had played skittles with Philip. The commentator remarked that 'all the locals knew him – and our reporter learnt how much they admired him'. *Pathé's* scenes inside the pub showed the interviewer drinking from a pint of beer with a man named Joe, who then, speaking directly to the cameraman, remarked that Philip was 'the most charming fellow' and that they had enjoyed 'many a tussle' on the skittles alley together. The reporter then asked a man called Paul what he thought of the prince's engagement. The latter replied that he was 'highly delighted to hear about it' and the men then toasted the royal couple's health. Another skittles player concluded with an anecdote about Philip's unassuming qualities, stating that he had visited the pub 'for about three or four weeks before [he] knew he was a prince'.[83]

The pub sequence presented Philip as an affable, everyman figure who enjoyed the company of other ordinary men. In media portrayals like this one, royal celebrity took on a much more democratic character than before 1939, with Philip personifying the more egalitarian post-war social order. *Pathé's* exposure of the Wiltshire skittles players' opinions echoed the interwar human-interest focus on the House of Windsor but combined it with a new kind of 'bottom-up' royal coverage that explored 'ordinary' people's views on royalty.

Philip simultaneously embodied other forms of royal celebrity, with newspapers and newsreels focusing attention on his good looks. This attention reflected a wider, growing obsession with physical attraction as a defining feature of British celebrity culture.[84] The *Daily Sketch* noted that the American press had labelled Philip 'a handsome guy', while the usually sober *British Movietone News* referred to him as the princess's 'very good-looking husband-to-be'.[85] His attractive appearance sat comfortably alongside his persona as a fashionable modernizer who enjoyed the pursuits

[82] CC, SOC. Driberg Supplementary 4, 'Notes on Prince Philip'.

[83] 'The Royal Romance', *Pathé News*, 14 July 1947.

[84] On post-war physical and sexual culture, see S. Szreter and K. Fisher, *Sex Before the Sexual Revolution: Intimate Life in England, 1918–1963* (Cambridge, 2010), pp. 286–93; I. Zweiniger-Bargielowska, *Austerity in Britain: Rationing, Controls, and Consumption, 1939– 1955* (Oxford, 2000), pp. 91–2.

[85] *Daily Sketch*, 10 July 1947, p. 12; 'Royal Betrothal', *British Movietone News*, 14 July 1947. See also 'The Royal Wedding', *Gaumont British News*, 24 Nov. 1947; *News Chronicle*, 20 Nov. 1947, p. 6; *Sunday Pictorial*, 13 July 1947, p. 7.

of driving, dancing and drinking cocktails. Philip's multifaceted public image thus drew on the symbolic economy of what historian Martin Francis has termed 'romantic Toryism'. Like his uncle Lord Mountbatten, Philip was celebrated for his patrician elegance and military prowess.[86] The *Sunday Express* compared the prince's glamour to that of the late duke of Kent, who, the newspaper stated, had been 'one of the most popular of the Royal Family'.[87] Moreover, as with Prince George's celebrity and that of the prince of Wales in the 1930s, part of Philip's charisma lay in his outgoing behaviour. The newsreels that filmed him at the navy training school in Corsham presented viewers with scenes of him joking with his colleagues over lunch. The *Gaumont British News* commentator stated that, 'chatting with fellow officers in the wardroom, Lieutenant Mountbatten seems to be glad to be back at work again after a very happy leave'.[88] Notably, a *Pathé* news editor prepared a list of camera shots for the same story and remarked on the 'good informal shots of Philip in the wardroom, chatting to companions between mouthfuls of food', which suggests that he thought the scene conveyed a natural image.[89]

Lord Mountbatten and the media thus worked in tandem to promote Philip's popular image by combining traditional and newer forms of royal celebrity to fashion a reputation that was distinguished by its modern style and egalitarianism. The prince seemed to mix as easily with West Country villagers as with royalty at Buckingham Palace. Moreover, to judge from Mass Observation personal testimonies, members of the public appear to have responded positively to this image as well, with more than twenty respondents remarking on him in admiring terms and invoking in their descriptions phrases used by the media. One thirty-year-old female secretary commented: 'I think Philip an ideal choice – a Prince, and far more important an English gentleman in education and career'.[90] Similarly, a man from London suggested that 'Philip ... even tho' Greek by birth is probably as British as any of us by reason of his upbringing and for my part I look on him as English'.[91] While Philip's

---

[86] M. Francis, 'Cecil Beaton's romantic Toryism and the symbolic economy of wartime Britain', *Jour. Brit. Stud.*, xlv (2006), 90–117.

[87] *Sunday Express*, 16 Nov. 1947, p. 2. For other media examples of Philip's highly modern persona, see *Manchester Guardian*, 10 July 1947, p. 5; *Daily Herald*, 10 July 1947, p. 2.

[88] 'Lieutenant Mountbatten Returns to Duty', *Gaumont British News*, 7 Aug. 1947. See also 'Lieut. Mountbatten Back at Duty', *British Movietone News*, 7 Aug. 1947; 'Philip Mountbatten Goes Back to Work', *Pathé News*, 7 Aug. 1947.

[89] <http://bufvc.ac.uk/newsonscreen/search/index.php/document/101910_shotlist> [accessed 12 Aug. 2018].

[90] MOA, 4223.

[91] MOA, 3887.

schooling at Gordonstoun and Royal Navy career appealed to some of the Mass Observation panel and helped to eclipse his foreign background, other respondents seemed to admire him for his egalitarian personality. One woman from Wembley approved of him because he was 'young and personable and not too rich'; and a female civil servant commented that, 'I think Philip is very suitable as he is very handsome and a good sort. He seems to have a great sense of humour, he isn't a snob and I think he will keep Elizabeth in her place if she gets carried away by her important position'.[92] While this woman's remarks conveyed her concern about upper-class snobbery, her descriptions of Philip's likeable character and good looks were echoed in other respondents' comments on the way he had appeared to them in visual media: he 'looked' a 'delightful person', a 'nice lad', a 'decent chap' and a 'sport'. But, most of all, he was 'attractive' and 'handsome'.[93]

A minority of twelve Mass Observation respondents recorded either a mild uncertainty about Philip, or a stronger dislike of him. There was some cynicism about how the media had tried to disguise his foreign connections which echoed the public distrust of official propaganda during the Second World War.[94] One man stated that he did not believe the 'drivel' published about Philip.[95] Another man from Thetford in Norfolk thought it was 'strange … that Prince Philip, who, despite his relationship to the Royal Family, is a foreigner, should be so readily acclaimed as one of the figureheads of all that is British, because he happens to marry the Heir to the throne'.[96] Some Mass Observation respondents were more explicit in criticizing his background, however, a young housewife from Bradford labelling him a 'ruddy Greek', while a forty-two-year-old domestic worker from Dartmouth in Devon noted that she was 'disgusted' with the royal wedding, labelling Philip 'a Greek of the parasitic class': 'Because of him and his relative Marina, Duchess of Kent, this country finds itself against the Greek patriots. The royal couple will be over-paid and under-worked and live luxuriously; also they will breed child parasites who will be granted huge allowances and be reared expensively'.[97] This woman drew on the kind of language used by the *Daily Worker* in its criticism of the monarchy in the 1930s to present a broader

[92] MOA, 3034 and 4271.
[93] E.g., MOA, 4203, 4273, 3015, 3121, 3642, 3816, 3434, 4153.
[94] See ch. 4.
[95] MOA, 3841.
[96] MOA, 3808.
[97] MOA, 1642 and 4214. For other concerns about Philip's Greek background, see MOA, 3893, 1980, 2567, 3790.

socialist attack on the prince and the House of Windsor's privileges. She also thought that because of the royal wedding Britain found itself aligned against the Greek communists – referred to here as 'patriots'.

International politics did, therefore, continue to shape some people's attitudes to the royal romance as it played out over the course of 1947. It is significant that the *Daily Mirror*, with its high circulation figures, maintained an ambiguous stance towards the marriage from the announcement of the engagement right through to the wedding itself.[98] Ten days before the marriage the *Mirror* published front-page photographs of Greek communists who had been beheaded by royalist forces in the civil war.[99] Carrying the headline 'What are We British Doing?', the *Mirror*'s report complained that British troops stationed in Greece were 'standing by' as 'cruelties and atrocities [were] taking place around them'. This coverage could be interpreted as a coded criticism of the royal wedding with its implicit questioning of the marriage links between the British and Greek royal families. In a similar way, the *Mirror* was the only mainstream newspaper to publish a picture of Philip as a boy wearing traditional Greek national dress on the day of his wedding.[100]

The royal biographer, Philip Ziegler, has claimed there was 'widespread' belief that Philip was 'amiable but dim'; however, this is not supported by the Mass Observation evidence. Descriptions of the prince's 'dimness', or similar traits, do not feature at all in the personal testimonies.[101] Anxieties about Philip's German connections (all his sisters had married German aristocrats who had supported the Nazis) also remained the concern of the few rather than the many: just two Mass Observation respondents criticized his ties to Germany.[102] This silence on Philip's Teutonic links is significant and again attests to the media's power in suppressing negative details. At a time when there was severe anti-German sentiment in Britain, the media chose not to dwell on Philip's relatives.[103] In all the 1947 news reports surveyed here, there were just four references to the prince's German associations, all from the left-wing or liberal press and published either before the engagement or on the day it was officially announced. After

---

[98] See n. 77.

[99] *Daily Mirror*, 10 Nov. 1947, p. 1; *Daily Mirror*, 11 Nov. 1947.

[100] *Daily Mirror*, 20 Nov. 1947, p. 1. For a discussion of the circulation of the *Mirror* in these years, see Bingham, *Family Newspapers?*, pp. 7–9 and 16–20.

[101] Ziegler, *Crown and People*, p. 81.

[102] MOA, 1654 and 3893. On elite concerns about Philip's German links, see Pimlott, *Elizabeth II*, pp. 104–5.

[103] B. Harrison, *Seeking a Role: the United Kingdom, 1951–1970* (Oxford, 2011), pp. 536–7; Kushner, *We Europeans?*, pp. 192–201.

this there were no more references, which may indicate that royal officials or Lord Mountbatten successfully prevented further inquiries into the prince's family connections. This fact was not lost on everyone, though, with one Mass Observation respondent remarking that the *Daily Mail* had conveniently erased from its picture of Philip's family tree the relatives 'who helped Germany during the war'.[104]

*

Following the royal engagement, the British media projected Elizabeth and Philip as exemplars of a post-war culture of love and domesticity to sustain the idea first mobilized by the *Pictorial* that the relationship was a true romance and not a political move. Historians who have explored the meanings of companionate marriage in the post-war period have argued that it prioritized mutual emotional and sexual satisfaction and was located within an increasingly private conception of the home.[105] With the help of courtiers, the media projected an idealized image of companionate love around Elizabeth and Philip to emphasize the emotional reality of their romance in order to encourage media audiences to empathize with them. Louis Wulff, the Press Association's accredited court correspondent, led in publicizing this narrative through a 'behind-the-scenes' article that was printed in the *Sunday Express*.[106] Given Wulff's close links to the palace, we might assume that George VI and his advisers approved the article before publication. Like Morrah, Wulff promoted the public image of a down-to-earth, fun-loving princess who was 'as romantic as any girl' and well matched in the modern, good-looking prince. The *Express* published the article the Sunday after the engagement was announced and it included an intimate portrayal of the princess's thoughts on love that set the tone for what was to come:

> All girls discuss young men, and Elizabeth and her friends were no exception. So it soon became common knowledge that a tall, blond and handsome naval officer called Philip was her favourite. Luckily his appearance came up to the high standard she had once set herself many years before when she said, 'when I marry, my husband will have to be very tall and very good-looking.' Some

[104] MOA, 3893. This might have referred to the family tree presented in the *Daily Mail*, 10 July 1947, p. 4.
[105] Langhamer, *The English in Love*, pp. 47–8; Finch and Summerfield, 'Social reconstruction'.
[106] *Sunday Express*, 13 July 1947, p. 2.

time later, when a friend pointed out that she might have to marry for political reasons, she replied, 'I couldn't marry a man I didn't love.'[107]

Wulff's commentary on the princess's romantic ideals was innovative: his first-hand revelations ascribed direct speech to Elizabeth to emphasize both her 'normality' and her desire to find love with a suitable partner. Like 'all girls' she talked about 'young men' with her friends and placed special importance on 'good looks'. Furthermore, these insights substantiated the idea that Elizabeth's romantic ambitions were more important than constitutional politics. Subsequent press reports echoed Wulff's stories and he prepared a series of articles for the *Sunday Express* in the weeks leading up to the wedding that struck the same revelatory notes as his earlier exposé.[108]

The royal household also helped the media to construct visual images that conveyed an idealized love story to audiences. The day after the couple's engagement was announced, courtiers arranged for Elizabeth and Philip to be filmed and photographed at a special sitting in the gardens of Buckingham Palace. All five major newsreel distributors used Graham Thompson's footage from this sitting and, in keeping with the cameraman's intimate style, it included new emotional gestures that would have been deemed unsuitable thirteen years earlier in 1934. George and Marina had readily posed for the newsreels, but had not initially physically touched one another. Now, in the more expressive mid 1940s, the princess and her naval-officer fiancé strolled together arm-in-arm, exchanged smiles, laughed inaudibly and talked between glances at the camera (Figure 5.5).[109] The newsreels used romantic soundtracks to heighten the ambiance of these scenes, which included close-up images of the engagement ring worn by Elizabeth. The *British Movietone News* commentator drew special attention to the princess's facial expression: 'In these, the first special studies of the pair since the news of their engagement, it is easy to see the radiant happiness of the princess'. Elizabeth's smile received extensive coverage in the press as well, with popular and quality newspapers often noting and illustrating how happy she looked.[110] In this way, then, her smile became a symbol of her emotional transformation and some members of the public interpreted it as such. One seventy-two-year-old widow from London who responded

---

[107] *Sunday Express*, 13 July 1947, p. 2.

[108] *Sunday Express*, 9 Nov. 1947, p. 2 and 16 Nov. 1947, p. 2.

[109] Compare 'The Royal Engagement', *Gaumont British News*, 14 July 1947, in which Philip and Elizabeth strolled arm-in-arm, with the film of George and Marina from 1934 that showed the couple walking side-by-side but not physically touching one another ('Royal Honeymoon', *British Movietone News*, 6 Dec. 1934).

[110] 'Royal Betrothal', *British Movietone News*; *Daily Telegraph*, 10 July 1947, p. 1; *Daily Mail*, 11 July 1947, p. 5; *Daily Mirror*, 21 Nov. 1947, p. 1.

Figure 5.5 'It is easy to see the radiant happiness of the princess', 10 July 1947 (RCIN 2002364). Royal Collection Trust / © Her Majesty Queen Elizabeth II 2019.

to the Mass Observation survey on the royal wedding commented that she was 'glad Princess Elizabeth married such a good man, for rumour had it that he was objected to at first, hence the sullen looks when abroad. Her happy marriage has completely changed her look'.[111] This woman had detected from pictures of the princess taken during the South Africa tour that she was 'sullen' because of complications with her engagement and contrasted this downcast appearance to her happier 'look' since her marriage. Another female respondent similarly described how visual media had evoked in her an empathy for Elizabeth and Philip. Despite her misgivings about Britain's new links to Greece, she noted that, 'when I look at their photographs they look such a nice couple – I just have to wish them joy'.[112] These examples demonstrated how media audiences sought to comprehend the royal protagonists' inner feelings from pictures and suggest that the emphasis which commentators like *Movietone*'s Lionel Gamlin placed on the princess's facial expressions may have helped to influence public attitudes.

[111] MOA, 1015.
[112] MOA, 4161.

The royal lovers also made a balcony appearance together with the princess's family on the evening their engagement was announced. The newsreel coverage of this interaction was again designed to convey the couple's happiness to audiences while dispelling any lingering doubt about the prince's suitability. Boasting to cinema viewers that it had waited 'with the film industry's biggest lens trained on the palace balcony', *Pathé News* presented audiences with images of the couple stepping out onto the veranda and waving to the crowds that had assembled outside the gates of Buckingham Palace. These scenes were interspersed with images of the large crowd waving back at the royals. The commentator remarked over a soundtrack of cheering that the 'heiress to the throne and her future husband met the British people' and added that George VI looked 'particularly happy' as he, the queen and Princess Margaret joined the couple on the balcony.[113] As with the press reports that highlighted how the king had 'gladly given his consent' to the marriage, this comment acted as a seal of approval designed to ease public anxieties about the international politics involved.[114]

The media would repeatedly emphasize the emotional dimensions of the royal romance until the couple's wedding day and a number of Mass Observation respondents notably commented on how this worked to evoke their empathy for the couple. One man from Nottingham recorded that he was 'pleased and proud that a Princess of England … had married someone of her choice'; and although 'naturally sceptical of this true love in Royal marriages … eventually the Daily Press broke a lot of that down. The newsreel in the cinema also helped … Gradually there emerged a feeling that behind the pageantry there was just a domestic family celebrating a great event in their private lives'.[115] A woman from London similarly noted that 'the little I have read about the Royal Couple gives me the impression that they are genuinely in love'.[116] The emotional focus of the media's royal love story thus helped to dissipate lingering concerns about the possible dynastic motives that had brought Elizabeth and Philip together. Out of 360 directive replies, more than fifty respondents commented that the prince and princess 'suited one another', that their relationship was 'not of political significance' or an 'arranged marriage' but instead the outcome of 'genuine' affection and a 'real love match'.[117]

---

[113] 'The Royal Romance', *Pathé News*. See also 'The Royal Engagement', *Gaumont British News*, 14 July 1947.

[114] *Daily Express*, 10 July 1947, p. 1; *Daily Mail*, 10 July 1947, p. 1; *Daily Telegraph*, 10 July 1947, p. 1; *News Chronicle*, 10 July 1947, p. 1.

[115] MOA, 4303.

[116] MOA, 4202.

[117] E.g., MOA, 3840, 1325, 2984, 3796, 4008, 4223, 3121, 4292, 4267, 4246, 3005, 3806, 3810. The following accounts are typical. One 55-year-old woman from Morcambe (Lancashire)

The fact that the couple looked as though they were in love appealed to Mass Observation respondents who identified with free choice and emotional fulfilment in marriage. The recurrence of positive expressions like these in the Mass Observation files pointed to the importance of new companionate forms of love in influencing both the projection and reception of the romance. With the help of the media, royal aides and the shadowy figure of Lord Mountbatten, Elizabeth and Philip were made to appear like-minded, well-suited, good-looking and as though they would love and support each other.[118] In contrast with the many positive responses, only eleven Mass Observation respondents expressed uncertainly over whether Elizabeth and Philip were in love (and, indeed, most hoped they were) and just three recorded complete disbelief that it was a real romance.[119] The relatively small size of this section of opinion suggests that the official narrative on the emotional authenticity of the princess and prince's love story, which was popularized by the media, resonated with members of the public and helped to generate support for the royal couple.

'Part of that great British family tradition'
One of the messages at the heart of post-war reconstruction was that family life was central to both social order and citizenship, with the home presented as a crucial space for adult and child socialization.[120] Moral campaigners argued that domesticity had always been a key tenet of the national character and that it helped to account for the country's strength. For example, the general secretary of the National Marriage Guidance Council proclaimed in 1946 that 'Britain has always been proud of her family life. It has been the backbone of her national greatness ... the only lasting foundation for a

---

(MOA, 2675) stated: 'I'm very pleased that it is a real love match and not a diplomatic one; and I think they really are a lovely couple'. A woman from Truro (Cornwall) (MOA, 4247) noted that she was 'glad Princess Elizabeth was marrying someone she loved [instead of] having one of these arranged marriages which has so often been the lot of heir and heiresses to the throne'. One (MOA, 2068) of the 20 men who empathized with the royal romance described how, despite having originally been troubled by Philip's Greek background, he realized that 'political marriages were out of date and could no longer determine political allegiances'. He concluded that 'Elizabeth was lucky to find a man with whom she was in love and who was eligible to marry her'.

[118] A good example of this came from a middle-aged woman from Watford (MOA, 4203) who wrote that 'the young couple should be very happy, the bridegroom seems gay, looks attractive and should be a source of strength to the Princess as she undertakes more of the causes of the State'.

[119] For examples of uncertain respondents, see MOA, 3913, 2475, 1099. For disbelievers, see MOA, 3009, 3667, 3789.

[120] C. Langhamer, 'The meanings of home in postwar Britain', Jour. Contemp. Hist., xl (2005), 341–62, at pp. 342–4.

sound national life is sound family life'.[121] This polemic was indicative of a post-war political culture that sought to impress upon the working classes in particular the value of the nuclear family in order to reverse the rise in divorce and illegitimacy and the decline in population.[122] Sensitive to these social and moral changes, the royal household saw the 1947 royal wedding as an opportunity to reaffirm the House of Windsor's role as a symbol of domestic virtue by promoting Christian family values to new audiences. Supported by the Church of England, which was also keen to reassert its function as a moral guiding force, royal officials elevated Elizabeth and Philip as a model couple in order to appeal to a less deferential and more democratic generation.[123]

The monarchy's successful orchestration of a family-centred royal wedding relied on courtiers navigating the competing demands of different interest groups. The royalist media spearheaded the campaign for a day of popular celebration and the BBC and newsreels fought to bring their audiences a visual illustration of the wedding from inside Westminster abbey. Meanwhile, the liberal and left-wing press expressed concerns about the economic costs of the wedding at a time of austerity, some of which were shared by a Labour administration that was torn between thrift and a desire to put on a good show should it help to boost national morale.[124] A notable example of these tensions coming to a head was the government's decision that it would not call a public holiday to celebrate the wedding. Clement Attlee's private secretary, Laurence Helsby, wrote to Alan Lascelles confirming this position:

> While a holiday would certainly have been appropriate in more normal times and in accordance with the wishes of the people, in the present economic difficulties of the country [the Prime Minister] is driven to the conclusion that a general stoppage of work would be unwise and open to misconstruction. This conclusion is, he hopes, consistent with the known wishes of The King and of Princess Elizabeth herself that the wedding should not give rise to any

[121] Langhamer, *The English in Love*, p. 10.
[122] Field, *Blood, Sweat, and Toil*, p. 216; 'Thane, 'Unmarried motherhood', pp. 20–3; Langhamer, 'The meanings of home', p. 345.
[123] E.g., the 3 opinion polls conducted by the weekly magazine *News Review* on the role and relevance of the Church of England in post-war Britain: *News Review*, 23 Oct. 1947, pp. 1, 5, 19–22; 30 Oct. 1947, pp. 22–4; 6 Nov. 1947, pp. 22–4. The pessimistic findings of the *News Review*'s opinion polls complemented the analysis of Mass Observation's own study of the religiosity of a metropolitan district in *Puzzled People: a Study in Popular Attitudes to Religion, Ethics, Progress and Politics in a London Borough* (London, 1947). For a more optimistic historical perspective, see C. Brown, *The Death of Christian Britain: Understanding Secularisation, 1800–2000* (London, 2009), pp. 170–5.
[124] Pimlott, *Elizabeth II*, pp. 132–3 and 142–3.

expenditure or work which is not in keeping with the spirit of these hard times. Indeed, it has occurred to the Prime Minister that Princess Elizabeth might feel disposed to let it be known as her own wish that, in view of the country's needs, there should be no interruption to work.[125]

The letter indicates that the king had previously advised Attlee that he and the princess thought a public holiday would be out of step with the austere times. This approach was in keeping with a royal public relations strategy that sought to prevent criticism of royal profligacy arising by limiting both the expense and scale of the wedding. At a time when the British press were diligently reporting on the additional ration coupons the princess would receive for her dress, the new home she and Philip would live in and the large annuity payments the couple would receive from the government, it was crucial for the royal family to avoid controversy wherever possible.[126] Lascelles was naturally of this mind, too. He telephoned Helsby to inform him that, while it was customary to announce a holiday for schoolchildren in connection with royal weddings, there was no precedent for calling a national holiday and 'that The King did not favour the [Prime Minister's] suggestion that Princess Elizabeth might express a wish that there should be no public holiday … this threw upon her the responsibility for a decision which expressed in this form might arouse criticism'.[127] This conversation reveals that George VI and his courtiers sought to protect Elizabeth's reputation from adverse public reaction; and it was decided that the Ministry of Education would announce the school holiday in a press release which would include a short reference to the fact that there would not be a national holiday.

The official emphasis on moderation not only accorded with the nation's economic circumstances but also contributed to the idea that the princess and prince entertained the same 'normal' domestic aspirations as other young British people and would be married with the same ritual that united other Christian couples. This was, of course, all relative. The royals would still parade through central London to the cheering of thousands of excited spectators; the bridal couple would participate in all the usual ceremonial customs associated with royal occasions, including the now obligatory balcony appearance; and the marriage would be consecrated in the nation's symbolic spiritual centre, Westminster abbey. And yet, despite what was

[125] TNA, PREM 8/656, L. N. Helsby to A. Lascelles, 22 Sept. 1947.
[126] Pimlott, *Elizabeth II*, pp. 127–36. Also see *Sunday Pictorial*, 16 Nov. 1947, p. 1; *Manchester Guardian*, 23 Oct. 1947, p. 5 and 20 Nov. 1947, p. 3; *Daily Mirror*, 20 Nov. 1947, p. 2.
[127] TNA, PREM 8/656, L. N. Helsby's written record of conversation with A. Lascelles, 25 Sept. 1947.

clearly the *extraordinary* nature of the royal wedding and its protagonists, the notion that Elizabeth and Philip were ordinary people, representative of their generation in their hopes and desires, left a deep impression on many Mass Observation respondents who went on to write about the marriage. To understand the popular appeal of this message, we must look beyond press discourse to the wider chorus of voices that championed this idea in order to generate personal identification with the royal lovers.

The archbishop of Canterbury, Geoffrey Fisher, was a conservative moralist who championed a traditional vision of family life and he became a vocal proponent of the notion that Elizabeth and Philip were characteristic of other couples their age.[128] In a speech he delivered as part of the House of Lords' address of congratulation to George VI on the forthcoming marriage of his daughter, he drew attention to the modern emotional dimensions of Elizabeth and Philip's relationship: 'It is no politically arranged marriage such as the past once knew. It springs from a true accord of hearts between two young persons who have grown up together, knowing each other well, and have made their own decisions'.[129] Fisher thus projected an image of the royal couple as exemplars of their generation in their desire for personal enrichment, but he also seized on the wedding as an opportunity to promote a model of Christian family life to the nation at large. The secretary of King George's Jubilee Trust, Commander J. B. Adams, wrote to the archbishop a week after the royal engagement was announced, stating that the king had authorized the publication of a souvenir programme like the ones produced for the 1935 silver jubilee and 1937 coronation.[130] Adams asked Fisher if he would write an introduction to the wedding ceremony 'underlining its religious significance as did the late Archbishop of Canterbury on the Coronation Service'. In reply, Fisher initially indicated that he did not think an introduction necessary as 'the Marriage Service will be precisely the same Marriage Service as everybody is married with in every church in the land'.[131] However, after finally agreeing to write the piece, he chose to use the introduction to expand on the very idea that marriage was a common rite of passage shared by Christians and that it was of great importance to British national life:

> The Marriage Service of the Book of Common Prayer is entitled 'The Form of Solemnization of Matrimony' that is to say, the form by which, besides being made legally valid, a marriage is made before God to be blessed by Him, is

[128] A. Webster, 'Fisher, Geoffrey Francis, Baron Fisher of Lambeth', in *ODNB* <https://doi.org/10.1093/ref:odnb/31108> [accessed 12 Oct. 2018].

[129] LPL, Fisher 34, fo. 93, 'Archbishop of Canterbury's speech in support of the House of Lords' Address of Congratulations on 22nd October 1947'.

[130] LPL, Fisher 34, fo. 51, J. B. Adams to G. Fisher, 18 July 1947.

[131] LPL, Fisher 34, fo. 53, G. Fisher to J. B. Adams, 25 July 1947.

'christened' and made holy. Marriage intimately concerns the parties to it, but it is not their concern alone. It has a social significance also. The community is concerned, since the family is the unit of society and the community depends for its strength and stability upon its families. Therefore the State, as the guardian of the well-being of the community, has its marriage laws ... This Form of Service, which contains embedded in it many ancient elements, has the simplicity and restraint which is characteristic of the Church of England. Whether used in Westminster Abbey or in a simple parish church, unmistakably it declares the dignity of Christian marriage and surrounds it with the loving purpose and continuing grace of Christ.[132]

Fisher's words presented Elizabeth and Philip as a model Christian couple and he used a progressive sociological lexicon to draw a direct link between the importance of the family 'unit' and the well-being of the entire nation.[133] This message was also promoted by the archbishop of York, Cyril Garbett, who delivered a sermon as part of the 1947 royal wedding ceremony, which was broadcast live to listeners, and emphasized that the bride and groom were no different to other couples:

In the presence of this congregation and in the hearing of an invisible audience in all parts of the world, you have now become man and wife. Notwithstanding the splendour and national significance of the service in this Abbey, it is in all essentials the same as it would be for any cottager who might be married this afternoon in some small country church in a remote village in the dales. The same vows are taken; the same prayers are offered; and the same blessings are given ... A happy and unselfish home life of your own will enable you to enter more readily into the joys and sorrows of a people who have a deep and instinctive love for their homes.[134]

The archbishop's famous likening of the royal wedding to that of a 'cottager' received much media attention the day after the service.[135] As well as printing the sermon, the *Daily Mirror* presented an article on the 'simple story' at the centre of the wedding which began with the line, 'A young English girl was married yesterday in the family church'.[136] Reports like this one compared the princess's experience to that of other young women, with Westminster abbey characterized as the nation's 'family church'. Hannen Swaffer, writing for the left-wing *Daily Herald*, also claimed that royalty

[132] King George's Jubilee Trust, *The Wedding of Her Royal Highness Princess Elizabeth and Lieutenant Philip Mountbatten* (London, 1947), p. 19.
[133] E.g., M. Young and P. Willmott, *Family and Kinship in East London* (London, 1957), appendix 4: 'Kinship terms used in the study'.
[134] Quoted in *The Times*, 21 Nov. 1947, p. 4.
[135] E.g., *Daily Mirror*, 21 Nov. 1947, p. 2; *Daily Mail*, 21 Nov. 1947, p. 2.
[136] *Daily Mirror*, 21 Nov. 1947, p. 2.

shared in a common domesticity with their subjects when he stated that Elizabeth's nuptials 'differed' from earlier royal weddings because 'in spite of the pageantry and pomp, there was such an emphasis laid upon the fact that the marriage, in its significance, differed in no way from one in which two of the humblest folk were united in matrimony'.[137]

*

The BBC and newsreel companies joined with the Church of England in projecting an image of the prince and princess as exemplars of a national culture of Christian marriage and romantic fulfilment. In its coverage the broadcaster sought to balance the dignity of the occasion with its desire to bring audiences closer to proceedings and to convey to them the celebratory mood of the event. In particular, it wanted to use its new television service to bring viewers a live programme of the royal wedding.[138] The immediate post-war years witnessed a growing tension emerge between the BBC and the Newsreel Association as the broadcaster sought to bring its viewers visual news – the traditional terrain of the newsreels. To begin with, the BBC applied to the NRA to use Graham Thompson's accredited footage of royal events as part of its television coverage, but newsreel officials consistently rejected the BBC's requests, a revealing entry in the NRA's minute books recording that the managing director of *British Movietone*, Sir Ernest Gordon Craig, met with Buckingham Palace's new press secretary, Richard Colville, to explain that the newsreel companies were 'fundamentally opposed to any co-operation with the BBC'.[139] This policy of non-cooperation ultimately led the broadcaster to establish its own film unit, which accompanied the royal family on their 1947 tour of South Africa.

In a memo dated 4 September 1947 the head of outside television broadcasts, Ian (later Lord) Orr-Ewing, noted that 'following a chance meeting with Cmdr. Colville' ('an old school acquaintance'), he had 'visited Buckingham Palace to explain further what the televising of the Royal Wedding really involved'. Colville had asked that 'nothing should at present leak out to the press', clearly anxious to prevent the kind of disclosure that had pre-empted the announcement of the sound broadcast of the 1934 royal wedding thirteen years previously. Orr-Ewing outlined that Colville

[137] *Daily Herald*, 21 Nov. 1947, p. 2. For similar examples, see *Daily Express*, 21 Nov. 1947, p. 2; *Daily Sketch*, 20 Nov. 1947, p. 6.

[138] BBCWA, R30/845/1-3 and T14/1350/1-2.

[139] BFINA, NRA vol. 3, m.2511, 'Television and the Royal Rota', 26 Feb. 1948. See also m.2236, 'Buckingham Palace and Television', 26 Sept. 1946.

thought it 'probable that the King would agree to television and newsreels, but would not agree to a full length Technicolor film, in view of the extra lighting required. [Colville] also confirmed that the King has an inherent objection to having spotlights focused on him, general lighting being much more acceptable, but we would have to keep the intensity within reasonable limits'.[140] This memo is worth quoting at length as it demonstrates how George VI's aversion to artificial lighting dictated the media's access to royal events in the immediate post-war years. Indeed, the BBC files for the wedding reveal that the broadcaster entered into protracted negotiations to acquire highly sensitive 'image-orthicon' television cameras – which required less light – as part of its campaign to secure permission to televise the marriage ceremony.[141] However, when Orr-Ewing filed his next memorandum on 8 September it was to report a telephone call with Colville, the latter having informed him that George VI 'considered the wedding of his daughter to be a private and religious matter which should not, under present conditions, form a subject to be taken by newsreels and television cameras'.[142] Like his father before him, the king was concerned about the technical arrangements for royal events. Not only did he forbid the filming of the service, he also prevented HMV and the BBC from making recordings of the ceremony for commercial sale, thus preserving the sacred and intimate character of the occasion.[143]

George VI's attitude accorded with his vision of his daughter's wedding as a more modest event compared to the royal spectacles of the interwar years. Still, Graham Thompson managed to use his influence within the royal household to persuade the king to allow him to arrange the filming of the return procession up the aisle after the marriage service had ended. In his 1992 interview Thompson described how he had resorted to deceit and 'quite a bit of trickery' in convincing the dean of Westminster, who acted as the king's proxy, that additional lighting at the abbey's west door would be acceptable. Thompson had dimmers installed on his lighting rig to disguise the full extent of the artificial illumination required to record the wedding procession as it left the abbey and Dean Alan Don unwittingly agreed that the system could remain in place.[144] The result was that the

[140] BBCWA, T14/1350/1, Record of Interview at Buckingham Palace on 4th September with Cmdr. R. Colville, Press Secretary to H.M. King on the subject of Televising the Royal Wedding, 22nd Nov. 1947.
[141] BBCWA, T14/1350/1, Private memo from P. H. Dorté, 16 Sept. 1947.
[142] BBCWA, T14/1350/1, private memo from C. I. Orr-Ewing, 8 Sept. 1947.
[143] BBCWA, R30/845/2, R. Colville to B. E. Nicolls, 10 Oct. 1947; 'The Royal Wedding: Prospective Unauthorised Commercial Recordings', 17 Oct. 1947.
[144] Interview with G. Thompson, 28 Jan. 1992, side 2 (08:45–15:00).

newsreels presented to cinemagoers scenes of a royal wedding from inside Westminster abbey for the first time.[145] However, arguably a more significant innovation resulted from Orr-Ewing's successful application to Colville for a camera position on Thompson's platform, something which enabled the BBC to transmit live television images of the return procession to those viewers watching at home. The estimated number of people who tuned in for the BBC's television coverage of the royal wedding was 500,000 and included one Mass Observation respondent – a forty-one-year-old clerk from north-west London – whose remarks on the effect television had in making her feel included in a national event anticipated the responses of viewers to the 1953 coronation: 'I saw and heard it on the television, and was excited and moved as if I'd been there. I think it was a very impressive occasion, beautifully arranged and worthy of all the best British traditions. The simplicity of the ceremony was exactly right in perfect taste and so was the glorious pageantry'.[146]

The restrictions on the filming of Elizabeth and Philip's wedding meant the BBC's main focus was its radio coverage of the ceremony, which was officially sanctioned by the king.[147] Here, again, the BBC seems to have succeeded in projecting an image of the couple that encouraged listeners to identify with them and their marriage as symbolic of a national culture. The broadcaster's elaborate technical preparations were key to the transmission of an intimate scene from the abbey which defined how many experienced the event. Seymour de Lotbinière, who had succeeded Gerald Cock as director of outside broadcasts, oversaw the installation of thirty-two microphones in the abbey, roughly the same number as used during the 1937 coronation.[148] Whereas just one microphone had been used at the wedding of George and Marina to record their words in reply to Cosmo Lang's prompts, four microphones were installed in 1947 to cover Archbishop Fisher's voice and the royal responses. The mics were displayed more prominently, too, enabling better sound transmission than at George VI's coronation because there was no need to conceal them for fear they would be caught on camera. These important improvements in the quality of the broadcast helped to create a strong connection between listeners and the royal couple as they recited their marriage vows.

---

[145] 'The Royal Wedding', *British Movietone News*, 24 Nov. 1947; 'The Princess Weds', *Pathé News*, 21 Nov. 1947.

[146] MOA, 4182. On the BBC's televising of the return procession up the aisle to viewers, see BBCWA, T14/1350/2, C. I. Orr-Ewing to R. Colville, 26 Nov. 1947.

[147] BBCWA, R30/845/1, E. Ford to B. E. Nicolls, 13 Sept. 1947.

[148] BBCWA, R30/845/2, 'Royal Wedding Notes on Engineering Arrangements', undated.

Historians who have studied soundscapes have suggested that listening differs from viewing in that sound places the subject at the centre of the sensory experience, while the visual form is consumed from a peripheral position, looking on.[149] According to this argument, radio can be a highly immersive experience. These ideas find some support in more than twenty reports by Mass Observation respondents, who admitted that the sound broadcast of the 1947 wedding service had exercised a powerful effect on them, several noting they were 'moved' by it, others saying they were 'touched emotionally'.[150] The princess's marriage vows were the most commented-on feature of the broadcast and evoked empathy for her among listeners. The experience of a woman from London who was 'just a bit' older than Elizabeth and who listened to the service at her home in Twickenham attested to the affective dimensions of the broadcast. She originally thought that the princess 'through no particular inherent quality of her own, but through being born to the right parents, had had the sort of wedding that every girl dreams of but few obtain'. However, she went on to explain how the broadcast had quickly dispelled her jealous feelings:

> While listening to the ceremony envy disappeared in the sentimental glow one felt at the thought that a young girl was going through the most important ceremony of her life – provided she really is in love with Prince Philip and somehow one feels she is. The radio served us gallantly on this occasion, as on so many others, and my husband and I sat enthralled for an hour listening alternately to the cheering crowds, the lovely music, the frightened schoolgirl 'I will', and the strong pleasant voice of Prince Philip. I'm alternately swayed by the arguments on both sides as to whether public money should have been more or less lavishly spent on the Royal Wedding. The Socialist in me says it should not have been so extravagantly done at a time of national crisis, but the woman in me says 'don't spoil her happiness by bickering about amounts of money which, compared [to] our debts, are infinitesimal' – I think the woman wins![151]

This respondent's description of Elizabeth as a 'young girl' and of her 'frightened schoolgirl "I will"' shows the writer empathized with the princess because of the vulnerable image conveyed by the radio as she recited her vows. Indeed, these emotions were strong enough to dispel her grudge about royal privilege and her socialist concerns about the cost

---

[149] R. M. Schafer, 'Acoustic space', in *Dwelling, Place and Environment: Towards a Phenomenology of Person and World*, ed. D. Seamon and R. Mugerauer (New York, 1989), pp. 87–99.
[150] E.g., MOA, 3815, 3371, 3589.
[151] MOA, 4162. For other expressions of jealousy, see MOA, 4301, 3817, 3635.

of the event. A forty-four-year-old woman from Beckenham expressed a similar empathy for Elizabeth: '[Hearing the princess] say the response in rather a trembling voice, I realised for the first time that she is only just twenty-one, and the whole thing must have been a bit of an ordeal for her. I felt almost as if she was being sacrificed to make the nation prosperous and happy'.[152] This woman drew on the pre-war imagery of the suffering royal to describe how she identified with the vulnerable character of the princess as communicated by radio. This type of response suggests that the broadcast enabled listeners to experience intimate moments of the wedding service, with the audial exposure of Elizabeth's emotions intensifying the empathy many felt for her. Crucially, this kind of reaction was not restricted to a female listenership, either. A married man from Nottingham, who felt 'ashamed' of his behaviour, recorded that he had tuned into the broadcast in a 'casual state of mind', only to find himself 'in a highly emotional state and … on the verge of tears during the whole of the ceremony in the Abbey. Fortunately, I was alone, my wife was busy in the kitchen'.[153] While this respondent thought his crying would undermine his masculinity, his report signalled the profound emotional impact that radio could have on male and female listeners alike.

The sound broadcast also evoked personal forms of identification with the House of Windsor as a family group. A sixty-three-year-old woman noted that she thought the ceremony a 'heart-warming showing of a natural and necessary stage in the life of Elizabeth and the Royal Family as to remind us of their humanness. All married women knew how she felt and all parents with married daughters knew how the King and Queen felt'.[154] This description again reveals that members of the public identified with royalty through the emotions associated with common rites of passage like marriage. A housewife from Truro in Cornwall recorded that she became very interested as the wedding day approached, planning her work so that she 'could listen to almost all of it' on the radio:

> This I did and found myself going through the whole ceremony with her. I thought how if I were her I should at this moment feel a pit in my stomach. I also felt that it brought back to all the millions listening their own wedding-day, and all their young ideals and hopes and aspirations. For the first time I understood the fascination of weddings for older people – especially women – something I had never quite understood before.[155]

[152] MOA, 1054.

[153] MOA, 4383.

[154] MOA, 1014 (respondent's own underlining). For other descriptions of the 'humanness' of the event, see MOA, 3426, 3371, 3391.

[155] MOA, 4247.

This respondent revealed that the broadcast evoked from her an empathy for the princess and a nostalgia about marriage in general which she felt she shared with 'millions' of other people who she imagined were listening. The broadcast thus encouraged affective integration around Elizabeth, with the listener experiencing a sense of collective emotional identification which she believed was particularly strong among older people and women.

One sixty-year-old woman from Coventry who sympathized politically with communism but was disappointed at the way the *Daily Worker* had criticized the royal wedding, described how the emotional 'reality' of the marriage influenced her feelings: 'I think the Royal Wedding demonstrates a hunger for something beautiful and <u>real</u> as against the eternal phoney sentiment of films. A real princess, really in love with a real prince, married with a real service, with real royalty for parents and relations'.[156] For her, the ostensible emotional authenticity of this family occasion set it apart from the 'unreality' of popular films. She went onto note that she and two elderly female friends had tearfully listened 'as the responses of Philip and Elizabeth came through' and even invoked the old adage that the media had repeatedly used to describe the royal love stories of the interwar period when she proclaimed that 'in fact, all the world loves a lover, which I suppose sums it up'.

We might interpret this woman's response as evidence of both the impact of the prolonged media campaign that drew attention to the 'true love match' in 1947 and the success of radio in communicating what sounded like the feelings of the royal couple during their marriage ceremony. In the lead-up to the wedding, BBC executives had also planned the sound broadcast to ensure it conveyed some of the emotions expressed by the crowds. It now had an 'Actuality Unit' in charge of 'effects' microphones which would record 'the cheers of the crowd and the noise of trotting horses' on the processional route and outside Buckingham Palace.[157] The celebratory mood of the royal wedding broadcast was captured in the way it was designed to mirror the Victory Day programmes, with the BBC calling in the same team of 'observers' to offer commentary on the wedding that had contributed to its VE and VJ Day coverage.[158] Furthermore, these speakers were instructed to address a 'non-London audience' in order to appeal to listeners in the regions who might otherwise feel excluded from the national social imaginary constructed by the broadcast.[159]

---

[156] MOA, 1644 (original emphasis).

[157] BBCWA, R30/845/2, E. M. Peacock to Mr Glassborow, 24 Oct. 1947; R30/845/3, 'Royal Wedding Appendix', 14. Nov. 1947.

[158] BBCWA, R30/845/1, Memo from Senior Superintendent Engineer, 5 Sept. 1947; R30/845/3, 'The Royal Wedding', undated.

[159] BBCWA, R30/845/3, 'Draft Lay-out for Royal Wedding Broadcast'.

It was, perhaps, testament to the success of these policies that a thirty-three-year-old Scottish housewife noted that, despite not 'car[ing] two pins about [the royal wedding]', to her 'astonishment' she was powerfully affected by the broadcast: '[S]o tense and electric was the emotion of the crowds, that the microphones picked it up and transmitted it, so that I, doing a prosaic morning's ironing in Glasgow, was moved to tears. I discussed this afterwards with some friends of mine, and they admitted to the same experience'. She went on to explain that the 'sensation wasn't nearly so strong' when she watched the newsreel coverage of the wedding and questioned whether the 'emotion [was] lost in the canning of the soundtrack' or 'because I knew it was coming'.[160] Her words suggest that the immediacy of radio with its successful transmission of the atmosphere in London on wedding day had had a profound emotional impact that had caught her off guard.

The Glaswegian housewife was not very impressed by the film record of the wedding, but it is worth noting that most Mass Observation respondents who watched newsreel coverage of the event commented positively on it (this was not the case with the Technicolor film that was made).[161] One fifty-six-year-old housewife from Burnley in Lancashire remarked on the inclusive effects of newsreel: 'I felt sure that I watching the film saw more than any spectator at one particular point on the route'.[162] Editors went to special lengths to convey to newsreel viewers an image of a nation joined in celebration of the marriage. *British Paramount News*'s commentary was typical in highlighting royalty's symbolic association with the nation's domestic culture: 'This day Great Britain rejoiced and lifted up its heart. A harassed nation forgot its worries. The twin appeal of Monarchy and Marriage was a reminder, welcome indeed, of all that is fundamental and enduring in a world of change'.[163] As with earlier royal events, newsreel cameras also captured vast panoramas of the crowds that assembled in central London and imposed on these scenes soundtracks of wild cheering'; and, as with the interwar coverage of the crowds that gathered outside Buckingham Palace for the royal balcony appearance, newsreels placed special emphasis on the breaking of the police cordon and the rush to the palace gates as

[160] MOA, 4153.

[161] Those who recorded seeing newsreel coverage of the royal wedding included MOA, 3388, 4292, 4322, 4004, 4160, 2895, 3957, 4255, 3827, 3853, 3188, 4383. Those who recorded seeing the Technicolor film included MOA, 4317, 3053, 4301, 3815, 2899, 4123, 4230, 3873.

[162] MOA, 1032.

[163] 'The Royal Wedding', *British Paramount News*, 24 Nov. 1947. See also 'The Royal Wedding', *British Movietone News*, 24 Nov. 1947; 'The Princess Weds', *Pathé News*, 21 Nov. 1947.

visual indicators of royal popularity. *British Paramount*'s commentator exclaimed to cinemagoers that, 'strong as was the police cordon outside the Palace, the great mass of people overcame it in their determination to be as near as possible when the bride and bridegroom and other members of the royal family should appear on the balcony'.[164]

The newsreels used other narrative devices to communicate the impression that the entire country had gathered to participate in the wedding. *Pathé News* included scenes of women and men gathered in shops and other public spaces listening to the marriage service by way of the broadcast: 'In this moment, charged with great meaning, the people of Britain and the Commonwealth joined. They listened, and remembered in towns and villages, in shops, in streets, in homes'.[165] *Pathé* then juxtaposed footage of a normal-looking family listening to the broadcast in their living room with still photographs of the royal wedding ceremony. Choral music played over this sequence to create a seamless story connecting the royal wedding to the domesticity of an 'ordinary' British home. The accompanying shot list shows that the *Pathé* editor sought to create this image of normality through the scenes he selected: 'A married couple, and small daughter listening to the service. Fire burns in the grate (a typical family scene)'. In this way, then, newsreels projected the message that Elizabeth and Philip's wedding was symbolic of a national culture of domesticity and that their marriage was fundamentally British in nature and heritage. As *Movietone* told its viewers: 'This day will long be remembered as a vivid and important episode in the story of the nation'.[166]

*

Approximately two thirds of the Mass Observation respondents who remarked on the emotional dimensions of either the BBC radio broadcast or the newsreel films were women. To some extent this gendered disparity reflected the straightforward fact that, for most men and some women,

[164] The aforementioned housewife from Burnley (MOA, 1032) commented on these scenes: 'The most interesting part of the film was where the crowd breaks through the police cordon and rushes up near the Palace and the Royal group appears. This must be puzzling to foreigners. These are not victorious captains, famous actors or writers or singers, to be acclaimed by the crowd'. Her words attested to the enduring nature of this ritual between crown and people and what she perceived as its peculiarly British quality.

[165] 'The Princess Weds', *Pathé News*. For the accompanying shot list, see <http://bufvc.ac.uk/newsonscreen/search/index.php/document/102085_shotlist> [accessed 6 Oct. 2018].

[166] 'The Royal Wedding', *British Movietone News*, 24 Nov. 1947. See also *Daily Telegraph*, 21 Nov. 1947, p. 1; *The Times*, 21 Nov. 1947, p. 1; *Daily Mail*, 21 Nov. 1947, p. 1.

the royal wedding day was a normal working day, meaning that a greater number of women, like the aforementioned housewives, were able to listen live to the marriage ceremony within their homes. As noted in chapter 2 in relation to King George V's Christmas messages, the ability to listen to broadcasts at home with one's family or friends enabled personal forms of listening, something which may help to account for some of the emotionally engaged responses that Mass Observation respondents recorded in 1947. However, as with George and Marina's wedding in 1934, the media targeted women more than men as an audience susceptible to the appeal of the royal romance. The wedding dress that would be worn by the princess was the main topic of interest used by the media to achieve this kind of audience identification. The senior controller of the BBC, Basil (later Sir Basil) Nicolls, corresponded with Richard Colville at the palace to gain details about the dress from designer Norman Hartnell. Colville granted the BBC an exclusive preview of the dress on the condition that it withhold all its information until the official press release date on wedding day.[167] The BBC recruited Audrey Russell from its eastern service to 'give a woman's point of view' and she visited Hartnell's studio to prepare the descriptions of the dress that she would use in her commentary in the wedding broadcast.[168] BBC production files show that the broadcaster positioned another female observer, Joan Gilbert, inside Westminster abbey 'so that the ladies in our audience may hear all about the dresses' she saw from her vantage point;[169] and the BBC's Welsh division also managed to obtain a place in the abbey for Myfanwy Howell, the editor of its regional women's programme, so that she could later broadcast an eyewitness account of the event (she would sit next to the Women's Hour correspondent, who would go on to do the same for a national audience).[170]

As with Marina's marriage thirteen years earlier, the BBC thus helped to frame the 1947 royal wedding as a feminine occasion by encouraging women to take an active interest in the event through consumer fantasies connected to fashion. Newspapers also helped to perpetuate this gendered emphasis, with journalists resorting to subterfuge in order to gain access to information on the wedding dress. Writing to Lord Beaverbrook in mid October, the editor of the *Sunday Express*, John Gordon, noted that:

[167] BBCWA, R30/845/1, B. E. Nicolls to R. Colville, 25 Sept. 1947 and reply on 25 Sept. 1947; R30/845/2, C. Max-Muller to J. Dunbar, 16 Oct. 1947.
[168] BBCWA, R30/845/3, 'The Royal Wedding', undated.
[169] BBCWA, R30/845/3, 'The Royal Wedding – draft programme', p. 5.
[170] BBCWA, R30/845/2, Memo from A. Llywelyn-Williams to G. M. Bowen, 8 Oct. 1947, 'Seats for Broadcasters at the Royal Wedding', 16 Oct. 1947.

In all the bother now going on over the Princess' wedding I had the King's Secretary on the telephone this morning, saying very diffidently that he had been asked to try and get us to keep our reporters off the story. Apparently Hartnell had been complaining that Sunday Express reporters had been round his place. I said I was very sorry if I was causing Mr. Hartnell any perturbation but that my reporters' business was to get news, whether Mr. Hartnell liked it or not. There is so much stupid secrecy over the wedding arrangements that some of the leakages – most probably untrue – look like doing the Royal Family a great deal of harm.[171]

Gordon's words hinted at the journalistic resentment that royal secrecy aroused – indeed, Richard Colville's policy of keeping the British press firmly at arm's length was quickly to become the norm.[172]

Another of Beaverbrook's editors, Herbert Gunn at the *Evening Standard*, reported to his employer the day before the wedding that he had secured the popular novelist and author Rebecca West to write the newspaper's main story on the event – again signalling the importance of reaching a female audience – and noted that the palace had finally circulated information on the dress to newspapers:

The wedding has aroused more public interest than I believed possible a month ago, and despite the fog and rain with which we are now afflicted, I think there will be a tremendous crowd in the streets. Incidentally, we were able last week to give a number of exclusive details of the wedding dress which were quoted widely. Although we had the pictures of the wedding dress designs a week ago, I decided against using them because I thought there would be a great deal of public resentment if the Evening Standard had gone against what has become known, sentimentally, as 'the wish of a young girl to keep her wedding dress secret.'[173]

Despite his cynicism Gunn's letter again attests to the significance of Elizabeth's dress as a newsworthy item and shows how his sense of the popular anticipation which had built up around her marriage informed his decision to withhold pictures of the robe until wedding day. Even the Labour government expressed an interest in the dress. Spotting a public relations opportunity, the MP and president of the Board of Trade, Harold Wilson, entered into negotiations with the princess's private secretary, Sir John Colville, to have the dress – 'which is not only an object of loyal interest to the people of Great Britain but also one of the finest examples of British art, skill and workmanship' – displayed in the UK's main textile centres and in the Celtic nations' capitals in the months after the marriage, believing that

[171] PA, BBK/H/121, J. Gordon to Lord Beaverbrook, 10 Oct. 1947.
[172] Pimlott, *Elizabeth II*, p. 165.
[173] PA, BBK/H/250, H. Gunn to Lord Beaverbrook, 19 Nov. 1947.

it would 'arouse pride and interest in the industries which contributed to its production' and act as 'an invaluable stimulant to morale and recruitment in the textile industries'.[174] At a time when the government was investing heavily in British manufacturing and exports, Wilson's message was taken up and promoted by the media and the public seem to have responded positively: one Mass Observation respondent echoed the Labour MP's words in her appraisal of the dress as a 'magnificent example of the best artistry and workmanship in the world, and [it] shows what can be done in this country if we try'.[175]

Although Mass Observation personal testimonies revealed a heightened interest among female respondents in the heavily gendered elements of the royal wedding, such as the princess's clothing, men and women alike proved to be deeply invested in the idea that Elizabeth and Philip's marriage symbolized a family-centred national culture. At a time when men, as well as women, increasingly saw the home as an important space for emotional enrichment, the royal wedding provided a spectacular and reassuring example of what many people perceived to be a pillar of modern British life.[176] More than twenty Mass Observation respondents noted that they thought the royal marriage symbolized a national moral culture focused on domesticity. One twenty-seven-year-old research worker recorded that 'regarding Royalty mainly as a symbol of Respectability and Permanence and Family Institutions seems the most sensible attitude'.[177] A twenty-six-year-old man also interpreted the wedding as 'part of that great British family tradition', while a forest worker of the same age from Newmarket wrote that he thought 'these things tend to endear the family to us, and that in turn strengthens and supports the British way of life'.[178] Another young man, aged twenty-five, similarly thought that the royal wedding set a good example in an 'age of increasing divorce and domestic unrest'.[179] And, despite expressing the view that monarchy was incompatible with his left-wing republican politics, a twenty-six-year-old railway clerk from Northwich recorded that 'as a firm believer in the value of the family and monogamy as the basis for communal order and social progress I wish the newly married couple well'.[180]

---

[174] TNA, BT 64/1026, J. H. Wilson to J. Colville, 3 Feb. 1948 and reply on 4 Feb. 1948.
[175] MOA, 4182.
[176] C. Langhamer, 'Love and courtship in mid-twentieth-century England', *Hist. Jour.*, l (2007), 173–96, at p. 179; L. King, *Family Men: Fatherhood and Masculinity in Britain, 1914–1960* (Oxford, 2015), pp. 5–7.
[177] MOA, 3434.
[178] MOA, 1388 and 2511.
[179] MOA, 2921.
[180] MOA, 4098.

It is tempting to argue, based on these men's testimonies, that the younger generation in particular had internalized the symbolic association of monarchy with family life that was elevated through the palace's media strategy in the 1930s and 1940s. The most similar sentiment articulated by an older male respondent came from a forty-six-year-old chemist who expressed irritation at the 'humbug which suggests that [the princess] fares no better than I' – signalling that the public relations effort to equate the bridal couple with ordinary people was by no means entirely successful – but then went onto note that without royalty 'there could be a regrettable decline of sentimental association' as they offered a 'backbone of stability and an atmosphere of tradition and history in times of change'.[181] Although the Mass Observation sample is too small to make any definite assertions, it could well be that younger men, who more readily identified with a domesticated masculinity than their fathers' generation, valued the House of Windsor's promotion of family values particularly highly.[182]

Female respondents identified with the family model set by royalty but tended to express less specific sentiments in connecting the wedding to national life. A bank clerk from London described how the royal family 'do somehow represent a certain spiritual value of family life in this country', while a fifty-six-year-old poultry farmer from Arborfield Cross in Berkshire expressed her delight that Elizabeth had married for love and presented the royal nuptials as an 'epitome of all the lovely weddings that one would like every pretty girl to have – and indeed, any girl pretty or otherwise'.[183] Meanwhile, a forty-two-year-old schoolmistress from East Sussex noted the wedding's 'symbolic value – of family life, of youth growing up and taking responsibilities, of plans for the future'. She continued by remarking on both the political value of monarchy and the role the media played in influencing her emotions:

> I thought the general excitement showed the value to us as a people of having an institution like our limited monarchy: it provides a most useful outlet for the expression of emotion and is something tangible symbolising various values, to which it is easier to be loyal than to ideas … The BBC broadcast was remarkably good, and contributed a great deal to the feeling I have tried to express, that it was an event that mattered to ordinary people, and particularly to-day when death and destruction seem commoner than marriage and new life.[184]

---

[181] MOA, 3009. For similar examples, see MOA, 4186, 4202, 4269, 4383.
[182] King, *Family Men*, pp. 117–8.
[183] MOA, 4202 and 3388.
[184] MOA, 4256.

The broadcast enabled the schoolteacher to identify with a wider community, constituted of 'ordinary people', to whom she thought the wedding really 'mattered'. Significantly, her appreciation of the royal wedding was influenced by the shadow of wartime losses, with the symbolism of Elizabeth's marriage evoking optimism in her through its representation of family and 'new life'. This view was shared by a fifty-four-year-old farmer's wife from Wrexham in North Wales, who noted that she and her husband 'listened to the broadcast from start to finish and were very impressed and found it very moving. The whole thing was so completely British and would only have happened here – it was so sane and human, so like things ought to be if more were decent, friendly and honest'.[185]

These upbeat appraisals were echoed in other Mass Observation testimonies which either presented the wedding as a turning point in the nation's fortunes or contrasted Britain's celebratory mood with national cultures abroad. A twenty-four-year-old Cambridge student described her sense of pride in the wedding, noting that '[w]e, Britain, could produce something lovely and fairy tale in spite of war and aftermath, that the USA with all wealth and self-assurance just couldn't. Of course the whole thing was lit up from within by the fact that Liz and Phil seemed so gorgeously happy and genuine about it'.[186] Although the student's words betrayed an anxiety about Britain's diminished status as a world power following the war, a fifty-seven-year-old man from Colwyn Bay in North Wales was full of confidence when he described how he was 'proud to belong at this time to the one nation in the whole world which can stage a Royal Wedding like ours, the nation to which all the world at this time looks up'.[187] A thirty-four-year-old production manager from Caerleon in South Wales noted his 'feeling that in later years we will be able to look back and point to this occasion as the moment when for no precise reason people felt things were going to get better for the first time'.[188] This view was shared by a forty-six-year-old woman from Birmingham who looked back further than the war to 1936 and the abdication crisis as the key moment when Britain's fortunes began to slide: 'I feel the Royal Wedding has put us back where we were in the world's estimation before the Duke of Windsor threw his crown away. I feel it was the beginning of a new era. Already the impetus to do better, to create, to start, to live, not exist from day to day, has begun to manifest itself'.[189] While this woman's response hints at a longer-term sense of British

---

[185] MOA, 3371.
[186] MOA, 3005. See also MOA, 4271, 3015, 2746, 4236.
[187] MOA, 1679.
[188] MOA, 3878.
[189] MOA, 2253.

decline that stemmed from Edward VIII's sudden departure, these personal testimonies point to a perception of national renewal associated with Elizabeth and Philip which would find wider popular resonance when the princess acceded to the throne in 1952.

It is significant that even negative reactions recorded by the Mass Observation panel about the wedding attested to the pervasive symbolism of royal domesticity and the public image of the 'ordinary' princess. A twenty-two-year-old General Post Office engineer remarked that he thought 'the whole performance is staged by Church and State to enhance the concept of family life, yet what relation the general standard of family life has to a couple who start with every circumstance of wealth and luxury is never questioned'.[190] A thirty-five-year-old journalist seemed to share in the belief that officials had staged the wedding to set a moral example to the nation when she wrote that 'royal functions' were used to 'foster fake sentiments' and that the 'symbols of family are all nonsense'.[191] A forty-seven-year-old housewife from Otley in West Yorkshire detected a similar inconsistency between the House of Windsor's mode of living and that of other British families. She criticized 'the attempt that was made to glamourise the whole affair and at the same time to make people believe that it was just an ordinary wedding and that the royal family practically had to make do and mend like other people'.[192] An elderly woman from the same area also thought that an 'absurd fuss [had] been made about the Royal family, a very ordinary set of people really'. She continued:

> I rather like the Queen with her smile. But her daughter is so plain, and has such an ugly voice. I did not bother to listen to the service but I heard some of the BBC records in the afternoon … To the BBC or whoever is behind it trying to work up the Royal family as important again, as they did after George V had that illness in the twenties? Surely the thing to do in these revolutionary days is to empathise with the *unimportance* of the King in our Constitution, that he is more a figurehead than anything else.[193]

This complex, shifting personal testimony, with its presentation of the princess as 'plain' and her voice as 'ugly', ran counter to the vast majority of opinion recorded by Mass Observation. The elderly writer also expressed her cynicism at the way shadowy officials had 'worked up' the royal wedding to generate popular support for the House of Windsor, comparing it unfavourably to the way royalty had been promoted by the media in

[190] MOA, 3795.
[191] MOA, 3320.
[192] MOA, 1362.
[193] MOA, 3120 (original emphasis).

the early 1930s. Like several others, this respondent saw the wedding for what it was: an attempt by an elite to reassert the cultural power of the royal family at a time of significant social and political change. However, it is important that we place these critical, discerning voices in context, as a large majority of Mass Observation commentators did not question the meaning of the wedding but instead remarked positively on the 'real family feeling' it created and the way it helped to crystallize their awareness of a national emotional community that seemed united in its appreciation of domesticity and companionate love.[194]

'Honeymooning "in a gold-fish bowl"'

The single most commented-on feature in all the Mass Observation personal testimonies written in reply to the December 1947 directive was the way the media coverage of the royal wedding and subsequent honeymoon intruded on Elizabeth and Philip's private lives. Nearly a fifth of all respondents either recorded their sympathy for 'the couple having to suffer all that publicity', expressed revulsion at the media's 'vulgar curiosity' about a 'purely private family affair' or vehemently castigated the press for publishing 'sordid details'.[195] While this criticism forms part of the wider disapproval voiced by Mass Observation respondents about the scale of the royal wedding coverage, it also reveals a strong attachment to the family values exemplified by the House of Windsor as part of Britain's culture of domesticity. This was particularly the case with the issue of sex: within the chorus of outrage there were forty comments aimed at the media-led interest in the royal couple's honeymoon activities. The honeymoon was a rite of passage defined by private conjugal happiness and consummation; and the Mass Observation panel's criticism of the media's prurient coverage of the honeymoon (and the public's interest in the royal honeymooners) suggests there was a deep concern for Elizabeth and Philip's intimate lives. This moment was significant as it witnessed the merging of an older belief in the burdens of royal *public* life with a new concept of royal suffering that was rooted in the over-exposure of royal *private* life. This media-induced narrative of suffering was not only symptomatic of the more irreverent post-war press culture, with news editors becoming increasingly brazen in revealing royal intimacy, but also reflected the growing popular belief that private home life was sacrosanct and a right to which everyone was entitled.[196]

Elizabeth and Philip left London on the afternoon of their wedding day

---

[194] MOA, 3900. See also Ziegler, *Crown and People*, pp. 83–4; and MOA, 4221.
[195] E.g., MOA, 1682, 3810, 3891, 4172, 3856, 3891, 2142, 4308, 4236, 3895, 2979, 3960, 4247.
[196] Szreter and Fisher, *Sex Before the Sexual Revolution*, pp. 36 and 348–62.

for Lord Mountbatten's Broadlands country home in Romsey, Hampshire. The wife of the archbishop of Canterbury, Mrs Rosamond Fisher, went to watch the couple on their drive to Waterloo station. She recorded that 'it was very romantic to see them come by in the open landau ... They both looked very gay and jolly. She was in a powder-blue hat and coat. I should think they must have been thankful to reach the sanctuary of their train and have an hour or so's quiet before facing crowds again at Winchester'. Mrs Fisher also reported that her husband had enjoyed a 'very nice meal' as part of the wedding breakfast served at the palace, but that the *Mirror* had published a 'speech which the Princess never made and presumably ... invented the other speeches as well; as there were no Press men present'.[197] This kind of misreporting would come to define the media coverage of the royal honeymoon. In 1934 courtiers had managed to limit press coverage of George and Marina's honeymoon through negotiations with the chairman of the Newspaper Proprietors' Association, but this was not an option in the less deferential atmosphere of 1947.[198] Under the enticing headline, 'My Wonderful Wedding', the *Daily Mail* provided a moment-by-moment account of the royal couple's arrival at Broadlands:

> Princess Elizabeth and Prince Philip jumped out of the car at the door of Broadlands like 'teen-agers, before the chauffeur could open the car door for them. Hand-in-hand they ran up the five stone steps to the open glazed doors of the south wing. They were greeted with smiling courtesy by the butler Mr. Frank Randell. As they crossed the threshold the Princess squeezed the Duke's hand. 'It's been a wonderful wedding but it's lovely to be here at last,' she said.[199]

These allegedly first-hand insights were augmented by descriptions of the layout of the house and the food the lovers ate on their arrival. The intimate perspective the *Mail* offered into the honeymoon retreat was notably captured in the conversation between the royal lovers: it is highly unlikely it ever took place but it provided a personal view into the princess's emotional state and this kind of revelation persisted for several days in the popular press.[200]

It was not to everyone's liking, though. One twenty-year-old Mass Observation respondent who studied at Bristol university noted that she was 'really cross' with 'the pursuing of the Duke of Edinburgh and the Princess

[197] LPL, Fisher 276, fos. 1–11, 'An Account of the Wedding of HRH Princess Elizabeth and the Duke of Edinburgh' (original emphasis).
[198] RA, PS/PSO/GV/MAN/SS340, F. H. Mitchell to T. McAra, 20 Nov. 1934.
[199] *Daily Mail*, 21 Nov. 1947, p. 1.
[200] For similar examples, see *Daily Sketch*, 21 Nov. 1947, p. 1; *Daily Mirror*, 22 Nov. 1947, pp. 1 and 8.

at Broadlands. The "Daily Mirror" was guilty of the most deplorable lack of taste in publishing descriptions of the Royal couple's room, their arrival, and hour-by-hour accounts of the first few days after their arrival'.[201] A male Mass Observation respondent, who criticized what he saw as the 'nauseating publicity', wryly commented that the prince and princess should have gone 'to bed together in the Glass Coach in full public view' as part of a 'fertility ceremony' in an effort to satiate the media-led interest in their honeymoon activities.[202] A housewife from Buckingham similarly stated that she was 'sure that many would have entered the bedroom before their curiosity had been alleviated – if then'.[203]

The many responses like these demonstrate that members of the public were concerned about the royal lovers' domestic lives. Two days into their honeymoon the BBC revealed that Elizabeth and Philip would be attending the local Sunday church service at Romsey abbey. As one Mass Observation respondent remarked, this was a 'mistake', because tens of thousands of people flocked to the abbey to participate in the service with the princess and prince.[204] The *Mirror* described how 'when regular church-goers reached the Abbey they found that enthusiastic sightseers from all parts of England had forestalled them. Many were unable to get into the service, because visitors filled the pews'.[205] Most of those who had travelled long distances to the abbey found they were spectators to the event, newsreels showing that multitudes of people clambered onto gravestones and climbed up trees in order to glimpse the royal couple on their entry to and exit from the service.[206] The commentator on the *British Paramount* newsreel told cinemagoers that the princess and prince 'might well have resented a mass intrusion on their honeymoon but very graciously accepted it all as perfectly natural. To be royal is to be denied the full advantage of private life'.[207] Reports like this one communicated the idea that the House of Windsor readily engaged with their people despite the imposition this placed on them personally. However, this perspective, which sought to justify and legitimize the media's intrusive coverage of the royal couple, was contested by many Mass Observation respondents, who voiced stern opposition to the scenes at Romsey.

---

[201] MOA, 4170.
[202] MOA, 3806.
[203] MOA, 4260.
[204] MOA, 3572.
[205] *Daily Mirror*, 24 Nov. 1947, p. 1. See also *Daily Express*, 24 Nov. 1947, p. 1.
[206] 'Royal Honeymooners Attend Romsey Abbey', *British Movietone News*, 27 Nov. 1947.
[207] 'The Royal Honeymoon – A Glimpse', *British Paramount News*, 27 Nov. 1947.

One schoolmistress from London 'deplored the bad behaviour at Romsey Abbey' while a schoolmaster from Manchester noted it was a 'pity' the church service had become an event for a 'sightseeing mob'.[208] A twenty-one-year-old man from Nottingham recorded his disapproval in similar terms: 'I deplore the publicity given to the young couple's romance and to the prying, sightseeing and reporting carried out on their honeymoon. To spoil the privacy of two young people – who probably would gladly be common citizens rather than royal personages – just for the sake of tradition and "glorious" ceremony is cruel'.[209] This respondent viewed royal life as unenviable because of its public nature and the way publicity constrained a normal existence. A teacher from Brighton was among several on the Mass Observation panel who expressed the same view, recording that he was 'sorry for the couple honeymooning "in a gold-fish bowl"'.[210] These sorts of comment clearly show that some Mass Observation respondents sympathized with royalty because of their perceived lack of privacy.

This type of sympathy was most strongly articulated by a group of female Mass Observation respondents, all aged below thirty, who wrote that they would 'hate to have been born in to such a public position' as Elizabeth.[211] As seen in some of the letters that were published by the *Sunday Pictorial* at the beginning of 1947, this compassion seems to have stemmed from a wider concern about the princess's emotional fulfilment; and, as with the *Pictorial*'s poll, many women who responded to Mass Observation's directive thought the princess's personal happiness in marriage would help to compensate for her difficult role. A twenty-nine-year-old woman from Cambridge was clearly heartened by the companionate partnership she detected between the royal couple when she stated that 'there seems little doubt that [Elizabeth and Philip] are in love. This makes me glad for the Princess's sake, for her job is difficult enough and her chance of privacy and personal joy so small it is good to know she has someone for whom she has an affection to stand by her'.[212] A thirty-year-old woman from Oxford similarly expressed that she was 'glad that Princess Elizabeth has married young and apparently happily so that she can have some home life and probably be with her children before she need assume even greater responsibility'.[213] As the next chapter argues, the image of *Queen* Elizabeth

[208] MOA, 246 and 1118. For other, similar examples, see MOA, 3462, 2267, 1066, 2475, 4186, 3799, 1014, 4419.
[209] MOA, 3820.
[210] MOA, 3920. For similar examples, see MOA, 1054, 3913, 3841, 4260, 2694, 3856, 4186.
[211] MOA, 1668; also MOA, 4161, 3462, 4247.
[212] MOA, 4186.
[213] MOA, 4299.

II as a wife and mother evoked a range of emotional responses from British television viewers who tuned in to watch the new monarch's coronation on 2 June 1953. However, one of the recurrent reactions was that the queen's emotional fulfilment was eclipsed by increasingly heavy duties made worse by the increased media exposure of her personal life. In tracing the emergence of these kinds of sentiment, we should look to the events of 1947 as a key moment of change when a new, media-inspired discourse of royal suffering helped to transform how members of the public perceived royalty.

Conclusion

Mass Observation respondents invested Princess Elizabeth's position as heiress presumptive to the throne with emotional meaning that centred on her achieving personal fulfilment at home. The many reports which included the view that she had a 'rotten job', a 'rotten sort of life', 'trying public duties' and a 'harder task than any previous ruler' reveal the kind of anxiety that sections of the public expressed about the princess's private life.[214] Women of a similar age to Elizabeth in particular seem to have articulated this kind of sympathy because they identified closely with her domestic ambitions. However, it also connected with a broader public belief, uninfluenced by gender, that royalty had a right to enjoy a private home life at a time when this was a central tenet of a national culture of domesticity. Notably, more than double the number of Mass Observation respondents criticized the intrusion into the royal honeymoon than opposed the expense of Elizabeth and Philip's wedding, demonstrating the special concern that members of the public had for the princess and prince's personal fulfilment.

The emergence of a powerful emotional identification with royal domesticity can be located to the early 1930s and wartime, with members of the British public equating the royal family's suffering with that of the nation at large. However, we should see 1947 as a crucial moment when the Church, crown and royalist media renewed their triumvirate in order to promote the House of Windsor's symbolic leadership of the nation's family-centred culture against a backdrop of declining deference, increasingly critical media coverage and anxieties regarding the British public's morality. Writing to George VI after the wedding, the archbishop of Canterbury boasted of this triumvirate's achievement:

> I have heard from all sides how profoundly those who were present at the Service were moved, while those who heard it broadcast were no less impressed by the solemn dignity and simplicity of the proceedings. Many of them have

[214] E.g., MOA, 1061, 3388, 4221, 4223, 4241, 1095, 4235, 3434, 1034, 4161, 4279, 3900, 2511.

said to me that they felt as though they were worshippers in the Abbey itself. I think there never was a Royal Wedding which so profoundly engaged the affection and emotions of Your Majesty's people. It has brought a real uplift of spirit to aid them at a difficult time.[215]

As we have seen, the emphasis not only on the religiosity of the event but also its 'simplicity' and egalitarian appeal to ordinary British people was a note regularly sounded by officials and the media in the build up to the marriage and the coverage of the wedding day itself. Although there was some dissent on the Mass Observation panel, the overwhelming belief contained in the personal testimonies was that the wedding did indeed reinvigorate royalty's moral and emotional role at the heart of society. New broadcasting techniques immersed listeners more deeply in a royal wedding programme than ever before and strengthened the empathetic feelings that linked them to the bridal couple. And, at a time not only of austerity but also of growing concern about public morality, the blanket media coverage heightened public awareness of a nation united around the monarchy, with Mass Observation respondents conflating royal family life with the symbolic continuity of national life.

The journalist Harry Hopkins later stated that 'in a febrile world of apparently collapsing moral values, the unselfconscious picture of domestic normality presented [by the royal family] was inevitably reassuring'.[216] The 'normality' he singled out is significant because, as this chapter has shown, it was part of a carefully crafted public image designed to enhance the House of Windsor's popular appeal. In part, the emphasis on royal 'ordinariness' seems to have come in response to attacks on Philip's 'foreignness'. Lord Mountbatten understood that, following a socially levelling war, the monarchy needed to extend its reach through new democratic channels if it was to overcome public criticism both of older hierarchies and its dynastic links to Europe. As we have seen, a number of the Mass Observation panel responded positively to the prince's public image as an 'ordinary' English naval officer. Mountbatten's public relations triumph was mirrored in the success of courtiers and the journalist Dermot Morrah in projecting an image of Elizabeth that deliberately paired her apparent desire for an 'ordinary' fulfilling home life with a discursive emphasis on the 'extraordinary' onerous duties bequeathed on her by birth. These characteristics naturally existed in an uneasy tension and evoked deep public sympathy for the princess and her ostensibly inhibited existence.

[215] LPL, Fisher 34, fo. 557, G. Fisher to King George VI, 27 Nov. 1947.
[216] H. Hopkins, *The New Look: a Social History of the Forties and Fifties in Britain* (London, 1963), p. 290.

The *Sunday Pictorial*'s poll on the rumoured royal engagement in January 1947 had first uncovered this kind of empathy for Elizabeth, as well as some initial opposition to her relationship with Philip which hinged on the constitutional question of whether it was sensible for the British monarchy once again to tie itself to Greek royalty. However, from the many responses to the Mass Observation royal wedding directive of December 1947 it appears that, where opposition persisted, it tended to do so in relation to the economic advantages afforded the royal lovers, while the prevailing attitude was one of sympathy for a couple whose personal enrichment was constrained not only by their demanding public lives but also by an increasingly outspoken media that seemed intent on exposing royal private life at all costs.

6. 'This time I was THERE taking part': the television broadcast of the 1953 coronation

This final chapter examines how both the temporal immediacy of television as a new medium of mass communication and the domestic settings in which most British viewers watched it transformed the emotional dimensions of monarchy on coronation day in 1953. It draws on 163 Mass Observation directive reports written by respondents about their experience of the coronation and more than 200 school essays composed by adolescents between the ages of twelve and sixteen on their involvement in the event in order to analyse some of the effects the television coverage of Queen Elizabeth II's crowning had on viewers' feelings. This chapter builds on the work of royal biographer Ben Pimlott and others who have argued that the television broadcast enabled a greater number of people to participate in a royal event than ever before and that this large-scale involvement engendered a heightened sense of national community among audiences.[1] However, this idea is taken one step further here. As well as tightening the imagined bonds of nation that linked viewers around the country, the televised coronation enriched the social relationships of those who gathered as collectives to watch the broadcast. The coronation was generally viewed from the informal setting of the home alongside family or friends and often evoked intimate and highly personal responses from audience members. And yet, this was also a unique *shared* experience because, for the first time ever, kinship and friendship groups across the country were able, via the BBC's live transmission, to visually consume and interpret the meanings of monarchy *together*. Their shared identification with the event and the royal family at its centre reaffirmed the empathetic bonds that connected them to the House of Windsor and strengthened their own relationships with one another. Indeed, this chapter shows how the BBC and British media managed to intensify the emotions expressed by viewers in response to the television broadcast of the queen's crowning by drawing attention to the familial aspects of the coronation story: Mass Observation personal testimonies reveal that audiences responded positively to maternal images

---

[1] B. Pimlott, *The Queen: Elizabeth II and the Monarchy* (London, 2002), p. 207; M. Aldridge, *The Birth of British Television: a History* (Basingstoke, 2012), pp. 169 and 178–9.

of the queen, with adults and children expressing a shared loyalty to and affection for her which consolidated the emotional meanings they associated with the monarchy while strengthening their own interpersonal bonds.[2]

The 1953 coronation has received more historical attention than any of the earlier case studies examined as part of *The Family Firm*. Some scholars have interpreted the event as a moment of national renaissance following the Second World War: according to this idea, the youthful queen personified the post-war generation's hopes for a brighter, more affluent future and her crowning on 2 June exemplified a cluster of uniquely British moral and spiritual beliefs.[3] Recent historical work has also emphasized the Commonwealth dimensions of the occasion and the way the media projected a renewed vision of a group of post-imperial nations that remained closely united through their shared ties to the crown.[4] The suggestion has been that, with the rise of the USA and USSR on the world stage, the coronation acted to reassert Britain's global position by fusing established traditions with newer, modern symbols like the television broadcast of the ceremony.[5]

Historians have also devoted more attention to the public's response to the coronation than to any other aspect of the popular reception of the modern monarchy. In particular, scholars have sought to test contemporary arguments made by the sociologists Edward Shils and Michael Young that the event was 'an act of national communion' in which the public joined with the queen in reaffirming the moral values at the heart of society.[6] Shils and Young's analysis was over-functionalist in its emphasis on national unity and, while it helped to spawn a significant body of scholarship in

[2] Elizabeth II will be referred to as 'the queen' in this chapter, while her mother, also known as Queen Elizabeth, will be referred to as the queen mother or queen dowager. Queen Mary died in March 1953, so George VI's consort was the only member of the royal family known as the queen mother by the time of her daughter's coronation in June.

[3] J. Anderson, 'The Tory party at prayer? The Church of England and British politics in the 1950s', *Jour. Church and State*, lviii (2015), 417–40, at pp. 420–2; E. Shils and M. Young, 'The meaning of the coronation', *Sociological Rev.*, i (1953), 63–81; I. Bradley, *God Save the Queen: the Spiritual Dimension of Monarchy* (London, 2002), pp. 85–7.

[4] W. Webster, *Englishness and Empire 1939–1965* (Oxford, 2005), pp. 96–8 and 105–13; T. Hajkowski, *The BBC and National Identity in Britain, 1922–53* (Manchester, 2010), pp. 100–4. See also D. Cannadine, 'The context, performance and meaning of ritual: the British monarchy and the "invention of tradition", c.1820–1977', in *The Invention of Tradition*, ed. E. Hobsbawm and T. Ranger (Cambridge, 1983), pp. 101–64, at pp. 153–5; P. Murphy, *Monarchy and the End of Empire: the House of Windsor, the British Government, and the Postwar Commonwealth* (Oxford, 2013), pp. 54–60.

[5] F. Mort, *Capital Affairs: London and the Making of the Permissive Society* (New Haven, Conn., 2010), p. 18; Pimlott, *Elizabeth II*, pp. 206–7; Webster, *Englishness and Empire*, pp. 115–8; Cannadine, 'Context, performance and meaning', pp. 150–4.

[6] Shils and Young, 'The meaning of the coronation', pp. 66–7.

the field of media studies on the nature of televised national events, it failed to account for expressions of dissent or disaffection experienced by members of the public on coronation day.[7] Mass Observation respondents notably articulated a range of opinions, including critical perspectives. For example, several complained that the coronation was London-focused and that their communities were too far-removed geographically to enable them to feel as though they were participating in it.[8] In a similar vein, historian Joe Moran's recent study of television viewership on coronation day has assessed the varying reactions of Mass Observation respondents to the BBC's coverage, which ranged from awed attentiveness through irreverent derision to indifference.[9] Nevertheless, one idea hidden away in Shils and Young's wide-ranging analysis that has stood the test of time is that Elizabeth II's coronation was, in essence, the day of the 'family unit': it brought 'vitality into family relationships' and 'was a time for drawing closer the bonds of the family, for re-asserting its solidarity and for re-emphasizing the values of the family – generosity, loyalty, love'.[10] This chapter builds on this idea by arguing that 2 June 1953 witnessed not only a reinvigoration of the empathy that linked media audiences to the House of Windsor (and the viewing nation at large) but also a deepening of the shared understanding of the monarchy that connected families and friends.

The first section examines the fractious debates that unfolded publicly and privately regarding the televising of the Westminster abbey coronation service and how, once the committee responsible for overseeing its organization finally, and reluctantly, agreed to allow the BBC to broadcast a live transmission of most of the ceremony, the prospect of the television coverage exercised a powerful hold over media audiences and helped to generate enthusiasm for the occasion. The sense of anticipation can be discerned from a collection of more than 200 school essays, most of which were written in the month before 2 June by girls at grammar schools in

---

[7] D. Dayan and E. Katz, *Media Events: the Live Broadcasting of History* (Cambridge, Mass., 1992) is the key text in this area of media studies.

[8] H. Örnebring, 'Revisiting the coronation: a critical perspective on the coronation of Queen Elizabeth II in 1953', *Nordicom Rev.*, xxv (2004), 175–95. See also H. Örnebring, 'Writing the history of television audiences: the coronation in the Mass-Observation archive', in *Re-viewing Television History: Critical Issues in Television Historiography*, ed. H. Wheatley (London, 2008), pp. 170–183; Mort, *Capital Affairs*, p. 31. See also P. Ziegler, *Crown and People* (London, 1978), p. 104.

[9] J. Moran, *Armchair Nation: an Intimate History of Britain in Front of the TV* (London, 2013), pp. 77–81. In highlighting the varied nature of MO reactions, Moran built on D. Kynaston, *Family Britain: 1951–57* (London, 2010), pp. 299–307 and Ziegler, *Crown and People*, pp. 114–8.

[10] Shils and Young, 'The meaning of the coronation', pp. 71–3.

west London and Cheshire and by boys from schools of unknown status in Bury St. Edmunds and Surrey.[11] The essays reveal royalist identities in formation under influences exerted on them in the classroom (that is, by a teacher, their peers and the educational setting) and external influences such as family, friends and personal beliefs.[12] All the essays examined here contain traces of a pedagogic influence in the form of repeated themes and attitudes; unfortunately there are no accompanying documents that illuminate the activities or discussions on which the essays were based, nor is it always clear to what questions the pupils were responding. However, there are many personal and idiosyncratic features in the essays which reveal

[11] Approximately 500 school essays are contained in the Mass Observation online archive under the file reference TC/69/3/A–E. These can be located through the keyword search '1953 coronation', which leads to the coronation study, all of which has been digitized. MO's 1953 coronation project was extremely ambitious and yielded an unwieldy amount of information, most of which is yet to receive historical analysis. This chapter revisits 2 sets of records, both of which have been touched on by Kynaston and Ziegler in their respective studies on the 1953 coronation (Kynaston, *Family Britain*; Ziegler, *Crown and People*). It focuses on the first 7 sets of essays contained in files TC/69/3/A and B, batches A to G. These include essays written before and after the event by girls aged 13 to 16 at a grammar school in west London (A, F and G); by girls of the same age at West Kirby girls' grammar school in Cheshire (B and C); by a group of boys aged 14 to 16 at a school of unknown status in Surrey (D); and by a group of boys aged 12 to 14 at an unknown school in Bury St. Edmunds (E). Essays from other batches (H to P) are sometimes used to support the arguments posited in this chapter, but the analysis presented here has focused on the first 7 batches due to the large size of the archive and because they reflect the opinions of girls and boys of roughly the same age. The essays are separately numbered in the archive and are referred to here using their file reference, batch letters and numbers, e.g., 3/A/A1. The second group of records examined here are the directive replies to the day survey for 2 June 1953, located in TC/69/7/A–H. Seventy-six women and 87 men replied to this survey, discussing what they had done over the course of coronation day as prompted by a set of questions that also asked them to report on any local celebrations, the most 'stirring', 'peculiar' and 'funniest' incidents of the day, whether those watching or listening to the BBC programmes remained silent for the anointing of the queen and how they thought the 1953 coronation compared with that of George VI in 1937. These questions shaped the responses recorded by the MO respondents and this influence is considered throughout the analysis presented in this chapter. Some of the 163 directive replies include index numbers and, where this is the case, they are referred to using their file letters (A–H) and index number, e.g., 7/A/2077. Where there is no index number, the reports are referred to according to their file letter and occupation when stated, e.g., 7/A/Youth Employment Officer. The original hardcopies of both sets of records can be found in the MO archive at The Keep (University of Sussex) under the references SxMOA1/2/69/3 and 7.

[12] For further discussion regarding the use of school essays as sources, see H. Barron and C. Langhamer, 'Feeling through practice: subjectivity and emotion in children's writing', *Jour. Social Hist.*, li (2017), 101–23, at pp. 103–6; J. Greenhalgh, '"Till we hear the last all clear": gender and the presentation of self in young girls' writing about the bombing of Hull during the Second World War', *Gender & History*, xxvi (2014), 167–83, at pp. 169–71.

how the girls and boys considered television to be a new conduit of mass participation through which they expected to share in the coronation. In particular, the national dimensions of the event generated deep interest among these adolescents, who envisaged themselves forming part of a privileged viewership on coronation day.

The second section draws on a wider range of Mass Observation personal testimonies to explore how members of the public internalized and responded to television images of the coronation. Examining the directive replies of the regular Mass Observation panel in response to a special coronation-day survey and essays written by the girls from the west London and Cheshire grammar schools after the event, this section gauges how television coverage of the ceremony affected viewers' emotions by enabling them to visually experience first-hand what had hitherto been an exclusive occasion. Adults and children notably remarked that television allowed them 'to feel' as though they had participated in the coronation service as part of a national community of viewers. However, at the same time the domestic settings in which most respondents and essayists watched the coronation shaped their experiences of the event: quotidian domestic rituals and informal conversations overlapped with the unique television images, producing a dynamic media environment in which families and friends interpreted the meanings of the event together, strengthening their shared understanding of monarchy and the emotional connections that underpinned their social relationships.[13]

The third and final section examines the many descriptions in the Mass Observation records of Elizabeth II's domestic role on coronation day. It begins by analysing the symbolic visual economy of the queen and her young children as constructed by Pitkin's official royal souvenir magazines and the press in the years leading up to the coronation. It then moves on to examine how the BBC carefully choreographed images of the queen's relationship to her son and heir, Prince Charles, on coronation day and the way these scenes prompted a large number of comments from the Mass Observation panel and school essayists. The public reactions to Elizabeth II's motherly image reflect the special investment adults and children had in her maternal role as queen. These comments also suggest that the BBC's deliberate focus on this aspect of the monarch's public image evoked from media audiences personal identification with her which not only invigorated the shared emotions that linked groups of television viewers but also strengthened a national emotional community that empathized with

---

[13] On the dynamic, self-reflexive qualities of television viewing, see H. Wood, *Talking with Television: Women, Talk Shows, and Modern Self-Reflexivity* (Chicago, Ill.,2009).

the queen. The words of the Mass Observation respondents and schoolgirls who wrote about the coronation also clearly reveal the enduring legacy of the concept that royal life was an unenviable burden, with many discussing either the queen's vulnerability during the ceremony or the way that she had to make personal sacrifices which affected her domestic happiness in order to serve her peoples.

'I shall have my eyes glued to the Television set'

Preparations for Elizabeth II's coronation began almost immediately after her father died on 6 February 1952.[14] The most contentious element in all the planning for the event was whether or not the BBC would be permitted to televise the queen's crowning from Westminster abbey. By 1952, television had achieved maturity as a form of mass communication, benefiting from the rapid construction of television masts and transmitters across Britain in the late 1940s and early 1950s. It also gained in popularity as better quality television sets became available to consumers and as the BBC diversified its programming as the nation's one and only television broadcaster (ITV was launched in 1955).[15] However, Buckingham Palace and its allies remained deeply distrustful of the new medium – a scepticism that can in part be explained with reference to the prevailing attitude among the British elite and intelligentsia that television was a 'low' form of entertainment which had a corrupting influence on public life.[16] As we know, the BBC was prevented from televising the 1947 royal wedding ceremony out of concern for the privacy of the royal family and, since becoming queen, Elizabeth II had refused to let her Christmas broadcast be recorded for TV or have 'close-up' images of her face televised during royal public appearances.[17]

In spite of the condescending strain of opinion that presented television as a source of social harm, the BBC wanted to provide its rapidly growing viewership with new kinds of access to the monarchy – a policy that both adhered to its longstanding aim to bring the House of Windsor closer to media audiences while lending the new medium of TV a veneer of

[14] LPL, Fisher 123, fos. 1–2, 'Diary of Coronation Events'; Pimlott, *Elizabeth II*, p. 204. For an analysis of the public response to the death of George VI, see I. Zweiniger-Bargielowska, 'Royal death and living memorials: the funerals and commemoration of George V and George VI, 1936–52', *Hist. Research*, lxxxix (2015), 158–75.

[15] Moran, *Armchair Nation*, pp. 63–71, 86–7.

[16] S. Nixon, *Hard Sell: Advertising, Affluence and Transatlantic Relations, c.1951–69* (Manchester, 2013), pp. 95–9 and 143–4; L. Black, 'The impression of affluence: political culture in the 1950s and 1960s', in *An Affluent Society? Britain's Post-War 'Golden Age' Revisited*, ed. L. Black and H. Pemberton (Aldershot, 2004), pp. 85–106, at p. 90.

[17] Moran, *Armchair Nation*, p. 74.

respectability that might help to offset critical views. In this vein, at the beginning of June 1952 BBC executives approached the official coronation commission, which was chaired by Prince Philip and tasked with overseeing the organization of the event, to suggest that radio and television be allowed to transmit the coronation service live to the nation and the world.[18] Anticipating the commission's objections to the use of new technical equipment and artificial lighting in the abbey (as had been the case at earlier royal events), the BBC made it clear to the officials involved in the staging of the ceremony that its television crews were highly professional, that its apparatus could be kept to a bare minimum and that the television cameras required less illumination than newsreel cameras.[19] This put the commission in a difficult position because if they were to grant newsreel film crews access to record the service along with radio broadcasters, as they had done in 1937, then why should television cameras be excluded?

Reporting on the first meeting of the executive coronation committee (the managerial offshoot of the commission), which took place on 16 June 1952, the archbishop of Canterbury, Geoffrey Fisher, recorded that he and the duke of Norfolk (also officially titled the earl marshal and the man responsible for overseeing the organization of the secular parts of the coronation) agreed that the BBC's proposal for television should be 'resist[ed] ... altogether' to begin with. However, both realized that should the television cameras require 'no more lighting and no more space than cinematograph apparatus', as the BBC had suggested, then it would be 'extremely difficult to say that what can be filmed cannot be televised'.[20] Nevertheless, at subsequent meetings of the executive and joint coronation committees, Fisher and the earl marshal formed a united front in opposing the BBC's plans for television and were successful in winning over other committee members to their point of view. As well as repeatedly questioning the feasibility of the broadcast on technical grounds, they presented a number of other arguments, including that television would place an 'intolerable strain on the Queen and everybody else', believing that 'no mistake [made in front of the cameras could] ever be rectified'. They also thought that some Christians might find the televising of the ceremony 'offensive' because of its sacred character – although they conceded this was

[18] BBCWA, T16/169, 'Copy of letter sent by D. H. S. B. to the Coronation Commission', 3 June 1952.
[19] BBCWA, T16/169, S. J. de Lotbinière to T. F. Clark, 11 July 1952; Rev. F. H. House to A. C. Don, Dean of Westminster, 17 July 1952.
[20] LPL, Fisher 123, fos. 3–4, 'Diary of Coronation Events'. The executive and joint coronation committees were both chaired by the duke of Norfolk and reported back to the larger coronation commission headed by the duke of Edinburgh.

a weak point with which to oppose television given that a newsreel film had been made of George VI's coronation sixteen years previously.[21]

The problem the archbishop and earl marshal had was that every argument they presented against television met with a counterargument from the BBC, which intended to persuade them of the important and respectful role television could play in bringing the ceremony to the nation at large. Leading the BBC's campaign was director of television George Barnes, who met with Fisher and other members of the various coronation committees to try to convince them that his team would not only televise a reverent vision of the ceremony to viewers, but that any 'untoward incident' that might occur during the service could be hidden from the audience at home through the careful editing of the live transmission by a BBC producer stationed at a control desk in the abbey.[22] By the beginning of October 1952 it seemed that Barnes was winning the battle and that pressure was building on the royal household and coronation committees to agree to television. Fisher noted in his diary that should he and the duke of Norfolk be forced to allow the whole ceremony to be televised, then the consecration and communion would have to be concealed from the cameras because of the sacredness of these parts of the service.[23] However, on 20 October Buckingham Palace suddenly announced to the press that, after very careful consideration and further consultation with Prime Minister Winston Churchill and his cabinet, it had been agreed that television coverage would be restricted to the procession in and out of the Abbey.[24]

Barnes was surprised and disappointed as he thought he had managed to convince those in charge of the coronation that television was a good thing.[25] Indeed, Pimlott has suggested that the main reason the royal household turned television down at this point was that the queen herself was against it and had expressed grave reservations about the broadcast to Churchill, who reluctantly agreed to take her side.[26] However, the prime minister proved to be sensitive to public and political opinion: the press complained about the palace's decision to exclude television viewers from the service, with the *Daily Express* going so far as to undertake a poll on the issue that resulted in a front-page headline announcing that four out of five of its readers

[21] LPL, Fisher 123, fo. 5, 'Diary of Coronation Events'.
[22] LPL, Fisher 123, fo. 6, 'Diary of Coronation Events'.
[23] LPL, Fisher 123, fo. 6, 'Diary of Coronation Events'.
[24] *Daily Mirror*, 21 Oct. 1952, pp. 1 and 16.
[25] BBCWA, T16/169, Rev. F. H. House to D. Tel. B., 22 Oct. 1922; *Daily Mirror*, 21 Oct. 1952, pp. 1 and 16.
[26] Pimlott, *Elizabeth II*, p. 205.

favoured televising the entire ceremony.[27] Meanwhile, Churchill became
the target of a barrage of angry criticism from opposition MPs who claimed
to have received large numbers of letters from constituents outraged that
they would not be able to see their new queen crowned.[28] In response to
these concerns, the prime minister arranged an informal conference at 10
Downing Street on 24 October with members of the executive coronation
committee, including the archbishop of Canterbury, the earl marshal and
the monarch's private secretary, Sir Alan Lascelles. As Fisher recounted in
his diary:

> From the first word it was quite obvious that [Churchill] had made up his mind
> that everything should be televised except possibly the Consecration and the
> Communion ... I said that my own position was that I was willing that the
> whole ceremony should be filmed, but that I could not agree to television of
> those entirely spiritual parts of the Service ... [I said] that the precedent of the
> last Coronation should be followed by which the Anointing, the Consecration
> and the Communion were not filmed. Lascelles strongly supported this from
> the Queen's point of view.[29]

As already noted, the hallowed nature of the rituals referred to by the
archbishop helps to explain why he and the private secretary thought these
elements of the ceremony should be concealed from television audiences.
This view eventually won the day and, although the duke of Norfolk was
still far from happy about the prospect of a television broadcast, it was
agreed by those who attended Churchill's meeting that the BBC would
be afforded the same access as the newsreels to record the entire abbey
ceremony – apart from the anointing and communion – on the condition
that cameramen did not take any close-up images of the queen at any point
during the service.[30]

On 28 October 1952 Churchill was able to report to the House of
Commons that it was probable that the restrictions on television would
be lifted. Responding to questions put to him by his political opponents,
he outlined his support for television and suggested it would enable the
public to participate in the coronation in a new, positive way. He then
went on to stress to his audience that the broadcast should not be viewed
irreverently or as a 'theatrical piece', but as an occasion of the utmost moral
seriousness – a refrain that would continue to dominate discussions of the

---

[27] *Daily Express*, 22 Oct. 1952, p. 4; 23 Oct. 1952, p. 1; 24 Oct. 1952, p. 1; 28 Oct. 1952, p. 1.
[28] *Daily Mirror*, 21 Oct. 1952, pp. 1 and 16; 24 Oct. 1952, p. 1; 29 Oct. 1952, p. 4; *Daily Mail*, 24 Oct. 1952, p. 5.
[29] LPL, Fisher 123, fo. 8, 'Diary of Coronation Events'.
[30] LPL, Fisher 123, fos. 8–11, 'Diary of Coronation Events'.

televised ceremony until coronation day.[31] After this parliamentary sitting, the earl marshal duly stated that the executive coronation committee would reconsider the question of television and, finally, on 8 December 1952 it was officially announced that the ceremony would be televised according to the plans first outlined at 10 Downing Street back in October.[32] The newspapers were ecstatic and celebrated the volte-face as a triumph of the public's will over an unpopular royal decision. The *Daily Express* even suggested that it was now the queen's desire to be 'crowned in the sight of all the people'.[33] Whether or not this was true, reports like this one gave the impression that a compassionate monarch listened to and cared for her subjects and wanted them to participate in her coronation.

*

The effects of the decision to grant the BBC permission to televise the coronation service were twofold. First, and most straightforwardly, in the run-up to 2 June 1953 the coronation was heralded as a landmark moment in the history of broadcasting, with the media celebrating Elizabeth II's crowning for the way it would witness a majority of the British population coming together around television sets in order to partake in a royal public spectacle. But, at the same time the presence of the BBC's television cameras meant there were added pressures on the stage-managers of the coronation to ensure everything was just right. In this respect, new kinds of mass communication once again stimulated a professionalization in the way royal public events were orchestrated for media audiences – as had been the case with royal occasions in the 1930s, although then they had primarily been arranged for radio listeners rather than television viewers. Of course, the 1953 coronation service was also broadcast live from the abbey for wireless listeners who were either unable or unwilling to watch it unfold on television. However, those most intimately involved in the preparations for the coronation, including the archbishop of Canterbury, the earl marshal and the monarch herself, focused their attention on how it would appear on television screens and did all they could in the months and weeks before the big day to ensure that it ran smoothly. For example, special lighting tests were conducted by the BBC for Fisher, Prince Philip and the

---

[31] *Daily Mail*, 29 Oct. 1952, pp. 1–2; *Daily Mirror*, 29 Oct. 1952, p. 1; *Daily Express*, 29 Oct. 1952, p. 1.

[32] *Daily Mirror*, 9 Oct. 1952, p. 1.

[33] *Daily Express*, 9 Oct. 1952, pp. 1 and 4. Pimlott also raises this possibility of a royal about-face (Pimlott, *Elizabeth II*, p. 206).

queen, who had the final say over the artificial illumination that would be used for the television broadcast.[34] Similarly, the royal household worked with the abbey authorities to try to ensure that the television cameramen stuck to the agreed 'no close-ups' policy.[35] And, on 15 May – just over two weeks before the coronation – an intensive daily rehearsal schedule began in order to familiarize the royal and religious protagonists with the many movements and rituals involved in the ceremony. When the queen was unable to attend, the duchess of Norfolk stood in for her as the central performer and Fisher recorded with satisfaction in his diary that he and the earl marshal led the rehearsals together – a partnership that turned out to be a great success.[36]

While all this was going on at Westminster, schoolchildren across the country were completing classroom exercises that focused on the upcoming royal event. In answer to the question, 'What do you think about the coronation?', a thirteen-year-old girl at a west London grammar school wrote that 'the government is always having a moan about housing, but never thinks of ways in which it can cut down in pomp and ceremony and save money for more important things'. But despite her criticism of the cost of the coronation, she expressed a keen desire to participate in it:

> Although I say all these things against it, I am longing to see it. It gives me a thrill to think that in so many days and so many weeks we will see the queen ride down to Westminster Abbey. I think the queen has been very gracious in letting us see her Coronation on television. It will be the first time in History that the ordinary people have seen one and it will be a great thrill.[37]

The themes contained in this quotation are characteristic of those that shaped many of the essays written by adolescent children on the meaning of the coronation. First, this schoolgirl was typical in opposing government expenditure while nevertheless stating a strong desire to see the coronation.[38] To explain this contradiction, she invested the event with a special historical meaning which related to the fact it was the first time 'ordinary people' could see it.[39] Other children similarly characterized it as the 'greatest

---

[34] LPL, Fisher 123, fo. 21, 'Diary of Coronation Events'.

[35] LPL, Fisher 123, fos. 23–4, 'Diary of Coronation Events'.

[36] LPL, Fisher 123, fos. 25–7 and 32, 'Diary of Coronation Events'.

[37] MOA, 3/B/G2.

[38] For other essays which expressed concerns about cost but articulated the writers' desire to participate, see MOA, 3/A/C9, 3/A/C8, 3/A/C18, 3/A/C22, 3/A/D7, 3/A/D9, 3/B/G6, 3/B/G10, 3/B/G11, 3/B/G18 3/B/G27. On media criticism of the cost of the event, see Örnebring, 'Revisiting the coronation', pp. 187–9.

[39] For other examples which emphasize either the innovatory significance of the televisualization of the event or its historical connotations, see MOA, 3/A/B12, 3/A/C19,

occasion' or 'spectacle' they would ever see because of the innovative access provided by television. For them it signified a landmark moment in a longer tradition of royal events.[40] The girl's comment on Elizabeth II's benevolence in letting television viewers see the coronation is indicative of the way the media helped to popularize the idea that the queen personally wanted to be crowned in front of her people when, in fact, she had initially opposed television.[41] Notably, the schoolgirl also believed that television would create a national community around the focal point of the coronation, using the personal pronouns 'we' and 'us' to convey the inclusive nature of television viewing.[42] Many other children articulated a heightened awareness of a national collective when they asserted that 'everywhere', 'all over Britain', 'everyone' would be joining in the coronation celebrations.[43] The account of one fourteen-year-old schoolboy from Surrey was typical: 'The coronation is being telivized [sic] and then projected on to the cinema screens throughout the country so that practically *everybody* will hear or see the coronation'.[44]

The essayists' desire to participate in the coronation through the BBC's television broadcast was informed by a popular belief that it would offer privileged access to the spectacle. In this respect, their expectations were shaped by the wider media-led discourse on the unique opportunities created by television for mass participation.[45] A number of the west London schoolgirls also claimed that television offered a preferable means of joining in with the coronation rather than spectating from the procession route. One fourteen-year-old girl was typical when she stated that 'as we are lucky enough to have a television, I will be watching the screen for most of the day. I would very much like to see the Procession in life, but I know that I would only see a very little after waiting many hours'.[46] She suggested that TV offered superior and more comfortable access to the coronation spectacle and one of her classmates agreed that television offered comprehensive

---

3/A/C20, 3/A/C30, 3/A/C33, 3/A/D2, 3/A/D6, 3/A/D8, 3/B/E7, 3/B/E38, 3/B/F12, 3/B/F24, 3/B/G14, 3/B/G17.

[40] E.g., MOA, 3/A/C9, 3/A/C11, 3/A/C17, 3/A/D2, 3/A/D8, 3/A/D16, 3/B/E12, 3/B/F8, 3/B/G18.

[41] Pimlott, *Elizabeth II*, pp. 204–7; Moran, *Armchair Nation*, pp. 73–4.

[42] For other examples in which essayists presented themselves as part of a British community, see MOA, 3/A/C9, 3/A/C32, 3/A/D1, 3/A/D2, 3/B/E15, 3/B/E23, 3/B/37, 3/B/F3, 3/B/20, 3/B/G3, 3/B/G17, 3/B/G23.

[43] E.g., MOA, 3/A/C5, 3/A/C15, 3/A/C26, 3/A/D2, 3/A/D16, 3/B/E12, 3/B/E27, 3/B/E45, 3/B/F3, 3/B/G12, 3/B/G17, 3/B/G28.

[44] MOA, 3/A/D4 (this author's emphasis).

[45] E.g., *Daily Mirror*, 22 Oct. 1952, p. 7; 9 Dec. 1952, p. 1; 2 June 1953, p. 2; *Daily Express*, 9 Dec. 1952, pp. 1 and 4.

[46] MOA, 3/B/F6.

coverage: 'On Coronation day, I shall have my eyes glued to the Television set, so that I do not miss one single thing ... I expect that if I did go [in person] I would hardly see anything. But by going to my friend's house, I shall be able to see everything and to hear everything as well'.[47] These responses were characteristic of many of the reactions recorded by the girls at the west London grammar school, informed as they were by a belief in the obstructive nature of crowds on the procession route and, more notably, by the pervasive idea circulated by the media that television had created new and improved opportunities for popular spectatorship.

The desire to publicly participate through the television coverage was particularly acute among schoolchildren who lived far away from London and whose families did not intend to travel there to see the coronation. In contrast to their London counterparts, pupils at West Kirby girls' grammar school in Cheshire tended to think it was preferable to see the spectacle first-hand and that television coverage was 'the next best thing'.[48] One schoolgirl from Cheshire, whose family had planned a trip to the capital to see the procession, remarked that she would be 'one of the lucky people who will be in London', which suggests that there was a certain amount of social prestige attributed to her position by her classmates.[49] The Cheshire girls' value system was informed by their provincial status; their desire to participate in person differed from the attitudes of the schoolgirls in the capital, who took for granted their access to central London. For the girls from north-west England, television thus acted as the key conduit through which they could experience a sense of national inclusion and took on a powerful imaginative role. One fourteen-year-old girl was typical in her description of the sense of expectation that she and her peers ascribed to the television broadcast:

> As this will be the first Coronation in my time I naturally feel a great thrill and I think all the many preparations and colourful decorations are very exciting. But I wish I could go to London and actually see the Coronation and the procession in all the magnificent colour and glory. I think however that it is very fortunate that many people who cannot see the Coronation in London will be able to watch it on Television.[50]

---

[47] MOA, 3/B/F13. For similar examples, see MOA, 3/B/F/4, 3/B/F/8, 3/B/F/10, 3/B/F/11, 3/B/F/14, 3/B/F/16.
[48] E.g., MOA, 3/A/C1, 3/A/C4, 3/A/C8, 3/A/C10, 3/A/C11, 3/A/C15, 3/A/C24, 3/A/C37, 3/A/C29.
[49] MOA, 3/A/C3.
[50] MOA, 3/A/C7.

This girl was enthused by the coronation preparations in London but lamented that her own provincial location meant she was unable to join the festivities in the capital. Her repeated longing for 'colour' typified the responses of schoolgirls from Cheshire, some of whom stated that television's monochrome pictures would not fully convey the coronation spectacle – a complaint that could be interpreted as a symptom of the austere nature of the early post-war period and the longing for more affluent times.[51] For adolescent girls like this one, television provided access to an event from which they otherwise felt excluded and the prospect of her participation through television was crucial to sustaining her enthusiasm for the coronation.

Against this backdrop of anticipation, children who did not expect to be able to watch the televised coronation experienced a sense of exclusion from the imagined national community of viewers. One of the girls at school at West Kirby grammar was typical in the way she articulated this anxiety: 'We are not lucky enough to have a television, but I am hoping that a kind friend of mine will let me watch hers. I would be very disappointed if I missed it'.[52] An essay written by the same girl after the event reveals that she managed to watch television on coronation day and the opening sentence of her composition shows the sense of inclusion she experienced seeing it: '*We* saw everything very clearly, and I only wish it was in colour'.[53] One of her classmates was not so fortunate. Out of all the girls at the Cheshire grammar school who wrote essays before the coronation, just one unequivocally criticized the occasion and her disapproval might have stemmed from the fact that she did not expect to be able to watch television, although she did not freely admit this was the case. She complained that 'there is too much display about [the coronation]' and 'too much "hero-worship" about the royal family'. She thought she would spend 2 June 'either out for a country walk with [her] family, or gardening, or going to the nearest baths': 'We are not listening to anything connected with the Coronation on our radio, or going to neighbours television [*sic*]. The seats for the route are too dear to waste money on and I can think of far more pleasant things to do than stand in a crowd, which I hate anyway all pushing for a view'.[54] But her objections to the coronation had softened by the time she wrote

<hr/>

[51] I. Zweiniger-Bargielowska, *Austerity in Britain: Rationing, Controls, and Consumption, 1939–1955* (Oxford, 2000), pp. 60–98. For other examples of schoolgirls who were concerned about television's lack of colour, see MOA, 3/A/C2, 3/A/C3, 3/A/C4, 3/A/C27, 3/A/C29, 3/A/C30.

[52] MOA, 3/A/C14. For very similar examples, see MOA, 3/B/F27, 3/C/I4, 3/C/J19.

[53] MOA, 3/A/B17 (this author's emphasis).

[54] MOA, 3/A/C18.

her second essay after it. She had, in fact, spent all 2 June listening to the wireless broadcast of the event while knitting and described how she had been captivated by the event: 'The service was quite a nice one, the singing was lovely, especially the first anthem. The description of the dresses and uniforms was fascinating. I would have loved to have seen the colours and decorations'.[55] Her participation as a listener and her longing to have seen the colour and pageantry reveal that she, too, was inspired by a desire to experience the coronation and suggest that her original criticism of the event may have partly sprung from a sense of exclusion from the televised spectacle.

Some schoolchildren were more cynical of what they perceived as the pressures to partake in the event. Eight boys aged fourteen to sixteen, out of a class of sixteen boys at a Surrey school of unknown status, complained that the coronation had become a focal point of national curiosity and criticized the popular attitude to spectatorship on the procession route in London: 'I for one would not get crushed and trodden on just to get a glimpse of a horse drawn carriage going by. Many people will get badly hurt in the crowds that will go to see the coronation and those that see it will just be able to talk to others and say, "I saw the coronation"'.[56] This fourteen-year-old boy's opinion was shared by a number of his peers, something which may indicate their essays were influenced by an in-class discussion that preceded the writing exercise. All the same, this quotation illustrates the fact that some adolescents were very critical of what they deemed the self-gratifying motivations behind the popular interest in the coronation. They thought that those who would go to see the procession would do so just so they could tell others they had 'seen it' – a theme famously satirized by the 1950s Trinidadian calypso artist Young Tiger in his song 'I Was There (At the Coronation)'.[57]

The superior tone of the schoolboys' criticism and the disdain they expressed for the behaviour of what they implicitly presented as the self-indulgent masses also possibly points to their middle- or upper-class social status. This kind of class-focused condescension was even more apparent in the set of essays written by a group of boys at a school of unknown status in Bury St. Edmunds. One fourteen-year-old captured the tone of many of the essays:

[55] MOA, 3/A/B22.
[56] MOA, 3/A/D15. For other examples, see MOA, 3/A/D1, 3/A/D5, 3/A/D9, 3/A/D10, 3/A/D12, 3/A/D14, 3/A/D16.
[57] L. Bradley, *Sounds Like London: 100 Years of Black Music in the Capital* (London, 2013), pp. 47–8.

> I feel that the crowning of our Queen should be taken seriously and reverently; not like a Saturday afternoon football match or the pictures, as entertainment. During the Queen's prayer and the other really holy parts, the television will be turned away, not because it is too holy, but because the majority of people will not realise it is a service of tremendous importance, but will take it like any entertainment.[58]

Echoing Churchill's earlier warning about how the coronation should and should not be viewed, this boy discussed how television had the potential to desacralize the religious elements of the coronation service and claimed that a 'majority of people' did not appreciate its spiritual significance. One of his classmates recorded that he and his peers had had two history lessons and three scripture lessons on the 'religious side' of the event, which almost certainly informed their outlook.[59] Meanwhile, several others alluded pejoratively to the ignorance of what they perceived as the 'majority' by comparing them to football spectators – a theme echoed in essays written by girls at the grammar school in west London.[60] These condescending sentiments were indicative of the wider elite and intellectual anxieties about television as symptomatic of a 'low' mass culture which allegedly worked to debase public life.[61] However, like their female counterparts, despite having reservations about mass spectatorship most of the boys at Bury St. Edmunds still expressed a longing to watch the television coverage so that they did not miss out on what they deemed a unique national event. A thirteen-year-old captured this tension when he stated that 'Televiewers are lucky it is to be televised', although he added 'some viewers might take it as an entertainment, not as … a religious service'.[62]

The school essays thus reflect adolescent children's beliefs – instilled either inside or outside the classroom – that most British people planned to join in the coronation, with television facilitating mass popular involvement. While some essayists expressed concerns about the cost involved in staging the event, the obstructive crowds on the procession route, the distance that separated them from the London-based celebrations or the nature of the mass spectatorship that television would generate, they also noted their longing to participate personally through the television coverage of the

[58] MOA, 3/B/E8. For other examples, see MOA, 3/B/E2, 3/B/E6, 3/B/E10, 3/B/E11, 3/B/E12, 3/B/E16, 3/B/E18, 3/B/E20.
[59] MOA, 3/B/E4.
[60] MOA, 3/B/F14, 3/B/F18, 3/B/F27.
[61] Nixon, *Hard Sell*, pp. 95–9, 143–4; Black, 'The impression of affluence', p. 90.
[62] MOA, 3/B/E4. For similar examples that express contradictory attitudes towards the televising of the event, see MOA, 3/B/E2, 3/B/E5, 3/B/E10, 3/B/E11, 3/B/E15, 3/B/E17, 3/B/E19, 3/B/E21, 3/B/E23, 3/B/E26.

coronation. In this way the new medium and its innovatory significance offset other criticisms of the coronation and stimulated broad interest in the royal event among media audiences, which ensured that a national viewership would gather in expectation around television sets to watch the crowning of Elizabeth II.

'Looks like her mother'

On 2 June 1953 there were 2.7 million television sets operating across Britain with an average of seven and a half adults to a set. The BBC estimated that 20.4 million adults saw at least half an hour of the service, which was almost double the radio audience. This equated to 56 per cent of Britain's adult population – these figures excluding children.[63] This section examines how adults and children who watched the coronation on television thought they were sharing in a special moment as part of a national collective. It also analyses how, at the same time, television viewing was characterized by highly personal modes of consumption and a tension between national and more intimate experiences that seems to have been the defining feature of the televised event. This tension was animated by the domestic settings in which most viewers watched the coronation, as well as by the people with whom they saw it. Commonplace activities and conversations overlapped with the extraordinary scenes transmitted from Westminster abbey, with audience members engaging with the live moving images in novel ways. Notably, this home-based spectatorship witnessed audiences empathizing with the protagonists of the House of Windsor, expressing their thoughts and feelings in ways that were mutually reinforcing, which in turn evoked an affirming emotional experience among groups of viewers around the national focal point of the family monarchy.

Out of the seventy-six women who documented their coronation day activities for Mass Observation, thirty-five noted that they watched the televised procession and ceremony. This was roughly proportionate to the number of male respondents who saw it: forty out of eighty-seven men stated that they had seen the television broadcast. That almost half of all Mass Observation respondents watched the coronation coverage is, in itself, indicative of the mass participation created by television. A further thirty women and men listened to the service by wireless. A striking feature in all the directive replies are the negligible levels of opposition or apathy noted by respondents about the occasion: only fifteen out of 163 expressed disdain or disinterest in it. Given Mass Observation's progressive, anti-establishment

[63] A. Briggs, *The History of Broadcasting in the United Kingdom* (5 vols. Oxford, 1965–95), iv. 221; Moran, *Armchair Nation*, p. 77.

origins, the lack of criticism is significant.[64] As with the correspondence sent by readers to the *Manchester Guardian* censuring David Low's famously derisive 'Morning After' cartoon, or the letters sent to Kingsley Martin criticizing the *New Statesman*'s flippant coronation coverage, the Mass Observation reports indicated that a broad consensus existed that the queen's crowning was an important national event which should be treated with respect.[65]

Some of the Mass Observation respondents who watched television were influenced by the belief that the coronation met with broad acceptance, if not admiration, among the public and that the nation was united in celebrating it. The description of a thirty-six-year-old male clerk was typical. Comparing the 1953 coronation of the queen to that of her father in 1937, he recorded that it was distinguished by 'the fact that the whole nation joined in', indirectly indicating that the divisive events of December 1936 had turned people off the coronation of George VI.[66] He described how 'radio and TV made this an awe-inspiring ceremony. In 1937 I was an eavesdropper by radio, but this time I was THERE taking part'.[67] For this respondent, television facilitated a more national *and* a more intimate experience, the temporal simultaneity of the images from central London enhancing his sense of personal involvement while also heightening his awareness of a British community of viewers. A man from Cheshire who watched television with his children also commented that they 'took part in the actual service' and, contrasting the 1953 coronation to that of George VI, remarked that he 'remember[ed] little of the 1937 Coronation as it was a thing apart – not like this one where one was actually present through T.V.'.[68] Like the clerk above, this man expressed that he felt more involved through television and that by watching he had joined in an event which was for the first time accessible to the entire country. The socially integrative effect television had in overcoming regional differences was most explicitly articulated by an accountant from Sheffield when he stated: 'This year we seem to have actually taken part in the ceremony, and it was not just something that happened in far away London for the benefit solely of the

[64] N. Hubble, *Mass Observation and Everyday Life: Culture, History, Theory* (Basingstoke, 2006), pp. 4–8.

[65] Kynaston, *Family Britain*, pp. 306–7.

[66] MOA, 7/H/099.

[67] Emphasis in original.

[68] MOA, 7/F/Chief Inspector. For an almost identical response, see MOA, 7/H/ Agricultural Researcher; and for similar examples which stress a personalized sense of participation as well as a national dimension to their television experience, see MOA, 7/A/01, 7/A/0161, 7/B/793, 7/B/Retired Civil Servant, 7/B/Housewife, 7/D/202, 7/E/4019, 7/F/4037, 7/F/Lecturer, 7/G/4137, 7/H/2, 7/H/03.

inhabitants of that city'.[69] These Mass Observation respondents described how television had brought a national community together in celebration of the coronation, while acknowledging a personal sense of participation as well. Indeed, the tension in these descriptions between the collective and the intimate experience of television viewing was succinctly recorded by a schoolteacher from Weald in Sussex when she reflected that 'this Coronation was much more intimately and deeply shared by the whole people'.[70]

Adolescent schoolgirls who wrote essays about their coronation experience also discussed how television had heightened their personal sense of involvement in the event. Asked to record how they had spent coronation day, one girl from the grammar school in Cheshire responded at length:

> On Coronation day, after an early breakfast, I went to my friend's house, as I had been invited to see television. We all sat in a group around the television and watched the picturesque procession make its way from Buckingham Palace to Westminster Abbey. Thanks to the wonders of science we were able to see, like millions of British and continental viewers, the impressive Abbey service, the anointing and the crowning, and to really feel Elizabeth is Queen. The magnificent procession on the return route was so perfectly transmitted, that we were able to feel we were too, were taking part [*sic*]. We saw, also, the cheering, excited crowds, who had waited patiently for the wonderful moment of seeing their newly crowned queen pass in the State Coach, accompanied by the Duke of Edinburgh, her husband, who looked very proud of the fairy-tale Queen at his side. I shall always remember the way I spent my first coronation day, and I will have in my mind forever the day I saw new history being made.[71]

This full and complex response shows that the girl thought a community of viewers had formed around the focal point of the televised coronation and that European audiences shared in it, too. She stated that she and 'millions' of others had been immersed in the event, with the 'perfectly transmitted' television images allowing them 'to really feel Elizabeth is Queen' and that they also 'were taking part' – the new medium, with its moving pictures, clearly enhancing the authenticity of the experience. As with Mass Observation respondents who listened to the radio broadcasts of previous royal events like the 1947 royal wedding and 1937 coronation, her sense of participation and feelings seem to have been enlivened by the sounds and images of the 'cheering, excited crowds' – a feature regularly

---

[69] MOA, 7/F/093.
[70] MOA, 7/C/Teacher.
[71] MOA, 3/A/B4.

Figure 6.1. A photograph of a television screen showing Queen Elizabeth II as the coronation service unfolded, taken by a man from Southend-on-Sea on 2 June 1953.

noted by the schoolgirls who wrote about their coronation experience.[72] Furthermore, her description of the occasion as 'new history' in the making corresponded with the earlier essays that invested the coronation with special status because of its landmark associations. In this vein, adults and children also sought to memorialize the television broadcast by photographing the screens of television sets as the coronation played in front of them. One man in Southend-on-Sea in Essex photographed his television, investing the coronation broadcast with special historical meaning by generating a material record through which he and members of his family could later commemorate the event (Figure 6.1).[73]

[72] For an adult respondent's interesting description of the immersive quality of the 1953 coronation wireless broadcast, see MOA, 7/F/Retired Farmer. For children's essays that describe the experience of seeing and hearing crowds on TV, see MOA, 3/A/A4, 3/A/A12, 3/A/A24, 3/A/A30, 3/A/A31 3/A/A34, 3/A/A35, 3/A/A37, 3/A/A40.
[73] One of the schoolgirls from Cheshire noted that a boy at her television party was taking photographs of the TV screen (MOA, 3/A/B27), while the photograph presented

The one grievance occasionally expressed by adolescents about the television coverage which detracted from their sense of involvement related to the lack of colour images.[74] Schoolgirls from Cheshire complained about this more often than the pupils in west London, probably because they knew it was unlikely they would ever see the colourful decorations on the procession route for themselves. Adult Mass Observation respondents rarely complained about the television coverage, with just a handful of criticisms aimed at the size of television and its inability to fully convey the scale of the coronation spectacle.[75] Most of those who watched television instead praised the engaging qualities of the broadcast: its captivating effect was recorded by a thirty-nine-year-old housewife who stated that, when 'the camera caught [the queen] as she waved out the window and smiled, two women [with whom she sat] spontaneously and quite unself-consciously waved back as though they had been present [sic]'.[76] Clearly, television had the capacity to engross audiences who impulsively responded to the visual images they consumed.

The domestic settings in which most people watched the televised coronation and the company with whom they saw it were crucial factors in shaping the experiences reported by the Mass Observation respondents. One seventy-one-year-old woman who saw the coronation on television with her tenant and his relatives stated that she had worried before the event that she might not have been invited to watch television. Then, on the day itself, she wrote with pleasure that while watching 'a sense of the continuity of history gripped me, and I felt glad that I belonged to this country, and was no outsider'.[77] The feeling of involvement she experienced while watching television needs to be interpreted in relation to the sense of participation she felt because of her inclusion in her tenant's party. As well as the sense of collective viewing created around television sets, Mass Observation respondents who watched the coronation in their own or others' homes alongside family or friends experienced a heightened *personal* involvement because of the informal atmosphere of domestic settings. The

---

in Figure 6.1 comes from the private collection of B. Knowles and was taken by his great-grandfather on coronation day in 1953. Notably, one of the MO respondents noted that the *News Chronicle* had published an article providing readers with 'advice on taking photos from the T.V. screen' (MOA, 7/E/4250). For a useful analysis of commemorative processes and photography, see A. Kuhn, 'Memory texts and memory work: performances of memory in and with visual media', *Memory Studies*, xx (2010), 1–16; F. Trentmann, 'Materiality in the future of history: things, practices and politics', *Jour. Brit. Stud.*, xlviii (2009), 283–307.

[74] E.g., MOA, 3/A/A32, 3/A/A36, 3/A/A40, 3/A/B12, 3/A/B14, 3/A/B17, 3/A/B19, 3/A/B22.

[75] E.g., MOA, 7/A/1462, 7/C/023, 7/C/1971, 7/F/050, 7/H/School Teacher.

[76] MOA, 7/A/53.

[77] MOA, 7/C/023.

broadcast had the simultaneous effect of stimulating imagined identification with a national community of other television viewers while deepening the shared emotional experience of the coronation among groups who watched it together. Mass Observation had asked the respondents to 'give a short hour-by-hour description of [their] day' on 2 June and, although this meant they listed their normal activities alongside the more unique aspects related to television viewing, their reports reveal how the special qualities of the coronation were transformed by the constant ebb and flow of quotidian domestic rituals.

One forty-seven-year-old housewife who lived in Scotland hosted a television party for twenty people at her home. Her preoccupation over the course of coronation day was providing hospitality for her guests and she concluded her Mass Observation report by noting that 'although I had felt anxious about feeding all the guests I felt we had all had a happy day and that television had indeed made all the difference'.[78] This woman clearly found gratification in the positive experience of hosting a television party. One of the essays written by a schoolgirl from west London also revealed in two sentences the ease with which television viewers had transferred their attention between the coronation and ordinary home life:

> When I switched the television on my family were all silent. We listened with interest until I went outside into the kitchen and put the vegetables on the gas. All through the Coronation I thought how right it was for Princess Elizabeth to be the Queen. When the Queen was anointed my mother and I put the dinner onto plates and took it into the dining room. We ate it while we were listening to the singing.[79]

Mealtimes like this one interrupted the experience of the televised coronation for many adults and children who watched the broadcast in domestic environments. Women in particular stressed that they spent considerable time preparing food and girls often stated that they helped female relatives prepare for the day's events. In this respect it seems that gender helped to determine how people experienced the coronation. As historians Hester Barron and Claire Langhamer have noted, 'the shared experience of the everyday could create an emotional intimacy between mother and daughter', something which is evident from a number of the personal testimonies collected by Mass Observation in connection to the coronation.[80] A forty-one-year-old male agricultural researcher from Crawley noted that, at his television party, the 'womenfolk busied

[78] MOA, 7/A/Housewife.
[79] MOA, 3/A/A20.
[80] Barron and Langhamer, 'Feeling through practice', p. 114.

themselves before viewing commenced with the preparation of food'.[81] Meanwhile, a twenty-seven-year-old housewife from Portsmouth, who spent some of 2 June listening to the radio coverage, stated that her other coronation activities revolved around her domestic work and two young children, which included feeding her baby, washing nappies and keeping her toddler entertained.[82]

As we have seen, the potential for desacralization generated by the television broadcast of the coronation worried Church leaders like the archbishop of Canterbury, courtiers like Alan Lascelles and politicians like Churchill, all of whom thought that the spiritual significance of the ceremony might be lost on viewers.[83] It was made clear to the public that the very sacred moments of the coronation service would not be shown on television, the most important of which was the sovereign's anointing. Newspapers also issued readers with instructions to join in the prayers and spoken ritual with the congregation in the abbey.[84] But Mass Observation personal testimonies show that reverent silence was not always observed in front of television sets. The aforementioned schoolgirl from London was typical when she recorded that she and her mother used the moment of anointing to plate up the family's dinner.[85] In accordance with Mass Observation's longstanding policy to reveal how the British public's behaviour differed from its official representation, it asked its respondents whether they and the group with whom they watched television had observed silence as officially requested. The question naturally elicited a range of replies, most of which suggest that viewers paid little heed to the calls for quiet.[86] Where silence did prevail, it was usually out of respect for other guests who were watching. A forty-year-old accountant who was one of the few respondents to visit a public venue to watch the coronation stated that he, and the strangers around him, kept quiet for the duration of the broadcast. Viewing at a large television party at a primary school in Heaton Mersey in Stockport, he noted that during the queen's anointing 'the whole hall was silent … apart from the children

[81] MOA, 7/H/Agricultural Researcher.
[82] MOA, 7/A/1826. For other examples of girls' and women's domestic-themed experiences of coronation day, see MOA, 3/A/A3, 3/A/A18, 3/A/A22, 3/A/A35, 3/A/A44, 3/A/B2, 3/A/B10, 3/A/B12, 3/B/G22, 7/A/757, 7/A/4696.
[83] Pimlott, *Elizabeth II*, pp. 205 and 211–2.
[84] Moran, *Armchair Nation*, pp. 77–8.
[85] MOA, 3/A/A20.
[86] For examples of television parties that did not observe a silence, see MOA, 7/A/01, 7/A/School Teacher, 7/A/Youth Employment Officer, 7/A/757, 7/B/0177, 7/C/Teacher, 7/D/0857, 7/E/Chain Store Executive, 7/E/4250, 7/E/4019, 7/E/0708, 7/G/School Master, 7/G/4566.

who had become bored and were running up and down in the corridors'.[87] Just down the road in Northenden an Anglican vicar commented that at his television party 'there was a reverent silence during the anointing but [he thought] with most ordinary people it would have been more so had it been visible'.[88] A similar complaint was levelled by several of the respondents at the way the BBC censored the communion – the other sacred moment of the service – from its viewers. Experiencing a sudden sense of exclusion from the ceremony, they remarked that they and their company had deemed it a fitting moment to engage in their own activities. An accountant from Sheffield recorded that he and his brother's family had used the 'awkward part [with] the blank at the sacrament ... to exchange ideas about what had happened', while a twenty-five-year-old student who watched with seven of his friends reported that the moment of communion 'was considered suitable for handing round cigarettes'.[89] Every-day rituals like these were significant, with the televised coverage encouraging a shared desacralization of royal ceremony in the space of the home, be it through serving lunch with one's mother, chatting about the meaning of the royal spectacle or lighting cigarettes. Ironically, official efforts to protect the sanctity of the service by hiding parts of it from viewers thus seem to have led to an increase in irreverent, every-day activity among some groups.

The level of informality that characterized television parties was always greatest when those present were all close family. A railway clerk who watched with his wife, baby and his brother's family in Ealing, London, recorded the jocular comments made by the group during the television broadcast:

> The old Duke swears to her 'Not rude words I hope' 'Look at moth-holes at the back' – of cloaks. To be lifted into throne 'Want to see that – what if they drop her – hope they're strong' 'Here she comes – looks like her mother – calmer look' 'Very disappointing' – as they don't lift her. To baby 'Here's your queen, oi!' 'Thought Duke would pay homage first – only a relative' 'Nice close-up' – as he kisses left cheek. 'Duke of Gloucester – looks so old now' 'Duke of Kent – bless his little heart – I like that kid – ordeal for a youngster' 'Norfolk – don't like him'.[90]

The familiar tone of these remarks shows that television enabled media audiences to engage with the monarchy in a new way. They could consume television images without paying undue attention to the official soundtrack, instead offering their own audible running commentary. Unlike cinema and

---

[87] MOA, 7/G/4137.
[88] MOA, 7/E/1948.
[89] MOA, 7/F/093 and 7/F/Student. See also 7/H/School Teacher and 7/H/1478.
[90] MOA, 7/E/4250.

radio, in which silence was imperative to understanding what was going on, those who gathered to see the BBC's coronation programme were usually sitting upright in a cluster or 'viewing circle' around television sets and could openly converse and discuss the experience as events took place in front of them.[91] The remarks made by the Ealing family reveal how emotional reactions to the coronation became embedded in the affective economy of everyday life, with the group's conversation undermining the sanctity of the service through irreverent banter that focused on the character traits and foibles of the royal protagonists. The family's commentary suggests they had developed a personal familiarity with the royals: observations like 'looks like her mother' and 'looks so old now' show how the speakers casually indicated to one another their knowledge of the House of Windsor's main actors. The experience of the coronation for this group (and presumably many others) thus witnessed the deepening of a shared understanding and identification with the royal family as the coronation unfolded.

Although more respectful in tone, the directive reply of a retired civil servant who watched the television coverage with a group of her friends at home in Lancaster also reveals the spontaneous communal reactions inspired by the television broadcast:

> We were so much impressed … by the dignity and grace and composure of the Queen – someone remarked on her clear responses, and someone on the grace with which she sat down. One or two said how grave and unsmiling she was – but we felt this was fitting to the solemnity of the occasion. (At the end, when the coach turned into Buckingham Palace she was smiling and someone said, 'That's the best smile we've seen'). We all thought how small and how young she looked and thought of the weight she had to carry in the crown – all the regalia and heavy robes.[92]

This quotation again indicates that the civil servant and the company with whom she had watched television underwent a shared experience. Just like the family in Ealing, she and her friends discussed, contested and affirmed one another's opinions about the visual images in front of them. The civil servant's sense of participation was conveyed through her recurring use of the inclusive pronoun 'we', whereby she conflated her experience of television viewing with that of the rest of the group – a rhetorical device often used by Mass Observation respondents and schoolgirls in their essays.[93] These

[91] For the term 'viewing circle', see MOA, 7/H/Agricultural Researcher and 3/A/B27.
[92] MOA, 7/B/0137.
[93] For examples of these kinds of inclusive description, see MOA, 7/A/4398, 7/B/631, 7/E/4019, 7/H/052, 3/A/10, 3/A/14, 3/A/20, 3/A/29, 3/A/33, 3/A/36, 3/B/4, 3/B/16, 3/B/28, 3/B/29, 3/B/31.

shared, informal conversations point to the way viewers could experience an emotional unity around television sets, with the consumption of mass-mediated royalty leading to a tightening of interpersonal relationships as audiences picked over the meanings of monarchy together.

The television coverage of the queen's coronation generated a more intimate and more inclusive sense of participation in a royal ceremony than ever before. Mass Observation directive respondents and schoolgirls from across the country felt they formed part of a national community of viewers linked together around television sets. While the informal atmosphere of the domestic settings in which most viewers watched television transformed (and often undermined) the spiritual dimensions of the coronation, the conversational mood that characterized these spaces encouraged audiences to verbalize their thoughts and feelings on Elizabeth II and her family and, in so doing, they articulated a shared identification with royalty that connected them to the groups of people with whom they sat. The Ealing and Lancaster television parties were typical in their focus on the personalities of the royals, who formed a shared point of reference. A national community of viewers was thus united through their shared empathetic ties to the queen and her kin and, as the next section reveals, the BBC deliberately elevated this familial element to strengthen the emotional bonds that linked members of the public to the House of Windsor and to one another.

'My mummy is coming back'

The photographic coverage of Elizabeth II's children had antecedents in the intense visual exposure of her own childhood in the 1920s and 1930s and before that in images of the youthful Edward, prince of Wales, in the 1910s. However, this earlier coverage did not compare in volume or intimacy to the photographs of Prince Charles and Princess Anne produced for public consumption in the late 1940s and early 1950s. Somewhat ironically, the vast photographic souvenir industry that emerged around the monarch and her children in these years can be explained by a desire on the part of the royal family to exercise tighter control over their public image. In January 1950 the former royal governess, Marion Crawford, who had cared for Princesses Elizabeth and Margaret when they were children, went rogue and sold her memoirs about her time in the service of the royal family to an American publication, the *Ladies' Home Journal*.[94] The memoirs were then published by *Woman's Own* magazine in Britain and proved a roaring success with readers – although the palace worked hard to cast doubt on

---

[94] On Crawford's memoirs, see Pimlott, *Elizabeth II*, pp. 163–4. See also M. Crawford, *The Little Princesses* (London, 1950).

the accuracy of Crawford's recollections. Notably, this betrayal (which was never forgiven) came in the same year that the royal family was scandalized for a second time by the activities of the duke of Windsor. At the end of the war, Edward had once again become a thorn in the side of the monarchy. In 1944 the king's private secretary, Alan Lascelles, began to enquire secretly whether some unofficial post could be found for the duke in the USA that would keep him out of Britain and away from politics and the public.[95] However, to the frustration of the courtier, Edward rejected all his offers of unofficial posts, believing instead that his abilities would be better put to use in an official capacity on the other side of the Atlantic. The result was another souring of relations between the duke and the royal household, which led to him and the duchess moving to France where, with debts – personal and financial – to settle, he set about writing his memoirs. These were originally commissioned by the USA's *Life* magazine but were also purchased by Lord Beaverbrook's *Sunday Express*, which published them in mid December 1947, less than a month after Princess Elizabeth's wedding. As Edward's biographer has noted, these were 'good-tempered and colourful pieces that painted an attractive picture of the royal family and its daily life' in the period up until 1914.[96] They were not very revelatory but, according to the *Sunday Express*'s editor John Gordon, the palace sought to have them withdrawn from publication, although they were unsuccessful in their efforts.[97] The memoirs sent the newspaper's sales figures and the duke's popularity rocketing and so it was that the Express group set about securing the second instalment of Edward's recollections, which he had already begun writing.[98] He eventually completed these and they were subsequently purchased and published by the *Sunday Express* in 1950 to great acclaim; they brought the duke's story up as far as his romance with Wallis Simpson, his accession as king and his abdication. Gordon reported to his boss Beaverbrook that the newspaper achieved record consecutive sales increases every week the serialization of the memoirs continued, as well as the highest sales figures ever recorded by a Sunday paper.[99] He also noted that 'the Windsor instalment last week which brought Mrs. Simpson into the picture produced a heavy correspondence – heavier than any instalment since the earliest ones. And all very favourable. Indeed if we are not careful we shall

---

[95] P. Ziegler, *King Edward VIII: the Official Biography* (London, 2012), pp. 501–8; *King's Counsellor: Abdication and War: the Diaries of Sir Alan Lascelles*, ed. D. Hart-Davis (London, 2006), pp. 222–4, 239, 269, 355–60, 367, 372.
[96] Ziegler, *King Edward VIII*, p. 523.
[97] PA, BBK/H/121, J. Gordon to Lord Beaverbrook, 16 Dec. 1947.
[98] Also see Ziegler, *King Edward VIII*, p. 524.
[99] PA, BBK/H/121, J. Gordon to Lord Beaverbrook, 4 July and 11 July 1950.

be putting the Duke back on the throne'.[100] Clearly the memoirs aroused interest among British readers and evoked positive emotional identification with Edward and his wife. When the articles were later published in book form in 1951 they were also extremely popular, *A King's Story* selling more than 80,000 copies in its first month alone in the UK.[101]

The duke of Windsor thus remained a prominent and well-liked member of the royal family despite the best efforts of courtiers to keep him out of the limelight. As had been the case during the first year of the Second World War, he acted as a distraction from George VI's domestic group and his activities threatened to undermine the prestige of the monarchy by tarnishing its reputation after palace officials and the king had worked so hard to regain the public's support after the abdication. This was undoubtedly the reason why Elizabeth II expressly forbade Edward from attending her coronation in 1953.[102] It is no coincidence that, in the period when the duke was publishing his memoirs, the royal household developed a new media strategy that involved providing trusted photographers with more intimate access to life at the palace, particularly the domesticity of the queen and her young family, in an effort to refocus the public's attention on the line of succession. These photographs were issued to the press, reproduced as collectibles and also published by Pitkin as part of official souvenir magazines.[103] The first Pitkin royal souvenir magazine was published to celebrate Princess Elizabeth's twenty-first birthday in 1947 and another shortly followed to commemorate her and Prince Philip's wedding. However, it was the birth of their first son, Prince Charles, in 1948 that initiated a sustained photographic public relations campaign that focused on the younger members of the House of Windsor. Pitkin was given permission to reproduce images taken by royal photographers like Marcus Adams and Lisa Sheridan, who were granted special access to Charles and later on to his sister, Princess Anne. The images were subsequently printed in souvenir magazines such as the annual 'Golden Gift Books' of the royal children, which were published to coincide with their birthdays. The images in these souvenirs ranged from formal shots with Charles and

[100] PA, BBK/H/121, J. Gordon to Lord Beaverbrook, 11 July 1950.

[101] Ziegler, *King Edward VIII*, p. 527. See also S. Bradford, *King George VI* (London, 2011), pp. 590–3.

[102] LPL, Fisher 123, fo. 13, 'Diary of Coronation Events'.

[103] Very little is known about Pitkin's role as the publisher of official royal souvenir magazines in this period. This author's enquiries discovered that Pitkin no longer has an archive, having been subsumed into Pavilion Books. For reproductions of photographs of the royal children in the press, see *Daily Express*, 14 Nov. 1952, p. 1; *Daily Mirror*, 14 Nov. 1952, p. 1. For examples of photographs of the royal children printed as souvenir postcards, see RCIN, 2943746, 'Tuck post card of Prince Charles and Princess Anne', 24 Oct. 1952.

Figure 6.2. Marcus Adams, 'Princess Elizabeth and Prince Charles', 1948/49 (RCIN 2808647). Reproduced by Pitkin in *H.R.H. Princess Elizabeth: Silver Souvenir* (London, 1949), p. 26. Royal Collection Trust / © Her Majesty Queen Elizabeth II 2019.

Figure 6.3. Marcus Adams, 'Prince Charles and Princess Anne', 24 October 1952 (RCIN 2014220). Reproduced by Pitkin in *The Second Golden Gift Book of Prince Charles and Princess Anne* (London, 1952), p. 3. Royal Collection Trust / © Her Majesty Queen Elizabeth II 2019.

Anne sitting together in front of the camera to more natural images of them playing to pictures of them posing happily alongside their parents (Figures 6.2 and 6.3).[104] The message conveyed by these souvenirs, which replicated the visual codes from family photographs of ordinary British people during the 1950s, was that Charles and Anne were 'normal' children and that their mother and father loved and cared for them like all parents would.

The Pitkin souvenirs also regulated the exposure of the royal children. Courtiers were haunted by the media feeding-frenzy that had upset the royal honeymoon in 1947 and therefore tried to exercise tighter control over the media's access to the royal family's private lives.[105] As already noted, this move towards a more professionalized royal public relations system had been spearheaded by Lascelles after the abdication crisis and was later fronted by Richard Colville, the palace's press secretary. After Prince Charles's birth only the accredited cameraman Graham Thompson was given permission to film the royal baby.[106] Two years later, in 1950, following his sister's birth, Princess Elizabeth made it known through Colville that she 'objected to photographers taking unauthorized pictures of her children'.[107] Indeed, Thompson, who by this point had moved to the BBC's television department, was reprimanded by his new employers for making an unauthorized film 'of Prince Charles at play' which contravened 'the tacit agreement with the Press, Newsreel Companies, and other interests, to respect the Prince's privacy'.[108] Official royal photography and the Pitkin magazines thus enabled the monarchy to exercise control over the scenes of royal family life that were made public; and the souvenirs created an idealized visual iconography that simultaneously drew attention to the royal group's 'normal' characteristics by presenting them in informal, domestic poses.

Britain's newspapers helped to popularize this iconography by reproducing an idealized image of the monarch and her children. In the weeks before the coronation the press published many stories and photographs that presented Elizabeth II in her maternal role and emphasized that Prince Charles and Princess Anne were ordinary children.[109] For example, the *Daily Mirror*

---

[104] By the end of 1953, Pitkin had released more than 70 separate royal souvenir magazines, focusing on the private lives and public roles of Queen Elizabeth II and her closest relatives.

[105] See ch. 5.

[106] BBCWA, R34/862/7, Memo from P. H. Dorté to D. H. B, 3 Nov. 1948.

[107] BFINA, NRA vol.4, m.3429, 'Film of Princess Elizabeth's Children', 16 Nov. 1950.

[108] BBCWA, R34/862/9, B. E. Nicolls to R. Colville, 18 Aug. 1950. Thompson was replaced by the NRA with another accredited newsreel cameraman, P. J. Turner, in 1950 (BFINA, NRA vol. 4, m.3234, 'Royal Rota', 7 June 1950; m.4074, 'Royal Rota', 14 Aug. 1952; m.4101, 'Royal Rota', 18 Sept. 1952).

[109] E.g., *Daily Express*, 14 Apr. 1953, p. 1. This kind of photograph also appeared in popular

Figure 6.4. 'Let's Play In-And-Out-The Window', *Daily Mirror*,
1 May 1953, pp. 8–9. © The British Library Board.

dedicated a central spread to three large photographs taken by Lisa Sheridan of the queen playing 'in-and-out-the-window' with Charles and Anne at Balmoral (Figure 6.4).[110] In its caption the *Mirror* explained to its readers what was taking place in the 'wonderful new pictures', providing a dialogue between the queen and her children to animate their personalities and relationship. In view of this romanticized presentation of the royal family, a Mass Observation directive report written by a Manchester university student is pertinent. On coronation day he went for a half-mile walk through 'side streets' in the city, which he suggested were 'all more or less slums' and only '2 front-room windows were not decorated with a picture of the Queen, and/or [her] children', with 'the Duke less in evidence'.[111] The

magazines: *Picture Post*, 2 May 1953, p. 27; *Woman*, 9 May 1953, pp. 10–1; *Woman's Own*, 28 May 1953, pp. 24–5; *Modern Woman*, Apr. 1953, pp. 41–3.

[110] *Daily Mirror*, 1 May 1953, pp. 8–9. See also *Daily Express*, 1 May 1953, p. 3.

[111] MOA, 7/G/1873. On the importance of this kind of maternal identification within a Commonwealth context, see R. Feingold, 'Marketing the modern empire: Elizabeth II and the 1953–54 world tour', *Antipodes*, xxiii (2009), 147–54.

implication of this respondent's comments – that the people in these homes venerated the personalities of the queen and her children – is indicative of the post-war culture of royal maternalism that had been generated around Elizabeth II.

In light of the extensive media coverage of the queen's maternal image before her coronation, it is unsurprising that the BBC sought to draw attention to her children and particularly to her relationship with her son and heir in its television broadcast on 2 June. In so doing, the BBC encouraged emotional identification between audiences and the royals, elevating a common reference point to unite viewers around the bond between mother and son. The Mass Observation respondents and school essayists noted that, on three separate occasions during the day's broadcasting, they or those people with whom they watched reacted very positively to the televised scenes of the prince.

The first time adults and adolescent children reacted positively to Charles on 2 June was when he first appeared during the coronation service. In the week before the coronation the media speculated whether or not he would be present in the abbey to witness his mother's crowning.[112] This speculation had raised some concerns among the public, one fourteen-year-old schoolgirl from west London writing in an essay that she thought 'Prince Charles … ought to see his mother's actual crowning as it would show the significance that his mother is Queen'.[113] One of her classmates also thought he should be present as it would 'prepare [him] for his'.[114] The queen's maternal role and Charles's position as heir influenced how the BBC designed the scene in which he appeared during the service. Outside broadcast producer Peter Dimmock learnt that the prince would be present in the royal box with the queen mother and Princess Margaret at the moment the queen was crowned. He instructed his cameraman, B. P. Wilkes, who was in charge of filming the royal box, to focus in on Charles and, immediately after the archbishop of Canterbury finished the prayer that preceded the queen's crowning, the television broadcast cut to a scene of the prince looking down at his mother.[115] The implication was clear: here was the heir to the throne watching his mother undergo the ritual he would one day experience himself.

Charles's sudden appearance on television screens around the country elicited powerful reactions from viewers. Schoolgirls from Cheshire and west

[112] *Daily Express*, 2 June 1953, p. 12; *Daily Mirror*, 1 June 1953, p. 6.
[113] MOA, 3/B/G8.
[114] MOA, 3/B/G3.
[115] BBCWA, T14/869/2, 'The Coronation of Her Majesty Queen Elizabeth II: Producer's Script', p. 16.

Figure 6.5. A photograph of a television screen showing
Prince Charles and the Queen Mother in the royal box, taken
by a man from Southend-on-Sea on 2 June 1953.

London noted in their essays that they thought his arrival in the royal box
was particularly exciting, one remarking that 'when we saw Prince Charles
sitting with the Queen Mother ready for the crowning it was certainly one
of the happiest moments'.[116] This essay writer clearly acknowledged that
Charles's arrival had stimulated viewers' interest. Several adult respondents
also suggested that the television images of the prince in the abbey were the
'most stirring' or 'touching' they witnessed on 2 June, while others made
sense of these scenes through the maternal story on show.[117] For example,
the retired civil servant who had watched at a television party in Lancaster
commented that 'we were all pleased when we saw Prince Charles in the
Abbey and someone said she wondered whether the one time when the

[116] MOA, 3/A/B16. For other examples, see MOA, 3/A/A28 and 3/A/A4.
[117] E.g., MOA, 7/A/0219, 7/B/anon, 7/D/195, 7/E/4250, 7/F/806, 7/F/RAF Engineer
Officer.

Queen looked up for a moment was when he came in'.[118] The media actively mobilized this story of motherly care through these scenes, with the BBC's television commentator Richard Dimbleby stating at a later point in the abbey broadcast that the monarch had briefly glanced at her son; and the following day the press also suggested that her fleeting look aside had been at him.[119] One Mass Observation respondent identified as one of the 'most stirring incidents' she witnessed on 2 June 'the one and only sideways glance and smile [of the queen], the only moment which television showed us when she was not wholly engrossed in the ceremonial. This according to newspapers was directed to her son perhaps as he was leaving the Royal Box'.[120] Viewers also chose to photograph their television sets while Charles was on screen, which again suggests they thought these were special moments worth recording for posterity (Figure 6.5).[121]

The second time the prince appeared as part of the television coverage also prompted enthusiastic responses from British viewers. As already indicated, he left the royal box and returned to Buckingham Palace before the coronation ceremony had ended. Two hours later the BBC was televising scenes of his mother inside the gold state coach as she completed the final stretch of her return journey from the abbey. As the procession rounded the Victoria memorial at the end of the Mall, the television transmission switched to images of Charles and Anne looking down from the palace windows and pointing at the queen's carriage. The media had frequently reproduced this image of the royal children watching their mother from a distance as she performed her public role in the early 1950s.[122] One girl in a class of eight- and nine-year-old children at Northumberland Heath junior school in Kent recorded in an essay written about what she anticipated seeing on coronation day that 'the two children will be looking at [the queen] through the palace window'.[123] This girl thus acknowledged that this type of image of Charles and Anne was part of the recognizable canon of photographic scenes associated with the royal family in this period. Several of the adolescent schoolgirls from London and Cheshire commented that they particularly enjoyed these images on coronation day, one typically

[118] MOA, 7/B/0137.

[119] E.g., *Daily Mirror*, 3 June 1953, p. 5; *Daily Express*, 3 June 1953, p. 12. See also Ziegler, *Crown and People*, p. 111.

[120] MOA, 7/B/631.

[121] See also n. 73.

[122] E.g., *Daily Mirror*, 5 Nov. 1952, pp. 8–9; 28 Apr. 1953, p. 9; 1 June 1953, p. 16; E. Scott, *The Second Golden Gift Book of Prince Charles and Princess Anne* (London, 1952), p. 26 (also published by Pitkin). MOA, 3/A/A18; also 3/A/B14, 3/A.

[123] MOA, 3/D/N2/N27.

recording that she 'liked it when Prince Charles and Princess Ann [*sic*] saw their mother come home. Princess Ann got very excited and Prince Charles kept banging on the window'.[124] Adult respondents also expressed pleasure at these scenes: a thirty-four-year-old religious minister recorded his 'delight' at the 'unconscious reactions of the royal children as caught in the window by the TV camera'.[125] A teacher from Hertfordshire was even more enthusiastic, making a special point about these images: 'I should like to mention Prince Charles's excitement when he caught sight of the Coach from the window. He kept pointing as if he would like to push through the glass, as much to say "Look, there's my mummy in her coach. My mummy is coming back"'.[126] This woman empathized with the royal actors, investing the images with a special emotional meaning that focused on the children's desire to be reunited with their mother. As the religious minister stated, the charm of this scene lay in its appearing natural and 'unconscious', with Charles and Anne behaving as though they were normal children. The images, of course, had a deeper symbolic significance to which the Mass Observation evidence attests. The early 1950s were characterized by heated public debates on the roles women should occupy in British society. The welfare state, with its system of tax allowances, benefits and national insurance, had incentivized the idea that a women's primary role was as home-maker and mother. As historian Sean Nixon has noted, 'expert' psychologists like John Bowlby and Donald Winnicott 'gave additional intellectual weight to the idea that women's key responsibility was as a full-time mother who took exclusive care of the developing child'.[127] The lonely figure of the 'latch-key child' waiting for mother to return home from paid work outside the domestic sphere loomed large in the public's imagination and contributed to a rise in social anxieties about maternal deprivation.[128] The scenes of the royal children watching their mother from the palace windows, expectantly waiting to be reunited with her, acted as a stark reminder that the queen's public duties prevented her from fulfilling her domestic role, as she was unable to be at home with her children. Charles and Anne's separation from their mother and their visible happiness on

---

[124] MOA, 3/A/A18. See also MOA, 3/A/B14, 3/A/A11, 3/A/A27, 3/D/O8.

[125] MOA, 7/F/Minister of Religion.

[126] MOA, 7/A/Schoolteacher. For similar examples, see MOA, 7/C/HW, 7/C/0142, 7/D/195, 7/E/4019.

[127] S. Nixon, 'Life in the kitchen: television advertising, the housewife and domestic modernity in Britain, 1955–1969', *Contemporary British Hist.*, xxxi (2017), 69–90, at pp. 80–1.

[128] P. Summerfield, 'Women in Britain since 1945: companionate marriage and the double burden', in *Understanding Post-War British Society*, ed. J. Obelkevich and P. Catterall (London, 2002), pp. 58–72, at pp. 62–3.

her return home thus amplified the public discourse on the burdensome nature of royal status and the sacrifices it required of its protagonists. The duties imposed on royalty also symbolically manifested themselves through Charles's presence in Westminster abbey on coronation day. It was unusual for a child aged just four to be present at such a service, but the images of him alongside his grandmother, the queen mother, conveyed how a long life of public service lay ahead of him.

The final time the Mass Observation respondents and schoolchildren reacted enthusiastically to scenes of the prince and his interaction with his mother was the climactic balcony appearance after the latter's return to Buckingham Palace. Charles's behaviour on the balcony received more positive comments from adults and adolescents than any other aspect of the royal family's conduct on 2 June.[129] A thirty-four-year-old printer from Newtown, mid Wales, was typical in his remarks on 'the antics of Prince Charles on the balcony' as the 'funniest incident' of the day, with the heir to the throne grasping at his mother's bracelets as she and her family waved to the crowds gathered below them.[130] Again, it was the 'natural' quality of this scene that appealed to viewers – the prince's unplanned 'antics' lacking royalty's usual formality.[131] A housewife from Leeds also suggested that the 'funniest incident' from 2 June was the moment 'on the balcony before the fly-past [when] Prince Charles reached over, took his mother's right hand and put it up, as much to say, "Practice what you preach" – and she waved'.[132] As with the queen's sideways glance that was caught on camera during the coronation service, television viewers invested these moments with emotional meaning to emphasize an affection between mother and son. And, to augment the public's personal identification with the royals, the popular press published stories and photographs on the prince's behaviour on the balcony which used an intimate language to animate the relationship between him and his mother. The *Daily Mirror* was typical in using the caption 'Mummy – Mummy' to conjure this informal royal image (Figure 6.6).[133]

On the one hand, the BBC's television coverage of Prince Charles's interaction with his mother clearly encouraged audiences to identify personally with scenes of royal maternalism, invigorating an emotional

[129] E.g., MOA, 3/A/A27, 3/A/A30, 3/A/A38, 3/A/B6, 3/A/B14, 3/A/B17, 3/A/B21, 3/A/B27, 7/D/1090, 7/H/Schoolteacher.

[130] MOA, 7/E/Printer. See also 7/E/4019 and 7/F/Minister of Religion for almost identical responses.

[131] See also MOA, 7/E/4250.

[132] MOA, 7/D/0143. See also 3/A/A30.

[133] E.g., *Daily Express*, 3 June 1953, p. 12; *Daily Mirror*, 4 June 1953, pp. 8–9.

't keep still for a moment.

The full-of-beans boy of Buckingham Palace suddenly gets inquisitive, asking his mother about the Armill — the bracelet of Sincerity and Wisdom —she is wearing on her wrist. Television viewers saw him ask the Queen to move her arm, so he could see it flash, making the sort of picture millions of people like to keep. And here it is— caught by the candid camera.

Smiling, waving to the crowds, frowning in perplexity as the planes flash overhead . . . the candid camera was there to capture all the Royal Children's expressions as they stood on stools on the Palace balcony. Prince Charles wears his Coronation Medal, presented to him by the Queen.

MUMMY— MUMMY!

Figure 6.6. 'Mummy – Mummy!', *Daily Mirror*, 4 June 1953, p. 9. © The British Library Board.

community of viewers who empathized with the domesticity of the House of Windsor. On the other, this focus on royal familialism accentuated the public narrative on the unenviable character of royal life. In a similar vein to the coronation of her father sixteen years earlier, media audiences also expressed special concern for the queen's wellbeing during the coronation ceremony. In part we should interpret this in relation to the stress that both the media and Archbishop Geoffrey Fisher placed on the burdens of royal duty and the pressures of the coronation service in advance of the event, much like Cosmo Lang had in 1937.[134] The queen had also drawn attention to the personal difficulties she would encounter as monarch when she told listeners at the end of her 1952 Christmas broadcast that she would dedicate herself anew to their service on coronation day. Having vocally reaffirmed her commitment to serve her subjects, she then asked listeners to support her in her onerous role, just as her grandfather had done in his final royal broadcasts two decades previously: 'I want to ask you all, whatever your religion, to pray for me on that day – to pray that God may give me wisdom and strength to carry out the solemn promises I shall be making, and that I may faithfully serve Him and you, all the days of my life'.[135] The monarch's words were widely reported by newspapers that emphasized her commitment to her difficult position and even claimed she had written the broadcast herself – thus implying that the feelings she expressed were real.[136]

The public's sympathetic reactions to the queen on 2 June 1953 suggested that they were moved by the vulnerable image of her that had been carefully crafted in the lead-up to the coronation. For example, a group of thirteen-year-old girls from the grammar school in west London recorded in their essays that they thought Prince Philip should be with the queen in the service to support her.[137] One of these girls couched her concern in broader terms relating to the personal hardships endured by the monarch: 'I don't think that the Queen should be always working. Many others will agree that the Queen has a hard time, after all she is a human being. The Royal Family are not together enough, is what many say'.[138] This kind of anxiety, which focused on the personal sacrifices made by Elizabeth II, was communicated implicitly by Mass Observation respondents and essayists who expressed disquiet that she was separated from her family during the coronation service, with several stating that she looked 'lonely' or 'weighed down' by the crown on her head.[139] Although royal and religious officials had expressly prohibited television close-ups before the event, it is notable that the BBC cameramen in the abbey disregarded this rule on the day itself in order

---

[134] Pimlott, *Elizabeth II*, pp. 209–10; Anderson, 'The Tory party at prayer', p. 421.

[135] Quoted in T. Fleming, *Voices Out of the Air: the Royal Christmas Broadcasts, 1932–1981* (London, 1981), pp. 70–1.

[136] *Daily Express*, 27 Dec. 1952, p. 1; *Daily Mirror*, 27 Dec. 1952, p. 1; *Daily Mail*, 27 Dec. 1952, p. 1.

[137] MOA, 3/B/G18, 3/B/G19, 3/B/G20. For a similar adult view, see MOA, 7/A/1605. This concern about Philip's place in the service was probably shaped by press articles which, since February 1953, had speculated about the specific role he would perform in relation to the queen. Mischievously, the *Daily Mirror* undertook a public poll on this question (*Daily Mirror*, 24 Feb. 1953, p. 1; *Daily Mirror*, 20 Apr. 1953, p. 1).

[138] MOA, 3/B/G18.

[139] E.g., MOA, 7/A/1462, 7/A/4398, 7/E/1858, 7/F/Minister of Religion, 7/H/048.

to present audiences with large pictures of the queen's face that enabled viewers to scrutinize it and identify with the emotions it conveyed.[140] In respect of these close-ups, it is perhaps unsurprising that Mass Observation respondents and schoolgirls noted concerns about the queen's 'youth' and the way she 'looked very nervous'.[141] The phrases recorded by viewers about the queen's apparent unease echoed the responses of many of those who had listened to the radio broadcast of her father's coronation sixteen years before. As in 1937, it is clear that the narrative of the burdens of royal public life took on a very literal form through the monarch as she endured a seemingly torturous coronation service that was being transmitted live not only to Britain but to audiences spread across the rest of the world.

The public's sympathy for Elizabeth II should also be interpreted in relation to the popular belief that she was placing public duty ahead of personal ambition, sacrificing fulfilment as a young woman to undertake her role as sovereign. A large number of school essayists specifically focused on this story of sacrifice. Girls at the Cheshire and London grammar schools seemed to be reflecting on a previous classroom discussion on the meaning of the coronation when they wrote that they thought the queen was 'dedicating her life' to the 'service of her people' and 'her country' and that she was thus owed 'our loyalty and support'.[142] Some explicitly asserted that the queen's dedication involved her forsaking her personal ambitions: a fourteen-year-old girl stated that 'she must always put other people's desires before hers, no matter how she feels about it'.[143] These examples show that adolescent children were educated on the meaning of the coronation and that this helped to popularize the normative discourse on the burdens of royal life. These essays also reveal that members of the public envisioned the queen's national duty in relation to the constraints it placed on her personal development; and that the formation of royalist identities in the classroom was partly rooted in empathy for the monarch at a time when fulfilment in domestic life was deemed to be a core tenet of modern selfhood.[144]

[140] Moran, *Armchair Nation*, pp. 73–4 and 80. See also Pimlott, *Elizabeth II*, pp. 190–1 and 205.

[141] E.g., MOA, 3/A/A34, 7/C/023, 7/C/HW, 7/C/0142, 7/D/2029, 7/E/4250, 7/G/948, 7/E/1948.

[142] MOA, 3/A/B17, 3/A/B24, 3/A/C3, 3/A/C20, 3/A/C21, 3/B/F1, 3/B/F6, 3/B/F11, 3/B/F21, 3/B/F23, 3/B/G15. For similar sentiments, see MOA, 3/A/C11, 3/B/G3, 3/B/F15, 3/B/F17.

[143] MOA, 3/A/B22. See also 3/A/F3.

[144] C. Langhamer, 'Love, selfhood and authenticity in post-war Britain', *Cult. and Soc. Hist.*, ix (2012), 277–97, esp. at pp. 277–82; J. Finch and P. Summerfield, 'Social reconstruction and the emergence of companionate marriage, 1945–1959', in *Marriage, Domestic Life and Social Change: Writings for Jacqueline Burgoyne*, ed. D. Clark (London, 1991), pp. 7–32.

Conclusion

On 9 June, exactly one week after the coronation, Geoffrey Fisher wrote to George Barnes at the BBC's television department to congratulate him and his team on the broadcast:

> On my side may I say that from what I have heard from far and near, I am satisfied that T.V. did a really superb job ... You know that I am no great supporter of T.V., regarding it as an extravagance and a supreme time waster. But I admit that for certain occasions it is a great benefit. And I freely say that thanks to T.V. the Coronation Service got into countless homes and brought to the viewers a realization of the Queen's burden, the Queen's dedication, God's presence and God's consecration, of religion and of themselves – which otherwise they would not even have guessed at.[145]

Fisher similarly confided in his diary that he thought the 'religious significance' of the event had been 'much more generally appreciated than at the last Coronation' and added that he thought the 'Queen's request for the prayers of everybody in her Christmas broadcast made a very deep impression'.[146] The archbishop thus seems to have warmed to television as a form of mass communication as a result of the coronation broadcast, recognizing in it the potential to strengthen the religious beliefs of viewers and to make more visible the popular meanings that underpinned the monarchy's public image. For Fisher, this primarily concerned Elizabeth II's commitment to serve her subjects. As we have seen, the queen's ostensible burdens and her domestic role were more integral to her public presentation on her coronation day than historians have previously acknowledged. While the media and other public voices heralded a New Elizabethan Age and the dawn of Commonwealth, Mass Observation sources suggest that public attitudes to the monarch on 2 June focused mainly on her personality and family life. The respondents who partook in Mass Observation's coronation-day survey had also participated in an earlier survey that had asked them whether they 'ever [had] personal thoughts about the Queen [and] if so, what sort of thoughts [these were]'.[147] It is a great shame that all but one of the original replies to this directive have since been lost, but the one surviving reply, oddly enclosed with the 2 June responses and written by the same retired civil servant who had watched the coronation at a television party in Lancaster, illuminated the strong empathetic connection that mass media facilitated between members of the public and the royal family:

---

[145] LPL, Fisher 124, fo. 217, G. Fisher to G. Barnes, 9 June 1953.
[146] LPL, Fisher 124, fo. 33, 'Diary of Coronation Events'.
[147] MOA, TC/69/2/A, 'Code List Survey 167', p. 3.

I do think in personal terms about the Queen. I regard her with affection and pride and admiration, much as I might do a distinguished younger member of my own family or circle of acquaintances. I suppose it is rather foolish, seeing she is so far removed from me. But we see so many photos and read and hear so much of her intimate personal family and private life that one can't help feeling that one knows her personally – even without seeing her in the flesh.[148]

Clearly recognizing the key role played by the media as the organizing force in her para-social emotional relationship with the queen, this woman was among a number of respondents who expressed loyalty to the monarch which was rooted in the ability to identify with her personally.[149] For some Mass Observation respondents it was this intimate identification that distinguished Elizabeth II from her father. Several compared the 1953 coronation to that of George VI and noted that the abdication of Edward VIII had tarnished the 1937 event, but a forty-two-year-old primary school teacher went one step further when she stated that, while the new queen was 'young and the family appeared romantic', her father had been 'a sincere but not a romantic figure'.[150]

This chapter has shown that the media and BBC television in particular played a crucial part in generating a popular appeal around the post-war royal family. The prospect of seeing the television broadcast of the coronation notably offset other public criticism about the event, with adolescent schoolchildren acknowledging a strong desire to participate in what they perceived as a historic occasion. On the day itself, television facilitated new modes of participation by enabling viewers to conceive of themselves as part of a national community linked together around television sets in the home. Across the country Mass Observation respondents and school essayists recorded that they experienced an increased sense of involvement as part of a collective British viewership. Equally, the informal domestic settings in which most people watched television enhanced the shared and intimate qualities of the coronation experience by encouraging viewers to relate personally, and as part of groups, to the images they consumed, deepening their mutual emotional identification with the royal family. Furthermore, we have seen how the BBC elevated the familial aspects of the coronation by focusing on the queen's maternal image, which, in turn, stimulated shared feelings among its national viewership and fostered sympathy for the monarch's ostensibly onerous public role.

[148] MOA, 7/B/0137, Part A, May 1953.
[149] E.g., MOA, 7/A/0161, 7/A/anon (Edenbridge), 7/C/Housewife, 7/C/anon (Brighton).
[150] MOA, 7/A/0161. For other examples that discuss the negative impact of the abdication crisis on the 1937 coronation, see MOA, 7/B/Housewife, 7/B/0137, 7/B/924, 7/C/0214, 7/D/1587, 7/G/Schoolmaster, 7/H/055.

Conclusion

In the last years of King George V's reign, the royal family developed a new public relations strategy in order to promote a set of moral values that were instrumental in shaping how the monarch's second son, King George VI, and his granddaughter, Queen Elizabeth II, sought to perform their public roles. The BBC television coverage of the 1953 coronation articulated these values, including the Christian ideals of family, duty and self-sacrifice, through the sacred ritual involved in the Westminster abbey service. Television provided royal stage-managers with a new platform through which to popularize among a mass audience the religious symbolism that had come to underpin the crown's public image in the preceding decades. Where radio had enabled courtiers, clergy and BBC editors to craft broadcasts that immersed listeners in royal events that highlighted the monarchy's commitment to domesticity and to serving the public, television created a more vivid, immediate and intimate experience for viewers, who were now able to participate in royal family occasions as spectators. However, as we have seen from reports written by Mass Observation respondents who spent coronation day at home with friends and family, watching the events in central London unfold on television sets, it is clear the religious elements of the coronation did not always resonate with audiences. TV could provide new kinds of instruction on the meanings attached to royalty and religion, but it also had the potential to desacralize the crown and Church by facilitating more informal, irreverent patterns of media consumption. This is what the organizers of the coronation had feared when they originally tried to prevent the BBC from televising the crowning ceremony, but now it was too late – the proverbial genie had been let out of the bottle – and from 1953 onwards royal personalities would be subject to new kinds of scrutiny as their images were visually dissected and devoured within the relaxed, communal setting of the post-war home.

Viewers' responses to the 1953 coronation also reveal that members of the public had forged powerful empathetic relationships with the main protagonists of the House of Windsor. These imagined connections had intensified in the years between 1932 and 1953 with readers, listeners and viewers increasingly identifying with the private lives and feelings of the royal family. This empathy was deliberately fostered by the royal household and allies of the throne, who sought to project an idealized image of royal

'Conclusion', in E. Owens, *The Family Firm: Monarchy, Mass Media and the British Public, 1932–53* (London, 2019), pp. 373–87. License: CC-BY-NC-ND 4.0.

domestic life to media audiences as part of a wider strategy to strengthen the public's loyalty to the crown and adherence to the royal status quo through new emotional bonds. In particular, the language used by members of the House of Windsor to communicate with the public in this period became more informal and personal: under the authorship of archbishop of Canterbury Cosmo Lang, royal broadcasts and messages incorporated a more reflective, intimate register that provided audiences with what seemed like insights into the emotions felt by the royal family. The impact this language had on sections of the public is apparent in letters written by listeners in response to broadcasts in which the writer identified with the royal speaker's feelings. Equally, the public affection that Mass Observation recorded at the time of the 1937 coronation for the forlorn figure of Queen Mary suggests that the kind of expressive, personal messages she issued to the public (the first coming after her husband's death, the second following the abdication of her eldest son) evoked empathy and support for the royal family – in this case, at an extremely difficult moment of transition.

Courtiers and churchmen quickly came to appreciate the power of mass media for engendering public loyalty to the royal family through a new kind of top-down emotional programming that emerged in other European nations in the interwar years, too. With the outbreak of another global conflict in 1939, the monarchy's public relations strategy evolved again but this time in response to a rise in criticism and apathy towards the crown, a development the royal household tried to counter by highlighting the monarchy's contribution to the war effort and the way George VI, Queen Elizabeth and their children seemed to share emotionally in the hardships of the home front alongside their people. This royal media image was shaped by government propagandists, who tried to use the House of Windsor as a mouthpiece in order to further their own aims. However, royal officials ultimately managed to maintain control of the monarchy's image in order to promote a narrative consistent with the crown's pre-war activities. In the years immediately before and after the conflict, the palace also had to contend with intrepid news reporters and editors who sought to bring royal personalities and their feelings closer to media audiences through exposés that revealed the House of Windsor's private life to public view. There was particularly intense media scrutiny of royalty at the time of Princess Elizabeth's engagement and marriage to Philip Mountbatten and again after the births of their first two children. Tensions therefore existed between the various actors involved in the projection of the House of Windsor's image, but the intimate vision of royal domesticity that steadily emerged in these years helped to generate a sense of national unity among members of the public through new kinds of affective integration around the focal point of the family monarchy.

The dynamic relationship between British journalists, the public they claim to represent and the royal household has continued to shape the projection of the monarchy's media image to the present day. Those sections of the popular press that broke the mould by interrogating the royal family's behaviour in the 1930s and 1940s became even more outspoken as the decline in deference towards elite institutions like the government, Church and crown accelerated through the 1950s and 1960s. No longer did reporters and news editors take for granted royal privilege and power, but instead increasingly questioned the roles that royalty played in society and the wider world and developed a more irreverent approach to royal private life that saw them simultaneously venerating the idealized image of the family monarchy while hunting for scandalous stories to destabilize the domestic narrative. Despite the mixed media coverage that enveloped the House of Windsor in the second half of the twentieth century, many of the trends set in motion in the period from 1932 to 1953 can be seen at work in the methods used by Elizabeth II's household to try to win the affection and loyalty of her subjects. The queen's watchword during her reign has been 'duty'; and the language of self-sacrifice and service has been intrinsic to her public presentation – just as it was for her father and grandfather. Equally, she has repeatedly stressed the importance of 'the family' as the key social institution at the heart of the British nation. Whatever reservations critics of monarchy have expressed about the queen, it is clear she has taken these ideas of duty and domesticity seriously and has sought – with varying results – to impart the same values to her children and grandchildren.

The monarchy's history since Elizabeth II's coronation has been defined by a group of individuals who have either succeeded in championing the queen's high moral ideals or who have failed (often very publicly) to live up to them. This story of successes and failures is testament to the durability of the values and contradictions that came to underpin the royal media image in the two decades examined in this book. An important case in point, one in which these values and contradictions came to a head but which also signalled the beginning of a new phase in the monarchy's evolution and set the course for much of what was to come in the later twentieth century, was the romantic drama involving the queen's sister, Princess Margaret, in the weeks immediately after the coronation. On 14 June 1953 the Sunday newspaper *The People* announced to British readers that foreign news outlets were claiming Margaret was in love with a divorced man. It was unlikely that the princess, as third in line to the throne, would ever succeed her sister as queen, but if some tragedy befell Elizabeth II and her child heirs then Margaret would become monarch and would be expected to uphold the Christian values required of the defender of the faith.[1] As we have seen, marital impropriety was not tolerated by the Church of England and the archbishop of Canterbury, Geoffrey Fisher, was a staunch opponent of divorce and outspoken supporter of the monarchy's family-centred image. The sections of the media that criticized Margaret's romantic entanglement with a divorcé noted that it was highly unlikely she would ever be called upon to become queen, but it was the way her behaviour challenged the religious principles embodied by her elder sister that was the sticking point.[2] However, as one might expect, having witnessed how members of the public responded to the romantic quandaries of King Edward VIII in 1936 and the then Princess Elizabeth in 1947, there was another side to Margaret's story that once again highlights the significant changes the monarchy and British society underwent in the years between 1932 and 1953.

To begin with, Margaret was a popular figure with the media and, in the vein of younger royals of the interwar generation, she had been transformed into a celebrity who was renowned for her modern style, glamour and dynamic personality.[3] As in the case of Edward VIII when he was prince of Wales and Prince George and Princess Marina in 1934, courtiers and the press had encouraged the public to take a personal interest in Margaret's development: since her father's coronation sixteen years previously, she had been presented as a charismatic figure to whom the public could relate and whom it could admire. Although she was overshadowed by her sister, especially after Elizabeth started a family, news editors deemed Margaret's love life to be of great interest to their readerships.[4] The celebrity journalism of the mid twentieth century placed special emphasis on the revelation of private life as a way of getting to know the 'real' person behind the famous individual's public image. When combined with the more critical attitude developed by left-wing newspapers to the monarchy in the late 1930s, which partly sprung from the uncomfortable knowledge that they had conspired to keep Edward VIII's relationship with Wallis Simpson concealed from readers, these new kinds of exposure led to increased scrutiny of the personal lives and decisions made by the royal family, as well as a growing disregard for older notions of social propriety.[5] George V's monarchy had been revered by the mainstream media and his political contemporaries as sacrosanct; any

[1] For a good overview of the Margaret-Townsend episode, see B. Pimlott, *The Queen: Elizabeth II and the Monarchy* (London, 2002), pp. 217–20, 232–9.

[2] Pimlott, *Elizabeth II*, pp. 236–9.

[3] C. Warwick, *Princess Margaret: a Life of Contrasts* (London, 2002), pp. 137–44.

[4] Warwick, *Princess Margaret*, pp. 135–8.

[5] A. Bingham, *Family Newspapers? Sex, Private Life, and the British Popular Press, 1918–1978* (Oxford, 2009), pp. 230, 244–6.

kind of private royal indiscretion was kept secret out of respect for the king and the gentlemanly codes of decorum that governed upper-class society during his reign. But the post-abdication years were made more difficult for royalty by a decline in deference that coincided with, but was also propelled by, the media's attempts to democratize national life.

Perhaps unsurprisingly, that self-appointed voice of Britain's post-war social democracy, the *Daily Mirror*, took the brazen step of polling its readers' opinions on the issue of Margaret's romance. In the wake of *The People*'s exposé and in the absence of any official denial from Buckingham Palace, journalists took a lead in announcing to readers that the man with whom the princess was in a relationship was Group-Captain Peter Townsend, a handsome RAF veteran whose family had long-standing ties to the British military. In 1944 he had been appointed equerry to George VI and had risen through the ranks of the royal household to become comptroller to the king's consort, Queen Elizabeth, in 1952 – the same year his first marriage ended in divorce. According to Margaret's biographers, it was in the wake of George VI's death in February 1952 that she and Townsend began their relationship, with the couple finding comfort in one another's arms at a difficult time in both their lives.[6] Following the initial media revelations, Elizabeth II's private secretary, Sir Alan Lascelles, hastily arranged with the help of Prime Minister Winston Churchill for the RAF veteran to be posted as an air attaché to the British embassy in Brussels, a move widely interpreted by the popular press as a ham-fisted attempt to separate the lovers. But now the *Mirror* came to the princess's rescue, inviting its readers to decide for themselves whether Margaret should be allowed to marry a man whom the newspaper sympathetically described as a heroic 'Battle of Britain pilot', as the 'innocent party in a divorce' and as father to two children over whom he had retained custody from an ex-wife who had already remarried.[7]

The *Mirror*'s poll built on the innovations of its sister paper, the *Sunday Pictorial*, back in 1947 when it canvassed its readers' opinions on the matter of Princess Elizabeth's rumoured engagement to Prince Philip of Greece. As in 1947, the *Mirror* found that its readers supported the royal romance so long as it was a love match, but this time by an overwhelming majority. Whereas members of the public had taken issue with Philip's foreign background, fearing that his marriage to the heiress to the throne might complicate Britain's international relations in the first years of the Cold War, no diplomatic obstacles stood in the way of Margaret and Townsend and, for those readers who responded to the *Mirror*'s poll, the moral questions

---

[6] Warwick, *Princess Margaret*, pp. 182–3.
[7] Bingham, *Family Newspapers?*, pp. 246–7; *Daily Mirror*, 13 July 1953, p. 1.

their relationship raised did not seem to matter much either: out of just over 70,000 responses, more than 68,000 expressed support for the couple.[8]

As *The Family Firm* has made clear, contradictory ideas of self-fulfilment and self-denial became fundamental to the monarchy's public image in the mid 1930s. George and Marina's royal wedding was projected to the public as an event characterized by a more demonstrative form of romance and a new emotional culture which stressed that love and domesticity were key to personal happiness. This emotional culture had extended its reach across society by the end of the Second World War and informed how many respondents to the *Pictorial* poll and the Mass Observation directive on the 1947 royal engagement and wedding identified with Princess Elizabeth's apparent desire to marry for love. Indeed, the widespread belief that a happy home life might make up for the onerous nature of her public duties seems to have won the day; and we know that this narrative was actively promoted by the royal household and the media in an effort to generate support for her choice of Philip.

The underlying tension between self-fulfilment and self-sacrifice that characterized Elizabeth and Philip's royal love story had gathered momentum because of the actions of Edward VIII when he chose to renounce the throne and his duty to his people in order to marry the woman he loved in 1936. The abdication threw into sharp relief not only the increasingly widespread perception that to be royal was to be burdened with heavy responsibilities to the nation and empire, but also that one's emotional desires were constrained by the strict moral code upheld by the Church. While this was fine for Edward's father George V, who, in his last years on the throne, vocally championed the virtues of Christian domesticity and public service in order to unite his subjects around the media image of a dutiful family monarchy, for younger royals whose romantic aspirations lay outside this strict moral formula it was much trickier. George VI's subsequent coronation and reign alongside Queen Elizabeth was characterized by a revived emphasis on constitutionalism and a royal public relations narrative that highlighted the satisfaction the royal family derived from their happy home lives, but which simultaneously stressed that the ostensible burdens of royal public duty worked to circumscribe personal fulfilment. Indeed, this tension was at the heart of the media campaigns waged by stage-managers like Archbishop Cosmo Lang in the lead-up to the king's crowning in May 1937. During the Second World War, the Ministry of Information and the BBC helped to project a narrative of royal suffering in order to generate popular identification with the House of Windsor's leadership on the home front.

---

[8] Bingham, *Family Newspapers?*, p. 247; *Daily Mirror*, 17 July 1953, p. 1.

After 1945 this idea was taken a step further by other loyal disciples like *The Times* journalist Dermot Morrah, who sought to perpetuate the perception that royal life was demanding and unenviable right at the moment when other sections of the media were lending this narrative credibility: the invasive reporting witnessed during Princess Elizabeth and Prince Philip's honeymoon in 1947 was met with outrage from members of the public who identified with the royal couple's desire for privacy.

At a time when modern ideas of self-enrichment were gaining ground throughout Britain, and in particular the belief that personal fulfilment could be achieved through domestic private life, a coterie of courtiers, clerics and journalists therefore popularized the idea that the royal family wanted to enjoy 'ordinary' home lives but that their 'extraordinary' public roles often prevented them from achieving personal fulfilment. This contradictory narrative took on various forms across the period and evoked a potent mixture of empathy and compassion for the House of Windsor from sections of the population, as seen in the many letters, school essays and Mass Observation personal testimonies examined in this book. Indeed, it was a sympathetic kind of emotional identification that characterized many *Mirror* readers' responses to Princess Margaret's romantic dilemma in July 1953.[9] Moreover, echoing the anger that had been levelled at Lang following Edward VIII's abdication almost two decades before, it was the Church of England and its teachings on divorce that bore the brunt of the public criticism which erupted when Margaret and Townsend's relationship came to an end. Two years later, in 1955, following a fleeting reunion after the RAF veteran returned from Belgium and another unparalleled display of frenzied media speculation, the princess finally decided she would not marry him because it would go against her duty, contravening the Christian ideals of marriage, domesticity and self-sacrifice that the family monarchy held so dear.[10]

We have seen that from 1932 to 1953 the crown and Church developed a formidable partnership in the way they expertly orchestrated royal occasions as national events that elevated royal family life as a model for popular emulation. However, by the mid 1950s, British people's views on divorce were rapidly changing and in many ways the public response to the Margaret-Townsend affair seems to have pointed to a deepening disillusionment with the Church's attitude to the sanctity of marriage that would take on fuller form in the early 1960s. This famous decade witnessed

[9] E.g., the sample of readers' letters published by the *Daily Mirror* on 13 July 1953, p. 2. For other interpretations of public opinion, including that of MO, see C. Langhamer, *The English in Love: the Intimate Story of an Emotional Revolution* (Oxford, 2013), pp. 2–3.
[10] Pimlott, *Elizabeth II*, pp. 236–8; Bingham, *Family Newspapers?*, pp. 247–50.

the rise of secular individualism which, although its origins can be located in the interwar years, saw a sudden and irreversible decline in religious observance and church attendance that was matched by a liberalization of Britain's laws and customs in ways that enabled and encouraged new kinds of self-expression and self-fulfilment.[11] At a time when the nation's political, social and cultural life was characterized by a pervasive sense of progress and modernity, the public image of the self-sacrificing family monarchy seemed old fashioned. However, rather than move with the times, it appears the royal household chose to proceed with caution by instead clinging to many of the traditional moral values upon which the monarchy had for so long relied, while only adapting to wider changes when necessary.

This blend of the old and the new was on show in 1960 when Margaret was finally married – but to the celebrity portrait photographer, Antony Armstrong-Jones – as part of a royal wedding that looked and felt much like those of the 1930s and 1940s. In 1934, BBC broadcasters had worked with the Church and royal household to project George and Marina's wedding as a nation-building event in an effort to unite the public around the centrepiece of a royal love story at a time of crisis both at home and abroad. To this end, radio provided listeners with a new kind of access to a royal marriage ceremony and enabled shared emotional participation in a royal family event for the first time. Similarly, against the backdrop of post-war austerity Princess Elizabeth's marriage to Philip Mountbatten was staged in order to brighten hard times and to engender public loyalty to the heiress to the throne through emotional identification with her romantic aspirations. Again, there was notable innovation in 1947 when the king allowed his personal newsreel cameraman to film inside Westminster abbey, providing cinemagoers with memorable scenes of a smiling princess as she walked back down the aisle hand-in-hand with her new husband. Margaret's marriage to Armstrong-Jones built on the templates established by the earlier events, but there were also differences which included the fact that, despite his recently-acquired fame as part of London's bohemian set, the bridegroom was a commoner and had no direct blood ties to the British aristocracy or European royalty – the groups that most young Windsor royals had looked to for spouses since 1918. Most notably of all, however, Margaret and Armstrong-Jones's wedding was the first to be televised to Britain and the rest of the world from the abbey. In keeping with the royal romances of the interwar years, the theme of true love dominated the coverage of the couple's marriage ceremony, which was expertly choreographed by the

[11] C. Brown, *The Death of Christian Britain: Understanding Secularisation 1800–2000* (London, 2009), pp. 6–8.

BBC, royal household and Church in order to provide media audiences with more intimate access to a royal wedding than ever before: it was also the first time television viewers saw inside Buckingham Palace when the newlyweds arrived there for the marriage reception.[12]

In the mould of earlier royal events, including the 1937 coronation and the VE Day celebrations, the media coverage of Margaret's wedding was also characterized by a visual and discursive emphasis on mass participation as communicated through the scenes and sounds of large crowds that gathered in central London, a climactic balcony appearance when the royal family group met with a loud roar of cheering and an emotionally expressive couple who, like the princess's Aunt Marina a quarter of a century before, engaged with the public by smiling and waving to them.[13] These rituals highlighted the popularity of the crown in the years either side of the Second World War and have remained part of the canon of images associated with the House of Windsor into the twenty-first century. These customs have worked symbolically to convey the nation's royalism by conjuring an illusion of intimacy between the monarchy and public and yet they crystallized in the 1930s at a time when Britain's royal democracy seemed threatened by a new wave of totalitarian politics. Indeed, the European fascist regimes, just like the monarchy and its allies, used new kinds of media to create scenes of the 'masses' loyally joined together around the focal point of the nation's leader – be it Adolf Hitler or George V – in order to outwardly communicate the impression that the public supported the status quo.

It might seem strange that this highly-charged imagery has persisted through to the twenty-first century, especially given the fact there has been no existential political, social or economic crisis since 1945 that has required the House of Windsor to adopt such an overt nation-building role as was the case in the years before and during the Second World War. Nevertheless, the monarchy has retained its place at the heart of the British nation's symbolic economy by offering a sense of continuity with past events through regular repetition of the rituals and public performances that became so essential to its existence in the years between 1932 and 1953, a key example being royal weddings, two of which took place in 2018. Indeed, the royal family's importance to ideas of national identity and tradition may even have increased since 1953 in response to the significant transformations of the second half of the twentieth century and first decades of the twenty-first century. Decolonization, immigration, affluence, the liberalization

---

[12] On Margaret and Armstrong-Jones's engagement and wedding, see Warwick, *Princess Margaret*, pp. 225–32.

[13] E.g., 'The Wedding of HRH Princess Margaret and Antony Armstrong-Jones', *British Movietone News*, 9 May 1960.

of the UK's laws and customs and, more recently, the reinvention, for good or ill, of politics and the economy in response to technological and globalizing shifts have changed British culture, society and identities almost beyond recognition – and yet the one major constant has been Elizabeth II's monarchy as the identifiable link with the past that has continued to bring members of the public together.

Given the significant changes of the sixty-five-year period from 1953 to 2018, it is little wonder that the crown has, at times, had to justify its relevance to a more democratic society and people. This is also because, as commentators recorded at the time and as historians have suggested more recently, the years since Elizabeth II's coronation have witnessed the House of Windsor descend into a kind of 'soap opera' in which the dysfunctional elements of the royals' private lives have routinely been brought into sharp focus through media exposés.[14] Indeed, the royal reportage that increasingly emerged after 1953 had two distinctive and contradictory sides to it: on the one hand, it was reverent, fawning and celebrated the domesticity and duty of the monarch and her family; on the other hand, it was aggressive, disrespectful and set on revealing the behaviour of the personalities who made up the royal group in ways that destabilized the idealized narrative. The first signs of this more combative approach between the media and the royals could be detected back in 1947 during Princess Elizabeth and Prince Philip's honeymoon, but it was clearly in action again during the Margaret-Townsend episode and led the newly formed press council to publicly condemn the conduct of newspapers like the *Mirror*.[15]

Unfortunately for Princess Margaret, she remained the lead protagonist in the royal soap opera as it unfolded over the course of the 1960s and 1970s. An increasingly hostile popular press, led by *The Sun* after it was relaunched by the Australian press baron Rupert Murdoch in 1969, reported on her and her husband's extramarital affairs, which led to their separation and eventual divorce in 1978 – the first ever directly involving a member of the House of Windsor, although by no means the last.[16] Shortly after this, Margaret was succeeded in the principal role by Princess Diana who, following her marriage to Charles, prince of Wales, in what was widely feted

---

[14] J. Richards, 'The monarchy and film, 1900–2006', in *The Monarchy and the British Nation 1780 to the Present*, ed. A. Olechnowicz (Cambridge, 2007), pp. 258–79, at pp. 278–9; R. Coward, 'The royals', in *Female Desire*, ed. R. Coward (London, 1984), pp. 161–71, at p. 171; M. Muggeridge, 'Royal Soap Opera', *New Statesman and Nation*, l, 22 Oct. 1955, pp. 499–500.

[15] Bingham, *Family Newspapers?*, p. 247.

[16] Warwick, *Princess Margaret*, pp. 245–59; A. Bingham and M. Conboy, *Tabloid Century: the Popular Press in Britain, 1896 to the Present* (Oxford, 2015), pp. 121–2.

as a true love story in 1981, became the centre of a toxic media frenzy as it became apparent that their relationship was, in fact, doomed. In the later 1980s and early 1990s, journalists claimed that the couple were desperately unhappy, with sensational exposés revealing extramarital affairs, along with the princess's mental health problems and eating disorders.[17] There was also intense media scrutiny of the effect Charles and Diana's failing marriage was having on their sons, Princes William and Harry, until the couple finally petitioned for divorce in 1996 following a direct intervention from the prince's mother, Elizabeth II, who wanted to put an end to a scandal that was rapidly undermining the monarchy's respectability. However, the queen's second son would also file for divorce later that same year after another series of scandalous revelations, meaning three of her four children had now sought annulments, the first coming when her daughter, Princess Anne, divorced her husband after a prolonged separation in 1992.[18]

According to opinion polls, the monarchy's overall popularity in the period from 1953 to 2018 has never really wavered.[19] Indeed, with the steady rise in divorce among the British public since the 1960s, the defining (and dysfunctional) features of the royal family's domestic lives have in some ways continued to mirror those of society at large. Nevertheless, it is perhaps unsurprising that the series of scandals that rocked the monarchy in the 1990s, in particular Diana's famous television interview in 1995 when she talked about the breakdown of her marriage, followed two years later by her sudden death, led to serious questions arising about the future of the crown.[20] When the family monarchy has not worked – that is to say, when it is has failed to uphold the moral values that became so central to its public image in the years between 1932 and 1953 – it has met with public disapproval. It is notable that in the decade from 2008 to 2018 the House of Windsor enjoyed a resurgence in its popularity precisely because it was led by a younger generation of individuals who have enthusiastically promoted Christian domesticity in ways reminiscent of the royal family in the mid twentieth century. The royal household's reorientation of the monarchy's public image around the figures of Princes William and Harry and their home lives has done much to repair a crown that was deeply shaken by the humiliating exposés of the 1980s and 1990s and has helped to focus positive attention on the future of the Windsor dynasty as the reign of Elizabeth II comes to an end.

[17] Bingham and Conboy, *Tabloid Century*, pp. 123–4.
[18] Pimlott, *Elizabeth II*, pp. 548–55.
[19] A. Olechnowicz, '"A jealous hatred": royal popularity and social inequality', in Olechnowicz, *The Monarchy and the British Nation*, pp. 280–314, at pp. 291–2.
[20] Olechnowicz, '"Jealous hatred"', pp. 291–3.

William and Harry's story has also been one of public duty in the face of personal suffering, not only with the loss of their mother but also in their constant (and highly publicized) battle with the press and 'paparazzi' – the belligerent group of photographic news reporters that emerged in the second half of the twentieth century. As we have seen, the royal public relations narrative that highlighted how the intrusive nature of media coverage prevented younger members of the House of Windsor from enjoying fulfilling personal lives caught on at the time of the royal honeymoon in 1947. However, it has remained an integral part of the royal family's approach to the media ever since. The notion that royal public life is burdensome has continued to play a crucial part in the strategy and language developed by courtiers in their attempts to foster public emotional identification with individual royals and the monarchy as an institution. The impression that many members of the public are left with is that royal life (despite its huge range of privileges) is in fact unenviable – that it is a 'rotten job'.[21] Scholars have suggested that it is this perception of undesirability that has been essential to the way the British public have rationalized supporting a royal family and an elite institution that are economically and socially far-removed from their own, often difficult, everyday lives.[22] According to this argument, privilege has come at the price of unrelenting public duties, the prying of reporters into one's personal life and the constant sense of expectation that comes with being a national celebrity from the moment one is born to the moment one dies, whether one likes it or not.

Mass Observation has provided rich insights into the range of public emotions developed and articulated in relation to royal personalities in the years between 1937 and 1953. Most of these emotions seem to have been positive and were regularly rooted in an empathy with the family-centred trials and tribulations of the House of Windsor. Of course, there was dissent and it has been one of the aims of *The Family Firm* to highlight conflicting interpretations of the monarchy's public role that did not align with the media's largely celebratory narrative or the bulk of public opinion that at least outwardly (and as often measured through emotionally charged polls) seems to have held the crown in high regard. When looked at in connection with other kinds of personal testimony, such as letters written to the royal family, Mass Observation has shown that gender has historically shaped the kinds of emotions that have underpinned the para-social relationships developed by men and women with the House of Windsor. Female writers

---

[21] Observation of a fifty-year-old male MO respondent (MOA, TC/14 154-186, M50C, p. 3); see ch. 4.

[22] Olechnowicz, '"Jealous hatred"', pp. 305–7; M. Billig, *Talking of the Royal Family* (London, 1992), pp. 124–5, 140–2.

tended to empathize more readily with the domestic ordeals of the royals, although by the late 1940s young men were also expressing strong feelings in relation to the family monarchy. Meanwhile, school essays have illuminated the way royalist identities were shaped from the earliest stages of life and that boys and girls identified differently with the cast of royal personalities. These personal documents have also shown that the structural properties of different media like photographs, film, radio and television have transformed how readers, listeners and viewers imagined and responded to the royal public image they consumed. In particular, broadcasting created a heightened sense of national participation around radio and television sets, with the temporal simultaneity of the media creating emotional experiences that were highly personal but at the same time collective in nature.

We must not take for granted Mass Observation's efforts to gauge public opinion. It was clear after the fallout of the abdication crisis that public attitudes to the monarchy had often been misrepresented by the press and politicians in order to maintain a misleading vision of a modern British nation that was peaceable and unified but which paid little heed to the opinions of ordinary people. Mass Observation's unique approach to ethnography had precursors in the BBC's attempts to engage with crowds and the newsreel interviews conducted with working-class people in the lead-up to the 1937 coronation. As we have seen, the abdication also encouraged new press-led interventions into public opinion on royal matters via national polls. In this way, then, questions about the monarchy's place in Britain have had a consistently democratizing influence on society, motiving new kinds of investigation that have tried to understand what the public really think of their royal rulers. Unfortunately for historians, Mass Observation wound down its activities in the mid 1950s, the queen's coronation being its last major study, although was relaunched as the 'Mass Observation Project' in 1981 at the time of Charles and Diana's wedding (a major royal family event was again judged an opportune moment to gauge the public's temperament). The Mass Observation Project has undertaken qualitative studies of many royal events from the early 1980s through to the 2018 royal wedding, although there is no Mass Observation evidence for the almost three-decade period that separates Elizabeth II's coronation from the marriage of her first son and heir. These years were not only defined by post-colonial immigration and significant shifts in the cultural, religious and ethnic make-up of the British population, but also by de-industrialization, a resurgence in Celtic nationalism, advances in gender equality and the emergence of a new identity politics that in many ways superseded older class-based loyalties. In the absence of first-hand evidence like Mass Observation personal testimonies, scholars could look to the methods employed by oral historians in order to gauge how public feelings towards the monarchy evolved in this eventful period.[23]

Other histories of the British monarchy also urgently require attention. Analysis of the attitudes and emotions of subjects-cum-citizens towards the royals in the empire and, later, the Commonwealth would complement recent important interventions which have examined how the House of Windsor navigated the reformulation of the imperial state in the wake of two world wars and decolonization. These studies have shown that the monarchy has retained a crucial symbolic role at the centre of a Commonwealth system that now exists only because of the enthusiastic approach that Elizabeth II has adopted to it and, seemingly, the popular respect this has commanded at ground level within the diverse constituent nations of which it is formed.[24] More historical attention could also be devoted to analysing the British monarchy's links to other crowned heads of state in the twentieth century. We hear less and less in the twenty-first century about the royal family's European cousinhood and yet, as this book has shown, the House of Windsor is connected through ties of kinship to many continental monarchies that still exist, most notably the Scandinavian royal dynasties. The idea that the British monarchy's survival instinct caused it to distance itself from other royal houses after 1917 is often repeated, but the royal weddings of the 1930s and 1940s, and the care and trouble George VI later took with the exiled kings and queens of northern Europe and the Balkans during the Second World War, suggest that we should not exaggerate the House of Windsor's insularity in the mid twentieth century. Further analysis of the crown's ties to the old continental order would enhance our understanding of a complex period when global international relations were undergoing rapid change that dramatically altered the way the British saw themselves in relation to the rest of the world.

Writing at the end of 2018, it seems that the family firm is soon destined to pass from one monarch to another: the current heir to the throne, Prince Charles, will probably become King Charles III and, on succeeding his mother, will doubtless aim to leave his mark on the institution of monarchy. And yet one thing will not change. In light of possible constitutional impropriety involving secret lobbying, or 'motivating' as he puts it, of government ministers in his role as prince of Wales on issues close to his

---

[23] For more information on the Mass Observation Project, see <http://www.massobs.org.uk/about/mass-observation-project> [accessed 12 Oct. 2018].

[24] F. Mort, 'On tour with the prince: monarchy, imperial politics and publicity in the prince of Wales's dominion tours 1919–20', *Twentieth Century British Hist.*, xxix (2018), 25–57; P. Murphy, *Monarchy and the End of Empire: the House of Windsor, the British Government, and the Postwar Commonwealth* (Oxford, 2013).

heart like the environment, architecture and wildlife, Charles has with increasing vigour projected an image in which he is cast as a loving father figure to his sons, William and Harry, and, more recently, as a devoted grandfather to a growing brood of child princes and princesses.[25] This image resembles that of the prince's great-grandfather George V, who in his final years on the throne spoke to wireless listeners on Christmas Day to tell them that it was his home life and personal relationships with his children and grandchildren that linked him to his subjects, not only through a shared identification with the individual personalities who made up the House of Windsor, but also through a mutual appreciation of domesticity. Family is symbolically and literally the lifeblood of the crown. Since the mid 1930s, Buckingham Palace's public relations strategy has emphasized that members of the royal family have found it difficult to achieve personal fulfilment in the domestic setting because of their onerous public roles; and this juxtaposition has consistently evoked powerful emotional responses from their subjects and, crucially, adherence to Britain's unique royal democracy. It is clear that the current group of royals and their advisors working behind the scenes understand the appeal the image of the dutiful family monarchy continues to have among the public. One thing thus remains certain and that is the important role the combination of domesticity and duty will play as the House of Windsor continues to adapt to the metamorphoses of the twenty-first century.

[25] 'Prince, Son and Heir: Charles at 70', dir. John Bridcut (Crux Productions Ltd., BBC 1, 8 Nov. 2018).

Bibliography

Aitkin, M., *The Abdication of King Edward VIII* (London, 1966).

Aldgate, T., 'The newsreels, public order, and the projection of Britain', in *Impacts and Influences: Essays on Media Power in the Twentieth Century*, ed. J. Curran, A. Smith and P. Wingate (London, 1987), pp. 145–56.

Aldridge, M., *The Birth of British Television: a History* (Basingstoke, 2012).

Anderson, B., *Imagined Communities: Reflections on the Origin and Spread of Nationalism* (London, 1986).

Anderson, J., 'The tory party at prayer? The Church of England and British politics in the 1950s', *Journal of Church and State*, lviii (2015), 417–40.

Andrews, M., *Domesticating the Airwaves: Broadcasting, Domesticity and Femininity* (London, 2012).

Andrews, M., 'Homes both sides of the microphone: wireless and domestic space in interwar Britain', *Women's History Review*, xxi (2012), 605–21.

Anthony, S., *Public Relations and the Making of Modern Britain: Stephen Tallents and the Birth of a Progressive Media Profession* (Manchester, 2012).

Bagehot, W., *The English Constitution* (London, 1867).

Baldwin, S., *Service of Our Lives: Last Speeches as Prime Minister* (London, 1938).

Ball, S., *Portrait of a Party: the Conservative Party in Britain 1918–1945* (Oxford, 2013).

Barron, H. and C. Langhamer, 'Children, class, and the search for security: writing the future in 1930s Britain', *Twentieth Century British History*, xxviii (2017), 367–89.

— 'Feeling through practice: subjectivity and emotion in children's writing', *Journal of Social History*, li (2017), 101–23.

Baxter, A. B., *Destiny Called to Them* (Oxford, 1939).

Beaken, R., *Cosmo Lang: Archbishop in War and Crisis* (London, 2012).

Beers, L., 'Whose opinion? Changing attitudes towards opinion polling in British politics, 1937–1964', *Twentieth Century British History*, xvii (2006), 177–205.

— *Your Britain: Media and the Making of the Labour Party* (Cambridge, Mass., 2010).

— 'A model MP? Ellen Wilkinson, gender, politics and celebrity culture in interwar Britain', *Cultural and Social History*, x (2013), 231–50.

Berenson, E. and E. Giloi, *Constructing Charisma: Celebrity, Fame and Power in Nineteenth-Century Europe* (Oxford, 2010).

Bergmeier, H., *Hitler's Airwaves: the Inside Story of Nazi Radio Broadcasting and Propaganda Swing* (New Haven, Conn., 1997).

Bernini, S., *Family Life and Individual Welfare in Post-War Europe: Britain and Italy Compared* (Basingstoke, 2007) .

Billig, M., *Talking of the Royal Family* (London, 1992).

Bingham, A., '"An era of domesticity"? Histories of women and gender in interwar Britain', *Cultural and Social History*, i (2004), 225–33.

— *Gender, Modernity and the Popular Press in Inter-War Britain* (Oxford, 2004).

— *Family Newspapers? Sex, Private Life, and the British Popular Press 1918–1978* (Oxford, 2009).

Bingham, A. and M. Conboy, *Tabloid Century: the Popular Press in Britain, 1896 to the Present* (Oxford, 2015).

Birdsall, C., *Nazi Soundscapes: Sound, Technology and Urban Space in Germany, 1933–1945* (Amsterdam, 2012).

Birmingham Feminist History Group, 'Feminism as femininity in the 1950s', *Feminist Review*, iii (1979), 48–65.

Birnbaum, N., 'Monarchy and sociologists: a reply to Professor Shils and Mr Young', *The Sociological Review*, iii (1955), 5–23.

Black, L., 'The impression of affluence: political culture in the 1950s and 1960s', in *An Affluent Society? Britain's Post-War 'Golden Age' Revisited*, ed. L. Black and H. Pemberton (Aldershot, 2004), pp. 85–106.

Bogdanor, V., *The Monarchy and the Constitution* (Oxford, 1995).

Bolitho, H., *Edward VIII: His Life and Reign* (London, 1937).

Borch, C., *The Politics of Crowds: an Alternative History of Sociology* (Cambridge, 2012).

Bottomore, S., '"She's just like my granny! Where's her crown?" Monarchs and movies, 1896–1916', in *Celebrating 1895: the Centenary of Cinema*, ed. J. Fullerton (London, 1998), pp. 172–81.

Bradford, S., *King George VI* (London, 2011).

Bradley, I., *God Save the Queen: the Spiritual Dimension of Monarchy* (London, 2002).

Bradley, L., *Sounds Like London: 100 Years of Black Music in the Capital* (London, 2013).

Braybon, G. and P. Summerfield, *Out of the Cage: Women's Experiences in Two World Wars* (London, 2013).

Brazier, R., 'The monarchy', in *The British Constitution in the Twentieth Century*, ed. V. Bogdanor (Oxford, 2003), pp. 69–98.

Breward, C., *The Culture of Fashion* (Manchester, 1995).

Briggs, A., *The History of Broadcasting in the United Kingdom* (5 vols., Oxford, 1961–95), ii: *The Golden Age of Wireless* (Oxford, 1965).

— *The History of Broadcasting in the United Kingdom* (5 vols., Oxford, 1961–95), iii: *The War of Words, 1939–1945* (Oxford, 1970).

— *The History of Broadcasting in the United Kingdom* (5 vols., Oxford, 1961–95), iv: *Sound and Vision* (Oxford, 1995).

Brown, C. G., *The Death of Christian Britain: Understanding Secularisation 1800–2000* (London, 2009).

Brown, R., '"It's a very wonderful process ...": film and British royalty, 1896–1902', *Court Historian*, viii (2003), 1–22.

Brown, S., 'Cecil Beaton and the iconography of the House of Windsor', *Photography and Culture*, iv (2011), 293–308.

Brunt, R., 'A divine gift to inspire? Popular cultural representations, nationhood and the British monarchy', in *Come on Down? Popular Media Culture in Post-War Britain*, ed. D. Strinati and S. Wagg (London, 1992), pp. 285–301.

— 'The family firm restored: newsreel coverage of the British monarchy, 1936–45', in *Nationalising Femininity: Culture, Sexuality and British Cinema in the Second World War*, ed. C. Gledhill and G. Swanson (Manchester, 1996), pp. 140–51.

Bryant, A., *King George V* (London, 1937).

Buettner, E., *Europe After Empire: Decolonization, Society, and Culture* (Cambridge, 2016).

Bush, B., *Imperialism, Race and Resistance: Africa and Britain, 1919–1945* (London, 1999).

Calder, A., *The People's War: Britain 1939–1945* (London, 1992).

Cannadine, D., 'The context, performance and meaning of ritual: the British monarchy and the "invention of tradition", *c*.1820–1977', in *The Invention of Tradition*, ed. E. Hobsbawm and T. Ranger (Cambridge, 1983), pp. 101–64.

— 'Introduction: divine rites of kings', in *Rituals of Royalty: Power and Ceremonial in Traditional Societies*, ed. D. Cannadine and S. Price (Cambridge, 1987), pp. 1–19.

— 'The last Hanoverian sovereign? Victorian monarchy in historical perspective, 1688–1988', in *The First Modern Society*, ed. A. Beier, D. Cannadine and J. M. Rosenheim (Cambridge, 1989), pp. 127–65.

— *The Decline and Fall of the British Aristocracy* (New Haven, Conn., 1990).

— *History in Our Time* (New Haven, Conn., 1998).

— 'Churchill and the British monarchy', *Transactions of the Royal Historical Society*, xi (2001), 249–72.

— *Ornamentalism: How the British Saw Their Empire* (Oxford, 2002).

— 'From biography to history: writing the modern British monarchy', *Historical Research*, lxxvii (2004), 289–312.

— *George V: the Unexpected King* (London, 2014).

Cardiff, D., 'The serious and the popular: aspects of the evolution of style in radio talk 1928–1939', in *Media Culture and Identity: a Critical Reader*, ed. R. Collins (London, 1986), pp. 228–41.

Ceadel, M., 'The first British referendum: the Peace Ballot, 1934–5', *English Historical Review*, xcv (1980), 810–39.

— *Semi-Detached Idealists: the British Peace Movement and International Relations, 1854–1945* (Oxford, 2000).

Chamberlain, M., 'George Lamming', in *West Indian Intellectuals in Britain*, ed. B. Schwarz (Manchester, 2003), pp. 175–95.

Chambers, C., *Ireland in the Newsreels* (Dublin, 2012).

Chapman, J., 'Cinema, monarchy and the making of heritage: *A Queen is Crowned* (1953)', in *British Historical Cinema: the History, Heritage and Costume Film*, ed. C. Monk and A. Sargeant (London, 2002), pp. 82–91.

Churchill, W. S., *The Second World War: Abridged Edition with an Epilogue on the Years 1945 to 1957* (London, 2002).

Colley, L., *Britons: Forging the Nation, 1707–1837* (London, 1994).

Collins, M., *Modern Love: an Intimate History of Men and Women in Twentieth Century Britain* (London, 2002).

Colls, R., 'The constitution and the English', *History Workshop Journal*, xlvi (1998), 27–128.

Colpus, E., 'The week's good cause: mass culture and cultures of philanthropy at the interwar BBC', *Twentieth Century British History*, xxii (2011), 305–29.

Conekin, B., F. Mort and C. Waters, 'Introduction', in *Moments of Modernity: Reconstructing Britain, 1945–64*, ed. B. Conekin, F. Mort and C. Waters (London, 1999), pp. 1–21.

Connelly, M., *We Can Take It! Britain and the Memory of the Second World War* (London, 2004).

— *Christmas: a History* (London, 2012).

Cooke, C., *The Life of Richard Stafford Cripps* (London, 1957).

Coontz, S., *Marriage, a History: from Obedience to Intimacy or How Love Conquered Marriage* (London, 2005).

Couldry, N., *Media Rituals: a Critical Approach* (London, 2003).

Coward, R., 'The royals', in *Female Desire*, ed. R. Coward (London, 1984), pp. 161–71.

Craig, D. M., 'The crowned republic? Monarchy and anti-monarchy in Britain, 1760–1901', *Historical Journal*, xlvi (2003), 167–85.

Crawford, M., *The Little Princesses* (London, 1993).

Dacre, N., 'The funeral of Diana, princess of Wales', *Court Historian*, viii (2003), 85–90.

Davidoff, L. et al., *The Family Story: Blood, Contract, and Intimacy, 1830–1960* (London, 1999).

Day, J. W., *H.R.H. Princess Marina, Duchess of Kent: the First Authentic Life Story* (London, 1969).

Dayan, D., 'Rituels populistes: public et television aux funerailles de Lady Diana', *Bulletin D'Histoire Politique*, xiv (2005), 89–107.

Dayan, D. and E. Katz, 'Electronic ceremonies: television performs a royal wedding', in *On Signs*, ed. M. Blonsky (Baltimore, 1985), pp. 16–32.

— *Media Events: the Live Broadcasting of History* (Cambridge, Mass., 1992).

— 'Defining media events', in *News: a Reader*, ed. H. Tumber (Oxford, 1999), pp. 49–60.

Dimbleby, R., *Elizabeth: Our Queen* (London, 1975).

Dixon, T., *Weeping Britannia: Portrait of a Nation in Tears* (Oxford, 2015).

Donaldson, F., *Edward VIII* (London, 1974).

Donnelly, M., *Britain in the Second World War* (Oxford, 1999).

Douglas-Home, C., *Dignified and Efficient: the British Monarchy in the Twentieth Century* (Brinksworth, 2000).

Dudley Edwards, R., *Newspapermen: Hugh Cudlipp, Cecil Harmsworth King and the Glory Days of Fleet Street* (London, 2003).

Dyer, R., *Stars* (London, 1998).

— *Heavenly Bodies: Film Stars and Society* (London, 2004).

Easen, S., 'A game women cannot play? Women and British newsreels', in *Yesterday's News: the British Cinema Newsreel Reader*, ed. L. McKernan (London, 2002), pp. 281–9.

Edgerton, D., *Warfare State: Britain, 1920–1970* (Cambridge, 2006).

Edwards, A., *Royal Sisters: Elizabeth and Margaret, 1926–1956* (London, 1990).

Edwards, B., 'Edward VII becomes king', in *The Edwardian Sense: Art, Design and Performance in Britain, 1901–1910*, ed. M. O'Neill and M. Hall (New Haven, Conn., 2010), pp. 23–31.

Ehrman, E., 'Broken traditions: 1930–55', in *The London Look: Fashion From Street to Catwalk*, ed. C. Breward, E. Ehrman and C. Evans (London, 2004), pp. 97–117.

Eley, G., *Nazism as Fascism: Violence, Ideology, and the Ground of Consent in Germany 1930–1945* (New York, 2013).

Ellis, J., *The Duchess of Kent: an Intimate Portrait* (London, 1952).

Ellis, J. S., 'Reconciling the Celt: British national identity, empire, and the 1911 investiture of the prince of Wales', *Journal of British Studies*, xxxvii (1998), 391–418.

— *Investiture: Royal Ceremony and National Identity in Wales, 1911–1969* (Cardiff, 2008).

Ellison, G., *The Authorised Life Story of Princess Marina* (London, 1934).

Ellul, J., *Propaganda: the Formation of Men's Attitudes* (New York, 1971).

Encyclopaedia of Recorded Sound, ed. F. Hoffmann (2 vols., New York and London, 2005).

Evans, T., 'The other woman and her child: extra-marital affairs and illegitimacy in twentieth-century Britain', *Women's History Review*, xx (2011), 47–65.

Evans, T. and P. Thane, 'Lone mothers', *Women's History Review*, xx (2011), 3–9.

Field, G. G., *Blood, Sweat, and Toil: Remaking the British Working Class, 1939–1945* (Oxford, 2011).

Fielding, S., P. Thompson and N. Tiratsoo, *England Arise! The Labour Party and Popular Politics in 1940s Britain* (Manchester, 1995).

Finch, J. and P. Summerfield, 'Social reconstruction and the emergence of companionate marriage, 1945–1959', in *Marriage, Domestic Life and Social Change: Writings for Jacqueline Burgoyne*, ed. D. Clark (London, 1991), pp. 7–32.

Fleming, T., *Voices Out of the Air: Royal Christmas Day Broadcasts, 1932–1981* (London, 1981).

Ford, C. and B. Harrison, *A Hundred Years Ago* (London, 1994).

Fox, J., 'Winston Churchill and the "Men of Destiny": leadership and the role of the prime minister in wartime feature films', in *Making Reputations: Power, Persuasion and the Individual in Modern British Politics*, ed. R. Toye and J. V. Gottlieb (London, 2005), pp. 92–108.

— 'Careless talk: tensions within British domestic propaganda during the Second World War', *Journal of British Studies*, li (2012), 936–66.

— 'The propaganda war', in *The Cambridge History of the Second World War* (3 vols., Cambridge, 2015), ii: *Politics and Ideology*, ed. R. J. B. Bosworth and J. A. Maiolo, pp. 91–116.

Francis, M., 'The domestication of the male? Recent research on nineteenth- and twentieth-century British masculinity', *Historical Journal*, xlv (2002), 637–52.

— 'Tears, tantrums, and bared teeth: the emotional economy of three Conservative prime ministers, 1951–1963', *Journal of British Studies*, xli (2002), 354–87.

— 'Cecil Beaton's romantic toryism and the symbolic economy of wartime Britain', *Journal of British Studies*, xlv (2006), 90–117.

— *The Flyer: British Culture and the Royal Air Force 1939–1945* (Oxford, 2008).

Fujitani, T., *Splendid Monarchy: Power and Pageantry in Modern Japan* (London, 1996).

Gardiner, J., *The Thirties: an Intimate History* (London, 2011).

Geertz, C., *The Interpretation of Cultures* (New York, 1973).

Giles, D., *Illusions of Immortality: a Psychology of Fame and Celebrity* (Basingstoke, 2000).

Giles, J., *The Parlour and the Suburb: Domestic Identities, Class, Femininity and Identity* (Oxford, 2004).

Gore, J., 'Clive Wigram', in *Royal Lives: Portraits of the Past Royals by Those in the Know*, ed. F. Prochaska (Oxford, 2002), pp. 557–9.

Gorer, G., *Exploring English Character* (London, 1955).

Gorman, J. T., *George VI: King and Emperor* (London, 1937).

Gottlieb, J. V., *'Guilty Women', Foreign Policy, and Appeasement in Inter-War Britain* (Basingstoke, 2015).

Grandy, C., 'Paying for love: women's work and love in popular film in interwar Britain', *Journal of the History of Sexuality*, xix (2010), 483–507.

— *Heroes and Happy Endings: Class, Gender, and Nation in Popular Film and Fiction in Interwar Britain* (Manchester, 2014).

Graves, R. and A. Hodge, *The Long Week-End: a Social History of Great Britain 1918–1939* (London, 1940).

Green, M., *Children of the Sun: a Narrative of 'Decadence' in England after 1918* (London, 1977).

Greenhalgh, J., '"Till we hear the last all clear": gender and the presentation of self in young girls' writing about the bombing of Hull during the Second World War', *Gender and History*, xxvi (2014), 167–83.

Grimley, M., *Citizenship, Community and the Church of England: Liberal Anglican Theories of the State Between the Wars* (Oxford, 2004).

— 'The religion of Englishness: puritanism, providentialism, and "national character", 1918–1945', *Journal of British Studies*, xlvi (2007), 884–906.

Gunning, T., 'Reproducing royalty: filming the coronation of Edward VII', in *The Edwardian Sense: Art, Design and Performance in Britain, 1901–1910*, ed. M. O'Neill and M. Hall (New Haven, Conn., 2010), pp. 15–22.

Hajkowski, T., *The BBC and National Identity in Britain, 1922–53* (Manchester, 2010).

Hammerton, E. and D. Cannadine, 'Conflict and consensus on a ceremonial occasion: the diamond jubilee in Cambridge in 1897', *Historical Journal*, xxiv (1981), 111–46.

Hampton, M., *Visions of the Press in Britain* (Chicago, Ill., 2004).

Harold Nicolson: Diaries and Letters, ed. N. Nicolson (3 vols., London 1962–8), ii: *the War Years 1939–45* (London, 1967).

Harold Nicolson: Diaries and Letters, ed. N. Nicolson (3 vols., London 1962–8), iii: *the Later Years 1945–62* (London, 1968).

Harper, S., 'The years of total war: propaganda and entertainment', in *Nationalising Femininity: Culture, Sexuality and British Cinema in the Second World War*, ed. C. Gledhill and G. Swanson (Manchester, 1996), pp. 193–212.

Harper, S. and V. Porter, *British Cinema of the 1950s: the Decline of Deference* (Oxford, 2007).

Harris, K., *The Queen* (London, 1994).

Harris, L. M., *Long to Reign Over Us? The Status of the Royal Family in the Sixties* (London, 1966).

Harrison, B. H., *Peaceable Kingdom: Stability and Change in Modern Britain* (Oxford, 1982).

— *The Transformation of British Politics, 1860–1995* (Oxford, 1996).

— *Seeking a Role: the United Kingdom, 1951–1970* (Oxford, 2011).

Harrisson, T., 'What is public opinion?', *Political Quarterly*, xi (1940), 368–83.

— *Living Through the Blitz* (London, 1978).

Hennessy, P., *The Hidden Wiring: Unearthing the British Constitution* (London, 1995).

Hiley, N., 'The candid camera of the Edwardian tabloids', *History Today*, xliii (1993), 16–22.

Hiley, N. and L. McKernan, 'Reconstructing the news: British newsreel documentation and the British universities newsreel project', *Film History*, xiii (2001), 185–99.

Hilmes, M., *Radio Voices: American Broadcasting, 1922–1952* (Minneapolis, Minn., 1997).

Hinton, J., *Nine Wartime Lives: Mass-Observation and the Making of the Modern Self* (Oxford, 2010).

— *The Mass Observers: a History, 1937–1949* (Oxford, 2013).

— 'Self-reflections in the mass', *History Workshop Journal*, lxxv (2013), 251–9 .

Holman, V., 'Carefully concealed connections: the Ministry of Information and British publishing, 1939–1946', *Book History*, viii (2005), 197–226.

Hopkins, H., *The New Look: a Social History of the Forties and Fifties in Britain* (London, 1963).

Houlbrook, M., '"A pin to see the peepshow": culture, fiction and selfhood in Edith Thompson's Letters, 1921–1922', *Past & Present*, ccvii (2010), 215–49.

— *Prince of Tricksters: the Incredible True Story of Netley Lucas, Gentleman Crook* (Chicago, Ill., 2016).

Howell, G., *In Vogue: Sixty Years of Celebrities and Fashion from British Vogue* (Harmondsworth, 1978).

Hubble, N., *Mass Observation and Everyday Life: Culture, History, Theory* (Basingstoke, 2006).

Hucker, D., *Public Opinion and the End of Appeasement in Britain and France* (Farnham, 2011).

Hulbert, J., 'Right-wing propaganda or reporting history?: the newsreels and the Suez crisis of 1956', *Film History*, xiv (2002), 261–81.

Inglis, F., *A Short History of Celebrity* (Oxford, 2010).

Jackson, K., *George Newnes and the New Journalism in Britain, 1880–1910: Culture and Profit* (London and New York, 2016).

James, R. R., *A Spirit Undaunted: the Political Role of George VI* (London, 1998).

Jeffery, K., 'Crown, communication and the colonial post: stamps, the monarchy and the British empire', *Journal of Imperial and Commonwealth History*, xxxiv (2006), 45–70.

Jenkyns, R., *Westminster Abbey: a Thousand Years of National Pageantry* (London, 2011).

Johnes, M., *Christmas and the British: a Modern History* (London, 2016).

Jones, E., 'The psychology of constitutional monarchy', in E. Jones, *Essays in Applied Psychoanalysis*, i (London, 1951), 227–33.

Jones, H., 'The nature of kingship in First World War Britain', in *The Windsor Dynasty 1910 to the Present: 'Long to Reign Over Us'?*, ed. M. Glencross, J. Rowbotham and M. D. Kandiah (Basingstoke, 2016), pp. 195–216.

— 'A prince in the trenches? Edward VIII and the First World War', in *Sons and Heirs: Succession and Political Culture in Nineteenth-Century Europe*, ed. F. L. Müller and H. Mehrkens (Basingstoke, 2016), pp. 229–46.

Jones, M., '"The surest safeguard of peace": Technology, navy and the nation in boys' papers, c.1905–1907', in *The Dreadnought and the Edwardian Age*, ed. R. J. Blyth, A. Lambert and J. Rüger (Farnham, 2011), pp. 109–31.

Jonsson, S., *Crowds and Democracy: the Idea and Images of the Masses from Revolution to Fascism* (New York, 2013).

Kandiah, M. D. et al., 'The ultimate Windsor ceremonials: coronations and investitures', in *The Windsor Dynasty 1910 to the Present: 'Long to Reign Over Us'?*, ed. M. Glencross, J. Rowbotham and M. D. Kandiah (Basingstoke, 2016), pp. 59–86.

Kaul, C., *Reporting the Raj: the British Press and India, c. 1880–1922* (Manchester, 2003).

— 'Monarchical display and the politics of empire: princes of Wales and India, 1870–1920s', *Twentieth Century British History*, xvii (2006), 464–88.

Kelley, K., *The Royals* (New York, 2008).

Kent, S. K., *Gender and Power in Britain, 1640–1990* (London, 1999).

— *Queen Victoria: Gender and Empire* (Oxford, 2016).

King George's Jubilee Trust, *Official Programme of the Jubilee Procession* (London, 1935).

— *The Coronation of Their Majesties King George VI & Queen Elizabeth: Official Souvenir Programme* (London, 1937).

— *The Royal Family in Wartime: the Illustrated Story of the activities of the Royal Family in the Service of People and Empire* (London, 1945).

— *The Wedding of Her Royal Highness Princess Elizabeth and Lieutenant Philip Mountbatten* (London, 1947).

King, L., *Family Men: Fatherhood and Masculinity in Britain, 1914–1960* (Oxford, 2015).

King, S., *Princess Marina: Her Life and Times* (London, 1969).

King's Counsellor: Abdication and War: the Diaries of Sir Alan Lascelles, ed. D. Hart-Davis (London, 2006).

Kirkham, P., 'Fashioning the feminine: dress, appearance and femininity in wartime Britain', in *Nationalising Femininity: Culture, Sexuality and British Cinema in the Second World War*, ed. C. Gledhill and G. Swanson (Manchester, 1996), pp. 152–74.

Kuhn, A., 'Cinema culture and femininity in the 1930s', in *Nationalising Femininity: Culture, Sexuality and British Cinema in the Second World War*, ed. C. Gledhill and G. Swanson (Manchester, 1996), pp. 177–92.

— *Family Secrets: Acts of Memory and Imagination* (London, 2002).

— 'Memory texts and memory work: performances of memory in and with visual media', *Memory Studies*, xx (2010), 1–16.

Kushner, T., *We Europeans? Mass-Observation, 'Race' and British Identity in Twentieth-Century Britain* (Oxford, 2004).

Kynaston, D., *Austerity Britain: 1945–51* (London, 2008).

— *Family Britain: 1951–57* (London, 2010).

Lacey, K., *Feminine Frequencies: Gender, German Radio, and the Public Sphere 1923–1945* (Michigan, 1996).

Lacey, R., *Majesty: Elizabeth II and the House of Windsor* (London, 1979).

— 'Made for the media: the twentieth-century investitures of the prince of Wales', *Court Historian*, viii (2003), 31–40.

Langhamer, C., 'The meanings of home in postwar Britain', *Journal of Contemporary History*, xl (2005), 341–62.

— 'Love and courtship in mid-twentieth-century England', *Historical Journal*, l (2007), 173–96.

— 'Love, selfhood and authenticity in post-war Britain', *Cultural and Social History*, ix (2012), 277–97.

— *The English in Love: the Intimate Story of an Emotional Revolution* (Oxford, 2013).

Lawrence, J., 'The transformation of British public politics after the First World War', *Past & Present*, cxc (2006), 185–216.

— *Electing Our Masters: the Hustings in British Politics from Hogarth to Blair* (Oxford, 2009).

LeMahieu, D. L., *A Culture for Democracy: Mass Communication and the Cultivated Mind in Britain in Between the Wars* (Oxford, 1998).

Lewis, J., 'Marriage', in *Women in Twentieth-Century Britain*, ed. I. Zweiniger-Bargielowska (Harlow, 2001), pp. 69–85.

Light, A., *Forever England: Femininity, Literature and Conservatism Between the Wars* (London, 1991).

Linkof, R., '"The photographic attack on His Royal Highness": the prince of Wales, Wallis Simpson and the prehistory of the paparazzi', *Photography and Culture*, iv (2011), 277–92.

Loughlin, J., 'Crown, spectacle and identity: the British monarchy and Ireland under the Union, 1800–1922', in *The Monarchy and the British Nation, 1780 to the Present*, ed. A. Olechnowicz (Cambridge, 2007), pp. 108–37.

Loviglio, J., 'Vox pop: network radio and the voice of the people', in *Radio Reader: Essays in the Cultural History of Radio*, ed. M. Hilmes and J. Loviglio (New York, 2002), pp. 89–111.

— *Radio's Intimate Public: Network Broadcasting and Mass-Mediated Democracy* (London, 2005).

Lowe, R., 'The Second World War, consensus, and the foundation of the welfare state', *Twentieth Century British History*, i (1990), 152–82.

Lüdtke, A., 'Love of state – affection for authority: politics of mass participation in twentieth century European contexts', in *New Dangerous Liaisons: Discourses on Europe and Love in the Twentieth Century*, ed. L. Passerini, L. Ellena and A. C. T. Geppert (New York, 2010), pp. 58–74.

McCarthy, H., *The British People and the League of Nations: Democracy, Citizenship and Internationalism, c.1918–45* (Manchester, 2011).

—— 'Whose democracy? Historians of British political culture between the wars', *Historical Journal*, lv (2012), 221–38.

McCarthy, H. and P. Thane, 'The politics of association in industrial society', *Twentieth Century British History*, xxii (2011), 217–29.

McDowell, C., *A Hundred Years of Royal Style* (London, 1985).

McGuigan, J., 'British identity and the people's princess', *Sociological Review*, xlviii (2001), 1–18.

Mackay, R., *Half the Battle: Civilian Morale in Britain during the Second World War* (Manchester, 2002).

Mackenzie, C., *The Windsor Tapestry: Being a Study of the Life, Heritage and Abdication of H.R.H. the Duke of Windsor, K.G.* (London, 1938).

McKernan, L., 'The finest cinema performers we possess: British royalty and the newsreels, 1910–37', *Court Historian*, viii (2003), 59–71.

—— '"The modern elixir of life": Kinemacolor, royalty and the Delhi durbar', *Film History*, xxi (2009), 122–36.

—— 'The newsreel audience', in *Researching Newsreels: Local, National, and Transnational Case Studies*, ed. C. Chambers, M. Jönsson and R. Vande Winkel (Basingstoke, 2018), pp. 35–50.

McKibbin, R., 'Class and conventional wisdom: the Conservative party and the "public" in inter-war Britain', in R. McKibbin, *The Ideologies of Class: Social Relations in Britain 1880–1950* (Oxford, 1990), pp. 259–93.

—— *Classes and Cultures: England 1918–1951* (Oxford, 1998).

—— 'Introduction', in Marie Stopes, *Married Love*, ed. R. McKibbin (Oxford, 2004), pp. vii–li.

—— *Parties and People: England 1914–51* (Oxford, 2010).

Maclagan, M., 'Alan Frederick Lascelles', in *Royal Lives: Portraits of the Past Royals by Those in the Know*, ed. F. Prochaska (Oxford, 2002), pp. 570–2.

McLaine, I., *Ministry of Morale: Home Front Morale and the Ministry of Information in World War II* (London, 1979).

McLean, R., 'Kaiser Wilhelm II and the British royal family: Anglo-German dynastic relations in political context, 1890–1914', *History*, lxxxvi (2001), 478–502.

Macmillan, W. M., *Warning from the West Indies: a Tract for Africa and the Empire* (London, 1936).

Mandler, P., *The English National Character: the History of an Idea from Edmund Burke to Tony Blair* (London, 2006).

Marriot, S., 'The BBC, ITN and the funeral of Princess Diana', *Media History*, xiii (2007), 93–110.

Marshall, P. D., 'Intimately intertwined in the most public way: celebrity and journalism', in *The Celebrity Culture Reader*, ed. P. D. Marshall (London and New York, 2006), pp. 315–23.

Martin, K., *The Magic of Monarchy* (London, 1937).

— *New Statesman Pamphlet: Fascism, Democracy and the Press* (London, 1938).

Mass Observation, *May the Twelfth: Mass-Observation Day Surveys 1937, by Over Two Hundred Observers*, ed. H. Jennings et al. (London, 1937, 2nd edn., 1987).

— *Puzzled People: a Study in Popular Attitudes to Religion, Ethics, Progress and Politics in a London Borough* (London, 1947).

Matt, S. J., 'Current emotion research in history: or, doing history from the inside out', *Emotion Review*, iii (2011), 117–24.

Mayhall, L. N., 'The prince of Wales *versus* Clark Gable: anglophone celebrity and citizenship between the wars', *Cultural and Social History*, iv (2007), 529–43.

Melman, B., *Women and the Popular Imagination in the Twenties: Flappers and Nymphs* (Basingstoke, 1988).

Mirzoeff, N., *The Visual Culture Reader* (London, 2002).

Mole, T., *Byron's Romantic Celebrity: Industrial Culture and the Hermeneutic of Intimacy* (Basingstoke, 2007).

Moran, J., *Armchair Nation: an Intimate History of Britain in Front of the TV* (London, 2013).

— 'Vox populi?: the recorded voice and twentieth-century British history', *Twentieth Century British History*, xxv (2014), 461–83.

Morash, C., *A History of the Media in Ireland* (Cambridge, 2010).

Morgan, K. O., *Britain since 1945: the People's Peace* (Oxford, 2001).

— 'The Labour party and British republicanism', *E-rea: Revue* électronique *d'études sur le monde anglophone*, i (2003) <https://journals.openedition.org/erea/347> [accessed 12 Oct. 2018].

Morgan, S., 'Celebrity: academic "pseudo-event" or a useful concept for historians?', *Cultural and Social History*, viii (2011), 95–114.

Morrah, D., *Princess Elizabeth: the Illustrated Story of Twenty-one Years in the Life of the Heir Presumptive* (London, 1947).

— *The Work of the Queen* (London, 1958).

Mort, F., *Capital Affairs: London and the Making of the Permissive Society* (New Haven, Conn., 2010).

— 'Love in a cold climate: letters, public opinion and monarchy in the 1936 abdication crisis', *Twentieth Century British History*, xxv (2014), 30–62.

— 'On tour with the prince: monarchy: imperial politics and publicity in the prince of Wales's dominion tours 1919–20', *Twentieth Century British History*, xxix (2018), 25–57.

— 'Safe for democracy: constitutional politics, popular spectacle, and the British monarchy 1910–1914', *Journal of British Studies*, lviii (2019), 1–33.

Mullen, R., 'The last marriage of a prince of Wales, 1863', *History Today*, xxxi (1981), 10–14.

Murphy, P., *Monarchy and the End of Empire: the House of Windsor, the British Government, and the Postwar Commonwealth* (Oxford, 2013).

Nairn, T., *The Enchanted Glass: Britain and its Monarchy* (London, 1988).

Nicholas, S., 'The construction of a national identity: Stanley Baldwin, "Englishness" and the mass media in inter-war Britain', in *The Conservatives and British Society, 1880–1990*, ed. M. Francis and I. Zweiniger-Bargielowska (Cardiff, 1996), pp. 127–46.

— *The Echo of War: Home Front Propaganda and the Wartime BBC, 1939–45* (Manchester, 1996).

— 'Media history or media histories?', *Media History*, xviii (2012), 379–94.

Nicolson, H., *King George the Fifth: His Life and Reign* (London, 1952).

Nixon, S., *Hard Sell: Advertising, Affluence and Transatlantic Relations, c.1951–69* (Manchester, 2013).

— 'Life in the kitchen: television advertising, the housewife and domestic modernity in Britain, 1955–1969', *Contemporary British History*, xxxi (2017), 69–90.

Olechnowicz, A., '"A jealous hatred": royal popularity and social inequality', in *The Monarchy and the British Nation 1780 to the Present*, ed. A. Olechnowicz (Cambridge, 2007), pp. 280–314.

— 'Introduction: historians and the study of anti-fascism', in *Varieties of Anti-Fascism: Britain in the Inter-War Period*, ed. N. Copsey and A. Olechnowicz (Basingstoke, 2010), pp. 1–27.

— 'Britain's "quasi-magical" monarchy in the mid-twentieth century?', in *Classes, Cultures and Politics: Essays on British History for Ross McKibbin*, ed. C. V. J. Griffiths, J. J. Nott and W. Whyte (Oxford, 2011), pp. 70–84.

— 'Historians and the modern British monarchy', in *The Monarchy and the British Nation 1780 to the Present*, ed. A. Olechnowicz (Cambridge, 2007), pp. 6–44.

Örnebring, H., 'Revisiting the coronation: a critical perspective on the coronation of Queen Elizabeth II in 1953', *Nordicom Review*, xxv (2004), 175–95.

— 'Writing the history of television audiences: the coronation in the Mass-Observation archive', in *Re-viewing Television History: Critical Issues in Television Historiography*, ed. H. Wheatley (London, 2008), pp. 170–83.

Orr, C. C., 'The feminization of the monarchy, 1780–1910: royal masculinity and female empowerment', in *The Monarchy and the British Nation 1780 to the Present*, ed. A. Olechnowicz (Cambridge, 2007), pp. 76–107.

Overy, R., *The Morbid Age: Britain and the Crisis of Civilization, 1919–1939* (London, 2010).

Owens, E., 'The changing media representation of T. E. Lawrence and celebrity culture in Britain, 1919–1935', *Cultural and Social History*, xii (2015), 465–88.

Oxford Dictionary of National Biography (60 vols., Oxford 2004) <http://www.oxforddnb.com>.

J. Parry, 'Whig monarchy, whig nation: crown politics and representativeness, 1800–2000', in *The Monarchy and the British Nation 1780 to the Present*, ed. A. Olechnowicz (Cambridge, 2007), pp. 47–75.

Passerini, L., *Europe in Love, Love in Europe: Imagination and Politics in Britain Between the Wars* (London, 1999).

Paulmann, J., 'Searching for a "royal international": the mechanics of monarchical relations in nineteenth-century Europe', in *The Mechanics of Internationalism: Culture, Society and Politics from the 1840s to the First World War*, ed. M. H. Geyer and J. Paulmann (Oxford, 2001), pp. 145–76.

Perry, J., 'Christmas as Nazi holiday: colonising the Christmas mood', in *Life and Times in Nazi Germany*, ed. L. Pine (London, 2016), pp. 263–89.

Pickett, L., et al. *The War of the Windsors: a Century of Unconstitutional Monarchy* (Edinburgh, 2002).

Pimlott, B., *Labour and the Left in the 1930s* (Cambridge, 1977).

—— *The Queen: Elizabeth II and the Monarchy* (London, 2002).

Plamper, J., *The Stalin Cult: a Study in the Alchemy of Power* (London, 2012).

—— *The History of Emotions: an Introduction* (Oxford, 2015).

Plunkett, J., 'A media monarchy? Queen Victoria and the radical press, 1837–1901', *Media History*, ix (2003), 3–18.

—— *Queen Victoria: First Media Monarch* (Oxford, 2003).

Pocock, D., 'Afterword', in Mass Observation, *May the Twelfth: Mass-Observation Day Surveys 1937, by Over Two Hundred Observers* (London, 1987), pp. 415–23.

Ponce de Leon, C. L., *Self-Exposure: Human-Interest Journalism and the Emergence of Celebrity in America, 1890–1940* (London, 2002).

Pope-Hennessy, J., *Queen Mary, 1867–1953* (London, 1959).

Porter, B., *The Absent-Minded Imperialists: Empire, Society, and Culture in Britain* (Oxford, 2004).

Potter, S., 'The BBC, the CBC, and the 1939 royal tour of Canada', *Cultural and Social History*, iii (2006), 424–44.

—— *Broadcasting Empire: the BBC and the British World, 1922–1970* (Oxford, 2012).

Prochaska, F., *Royal Bounty: the Making of a Welfare Monarchy* (New Haven, Conn., 1995).

—— 'George V and republicanism, 1917–1919', *Twentieth Century British History*, x (1999), 27–51.

—— 'Wigram, Clive, first Baron Wigram', in *Oxford Dictionary of National Biography*, doi.org/10.1093/ref:odnb/36890 [accessed 12 Oct. 2018].

Pronay, N., 'The newsreels: the illusion of actuality', in *The Historian and Film*, ed. P. Smith (Cambridge, 1976), pp. 95–119.

Pugh, M., *We Danced All Night: a Social History of Britain Between the Wars* (London, 2009).

Reddy, W. M., *The Navigation of Feeling: a Framework for the History of Emotions* (Cambridge, 2001).

— 'The rule of love: the history of Western romantic love in comparative perspective', in *New Dangerous Liaisons: Discourses on Europe and Love in the Twentieth Century*, ed. L. Passerini, L. Ellena and A. C. T. Geppert (Oxford, 2010), pp. 33– 57.

Reed, D., 'What a lovely frock: royal weddings and the illustrated press in the pre-television age', *Court Historian*, viii (2003), 41–50.

Reinermann, L., 'Fleet Street and the Kaiser: British public opinion and Wilhelm II', *German History*, xxvi (2008), 469–85.

Richards, J., 'Imperial images: the British empire and monarchy on film', *Cultures*, ii (1974), 79–114.

— 'The coronation of Queen Elizabeth II and film', *Court Historian*, ix (2004), 69–79.

— 'The monarchy and film, 1900–2006', in *The Monarchy and the British Nation 1780 to the Present*, ed. A. Olechnowicz (Cambridge, 2007), pp. 258–79.

— *The Age of the Dream Palace: Cinema and Society in 1930s Britain* (London, 2010).

Richards, J. and D. Sheridan, *Mass-Observation at the Movies* (London, 1987).

Rieger, B., '"Fast couples": technology, gender and modernity in Britain and Germany during the nineteen-thirties', *Historical Research*, lxxvi (2003), 364–88.

Rieger, B. and M. Daunton, 'Introduction', in *Meanings of Modernity: Britain from the Late Victorian Era to World War II*, ed. B. Rieger and M. Daunton (Oxford, 2001), pp. 1–21.

Ring, A., *The Story of Princess Elizabeth: Told with the Sanction of her Parents* (London, 1930).

Roby, K., *The King the Press and the People: a Study of Edward VII* (London, 1975).

Roper, M., 'Slipping out of view: subjectivity and emotion in gender history', *History Workshop Journal*, lix (2005), 57–72.

Rose, K., *King George V* (London, 1983).

Rose, N., *Governing the Soul: the Shaping of the Private Self* (London, 1999).

Rose, S. O., *Which People's War? National Identity and Citizenship in Britain 1939–1945* (Oxford, 2003).

Rosenwein, B. H., 'Problems and methods in the history of emotions', *Passions in Context*, i (2010), 1–32.

— *Generations of Feeling: a History of Emotions, 600–1700* (Cambridge, 2016).

Rüger, J., *The Great Naval Game: Britain and Germany in the Age of Empire* (Cambridge, 2007).

Scannell, P. and D. Cardiff, *A Social History of British Broadcasting*, i. *1922–39: Serving the Nation* (Oxford, 1991).

Schafer, R. M., 'Acoustic space', in *Dwelling, Place and Environment: Towards a Phenomenology of Person and World*, ed. D. Seamon and R. Mugerauer (New York, 1989), pp. 87–99.

Schickel, R., *Intimate Strangers: the Cult of Celebrity in America* (Chicago, Ill., 2000).

Schnapp, J., 'The mass panorama', *Modernism/Modernity*, ix (2002), 243–81.

Schwarz, B., 'The language of constitutionalism: Baldwinite Conservatism', in *Formations of Nation and People*, ed. Formations Editorial Collective (London, 1984), pp. 1–18.

Schwarzenbach, A., 'Royal photographs: emotions for the people', *Contemporary European History*, xiii (2004), 255–80.

— 'Love, marriage and divorce: American and European reactions to the abdication of Edward', in *New Dangerous Liaisons: Discourses on Europe and Love in the Twentieth Century*, ed. L. Passerini, L. Ellena and A. C. T. Geppert (New York, 2010), pp. 137–57.

Seaton, J., 'Broadcasting and the blitz', in *Power without Responsibility: the Press, Broadcasting and New Media in Britain*, ed. J. Curran and J. Seaton (London, 2009), pp. 120–42.

Shapira, M., *The War Inside: Psychoanalysis, Total War, and the Making of the Democratic Self in Postwar Britain* (Cambridge, 2013).

Shawcross, W., *Queen Elizabeth, the Queen Mother: the Official Biography* (Basingstoke, 2009).

— *Counting One's Blessings: the Selected Letters of Queen Elizabeth The Queen Mother* (Basingstoke, 2012) .

Sheridan, D., 'Writing to the archive: Mass-Observation as autobiography', *Sociology*, xxvii (1993), 27–40.

Shils, E. and M. Young, 'The meaning of the coronation', *Sociological Review*, i (1953), 63–81.

Smith, H. L., 'The effect of the war on the status of women', in *War and Social Change: British Society in the Second World War*, ed. H. L. Smith (Manchester, 1986), pp. 208–29.

Smith, T., '"Almost pathetic … but also very glorious": the consumer spectacle of the diamond jubilee', *Social History*, xxix (1996), 333–56.

Stedman Jones, G., 'The "Cockney" and the nation', in *Metropolis: Histories and Representations since 1800*, ed. D. Feldman and G. Stedman Jones (London, 1989), pp. 272–324.

Steedman, C., *The Tidy House: Little Girls Writing* (London, 1982).

Strasdin, K., 'Empire dressing: the design and realization of Queen Alexandra's coronation gown', *Journal of Design History*, xxv (2012), 155–70.

Summerfield, P., 'Mass-Observation: social research or social movement?', *Journal of Contemporary History*, xx (1985), 439–52.

— *Reconstructing Women's Wartime Lives: Discourse and Subjectivity in Oral Histories of the Second World War* (Manchester, 1998).

— 'Women in Britain since 1945: companionate marriage and the double burden', in *Understanding Post-War British Society*, ed. J. Obelkevich and P. Catterall (London, 2002), pp. 58–72.

— 'Culture and composure: creating narratives of the gendered self in oral history interviews', *Cultural and Social History*, i (2004), 65–93.

— *Women Workers in the Second World War: Production and Patriarchy in Conflict* (London, 2013).

— *Histories of the Self: Personal Narratives and Historical Practice* (London, 2019).

Szreter, S. and Fisher, K., *Sex Before the Sexual Revolution: Intimate Life in England, 1918–1963* (Cambridge, 2010).

Taylor, A., 'Speaking to democracy: the Conservative party and mass opinion from the 1920s to the 1950s', in *Mass Conservatism: the Conservatives and the Public since the 1880s* (London, 2002), pp. 78–99.

Taylor, A. J. P., *English History 1914–1945* (Oxford, 1965).

Taylor, D. J., *Bright Young People: the Rise and Fall of a Generation: 1918–1940* (London, 2007).

Taylor, M., 'Introduction', in *Walter Bagehot: the English Constitution*, ed. M. Taylor (Oxford, 2001), pp. vii–xxx.

Thamer, H.-U., 'The orchestration of the national community: the Nuremberg party rallies of the NSDAP', in *Fascism and Theatre: Comparative Studies on the Aesthetics and Politics of Performance in Europe, 1925–1945*, ed. G. Berghaus (Oxford, 1996), pp. 172–90.

Thane, P., 'Unmarried motherhood in twentieth-century England', *Women's History Review*, xx (2011), 11–29.

— 'The impact of mass democracy on British political culture, 1918–1939', in *The Aftermath of Suffrage: Women, Gender, and Politics in Britain, 1918–1945*, ed. J. Gottlieb and R. Toye (Basingstoke, 2013), pp. 70–86.

Thane P. and T. Evans, *Sinners? Scroungers? Saints? Unmarried Motherhood in Twentieth-Century England* (Oxford, 2012).

Thomas, J., 'Beneath the mourning veil: Mass-Observation and the death of Diana' <http://www.massobs.org.uk/images/occasional_papers/no12_thomas.pdf> [accessed 12 Oct. 2018].

Thompson, D., *State Control in Fascist Italy: Culture and Conformity, 1925–43* (Manchester, 1991).

Thompson, J., *British Political Culture and the Idea of 'Public Opinion', 1867–1914* (Cambridge, 2013).

Thomson, M., 'Psychology and the "consciousness of modernity" in early twentieth-century Britain', in *Meanings of Modernity: Britain from the Late Victorian Era to World War II*, ed. B. Rieger and M. Daunton (Oxford, 2001), pp. 97–115.

— *Psychological Subjects: Identity, Culture and Health in Twentieth-Century Britain* (Oxford, 2006).

Thornton, M., *Royal Feud: the Queen Mother and the Duchess of Windsor* (London, 1985).

Tinkler, P., *Constructing Girlhood: Popular Magazines for Girls Growing up in England 1920–1950* (London, 1995).

Tinkler, P. and C. K. Warsh, 'Feminine modernity in interwar Britain and North America: corsets, cars, and cigarettes', *Journal of Women's History*, xx (2008) 113–43.

Titmuss, R. M., *Problems of Social Policy* (London, 1976).

Toye, R., *The Roar of the Lion: the Untold Story of Churchill's World War II Speeches* (Oxford, 2013).

Toye, R. and P. Clarke, 'Cripps, Sir (Richard) Stafford', in *Oxford Dictionary of National Biography*, doi.org/10.1093/ref:odnb/32630 [accessed 12 Oct. 2018].

Trentmann, F., 'Materiality in the future of history: things, practices and politics', *Journal of British Studies*, xlviii (2009), 283–307.

Turner, G., 'Approaching celebrity studies', *Celebrity Studies*, i (2010), 11–20.

Turnock, R., *Interpreting Diana: Television Audiences and the Death of a Princess* (London, 2000).

Turvey, G., 'Ideological contradictions: the film topicals of the British and Colonial Kinematograph Company', *Early Popular Visual Culture*, v (2007), 41–56.

Von-Der Hoven, H., *Intimate Life Story of H.R.H. the Duchess of Kent: Told for the First Time and Presented with the Personal Approval of Her Royal Highness* (London, 1937).

Wagner, K. A., 'Calculated to strike terror': the Amritsar massacre and the spectacle of colonial violence', *Past & Present*, ccxxxiii (2016), 185–225.

Ward, P., *Britishness Since 1870* (London, 2004).

Wardhaugh, J., 'Crowds, culture, and power: mass politics and the press in interwar France', *Journalism Studies*, xiv (2013), 743–58.

Warwick, C., *Two Centuries of Royal Weddings* (Worthing, 1980).

— *George and Marina: Duke and Duchess of Kent* (London, 1988).

— *Princess Margaret: a Life of Contrasts* (London, 2002).

Waters, C., 'Beyond Americanization – rethinking Anglo-American cultural exchange between the wars', *Cultural and Social History*, iv (2007), 451–9.

Watson, S., *Marina: the Story of a Princess* (London, 1997).

Weber, M., *On Charisma and Institution Building* (London, 1968).

Webster, W., *Englishness and Empire 1939–1965* (Oxford, 2005).

Wheeler-Bennett, J., *King George VI: His Life and Reign* (London, 1958).

Whiting, A., *The Kents* (London, 1985).

Wiener, J., 'How new was the new journalism?', in *Papers for the Millions: the New Journalism in Britain, 1850s to 1914*, ed. J. Wiener (New York, 1988), pp. 47–71.

Wilkinson, A., 'Lang, (William) Cosmo Gordon, Baron Lang of Lambeth', in *Oxford Dictionary of National Biography*, doi.org/10.1093/ref:odnb/34398 [accessed 12 Oct. 2018].

Williams, S., *The People's King: the True Story of the Abdication* (London, 2003).

Williams, V., *Women Photographers: the Other Observers, 1900 to the Present* (London, 1986).

Williamson, P., *National Crisis and National Government: British Politics, the Economy and Empire, 1926–1932* (Cambridge, 1992).

— 'The doctrinal politics of Stanley Baldwin', in *Public and Private Doctrine: Essays in British History Presented to Michael Cowling*, ed. M. Bentley (Cambridge, 1993), pp. 181–208.

— *Stanley Baldwin: Conservative Leadership and National Values* (Cambridge, 1999).

— 'The monarchy and public values, 1900–1953', in *The Monarchy and the British Nation 1780 to the Present*, ed. A. Olechnowicz (Cambridge, 2007), pp. 223–57.

— 'National days of prayer: the churches, the state and public worship in Britain, 1899–1957', *English Historical Review*, cxxviii (2013), 323–66.

— 'Cripps, Charles Alfred, first Baron Parmoor', in *Oxford Dictionary of National Biography*, doi.org/10.1093/ref:odnb/32629 [accessed 12 Oct. 2018].

Willis-Tropea, L., 'Glamour photography and the institutionalization of celebrity', *Photography and Culture*, iv (2011), 261–76.

Wilson, E., *Women and the Welfare State* (London, 1977).

Winkler, M. M., *The Roman Salute: Cinema, History, Ideology* (Columbus, O., 2009).

Winship, J., *Inside Women's Magazines* (London, 1987).

Wolffe, J., 'The religions of the silent majority', in *The Growth of Religious Diversity: Britain from 1945* (2 vols., London, 1993), i: *Traditions*, ed. G. Parsons, pp. 305–46.

— *Great Deaths: Grieving, Religion, and Nationhood in Victorian and Edwardian Britain* (Oxford, 2000).

— 'The people's king: the crowd and the media at the funeral of Edward VII, May 1910', *Court Historian*, viii (2003), 23–30.

Wood, H., *Talking with Television: Women, Talk Shows, and Modern Self-Reflexivity* (Chicago, Ill., 2009).

Wrench, J., *Geoffrey Dawson and Our Times* (London, 1955).

Wynn, M., 'A royal romance: the marriage of Princess Marina of Greece', *Royalty Digest*, vii (2012), 51–8.

Young, M. and P. Willmott, *Family and Kinship in East London* (London, 1957).

Ziegler, P., *Crown and People* (London, 1978).

— 'Edward VIII: the modern monarch?', *Court Historian*, viii (2003), 73–83.

— *King Edward VIII* (London, 2012).

— *George VI: the Dutiful King* (London, 2014).

Zweiniger-Bargielowska, I., 'Royal rations', *History Today*, xliii (1993), 13–15.

— *Austerity in Britain: Rationing, Controls, and Consumption 1939–1955* (Oxford, 2000).

— 'The body and consumer culture', in *Women in Twentieth-Century Britain: Social, Cultural and Political Change*, ed. I. Zweiniger-Bargielowska (Harlow, 2001), pp. 183–97.

— 'Keep fit and play the game: George VI, outdoor recreation and social cohesion in interwar Britain', *Cultural and Social History*, xi (2014), 111–29.

— 'Royal death and living memorials: the funerals and commemoration of George V and George VI, 1936–52', *Historical Research*, lxxxix (2015), 158–75.

Index